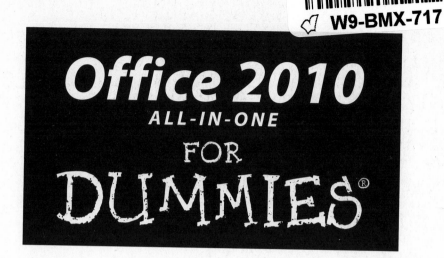

Office 2010

ALL-IN-ONE

FOR DUMMIES®

by Peter Weverka

WITHDRAWN

WILEY

Wiley Publishing, Inc.

Office 2010 All-in-One For Dummies®

Published by
Wiley Publishing, Inc.
111 River Street
Hoboken, NJ 07030-5774

www.wiley.com

Copyright © 2010 by Wiley Publishing, Inc., Indianapolis, Indiana

Published by Wiley Publishing, Inc., Indianapolis, Indiana

Published simultaneously in Canada

For general information on our other products and services, please contact our Customer Care Department within the U.S. at 877-762-2974, outside the U.S. at 317-572-3993, or fax 317-572-4002.

For technical support, please visit www.wiley.com/techsupport.

Wiley also publishes its books in a variety of electronic formats. Some content that appears in print may not be available in electronic books.

Library of Congress Control Number: 2010922571

ISBN: 978-0-470-49748-7

Manufactured in the United States of America

10 9 8 7 6 5 4 3 2 1

WILEY

About the Author

Peter Weverka is the bestselling author of many *For Dummies* books, including *Office 2007 All-in-One Desk Reference for Dummies,* as well as 35 other computer books about various topics. Peter's humorous articles and stories — none related to computers, thankfully — have appeared in *Harper's, SPY,* and other magazines for grown-ups.

Dedication

For Aiko Sofia and Henry Gabriel.

Acknowledgments

This book owes a lot to many hard-working Indianapolis Colts fans at the offices of Wiley Publishing in Indiana. For the umpteenth time, I want to express my gratitude to Steve Hayes for his encouragement and the opportunity to write another *For Dummies* book.

Susan Christophersen knows the editing craft as well as any editor I have ever worked with. It was a pleasure — once again — to work with her.

Technical editor Lee Musick made sure that all the explanations in this book are indeed accurate, and I would like to thank him for his diligence and suggestions for improving this book. I would also like to thank Rich Tennant for the witty cartoons you will find on the pages of this book and Potomac Indexing, LLC for writing the index.

These people at the Wiley offices in Indianapolis gave their all to this book, and I want to acknowledge them by name:

Carl Byers, Ashley Chamberlain, Samantha Cherolis, Katherine Crocker, Joyce Haughey, Rebecca Denoncour, Bonnie Mikkelson

Finally, I owe my family — Sofia, Henry, and Addie — a debt for tolerating my vampire-like working hours and eerie demeanor at daybreak. How can I ever repay you?

Publisher's Acknowledgments

We're proud of this book; please send us your comments at http://dummies.custhelp.com. For other comments, please contact our Customer Care Department within the U.S. at 877-762-2974, outside the U.S. at 317-572-3993, or fax 317-572-4002.

Some of the people who helped bring this book to market include the following:

Acquisitions and Editorial

Project and Copy Editor:
Susan Christophersen

Executive Editor: Steve Hayes

Technical Editor: Lee Musick

Editorial Manager: Jodi Jensen

Editorial Assistant: Amanda Graham

Sr. Editorial Assistant: Cherie Case

Cartoons: Rich Tennant
(www.the5thwave.com)

Composition Services

Project Coordinator: Katherine Crocker

Layout and Graphics: Carl Byers,
Ashley Chamberlain, Samantha K. Cherolis,
Joyce Haughey

Proofreaders: Rebecca Denoncour,
Bonnie Mikkelson

Indexer: Potomac Indexing, LLC

Publishing and Editorial for Technology Dummies

Richard Swadley, Vice President and Executive Group Publisher

Andy Cummings, Vice President and Publisher

Mary Bednarek, Executive Acquisitions Director

Mary C. Corder, Editorial Director

Publishing for Consumer Dummies

Diane Graves Steele, Vice President and Publisher

Composition Services

Debbie Stailey, Director of Composition Services

Contents at a Glance

Table of Contents

Introduction

This book is for users of Office 2010 who want to get to the heart of the program without wasting time. Don't look in this book to find out how the different programs in the Office suite work. Look in this book to find out how *you* can get *your* work done better and faster with these programs.

I show you everything you need to make the most of the different Office programs. On the way, you have a laugh or two. No matter how much or how little skill you bring to the table, the guidance of this book will make you a better, more proficient, more confident user of the Office programs.

What's in This Book, Anyway?

This book is your guide to making the most of the Office programs. It's jam-packed with how-to's, advice, shortcuts, and tips. Here's a bare outline of the eight parts of this book:

✦ **Part I: Common Office Tools:** Looks into the many commands and features that are common to all or several of the Office programs. Master the material in Part I and you will be well on your way to mastering all the programs. Part I explains handling text, the proofing tools, charts, diagrams, and tables. It explores speed techniques that can make you more productive in most of the Office programs, as well as how to draw and manipulate lines, shapes, clip art, and other so-called objects.

✦ **Part II: Word:** Explains the numerous features in Office's word processor, including how to create documents from letters to reports. Use the techniques described here to turn Word into a desktop-publishing program and quickly dispatch office tasks such as mass mailings. You also discover how to get Word's help in writing indexes, bibliographies, and other items of interest to scholars.

✦ **Part III: Outlook:** Shows you how to send and receive e-mail messages and files, as well as track tasks, maintain an address book, and keep a calendar with Outlook. If you're one of those people who receive numerous e-mail messages each day, you will be delighted to discover all the ways to track and manage e-mail — and junk e-mail — in Outlook.

✦ **Part IV: PowerPoint:** Demonstrates how to construct a meaningful presentation that makes the audience say, "Wow!" Included in Part IV are instructions for making a presentation livelier and more original, both when you create your presentation and when you deliver it.

✦ **Part V: Excel:** Shows the many different ways to crunch the numbers with the bean counter in the Office suite. Along the way, you find out how to design worksheets that are easy to read and understand, use data-validation rules to cut down on entry mistakes, and analyze your data. You find out just how useful Excel can be for financial analyses, data tracking, and forecasting.

✦ **Part VI: Access:** Describes how to create a relational database for storing information, as well as query the database for information and gather information into meaningful reports. Don't be frightened by the word "database." You will be surprised to discover how useful Access can be in your work.

✦ **Part VII: Publisher:** Shows how to create brochures, pamphlets, newsletters, and other publications with the "print shop in a can."

✦ **Part VIII: Office — One Step Beyond:** For people who want to take full advantage of Office, Part VIII delves into customizing the Office programs, and recording and running macros. It looks into some auxiliary programs that come with Office, including OneNote, the Picture Manager, and the Clip Organizer. It also looks into alternative ways to distribute your work — in a blog or a Web page, for example, and devotes the final chapter to using Office Web Apps, which are the online versions of Word, Excel, PowerPoint, and OneNote. Online applications are the wave of the future, so be sure to check this chapter out.

What Makes This Book Different

You are holding in your hands a computer book designed to make mastering the Office programs as easy and comfortable as possible. Besides the fact that this book is easy to read, it's different from other books about Office. Read on to see why.

Easy-to-look-up information

This book is a reference, and that means that readers have to be able to find instructions quickly. To that end, I have taken great pains to make sure that the material in this book is well organized and easy to find. The descriptive headings help you find information quickly. The bulleted and numbered lists make following instructions simpler. The tables make options easier to understand and compare.

I want you to be able to look down the page and see in a heading or list the name of the topic that concerns you. I want you to be able to find instructions quickly. Compare the table of contents in this book to the book next to it on the bookstore shelf. The table of contents in this book is put together better and presents topics so that you can find them in a hurry.

A task-oriented approach

Most computer books describe what the software is, but this book explains how to complete tasks with the software. I assume that you came to this book because you want to know how to *do* something — print form letters, create a worksheet, or query a database. You came to the right place. This book describes how to get tasks done.

Meaningful screen shots

The screen shots in this book show only the part of the screen that illustrates what is being explained in the text. When instructions refer to one part of the screen, only that part of the screen is shown. I took great care to make sure that the screen shots in this book serve to help you understand the Office programs and how they work. Compare this book to the next one on the bookstore shelf. Do you see how clean the screen shots in this book are?

Foolish Assumptions

Please forgive me, but I made one or two foolish assumptions about you, the reader of this book. I assumed that:

+ You own a copy of Office 2010, the latest edition of Office, and you have installed it on your computer.

+ You use a Windows operating system. All people who have the Windows operating system installed on their computers are invited to read this book. It serves for people who have Windows 7, Windows Vista, Windows XP, and Windows NT.

+ You are kind to foreign tourists and small animals.

Conventions Used in This Book

I want you to understand all the instructions in this book, and in that spirit, I've adopted a few conventions.

Where you see boldface letters or numbers in this book, it means to type the letters or numbers. For example, "Enter **25** in the Percentage text box" means to do exactly that: Enter the number 25.

Sometimes two tabs on the Ribbon have the same name. To distinguish tabs with the same name from one another, I sometimes include one tab's "Tools" heading in parentheses if there could be confusion about which tab

I'm referring to. In PowerPoint, for example, when you see the words "(Table Tools) Design tab," I'm referring to the Design tab for creating tables, not the Design tab for changing a slide's appearance. (Book I, Chapter 1 describes the Ribbon and the tabs in detail.)

To show you how to step through command sequences, I use the ⇨ symbol. For example, on the Home tab in Word, you can click the Change Styles button and choose Style Set⇨Distinctive to change the look of a document. The ⇨ symbol is just a shorthand method of saying "Choose Style Set and then choose Distinctive."

To give most commands, you can press combinations of keys. For example, pressing Ctrl+S saves the file you're working on. In other words, you can hold down the Ctrl key and press the S key to save a file. Where you see Ctrl+, Alt+, or Shift+ and a key name or key names, press the keys simultaneously.

 Yet another way to give a command is to click a button. When I tell you to click a button, you see a small illustration of the button in the margin of this book (unless the button is too large to fit in the margin). The button shown here is the Save button, the one you can click to save a file.

Icons Used in This Book

To help you get the most out of this book, I've placed icons here and there. Here's what the icons mean:

 Next to the Tip icon, you can find shortcuts and tricks of the trade to make your visit to Officeland more enjoyable.

 Where you see the Warning icon, tread softly and carefully. It means that you are about to do something that you may regret later.

 When I explain a juicy little fact that bears remembering, I mark it with a Remember icon. When you see this icon, prick up your ears. You will discover something that you need to remember throughout your adventures with Word, Excel, PowerPoint, or the other Office program I am demystifying.

 When I am forced to describe high-tech stuff, a Technical Stuff icon appears in the margin. You don't have to read what's beside the Technical Stuff icons if you don't want to, although these technical descriptions often help you understand how a software feature works.

Good Luck, Reader!

If you have a comment about this book, a question, or a shortcut you would like to share with me, send an e-mail message to me at this address: peterwev@gmail.com. Be advised that I usually can't answer e-mail right away because I'm too darned busy. I do appreciate comments and questions, however, because they help me pass my dreary days in captivity.

Book I

Common Office Tools

The 5th Wave   By Rich Tennant

"The odd thing is he always insists on using the latest version of Office."

Contents at a Glance

Chapter 1: Office Nuts and Bolts

In This Chapter

✔ **Introducing the Office programs**

✔ **Running an Office program**

✔ **Exploring the Office interface**

✔ **Saving and automatically recovering your files**

✔ **Opening and closing an Office file**

✔ **Recording a file's document properties**

✔ **Clamping a password on a file**

Chapter 1 is where you get your feet wet with Office 2010. Walk right to the shore and sink your toes in the water. Don't worry; I won't push you from behind.

In this chapter, you meet the Office programs and discover speed techniques for opening programs and files. I show you around the Ribbon, Quick Access toolbar, and other Office program landmarks. I also show you how to open files, save files, and clamp a password on a file.

A Survey of Office Programs

Office 2010, sometimes called the *Microsoft Office Suite,* is a collection of computer programs. Why is it called Office? I think because the people who invented it wanted to make software for completing tasks that need doing in a typical office. When you hear someone talk about "Office" or the "Office software," they're talking about several different programs:

✦ **Word:** A word processor for writing letters, reports, and so on. A Word file is called a *document* (see Book II).

✦ **Outlook:** A personal information manager, scheduler, and e-mailer (see Book III).

✦ **PowerPoint:** A means of creating slide presentations to give in front of audiences. A PowerPoint file is called a *presentation,* or sometimes a *slide show* (see Book IV).

✦ **Excel:** A number cruncher for performing numerical analyses. An Excel file is called a *workbook* (see Book V).

✦ **Access:** A database management program (see Book VI).

✦ **Publisher:** A means of creating desktop-publishing files — pamphlets, notices, newsletters, and the like (see Book VII).

Office 2010 also comes with the *Clip Organizer,* for managing and inserting clip-art images in files and managing media files on your computer; the *Picture Manger,* for inserting and editing pictures; and *OneNote 2010,* a program for taking notes and brainstorming. These programs are explained in Book VIII.

If you're new to Office, don't be daunted by the prospect of having to study so many different computer programs. The programs have much in common. You find the same commands throughout Office. For example, the method of choosing fonts is the same in Word, Outlook, PowerPoint, Excel, Access, and Publisher. Creating diagrams and charts works the same in Word, PowerPoint, and Excel. Book I describes tasks that are common to all or most of the Office programs. Master one Office program and you're well on your way to mastering the next.

Starting an Office Program

Unless you start an Office program, you can't create a document, construct a worksheet, or make a database. Many have tried to undertake these tasks with mud and papier-mâché without starting a program first, but all have failed. Here are the various and sundry ways to start an Office program:

✦ **The old-fashioned way:** Click the Start button, choose All Programs⇨ Microsoft Office, and then choose the program's name on the submenu.

✦ **The Start menu:** Click the program's name on the Start menu, as shown in Figure 1-1. The *Start menu* is the menu you see when you click the Start button. By placing a program's name on the Start menu, you can open the program simply by clicking the Start button and then clicking the program's name. To place an Office program on the Start menu:

1. **Click the Start button and choose All Programs⇨Microsoft Office.**

2. **Move the pointer over the program's name on the submenu, but don't click to select the program's name.**

3. **Right-click the program's name and choose Pin to Start Menu on the shortcut menu that appears.**

To remove a program's name from the Start menu, right-click the name and choose Remove from This List.

Click a program name on the Start menu   Double-click a shortcut icon

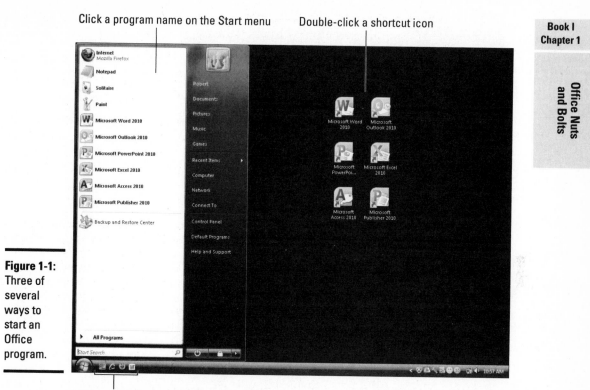

Figure 1-1:
Three of
several
ways to
start an
Office
program.

Click an icon on the Quick Launch toolbar

✦ **Desktop shortcut icon:** Double-click the program's shortcut icon (see
   Figure 1-1). A *shortcut icon* is an icon you can double-click to do something in a hurry. By creating a shortcut icon on the Windows desktop,
   you can double-click the icon and immediately start an Office program.
   To place an Office shortcut icon on the desktop:

   1. **Click the Start button and choose All Programs⇨Microsoft Office.**

   2. **Move the pointer over the program's name on the submenu, but
      don't click the program's name.**

   3. **Right-click the program's name and choose Send To⇨Desktop
      (Create Shortcut) on the shortcut menu that appears.**

   You can also right-click the name of a program you pinned to the
   Start menu and choose Send To⇨Desktop (Create Shortcut).

   To remove a desktop shortcut icon from the Windows desktop, right-
   click it, choose Delete, and click Yes in the Delete Shortcut dialog box.
   Don't worry about deleting a program when you delete its shortcut icon.
   All you do when you choose Delete is remove the program's shortcut
   icon from the desktop and make your desktop a little less crowded.

Starting a program along with your computer

Yet another way to start an Office program is to make the program start automatically whenever you turn on your computer. If you're the president of the Office Fan Club and you have to run, for example, Outlook each time your computer starts, create an Outlook shortcut icon and copy it into the Startup folder. Note which Windows operating system you have, and copy the shortcut icon into the Startup folder in one of these locations:

* **Windows 7 and Vista:** `C:\Users\`
  `Username\AppData\Roaming\`
  `Microsoft\Windows\Start`
  `Menu\Programs\Startup`

* **Windows XP:** `C:\Documents and`
  `Settings\Username\Start`
  `Menu\Programs\Startup`

✦ **Quick Launch toolbar (Windows Vista and XP only):** Click a shortcut icon on the Quick Launch toolbar (refer to Figure 1-1). The Quick Launch toolbar appears on the Windows taskbar and is easy to find. Wherever your work takes you, you can see the Quick Launch toolbar and click its shortcut icons to start programs. Create a shortcut icon and follow these steps to place a copy of it on the Quick Launch toolbar:

1. **Click the shortcut icon to select it.**

2. **Hold down the Ctrl key.**

3. **Drag the shortcut icon onto the Quick Launch toolbar.**

   To change an icon's position on the toolbar, drag it to the left or the right. To remove an icon, right-click it and choose Delete.

Finding Your Way Around the Office Interface

Interface, also called the *user interface,* is a computer term that describes how a software program presents itself to the people who use it (and you probably thought *interface* meant two people kissing). These pages give you a quick tour of the Office interface and explain what the various parts of the interface are. You will be glad to know that the interface of all the Office programs is pretty much the same. Click along with me as I describe the interface and you'll know what's what by the time you finish reading these pages.

The File tab

File

In the upper-left corner of the window is the File tab, as shown in Figure 1-2. Go to the File tab to find commands for creating, opening, and saving files, as well as doing other file-management tasks. Notice the Options command. You can choose Options to open the Options dialog box and tell the program you are working in how you want it to work.

File tab

Quick Access toolbar

Figure 1-2:
The File tab and Quick Access toolbar are always available.

To leave the File tab, click a different tab on the Ribbon — Home, Insert, or another tab. Be sure *not* to choose the Exit command on the File tab menu. Doing so closes the Office program you are working in.

The Quick Access toolbar

No matter where you travel in an Office program, you see the *Quick Access toolbar* in the upper-left corner of the screen (refer to Figure 1-2). This toolbar offers three necessary buttons: the all-important Save button, the trusty Undo button, and the convenient Repeat button. You can place more buttons on the Quick Access toolbar as well as move the toolbar lower in the window. I explain how to customize the Quick Access toolbar in Book VIII, Chapter 1.

By the way, Microsoft says that you can call the Quick Access toolbar the QAT, or "kwat," but I don't think you should do that. Others might think you have indigestion.

The Ribbon and its tabs

Across the top of the screen is the *Ribbon,* an assortment of different *tabs;* click a tab to undertake a task. For example, click the Home tab to format text; click the Insert tab to insert a table or chart. Figure 1-3 shows what you see in Word when you click the Home, Insert, and Page Layout tabs on the Ribbon. Each tab offers a different set of buttons, menus, and galleries.

The Ribbon   To visit a tab on the Ribbon, click its name

Figure 1-3:
The
commands
are different
on each
tab on the
Ribbon.

Practically speaking, your first step when you start a new task is to click a tab on the Ribbon. Knowing which tab to click takes awhile, but the names of tabs — Home, Insert, View, and so on — hint as to which commands you find when you visit a tab.

 To make the Ribbon disappear and get more room to view items on-screen, click the Minimize the Ribbon button (or press Ctrl+F1). This button is located on the right side of the Ribbon, to the left of the Help button. You can also right-click the Ribbon and choose Minimize the Ribbon on the shortcut menu, or double-click a tab on the Ribbon. To see the Ribbon again, click the Minimize the Ribbon button, press Ctrl+F1, double-click a Ribbon tab, or right-click a tab name or the Quick Access toolbar and deselect Minimize the Ribbon on the shortcut menu. While the Ribbon is minimized, you can click a tab name to display a tab.

 How many buttons appear on some of the tabs depends on the size of your monitor screen. On narrow 800 x 600 screens, Office sometimes can't find enough room to display all the buttons on a tab, so it presents you with a primary button to click in order to get to the other buttons. Throughout this book, I endeavor to tell you which button you click if your monitor has a narrow or a wide screen, but if the instructions in this book tell you to click a button and you don't see it, you have to click a primary button first. Look around for the primary button and then click it to get to the secondary button.

Context-sensitive tabs

Sorry for dropping the term *context-sensitive* on you. I usually steer clear of these horrid computer terms, but I can't help it this time because Microsoft calls some tabs context-sensitive, and by golly, I have to call them that, too.

To keep the Ribbon from getting too crowded with tabs, some tabs appear only in context — they appear on the Ribbon after you insert or click something. In Figure 1-4, for example, I inserted a table, and two additional tabs — the Design tab and the Layout tab — appear on the Ribbon under the heading "Table Tools." These context-sensitive tabs offer commands for designing and laying out tables. When I click the (Table Tools) Design tab, as Figure 1-4 shows, I see commands for putting colors and borders on tables. The idea behind context-sensitive tabs is to direct you to the commands you need and exclude all other commands.

Select or insert an item. . .   and you get context-sensitive tabs

Figure 1-4:
After you insert or select an item, context-sensitive tabs appear on the Ribbon.

Critter Population Levels

	Deer	Bear	Wombat
California	150,000	8,000	42,000
Nevada	45,000	2,000	23,000
Arizona	23,000	2,500	112,000

If you're looking for a tab on the Ribbon but can't find it, the tab is probably context-sensitive. You have to insert or select an item to make some tabs appear on the Ribbon. Context-sensitive tabs appear on the right side of the Ribbon under a heading with the word *Tools* in its name.

Context-sensitive tab names can be confusing because sometimes they repeat the names of other tabs. When I refer to a context-sensitive tab name in this book, I include its Tools heading in parentheses in case there is any confusion about which tab I'm referring to. In PowerPoint, for example, the Design tab that always appears on the Ribbon is the *Design tab,* but the context-sensitive Design tab is the *(Table Tools) Design tab.*

The anatomy of a tab

All tabs are different in terms of the commands they offer, but all are the same insofar as how they present commands. On every tab, you find groups and buttons. Some tabs also offer galleries. Groups, buttons, galleries — what's up with that?

Groups

Commands on each tab are organized into *groups*. The names of these groups appear below the buttons and galleries on tabs. For example, the Home tab in Excel is organized into several groups, including the Clipboard, Font, Alignment, Number, Styles, Cells, and Editing group, as shown in Figure 1-5.

Figure 1-5:
Each tab is organized into groups; some groups offer group buttons.

Group names

Group buttons

Groups serve two purposes:

✦ Groups tell you what the buttons and galleries above their names are used for. On the Home tab in Excel, for example, the buttons in the Font group are for formatting text. Read group names to help find the command you need.

✦ Many groups have a *group button* that you can click to open a dialog box or task pane (officially, Microsoft calls these little buttons *dialog box launchers,* but let's act like grownups, shall we?). Group buttons are found to the right of group names (refer to Figure 1-5). Moving the pointer over a group button opens a pop-up help box with a description and picture of the dialog box or task pane that appears when the button is clicked.

As with tabs on the Ribbon, group buttons are context-sensitive (there's that term again!). Whether you can click a group button to open a dialog box or task pane depends on the context in which you're working. Sometimes the buttons are grayed out because they don't pertain to the task you're currently doing.

Buttons

Go to any tab and you find buttons of all shapes and sizes. Square buttons and rectangular buttons. Big and small buttons. Buttons with labels and buttons without labels. Is there any rhyme or reason to these button shapes and sizes? No, there isn't.

What matters isn't a button's shape or size, but whether a down-pointing arrow appears on its face:

✦ **A button with an arrow:** Click a button *with* an arrow and you get a drop-down list with options you can select.

✦ **A button without an arrow:** Click a button *without* an arrow and you complete an action of some kind.

✦ **A hybrid button with an arrow:** Some buttons serve a dual purpose as a button and a drop-down list. By clicking the symbol on the top half of the button, you complete an action; by clicking the arrow on the bottom half of the button, you open a drop-down list. On the Home tab, for example, clicking the top half of the Paste button pastes what is on the Clipboard into your file, but clicking the bottom half of the button opens a drop-down list with Paste options.

You can find out what clicking a button does by moving the pointer over it. You see a pop-up description of what the button is for.

Galleries

Built into some tabs are galleries like the one shown in Figure 1-6. The gallery in the figure pertains to charts: The Chart Styles gallery is for formatting charts. A *gallery* presents you with visual options for changing an item. When you move the pointer over a gallery choice, the item on your page or slide — the table, chart, or diagram, for example — changes appearance. In this way, you can preview different choices before you click to select the choice you want.

Click the More button to open the gallery in a drop-down list

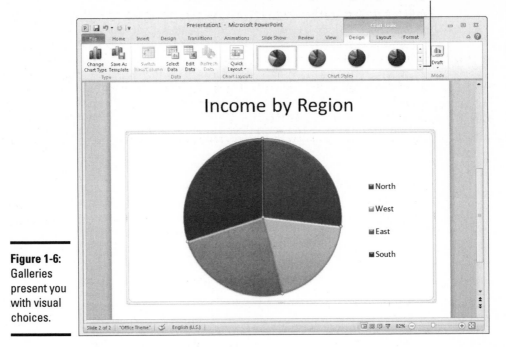

Figure 1-6:
Galleries
present you
with visual
choices.

To view and make choices on a gallery:

+ Move the pointer over gallery choices and watch how the item or items on-screen change.

+ Click a scroll arrow to see more gallery choices on the tab.

+ Click the More button (refer to Figure 1-6) to open the gallery choices in a drop-down list and see many choices simultaneously.

+ Click a gallery choice to apply it.

Live previewing

Thanks to *live previewing,* you can see the results of a menu or gallery choice before actually making the choice. Here's how live previewing works: Move the pointer over an option in a gallery or drop-down list and glance at your page or slide. You can see the results of selecting the option. For example, you see a different font or shape color. You can judge whether choosing the option is worthwhile without choosing the option first. Live previewing liberates you from repeatedly choosing commands, backtracking, and trying again until you get it right.

Right-clicking to open a shortcut menu

Similar to mini-toolbars are the shortcut menus you get when you right-click. *Right-click* means to click the right, not the left, mouse button. Right-click just about anywhere and you get a shortcut menu of some kind. The shortcut menus differ, depending on what you right-click.

Right-clicking sometimes gets you to the command you need without having to select a different tab. I right-click more than usual in Office to keep from switching from tab to tab on the Ribbon.

Mini-toolbars

A *mini-toolbar* is a ghostlike toolbar that appears on-screen to help you do a task, as shown in Figure 1-7. Move the pointer over the mini-toolbar, and it ceases being ghostlike, as Figure 1-7 demonstrates. Now you can select an option from a drop-down list or click a button on the mini-toolbar to complete a task.

Figure 1-7:
Move the pointer over the mini-toolbar to make it come alive.

All's well that ends well.   All's well that ends well.

The mini-toolbar, shown in Figure 1-7, appears when you select text and then move the pointer over selected text. Don't be frightened of these ghostlike mini-toolbars. Keep your eyes open for them. Mini-toolbars are very convenient, and they save you the trouble of going to a different tab to complete a task.

Office 2010 for keyboard lovers

People who like to give commands by pressing keyboard shortcuts may well ask, "Where are the keyboard shortcuts in Office?" The answer is: They're still there. For example, you can press Ctrl+B to boldface text and Ctrl+U to underline text.

Office offers Alt+key shortcuts as well. Press the Alt key and letters — they're called *KeyTips* — appear on tab names, as shown in Figure 1-8. After you press the Alt key, follow these instructions to make use of KeyTips:

✦ **Go to a tab.** Press a KeyTip on a tab to visit a tab.

✦ **Make KeyTips appear on menu items.** Press a KeyTip on a button or gallery to make KeyTips appear on menu items.

Figure 1-8:
Press the
Alt key to
see KeyTips.

Saving Your Files

Soon after you create a new file, be sure to save it. And save your file from time to time while you work on it as well. Until you save your work, it rests in the computer's electronic memory (RAM), a precarious location. If a power outage occurs or your computer stalls, you lose all the work you did since the last time you saved your file. Make it a habit to save files every ten minutes or so or when you complete an important task.

These pages explain how to save a file, name a file, choose the folder where you want to save a file, declare where you want to save files by default, save files for use in 97–2003 editions of Office, and handle files that were saved automatically after a computer failure.

Saving a file

To save a file:

✦ Click the Save button (you find it on the Quick Access toolbar).

✦ Press Ctrl+S.

✦ Go to the File tab and choose Save.

Saving a file for the first time

The first time you save a presentation, the Save As dialog box opens. It invites you to give the file a name and choose a folder in which to store it. Enter a descriptive name in the File Name text box. To locate a folder for storing your presentation, see "Navigating the Save As and Open Dialog Boxes," later in this chapter.

Declaring where you like to save files

When you attempt to save a file for the first time in the Save As dialog box, Office shows you the contents of the Document folder (in Windows 7 and Windows Vista) or the My Documents folder (in Windows XP) on the assumption that you keep most of your files in that folder. The Documents folder is the center of the universe as far as Office is concerned, but perhaps you keep the majority of your files in a different folder. How would you like to see it first in the Save As and Open dialog boxes?

To direct Office to the folder you like best and make it appear first in the Save As and Open dialog boxes, follow these steps:

File

1. **In Word, Excel, PowerPoint, or Access, go to the File tab and choose Options.**

You see the Options dialog box.

2. **In Word, Excel, and PowerPoint, select the Save category; in Access, select the General category.**

Figure 1-9 shows the topmost options in this category.

3. **In the Default File Location (or Default Database Folder) text box, enter the address of the folder where you prefer to keep your files.**

For example, if you're fond of keeping files in the My Stuff folder on the C drive of your computer, enter **C:\My Stuff**, or click the Browse button (if it's available) and select the My Stuff folder in the Modify Location dialog box.

4. **Click OK.**

Figure 1-9:
The Save options in the Options dialog box.

Customize how documents are saved.

Save documents

| Save files in this format: | Word Document (*.docx) ▾ |
| Save AutoRecover information every | 10 minutes |
| Keep the last Auto Recovered file if I close without saving |
| AutoRecover file location: | C:\Users\Robert\AppData\Roaming\Microsoft\Word\ | Browse... |
| Default file location: | C:\My Stuff | Browse... |

Saving files for use in earlier versions of an Office program

Not everyone is a proud owner of Office 2010. Before you pass along a file to a co-worker who has Office 2003, XP, 2000, or 97, save your document so that your co-worker can open it. People with versions of Office prior to version 2010 and 2007 cannot open your Office files unless you save your files for earlier versions of Office.

You can tell whether a Word, PowerPoint, Access, or Excel file is formatted for a 2010 program or an earlier version of the program by glancing at its file extension. PowerPoint, Excel, Access, and Word files have four-letter, not three-letter file extensions. Table 1-1 lists Office program file extensions.

Table 1-1	Office Program File Extensions	
Program	*2010, 2007*	*97–2003*
Access	`.accdb`	`.mlb`
Excel	`.xlsx`	`.xls`
PowerPoint	`.pptx`	`.ppt`
Publisher	`.pub`	`.pub`
Word	`.docx`	`.doc`

Saving a file for use in Office 97–2003

Follow these steps to save a file so that someone with Office 97, 2000, XP, or 2003 can open it:

1. **Go to the File tab.**

2. **Choose Save & Send.**

   You see the Share window.

3. **Under File Types, choose Change File Type and then choose the 97–2003 option for saving files.**

   The Save As dialog box opens.

4. **Enter a new name for the file, if necessary.**

5. **Click the Save button.**

   You can tell when you're working on a file saved in the 97–2003 format because the words "Compatibility Mode" appear in the title bar next to the file's name. The title bar is located at the top of the screen.

Files saved in the 97–2003 format have a different file extension. Rather than a four-letter file extension that ends in *x*, they have a three-letter extension without the *x* (see Table 1-1, shown previously).

Saving files by default for earlier versions of Office

If you're way ahead of the pack and you always have to save files in a different format so that co-workers can open them, make the different format the default format for saving all your files. That way, you don't have to choose a new format whenever you pass along a file to a co-worker.

Follow these steps to change the default format for saving files:

| File |

1. **Go to the File tab and choose Options.**

   The Options dialog box appears.

2. **In Word, Excel, and PowerPoint, select the Save category; in Access, select the General category.**

3. **In the Save Files in This Format drop-down list, choose the 97–2003 format.**

4. **Click OK.**

   Remember that you made 97–2003 the default format for saving files. At some point, when the world catches up to you and 97–2003 files have become obsolete, return to the Options dialog box and choose the most up-to-date format.

Saving AutoRecovery information

To insure against data loss due to computer and power failures, Office saves files on its own every ten minutes. These files are saved in an AutoRecovery file. After your computer fails, you can try to recover some of the work you lost by getting it from the AutoRecovery file (see the sidebar "When disaster strikes!").

Converting Office 97–2003 files to 2010

When you open a file made in an earlier version of Office, the program switches to *compatibility mode.* Features that weren't part of earlier versions of the program are shut down. You can tell when a file is in compatibility mode because the words *Compatibility Mode* appear in the title bar next to the file's name.

Follow these steps to convert a 97–2003 file for use in an Office 2010 program:

1. **Go to the File tab and choose Convert.**

   A dialog box informs you what converting means. If you don't see the Convert option, your file has been converted already.

2. **Click OK.**

Microsoft Word

This action will convert the document to the newest file format. The layout of the document may change.

Converting allows you to use all the new features of Word and reduces the size of your file. This document will be replaced by the converted version.

☐ Do not ask me again about converting documents

| Tell Me More... | | OK | Cancel |

When disaster strikes!

After your computer fails and you restart an Office program, you see the Document Recovery task pane with a list of files that were open when the failure occurred:

- *AutoSave* files are files that Office saves as part of its AutoRecovery procedure (see "Saving AutoRecovery information").

- *Original* files are files that you save by clicking the Save button.

The Document Recovery task pane tells you when each file was saved. By studying the time listings, you can tell which version of a file — the AutoRecovery file or the file you saved — is most up-to-date.

Open the drop-down list for a file and select one of these options:

- **View:** Opens the file so that you can examine and work on it. If you want to keep it, click the Save button.

- **Save As:** Opens the Save As dialog box so that you can save the file under a different name. Choose this command to keep a copy of the recovered file on hand in case you need it.

- **Close:** Closes the file.

- **Show Repairs:** Shows repairs made to the file (for use with repaired Word documents).

Document Recovery

PowerPoint has recovered the following files. Save the ones you wish to keep.

Available files

Marketing Report.pptx [Original]
Version created last time the user saved the file
11:53 AM Monday, October 19, 2009

High Flying.pptx [Autosa...
Version created from the...
11:36 AM Monday, Octob...

| View
| Save As...
| Close
| Show Repairs

High Flying.pptx [Origina...
Version created last time...
11:53 AM Monday, October 19, 2009

Which file do I want to save?

Close

Office saves AutoRecovery files every ten minutes, but if you want the program to save the files more or less frequently, you can change the AutoRecovery setting. Auto-recovering taxes a computer's memory. If your computer is sluggish, consider making AutoRecovery files at intervals longer than ten minutes; if your computer fails often and you're worried about losing data, make AutoRecovery files more frequently.

Follow these steps to tell Office how often to save data in an AutoRecovery file:

File

1. **On the File tab, choose Options.**

The Options dialog box appears.

2. **Select the Save category (refer to Figure 1-9).**

3. **Enter a Minutes setting in the Save AutoRecover Information Every box.**

4. **Click OK.**

Navigating the Save As and Open Dialog Boxes

The Open dialog box and Save As dialog box offer a bunch of different ways to locate a file you want to open or locate the folder where you want to save a file. Figure 1-10 shows the Open dialog box. I'm happy to report that both dialog boxes, Open and Save As, work the same way.

✦ **Retracing your search:** Click the Back and Forward buttons (or open the drop-down list on the Back button) to retrace your search for a folder or revisit a folder you previously visited.

Change views   Search for a file in a folder

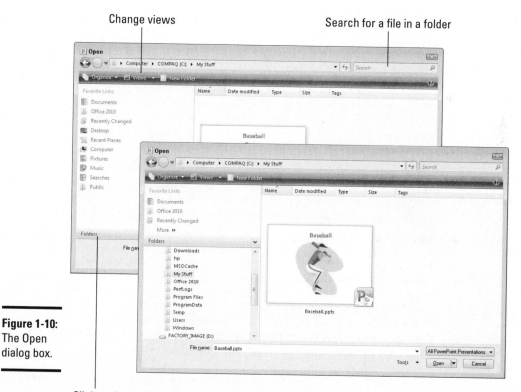

Figure 1-10:
The Open
dialog box.

Click to display the Navigation pane

Putting a favorite folder on the Favorites list

The Favorites list (or Favorite Links list) in the Open dialog box and Save As dialog box gives you the opportunity to go lickety-split to a folder on your computer or network. All you have to do is click a folder name on the list to see the contents of the folder. If there's a particular folder you visit often that deserves "favorite" status, you can put that folder on the Favorites list by following these steps:

1. **In the Open or Save As dialog box, locate and select the folder that you want to be a favorite.**

2. **Drag the folder into the Favorites list. That's right — just drag it. Moreover, you can slide it up or down the list to put it where you are most likely to find it.**

To remove a folder from the Favorites list, right-click it and choose Remove Link.

✦ **Searching for files in a folder:** Use the Search box to search for subfolders and files in the folder you're currently viewing. After you type the first few letters of a filename or subfolder, you see only the names of items that start with the letters you typed. To see all the files and subfolders again, click the Close button (the *X*) in the Search box.

✦ **Changing views:** Display folder contents differently by choosing a view on the Views drop-down list (in Windows 7, look for the View arrow in the upper-right corner of the dialog box). In Details view, you see how large files are and when they were last edited.

✦ **Creating a new folder:** Click the New Folder button to create a new subfolder for storing files. Select the folder that your new folder will be subordinate to and click the New Folder button. Then type a name for the saved file.

✦ **Open one of your favorite folders (Windows Vista):** Select a folder in the Favorite Links list to see its contents. Later in this chapter, the "Putting a favorite folder on the Favorite list" sidebar explains how to place the name of a folder in the list.

✦ **Navigate to different folders:** Click the Folders bar (in the lower-left corner of the dialog box) to open the Navigation pane and look for folders or presentations on a different drive, network location, or folder on your computer. If you don't see the Folders bar, click the Organize button and choose Layout⇨Navigation Pane.

Opening and Closing Files

To get to work on a file, you have to open it first. And, of course, you close a file when you're finished working on it and want to stop and smell the roses.

The following pages explain all the intricate details of opening and closing files. In these pages, you find many tips for finding and opening the file you want to work on.

Opening a file

Between the two of them, Office and Windows offer many shortcuts for opening files. To open a file, take the standard route — go to the File tab and choose Open — or take advantage of the numerous ways to open files quickly.

The slow, conventional way to open a file

If you can't open a file by any other means, you have to resort to the Open dialog box:

File

1. **On the File tab, choose Open (or press Ctrl+O).**

You see the Open dialog box (refer to Figure 1-10).

2. **Locate and select the file you want to open.**

Earlier in this chapter, "Navigating the Save As and Open Dialog Boxes" offers some tricks for locating a file in the Open dialog box.

3. **Click the Open button.**

Your file opens. You can also double-click a filename to open a file.

Speed techniques for opening files

As shown in Figure 1-11, the fastest way to open a file is to go to the File tab, choose Recent, and choose the file's name on the Recent Documents list. This list shows the names of the last 22 files you opened. By moving the pointer over a name, you can see which folder a file is stored in. Click the pin next to a name to make the name remain on the list even if it isn't one of the last several files you opened (click the pin a second time to "unpin" a name).

To make more (or fewer) than 22 filenames appear on the Recent Documents list, go the File tab in Word, Excel, or PowerPoint, and choose Options. In the Options dialog box, visit the Advanced category, scroll to the Display section, and enter a number in the Show This Number of Recent Documents text box.

Here are other speed techniques for opening files:

✦ **In Windows Explorer or Computer:** Locate the file in one of these file-management programs and double-click its name.

✦ **Shortcut icon:** Create a shortcut icon to a file and place the icon on the Windows desktop. In Windows Explorer or the Open dialog box, right-click the file's name and choose Send To⇨Desktop (Create Shortcut). To quickly open the file, double-click its shortcut icon on the desktop.

Click to "pin" a name to the list

Figure 1-11:
Opening
a file on
the Recent
Documents
list.

Closing a file

Closing a file is certainly easier than opening one. To close a file, save your file and use one of these techniques:

+ On the File tab, choose Close. The program remains open although the file is closed.

+ Click the Close button — the *X* in the upper-right corner of the window. (Alternatively, press Alt+F4.) Clicking the Close button closes the program as well as the file.

+ Click the program icon (in the upper-left corner of the screen) and choose Close.

If you try to close a file without first saving it, a message box asks whether ditching your file is in your best interests, and you get a chance to click Save in the message box and save your file. Sometimes closing a file without saving the changes you made to it is worthwhile. If you made a bunch of editorial mistakes and want to start over, you can close the file without saving the changes you made. Next time you open the file, you see the version that you had before you made all those mistakes.

Reading and Recording File Properties

Properties are a means of describing a file. If you manage two dozen or more files, you owe it to yourself to record properties. You can use them later to identify files.

File

To read property descriptions, go to the File tab and examine the Information window. Property descriptions are found on the right side of the window, as shown in Figure 1-12.

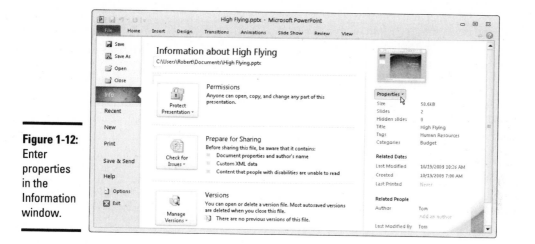

Figure 1-12:
Enter
properties
in the
Information
window.

To record even more descriptions, click the Properties button and choose one of these commands on the drop-down list:

✦ **Show Document Panel:** The Document Properties panel appears so that you can enter more descriptions and comments.

✦ **Advanced Properties:** The Properties dialog box appears. Enter information about your file on the Summary and Custom tab.

You can read a file's properties without opening a file. In Windows Explorer, Computer, or the Open dialog box, right-click a file's name and choose Properties. You see the Properties dialog box. Go to the Details tab to see descriptions you entered.

Word, Excel, and PowerPoint offer a command for erasing document properties. On the File tab, choose Info, click the Check for Issues button, and choose Inspect Document. In the Document Inspector dialog box, click the Inspect button, and then click the Remove All button if you want to remove document properties.

Locking a File with a Password

Perhaps you want to submit your file to others for critical review but you don't want any Tom, Dick, or Harry to look at your file. In that case, lock your file with a password and give out the password only to people whose opinions you trust. These pages explain how to password-protect a file, open a file that is locked with a password, and remove the password from a file.

Password-protecting a file

Follow these steps to clamp a password on a file, such that others need a password to open and perhaps also edit it:

1. **Go to the File tab.**

2. **In the Information window, click the Protect Document (or Workbook) button, and choose Encrypt with Password on the drop-down list.**

   The Encrypt Document dialog box appears, as shown in Figure 1-13.

Figure 1-13: Enter passwords for the file in this dialog box.

3. **Enter a password in the Password text box and click OK.**

   Others will need the password you enter to open the file. No ifs, ands, or buts. They have to enter the password.

   Passwords are case-sensitive. In other words, you have to enter the correct combination of upper- and lowercase letters to successfully enter the password. If the password is *Valparaiso* (with an uppercase *V*), entering **valparaiso** (with a lowercase v) is deemed the wrong password and doesn't open the file.

4. **In the Confirm Password dialog box, enter the password again.**

   Figure 1-13 shows the Confirm Password dialog box

5. **Click OK.**

   The Information window informs you that a password is required to open the file.

Removing a password from a file

Follow these steps to remove a password from a file:

1. **Open the file that needs its password removed.**

2. **Go to the File tab, and in the Information window, click the Protect Document button, and choose Encrypt with Password.**

   The Encrypt Document dialog box appears (refer to Figure 1-13).

3. **Delete the password and click OK.**

Chapter 2: Wrestling with the Text

In This Chapter

- Selecting, moving, copying, and deleting text
- Changing the appearance, size, and color of text
- Changing the case of letters
- Inserting foreign characters and symbols
- Finding text — and replacing it if you want
- Hyperlinking to Web pages and other places in a file

To enter text, all you have to do is wiggle your fingers over the keyboard. Everybody knows that. But not everyone knows all the different ways to change the look and size of text in an Office 2010 file. In this chapter, I explain how to do that as well as how to move, copy, and delete text. You find out how to quickly change a letter's case, enter a symbol or foreign character, and find and replace text in a file. Finally, I show you how to link your files to the Internet by fashioning a hyperlink.

Manipulating the Text

This short but important part of Chapter 2 describes the many techniques for selecting, deleting, copying, and moving text. You find an inordinate number of tips on these pages because there are so many shortcuts for manipulating text. Master the many shortcuts and you cut down considerably on the time you spend editing text.

Selecting text

Before you can do anything to text — move it, boldface it, delete it, translate it — you have to select it. Here are speed techniques for selecting text:

To Select	Do This
A word	Double-click the word.
A few words	Drag over the words.
A paragraph	Triple-click inside the paragraph (in Word, PowerPoint, and Outlook messages).
A block of text	Click the start of the text, hold down the Shift key, and click the end of the text. In Word you can also click the start of the text, press F8, and click at the end of the text.
All text	Press Ctrl+A.

Word offers a special command for selecting text with similar formats throughout a document. You can use this command to make wholesale changes to text. Select an example of the text that needs changing, and on the Home tab, click the Select button and choose Select Text with Similar Formatting (you may have to click the Editing button first). Then choose formatting commands to change all instances of the text that you selected.

Moving and copying text

Office offers a number of different ways to move and copy text from place to place. Drum roll, please. . . . Select the text you want to move or copy and then use one of these techniques to move or copy it:

✦ **Dragging and dropping:** Move the mouse over the text and then click and drag the text to a new location. *Drag* means to hold down the mouse button while you move the pointer on-screen. If you want to copy rather than move the text, hold down the Ctrl key while you drag.

✦ **Dragging and dropping with the right mouse button:** Drag the text while holding down the right, not the left, mouse button. After you release the right mouse button, a shortcut menu appears with Move Here and Copy Here options. Choose an option to move or copy the text.

✦ **Using the Clipboard:** Move or copy the text to the Clipboard by clicking the Cut or Copy button, pressing Ctrl+X or Ctrl+C, or right-clicking and choosing Cut or Copy on the shortcut menu. The text is moved or copied to an electronic holding tank called the *Clipboard*. Paste the text by clicking the Paste button, pressing Ctrl+V, or right-clicking and choosing Paste. You can find the Paste, Cut, and Copy buttons on the Home tab.

A look at the Paste options

 Text adopts the formatting of neighboring text when you move or copy it to a new location. Using the Paste options, however, you can decide for yourself what happens to text formatting when you move or copy text from one place to another. To avail yourself of the Paste options:

✔ On the Home tab, open the drop-down list on the Paste button to see the Paste Options submenu.

✔ Right-click to see the Paste options on the shortcut menu.

 (Ctrl) ▾ Click the Paste Options button to open the Paste Options submenu. This button appears after you paste text by clicking the Paste button or pressing Ctrl+V.

Choose a Paste option to determine what happens to text formatting when you move or copy text to a new location:

Keep Source Formatting: The text keeps its original formatting. Choose this option to move or copy text formatting along with text to a different location.

Merge Formatting (Word only): The text adopts the formatting of the text to where it is moved or copied.

Use Destination Theme (Word only): The text adopts the formatting of the theme you chose for your document (if you chose a theme).

 Keep Text Only: The text is stripped of all formatting.

Some people think that the Paste Options button is a bother. If you're one of those people, go to the File tab and choose Options. You see the Options dialog box. Go to the Advanced category and deselect the Show Paste Options Buttons When Content Is Pasted check box.

Taking advantage of the Clipboard task pane

The Windows Clipboard is a piece of work. After you copy or cut text with the Cut or Copy command, the text is placed on the Clipboard. The Clipboard holds the last 24 items that you cut or copied. You can open the Clipboard task pane and view the last 24 items you cut or copied to the Clipboard and cut or copy them anew, as shown in Figure 2-1.

To open the Clipboard task pane, go to the Home tab and click the Clipboard group button (it's to the right of the word *Clipboard*). Icons next to the items tell you where they came from. To copy an item, click it or open its drop-down list and choose Paste. The Clipboard is available to all Office programs; it's especially useful for copying text and graphics from one Office program to another.

Figure 2-1:
The
Clipboard
task pane in
action.

The Options pop-up list at the bottom of the Clipboard task pane offers these options:

✦ **Show Office Clipboard Automatically:** Choose this option if you want the Clipboard task pane to open automatically when you cut or copy two items consecutively or you copy the same item twice.

✦ **Show Office Clipboard When Ctrl+C Pressed Twice:** Choose this option if you want to open the Clipboard task pane by pressing Ctrl+C and Ctrl+C again.

✦ **Collect Without Showing Office Clipboard:** Choose this option to be notified when an item has been cut or copied to the Clipboard by an icon in the system tray and/or a pop-up notice. To be notified, you must have selected either or both of the preceding two options on the Options menu.

✦ **Show Office Clipboard Icon on Taskbar:** Choose this option to be notified when an item has been cut or copied to the Clipboard by an icon in the *system tray,* the part of the Windows taskbar by the clock. (The icon appears after you cut or copy the first item to the Clipboard.) You can double-click the icon to open the Clipboard task pane. After an item is cut or copied to the Clipboard, a tiny page glides across the icon.

✦ **Show Status Near Taskbar When Copying:** Choose this option to be notified when an item has been cut or copied to the Clipboard by a pop-up notice in the lower-right corner of the screen. It tells you how many items have been collected on the Clipboard.

Deleting text

To delete a bunch of text simultaneously, select the text you want to delete and press the Delete key. By the way, you can kill two birds with one stone by selecting text and then starting to type. The letters you type immediately take the place of and delete the text you selected.

You can always click the Undo button (or press Ctrl+Z) if you regret deleting text. This button is located on the Quick Access toolbar.

Changing the Look of Text

What text looks like is determined by its font, the size of the letters, the color of the letters, and whether text effects or font styles such as italic or boldface are in the text. The text's appearance really matters in Word, PowerPoint, and Publisher because files you create in those programs are meant to be read by all and sundry. Even in Excel, Access, and Outlook messages, however, font choices matter because the choices you make determine whether your work is easy to read and understand.

A *font* is a collection of letters, numbers, and symbols in a particular typeface, including all italic and boldface variations of the letters, numbers, and symbols. Fonts have beautiful names and some of them are many centuries old. Most computers come with these fonts: Arial, Tahoma, Times New Roman, and Verdana. By default, Office often applies the Calibri and Cambria fonts to text.

Format Painter: A fast way to change the look of text

When you're in a hurry to change the look of text and reformat paragraphs, consider using the Format Painter. This nifty tool works something like a paintbrush. You drag it over text to copy formats from place to place. Follow these instructions to use the Format Painter:

1. **Click a place with text and paragraph formats that you want to copy elsewhere (or select the text).**

2. **On the Home tab (or the Format Text tab in an Outlook message), click or double-click the Format Painter button (or press Ctrl+Shift+C).**

    You can find the Format Painter button in the Clipboard group. Click the button to copy formats once; double-click to copy formats to more than one location. The pointer changes into a paintbrush.

3. **Drag the pointer across text to which you want to copy the formats.**

   You can go from place to place with the Format Painter.

4. **Click the Format Painter button a second time or press Esc when you're finished with the Format Painter.**

   Press Esc or click the Format Painter button again to cease using the Format Painter if you used it to copy formats to more than one location.

   At the opposite end of the spectrum from the Format Painter button is the Clear Formatting button on the Home tab. You can select text and click this button to strip text of all its formats, whatever they may be.

Font styles include boldface, italic, and underline. By convention, headings are boldface. Italics are used for emphasis and to mark foreign words in text. Office provides a number of text effects. *Text effects,* also known as *text attributes*, include strikethrough and superscript. Use text effects sparingly.

The following pages look at the different ways to change the font, font size, and color of text, as well as how to assign font styles and text effects to text.

Choosing fonts for text

If you aren't happy with the fonts you chose, select the text that needs a font change and change fonts with one of these techniques:

✦ **Mini-toolbar:** Move the pointer over the selected text. You see the mini-toolbar. Move the pointer over this toolbar and choose a font in the Font drop-down list, as shown in Figure 2-2.

✦ **Shortcut menu:** Right-click the selected text and choose a new font on the shortcut menu.

✦ **Font drop-down list:** On the Home tab, open the Font drop-down list and choose a font.

✦ **Font dialog box:** On the Home tab, click the Font group button. You see the Font dialog box. Select a font and click OK.

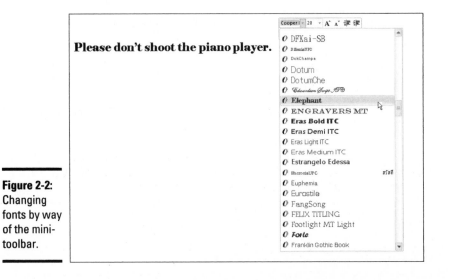

Figure 2-2: Changing fonts by way of the mini-toolbar.

Another way to change fonts is to select a different theme font. In the Page Layout tab (in Word and Excel) or the Design tab (in PowerPoint), open the drop-down list on the Theme Fonts button and choose a font combination.

Installing and removing fonts on your computer

If Windows is installed on your computer, so are many different fonts. The names of these fonts appear on the Font drop-down list, Font dialog box, and mini-toolbar. Do you have enough fonts on your computer? Do you want to remove fonts to keep the Font drop-down list from being overcrowded?

Font files are kept in the `C:\Windows\Fonts` folder on your computer. You can double-click the Fonts icon in the Control Panel to open this folder. Here are instructions for handling fonts:

✔ **Installing new fonts:** Place the font file in the `C:\Windows\Fonts` folder.

✔ **Removing a font:** Move the font file out of the `C:\Windows\Fonts` folder. Store font files you don't want in another folder where you can resuscitate them if need be.

✔ **Examining fonts:** Double-click a font file to examine a font more closely. A window opens, and you see precisely what the font looks like. Do you know why "The quick brown fox jumps over the lazy dog" appears in this window? Because that sentence includes every letter in the alphabet.

Century Gothic (TrueType)

Print   Properties

Font name: Century Gothic
Digitally Signed, TrueType Outlines

abcdefghijklmnopqrstuvwxyz ABCDEFGHIJKLMNOPQRSTUVWXYZ
1234567890.:,;'" (!?) +-*/=

12   The quick brown fox jumps over the lazy dog. 1234567890

18   The quick brown fox jumps over the lazy dog.

24   The quick brown fox jumps over the

36   The quick brown fox jum

Avoid using too many different fonts because a file with too many fonts looks like alphabet soup. The object is to choose a font that helps set the tone. An aggressive sales pitch calls for a strong, bold font; a technical presentation calls for a font that is clean and unobtrusive. Make sure that the fonts you select help communicate your message.

Changing the font size of text

Font size is measured in *points;* a point is $\frac{1}{72}$ of an inch. The golden rule of font sizes goes something like this: the larger the font size, the more important the text. This is why headings are larger than footnotes. Select your text and use one of these techniques to change the font size of the letters:

✦ **Mini-toolbar:** Move the pointer over the text, and when you see the mini-toolbar, move the pointer over the toolbar and choose a font size on the Font Size drop-down list (refer to Figure 2-2).

✦ **Shortcut menu:** Right-click the text and choose a new font size on the shortcut menu.

✦ **Font Size drop-down list:** On the Home tab, open the Font Size drop-down list and choose a font. You can live-preview font sizes this way.

✦ **Font dialog box:** On the Home tab, click the Font group button, and in the Font dialog box, choose a font size and click OK.

✦ **Increase Font Size and Decrease Font Size buttons:** Click these buttons (or press Ctrl+] or Ctrl+[) to increase or decrease the point size by the next interval on the Font Size drop-down list. You can find the Increase Font Size and Decrease Font Size buttons on the Home tab and the mini-toolbar. Watch the Font Size list or your text and note how the text changes size. This is an excellent technique when you want to "eyeball it" and you don't care to fool with the Font Size drop-down list or Font dialog box.

Click the Increase Font Size and Decrease Font Size buttons when you're dealing with fonts of different sizes and you want to proportionally change the size of all the letters. Drag the pointer over the text to select it before clicking one of the buttons.

If the font size you want isn't on the Font Size drop-down list, enter the size. For example, to change the font size to 13.5 points, type **13.5** in the Font Size box and press Enter.

Applying font styles to text

There are four — count 'em, four — font styles: regular, bold, italic, and underline:

✦ **Regular**: This style is just Office's way of denoting an absence of any font style.

✦ **Italic**: Italics are used for emphasis, when introducing a new term, and to mark foreign words such as *violà, gung hay fat choy,* and *Qué magnifico!* You can also italicize titles to make them a little more elegant.

✦ **Bold:** Bold text calls attention to itself.

✦ **Underline:** Underlined text also calls attention to itself, but use underlining sparingly. Later in this chapter, "Underlining text" looks at all the ways to underline text.

Select text and use one of these techniques to apply a font style to it:

✦ **Home tab:** Click the Bold, Italic, or Underline button.

✦ **Keyboard:** Press Ctrl+B to boldface text, Ctrl+I to italicize it, or Ctrl+U to underline it.

✦ **Mini-toolbar:** The mini-toolbar offers the Bold, Italic, and Underline button.

✦ **Font dialog box:** Select a Font Style option in the Font dialog box. To open this dialog box, visit the Home tab and click the Font group button.

To remove a font style, click the Bold, Italic, or Underline button a second time. You can also select text and then click the Clear Formatting button on the Home tab (in Word, PowerPoint, and Publisher).

Applying text effects to text

Text effects have various uses, some utilitarian and some strictly for yucks. Be careful with text effects. Use them sparingly and to good purpose. To apply a text effect, start on the Home tab (or the Format Text tab in Outlook messages) and do one of the following:

✦ Click a text effect button on the Home tab.

✦ Click the Font group button and choose a text effect in the bottom half of the Font dialog box, as shown in Figure 2-3.

Figure 2-3: Text effects in the Font dialog box (Word).

Here's a rundown of the different text effects (not all these effects are available in PowerPoint, Excel, Publisher, and Outlook):

 ✦ **Strikethrough and double strikethrough:** By convention, *strikethrough* is used to show where passages are struck from a contract or other important document. Double strikethrough, for all I know, is used to shows where passages are struck out forcefully. Use these text effects to demonstrate ideas that you reject.

 ✦ **Subscript:** A *subscripted* letter is lowered in the text. In this chemical formula, the 2 is lowered to show that two atoms of hydrogen are needed along with one atom of oxygen to form a molecule of water: H_2O. (Press Ctrl+=.)

 ✦ **Superscript:** A *superscripted* letter or number is one that is raised in the text. Superscript is used in mathematical and scientific formulas, in ordinal numbers (1st, 2nd, 3rd), and to mark footnotes. In the theory of relativity, the 2 is superscripted: $E = mc^2$. (Press Ctrl+Shift+plus sign.)

 ✦ **Small Caps:** A *small cap* is a small capital letter. You can find many creative uses for small caps. An all-small-cap title looks elegant. Be sure to type lowercase letters in order to create small caps. Type an uppercase letter, and Office refuses to turn it into a small cap. Not all fonts can produce small capital letters.

 ✦ **All Caps:** The All Caps text effect merely capitalizes all letters. Use it in styles to make sure that you enter text in all capital letters.

 ✦ **Equalize Character Height (PowerPoint only):** This effect makes all characters the same height and stretches the characters in text. You can use it to produce interesting effects in text box announcements.

Underlining text

You can choose from 15 ways to underline text, with styles ranging from Words Only to Wavy Line, and you can select a color for the underline in Word, PowerPoint, and Outlook. If you decide to underline titles, do it consistently. To underline text, select the text that you want to underline, go to the Home tab, and pick your poison:

 ✦ On the Home tab, click the Underline button. A single line runs under all the words you selected. In Word, you can open the drop-down list on the Underline button and choose from several ways to underline text.

 ✦ Click the Font group button to open the Font dialog box (refer to Figure 2-3) and then choose an underline style from the drop-down list. You can also choose an underline color from the Underline Color drop-down list (in Word, PowerPoint, and Outlook). The color you select applies to the underline, not to the words being underlined.

To remove an underline from text, select the text and then click the Underline button on the Home tab.

Changing the color of text

Before you change the color of text, peer at your computer screen and examine the background theme or color you chose. Unless the color of the text is different from the theme or color, you can't read the text. Besides choosing a color that contributes to the overall tone, choose a color that is easy to read.

Select the text that needs touching up and use one of these techniques to change its color:

✦ On the mini-toolbar, open the drop-down list on the Font Color button and choose a color, as shown in Figure 2-4.

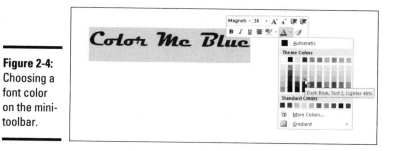

Figure 2-4:
Choosing a
font color
on the mini-
toolbar.

✦ Right-click, open the drop-down list on the Font Color button, and choose a color on the shortcut menu.

✦ On the Home tab, open the drop-down list on the Font Color button and choose a color.

✦ On the Home tab, click the Font group button to open the Font dialog box, open the Font Color drop-down list, and choose a color.

The Font Color drop-down list offers theme colors and standard colors. You are well advised to choose a theme color. These colors are deemed *theme colors* because they jive with the theme you choose for your file.

Quick Ways to Handle Case, or Capitalization

Case refers to how letters are capitalized in words and sentences. Table 2-1 explains the different cases, and Figure 2-5 demonstrates why paying attention to case matters. In the figure, the PowerPoint slide titles are presented using different cases, and the titles are inconsistent with one another. In one slide, only the first letter in the title is capitalized (sentence case); in another slide, the first letter in each word is capitalized (capitalize each word); in another, none of the letters is capitalized (lowercase); and in another, all the letters are capitalized (uppercase). In your titles and headings, decide on a capitalization scheme and stick with it for consistency's sake.

Table 2-1	Cases for Headings and Titles	
Case	*Description*	*Example Title*
Sentence case	The first letter in the first word is capitalized; all other words are lowercase unless they are proper names.	Man bites dog in January
Lowercase	All letters are lowercase unless they are proper names.	man bites dog in January
Uppercase	All letters are uppercase no matter what.	MAN BITES DOG IN JANUARY
Capitalize each word	The first letter in each word is capitalized.	Man Bites Dog In January

Figure 2-5: Capitalization schemes (clockwise from upper left): sentence case; capitalize each word; uppercase; lowercase.

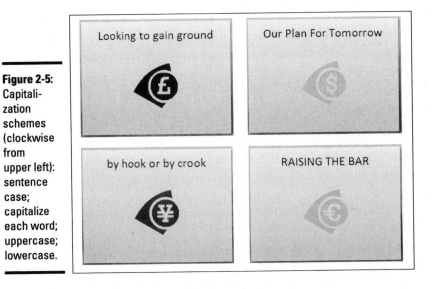

To change case in Word and PowerPoint, all you have to do is select the text, go to the Home tab, click the Change Case button, and choose an option on the drop-down list:

+ **Sentence case**: Renders the letters in sentence case.

+ **lowercase**: Makes all the letters lowercase.

+ **UPPERCASE**: Renders all the letters as capital letters.

✦ **Capitalize Each Word:** Capitalizes the first letter in each word. If you choose this option for a title or heading, go into the title and lowercase the first letter of articles *(the, a, an)*, coordinate conjunctions *(and, or, for, nor)*, and prepositions unless they're the first or last word in the title.

✦ **tOGGLE cASE:** Choose this option if you accidentally enter letters with the Caps Lock key pressed.

You can also change case by pressing Shift+F3. Pressing this key combination in Word and PowerPoint changes characters to uppercase, lowercase, each word capitalized, and back to uppercase again.

Entering Symbols and Foreign Characters

Don't panic if you need to enter an umlaut, grave accent, or cedilla because you can do it by way of the Symbol dialog box, as shown in Figure 2-6. You can enter just about any symbol and foreign character by way of this dialog box. Click where you want to enter a symbol or foreign character and follow these steps to enter it:

Figure 2-6:
To enter
a symbol
or foreign
character,
select it
and click
the Insert
button.

1. **On the Insert tab, click the Symbol button. (You may have to click the Symbols button first, depending on the size of your screen.)**

In Word, Outlook, and Publisher, click More Symbols after you click the Symbol button if no symbol on the drop-down list does the job for you. You see the Symbol dialog box (refer to Figure 2-6).

2. **If you're looking to insert a symbol, not a foreign character, choose Webdings or Wingdings 1, 2, or 3 in the Font drop-down list.**

   Webdings and the Wingdings fonts offer all kinds of weird and wacky symbols.

3. **Select a symbol or foreign character.**

   You may have to scroll to find the one you want.

4. **Click the Insert button to enter the symbol and then click Close to close the dialog box.**

   The Symbol dialog box lists the last several symbols or foreign characters you entered under Recently Used Symbols. See whether the symbol you need is listed there. It spares you the trouble of rummaging in the Symbol dialog box. In Word, Outlook, and Publisher, you see the last several symbols or foreign characters you entered on a drop-down list after you click the Symbol button.

Finding and Replacing Text

Use the Find command to locate a name or text passage. Use its twin, the powerful Replace command, to find and replace a name or text passage throughout a file. For an idea of how useful the Replace command is, imagine that the company you work for just changed its name and the old company name is in many different places. By using the Replace command, you can replace the old company name with the new name throughout a long file in a matter of seconds.

The basics: Finding stray words and phrases

To locate stray words, names, text passages, and formats, follow these basic steps:

1. **Press Ctrl+F or go to the Home tab and click the Find button. (In Excel, click the Find & Select button and choose Find on the drop-down list.)**

   A dialog box or pane appears so that you can enter search criteria. Figure 2-7 shows the Find dialog box in PowerPoint and the Find and Replace dialog box in Excel.

Figure 2-7: Conducting a Find operation in PowerPoint (left) and Excel (right).

2. **Enter the word or phrase in the Find What or Search Document text box.**

   After you enter the word or phrase in Word, the Navigation pane lists each instance of the term you're looking for and the term is highlighted in your document wherever it is found, as shown in Figure 2-8. You can click an instance of the search term in the Navigation pane to scroll to a location in your document where the search term is located.

   In Excel, PowerPoint, and Publisher, the Find What drop-down list shows words and phrases you looked for recently. You can make a selection from that list rather than enter a search term.

Enter a word or phrase

Choose a search option   Choose search criteria

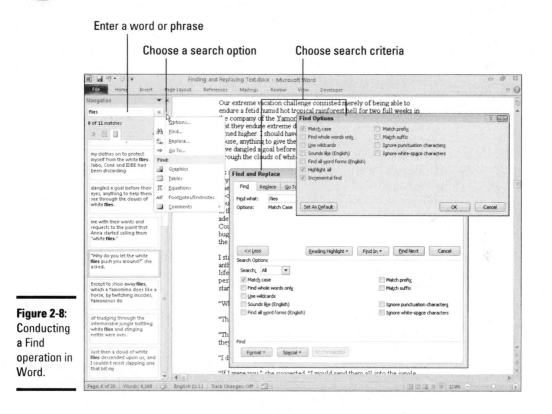

Figure 2-8:
Conducting a Find operation in Word.

3. **If you want, choose additional options for narrowing your search.**

   To access these options in Excel, click the Options button (refer to Figure 2-7); in Word, click the Find Options button — it's located to the right of the Search Document text box in the Navigation pane — and make a choice on the drop-down list (refer to Figure 2-8).

Later in this chapter, "Narrowing your search" explains how to make searches more efficient.

4. **Click the Find Next button if you're looking for a simple word or phrase, or the Find All button to locate all instances of a word or phrase in your file.**

   In PowerPoint, the Find All button is available only if you start your search in Slide Sorter view.

5. **To find the next instance of the thing you're looking for, click Find Next again.**

   In Word, either click an instance of the search word in the Navigation pane or click the Previous Find/Go To or Next Find/Go To button at the bottom of the scroll bar (or press Ctrl+Page Up or Ctrl+Page Down) to go to the previous or next instance of the thing you're looking for.

Narrowing your search

All the Office programs offer techniques for narrowing a search and making it more efficient. You can choose criteria for narrowing your search as well as search for text that has been formatted a certain way.

To narrow your search in Word, click the Find Options button, choose Options or Find on the drop-down list, and make choices in the Find Options or Find and Replace dialog box (refer to Figure 2-8). In Excel, click the Options button in the Find and Replace dialog box (refer to Figure 2-7).

Match Case and Find Whole Words Only

These options are your first line of defense in narrowing a search:

✦ **Match Case:** Searches for words with upper- and lowercase letters that exactly match those in the Find What or Search Document text box. When the Match Case option is selected, a search for *bow* finds *bow,* but not *Bow* or *BOW.*

✦ **Find Whole Words Only (not available in Excel):** Normally, a search for *bow* yields *elbow, bowler, bow-wow,* and all other words with the letters *b-o-w* (in that order). Click this option and you get only *bow.*

Searching for formats in Word and Excel

In Word and Excel, you can search for formats or text that was formatted a certain way with these techniques:

✦ **In Word:** Click the Format button in the Find and Replace dialog box (refer to Figure 2-8), and on the drop-down list, choose a Format type — Font, Paragraph, Tabs, Language, Frame, Style, or Highlight. A Find dialog box opens so that you can describe the format you're looking for. Select options in the dialog box to describe the format and click OK.

✦ **In Excel:** Click the Format button and choose a format in the Find Format dialog box. You can also open the drop-down list on the Format button, select Choose Format from Cell on the drop-down list, and click a cell to describe the format you're looking for.

After you finish conducting your search for formatted text, don't forget to click the No Formatting button (in Word) or open the Format drop-down list and choose Clear Find Format (in Excel). You can't conduct a normal search again unless you turn format searching off.

Taking advantage of search criteria in Word

Above and beyond the other Office programs, Word offers a bunch of ways to narrow a search. To take advantage of the search options in Word, click the Find Options button (it's located to the right of the Search Document box in the Navigation pane) and choose Options or Advanced Find on the drop-down list:

✦ Choose Options to open the Find Options dialog box and describe search criteria. With this technique, search terms when they are found are highlighted in the Navigation pane (provided that you select the Highlight All check box).

✦ Choose Advanced Find to open the Find tab of the Find and Replace dialog box and describe search criteria. With this technique, you click the Find Next button in the dialog box and locate search terms one at a time.

Word search options

Word offers these check box options for narrowing a search.

✦ **Use Wildcards:** Click here if you intend to use wildcards in searches. (See "Using wildcard operators to refine searches," later in this chapter.)

✦ **Sounds Like:** Looks for words that sound like the one in the Find What box. A search for *bow* with this option selected finds *beau*, for example. However, it doesn't find *bough*. This command isn't very reliable.

✦ **Find All Word Forms:** Takes into account verb conjugations and plurals. With this option clicked, you get *bows, bowing,* and *bowed* as well as *bow.*

✦ **Match Prefix:** A *prefix* is a syllable appearing before the root or stem of a word to alter its meaning. For example, *co, mid, non,* and *un* are prefixes in the words *coauthor, midtown, nonviolent,* and *unselfish.* Choose this option and enter a prefix in the Find What text box to locate words that begin with the prefix you enter.

✦ **Match Suffix:** A *suffix* is a syllable or two appearing at the end of a word that alters its meaning. For example, *age, ish,* and *ness* are suffixes in the words *spillage, smallish,* and *darkness.* Choose this option and enter a suffix in the Find What text box to find words that end with the same suffix.

✦ **Ignore Punctuation Characters:** Search in text for word phrases without regard for commas, periods, and other punctuation marks. For example, a search for *Yuma Arizona* finds *Yuma, Arizona* (with a comma) in the text.

✦ **Ignore White-Space Characters:** Search in text for word phrases without regard for white space caused by multiple blank spaces or tab entries.

Using wildcard operators to refine searches

Word permits you to use wildcard operators in searches. A *wildcard operator* is a character that represents characters in a search expression. Wildcards aren't for everybody. Using them requires a certain amount of expertise, but after you know how to use them, wildcards can be invaluable in searches and macros. Table 2-2 explains the wildcard operators you can use in searches. Click the Use Wildcards check box if you want to search using wildcards.

Table 2-2	Wildcards for Searches	
Operator	*What It Finds*	*Example*
?	Any single character	**b?t** finds *bat*, *bet*, *bit*, and *but*.
*	Zero or more characters	**t*o** finds *to*, *two*, and *tattoo*.
[*xyz*]	A specific character, *x*, *y*, or *z*	**t[aeiou]pper** finds *tapper*, *tipper*, and *topper*.
[*x-z*]	A range of characters, *x* through *z*	**[1-4]000** finds *1000*, *2000*, *3000*, and *4000*, but not *5000*.
[!*xy*]	Not the specific character or characters, *xy*	**p[!io]t** finds *pat* and *pet*, but not *pit* or *pot*.
<	Characters at the beginning of words	**<info** finds *information*, *infomaniac*, and *infomercial*.
>	Characters at the end of words	**ese>** finds *these*, *journalese*, and *legalese*.
@@	One or more instances of the previous character	**sho@@t** finds *shot* and *shoot*.
{*n*}	Exactly *n* instances of the previous character	**sho{2}t** finds *shoot* but not *shot*.
{*n,*}	At least *n* instances of the previous character	**^p{3,}** finds three or more paragraph breaks in a row, but not a single paragraph break or two paragraph breaks in a row.
{*n,m*}	From *n* to *m* instances of the previous character	**10{2,4}** finds *100*, *1000*, and *10000*, but not *10* or *100000*.

You can't conduct a whole-word-only search with a wildcard. For example, a search for **f*s** not only finds *fads* and *fits* but also all text strings that begin with *f* and end with *s,* such as *for the birds.* Wildcard searches can yield many, many results and are sometimes useless.

To search for an asterisk (*), question mark (?), or other character that serves as a wildcard search operator, place a backslash (\) before it in the text box.

Searching for special characters in Word

Table 2-3 describes the *special characters* you can look for in Word documents. To look for the special characters listed in the table, enter the character directly in the text box or click the Special button in the Find and Replace dialog box, and then choose a special character from the pop-up list. Be sure to enter lowercase letters. For example, you must enter **^n**, not **^N**, to look for a column break. *Note:* A caret (^) precedes special characters.

Table 2-3	Special Characters for Searches
To Find/Replace	*Enter*
Manual Formats That Users Insert	
Column break	^n
Field[1]	^d
Manual line break (↵)	^l
Manual page break	^m
No-width non break	^z
No-width optional break	^x
Paragraph break (¶)	^p
Section break[1]	^b
Section character	^%
Tab space (→)	^t
Punctuation Marks	
1/4 em space	^q
Caret (^)	^^
Ellipsis	^i
Em dash (—)	^+
En dash (–)	^=
Full-width ellipses	^j
Nonbreaking hyphen	^~
Optional hyphen	^-

(continued)

Table 2-3 *(continued)*

To Find/Replace	Enter
White space (one or more blank spaces)[1]	^w
Characters and Symbols	
Foreign character	You can type foreign characters in the Find What and Replace With text boxes.
ANSI and ASCII characters and symbols	^*nnnn*, where *nnnn* is the four-digit code
Any character[1]	^?
Any digit[1]	^#
Any letter[1]	^$
Clipboard contents[2]	^c
Contents of the Find What box[2]	^&
Elements of Reports and Scholarly Papers	
Endnote mark[1]	^e
Footnote mark[1]	^f
Graphic[1]	^g

[1]*For use in find operations only*
[2]*For use in replace operations only*

Before searching for special characters in Word, go to the Home tab and click the Show/Hide¶ button. That way, you see special characters — also known as *hidden format symbols* — on-screen when Word finds them.

Creative people find many uses for special characters in searches. The easiest way to find section breaks, column breaks, and manual line breaks in a document is to enter **^b**, **^n**, or **^l**, respectively, and start searching. By combining special characters with text, you can make find-and-replace operations more productive. For example, to replace all double hyphens (–) in a document with em dashes (—), enter – in the Find What text box and **^m** in the Replace With text box. This kind of find-and-replace operation is especially useful for cleaning documents that were created in another program and then imported into Word.

Conducting a find-and-replace operation

Conducting a find-and-replace operation is the spitting image of conducting a find operation. Figure 2-9 shows (in PowerPoint) the Replace dialog box, the place where you declare what you want to find and what to replace it with. Do the options and buttons in the dialog box look familiar? They do if you read the previous handful of pages about searching because the Replace options are the same as the Find options.

Figure 2-9:
Using the
powerful
Replace
command in
PowerPoint.

Replace		
Find what:		Find Next
catsup	▼	
Replace with:		Close
ketchup	▼	
☐ Match case		Replace
☐ Find whole words only		Replace All

The key to a successful find-and-replace operation is making sure that you *find* exactly what you want to find and replace. One way to make sure that you find the right text is to start by running a Find operation. If the program finds precisely the text you want, you're in business. Click the Replace tab or Replace button in the Find dialog box and then enter the replacement text.

To locate and replace words, names, or text passages with the Find command, follow these steps:

1. **Press Ctrl+H or go to the Home tab and click the Replace button (in Excel, click the Find & Select button and choose Replace on the drop-down list).**

    The Replace (or Find and Replace) dialog box appears (refer to Figure 2-9).

2. **Describe the text that needs replacing.**

    Earlier in this chapter, "The basics: Finding stray words and phrases" explains how to construct a search. Try to narrow your search so that you find only the text you are looking for.

3. **Click the Find Next button.**

    Did your program find what you're looking for? If it didn't, describe the search again.

4. **Enter the replacement text in the Replace With text box.**

    You can select replacement text from the drop-down list.

5. **Either replace everything simultaneously or do it one at a time.**

    Click one of these buttons:

    -   Click Replace All to make all replacements in an instant.
    -   Click Find Next and then either click Replace to make the replacement or Find Next to bypass it.

Click the Replace All button only if you are very, very confident that the thing your program found is the thing you want to replace.

Be sure to examine your file after you conduct a find-and-replace operation. You never know what the powerful Replace command will do. If the command makes a hash of your file, click the Undo button.

Creating Hyperlinks

A *hyperlink* is an electronic shortcut from one place to another. If you've spent any time on the Internet, you know what a hyperlink is. Clicking hyperlinks on the Internet takes you to different Web pages or different places on the same Web page. In the Office programs, you can use hyperlinks to connect readers to your favorite Web pages or to a different page, slide, or file. You can fashion a link out of a word or phrase as well as any object — a clip-art image, text box, shape, or picture.

These pages explain how to insert a hyperlink to another place in your file as well as create links to Web pages. You also discover how to enter an e-mail hyperlink that makes it easy for others to e-mail you. By the way, the Office programs create a hyperlink for you automatically when you type a word that begins with *www* and ends with *.com* or *.net*. The programs create an automatic e-mail hyperlink when you enter letters that include the symbol (@) and end in *.com* or *.net*.

Linking a hyperlink to a Web page

It could well be that a Web page on the Internet has all the information your readers need. In that case, you can link to the Web page so that viewers can visit it in the course of viewing your file. When a viewer clicks the link, a Web browser opens and the Web page appears.

Follow these steps to hyperlink your file to a Web page on the Internet:

1. **Select the text or object that will form the hyperlink.**

   For example, select a line of text or phrase if you want viewers to be able to click it to go to a Web page.

Hyperlink

2. **On the Insert tab, click the Hyperlink button (or press Ctrl+K).**

   Depending on the size of your screen, you may have to click the Links button before you can get to the Hyperlink button. You see the Insert Hyperlink dialog box, as shown in Figure 2-10. You can also open this dialog box by right-clicking an object or text and choosing Hyperlink on the shortcut menu.

3. **Under Link To, select Existing File or Web Page.**

4. **In the Address text box, enter the address of the Web page to which you want to link, as shown in Figure 2-10.**

Choose a Web page   Click to go on the Internet to a Web page

Figure 2-10:
Enter the
Web page
target in the
Address
text box to
create a
hyperlink to
a Web page.

From easiest to hardest, here are techniques for entering Web page addresses:

- *Click the Browse the Web button:* Your Web browser opens after you click this button. Go to the Web page you want to link to and return to your program. The Web page's address appears in the Address text box. (Figure 2-10 shows where the Browse the Web button is.)

- *Click Browsed Pages:* The dialog box lists Web pages you recently visited after you click this button, as shown in Figure 2-10. Choose a Web page.

- *Type (or copy) a Web page address into the Address text box:* Enter the address of the Web page. You can right-click the text box and choose Paste to copy a Web page address into the text box.

5. **Click the ScreenTip button, enter a ScreenTip in the Set Hyperlink ScreenTip dialog box, and click OK.**

Viewers can read the ScreenTip you enter when they move their pointers over the hyperlink.

6. **Click OK in the Insert Hyperlink dialog box.**

I would test the hyperlink if I were you to make sure that it takes viewers to the right Web page. To test a hyperlink, Ctrl+click it or right-click it and choose Open Hyperlink on the shortcut menu.

Creating a hyperlink to another place in your file

Follow these steps to create a hyperlink to another place in your file:

1. **Select the text or object that will form the hyperlink.**

2. **On the Insert tab, click the Hyperlink button (or press Ctrl+K).**

You see the Insert Hyperlink dialog box. (Depending on the size of your screen, you may have to click the Links button before you see the Hyperlink button.) Another way to open this dialog box is to right-click and choose Hyperlink in the shortcut menu.

3. **Under Link To, select Place in This Document.**

What you see in the dialog box depends on which program you're working in:

- *Word:* You see bookmarks and headings to which you've assigned a heading style.

- *PowerPoint:* You see a list of slides in your presentation, as well as links to the first, last, next, and previous slide, as shown in Figure 2-11.

- *Excel:* You see boxes for entering cell references and defined cell names.

- *Publisher:* You see page number and page titles, as well as links to the first, last, next, and previous page.

Select Place in This Document

Select a target   Click to enter a ScreenTip

Figure 2-11:
You can also create a hyperlink to a different place in a file.

4. **Select the target of the hyperlink.**

5. **Click the ScreenTip button.**

   You see the Set Hyperlink ScreenTip dialog box, as shown in Figure 2-11.

6. **Enter a ScreenTip and click OK.**

   When viewers move their pointers over the link, they see the words you enter. Enter a description of where the hyperlink takes you.

7. **Click OK in the Insert Hyperlink dialog box.**

   To test your hyperlink, move the pointer over it. You should see the ScreenTip description you wrote. Ctrl+click the link to see if it takes you to the right place.

Creating an e-mail hyperlink

An *e-mail hyperlink* is one that opens an e-mail program. These links are sometimes found on Web pages so that anyone visiting a Web page can conveniently send an e-mail message to the person who manages the Web page. When you click an e-mail hyperlink, your default e-mail program opens. And if the person who set up the link was thorough about it, the e-mail message is already addressed and given a subject line.

Include an e-mail hyperlink in a file if you're distributing the file to others and you would like them to be able to comment on your work and send the comments to you.

Follow these steps to put an e-mail hyperlink in a file:

1. **Select the words or object that will constitute the link.**

2. **On the Insert tab, click the Hyperlink button (or press Ctrl+K).**

   The Insert Hyperlink dialog box appears.

3. **Under Link To, click E-Mail Address.**

   Text boxes appear for entering an e-mail address and a subject message.

4. **Enter your e-mail address and a subject for the messages that others will send you.**

   Office inserts the word *mailto:* before your e-mail address as you enter it.

5. **Click OK.**

   Test the link by Ctrl+clicking it. Your default e-mail program opens. The e-mail message is already addressed and given a subject.

Repairing and removing hyperlinks

From time to time, check the hyperlinks in your file to make sure that they still work. Clicking a hyperlink and having nothing happen is disappointing. Hyperlinks get broken when Web pages and parts of files are deleted.

To repair or remove a hyperlink, right-click the link and choose Edit Hyperlink on the shortcut menu (or click in the link and then click the Hyperlink button on the Insert tab). You see the Edit Hyperlink dialog box. This dialog box looks and works just like the Insert Hyperlink dialog box.

+ **Repairing a link**: Select a target in your file or a Web page and click OK.

+ **Removing a link:** Click the Remove Link button. You can also remove a hyperlink by right-clicking the link and choosing Remove Hyperlink on the shortcut menu.

Chapter 3: Speed Techniques Worth Knowing About

In This Chapter

✔ Undoing mistakes and repeating actions

✔ Zooming to get a better view of your work

✔ Working with two different files at the same time

✔ Instructing Office to correct typos automatically

✔ Entering hard-to-type text with the AutoCorrect command

This brief chapter takes you on a whirlwind tour of shortcut commands that can save you time and effort no matter which Office program you're working in. This chapter is devoted to people who want to get it done quickly and get away from their computers. It explains the Undo and Repeat commands, zooming in and out, and opening more than one window on the same file. You also discover how to display windows in different ways, correct your typos automatically, and enter hard-to-type terminology with a simple flick of the wrist.

Undoing and Repeating Commands

If I were to choose two commands for the Hall of Fame, they would be the Undo command and the Repeat command. One allows you to reverse actions you regret doing, and the other repeats a previous action without you having to choose the same commands all over again. Undo and Repeat are explained forthwith.

Undoing a mistake

Fortunately for you, all is not lost if you make a big blunder because Office has a marvelous little tool called the Undo command. This command "remembers" your previous editorial and formatting changes. As long as you catch your error in time, you can undo your mistake.

 Click the Undo button on the Quick Access toolbar (or press Ctrl+Z) to undo your most recent change. If you made your error and went on to do something else before you caught it, open the drop-down list on the Undo button.

It lists your previous actions, as shown in Figure 3-1. Click the action you want to undo, or if it isn't on the list, scroll until you find the error and then click it.

Figure 3-1: Fixing a mistake with the Undo drop-down list.

Remember, however, that choosing an action far down the Undo list also reverses the actions before it on the list. For example, if you undo the 19th action on the list, you also undo the 18 more recent actions above it.

Repeating an action — and quicker this time

The Quick Access toolbar offers a button called Repeat that you can click to repeat your last action. This button can be a mighty, mighty timesaver. For example, if you just changed fonts in one heading and you want to change another heading in the same way, select the heading and click the Repeat button (or press F4 or Ctrl+Y). Move the pointer over the Repeat button to see what clicking it does.

You can find many creative uses for the Repeat command if you use your imagination. For example, If you had to type "I will not talk in class" a hundred times as a punishment for talking in class, you could make excellent use of the Repeat command to fulfill your punishment. All you would have to do is write the sentence once and then click the Repeat button 99 times.

After you click the Undo button, the Repeat button changes names and becomes the Redo button. Click the Redo button to "redo" the command you "undid." In other words, if you regret clicking the Undo button, you can turn back the clock by clicking Redo.

Zooming In, Zooming Out

Eyes weren't meant to stare at the computer screen all day, which makes the Zoom controls all the more valuable. You can find these controls in the lower-right corner of the window and on the View tab, as shown in Figure 3-2. Use them freely and often to enlarge or shrink what is on the screen and preserve your eyes for important things, such as gazing at the sunset.

Figure 3-2:
The Zoom
controls.

Meet the Zoom controls:

✦ **Zoom dialog box:** Click the Zoom button on the View tab or the Zoom box (the % listing) to display the Zoom dialog box, as shown in Figure 3-2. From there, you can select an option button or enter a Percent measurement.

✦ **Zoom button:** Click the Zoom In or Zoom Out button on the Zoom slider to zoom in or out in 10-percent increments.

✦ **Zoom slider:** Drag the *Zoom slider* left to shrink or right to enlarge what is on your screen.

✦ **Mouse wheel:** If your mouse has a wheel, you can hold down the Ctrl key and spin the wheel to quickly zoom in or out.

Each Office program offers its own special Zoom commands in the Zoom group on the View tab. In Word, for example, you can display one page or many pages; in Excel, you can click the Zoom to Selection button and enlarge a handful of cells. Make friends with the Zoom commands. They never let you down.

Viewing a File through More Than One Window

By way of the commands in the Window group in the View tab, you can be two places simultaneously, at least where Office is concerned. You can work on two files at once. You can place files side by side on the screen and do a number of other things to make your work a little easier.

Word, Excel, and PowerPoint offer these buttons in the Window group:

✦ **New Window:** Opens another window on your file so you can be two places at once in the same file. To go back and forth between windows, click a taskbar button or click the Switch Windows button and choose a window name on the drop-down list. Click a window's Close button when you're finished looking at it.

✦ **Arrange All:** Arranges open windows side by side on-screen.

✦ **Switch Windows:** Opens a drop-down list with open windows so you can travel between windows.

You can also take advantage of these Window buttons in Word and Excel to compare files:

✦ **View Side by Side**: Displays files side by side so you can compare and contrast them.

✦ **Synchronous Scrolling:** Permits you to scroll two files at the same rate so you can proofread one against the other. To use this command, start by clicking the View Side by Side button. After you click the Synchronous Scrolling button, click the Reset Window Position button so both files are displayed at the same size on-screen.

✦ **Reset Window Position:** Makes files being shown side by side the same size on-screen to make them easier to compare.

Correcting Typos on the Fly

The unseen hand of Office 2010 corrects some typos and misspellings automatically. For example, try typing **accomodate** with one *m* — Office corrects the misspelling and inserts the second *m* for you. Try typing

perminent with an *i* instead of an *a* — the invisible hand of Office corrects the misspelling, and you get *permanent.* While you're at it, type a colon and a close parenthesis **:)** — you get a smiley face.

As good as the AutoCorrect feature is, you can make it even better. You can also add the typos and misspellings you often make to the list of words that are corrected automatically.

Opening the AutoCorrect dialog box

Office corrects common spelling errors and turns punctuation mark combinations into symbols as part of its AutoCorrect feature. To see which typos are corrected and which punctuation marks are turned into symbols, open the AutoCorrect dialog box by following these steps:

File

1. **On the File tab, choose Options.**

   You see the Options dialog box.

2. **Go to the Proofing category.**

3. **Click the AutoCorrect Options button.**

   The AutoCorrect dialog box opens.

4. **Click the AutoCorrect tab.**

   As shown in Figure 3-3, the AutoCorrect tab lists words that are corrected automatically. Scroll down the Replace list and have a look around. Go ahead. Make yourself at home.

Enter a typo and its replacement

Figure 3-3:
As you type, words in the Replace column are replaced automatically with words in the With column.

Telling Office which typos and misspellings to correct

No doubt you make the same typing errors and spelling errors time and time again. To keep from making these errors, you can tell Office to correct them for you automatically. You do that by entering the misspelling and its corrected spelling in the AutoCorrect dialog box (see Figure 3-3):

✦ Enter the misspelling in the Replace text box and its correct spelling in the With text box.

✦ Click the AutoCorrect button in the Spelling dialog box when you spell-check a file. This action automatically places the misspelling and its correction in the AutoCorrect dialog box so that the correction is made in the future.

You can also remove misspellings and typos from the list of words that are corrected automatically. To remove a word from the list of corrected words, select it in the AutoCorrect dialog box and click the Delete button.

Preventing capitalization errors with AutoCorrect

Near the top of the AutoCorrect dialog box (refer to Figure 3-3) are five check boxes whose job is to prevent capitalization errors. These options do their jobs very well, sometimes to a fault:

✦ **Correct TWo INitial Capitals:** Prevents two capital letters from appearing in a row at the start of a word with more than two letters. Only the first letter is capitalized. This option is for people who can't lift their little fingers from the Shift key fast enough after typing the first capital letter at the start of a word.

✦ **Capitalize first letter of sentences:** Makes sure that the first letter in a sentence is capitalized.

✦ **Capitalize first letter of table cells:** Makes sure that the first letter you enter in a table cell is a capital letter. A table cell holds one data item; it's the place in a table where a column and row intersect.

✦ **Capitalize names of days:** Makes sure that the names of the days of the week are capitalized.

✦ **Correct accidental usage of cAPS LOCK key:** Changes capital letters to lowercase letters if you press the Shift key to start a sentence while Caps Lock is on. The idea here is that if you press down the Shift key while Caps Lock is on, you don't know that Caps Lock is on because you don't need to hold down the Shift key to enter capital letters. AutoCorrect turns the first letter into a capital letter and the following letters into lowercase letters and then turns Caps Lock off.

Entering Text Quickly with the AutoCorrect Command

The preceding part of this chapter explains how you can use the AutoCorrect command to help correct typing errors, but with a little cunning you can also use it to quickly enter hard-to-type jargon, scientific names, and the like. To open the AutoCorrect dialog box, go to the File tab, choose Options, go to the Proofing category in the Options dialog box, and then click the AutoCorrect Options button. Select the AutoCorrect tab in the AutoCorrect dialog box, as shown in Figure 3-4.

Enter text to trigger AutoCorrect

What's entered when you type the text

Figure 3-4:
With a little cunning, you can use AutoCorrect to enter hard-to-type text.

In the Replace column in the AutoCorrect tab are hundreds of common typing errors and codes that Office corrects automatically. The program corrects the errors by entering text in the With column whenever you mistakenly type the letters in the Replace column. However, you can also use this dialog box for a secondary purpose to quickly enter text.

To make AutoCorrect work as a means of entering text, you tell Office to enter the text whenever you type three or four specific characters. In Figure 3-4, for example, Office is instructed to insert the words *Cordyceps sinensis* (a mushroom genus) whenever I enter the characters **/cs** (and press the spacebar). Follow these steps to use AutoCorrect to enter text:

1. **Open the AutoCorrect tab of the AutoCorrect dialog box (see Figure 3-4).**

2. **In the Replace text box, enter the three or four characters that will trigger the AutoCorrect mechanism and make it enter your text.**

   Don't enter a word, or characters that you might really type someday, in the Replace box. If you do, the AutoCorrect mechanism might kick in when you least expect it. Enter three or four characters that never appear together. And start all AutoCorrect entries with a slash (/). You might forget which characters trigger the AutoText entry or decide to delete your AutoCorrect entry someday. By starting it with a slash, you can find it easily in the AutoCorrect dialog box at the top of the Replace list.

3. **In the With text box, enter the hard-to-type name or word(s) that will appear when you enter the Replace text.**

4. **Click the Add button.**

5. **Click OK.**

   Test your AutoCorrect entry by typing the Replace text you entered in Step 2 (which, of course, includes the slash I recommend) and pressing the spacebar. (AutoCorrect doesn't do its work until you press the spacebar.)

To delete an AutoCorrect entry, open the AutoCorrect dialog box, select the entry, and click the Delete button.

Chapter 4: Taking Advantage of the Proofing Tools

In This Chapter

✔ Fixing spelling errors and customizing the spelling dictionary

✔ Repairing grammatical errors in Word documents

✔ Conducting outside research while you work in an Office program

✔ Looking for a better word in the thesaurus

✔ Working with and translating foreign language text

I was going to call this chapter "Foolproofing Your Work," but that seemed kind of presumptuous because keeping every error from slipping into your work is well-nigh impossible. Still, you can do a good job of proofing your work and eliminating errors by using the tools that Office provides for that purpose. This chapter describes how to proof your work for spelling and grammatical errors. It shows how to conduct research in reference books and on the Internet without leaving an Office program. You also find out how to translate text and proof foreign language text in an Office file. The Office proofing tools are not foolproof, but they're close to it.

Correcting Your Spelling Errors

Office keeps a dictionary in its hip pocket, which is a good thing for you. Who wants to be embarrassed by a spelling error? Office consults its dictionary when you enter text in Word, PowerPoint, Access, Excel, Outlook, and Publisher. To correct misspellings, you can either address them one at a time or start the spell checker and proof many pages or slides simultaneously. You can even create your own dictionary with the jargon and slang peculiar to your way of life and have Office check the spelling of your jargon and slang.

Don't trust the smell checker to be accurate all the time. It doesn't really locate misspelled words — it locates words that aren't in its dictionary. For example, if you write "Nero diddled while Rome burned," the spell checker won't catch the error. Nero *fiddled* while Rome burned, but because *diddle* is a legitimate word in the spelling dictionary, the spell checker overlooks the error. The moral: Proofread your files carefully and don't rely on the spell checker to catch all your smelling errors.

Getting rid of the squiggly red lines

More than a few people think that the squiggly red lines that appear under misspelled words are annoying. To keep those lines from appearing, press F7 to open the Spelling dialog box and click the Options button. You see the Proofing category of the Options dialog box. Deselect the Check Spelling As You Type check box.

Even with the red lines gone, you can do a quick spell-check of a word that you suspect has been misspelled. To do so, select the word (double-click it) and press F7. The Spelling dialog box appears if the word has indeed been misspelled. Select a word in the Suggestions box and click the Change button.

Correcting misspellings one at a time

In Word, PowerPoint, Publisher, and Outlook, you can practice the one-at-a-time method of spell-checking. As shown in Figure 4-1, you can right-click each word that is underlined in red and choose a correct spelling from the shortcut menu. After you choose a word from the shortcut menu, it replaces the misspelling that you right-clicked.

Figure 4-1: Right-click a word underlined in red to correct a typo or repeated word.

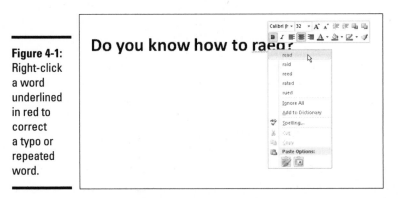

Words entered twice are also flagged in red, in which case the shortcut menu offers the Delete Repeated Word option so that you can delete the second word. You can also click Ignore All to tell Office when a word is correctly spelled and shouldn't be flagged, or click Add to Dictionary, which adds the word to the Office spelling dictionary and declares it a correctly spelled word.

Running a spell-check

Instead of correcting misspellings one at a time, you run a spell-check on your work. Start your spell-check with one of these methods:

✦ Press F7.

ABC
Spelling

✦ Go to the Review tab and click the Spelling (or Spelling & Grammar) button (you may have to click the Proofing button to get to the Spelling button). In Access, you can find the spelling button on the Home tab.

You see the Spelling and Grammar (or Spelling) dialog box, as shown in Figure 4-2. Misspellings appear in the Not In Dictionary text box. As I explain shortly, your Office program offers all sorts of amenities for handling misspellings, but here are options for correcting known misspellings in the Spelling dialog box:

Misspelled word   Choose the correct spelling and click Change

Figure 4-2:
Correcting a misspelling in the Spelling and Grammar dialog box.

✦ Select the correct spelling in the Suggestions box and click the Change button.

✦ Click in the page or slide you're working on and correct the spelling there; then click the Resume button, located where the Ignore or Ignore Once button used to be. (You can't do this in Excel.)

✦ In Word, Excel, or Access, correct the spelling inside the Not in Dictionary text box and then click the Change button. (In PowerPoint, correct the spelling in the Change To box and then click the Change button.)

If the word in question isn't a misspelling, tell your program how to handle the word by clicking one of these buttons:

✦ **Ignore (or Ignore Once):** Ignores this instance of the misspelling but stops on it again if the same misspelling appears later.

✦ **Ignore All:** Ignores the misspelling throughout the file you're working on and in all other open Office files as well.

✦ **Change/Delete:** Enters the selected word in the Suggestions box in the file where the misspelling used to be. When the same word appears twice in a row, the Delete button appears where the Change button was. Click the Delete button to delete the second word in the pair.

✦ **Change All/Delete All:** Replaces all instances of the misspelled word with the word that you selected in the Suggestions box. Click the Change All button to correct a misspelling that occurs throughout a file. When two words appear in a row, this button is called Delete All. Click the Delete All button to delete the second word in the pair throughout your file.

✦ **Add (or Add to Dictionary):** Adds the misspelling to the Office spelling dictionary. By clicking the Add button, you tell Office that the misspelling is a legitimate word or name.

✦ **Suggest (in PowerPoint only):** Changes the list of words in the Suggestions box. Select a word in the Suggestions box and then click the Suggest button to see whether you can find a correct spelling.

✦ **AutoCorrect:** Adds the spelling correction to the list of words that are corrected automatically. If you find yourself making the same typing error over and over, place the error on the AutoCorrect list and never have to correct it again. (See Chapter 3 of this mini-book for details.)

Office programs share the same spelling dictionary. For example, words you add to the spelling dictionary in PowerPoint are deemed correct spellings in Word documents, Excel spreadsheets, Publisher publications, Access databases, and Outlook e-mails.

Fine-tuning the spell checker

Especially if you deal in jargon and scientific terminology, you owe it to yourself to fine-tune the spell checker. No matter how arcane, it can make sure that your jargon gets used correctly. These pages explain the nuances of the spell checker.

Employing other dictionaries to help with spell-checking

To find spelling errors, Office compares each word on your page or slide to the words in its main dictionary and a second dictionary called `Custom. dic`. If a word you type isn't found in either dictionary, Office considers the word a misspelling. The main dictionary lists all known words in the English language; the `Custom.dic` dictionary lists words, proper names, and technical jargon that you deemed legitimate when you clicked the Add (or Add to Dictionary) button in the course of a spell-check and added a word to the `Custom.dic` dictionary.

From Office's standpoint, a dictionary is merely a list of words, one word per line, that has been saved in a `.dic` (dictionary) file. Besides the `Custom. dic` dictionary, you can employ other dictionaries to help with spell-checking. People who work in specialized professions such as law or medicine can also use legal dictionaries and medical dictionaries to spell-check their work. You can create dictionaries of your own for slang words, colloquialisms, or special projects. Before you start spell-checking, you can tell Office which dictionaries to use. You can edit dictionaries as well. All this magic is done by way of the Custom Dictionaries dialog box, shown in Figure 4-3, and explained in the pages that follow.

Click to edit or delete the words in a dictionary

Figure 4-3:
Adding a
word to
the custom
dictionary.

Opening the Custom Dictionaries dialog box

Starting in the Custom Dictionaries dialog box, you can create a new spelling dictionary, tell PowerPoint to use a third-party dictionary you acquired, edit words in a dictionary, and tell PowerPoint which dictionary to use in a spell-check. Better keep reading.

Follow these steps to open the Custom Dictionaries dialog box:

1. Press F7 or go to the Review tab and click the Spelling button.

You see the Spelling and Grammar (or Spelling) dialog box.

2. Click the Options button.

The Proofing category of the Options dialog box opens.

3. Click the Custom Dictionaries button.

Creating a new spelling dictionary

People who work in law offices, research facilities, and medical facilities type hundreds of arcane terms each day, none of which are in the main dictionary. One way to make sure that arcane terms are spelled correctly is to create or acquire a dictionary of legal, scientific, or medical terms and use it for spell-checking purposes. By Office's definition, a dictionary is simply a list of words saved in a dictionary (.dic) file.

Follow these steps to create a new spelling dictionary or tell Office that you want to use a secondary dictionary to check the spelling of words:

1. **Click the New button in the Custom Dictionaries dialog box (refer to Figure 4-3).**

   You see the Create Custom Dictionary dialog box.

2. **Enter a name for your new dictionary.**

3. **Click the Save button.**

   See "Entering and editing words in a dictionary," later in this chapter, to find out how to enter terms in your new spelling dictionary.

Using a third-party dictionary

Besides creating your own dictionary, you can acquire one and tell Office to use it by following these steps:

1. **Take note of where the dictionary file is located on your computer.**

   It doesn't have to be in the `C:\Users\User Name\AppData\Roaming\Microsoft\UProof` (Windows 7 and Windows Vista) or the `C:\Documents and Settings\`*User Name*`\Application Data\Microsoft\Proof` (or `UProof`) (Windows XP) folder along with the other dictionaries for PowerPoint to use it.

2. **Click the Add button in the Custom Dictionaries dialog box (refer to Figure 4-3).**

   The Add Custom Dictionary dialog box appears.

3. **Locate and select the dictionary on your computer.**

4. **Click Open.**

   The dictionary's name appears in the Custom Dictionaries dialog box. Ten dictionaries total can appear in the Dictionary List box.

Select a dictionary and click the Remove button to remove its name from the Dictionary List box. Removing a name in no way, shape, or form deletes the dictionary.

Entering and editing words in a dictionary

To edit the words in the `Custom.dic` dictionary or any other dictionary, select its name in the Custom Dictionaries dialog box (refer to Figure 4-3) and click the Edit Word List button. A dialog box opens with a list of the words in the dictionary, as shown in Figure 4-4. From there, you can delete words (by clicking the Delete button) and add words to the dictionary (by clicking the Add button).

Figure 4-4:
Edit the
words in
a custom
dictionary in
this dialog
box.

Preventing text from being spell-checked

Spell-checking address lists, lines of computer code, and foreign languages such as Spanglish for which Microsoft doesn't offer foreign language dictionaries is a thorough waste of time. Follow these steps in Word, PowerPoint, and Outlook to tell the spell checker to ignore text:

1. **Select the text.**

2. **In the Review tab, click the Language button and choose Set Proofing Language on the drop-down list.**

You see the Language dialog box.

3. **Select the Do Not Check Spelling or Grammar check box.**

4. **Click OK.**

Checking for Grammatical Errors in Word

Much of what constitutes good grammar is, like beauty, in the eye of the beholder. Still, you can do your best to repair grammatical errors in Word documents by getting the assistance of the grammar checker. The grammar checker identifies grammatical errors, explains what the errors are, and gives you the opportunity to correct the errors.

Figure 4-5 shows the grammar checker in action in the Spelling and Grammar dialog box. As long as the Check Grammar check box is selected, Word looks for grammatical errors along with spelling errors. To open the Spelling and Grammar dialog box, press F7 or go to the Review tab and click the Spelling & Grammar button.

Figure 4-5:
Fix
grammatical
errors
with the
grammar
checker.

Sentences in which grammatical errors appear are underlined in blue in your document. Meanwhile, the grammatical errors themselves appear in bright blue in the box at the top of the Spelling and Grammar dialog box (along with spelling errors, which are red). When Word encounters an error, take one of these actions to correct it:

✦ Select a correction in the Suggestions box and click the Change button.

✦ Delete the grammatical error or rephrase the sentence in the top of the dialog box, enter a correction, and click the Change button.

✦ Click outside the Spelling and Grammar dialog box, correct the grammatical error in your document, and then click the Resume button (you find it where the Ignore Once button used to be).

Click one of the Ignore buttons to let what Word thinks is a grammatical error stand.

If you want to fine-tune how Word runs its grammar checker, click the Options button in the Spelling and Grammar dialog box. You land in the Proofing category of the Word Options dialog box. Under When Correcting Spelling and Grammar in Word, choose whether to underline grammatical errors in your documents, whether to check for grammatical as well as spelling errors, and in the Writing Style drop-down list, how stringent you want the rules of grammar to be. Choose Grammar & Style, not Grammar Only, if you want Word to enforce style rules as well as the rules of grammar.

Researching a Topic Inside an Office Program

Thanks to the Research task pane, your desk needn't be as crowded as before. The Research task pane offers dictionaries, foreign language dictionaries, a thesaurus, language translators, and encyclopedias, as well as Internet searching, all available from inside the Office programs. As shown in Figure 4-6, the Research task pane can save you a trip to the library. Table 4-1 describes the research services in the Research task pane. Use these services to get information as you compose a Word document, Excel worksheet, Outlook message, Publisher publication, or PowerPoint presentation.

Enter what you want to research

Choose a search command or category

Figure 4-6:
The
Research
task pane is
like a mini-
reference
library.

Table 4-1   Research Services in the Research Task Pane

Research Service	*What It Provides*
All Reference Books	
Encarta dictionaries	Word definitions from the Microsoft Network's online dictionaries
Thesauruses	Synonyms from the Microsoft Network's online thesauruses
Translation	Translations from one language to another
All Research Sites	
Bing	Results from Microsoft's search engine

(continued)

Table 4-1 *(continued)*

Research Service	What It Provides
Factiva iWorks*	Business articles from Factiva (you must be a paid subscriber)
HighBeam Research*	Newspaper and magazine articles from the HighBeam Research Library (you must be a paid subscriber)
All Business and Financial Sites	
MSN Money Stock Quotes*	Stock quotes from the Microsoft Network's Money Web site
Thomas Gale Company Profiles*	Thumbnail company profiles, including tickers, revenue, and Web site information

*Requires an Internet connection.

Your computer must be connected to the Internet to run some of the services in the Research task pane. Bilingual dictionaries and thesauruses are installed as part of the Office software, but the research Web sites and the Encarta dictionaries and encyclopedia require an Internet connection.

In order to use some of the services offered by the Research task pane, you must pay a fee. These services are marked in search results with the Premium Content icon.

Using the Research task pane

The task pane offers menus and buttons for steering a search in different directions, but no matter what you want to research in the Research task pane, start your search the same way:

1. **Either click in a word or select the words that you want to research.**

   For example, if you want to translate a word, click it. Clicking a word or selecting words saves you the trouble of entering words in the Search For text box, but if no word in your file describes what you want to research, don't worry about it. You can enter the subject of your search later.

2. **On the Review tab, click the Research button (you may have to click the Proofing button first).**

   The Research task pane appears (refer to Figure 4-6). If you've researched since you started running your Office program, the options you chose for researching last time appear in the task pane.

3. **Enter a research term in the Search For text box (if one isn't there already).**

   If you weren't able to click a word or select words in Step 1, enter research terms now.

4. **Open the Search For drop-down list and tell Office where to steer your search (refer to Table 4-1).**

   Choose a reference book, research Web site, or business and financial Web site. To research in a category, choose a category name — All Reference Books, All Research Sites, or All Business and Financial Sites. Later in this chapter, "Choosing your research options" explains how to decide which researching options appear on the drop-down list.

5. **Click the Start Searching button (or press Enter).**

   The results of your search appear in the Research task pane.

If your search yields nothing worthwhile or nothing at all, scroll to the bottom of the task pane, click Can't Find It?, and try the All Reference Books or All Research Sites link. The first link searches all reference books — the dictionaries, thesauruses, and translation services. The second searches research sites — Bing, Factiva iWorks, and HighBeam Research.

You can retrace a search by clicking the Previous Search button or Next Search button in the Research task pane. These buttons work like the Back and Forward buttons in a Web browser.

Choosing your research options

Which research options appear in the Search For drop-down list is up to you. Maybe you want to dispense with the for-a-fee services. Maybe you want to get stock quotes from a particular country. To decide which research options appear in the Research task pane, open the task pane and click the Research Options link (at the bottom of the task pane). You see the Research Options dialog box. Select the research services you want and click OK.

Finding the Right Word with the Thesaurus

If you can't find the right word or if the word is on the tip of your tongue but you can't quite remember it, you can always give the thesaurus a shot. To find synonyms for a word, start by right-clicking the word and choosing Synonyms on the shortcut menu, as shown in Figure 4-7 (you can't do this in Excel). With luck, the synonym you're looking for appears on the submenu, and all you have to do is click to enter the synonym. Usually, however, finding a good synonym is a journey, not a Sunday stroll.

Figure 4-7:
Searching
for a
synonym.

To search for a good synonym, click the word in question and open the thesaurus on the Research task pane with one of these techniques:

✦ Press Shift+F7.

✦ Right-click the word and choose Synonyms⇨Thesaurus.

✦ Go to the Review tab and click the Thesaurus button.

The Research task pane opens. It offers a list of synonyms and sometimes
includes an antonym or two at the bottom. Now you're getting somewhere:

✦ **Choosing a synonym:** Move the pointer over the synonym you want,
open its drop-down list, and choose Insert.

✦ **Finding a synonym for a synonym:** If a synonym intrigues you, click it.
The task pane displays a new list of synonyms.

✦ **Searching for antonyms:** If you can't think of the right word, type its
antonym in the Search For box and then look for an "antonym of an antonym" in the Research task pane.

✦ **Revisit a word list:** Click the Back button as many times as necessary. If
you go back too far, you can always click its companion Forward button.

If your search for a synonym comes up dry, scroll to and click a link at the
bottom of the Research task pane. Clicking All Reference Books gives you
the opportunity to look up a word in the reference books you installed in
the task pane; clicking All Research Sites gives you a chance to search the
Internet (see "Researching a Topic inside an Office Program" earlier in this
chapter for details).

Proofing Text Written in a Foreign Language

In the interest of cosmopolitanism, Office gives you the opportunity to make foreign languages a part of Word documents, PowerPoint presentations, Publisher publications, and Outlook messages. To enter and edit text in a foreign language, start by installing proofing tools for the language. With the tools installed, you tell Office where in your file a foreign language is used. After that, you can spell-check text written in the language.

To spell-check text written in Uzbek, Estonian, Afrikaans, and other languages apart from English, French, and Spanish, you have to obtain additional proofing tools from Microsoft. These can be obtained at the Microsoft Product Information Center at `www.microsoft.com/products` (enter **proofing tools** in the Search box). Proofing tools include a spell checker, grammar checker, thesaurus, hyphenator, AutoCorrect list, and translation dictionary, but not all these tools are available for every language.

In PowerPoint and Word, the status bar along the bottom of the window lists which language the cursor is in. Glance at the status bar if you aren't sure which language Office is whispering in your ear.

Telling Office which languages you will use

Follow these steps to inform Word, PowerPoint, Publisher, and Outlook that you will use a language or languages besides English in your files:

1. **On the Review tab, click the Language button and choose Language Preferences.**

   The Options dialog box opens to the Language category.

2. **Open the Add Additional Editing Languages drop-down list, select a language, and click the Add button to make that language a part of your presentations, documents, and messages.**

3. **Click OK.**

Marking text as foreign language text

The next step is to tell Office where in your file you're using a foreign language. After you mark the text as foreign language text, Office can spell-check it with the proper dictionaries. Follow these steps to mark text so that Office knows in which language it was written:

1. **Select the text that you wrote in a foreign language.**

2. **Go to the Review tab.**

3. **Click the Language button and choose Set Proofing Language on the drop-down list.**

You see the Language dialog box, as shown in Figure 4-8.

4. **Select a language and click OK.**

Figure 4-8:
Identifying
foreign
language
words
for spell-
checking.

Translating Foreign Language Text

Office offers a gizmo for translating words and phrases from one language to another. The translation gizmo gives you the opportunity to translate single words and phrases as well as entire files, although, in my experience, it is only good for translating words and phrases. To translate an entire file, you have to seek the help of a real, native speaker.

Follow these steps to translate foreign language text:

1. **Select the word or phrase that needs translating.**

2. **On the Review tab, click the Translate button and choose a Translate option on the drop-down list.**

Office offers these ways to translate words:

- *Translate Document (Word only):* Word sends the text to a translation service at Bing Translator, and the translated text appears on a Web page. Copy the text and do what you will with it. (If the wrong translation languages are listed, choose the correct languages from the drop-down lists.)

- *Translate Selected Text:* The Research task pane opens, as shown in Figure 4-9. Choose a From and To option to translate the word from one language to another.

- *Mini Translator:* After you choose this option, move the pointer over the word you need translated. (If the Mini Translator command doesn't list the correct language, select the Choose Your Translation Language option and then select a language in the Translation Language Options dialog box.)

Figure 4-9:
Use the Research task pane to translate a word or phrase.

Chapter 5: Creating a Table

In This Chapter

- ✔ Understanding table jargon
- ✔ Creating a table and entering the text and numbers
- ✔ Aligning table text in various ways
- ✔ Merging and splitting cells to make interesting layouts
- ✔ Changing the size of rows and columns
- ✔ Decorating a table with table styles, colors, and borders
- ✔ Doing math calculations in a Word table
- ✔ Discovering an assortment of table tricks

The best way to present a bunch of data at once in Word, PowerPoint, or Publisher is to do it in a table. Viewers can compare and contrast the data. They can compare Elvis sightings in different cities or income from different businesses. They can contrast the number of socks lost in different washing machine brands. A table is a great way to plead your case or defend your position. On a PowerPoint slide, the audience can see right away that the numbers back you up. In a Word or Publisher document, readers can refer to your table to get the information they need.

As everyone who has worked on tables knows, however, tables are a chore. Getting all the columns to fit, making columns and rows the right width and height, and editing the text in a table isn't easy. This chapter explains how to create tables, enter text in tables, change the number and size of columns and rows, lay out tables, format tables, and (in Word) do the math in tables. You also discover a few tricks — including using a picture for the background — that only magicians know. And to start you on the right foot, I begin by explaining table jargon.

Talking Table Jargon

As with much else in Computerland, tables have their own jargon. Figure 5-1 describes this jargon. Sorry, but you need to catch up on these terms to construct the perfect table:

◆ **Cell:** The box that is formed where a row and column intersect. Each cell holds one data item.

◆ **Header row:** The name of the labels along the top row that explain what is in the columns below.

◆ **Row labels:** The labels in the first column that describe what is in each row.

◆ **Borders:** The lines in the table that define where the rows and columns are.

◆ **Gridlines:** The gray lines that show where the columns and rows are. Unless you've drawn borders around all the cells in a table, you can't tell where rows and columns begin and end without gridlines. To display or hide the gridlines, go to the (Table Tools) Layout tab and click the View Gridlines button.

Row labels   Header row

	Qtr 1	Qtr 2	Qtr 3	Qtr 4
East	4	8	5	6
West	3	4	4	9
North	3	8	9	6
South	8	7	7	9

Figure 5-1: The parts of a table.

Borders   Gridlines   Cells

Creating a Table

Word, PowerPoint, and Publisher offer several ways to create a table:

◆ **Drag on the Table menu.** On the Insert tab, click the Table button, point in the drop-down list to the number of columns and rows you want, click, and let go of the mouse button.

✦ **Use the Insert Table dialog box.** On the Insert tab, click the Table button and choose Insert Table on the drop-down list. The Insert Table dialog box appears. Enter the number of columns and rows you want and click OK. In PowerPoint, you can also open the Insert Table dialog box by clicking the Table icon in a content placeholder frame.

✦ **Draw a table (Word and PowerPoint).** On the Insert tab, click the Table button and then choose Draw Table on the drop-down list. The pointer changes into a pencil. Use the pencil to draw table borders, rows, and columns. If you make a mistake, click the Eraser button on the (Table Tools) Design tab and drag it over the parts of the table you regret drawing (you may have to click the Draw Borders button first). When you finish drawing the table, press Esc.

You can click the Pen Color button and choose a color on the drop-down list to draw your table in your favorite color.

✦ **Create a quick table (Word).** On the Insert tab, click the Table button and choose Quick Tables on the drop-down list. Then choose a ready-made table on the submenu. You have to replace the sample data in the quick table with your own data.

✦ **Convert text in a list into a table (Word).** Press Tab or enter a comma in each list item where you want the columns in the table to be. For example, to turn an address list into a table, put each name and address on its own line and press Tab or enter a comma after the first name, the last name, the street address, the city, the state, and the ZIP Code. For this feature to work, each name and address — each line — must have the same number of tab spaces or commas in it. Select the text you'll convert to a table, click the Table button on the Insert tab, and choose Convert Text to Table. Under Separate Text At in the Convert Text to Table dialog box, choose Tabs or Commas to tell Word how the columns are separated. Then click OK.

Constructing your table from an Excel worksheet

Fans of Microsoft Excel will be glad to know that you can construct an Excel worksheet in a Word document or PowerPoint slide. Excel worksheets, which present data in columns and rows, are very much like tables and can serve as such in documents and slides.

To create an Excel worksheet, go to the Insert tab, click the Table button, and choose Excel Spreadsheet. An Excel worksheet appears on the slide and — *gadzooks!* — you see Excel menus and commands where Word or PowerPoint menus and commands used to be. The worksheet you just created is embedded in your file. Whenever you click the worksheet, Excel menus and commands rather than Word or PowerPoint menus and commands appear on-screen. Click outside the worksheet to return to Word or PowerPoint. Book VIII, Chapter 7 explains how embedded objects work.

After you create a table, you get two new tabs on the Ribbon. The (Table Tools) Design tab offers commands for changing the look of the table; the (Table Tools) Layout tab is for changing around the rows and columns.

Entering the Text and Numbers

After you create the table, you can start entering text and numbers. All you have to do is click in a cell and start typing. Select your table and take advantage of these techniques to make the onerous task of entering table data a little easier:

✦ **Quickly changing a table's size:** Drag the bottom or side of a table to change its overall size. In Word, you can also go to the (Table Tools) Layout tab, click the AutoFit button, and choose AutoFit Window to make the table stretch from margin to margin.

✦ **Moving a table:** In Word, switch to Print Layout view and drag the table selector (the square in the upper-left corner of the table). In PowerPoint and Publisher, move the pointer over the table's perimeter, and when you see the four-headed arrow, click and drag.

✦ **Choosing your preferred font and font size:** Entering table data is easier when you're working in a font and font size you like. Select the table, visit the Home tab, and choose a font and font size there. In Word and PowerPoint, you can select a table by going to the (Table Tools) Layout tab, clicking the Select button, and choosing Select Table on the drop-down list.

✦ **Quickly inserting a new row:** Click in the last column of the last row in your table and press the Tab key to quickly insert a new row at the bottom of the table.

Here are some shortcuts for moving the cursor in a table:

Press	*Moves the Cursor to*
Tab	Next column in row
Shift+Tab	Previous column in row
↓	Row below
↑	Row above
Alt+Page Up	Top of column (Word and PowerPoint)
Alt+Page Down	Bottom of column (Word and PowerPoint)

Selecting Different Parts of a Table

It almost goes without saying, but before you can reformat, alter, or diddle with table cells, rows, or columns, you have to select them:

✦ **Selecting cells:** To select a cell, click in it. You can select several adjacent cells by dragging the pointer over them.

✦ **Selecting rows:** Move the pointer to the left of the row and click when you see the right-pointing arrow; click and drag to select several rows. You can also go to the (Table Tools) Layout tab, click inside the row you want to select, click the Select button, and choose Select Row on the drop-down list. To select more than one row at a time, select cells in the rows before choosing the Select Row command.

✦ **Selecting columns:** Move the pointer above the column and click when you see the down-pointing arrow; click and drag to select several columns. You can also start from the (Table Tools) Layout tab, click in the column you want to select, click the Select button, and choose Select Column in the drop-down list. To select several columns, select cells in the columns before choosing the Select Column command.

✦ **Selecting a table:** On the (Table Tools) Layout tab, click the Select button, and choose Select Table on the drop-down list. In PowerPoint, you can also right-click a table and choose Select Table on the shortcut menu.

Aligning Text in Columns and Rows

Aligning text in columns and rows is a matter of choosing how you want the text to line up vertically and how you want it to line up horizontally. Select the cells, columns, or rows, with text that you want to align (or select your entire table) and then align the text:

✦ **In Word and Publisher:** On the (Table Tools) Layout tab, click an Align button (you may have to click the Alignment button first, depending on the size of your screen). Word offers nine of them in the Alignment group.

✦ **In PowerPoint:** On the (Table Tools) Layout tab, click one Horizontal Align button (Align Left, Center, or Align Right), and one Vertical Align button (Align Top, Center Vertically, or Align Bottom). You may have to click the Alignment button first.

Merging and Splitting Cells

Merge and split cells to make your tables a little more elegant than run-of-the-mill tables. *Merge* cells to break down the barriers between cells and join them into one cell; *split* cells to divide a single cell into several cells (or several cells into several more cells). In the table shown in Figure 5-2, the cells in rows two, four, and six have been merged and a baseball player's name appears in each merged cell. Where rows two, four, and six originally had nine cells, they now have only one.

Merge and split cells

Figure 5-2:
Merge cells
to create
larger cells.

Select the cells you want to merge or split, go to the (Table Tools) Layout tab, and follow these instructions to merge or split cells:

✦ **Merging cells:** Click the Merge Cells button (in Word and PowerPoint, you can also right-click and choose Merge Cells).

✦ **Splitting cells:** Click the Split Cells button (in Word and PowerPoint, you can also right-click and choose Split Cells). In the Split Cells dialog box, declare how many columns and rows you want to split the cell into and then click OK. In Publisher, you can only split cells that were previously merged.

In Word and PowerPoint, you can merge and split cells by clicking the Draw Table or Eraser button on the (Table Tools) Design tab. Click the Draw Table button and then draw lines through cells to split them. Click the Eraser button and drag over or click the boundary between cells to merge cells. Press Esc when you finish drawing or erasing table cell boundaries. You can click the Pen Color button and choose a color on the drop-down list to draw in a particular color.

Split Table   Need to split a table? In Word, place the cursor in what you want to be the first row of the new table, go to the (Table Tools) Layout tab, and click the Split Table button.

Laying Out Your Table

Very likely, you created too many or too few columns or rows for your table. Some columns are probably too wide and others too narrow. If that's the case, you have to change the table layout by deleting, inserting, and changing the size of columns and rows, not to mention changing the size of the table itself. In other words, you have to modify the table layout. (Later in this chapter, "Decorating your table with borders and colors" shows how to put borders around tables and embellish them in other ways.)

Changing the size of a table, columns, and rows

The fastest way to adjust the width of columns, the height of rows, and the size of a table itself is to "eyeball it" and drag the mouse:

✦ **Column or row:** Move the pointer onto a gridline or border, and when the pointer changes into a double-headed arrow, start dragging. Tug and pull, tug and pull until the column or row is the right size.

In Word and PowerPoint, you can also go to the (Table Tools) Layout tab and enter measurements in the Height and Width text boxes to change the width of a column or the height of a row. The measurements affect entire columns or rows, not individual cells.

✦ **A table:** Select your table and use one of these techniques to change its size in Word and PowerPoint:

• *Dragging:* Drag the top, bottom, or side of the table. You can also drag the lower-right corner to change the size vertically and horizontally.

• *Height and Width text boxes:* On the (Table Tools) Layout tab, enter measurements in the Height and Width text boxes. In Publisher, these text boxes are found on the (Table Tools) Design tab. In PowerPoint, click the Lock Aspect Ratio check box if you want to keep the table's proportions when you change its height or width.

• *Table Properties dialog box (Word only):* On the (Table Tools) Layout tab, click the Cell Size group button, and on the Table tab of the Table Properties dialog box, enter a measurement in the Preferred Width text box.

Adjusting column and row size

Resizing columns and rows can be problematic in Word and PowerPoint. For that reason, Word and PowerPoint offer special commands on the (Table Tools) Layout tab for adjusting the width and height of rows and columns:

+ **Making all columns the same width:** Click the Distribute Columns button to make all columns the same width. Select columns before giving this command to make only the columns you select the same width.

+ **Making all rows the same height:** Click the Distribute Rows button to make all rows in the table the same height. Select rows before clicking the button to make only the rows you select the same height.

In Word, you can also click the AutoFit button on the (Table Tools) Layout tab, and take advantage of these commands on the drop-down list for handling columns and rows:

+ **AutoFit Contents:** Make each column wide enough to accommodate its widest entry.

+ **AutoFit Window:** Stretch the table so that it fits across the page between the left and right margin.

+ **Fixed Column Width:** Fix the column widths at their current settings.

Inserting and deleting columns and rows

The trick to inserting and deleting columns and rows is to correctly select part of the table first. You can insert more than one column or row at a time by selecting more than one column or row before giving the Insert command. To insert two columns, for example, select two columns and choose an Insert command; to insert three rows, select three rows and choose an Insert command. Earlier in this chapter, "Selecting Different Parts of a Table" explains how to make table selections.

Go to the (Table Tools) Layout tab and follow these instructions to insert and delete columns and rows:

+ **Inserting columns:** Select a column or columns and click the Insert Left or Insert Right button. If you want to insert just one column, click in a column and then click the Insert Left or Insert Right button. You can also right-click, choose Insert, and choose an Insert Columns command.

+ **Inserting rows:** Select a row or rows and click the Insert Above or Insert Below button. If you want to insert just one row, click in a row and click the Insert Above or Insert Below button. You can also right-click, choose Insert, and choose an Insert Rows command on the shortcut menu.

To insert a row at the end of a table, move the pointer into the last cell in the last row and press the Tab key.

✦ **Deleting columns:** Click in the column you want to delete, click the Delete button, and choose Delete Columns on the drop-down list. Select more than one column to delete more than one. (Pressing the Delete key deletes the data in the column, not the column itself.)

✦ **Deleting rows:** Click in the row you want to delete, click the Delete button, and choose Delete Rows. Select more than one row to delete more than one. (Pressing the Delete key deletes the data in the row, not the row itself.)

Sorting, or reordering a table (in Word)

On the subject of moving columns and rows, the fastest way to rearrange the rows in a Word table is to sort the table. *Sorting* means to rearrange all the rows in a table on the basis of data in one or more columns. For example, a table that shows candidates and the number of votes they received could be sorted in alphabetical order by the candidates' names or in numerical order by the number of votes they received. Both tables present the same information, but the information is sorted in different ways.

The difference between ascending and descending sorts is as follows:

✔ Ascending arranges text from A to Z, numbers from smallest to largest, and dates from earliest to latest.

✔ Descending arranges text from Z to A, numbers from largest to smallest, and dates from latest to earliest.

When you rearrange a table by sorting it, Word rearranges the formatting as well as the data. Do your sorting before you format the table.

Follow these steps to sort a table:

1. **On the (Table Tools) Layout tab, click the Sort button.**

You see the Sort dialog box. Depending on the size of your screen, you may have to click the Data button before you see the Sort button.

2. **In the first Sort By drop-down list, choose the column you want to sort with.**

3. **If necessary, open the first Type drop-down list and choose Text, Number, or Date to describe what kind of data you're dealing with.**

4. **Select the Ascending or Descending option button to declare whether you want an ascending or descending sort.**

5. **If necessary, on the first Then By drop-down list, choose the tiebreaker column.**

   If two items in the Sort By columns are alike, Word looks to your Then By column choice to break the tie and place one row before another in the table.

6. **Click OK.**

When you sort a table, Word ignores the *header row* — the first row in the table — and doesn't move it. However, if you want to include the header row in the sort, click the No Header Row option button in the Sort dialog box.

Moving columns and rows

Because there is no elegant way to move a column or row, you should move only one at a time. If you try to move several simultaneously, you open a can of worms that is best left unopened. To move a column or row:

1. **Select the column or row you want to move.**

   Earlier in this chapter, "Selecting Different Parts of a Table" explains how to select columns and rows.

2. **Right-click in the selection and choose Cut on the shortcut menu.**

   The column or row is moved to the Clipboard.

3. **Insert a new column or row where you want the column or row to be.**

   Earlier in this chapter, "Inserting and deleting columns and rows" explains how.

4. **Move the column or row:**

   - *Column:* Click in the topmost cell in your new column and then click the Paste button or press Ctrl+V.
   - *Row:* Click in the first column of the row you inserted and then click the Paste button or press Ctrl+V.

Formatting Your Table

After you enter text in the table, lay out the columns and rows, and make them the right size, the fun begins. Now you can dress up your table and make it look snazzy. You can change fonts, choose colors for columns and rows, and even land a graphic in the background of your table. You can also play with the borders that divide the columns and rows and shade columns, rows, and cells by filling them with gray shades or a black background. Read on to find out how to do these tricks.

Designing a table with a table style

The fastest way to get a good-looking table is to select a table style in the Table Styles gallery, as shown in Figure 5-3. A *table style* is a ready-made assortment of colors and border choices. You can save yourself a lot of formatting trouble by selecting a table style. After you've selected a table style, you can modify it by selecting or deselecting check boxes in the Table Style Options group.

Modify your table   Select a table style

	Wins	Losses	Ties	Goals Scored/ Scored on		Play-offs
Spiders	7	1	0	49	5	✓
Knights	5	2	1	15	12	✓
Bandits	4	2	2	9	14	
River Kings	3	4	1	6	19	
Bears	1	7	0	3	31	

Thanks everybody for a great football season!

Figure 5-3: You have many opportunities for designing tables.

Click anywhere in your table and follow these steps to choose a table style:

1. **Go to the (Table Tools) Design tab.**

2. **Open the Table Styles gallery and move the pointer over table style choices to "live-preview" the table.**

In Publisher, this gallery is called Table Formats.

3. **Select a table style.**

To remove a table style, open the Table Styles gallery and choose Clear (in Word) or Clear Table (in PowerPoint).

TIP

For consistency's sake, choose a similar table style — or better yet the same table style — for all the tables in your document or presentation. This way, your work doesn't become a showcase for table styles.

Calling attention to different rows and columns

On the (Table Tools) Design tab, Word and PowerPoint offer Table Style Options check boxes for calling attention to different rows or columns (refer to Figure 5-3). For example, you can make the first row in the table, called the header row, stand out by selecting the Header Row check box. If your table presents numerical data with total figures in the last row, you can call attention to the last row by selecting the Total Row check box. Select or deselect these check boxes on the (Table Tools) Design tab to make your table easier to read and understand:

✦ **Header Row and Total Row:** These check boxes make the first row and last row in a table stand out. Typically, the header row is a different color or contains boldface text because it is the row that identifies the data in the table. Click the Header Row check box to make the first row stand out; if you also want the last row to stand out, click the Total Row check box.

✦ **Banded Columns and Banded Rows:** *Banded* means "striped" in Office lingo. For striped columns or striped rows — columns or rows that alternate in color — select the Banded Columns or Banded Rows check box.

✦ **First Column and Last Column:** Often the first column stands out in a table because it identifies what type of data is in each row. Select the First Column check box to make it a different color or boldface its text. Check the Last Column check box if you want the rightmost column to stand out.

Decorating your table with borders and colors

Rather than rely on a table style, you can play interior decorator on your own. You can slap color on the columns and rows of your table, draw borders around columns and rows, and choose a look for borders. Figure 5-4 shows the drop-down lists on the (Table Tools) Design tab that pertain to table decoration. Use these lists to shade table columns and rows and draw table borders.

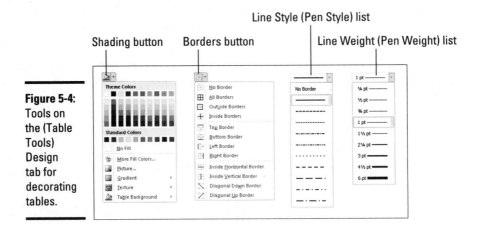

Figure 5-4:
Tools on the (Table Tools) Design tab for decorating tables.

Shading button   Borders button   Line Style (Pen Style) list   Line Weight (Pen Weight) list

Designing borders for your table

Follow these steps to fashion a border for your table or a part of your table:

1. **Go to the (Table Tools) Design tab.**

2. **Select the part of your table that needs a new border.**

To select the entire table, go to the (Table Tools) Layout tab, click the Select button, and choose Select Table.

3. **Open the Line Style drop-down list (in Word) or the Pen Style drop-down list (in PowerPoint) and choose a line style for the border (you may have to click the Draw Borders button first, depending on the size of your screen).**

Stay away from the dotted and dashed lines unless you have a good reason for choosing one. These lines can be distracting and keep others from focusing on the data presented in the table.

4. **Open the Line Weight drop-down list (in Word and Publisher) or the Pen Weight drop-down list (in PowerPoint) and choose a thickness for the border (you may have to click the Draw Borders button first).**

5. **If you want your borders to be a color apart from black, click the Pen Color button (Word and PowerPoint) or the Line Color button (Publisher) and choose a color on the drop-down list (you may have to click the Draw Borders button first).**

6. **Open the drop-down list on the Borders button and choose where to place borders on the part of the table you selected in Step 2.**

This is the tricky part. The Borders commands have different effects, depending on which part of the table you selected. For example, if you selected two rows and you choose the Top Border command, the command applies only to the top of the uppermost row. If you are anywhere near typical, you have to repeat Step 6 until you get it right.

In Word, you can also change borders by clicking the Draw Borders group button and making selections in the Borders and Shading dialog box, as shown in Figure 5-5.

Figure 5-5: In Word, you can draw borders with the Borders and Shading dialog box.

Selecting colors for columns, rows, or your table

Follow these steps to paint columns, rows, or your table a new color:

1. **Select the part of the table that needs a paint job.**

2. **In the (Table Tools) Design tab, open the drop-down list on the Shading button and choose a color (refer to Figure 5-5).**

This button is called Fill in Publisher.

Later in this chapter, "Using a picture as the table background" explains how to use a picture as the background in a table.

Using Math Formulas in Word Tables

No, you don't have to add the figures in columns and rows yourself; Word gladly does that for you. Word can perform other mathematical calculations as well. Follow these steps to perform mathematical calculations and tell Word how to format sums and products:

1. **Put the cursor in the cell that will hold the sum or product of the cells above, below, to the right, or to the left.**

2. **On the (Table Tools) Layout tab, click the Formula button.**

Depending on the size of your screen, you may have to click the Data button first. The Formula dialog box appears, as shown in Figure 5-6. In its wisdom, Word makes an educated guess about what you want the formula to do and places a formula in the Formula box.

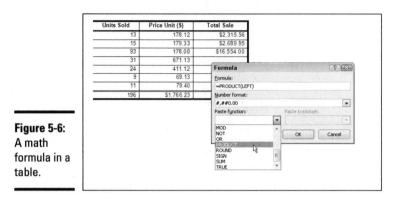

Figure 5-6:
A math
formula in a
table.

3. **If this isn't the formula you want, delete everything except the equal sign in the Formula box, open the Paste Function drop-down list, and choose another function for the formula.**

   For example, choose PRODUCT to multiply figures. You may have to type **left**, **right**, **above**, or **below** in the parentheses within the formula to tell Word where the figures that you want it to compute are.

4. **In the Number Format drop-down list, choose a format for your number.**

5. **Click OK.**

Word doesn't calculate blank cells in formulas. Enter 0 in blank cells if you want them to be included in calculations. You can copy functions from one cell to another to save yourself the trouble of opening the Formula dialog box.

Neat Table Tricks

The rest of this chapter details a handful of neat table tricks to make your tables stand out in a crowd. Why should all tables look alike? Read on to discover how to make text in the header row stand on its ear, put a picture behind a table, draw diagonal border lines, draw on top of a table, and wrap slide text around a table.

Changing the direction of header row text

In a top-heavy table in which the cells in the first row contain text and the cells below contain numbers, consider changing the direction of the text in the first row to make the table easier to read. Changing text direction in the first row is also a good way to squeeze more columns onto a table. Consider how wide the table shown in Figure 5-7 would be if the words in the first row were displayed horizontally.

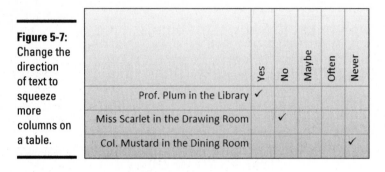

Follow these steps to change the direction of text on a table.

1. **Select the row that needs a change of text direction.**

   Usually, that's the first row in a table.

2. **Go to the (Table Tools) Layout tab.**

3. **Click the Text Direction button.**

   What happens next depends on whether you're operating in Word, Publisher, or PowerPoint:

   - *In Word and Publisher:* Keep clicking the Text Direction button until text lands where you want it to land. (You may have to click the Alignment button before you can see the Text Direction button.)

   - *In PowerPoint:* Choose a Text Direction option on the drop-down list. (You may have to click the Alignment button to get to the Text Direction button, depending on the size of your screen.)

4. **Change the height of the row to make the vertical text fit.**

   As "Changing the size of a table, columns, and rows" explains earlier in this chapter, you can change the height of a row by going to the (Table Tools) Layout tab and entering a measurement in the Height box.

Using a picture as the table background

As Figure 5-8 demonstrates, a picture used as the background in a table looks mighty nice. To make it work, however, you need a graphic that serves well as the background. For Figure 5-8, I got around this problem by recoloring my graphic (Book VIII, Chapter 3 explains how to recolor a graphic.) You also need to think about font colors. Your audience must be able to read the table text, and that usually means choosing a white or light font color for text so that the text can be read over the graphic. For Figure 5-8, I selected a white font color.

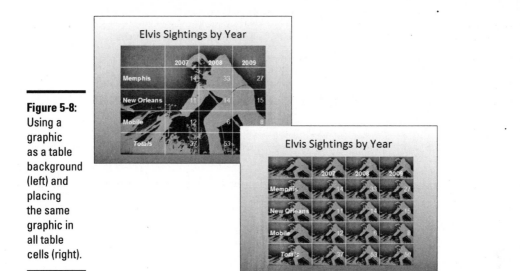

Figure 5-8:
Using a
graphic
as a table
background
(left) and
placing
the same
graphic in
all table
cells (right).

Besides putting a graphic behind a table, PowerPoint gives you the opportunity to make the graphic appear in every table cell, as shown on the right
side of Figure 5-8. Sorry, you can't do that feat in Word, but you can place a
picture behind a table, as the following pages explain.

Placing a picture behind a table

Placing a graphic behind a table requires a fair bit of work, but the results
are well worth the effort. First you insert the graphic and perhaps recolor it.
Then you create the table. Last, you make the table fit squarely on top of the
graphic and perhaps group the objects together.

In Word and PowerPoint, follow these steps to place a graphic behind a
table:

1. Insert the graphic, resize it, and format the graphic.

Book VIII, Chapter 3 explains how to insert and resize graphics. To insert
a graphic, go to the Insert tab and click the Picture button. To resize it,
drag a selection handle; make the graphic as big as you want your table
to be. To recolor a graphic similar to the job done to the graphic in
Figure 5-8, select the (Picture Tools) Format tab, click the Color button,
and choose an option.

2. Insert the table and make it roughly the same size as the graphic.

These tasks are explained earlier in this chapter. To change the size
of a table, drag a selection handle on its corner or side. Place the table
nearby the graphic, but not right on top of it.

3. **On the (Table Tools) Design tab, open the Table Styles gallery, and choose Clear (in Word) or Clear Table (in PowerPoint).**

   With the table styles out of the way, you can see the graphic clearly through your table.

4. **Enter the data in the table, select a font and font color, select a border and border color, and align the text.**

   These tasks (except for selecting fonts) are described throughout this chapter. The easiest way to choose a font and font color for a table is to select the table, go to the Home tab, and select a font and font size.

5. **Move the table squarely on top of the graphic and then make the table and graphic roughly the same size.**

Here are a few tricks that are worth knowing when you're handling a graphic and table:

+ In Word, you have to turn off text wrapping in order to bring the graphic behind the table. To do that, select your graphic, go to the (Picture Tools) Format tab, click the Wrap Text button, and choose Behind Text on the drop-down list.

+ If the graphic is in front of the table, select the graphic, go to the (Picture Tools) Format tab, open the drop-down list on the Send Backward button, and choose Send to Back (in PowerPoint) or Send Behind Text (in Word).

+ To make the graphic and table the same size, enter the same measurements for both. Select the table, go to the (Table Tools) Layout tab, and enter measurements for the table in the Height and Width boxes. Then select the graphic, go to the (Picture Tools) Format tab, and enter the same measurements in the Height and Width boxes (you may have to click the Size button to see these boxes, depending on the size of your screen).

Placing a background picture in each PowerPoint table cell

PowerPoint offers a special command for placing a picture in each table cell (refer to Figure 5-8). For this trick to work, you need a graphic of uniform color; otherwise, the text is too hard to read. (You might consult Book VIII, Chapter 3, which explains how to alter graphics with the Office Picture Manager.) Follow these steps to place a background picture in each PowerPoint table cell:

1. **Right-click your table and choose Select Table.**

2. **Go to the (Table Tools) Design tab.**

3. **Open the drop-down list on the Shading button and choose Picture.**

   The Insert Picture dialog box opens.

4. **Select a picture and click the Insert button.**

   To remove the background pictures from a table, open the drop-down list on the Shading button and choose No Fill or choose Clear Table in the Table Styles gallery.

Drawing diagonal lines on tables

Draw diagonal lines across table cells to cancel out those cells or otherwise make cells look different. In Figure 5-9, diagonal lines are drawn on cells to show that information that would otherwise be in the cells is either not available or is not relevant.

Figure 5-9:
Diagonal lines mark off cells as different.

	Mon.	Tues.	Wed.	Thurs.	Fri.	Sat.	Sun.
McKeef	8:00			3:00		8:00	2:15
Arnez	9:00	6:00	2:30	12:00	8:15		4:00
Danes	9:30		2:00	7:30		3:30	7:30
Minor		12:00	4:15	5:15	2:00		
Krupf	3:30	6:00		12:00	2:30	9:00	9:00
Gough	3:00			7:00	3:30	4:530	3:30
Gonzalez	12:00	7:15	8:30				10:15

Go to the (Table Tools) Design tab and use one of these techniques to draw diagonal lines across cells:

✦ **Draw Table button:** Click the Draw Table button (you may have to click the Draw Borders button first). The pointer changes into a pencil. Drag to draw the diagonal lines. Press Esc or click the Draw Table button a second time when you're finished drawing.

   Click the Pen Color button and choose a color before drawing on your table if you want the diagonal lines to be a certain color.

✦ **Borders button:** Select the cells that need diagonal lines, open the drop-down list on the Borders button, and choose Diagonal Down Border or Diagonal Up Border.

To remove diagonal lines, click the Eraser button and click or drag across the diagonals.

Drawing on a table

When you want to call attention to data in one part of a table, draw a circle around the data. By "draw" I mean make an Oval shape and place it over the data you want to highlight, as shown in Figure 5-10. Book I, Chapter 8 explains the drawing tools in detail. To spare you the trouble of turning to that chapter, here are shorthand instructions for drawing on a table in Word, PowerPoint, and Publisher:

Shapes

1. **On the Insert tab, click the Shapes button and select the Oval shape on the drop-down list.**

	April	May	June
Baltimore	$1.5 mil	$2.3 mil	$1.8 mil
New York	$1.2 mil	$3.2 mil	$4.1 mil
Philadelphia	$.8 mil	$1.8 mil	$1.7 mil
Newark	$2.1 mil	$2.2 mil	$2.1 mil

Figure 5-10:
You can circle data to highlight it.

2. **On a corner of your page or slide, away from the table, drag to draw the oval.**

Shape Fill ▾

3. **On the (Drawing Tools) Format tab, open the drop-down list on the Shape Fill button and choose No Fill.**

Shape Outline ▾

4. **Open the drop-down list on the Shape Outline button and choose a very dark color.**

5. **Open the drop-down list on the Shape Outline button, choose Weight, and choose a thick line.**

6. **Drag the oval over the data on your table that you want to highlight.**

If the oval is obscured by the table, go to the (Drawing Tools) Format tab, and click the Bring Forward button (click the Arrange button, if necessary, to see this button). While you're at it, consider rotating the oval a little way to make it appear as though it was drawn by hand on the table.

In the course of a live PowerPoint presentation, you can draw on slides with the Pen to highlight data. See Book IV, Chapter 4.

Chapter 6: Creating a Chart

In This Chapter

✔ Looking at the different parts of a chart

✔ Creating a chart

✔ Examining the different types of charts

✔ Entering chart data in an Excel worksheet

✔ Positioning a chart in Excel, Word, and PowerPoint

✔ Changing the appearance of a chart

✔ Saving a customized chart as a template so that you can use it again

✔ Exploring some fancy-schmancy chart tricks

✔ Fixing common problems with charts

*N*othing is more persuasive than a chart. The bars, pie slices, lines, or columns show instantaneously that production is up or down, that cats are better than dogs or dogs better than cats, or that catsup tastes better than ketchup. Fans of charts and graphs will be glad to know that putting a chart in a Word document, Excel worksheet, or PowerPoint slide is fairly easy.

This chapter explains how to create a chart. It looks at which charts are best for presenting different kinds of data, how to change a chart's appearance, and how to save charts in a template that you can use again. You discover some nice chart tricks, including how to make a picture the backdrop for a chart and how to annotate a chart. This chapter also addresses common chart problems.

A Mercifully Brief Anatomy Lesson

Throughout this chapter, I show you many ways to tinker with charts, but before you can begin tinkering, you need to know what you're tinkering with. In other words, you have to know what the different parts of a chart are. Here is a brief chart anatomy lesson. Figure 6-1 points out where some of the terms described here are found on a real, live chart:

✦ **Plot area:** The center of the chart, apart from the legend and data labels, where the data itself is presented.

✦ **Values:** The numerical values with which the chart is plotted. The values you enter determine the size of the *data markers* — the bars, columns, pie slices, and so on — that portray values. In the column chart in Figure 6-1, values determine the height of the columns.

✦ **Gridlines:** Lines on the chart that indicate value measurements. Gridlines are optional in charts (none are shown in Figure 6-1).

✦ **Worksheet:** Where you enter (or retrieve) the data used to plot the chart. The worksheet resembles a table. Figure 6-2 shows the worksheet I used to enter the data that produced the chart in Figure 6-1. Notice how the numbers at the top of the columns correspond to the numbers entered in the worksheet shown in Figure 6-2. A worksheet is called a *data table* when it appears along with a chart.

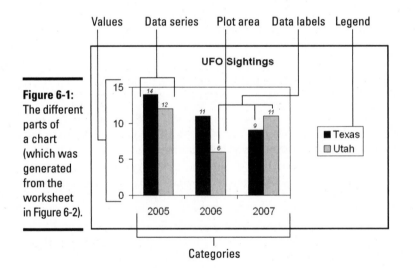

Figure 6-1: The different parts of a chart (which was generated from the worksheet in Figure 6-2).

Figure 6-2: The information entered in this worksheet produced the chart shown in Figure 6-1.

✦ **Data series:** A group of related data points presented by category on a chart. The chart in Figure 6-1 has two data series, one for Texas and one for Utah.

✦ **Categories:** The actual items that you want to compare or display in your chart. In Figure 6-1, the categories are the three years in which UFO sightings occurred in the two states.

✦ **Legend:** A text box located to the side, top, or bottom of a chart that identifies the chart's data labels.

✦ **Horizontal and vertical axes:** For plotting purposes, one side of the plot area. In the chart in Figure 6-1, UFO sightings are plotted on the *horizontal axis;* categories are plotted on the *vertical axis.* Sometimes these axes are called the *category axis* (or *x axis*) and the *value axis* (or *y axis*).

Axes can be confusing, but these axes aren't as evil as they seem. All you really need to know about them is this: You can label the axes in different ways and you can rotate the chart so that the horizontal becomes the vertical axis and vice versa (click the Switch Row/Column button).

✦ **Data point:** A value plotted on a chart that is represented by a column, line, bar, pie slice, dot, or other shape. Each data point corresponds to a value entered in the worksheet. In Figure 6-1, for example, the data points for Texas UFO sightings are 14 in 2005, 11 in 2006, and 9 in 2007. Hence the Texas columns in the table rise to the 14, 11, and 9 level.

✦ **Data marker:** Shapes on a chart that represent data points. Data markers include columns, lines, pie slices, bubbles, and dots. In Figure 6-1, columns are the data markers.

✦ **Data label:** A label that shows the actual values used to construct the data markers. In the chart in Figure 6-1, there are six data labels, one on the top of each column. Displaying data labels in charts is optional.

The good news where the anatomy of a chart is concerned is that you can click anywhere on a chart and see a pop-up box that tells you what part of the chart you just clicked. I wish biology class were that easy!

The Basics: Creating a Chart

Throughout this chapter, I explain the whys, wherefores, and whatnots of creating a chart. Before going into details, here are the basic steps that everyone needs to know to create a chart in Word, Excel, and PowerPoint:

1. **Go to the Insert tab.**

2. **If you're working in Excel, select the data you'll use to generate the chart (in Word and PowerPoint, skip to Step 3).**

In Excel, you select the data on a worksheet before creating the chart, but in Word and PowerPoint, you enter the data for the chart in Excel in Step 4. Yes, you heard me right — in Word and PowerPoint. Excel opens after you begin creating your chart so you can enter data for the chart in an Excel worksheet.

3. **Select the kind of chart you want.**

   How you select a chart type depends on which program you're working in:

   - *Excel:* Either open the drop-down list in one of buttons in the Chart group on the Insert tab (Column, Line, Pie, Bar, Area, Scatter, or Other Charts) and select a chart type, or click the Charts group button to open the Insert Chart dialog box and select a chart there. As shown in Figure 6-3, the Insert Chart dialog box shows all the kinds of charts you can create.

   - *Word and PowerPoint:* Click the Chart button. You see the Insert Chart dialog box shown in Figure 6-3. Select a chart and click OK. The Excel program opens on the right side of your computer screen. (In PowerPoint, you can also click the Chart icon on a placeholder frame to open the Insert Chart dialog box.)

   The next portion of this chapter, "Choosing the Right Chart," describes all the charts types and advises you which to choose.

Figure 6-3: Which chart do you want?

4. **In Word and PowerPoint, replace the sample data in the Excel work-sheet with the data you need for generating your chart.**

Later in this chapter, "Providing the Raw Data for Your Chart" explains how to enter data in an Excel worksheet. After you finish entering the data, you can close Excel by clicking the Close button in the Excel window or going to the File tab and choosing Close.

5. **To modify your chart, start by selecting it.**

Click a chart to select it. Selecting a chart makes the Chart Tools tabs appear in the upper-right corner of the window. Use these tabs — Design, Layout, and Format — to make your chart just-so.

In Word, you must be in Print Layout view to see a chart.

6. **Select the (Chart Tools) Design tab when you want to change the chart's layout, alter the data with which the chart was generated, or select a different chart type.**

Later in this chapter, "Changing a Chart's Appearance" explains how to change the design of a chart.

7. **Select the (Chart Tools) Layout tab when you want to change the chart's title, labels, or gridlines.**

You can add or remove parts of a chart starting on the Layout tab. Later in this chapter, "Changing the layout of a chart" describes how to change around the text and gridlines on a chart.

8. **Select the (Chart Tools) Format tab when you want to change the appearance of your chart.**

You can change colors and fills on your chart, as "Changing a chart element's color, font, or other particular" explains later in this chapter.

And if you decide to delete the chart you created? Click its perimeter to select it and then press the Delete key.

Choosing the Right Chart

If you're a fan of charts, the huge selection of charts can make you feel like a kid in a candy store, but if charts aren't your forte, the wealth of charts you can choose from can be daunting. You can choose among 6 dozen charts in 11 categories (refer to Figure 6-3). Which chart is best? The golden rule for choosing a chart type is to choose the one that presents information in the brightest possible light. The purpose of a chart is to compare information across different categories. Select a chart that draws out the comparison so that others can clearly make comparisons. Table 6-1 describes the 11 chart categories and explains in brief when to use each type of chart.

	Table 6-1	**Chart Types**
Symbol	*Chart Type*	*Best Use/Description*
	Area	Examine how values in different categories fluctuate over time, and see the cumulative change in values. (Same as a line chart except that the area between trend lines is colored in.)
	Bar	Compare values in different categories against one another, usually over time. Data is displayed in horizontal bars. (Same as a column chart except that the bars are horizontal.)
	Bubble	Examine data relationships by studying the size and location of the bubbles that represent the relationships. Bubble charts are often used in financial analyses and market research. (Similar to an XY scatter chart except that you can use three rather than two data series, and the data points appear as bubbles.)
	Column	Compare values in different categories against one another, usually over time. Data is displayed in vertical columns. (Same as a bar chart except that the bars are vertical.)
	Doughnut	See how values compare as percentages of a whole. (Similar to a pie chart except that you can use more than one data series and create concentric doughnut rings in the chart.)
	Line	Examine how values fluctuate over time. Data is displayed in a set of points connected by a line.
	Pie	See how values compare as percentages of a whole. Data from categories is displayed as a percentage of a whole. (Similar to a doughnut chart.)
	Radar	Examine data as it relates to one central point. Data is plotted on radial points from the central point. This kind of chart is used to make subjective performance analyses.
	XY (Scatter)	Compare different numeric data point sets in space to reveal patterns and trends in data. (Similar to a bubble chart except that the data appears as points rather than bubbles.)
	Stock	See how the value of an item fluctuates, as well as its daily, weekly, or yearly high, low, and closing price. This chart is used to track stock prices, but it can also be used to track air temperature and other variable quantities.
	Surface	Examine color-coded data on a 3-D surface to explore relationships between data values.

Providing the Raw Data for Your Chart

Every chart is constructed from *raw data* — the numbers and category names you select in an Excel worksheet (in Excel) or enter in an Excel worksheet (in Word and PowerPoint). If you're operating in Word or PowerPoint, you see, in the Excel worksheet, sample data in a *data range*. The information inside the data range is used to generate the chart. You can tell where the data range begins and ends because it is enclosed in a blue border. Your job is to replace the sample data in the data range with data of your own. As you enter your data, the chart on your slide or page takes shape.

Book V, Chapter 1 explains in detail how to enter data in an Excel worksheet, but here are the basics of entering data in case you're new to Excel:

+ **Entering the data in a cell:** A cell is the box in a worksheet where a column and row intersect; each cell can contain one data item. To enter data in a cell, click the cell and start typing. When you're finished, press Enter, press Tab, or click a different cell. You can also click in the Formula bar (above the worksheet) and enter the data there.

+ **Deleting the data in a cell:** To delete the data in a cell, including the sample data Excel provides for charts, click the cell and press Delete.

+ **Displaying the numbers:** When a number is too large to fit in a cell, Excel displays pound signs (###) or displays the number in scientific notation. Don't worry — the number is still recorded and is used to generate your chart. You can display large numbers by widening the columns in which the numbers are found. Move the pointer between column letters (A, B, and so on at the top of the worksheet) and when you see the double-headed arrow, click and drag to the right.

To enclose more or fewer cells in the data range, move the pointer to the lower-right corner of the data range, and when the pointer changes into a two-headed arrow, click and drag so that the blue box encloses only the data you want for your chart.

In Word and PowerPoint, click the Edit Data button on the (Chart Tools) Design tab at any time to open Excel and fiddle with the numbers and data from which your chart is generated.

Positioning Your Chart in a Workbook, Page, or Slide

To change the position of a chart, click to select it, click its perimeter, and when you see the four-headed arrow, start dragging. Otherwise, follow these instructions to land your chart where you want it to be:

✦ **Excel:** To move your chart to a different worksheet or create a new worksheet to hold your chart, go to the (Chart Tools) Design tab and click the Move Chart button. You see the Move Chart dialog box.

  • To move your chart to a different worksheet, click the Object In option button, choose the worksheet in the drop-down list, and click OK.

  • To create a new worksheet for a chart, click the New Sheet option button, enter a name for the new worksheet, and click OK.

✦ **Word:** Starting in Print Layout view, select your chart, and in the Page Layout or (Chart Tools) Format tab, click the Position button (you may have to click the Arrange button first, depending on the size of your screen). You see a drop-down list with text-wrapping options. Choose the option that describes how you want surrounding text to behave when it crashes into your chart. Book II, Chapter 4 looks in detail at wrapping text around charts and other objects in Word.

✦ **PowerPoint:** Select the chart and drag it on the slide to the right position.

Changing a Chart's Appearance

Charts are awfully nice already, but perhaps you want to redesign one. Perhaps you're an interior decorator type and you want to give charts your own personal touch. Excel, PowerPoint, and Word offer these Chart Tools tabs for redecorating charts:

✦ **Design tab:** For quickly changing a chart's appearance. Go to the Design tab if you're in a hurry. The ready-made gallery choices give you the opportunity to change a chart's layout and appearance in a matter of seconds. You can also choose a new chart type from the Design tab. See "Relying on a chart style to change appearances," later in this chapter.

✦ **Layout tab:** For rearranging, hiding, and displaying various parts of a chart, including the legend, labels, title, gridlines, and scale. Go to the Layout tab to tweak your chart and make different parts of it stand out or recede into the background. For example, you can display axis labels more prominently or make them disappear, enter a title for your chart, or display more or fewer gridlines. See "Changing the layout of a chart" and "Handling the gridlines," later in this chapter.

✦ **Format tab:** For changing the color, outline, font, and font size of various parts of a chart, including the labels, bars, and pie slices. You have to really know what you're doing and have a lot of time on your hands to change colors and fonts throughout a chart. See "Changing a chart element's color, font, or other particular," later in this chapter.

These pages explain how to change a chart's appearance, starting with the biggest change you can make — exchanging one type of chart for another.

Changing the chart type

The biggest way to overhaul a chart is to ditch it in favor of a different chart type. Luckily for you, Office makes this task simple. I wish that changing jobs were this easy. Follow these steps to change a pumpkin into a carriage or an existing chart into a different kind of chart:

1. **Click your chart to select it.**

2. **On the (Chart Tools) Design tab, click the Change Chart Type button, or right-click your chart and choose Change Chart Type on the short-cut menu.**

The Change Chart Type dialog box appears. Does it look familiar? This is the same dialog box you used to create your chart in the first place.

3. **Select a new chart type and click OK.**

Not all chart types can be converted successfully to other chart types. You may well have created a monster, in which case go back to Step 1 and start all over or click the Undo button.

Changing the size and shape of a chart

To make a chart taller or wider, follow these instructions:

✦ Click the perimeter of the chart to select it and then drag a handle on the side to make it wider, or a handle on the top or bottom to make it taller.

✦ Go to the (Chart Tools) Format tab and enter measurements in the Shape Height and Shape Width boxes. You can find these boxes in the Size group (you may have to click the Size button to see them, depending on the size of your screen).

Relying on a chart style to change appearances

The easiest way to change the look of a chart is to choose an option in the Chart Styles gallery in the (Chart Tools) Design tab, as shown in Figure 6-4. You can choose among 50 options. These gallery options are quite sophisti-cated. You would have a hard time fashioning these charts on your own.

Select a Chart style

Figure 6-4:
Redesign
your chart
in the Chart
Styles
gallery.

If your file includes more than one chart, make the charts consistent with one another. Give them a similar appearance so that your file doesn't turn into a chart fashion show. You can make charts consistent with one another by choosing similar options for charts in the Chart Styles gallery.

Changing the layout of a chart

Figure 6-5 identifies the chart elements that you can lay out in different ways. Some of these elements can be removed as well as placed on different parts of a chart. For example, you can display the legend on any side of a chart or not display it at all. Some of the elements can be labeled in different ways. To decide on the layout of a chart, select it and visit the (Chart Tools) Layout tab.

The following pages explain how to change the layout of a chart starting on the (Chart Tools) Layout tab. However, before hurrying to the Layout tab to change your chart's layout, you may consider taking a detour to the (Chart Tools) Design tab (refer to Figure 6-4). The Chart Layouts gallery on the Design tab offers ten ready-made layouts, one of which may meet your high expectations and spare you a trip to the Layout tab.

Figure 6-5:
The layout
elements of
a chart.

Deciding where chart elements appear and how they are labeled

On the (Chart Tools) Layout tab, open the drop-down list on these buttons and choose options to determine how and whether chart elements are labeled:

✦ **Chart Title:** The chart title appears above the chart and describes what the chart is about (refer to Figure 6-5). Place a centered title inside or above the chart. The Above Chart option shrinks the chart a bit to make room for the title. Click in the text box and enter the title after Office creates a chart title text box.

✦ **Axis Titles:** Axis titles list the series name and category name of the data being plotted in the chart (refer to Figure 6-5). You can select Rotated Title for the vertical axis to make the axis label read vertically rather than horizontally (refer to Figure 6-5).

✦ **Legend:** The legend is the box to the side, top, or bottom of the chart that describes what is being plotted (refer to Figure 6-5). Choose an option from the drop-down list to place the chart's legend above, below, or to the side of a chart.

✦ **Data Labels:** Data labels show the numeric values by which the data markers — the bars, columns, pie slices, or dots — in your chart are constructed (refer to Figure 6-5). For example, if a bar in your chart represents the number 28, the data label 28 appears in the bar. You can also label the series name or category name by choosing More Data Label Options on the drop-down list and making selections in the Format Data Labels dialog box.

✦ **Axes:** The axes labels are the series names and scale markers that appear in the chart. Choose Primary Horizontal Axis or Primary Vertical Axis and then select None to remove series names and scale markers from your chart. The other axes options are for deciding how to display axes labels (and are explained in the next section of this chapter).

Deciding how the chart's scale and axes labels are presented

The labels and scale on the horizontal and vertical axes of a chart tell viewers what is being plotted on the chart (refer to Figure 6-5). By clicking the Axes button on the (Chart Tools) Layout tab, you can fine-tune the axes labels and scale on your chart.

After you click the Axes button, you see options for changing around your chart's horizontal or vertical axis. What the horizontal and vertical axis options are depends on whether the axis you're dealing with presents text labels, expresses numerical values, or expresses date values.

Text axis options

Choose a text axis option on the drop-down list to remove the labels or present category name labels in reverse order from the way in which these labels are listed on the worksheet.

Numerical and date axis options

The axis options that pertain to numbers and dates are for declaring how to present the scale on your chart. You can present the numbers in thousands, millions, billions, or with a log scale. By opening the Format Axis dialog box shown in Figure 6-6, you can get quite specific about how the scale is presented on your chart. To open this dialog box, click the Axes button, select the appropriate axis option on the drop-down list, and choose More Options on the submenu. Which options you see in this dialog box depends greatly on which chart type you're dealing with.

The Format Axis dialog box offers these opportunities for changing around the scale of a chart:

✦ **Changing the scale's range:** By default, the scale ranges from 0 to 10 percent more than the largest value being plotted, but you can change the scale's range by selecting a Fixed option button and entering a new value in the Minimum and Maximum text box.

✦ **Changing the number of unit measurement labels:** Label measurements (and gridlines) appear at intervals on a chart according to the number entered in the Major Unit text box. For example, an entry of 10 tells Office to mark each 10 units with a measurement label. Select the Fixed option button and change the number in the Major Unit text box to draw fewer or more unit labels (and gridlines) on your chart. If your chart displays minor tick marks, do the same in the Minor Unit text box.

Figure 6-6:
Fashion a
numerical
scale for a
chart in the
Format Axis
dialog box.

✦ **Displaying numbers as thousandths, millionths, or billionths:** If your chart presents large numbers, consider listing these numbers in thousandths, millionths, or billionths by selecting an option in the Display Units drop-down list. You can also select the Logarithmic Scale check box to display numbers as logarithms.

✦ **Changing the tick-mark scale markers:** Choose Tick Mark options to tell Office where or whether to place *tick marks* — small unit markers — on the scale.

✦ **Changing the location of axis labels:** Choose an option in the Axis Labels drop-down list to tell Office where to place the unit labels on the scale.

✦ **Change the axis crosses:** Select the Axis Value option button and enter a measurement in the Axis Value text box if you want to change the baseline of your chart. Usually, the axis value is set to 0, and markers rise from 0 on the chart; but by entering a different measurement, you can make markers rise or fall from the baseline. For example, if the Axis Value baseline is 5, markers less than 5 fall from a baseline in the middle of the chart and markers greater than 5 rise above it.

Handling the gridlines

Gridlines are lines that cross a chart and indicate value measurements. Most charts include major gridlines to show where bars or columns meet or surpass a major unit of measurement, and you can also include fainter, minor gridlines that mark less significant measurements. Figure 6-7 shows a chart with gridlines displayed in different ways.

Figure 6-7:
Options for handling gridlines (clockwise from upper left): None, Major Gridlines, Major & Minor Gridlines, and Minor Gridlines.

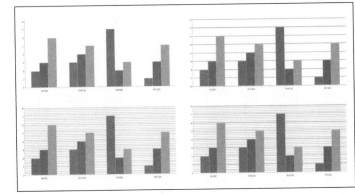

Select your chart and follow these instructions to hide or display gridlines, change the lines' width, or change the lines' color:

✦ **Hiding and choosing the frequency of gridlines:** On the (Chart Tools) Layout tab, click the Gridlines button, choose Primary Horizontal Gridlines or Primary Vertical Gridlines on the drop-down list, and choose an option on the submenu. You can hide gridlines (by choosing None), display major gridlines, display minor gridlines, or display major and minor gridlines (refer to Figure 6-7).

The frequency of gridlines on a chart is tied to the scale. If you want to control the frequency of the gridlines on your own without relying on a Gridlines option, change your chart's scale. The preceding section in this chapter explains how to handle scales.

✦ **Changing gridline width:** On the (Chart Tools) Format tab, open the Chart Elements drop-down list and choose Axis Major Gridlines or Axis Minor Gridlines (display gridlines on your chart if you don't see these options). Then click the Format Selection button, and in the Line Style category of the Format Gridlines dialog box, enter a measurement in the Width text box to make the gridlines heavier or thinner.

✦ **Changing gridline color:** On the (Chart Tools) Format tab, open the Chart Elements drop-down list and select Axis Major Gridlines or Axis Minor Gridlines. (Display gridlines on your chart if you don't see these options.) Then open the drop-down list on the Shape Outline button and choose a color. You can also click the Format Selection button, and in the Line Color category of the Format Gridlines dialog box, select the Solid Line option button and then click the Color button and choose a color there.

Gridlines are essential for helping read charts, but be very, very careful about displaying minor gridlines on charts. These lines can make your chart unreadable. They can turn a perfectly good chart into a gaudy pinstripe suit.

Changing a chart element's color, font, or other particular

Generally speaking, the (Chart Tools) Format tab is the place to go to change the color, line width, font, or font size of a chart element. As I explain shortly, you can do some interior decorating tasks on the (Chart Tools) Layout tab as well.

Follow these basic steps to change a color, line width, font, or font size in part of a chart:

1. Select the (Chart Tools) Format tab.

The tools on the (Chart Tools) Format tab are very similar to the tools found on the (Drawing Tools) Format tab. You can find all the tools you need here to change the color, outline, and size of a chart element. These tools are explained in detail in Book I, Chapter 8.

2. Select the chart element that needs a facelift.

To select a chart element, either click it or choose its name on the Chart Elements drop-down list, as shown in Figure 6-8. You can find this list in the upper-left corner of the window.

3. Format the chart element you selected.

Use one of these techniques to format the chart element:

Format Selection

- *Open a Format dialog box.* Click the Format Selection button to open a Format dialog box. The dialog box offers commands for formatting the element you selected.

- *Do the work on your own.* Format the chart element as you would any object. For example, to change fonts in the chart element you selected, right-click and choose a font on the shortcut menu. Or go to the Home tab to change font sizes. Or open the drop-down list on the Shape Fill button on the (Chart Tools) Format tab and select a new color.

Select a chart element so that you can format it

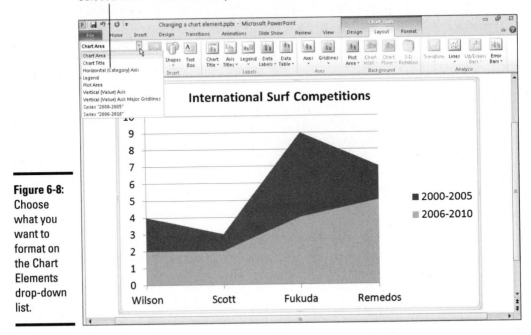

Figure 6-8:
Choose
what you
want to
format on
the Chart
Elements
drop-down
list.

The (Chart Tools) Layout tab also offers these convenient commands for
changing the color of a chart element:

✦ **Plot area:** The *plot area* is the rectangle in which the chart's gridlines, bars,
columns, pie slices, or lines appear. In some chart designs, the plot area is
filled with color. To remove this color or choose a different color, click the
Plot Area button and choose an option. Choose More Plot Area Options to
open the Format Plot Area dialog box and select a new fill color.

✦ **3-D chart wall and chart floor:** Three-dimensional charts have chart walls
and a chart floor. The *chart wall* forms the backdrop of a 3-D chart; the *chart
floor* forms the bottom of the chart. Click the Chart Wall button and choose
an option to remove the chart wall or change its color; click the Chart Floor
button and choose an option to remove the chart floor or change its color.

Saving a Chart as a Template So
That You Can Use It Again

If you go to the significant trouble of redecorating a chart and you expect to
do it again the same way in the future, save your chart as a template. This
way, you can call on the template in the future to create the same chart
and not have to decorate it again. Perhaps you've created charts with your

company's colors or you've created a chart that you're especially proud of. Save it as a template to spare yourself the work of reconstructing it.

A chart template holds data series colors, gridline settings, plot area colors, font settings, and the like. It doesn't hold data. These pages explain how to save a chart as a template and how to create a chart with a template you created.

Saving a chart as a template

Follow these steps to make a template out of a chart:

1. **Save your file to make sure that the chart settings are saved on your computer.**

2. **Select your chart.**

3. **Go to the (Chart Tools) Design tab.**

4. **Click the Save As Template button.**

You can find this button in the Type group. You see the Save Chart Template dialog box.

5. **Enter a descriptive name for the template and click the Save button.**

Include the type of chart you're dealing with in the name. This will help you understand which template you're selecting when the time comes to choose a chart template.

By default, chart templates are saved in this folder in Windows 7 and Windows Vista: `C:\Users\`*Username*`\AppData\Roaming\Microsoft\ Templates\Charts`. Chart templates are stored in this folder in Windows XP: `C:\Documents and Settings\`*Username*`\Application Data\ Microsoft\Templates\Charts`. The templates have the `.ctrx` extension. If you want to delete or rename a template, open the Charts folder in Windows Explorer or Computer and do your deleting and renaming there. You can open the Charts folder very quickly by clicking the Manage Templates button in the Insert Chart dialog box (refer to Figure 6-3).

Creating a chart from a template

To create a chart from your own customized template, open the Create Chart dialog box (click the Chart button) and go to the Templates category. The dialog box shows a list of templates you created. Move the pointer over a template to read its name in a pop-up box. Select a template and click OK.

Chart Tricks for the Daring and Heroic

This chapter wouldn't be complete without a handful of chart tricks to impress your friends and intimidate your enemies. In the pages that follow, you discover how to make charts roll over and play dead. You also find out how to decorate a chart with a picture, annotate a chart, display worksheet data alongside a chart, and create an overlay chart.

Decorating a chart with a picture

As shown in Figure 6-9, a picture looks mighty nice on the plot area of a chart — especially a column chart. If you have a picture in your computer that would serve well to decorate a chart, you are hereby encouraged to start decorating. Follow these steps to place a picture in the plot area of a chart:

1. **Select your chart.**

2. **On the (Chart Tools) Format tab, open the Chart Elements drop-down list and choose Plot Area.**

3. **Click the Shape Fill button and choose Picture on the drop-down list.**

You see the Insert Picture dialog box.

4. **Locate the picture you need and select it.**

Try to select a light-colored picture that will serve as a background. Book VIII, Chapter 3 explains how you can recolor a picture to make it lighter.

5. **Click the Insert button.**

The picture lands in your chart.

You may need to change the color of the *data markers* — the columns, bars, lines, or pie slices — on your chart to make them stand out against the picture. See "Changing a chart element's color, font, or other particular," earlier in this chapter.

Figure 6-9: Using a picture as the backdrop of a chart.

Annotating a chart

To highlight part of a chart — an especially large pie slice, a tall column, or a bar showing miniscule sales figures — annotate it with a callout text box and place the text box beside the pie slice, column, or bar. Figure 6-10 shows an example of an annotated chart. The annotation tells you that one sector isn't performing especially well and somebody ought to get on the ball.

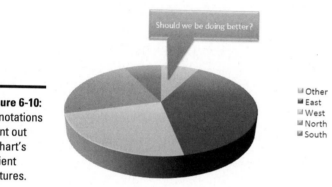

Figure 6-10:
Annotations
point out
a chart's
salient
features.

To annotate a chart, select a callout shape, enter text in the callout shape, and connect the shape to part of your chart. Follow these steps to annotate a chart:

1. **Select your chart and go to the (Chart Tools) Layout tab.**

2. **Click the Shapes button, scroll to the Callouts section of the drop-down list, and choose a callout.**

    Depending on the size of your screen, you may have to click the Insert button to get to the Shapes button.

3. **Drag on your slide to draw the callout shape.**

    Book I, Chapter 8 explains drawing shapes in gory detail.

4. **Type the annotation inside the callout shape.**

5. **Resize the callout shape as necessary to make it fit with the chart.**

6. **Drag the yellow diamond on the callout shape to attach the callout to the chart.**

    You probably have to do some interior decorating to make the callout color fit with the chart. Book I, Chapter 8 explains how to change an object's color.

Displaying the raw data alongside the chart

Showing the worksheet data used to produce a chart is sort of like showing the cops your ID. It proves you're the real thing. It makes your chart more authentic. If yours is a simple pie chart or other chart that wasn't generated with a large amount of raw data, you can display the data alongside your chart in a data table. Anyone who sees the table knows you're not kidding or fudging the numbers.

Select your chart and use of one of these techniques to place a table with the raw data below your chart:

 ✦ On the (Chart Tools) Layout tab, click the Data Table button and choose an option on the drop-down list.

 ✦ On the (Chart Tools) Design tab, open the Chart Layouts gallery and select a layout that includes a data table.

To format a data table, go to the (Chart Tools) Format tab, open the Chart Element drop-down list and choose Data Table. Then click the Format Selection button. You see the Format Data Table dialog box, where you can fill the table with color and choose colors for the lines in the table.

Creating an overlay chart

An *overlay chart* is a secondary chart that appears over another chart, the idea being to contrast two sets of data. Create an overlay chart by selecting one data series in a chart you already created and instructing Office to use the data in the series for the overlay chart. To create an overlay chart, the original chart must plot more than one data series. Figure 6-11 shows a bar chart overlaying a stacked area chart.

Figure 6-11:
An overlay chart, in this case a bar chart overlaying a stacked area chart.

Yields at Blue, Muddy, and Mirror Lake

Follow these steps to create an overlay chart:

1. **In a chart you created, click to select the data series that you will use to create the secondary chart.**

The easiest way to select a data series is to click the chart itself, but you can also go to the (Chart Tools) Format tab and select a series in the Chart Elements drop-down list.

2. **Right-click the data series you selected and choose Change Series Chart Type.**

You see the Change Chart Type dialog box.

3. **Choose a chart type for the overlay chart and click OK.**

Be sure to click a chart type different from the one in the other chart.

Placing a trendline on a chart

Especially on column charts, a *trendline* can help viewers more clearly see changes in data. Viewers can see, for example, that sales are going up or down, income is rising or falling, or annual rainfall is increasing or decreasing. Figure 6-12 shows an example of a trendline on a chart. In this case, the trendline shows that the deer population in Sacramento County is rising.

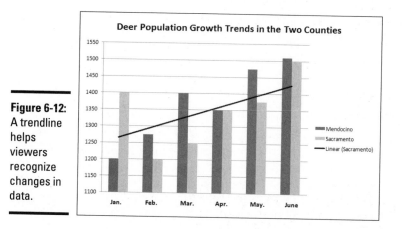

Figure 6-12:
A trendline
helps
viewers
recognize
changes in
data.

Follow these steps to put a trendline on a chart:

1. **On the (Chart Tools) Layout tab, open the Chart Elements drop-down list and choose the data series that you want to highlight with a trendline.**

2. Click the Trendline button and choose a trendline option on the drop-down list.

You can choose More Trendline Options on the drop-down list to open the Format Trendline dialog box and choose additional types of trendlines.

To change the look of a trendline, right-click it and choose Format Trendline. In the Format Trendline dialog box, choose a line color and line style.

To remove a trendline from a chart, go to the (Chart Tools) Layout tab, click the Trendline button, and choose None on the drop-down list.

Troubleshooting a Chart

Sometimes tinkering with a chart opens a Pandora's box of problems. You find yourself having to correct little errors that appear in charts. Here are some shorthand instructions for fixing common chart problems:

✦ **The dates in the chart aren't formatted right.** To change the way in which dates are formatted on a chart, go to the (Chart Tools) Format tab, open the Chart Elements drop-down list, and choose Horizontal (Value) Axis or Vertical (Value) Axis. Then click the Format Selection button, and in the Format Axis dialog box, go to the Number category, select Date in the Category menu, and choose a date format.

✦ **The numbers in the chart aren't formatted right.** To change the number of decimal places, include comma separators in numbers, display currency symbols, or do all else that pertains to numbers, go to the (Chart Tools) Format tab, open the Chart Elements drop-down list, and choose Horizontal (Value) Axis or Vertical (Value) Axis. Then click the Format Selection button. You see the Format Axis dialog box. Visit the Number category and select options for displaying numbers.

✦ **"Category 1" or "Series 1" appears in the chart legend.** To direct you to the right place to enter data in Excel worksheets, phantom names such as "Category 1" and "Series 1" appear in worksheets. Sometimes these phantoms wind up in chart legends as well. To remove them, go to the (Chart Tools) Design tab and click the Edit Data button. You see the Excel worksheet, where the data range used to generate the chart is enclosed in a blue box. Drag the lower-right corner of the box so that the box encloses only the data you want for your chart.

✦ **In 3-D charts, small markers are obscured by large markers in the foreground.** For all the data markers to be shown in a 3-D chart, the smaller ones have to be in the foreground. To rearrange data markers, go to the (Chart Tools) Design tab and click the Select Data button to open the Select Data Source dialog box. Then select a series and click the Up or Down button to rearrange the series in your chart. Series that are high on the list go to the back of the chart; series that are low on the list go to the front.

✦ **The chart doesn't gather all data from the worksheet.** On the (Chart Tools) Design tab, click the Edit Data button, and in the Excel worksheet that stores data for your chart, enlarge the blue data-range box so that it encloses all your data. You can enlarge the box by dragging its lower-right corner.

✦ **The scale is too big for my chart.** Especially if the scale range on a chart is small, the scale can be too big compared to the data markers. To change the scale range, go to the (Chart Tools) Layout tab, click the Axes button, choose the appropriate axis option on the drop-down list, and choose More Options. Then, in the Format Axis dialog box, select the Fixed option button and enter a Maximum value to establish the top of the scale for your chart. For more details, see "Deciding how the chart's scale and axes labels are presented," earlier in this chapter.

Chapter 7: Making a SmartArt Diagram

In This Chapter

✔ Creating a diagram

✔ Repositioning and resizing diagrams

✔ Laying out and changing the look of diagram shapes

✔ Entering text on a diagram shape

✔ Changing the appearance of a diagram

✔ Creating a diagram from shapes

Along with charts and tables, diagrams are the best way to present your ideas. Diagrams clearly show, for example, employees' relationships with one another, product cycles, workflow processes, and spheres of influence. A diagram is an excellent marriage of images and words. Diagrams allow an audience to literally visualize a concept, idea, or relationship.

This chapter explains how to construct diagrams from SmartArt graphics and how to create a diagram. It shows how to customize diagrams by changing the size of diagrams and diagram shapes, adding and removing shapes, and changing shapes' colors. You also discover how to change the direction of a diagram and enter the text. Finally, this chapter demonstrates how to create a diagram from scratch with shapes and connectors.

The Basics: Creating SmartArt Diagrams

In Word, PowerPoint, and Excel, diagrams are made from *SmartArt graphics*. These diagram graphics are "interactive" in the sense that you can move, alter, and write text on them. In other words, you can use them to construct diagrams. You can alter these diagrams to your liking. You can make a diagram portray precisely what you want it to portray, although you usually have to wrestle with the diagram a bit.

The first step in creating a diagram is to select a layout in the Choose a SmartArt Graphic dialog box, shown in Figure 7-1. After you create the initial diagram, you customize it to create a diagram of your own. About 120 diagrams are in the dialog box. They fall into these eight categories:

Diagram Type	Use
List	For describing blocks of related information, as well as sequential steps in a task, process, or workflow
Process	For describing how a concept or physical process changes over time or is modified
Cycle	For illustrating a circular progression without a beginning or end, or a relationship in which the components are in balance
Hierarchy	For describing hierarchical relationships between people, departments, and other entities, as well as portraying branchlike relationships in which one decision or action leads to another
Relationship	For describing the relationship between different components (but not hierarchical relationships)
Matrix	For showing the relationship between quadrants
Pyramid	For showing proportional or hierarchical relationships
Picture	For creating diagrams that include photographs and pictures (This catchall category presents picture diagrams from the other categories.)

Diagram types   Select a diagram   Diagram explanation

Figure 7-1:
To create
a diagram,
start by
selecting a
diagram in
this dialog
box.

WARNING! If you intend to construct a "flow chart type" diagram with many branches and levels, go to the Hierarchy category and select the Organization Chart or one of the hierarchy diagrams. As "Laying Out the Diagram Shapes" explains later in this chapter, only these choices permit you to make a diagram with many different branches and levels.

After you select a generic diagram in the Choose a SmartArt Graphic dialog box and click OK, the next step is to make the diagram your own by completing these tasks:

+ **Change the diagram's size and position:** Change the size and position of a diagram to make it fit squarely on your page or slide. See "Changing the Size and Position of a Diagram," later in this chapter.

+ **Add shapes to (or remove shapes from) the diagram:** Adding a shape involves declaring where to add the shape, promoting or demoting the shape with respect to other shapes, and declaring how the new shape connects to another shape. See "Laying Out the Diagram Shapes," later in this chapter.

+ **Enter text:** Enter text on each shape, or component, of the diagram. See "Handling the Text on Diagram Shapes," later in this chapter.

If you so desire, you can also customize your diagram by taking on some or all of these tasks:

+ **Changing its overall appearance:** Choose a different color scheme or 3-D variation for your diagram. See "Choosing a Look for Your Diagram," later in this chapter.

+ **Changing shapes:** Select a new shape for part of your diagram, change the size of a shape, or assign different colors to shapes to make shapes stand out. See "Changing the Appearance of Diagram Shapes," later in this chapter.

If you're comfortable creating a diagram of your own by drawing shapes and lines, no law says that you have to begin in the Choose a SmartArt Graphic dialog box. Later in this chapter, "Creating a Diagram from Scratch" looks into creating a diagram by making use of text boxes, lines, and shapes.

Creating the Initial Diagram

The first step in fashioning a diagram is to choose a SmartArt graphic in the Choose a SmartArt Graphic dialog box. After that, you roll up your sleeves, change the diagram's size and shape, and enter the text. If you select the wrong diagram to start with, all is not lost. You can choose another diagram in its place, although how successful swapping one diagram for another is depends on how lucky you are and how far along you are in creating your diagram. These pages explain how to create an initial diagram and swap one diagram for another.

Starting from a sketch

You can spare yourself a lot of trouble by starting from a sketch when you create a diagram. Find a pencil with a good eraser, grab a blank piece of paper, and start drawing. Imagine what your ideal diagram looks like. Draw the arrows or lines connecting the different parts of the diagram. Write the text. Draw the diagram that best illustrates what you want to communicate.

Later, in the Choose a SmartArt Graphic dialog box (refer to Figure 7-1), you can select the diagram that most resembles the one you sketched. The dialog box offers 120 types of diagrams. Unless you start from a sketch and have a solid idea of the diagram you want, you can get lost in the dialog box. Also, if you don't start from a sketch, adding shapes to the diagram and landing them in the right places can be a chore.

Creating a diagram

Follow these steps to create a diagram:

1. **On the Insert tab, click the SmartArt button.**

   You see the Choose a SmartArt Graphic dialog box (refer to Figure 7-1). In PowerPoint, you can also open the dialog box by clicking the SmartArt icon in a content placeholder frame.

2. **Select a diagram in the Choose a SmartArt Graphic dialog box.**

   Diagrams are divided into eight categories, as I explain earlier in this chapter. The dialog box offers a description of each diagram. Either select a type on the left side of the dialog box or scroll the entire list to find the graphic that most resembles the diagram you want.

   If you want to create a graph with many levels and branches, go to the Hierarchy category and select one of these charts: Organization Chart, Picture Organization Chart, or Name and Title Organization Chart. These three diagrams are much more complex than the others and allow for branching. See "Laying Out the Diagram Shapes" later in this chapter for details.

3. **Click OK.**

   The next topic in this chapter explains how to swap one diagram for another, in case you chose wrongly in the Choose a SmartArt Graphic dialog box.

Swapping one diagram for another

If the diagram you chose initially doesn't do the job, you can swap it for a different diagram. How successful the swap is depends on how far along you are in creating your diagram and whether your diagram is simple or complex. Follow these steps to swap one diagram for another:

1. **Click your diagram to select it.**

2. **Go to the (SmartArt Tools) Design tab.**

3. **Open the Layouts gallery (you may have to click the Change Layout button first).**

   You see a gallery with diagrams of the same type as the diagram you're working with.

4. **Select a new diagram or choose More Layouts to open the Choose a SmartArt Graphic dialog box and select a diagram there.**

You may have to click the trusty Undo button and start all over if the diagram you selected for the swap didn't do the job.

Changing the Size and Position of a Diagram

To make a diagram fit squarely on a page or slide, you have to change its size and position. Resizing and positioning diagrams and other objects is the subject of Book I, Chapter 8, but in case you don't care to travel that far to get instructions, here are shorthand instructions for resizing and positioning diagrams:

✦ **Resizing a diagram:** Select the diagram, move the pointer over a selection handle on the corner or side, and start dragging after the pointer changes into a two-headed arrow. You can also go to the (SmartArt Tools) Format tab and enter new measurements in the Width and Height boxes. (You may have to click the Size button to see these text boxes, depending on the size of your screen.)

✦ **Repositioning a diagram:** Select the diagram, move the pointer over its perimeter, and when you see the four-headed arrow, click and start dragging.

Notice when you resize a diagram that the shapes in the diagram change size proportionally. Most diagrams are designed so that shapes fill out the diagram. When you change the size of a diagram, remove a shape from a diagram, or add a shape, shapes change size within the diagram.

Laying Out the Diagram Shapes

At the heart of every diagram are the rectangles, circles, arrows, and whatnots that make the diagram what it is. These shapes illustrate the concept or idea you want to express to your audience. Your biggest challenge when creating a diagram is laying out the diagram shapes.

The following pages explain how to select diagram shapes, add shapes, reposition shapes, and remove shapes from diagrams. They also offer instructions specific to working with hierarchy diagrams.

Selecting a diagram shape

Before you can remove a shape from a diagram or indicate where you want to add a new shape, you have to select a diagram shape. To select a diagram shape, move the pointer over its perimeter and click when you see the four-headed arrow underneath your pointer.

You can tell when a diagram shape is selected because a solid line, not a dotted line, appears around the shape, as shown in Figure 7-2. When you see dotted lines around a shape, you're expected to enter text.

Selected diagram shape

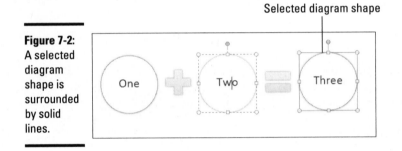

Figure 7-2: A selected diagram shape is surrounded by solid lines.

Removing a shape from a diagram

Removing a shape from a diagram is as easy as falling off a turnip truck as long as you correctly select the shape before you remove it. To remove a shape, select it and press Delete. Other shapes grow larger when you remove a shape, in keeping with the "fill out the diagram by any means necessary" philosophy.

Moving diagram shapes to different positions

If a shape in a diagram isn't in the right position, don't fret — you can change the order of shapes very easily by going to the (SmartArt Tools) Design tab and clicking the Move Up or Move Down button.

Select the diagram shape that needs repositioning and click the Move Up or Move Down button as many times as necessary to land the shape in the right place.

Adding shapes to diagrams apart from hierarchy diagrams

Unlike hierarchy diagrams, list, process, cycle, relationship, and matrix diagrams don't have branches. They always travel in one direction only. This makes adding shapes to these diagrams fairly straightforward. To add a shape, you select a shape in the diagram and then add the new shape so that it appears before or after the shape you selected, as shown in Figure 7-3.

Select a shape and choose an Add Shape option   The new shape

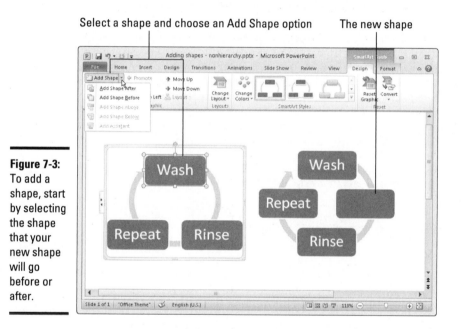

Figure 7-3:
To add a shape, start by selecting the shape that your new shape will go before or after.

Follow these steps to add a shape to a list, process, cycle, relationship, matrix, or pyramid diagram:

1. **In your diagram, select the shape that your new shape will appear before or after.**

   Earlier in this chapter, "Selecting a diagram shape" explains how to select diagram shapes.

2. **Choose the Add Shape After or Add Shape Before command.**

   To get to these commands, use one of these techniques:

   - On the (SmartArt Tools) Design tab, open the drop-down list on the Add Shape button and choose Add Shape After or Add Shape Before(refer to Figure 7-3).

   - Right-click the shape you selected, choose Add Shape on the shortcut menu, and then choose Add Shape After or Add Shape Before on the submenu.

Although the Add Shape drop-down list offers an Add Shape Above and Add Shape Below command (refer to Figure 7-3), these commands don't apply to list, process, cycle, relationship, or matrix diagrams. Ignore them. They're strictly for hierarchy and pyramid diagrams.

Adding shapes to hierarchy diagrams

Hierarchy diagrams are more complex than other diagrams because they branch out such that shapes are found on different levels. This branching out makes adding shapes to hierarchy diagrams problematic.

As shown in Figure 7-4, Office offers four Add Shape commands for adding shapes to hierarchy diagrams: Add Shape After, Add Shape Before, Add Shape Above, and Add Shape Below. What these commands do depends on whether the diagram is horizontally or vertically oriented, because what constitutes after, before, above, and below is different in vertical and horizontal diagrams. Suffice it to say that when you add shapes to hierarchy diagrams, you often have to try different commands, clicking the Undo button and starting all over until you get it right.

Select a shape and choose one of four Add Shape commands

Figure 7-4:
You can add a shape after, before, above, or below a shape in a hierarchy diagram.

Follow these steps to add a shape to a hierarchy diagram:

1. **In your diagram, select the shape to which your new shape will be connected.**

Earlier in this chapter, "Selecting a diagram shape" describes how to select a shape.

2. **Choose an Add Shape command.**

   Figure 7-4 shows what Add Shape commands do. You can choose Add Shape commands with one of these techniques:

   • On the (SmartArt Tools) Design tab, open the drop-down list on the Add Shape button and choose an Add Shape command (refer to Figure 7-4).

   • Right-click the shape you selected, choose Add Shape on the short-cut menu, and then choose an Add Shape command.

Adding shapes to Organization charts

An Organization chart diagram offers many opportunities for connecting shapes. The shapes can branch out from one another in four directions as well as appear to the side in the "assistant" position. When you place one shape below another shape, you can make the new shape *hang* so that it is joined to a line that drops, or hangs, from another shape. These pages explain how to add shapes and create hanging relationships between one shape and the shapes subordinate to it.

Adding an Organization Chart shape

Besides adding a shape after, before, above, or below a shape, you can add an assistant shape to an Organization Chart diagram, as shown in Figure 7-5. An *assistant shape* is an intermediary shape between two levels. Follow these steps to add a shape to an Organization Chart diagram:

1. **Select the shape to which you will add a new shape.**

   Earlier in this chapter, "Selecting a diagram shape" explains how to select shapes. As shown in Figure 7-5, shapes are surrounded by solid lines, not dotted lines, when you select them properly.

2. **Choose an Add Shape command.**

   You can choose Add Shape commands in two ways:

   • On the (SmartArt Tools) Design tab, open the drop-down list on the Add Shape button and choose an Add Shape command (refer to Figure 7-5).

   • Right-click the shape you selected, choose Add Shape on the short-cut menu, and then choose an Add Shape command on the submenu.

   Figure 7-5 demonstrates what the Add Shape commands do. Notice that Add Shape Before places a new shape to the left of the shape you selected; Add Shape After places a new shape to the right.

Select a shape and choose one of five Add Shape commands

Figure 7-5:
Adding a
shape to an
Organization
Chart
diagram.

Be careful about choosing the Add Shape Above command. This command effectively bumps the shape you selected to a lower level in order to make room for the new shape. In effect, you demote one shape when you place a new shape above it.

Shapes created by the Add Assistant command land on the left side of the line to which they're attached, but if you prefer the assistant shape to be on the right side of the line, you can drag it to the right.

Hanging a shape below another shape in an Organization Chart

Besides the standard relationship between shapes above and below one another, you can create a *hanging relationship* in an Organization Chart diagram. Figure 7-6 shows the three kinds of hanging relationships — Standard, Both, Left Hanging, and Right Hanging. In a hanging relationship, the line hangs from a shape, and subordinate shapes are connected to the line.

You can create a hanging relationship between shapes before or after you create the subordinate shapes. Follow these steps to create a hanging relationship:

1. **Select the shape to which other shapes will hang or are hanging.**

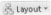

2. **On the (SmartArt Tools) Design tab, click the Layout button.**

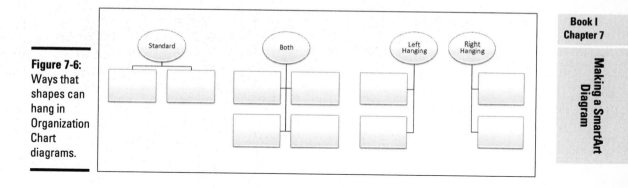

Figure 7-6:
Ways that
shapes can
hang in
Organization
Chart
diagrams.

3. **On the drop-down list, choose Both, Left Hanging, or Right Hanging.**

   The Standard option on the drop-down list is for creating a standard
   relationship, not a hanging relationship.

Promoting and demoting shapes in hierarchy diagrams

Shapes in hierarchy diagrams are ranked by level. If a shape is on the
wrong level, you can move it higher or lower in the diagram by clicking the
Promote or Demote button on the (SmartArt Tools) Design tab. Promoting
and demoting shapes can turn into a donnybrook if you aren't careful. If the
shapes being promoted or demoted are attached to subordinate shapes, the
subordinate shapes are promoted or demoted as well. This can have unforeseen and sometimes horrendous consequences.

Follow these steps to promote or demote a shape (and its subordinates) in a
hierarchy diagram:

1. **Select the shape that needs a change of rank.**

   You can select more than one shape by Ctrl+clicking.

2. **Go to the (SmartArt Tools) Design tab.**

3. **Click the Promote or Demote button.**

   Do you like what you see? If not, you may have to click the Undo button and
   start all over.

Handling the Text on Diagram Shapes

When you create a new diagram, "[Text]" (the word *Text* enclosed in brackets) appears on shapes. Your job is to replace this generic placeholder with something more meaningful and less bland. These sections explain how to enter text and bulleted lists on shapes.

Entering text on a diagram shape

Use one of these techniques to enter text on a diagram shape:

✦ **Click in the shape and start typing:** The words you type appear in the shape, as shown in Figure 7-7.

✦ **Enter text in the Text pane:** Enter the text by typing it in the Text pane, as shown in Figure 7-7. The text pane opens to the left of the diagram. To open the text pane:

- On the (SmartArt Tools) Design tab, click the Text Pane button.

- Click the Text Pane button on the diagram. This button is not labeled, but you can find it to the left of the diagram.

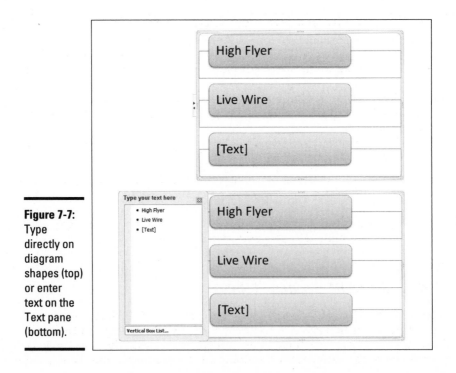

Figure 7-7:
Type
directly on
diagram
shapes (top)
or enter
text on the
Text pane
(bottom).

Turning a bulleted list into a diagram (PowerPoint)

Suppose you're working along in PowerPoint when suddenly the realization strikes you that a bulleted list in a text frame or text box would work much better as a diagram. For those occasions, you click the Convert to SmartArt button. By clicking this button, you can turn the text in a text frame or text box into a diagram. If the text frame or box contains a bulleted list, each bulleted item becomes a diagram shape.

Follow these steps to turn a text frame or text box into a diagram:

1. **Select the text frame or text box.**

2. **On the Home tab, click the Convert to SmartArt button.**

   You see a drop-down list with basic diagram choices.

3. **Either select a diagram on the list or choose More SmartArt Graphics to open the Choose a SmartArt Graphic dialog box and select a diagram there.**

The text in diagrams shrinks as you enter more text so that all text is the same size. If you want to make the text larger or smaller in one shape, see "Changing fonts and font sizes on shapes," later in this chapter.

Entering bulleted lists on diagram shapes

Some diagram shapes have built-in bulleted lists, but no matter. Whether a shape is prepared to be bulleted or not, you can enter bullets in a diagram shape. Here are instructions for entering and removing bullets:

✦ **Entering a bulleted list:** Select the shape that needs bullets, and on the (SmartArt Tools) Design tab, click the Add Bullet button. Either enter the bulleted items directly into the shape (pressing Enter as you type each entry) or click the Text Pane button to open the Text pane (refer to Figure 7-7) and enter bullets there.

✦ **Removing bulleted items:** Click before the first bulleted entry and keep pressing the Delete key until you have removed all the bulleted items. You can also start in the Text pane (refer to Figure 7-7) and press the Delete key there until you've removed the bulleted items, or drag to select several bulleted items and then press Delete.

Changing a Diagram's Direction

As long as your diagram is horizontally oriented, you can change its direction. As shown in Figure 7-8, you can flip it over such that the rightmost shape in your diagram becomes the leftmost shape, and what was the leftmost shape becomes the rightmost shape. If arrows are in your diagram, the arrows point the opposite direction after you flip the diagram. You can't flip vertically oriented diagrams this way. Sorry, but diagrams that run north to south, not west to east, can't be rolled over.

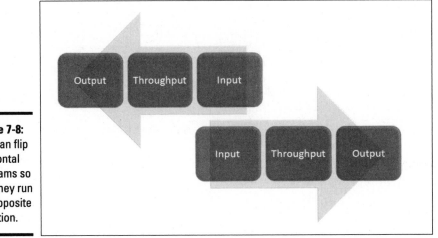

Figure 7-8:
You can flip horizontal diagrams so that they run the opposite direction.

Follow these steps to flip a horizontally oriented diagram:

1. **Select the diagram.**

 2. **On the (SmartArt Tools) Design tab, click the Right to Left button.**

If you don't like what you see, click the button again or click the Undo button.

Choosing a Look for Your Diagram

Decide how a diagram looks by starting on the (SmartArt Tools) Design tab. Starting there, you can choose a color scheme for your diagram and a different style. Between the Change Colors drop-down list and the SmartArt Styles gallery, you can find a combination of options that presents your diagram in the best light:

✦ **Change Colors button:** Click the Change Colors button to see color schemes for your diagram on the drop-down list, as shown in Figure 7-9. Point at a few options to live-preview them.

✦ **SmartArt Styles gallery:** Open the SmartArt Styles gallery to choose simple and 3-D variations on the diagram.

Select a color scheme

Select a diagram style

Figure 7-9:
Experiment
freely with
the Change
Colors and
SmartArt
Styles
gallery
options.

If you experiment too freely and want to backpedal, click the Reset Graphic button on the (SmartArt Tools) Design tab. Clicking this button reverses all the formatting changes you made to your diagram.

If your Word document, Excel worksheet, or PowerPoint presentation includes many diagrams, make sure that your diagrams are consistent in appearance. Choose similar colors for diagrams. If you like 3-D diagrams, make the majority of your diagrams 3-D. Don't let the diagrams overwhelm the ideas they are meant to express. The point is to present ideas in diagrams, not turn your work into a SmartArt diagram showcase.

Changing the Appearance of Diagram Shapes

To call attention to one part of a diagram, you can change the appearance of a shape and make it stand out. Any part of a diagram that is different from the other parts naturally gets more attention. To change the appearance of a shape, consider changing its size or color, exchanging one shape for another, or changing the font and font size of the text. These topics are covered in the following pages.

Changing the size of a diagram shape

A shape that is larger than other shapes in a diagram gets the attention of the audience. Select your shape and use one of these techniques to enlarge or shrink it:

✦ On the (SmartArt Tools) Format tab, click the Larger or Smaller button as many times as necessary to make the shape the right size.

✦ Move the pointer over a corner selection handle, and when the pointer changes to a two-headed arrow, click and start dragging.

Notice that the text inside the shape remains the same size although the shape is larger. To change the size of the text in a shape, see "Changing fonts and font sizes on shapes," later in this chapter.

To return a diagram shape to its original size after you've fooled with it, right-click the shape and choose Reset Shape.

Exchanging one shape for another

Another way to call attention to an important part of a diagram is to change shapes, as shown in Figure 7-10. Rather than a conventional shape, use an oval, block arrow, or star. You can substitute a shape in the Shapes gallery for any diagram shape (Book I, Chapter 8 explores the Shapes gallery). To exchange one shape for another in a diagram, select the shape and use one of these techniques:

✦ On the (SmartArt Tools) Format tab, click the Change Shape button and select a shape in the Shapes gallery.

✦ Right-click the shape, choose Change Shape on the shortcut menu, and select a shape on the submenu.

Figure 7-10: Using different shapes and different-sized shapes in a diagram.

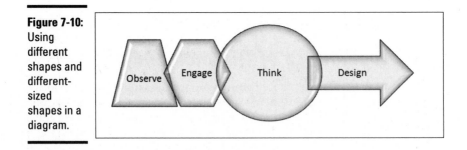

Changing a shape's color, fill, or outline

Yet another way to call attention to a shape is to change its color, fill, or outline border, as shown in Figure 7-11. Select a shape and go to the (SmartArt Tools) Format tab to change a shape's color, fill, or outline.

Shape style   Shape fill   Shape outline   Shape effect

Observe   Engage   Think   Design

Figure 7-11:
Ways to
make a
diagram
shape stand
out.

♦ **Restyling a shape:** Select an option in the Shape Styles gallery to give a shape a makeover.

♦ **Filling a shape with a new color:** Click the Shape Fill button and make a choice from the drop-down list to select a color, picture, two-color gradient, or texture for the shape.

♦ **Changing the outline:** Click the Shape Outline button and choose a color and weight for the shape's border on the drop-down list.

♦ **Applying a shape effect:** Click the Shape Effects button to select a shape effect for your shape.

Editing 3-D diagrams in 2-D

Three-dimensional diagrams are wonderful. You can impress your friends with a 3-D diagram. All you have to do to turn a mundane two-dimensional diagram into a three-dimensional showpiece is go to the (SmartArt Tools) Design tab, open the SmartArt Styles gallery, and select a 3-D option.

Unfortunately, editing a 3-D diagram can be difficult. The shapes and text are all aslant. It's hard to tell where to click or what to drag when you're editing a 3-D diagram.

Fortunately, you can get around the problem of editing a 3-D diagram by temporarily displaying it in two dimensions. On the (SmartArt Tools) Format tab, click the Edit in 2-D button to temporarily render a 3-D graphic in two dimensions. Click the button a second time to get the third dimension back.

Changing fonts and font sizes on shapes

To make a diagram shape stand out, try changing the font and font size of the text on the shape. Before you change fonts and font sizes, however, you should know that changing fonts in a shape effectively disconnects the shape from the other shapes in the diagram. Normally, text changes size throughout a diagram when you add or remove shapes, but when you change the font or font size in one shape, it is no longer associated with the other shapes; its letters don't change their size or appearance when shapes are added or removed from the diagram of which it is a part.

To alter the text on a diagram shape, select the text, go to the Home tab, and choose a different font, font size, and font color, too, if you want.

Creating a Diagram from Scratch

If you have the skill and the wherewithal, you can create a diagram from scratch by piecing together shapes, arrows, and connectors. The diagram in Figure 7-12, for example, was made not from SmartArt graphics but from shapes, arrows, and connectors. Book I, Chapter 8 explains how to draw shapes and lines between shapes. You can enter text on any shape merely by clicking inside it and wiggling your fingers over the keyboard.

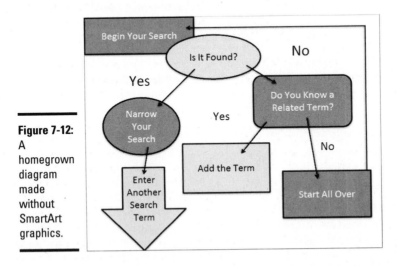

Figure 7-12: A homegrown diagram made without SmartArt graphics.

Making a diagram from scratch has some advantages. You can draw the connectors any which way. Lines can cross the diagram chaotically. You can include text boxes as well as shapes (the diagram in Figure 7-12 has four text boxes). Don't hesitate to fashion your own diagrams when a presentation or document calls for it.

Chapter 8: Drawing and Manipulating Lines, Shapes, and Other Objects

In This Chapter

- ✔ Drawing and manipulating lines, arrows, and connectors
- ✔ Creating and modifying shapes
- ✔ Creating WordArt images
- ✔ Selecting, resizing, moving, aligning, overlapping, rotating, and grouping objects
- ✔ Changing the color and border around an object

*W*hether you know it or not, Office 2010 comes with drawing commands for drawing lines, arrows, shapes, block arrows, stars, banners, and callout shapes. And Office provides numerous ways to manipulate these objects after you draw them. The drawing commands are meant to bring out the artist in you. Use them to make diagrams, fashion your own ideagrams, and illustrate difficult concepts and ideas. Lines and shapes give you a wonderful opportunity to exercise your creativity. A picture is worth a thousand words, so they say, and the drawing commands give you a chance to express yourself without having to write a thousand words.

In this chapter, you discover all the many ways to manipulate lines, shapes, text boxes, WordArt images, clip-art images, and graphics. You discover how to lay out these objects on a page or slide, flip them, change their colors, resize them, move them, and otherwise torture them until they look just right. You discover how to draw lines and arrows, draw connections between shapes, and draw ovals, squares, other shapes, and WordArt images. Use the techniques I describe in this chapter to bring something more to your Word documents, PowerPoint presentations, Publisher publications, and Excel worksheets: originality. With the techniques I describe in this chapter, you can bring the visual element into your work. You can communicate with images as well as words and numbers.

The Basics: Drawing Lines, Arrows, and Shapes

Figure 8-1 demonstrates how you can use lines, arrows, and shapes (not to mention text boxes) to illustrate ideas and concepts. Sometimes, saying it with lines and shapes is easier and more informative than saying it with words. Even in Excel worksheets, you can find opportunities to use lines, arrows, and shapes. For example, draw arrows and lines on worksheets to illustrate which cells are used to compute formulas.

Follow these basic steps to draw a line, arrow, or shape:

1. **Go to the Insert tab.**

   In Word, you must be in Print Layout view to draw and see lines and shapes.

2. **Click the Shapes button to open the Insert Shapes gallery.**

   As shown in Figure 8-2, the Shapes gallery appears. The shapes are divided into several categories, including Lines, Basic Shapes, and Block Arrows, as well as a category at the top of the gallery where shapes you chose recently are shown. (PowerPoint also offers the Shapes button on the Home tab.)

3. **Select a line, arrow, or shape in the Shapes gallery.**

4. **Drag on your page, slide, or worksheet.**

   As you drag, the line, arrow, or shape appears before your eyes.

5. **To alter your line, arrow, or shape — that is, to change its size, color, or outline — go to the (Drawing Tools) Format tab.**

   This tab offers many commands for manipulating lines and shapes. (Those commands are explained throughout this chapter.) You must select a line or shape to make the (Drawing Tools) Format tab appear.

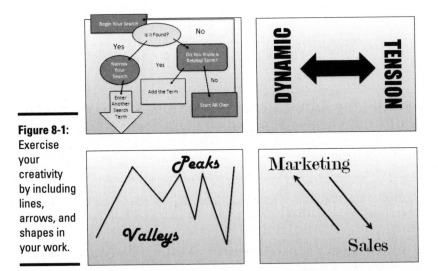

Figure 8-1: Exercise your creativity by including lines, arrows, and shapes in your work.

Figure 8-2:
To draw a
line, arrow,
or shape,
choose it in
the Shapes
gallery.

In the upper-left corner of the (Drawing Tools) Format tab is another
Shapes gallery for creating new shapes to go along with the one you
created.

Handling Lines, Arrows, and Connectors

Earlier in this chapter, Figure 8-1 shows examples of how you can use lines
and arrows to present ideas. As well as lines and arrows, the Insert Shapes
gallery offers *connectors,* the special lines that link shapes and can bend and
stretch as you move shapes around. Use connectors along with lines and
arrows to describe the relationships between the people or things in a diagram. These pages explain how to handle lines, arrows, and connectors.

Changing the length and position of a line or arrow

To change anything about a line or arrow, start by clicking to select it. You
can tell when a line has been selected because round selection handles
appear at either end. Follow these instructions to move a line or adjust its
length or angle:

+ **Changing the angle of a line:** Drag a selection handle up, down, or side-
ways. A dotted line shows where your line will be when you release the
mouse button.

+ **Changing the length:** Drag a selection handle away from or toward the
opposite selection handle.

✦ **Changing the position:** Move the pointer over the line itself and click when you see the four-headed arrow. Then drag the line to a new location.

Changing the appearance of a line, arrow, or connector

What a line looks like is a matter of its color, its *weight* (how wide it is), its *dash status* (it can be filled out or dashed), and its *cap* (its ends can be rounded, square, or flat). To change the appearance of a line, start by selecting it, going to the (Drawing Tools) Format tab, and opening the drop-down list on the Shape Outline button (this button is in the Shape Styles group). As shown in Figure 8-3, you see a drop-down list with commands for handling the appearance of lines, arrows, and connectors:

✦ **Color:** Select a color on the drop-down list (see Figure 8-3).

✦ **Width:** Choose Weight on the drop-down list (see Figure 8-3) and then choose a line width on the submenu. You can also choose More Lines on the submenu to open the Format Shape dialog box and change the width there. Enter a setting in points to make the line heavier or thinner.

✦ **Dotted or dashed lines:** Choose Dashes on the drop-down list (refer to Figure 8-3) and then choose an option on the submenu. Again, you can choose More Lines to open the Format Shape dialog box and choose from many dash types and compound lines.

✦ **Line caps:** Click the Shape Styles group button to open the Format Shape dialog box. In the Line Style category, select a cap type (Square, Round, or Flat).

You can also change the appearance of a line on the (Drawing Tools) Format tab by opening the Shape Styles gallery and selecting a style.

Figure 8-3: Open the drop-down list on the Shape Outline button to change the appearance of lines.

Choosing a default line style for consistency's sake

One of the secrets to making an attractive drawing is to make the lines consistent with one another. Lines should be the same width and color. They should be the same style. Unless you observe this rule, your drawings will be infested with lines of varying width and different colors. They will look like a confetti parade in a windstorm.

You can get around the problem of making lines consistent with one another by creating a model line and making it the default line style. After you declare a default style, all new lines you create are assigned the style. You don't have to spend as much time making the lines look alike.

Give a line the style, weight, and color that you want for all (or at least most) lines and then follow these steps to make that line the default style:

1. **Select and right-click the line.**

2. **Choose Set As Default Line on the shortcut menu.**

Attaching and handling arrowheads on lines and connectors

Arrows, of course, have arrowheads, and arrowheads on lines and connectors can go on either side or both sides of a line. What's more, arrowheads come in different sizes and shapes. To handle arrowheads on lines and connectors, select your line or connector and go to the (Drawing Tools) Format tab. Then use one of these techniques to handle the arrowheads:

✦ Open the drop-down list on the Shape Outline button, choose Arrows (refer to Figure 8-3), and select an arrow on the submenu.

✦ Click the Shape Styles group button to open the Format Shape dialog box. In the Line Style category, choose Arrow settings to describe where you want the arrowheads to be, what you want them to look like, and what size you want them to be.

To attach an arrowhead or arrowheads to a line or connector you've already drawn, select the line and proceed as though you were attaching arrowheads to a line that already has an arrow.

Connecting shapes by using connectors

Under Lines, the Shapes gallery offers six different connectors. Use *connectors* to link shapes and text boxes to form a diagram. Connectors differ from conventional lines in an important way: After you attach one to a shape, it stays with the shape when you move the shape. You don't have to worry about remaking all the connections after you move a shape. You can move shapes at will and let the connectors between shapes take care of themselves.

Figure 8-4 shows three types of connectors in action. (By the way, if you came here to explore how to make a diagram, be sure to check out Book I, Chapter 7 as well. It explains the Office SmartArt diagramming.)

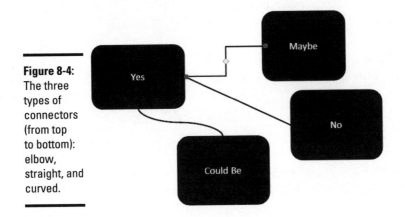

Figure 8-4:
The three types of connectors (from top to bottom): elbow, straight, and curved.

To connect shapes in Word, the shapes must be on the drawing canvas. Book II, Chapter 4 describes the Word drawing canvas. (Click the Shapes button and choose New Drawing Canvas to create one.)

Making the connection

Before you draw the connections, draw the shapes and arrange them on the slide where you want them to be in your diagram. Then follow these steps to connect two shapes with a connector:

1. **Select the two shapes that you want to connect.**

   To select the shapes, hold down the Ctrl key and click each one.

2. **On the (Drawing Tools) Format tab, open the Shapes gallery.**

3. **Under Lines, select the connector that will best fit between the two shapes you want to link together.**

4. **Move the pointer over a side selection handle on one of the shapes you want to connect.**

   The selection handles turn red.

5. **Click and drag the pointer over a selection handle on the other shape, and when you see red selection handles on that shape, release the mouse button.**

   Red, round selection handles appear on the shapes where they're connected. These red handles tell you that the two shapes are connected and will remain connected when you move them.

If your connector is attached to the wrong shape, don't despair. Select the connector, and on the (Drawing Tools) Format tab, click the Edit Shape button and choose Reroute Connectors. Then move the pointer over the red handle on the side of the connector that needs to be attached elsewhere, click, drag the connector elsewhere on the other shape, and release the mouse button when you see the red selection handles.

Adjusting a connector

Chances are, your connector needs adjusting to make it fit correctly between the two shapes. Click to select your connector and follow these techniques to adjust it:

✦ **Changing the shape of a connector:** Drag the yellow diamond on the connector. As you drag, the connector assumes different shapes.

✦ **Changing the connector type:** Right-click the connector, choose Connector Types, and choose Straight Connector, Elbow Connector, or Curved Connector on the submenu.

✦ **Handling arrows on connectors:** If the arrows on the connector aren't there, are pointing in the wrong direction, or shouldn't be there, change the arrowheads around using the same techniques you use with standard arrows. See "Attaching and handling arrowheads on lines and connectors," earlier in this chapter.

Make sure that the connector lines in your diagram are consistent with one another. Give them the same style and appearance, or else it will be hard to make sense of your diagram.

Handling Rectangles, Ovals, Stars, and Other Shapes

Figure 8-5 illustrates how shapes can come in very handy for illustrating concepts and ideas. You can combine shapes to make your own illustrations. Apart from the standard rectangle and oval, you can draw octagons and various other "-agons," arrows, stars, and banners. You are hereby encouraged to make shapes a part of your work, and you'll be glad to know that drawing shapes is not difficult. These pages explain how to draw a shape, exchange one shape for another, change a shape's symmetry, and enter words on a shape.

In Word, you must be in Print Layout view to draw and handle shapes. If you intend to draw more than one shape in Word, create a drawing canvas to hold the shapes (click the Shapes button and choose New Drawing Canvas). Book II, Chapter 4 describes the drawing canvas in Word.

Figure 8-5:
An example
of using
shapes (and
connectors)
to convey
an idea.

Drawing a shape

Follow these steps to draw a shape:

1. On the Insert tab, click the Shapes button to open the Shapes gallery.

You can also insert shapes from the Shapes gallery on the (Drawing Tools) Format tab.

2. Select a shape in the gallery.

If you've drawn the shape recently, you may be able to find it at the top of the gallery under Recently Used Shapes.

3. Click and drag slantwise to draw the shape, as shown at the top of Figure 8-6.

Hold down the Shift key as you drag if you want the shape to retain its proportions. For example, to draw a circle, select the Oval shape and hold down the Shift key as you draw.

Changing a shape's size and shape

Selection handles appear on the corners and sides of a shape after you select it. With the selection handles showing, you can change a shape's size and shape:

✦ Hold down the Shift key and drag a corner handle to change a shape's size and retain its symmetry.

✦ Drag a side, top, or bottom handle to stretch or scrunch a shape.

Choosing a different shape

To exchange one shape for another, select the shape and follow these steps:

1. On the (Drawing Tools) Format tab, click the Edit Shape button.

You can find this button in the Insert Shapes group.

2. Choose Change Shape on the drop-down list.

3. Select a new shape in the Shapes gallery.

Drag to draw a shape

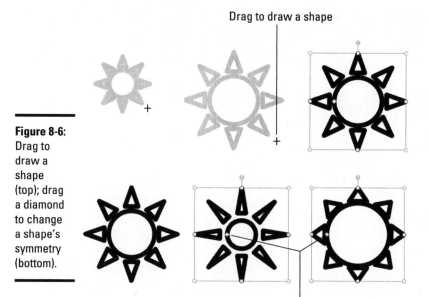

Figure 8-6:
Drag to
draw a
shape
(top); drag
a diamond
to change
a shape's
symmetry
(bottom).

Drag a diamond to change a shape's symmetry

Changing a shape's symmetry

A yellow diamond, sometimes more than one, appears on some shapes. By
dragging a diamond, you can change a shape's symmetry. Figure 8-6, for
example, shows the same shape — the Sun shape — altered to show different symmetries. Notice where the diamonds are. By dragging a diamond
even a short distance, you can do a lot to change a shape's symmetry.

Using a shape as a text box

Here's a neat trick: Rather than use the conventional rectangle as a text box,
you can use a shape. Figure 8-7 shows examples of shapes being used as text
boxes. By placing words on shapes, you can make the shapes illustrate ideas
and concepts.

Follow these instructions to handle text box shapes:

✦ **Entering the text:** Click in the shape and start typing. In Word, you can
right-click and choose Add Text if you have trouble typing in the shape.

✦ **Editing the text:** Click in the text and start editing. That's all there is to
it. If you have trouble getting inside the shape to edit the text, select the
shape, right-click it, and choose Edit Text on the shortcut menu.

✦ **Changing the font, color, and size of text:** Right-click in the text and
choose Font. Then, in the Font dialog box, choose a font, font color, and
a font size for the text.

✦ **Allowing the shape to enlarge for text:** You can allow the shape to enlarge and receive more text. Click the Shape Styles group button, and in the Text Box category of the Format Shape dialog box, select the Resize Shape to Fit Text option button.

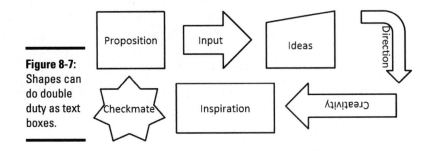

Figure 8-7:
Shapes can do double duty as text boxes.

WordArt for Bending, Spindling, and Mutilating Text

A *WordArt image* consists of a word that has been stretched, crumpled, or squeezed into an odd shape. Actually, a WordArt image can include more than one word. Figure 8-8 shows the WordArt gallery, where WordArt images are made, and an example of a WordArt image. After you insert a WordArt image, you can fool with the buttons on the WordArt toolbar and torture the word or phrase even further.

Figure 8-8:
Creating a WordArt image.

Turning a text box into a text box shape

To turn a conventional text box into a text box shape, follow these instructions:

1. **Select the text box by clicking its perimeter.**

2. **On the (Drawing Tools) Format tab, click the Edit Shape button, choose Change Shape, and then select a shape in the Shapes gallery.**

   After the conversion, you usually have to enlarge the shape to accommodate the text.

Creating a WordArt image

Follow these steps to create a WordArt image:

1. **On the Insert tab, click the WordArt button.**

   A drop-down list with WordArt styles appears.

2. **Select a WordArt style.**

   Don't worry about selecting the right style; you can choose a different one later on.

3. **Enter the text for the image in the WordArt text box.**

   Congratulations. You just created a WordArt image.

Editing a WordArt image

Usually, you have to wrestle with a WordArt image before it comes out right. Select the image, go to the (Drawing Tools) Format tab, and use these techniques to win the wrestling match:

✦ **Editing the words:** Click in the WordArt text box and edit the text there.

✦ **Choosing a new WordArt style:** Open the WordArt Styles gallery and select a style. Depending on the size of your screen and which program you're working in, you may have to click the Quick Styles button first (refer to Figure 8-8).

✦ **Changing the letters' color:** Click the Text Fill button and choose a color on the drop-down list.

✦ **Changing the letters' outline:** Click the Text Outline button and make choices to change the letters' outline.

To apply color or an outline to some of the letters or words in a WordArt image, select the letters or words before choosing options on the (Drawing Tools) Format tab.

Manipulating Lines, Shapes, Art, Text Boxes, and Other Objects

After you insert a shape, line, text box, clip-art image, graphic, diagram, WordArt image, chart, or embedded object in a file, it ceases being what it was before and becomes an *object*. Figure 8-9 shows eight objects. I'm not sure whether these eight objects resent being objectified, but Office objectifies them. As far as manipulating these items in Office is concerned, these are just objects.

Figure 8-9:
Examples of
objects.

The techniques for manipulating objects are the same whether you're dealing with a line, shape, graphic, clip-art image, diagram, or text box. The good news from your end is that you have to master only one set of techniques for handling these objects. Whether you want to move, change the size of, or change the outline of a text box, clip-art image, graphic, or shape, the techniques are the same.

In the remainder of this chapter are instructions for doing these tasks with objects:

✦ **Selecting:** Before you can do anything to objects, you have to select them. See "Selecting objects so that you can manipulate them," later in this chapter.

✦ **Making use of the rulers and grid:** Rulers (in Word, PowerPoint, Excel, and Publisher) and the grid (in Word and PowerPoint) can be very helpful for aligning and placing objects. See "Hiding and displaying the rulers and grid."

✦ **Changing an object's size and shape:** You can enlarge, shrink, stretch, and scrunch objects to make them wider or taller. See "Changing an object's size and shape."

✦ **Moving and positioning:** You can land objects with precision in a Word document, PowerPoint slide, or Excel worksheet. See "Moving and positioning objects."

✦ **Aligning and distributing:** Another way to move and position objects is to realign or redistribute them across a page, slide, or worksheet. See "Tricks for aligning and distributing objects."

✦ **Overlapping:** When you're dealing with several objects, they're bound to overlap — and sometimes overlapping objects make for an interesting effect. On the right side of Figure 8-9, for example, several objects overlap and give the impression that they were "dropped there." See "When objects overlap: Choosing which appears above the other," to handle overlapping objects.

✦ **Rotating and flipping:** Viewers turn their heads when they see an object that has been flipped or rotated. You can rotate and flip shapes, lines, text boxes, graphics, clip-art images, and WordArt images. See "Rotating and flipping objects."

✦ **Grouping:** To make working with several different objects easier, you can *group* them so that they become a single object. After objects have been grouped, manipulating them — manipulating it, I should say — is easier. See "Grouping objects to make working with them easier."

✦ **Applying outlines and fills:** Putting outlines and color fills on objects makes them stand out. You can also fill some kinds of objects with a color or pattern. See "Changing an Object's Color, Outline Color, and Transparency."

If you sighed after you finished reading this long list, I don't blame you. But be of good cheer: Most of these commands are easy to pick up, and including lines, shapes, text boxes, WordArt images, clip art, and graphics in your work is a good way to impress your friends and intimidate your enemies.

Selecting objects so that you can manipulate them

Before you can move or change the border of a graphic, text box, or other object, you have to select it. To select an object, simply click it. Sometimes, to align or decorate several objects simultaneously, you have to select more than one object at the same time. To select more than one object:

✦ Ctrl+click them. In other words, hold down the Ctrl key as you click the objects.

✦ On the Home tab, click the Select button and choose Select Objects on the drop-down list. (You may have to click the Find & Select button first, depending on the size of your screen.) Then click on one side of the objects you want to select and drag the pointer across the other objects. In Word, the objects must be on the drawing canvas for you to select them this way. (Book II, Chapter 4 describes the Word drawing canvas.)

✦ On the (Drawing Tools) Format tab, click the Selection Pane button. The Selection and Visibility pane opens, as shown in Figure 8-10. It lists objects on the drawing canvas (Word), slide (PowerPoint), or worksheet (Excel). Click or Ctrl+click object names in the pane to select objects.

You can also open the Selection and Visibility pane by clicking the Select button on the Home tab and choosing Selection Pane on the drop-down list. (You may have to click the Editing button first, depending on the size of your screen.)

Figure 8-10: Click an object in the Selection and Visibility pane to select it.

After you select an object, its selection handles appear. Objects have eight selection handles, one at each corner and one at each side. To tell whether an object is selected, look for its selection handles.

Hiding and displaying the rulers and grid

Word, PowerPoint, Excel, and Publisher offer two rulers, one along the top of the window and one along the left side. Use the rulers to help place and align objects. To display or hide these rulers, use one of these techniques:

✦ On the View tab, click the Ruler check box. (You may have to click the Show/Hide button first, depending on the size of your screen.) To see the rulers, you must be in Print Layout view In Word and Page Layout view in Excel.

✦ In PowerPoint, you can also hide or display rulers by right-clicking a slide (but not an object or frame) and choosing Ruler on the shortcut menu.

In Word and PowerPoint, the grid can come in very handy for aligning objects. On the View tab, click the Gridlines check box to see the grid. (You may have to click the Show/Hide button first.) The grid settings in PowerPoint are quite sophisticated (see Book IV, Chapter 4 for details).

By the way, fans of the metric system will be pleased to know that you can display centimeters (or millimeters, points, or picas) rather than inches on the ruler. On the File tab, choose Options. In the Options dialog box, go to the Advanced category, open the Show Measurements in Units Of drop-down list, and choose a unit of measurement.

Changing an object's size and shape

Usually when an object arrives on-screen, you have to wrestle with it. You have to change its size (and sometimes its shape as well). Figure 8-11 demonstrates how to resize an object. Select your object and use one of these methods to change its size and shape:

✦ **"Eyeball it":** Hold down the Shift key and drag a *corner* selection handle to make the object larger or smaller but maintain its proportions. Drag a selection handle on the *side* to stretch or crimp an object and change its shape as well as its size.

✦ **Enter height and width measurements:** On the Format tab, enter measurements in the Height and Width boxes (see Figure 8-11). Depending on the size of your screen, you may have to click the Size button before you can see these boxes.

✦ **Open the Format (or Layout) dialog box:** Click the Size group button on the Format tab to open the Format dialog box (in PowerPoint and Excel) or the Layout dialog box (in Word). Then change the Height and Width settings in the dialog box (refer to Figure 8-11).

Whether you can change an object's shape as well as its size depends on whether the object's aspect ratio is *locked.* If you're wrestling with an object and it won't do your bidding — if it refuses to change shape or it changes shape, and you don't want it to do that — unlock its aspect ratio setting. Click the Size group button, and in the dialog box that appears, select or deselect the Lock Aspect Ratio check box. When an object's aspect ratio is *locked,* it maintains its shape as you change its size, but when it's *unlocked,* you can change its shape as well as its size.

You can change the size and shape of several objects at one time by selecting all the objects before giving a command to change sizes. Being able to change objects' size this way is convenient when you want to change the size of many objects but maintain their relationships to one another.

Drag a selection handle. . .   or enter measurements

Figure 8-11:
Ways to
resize an
object.

Moving and positioning objects

Moving objects is considerably easier than moving furniture. Select the object you want to reposition and use one of these techniques to land it in the right place:

✦ **Dragging:** Move the pointer over the perimeter of the object, click when you see the four-headed arrow, and drag the object to a new location. Hold down the Shift key as you drag to move an object either horizontally or vertically in a straight line.

✦ **Using a dialog box (in PowerPoint and Word):** On the Format tab, click the Size group button. (Depending on the size of your screen, you may have to click the Size button first.) You see the Format or Layout dialog box. On the Position category or tab, enter Horizontal and Vertical position measurements to place the object on the slide or page.

✦ **Nudging:** If you can't quite fit an object in the right place, try using a Nudge command. Nudge commands move objects up, down, left, or right. Press one of the arrow keys (↑, ↓, ←, →) to move the object a little bit. Hold down the Ctrl key as you press an arrow key to make the object move by tiny increments.

TIP

Use the dialog box method of positioning objects when you want objects to be in the exact same position on different pages or slides.

Tricks for aligning and distributing objects

When several objects appear in the same place, use the Align and Distribute commands to give the objects an orderly appearance. You can make your Word page, PowerPoint slide, Excel worksheet, or Publisher publication look tidier by aligning the objects or by distributing them so that they are an equal distance from one another. Office offers special commands for doing these tasks.

Aligning objects

The Align commands come in handy when you want objects to line up with one another. Suppose you need to align several shapes. As shown in Figure 8-12, you can use an Align command to line up the shapes with precision. You don't have to tug and pull, tug and pull until the shapes are aligned with one another. In the figure, I used the Align Top command to line up the shapes along the top. In Word and PowerPoint, besides aligning objects with respect to one another, you can align objects with respect to the page (in Word) or the slide (in PowerPoint). For example, you can line up objects along the top of a slide.

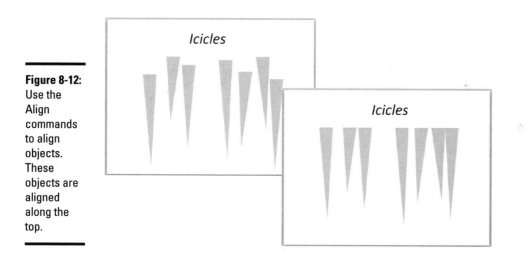

Figure 8-12:
Use the
Align
commands
to align
objects.
These
objects are
aligned
along the
top.

Follow these steps to line up objects:

1. **Move the objects to where, roughly, you want them to be, and if you want to align objects with respect to one another, move one object to a point that the others will align to.**

   When Office aligns objects with respect to one another, it aligns them to the object in the leftmost, centermost, rightmost, topmost, middlemost, or bottommost position, depending on which Align command you choose.

2. **Select the objects you want to align.**

   Earlier in this chapter, "Selecting objects so that you can manipulate them" looks at selection techniques.

3. **Go to the Format tab.**

   You can also click the Page Layout tab (in Word and Excel) or the Home tab (in PowerPoint).

4. **Click the Align button, and on the drop-down list, choose whether to align the objects with respect to one another or with respect to the page or page margin (in Word) or a slide (in PowerPoint).**

   Depending on the size of your screen, you may have to click the Arrange button to get to the Align button.

5. **Click the Align button again and choose an Align command — Left, Center, Right, Top, Middle, or Bottom (refer to Figure 8-12).**

6. **If necessary, drag the objects on the page.**

   That's right — drag them. After you give an Align command, the objects are still selected, and you can drag to adjust their positions.

Distributing objects so that they are equidistant

The Distribute commands — Distribute Horizontally and Distribute Vertically — come in handy for laying out objects on a page or slide. These commands arrange objects so that the same amount of space appears between each one. Rather than go to the trouble of pushing and pulling objects until they are distributed evenly, you can simply select the objects and choose a Distribute command.

Figure 8-13 demonstrates how the Distribute commands work. In the figure, I chose the Distribute Horizontally command so that the same amount of horizontal (side-by-side) space appears between the objects. Distributing objects such as these on your own, perhaps by entering measurements in the Layout or Format dialog box, is a waste of time when you can use a Distribute command.

Follow these steps to distribute objects horizontally or vertically on a page or slide:

1. **Arrange the objects so that the outermost objects — the ones that will go on the top and bottom or left side and right side — are where you want them to be.**

   In other words, if you want to distribute objects horizontally across a page, place the leftmost object and rightmost object where you want them to be. Office will distribute the other objects equally between the leftmost and rightmost object.

2. **Select the objects.**

3. **Go to the Format tab.**

   You can also go to the Page Layout tab (in Word and Excel) or the Home tab (in PowerPoint).

[⊫ Align ▾]

4. **Click the Align button and choose a Distribute option on the drop-down list.**

   To find the Align button, you may have to click the Arrange button first, depending on the size of your screen.

Figure 8-13: The Distribute commands rearrange objects so that the same amount of space is between them.

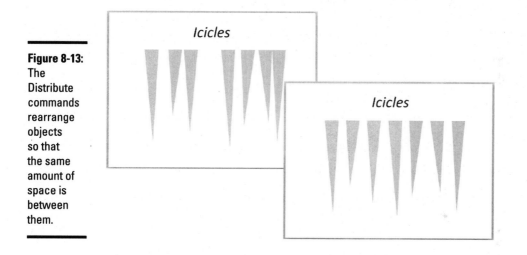

When objects overlap: Choosing which appears above the other

On a page or slide that is crowded with text boxes, shapes, graphics, and clip-art images, objects inevitably overlap, and you have to decide which object goes on top of the stack and which on the bottom. In a Word document, you have to decide as well whether text appears above or below objects.

Objects that deliberately overlap can be interesting and attractive to look at. On the right side of Figure 8-14, for example, a clip-art image and text box appear in front of a shape. Makes for a nice effect, no? These pages explain controlling how objects overlap with the Bring and Send commands and the Selection and Visibility pane.

Figure 8-14:
An example
of objects
overlapping.

Controlling overlaps with the Bring and Send commands

Word, PowerPoint, Excel, and Publisher offer these commands for handling objects in a stack:

✦ **Bring Forward:** Moves the object higher in the stack

✦ **Bring to Front:** Moves the object in front of all other objects in the stack

✦ **Send Backward:** Moves the object lower in the stack

✦ **Send to Back:** Moves the object behind all other objects

Word offers these additional commands:

✦ **Bring in Front of Text:** Moves the object in front of text on the page

✦ **Send Behind Text:** Moves the object behind text on the page so that the text appears over the object

Select an object and use one of these techniques to give a Bring or Send command:

✦ On the Format tab, click the Bring Forward or Send Backward button, or open the drop-down list on one of these buttons and choose a Bring or Send command (refer to Figure 8-14). Depending on the size of your screen, you may have to click the Arrange button before you can get to a Bring or Send command.

In Word, Excel, and Publisher, the Bring and Send commands are also available on the Page Layout tab; in PowerPoint, they are also available on the Home tab, although you may have to click the Arrange button first, depending on the size of your screen.

✦ Right-click an object and choose a Bring or Send command on the short-cut menu.

In Word, you can't choose a Bring or Send command unless you've chosen a text-wrapping option apart from In Line with Text for the object. Select your object, go to the Format tab, click the Text Wrap button, and choose an option on the drop-down list apart from In Line with Text. Book II, Chapter 4 looks at text wrapping in Word.

If an object on the bottom of the stack shows through after you place it on the bottom, the object on the top of the stack is transparent or semi-transparent. Transparent objects are like gauze curtains — they reveal what's behind them. If you want to make the object on the top of the stack less transparent, see "Making a color transparent," later in this chapter.

Controlling overlaps with the Selection and Visibility pane

Another way to control how objects overlap is to open the Selection and Visibility pane, select an object, and click the Bring Forward or Send Backward button as necessary to move the object up or down in the stack. The Bring Forward and Send Backward buttons are located at the bottom of the pane. Earlier in this chapter, "Selecting objects so that you can manipulate them" explains the Selection and Visibility pane. (On the Format tab, click the Selection Pane button to open it.)

Rotating and flipping objects

Rotating and flipping objects — that is, changing their orientation — is a neat way to spruce up a page or slide, as Figure 8-15 demonstrates. You can rotate and flip these kinds of objects: lines, shapes, text boxes, clip-art images, graphics, and WordArt images. To flip or rotate an object, select it and do one of the following:

✦ **Choose a Rotate or Flip command:** On the Format tab, click the Rotate button and choose an option on the drop-down list (refer to Figure 8-15). The Rotate commands rotate objects by 90 degrees; the Flip commands flip objects over. The Rotate button is also found on the Page Layout tab (in Word and Excel) and the Home tab (in PowerPoint and Publisher). You may have to click the Arrange button to see the Rotate button, depending on the size of your screen.

✦ **Roll your own:** Drag the object's *rotation handle,* the green dot that appears after you select it. Hold down the Shift key as you drag to rotate the shape by 15-degree increments.

✦ **Open the Format or Layout dialog box:** On the Rotate drop-down list, choose More Rotation Options to open the Format or Layout dialog box. Enter a degree measurement in the Rotation text box.

Drag the rotation handle. . .   or choose a Rotate or Flip command

Figure 8-15: Members of an audience turn their heads when objects are rotated or flipped.

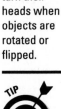

To rotate several objects simultaneously, Ctrl+click to select each object and then give a rotation command.

Grouping objects to make working with them easier

Consider the clip-art image, shape, and text box in Figure 8-16. To move, resize, or reshape these objects, I would have to laboriously move them one at a time — that is, I would have to do that if it weren't for the Group command.

The Group command assembles different objects into a single object to make moving, resizing, and reshaping objects easier. With the Group command, you select the objects that you want to "group" and then you wrap them into a bundle so that they become easier to work with. Office remembers which objects were grouped so that you can ungroup objects after you've moved or resized them.

Figure 8-16:
You can
move,
resize, and
reshape
grouped
objects
as though
they were
a single
object.

Grouping objects

Select the objects and do one of the following to group them into one happy family:

[Group ▾]

✦ On the Format tab (or the Page Layout tab in Word and Excel, and the Home tab in PowerPoint and Publisher), click the Group button and choose Group on the drop-down list. Depending on the size of your screen, you may have to click the Arrange button to get to the Group button.

✦ Right-click one of the objects you selected and choose Group⇨Group.

After objects are grouped, they form a single object with the eight selection handles.

To add an object to a group, select the object and the grouped objects by Ctrl+clicking and then choose the Group command.

Ungrouping and regrouping

[Group ▾]

To ungroup an object and break it into its components parts, perhaps to fiddle with one of the objects in the group, select the object, go to the Format tab, click the Group button, and choose Ungroup.

Office remembers which objects were in a group after you ungroup it. To reassemble the objects in a group, click an object that was formerly in the group and then choose the Regroup command. You can find this command on the Group button, and you can also give the Regroup command by right-clicking and choosing Group⇨Regroup.

Changing an Object's Color, Outline Color, and Transparency

If an object's color or outline color doesn't suit you, you have the right to change colors. For that matter, you can opt for a "blank" object with no color or remove the color from around the perimeter of the object. As the saying goes, "It's a free country."

Office has its own lingo when it comes to an object's color. Remember these terms when you make like Picasso with your shapes, text boxes, graphics, and clip-art images:

✦ **Shape fill colors:** The color that fills in an object is called the *shape fill.* You can apply shape fills to shapes, text boxes, and WordArt images, but not clip art or graphics. Besides colors, you can fill a shape with a picture, a gradient, or a texture. (See the next topic in this chapter, "Filling an object with a color, picture, or texture.")

✦ **Shape outline colors:** The line that goes around the perimeter of the object is called the *shape outline.* You can choose a color, style, and line width for outlines. (See "Putting the outline around an object," later in this chapter.)

The easiest way to decorate a shape, text box, or WordArt image is to visit the Format tab and make a selection in the Shape Styles gallery. These ready-made gallery selections can spare you the work of dealing with fill colors, outlines, and shape effects. Just remember not to mix and match different Shape Style options; use them with consistency.

Filling an object with a color, picture, or texture

Shapes, text boxes, and WordArt images are empty when you first create them, but you can fill them with a color, picture, gradient, or texture by following these basic steps:

1. **Select the object that needs a facelift.**

2. **On the Format tab, click the Shape Fill button.**

3. **On the drop-down list, choose a fill color, picture, gradient, or texture.**

Choose No Fill to remove the fill color, picture, gradient, or texture from an object.

Figure 8-17 shows the same object filled with a color, picture, gradient, and texture. Which do you prefer? Your choices are as follows:

✦ **Color:** Applies a single color to the object.

✦ **Picture:** Places a picture in the object. You see the Insert Picture dialog box. Choose a picture and click the Insert button.

✦ **Gradient (Word, PowerPoint, and Publisher only):** Applies gradient color shading to the object. You can choose between various shading styles.

✦ **Texture:** Offers 24 patterns meant to simulate various surfaces. The choices include Granite, Paper Bag, and Pink Tissue Paper. Be sure to use the scroll bar to see all the choices.

✦ **Pattern (Publisher only):** Applies a pattern to the object. Select a pattern on the Pattern tab of the Fill Effects dialog box.

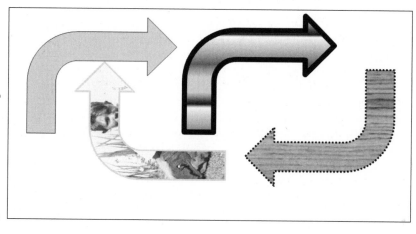

Figure 8-17: Shape fills (from left to right): color, picture, gradient, and texture.

Making a color transparent

A transparent color is like gauze because instead of being solid, it shows what's behind it. Transparent colors are especially useful in text boxes because the text shows through and can be read easily. Follow these steps to make the fill color in a text box, shape, or WordArt image transparent or semitransparent:

1. **Right-click the object and choose Format Shape (or Format AutoShape).**

   You see the Format Shape dialog box.

2. **In the Fill category, drag the Transparency slider to choose how transparent a color you want.**

   At 100%, the color is completely transparent and, in fact, not there; at 1%, the color is hardly transparent at all.

3. **Click the Close or OK button.**

You can also make a graphic transparent by recoloring it. See Book VIII, Chapter 3.

Designating a fill and outline color for all your objects

Instead of going to the significant trouble of giving all or most of your objects the same look, you can make one object the model for all others to follow and declare it the default style. After that, all new objects you insert appear in the same style, your objects have a uniform appearance, and you don't have to spend as much time formatting objects.

Select an object with a fill and an outline color that you want as your model, right-click the object, and choose Set As Default to make your object the default that all other objects start from.

Putting the outline around an object

The *outline* is the line that runs around the perimeter of an object. Put an outline color around an object to give it more definition or make it stand out. Figure 8-18 shows examples of outlines. What a shape outline looks like has to do with the color, weight, and dash style you choose for it.

Figure 8-18: An object's outline has to do with its color, weight, and dash style.

Select your object and follow these steps to change its outline:

Shape Outline ▾

1. **On the Format tab, click the Shape Outline button.**

A drop-down list appears.

2. **Choose a color, weight, or dash.**

You may have to return to the Shape Outline drop-down list more than once to make the outline just so.

- *Color:* Choose a theme color deemed right for borders by the makers of your program or choose a standard color.

- *Weight:* Choose how thick or thin you want the border to be. You can choose More Lines on the submenu to open the Format dialog box. In the Line Style category, you can choose compound lines and select point-size width for the outline.

- *Dashes:* Choose straight lines, dashed lines, or broken lines.

The (Picture Tools) Format tab — the one you see when you're dealing with pictures and clip art — offers the Picture Border drop-down list instead of the Shape Outline drop-down list, but the options on the lists are the same.

To remove an outline from an object, choose No Outline on the Shape Outline (or Picture Border) drop-down list.

Book II

Word

Contents at a Glance

Chapter 1: Speed Techniques for Using Word

In This Chapter

✓ Getting acquainted with the Word screen

✓ Creating a Word document

✓ Changing your view of a document

✓ Selecting text so that you can copy, move, or delete it

✓ Getting from place to place in long documents

✓ Pasting one Word document into another

✓ Creating data-entry forms

This chapter explains shortcuts and commands that can help you become a speedy user of Word 2010. Everything in this chapter was put here so that you can get off work earlier and take the slow, scenic route home. Starting here, you discover how to create and change your view of documents. You find out how to select text, get from place to place, and mark your place in long documents. You also explore how to insert one document into another and create data-entry forms to make entering information a little easier.

Introducing the Word Screen

Seeing the Word screen for the first time is like trying to find your way through Tokyo's busy Ikebukuro subway station. It's intimidating. But when you start using Word, you quickly find out what everything is. To help you get going, Figure 1-1 shows you the different parts of the screen. Here are shorthand descriptions of these screen parts:

✦ **Word button:** In the upper-left corner of the screen, the Word button offers a menu for restoring, moving, sizing, minimizing, maximizing, and closing the Word window.

✦ **Quick Access toolbar:** This toolbar offers the Save, Undo, and Repeat buttons. Wherever you go in Word, you see the Quick Access toolbar. Book I, Chapter 1 explains the toolbar in detail; Book VIII, Chapter 1 explains how to customize and move the Quick Access toolbar.

◆ **Title bar:** At the top of the screen, the title bar tells you the name of the document you're working on.

◆ **Minimize, Restore, Close buttons:** These three magic buttons make it very easy to shrink, enlarge, and close the window you are working in.

File

◆ **File tab:** Go to the File tab to do file-management tasks.

◆ **The Ribbon:** Select a tab on the Ribbon to undertake a new task. (Book I, Chapter 1 explains the Ribbon in detail, and Book VIII, Chapter 1 explains how to customize the Ribbon.)

◆ **Scroll bars:** The scroll bars help you get from place to place in a document.

◆ **Status bar:** The status bar gives you basic information about where you are and what you're doing in a document. It tells you what page and what section you're in, the total number of pages and words in your document, and what language the text is written in. Book VIII, Chapter 1 explains how to customize the status bar.

◆ **View buttons:** Click one of these buttons — Print Layout, Full Screen Reading, Web Layout, Outline, or Draft — to change your view of a document.

◆ **Zoom controls:** Use these controls to zoom in and out on your work.

File tab

Word button

The Ribbon

Quick Access toolbar   Title bar   Minimize, Restore, and Close buttons

Figure 1-1:
The Word
screen.

Status bar   View buttons   Zoom controls

Creating a New Document

Document is just a fancy word for a letter, report, announcement, or proclamation that you create with Word. When you first start Word, you see a new, blank document with the generic name *Document1*. You can start working right away on this document, or you can create a new document by choosing a template.

A *template* is a special kind of file that is used as the starting point for creating documents. Each template comes with many preformatted styles. If your aim is to create an academic report, flyer, newsletter, calendar, résumé, or other sophisticated document, see if you can spare yourself the formatting work by choosing the appropriate template when you create your document. (Chapter 3 of this mini-book explains templates in detail and how to create your own templates.)

File

No matter what kind of document you want, start creating it by going to the File tab and choosing New. The Available Templates window shown in Figure 1-2 appears. This window offers templates for creating many types of documents. Click a template in this window to see, on the right side of the window, a preview of the document you will create. Double-click a template (or select it and click the Create button) to create a document.

**Book II
Chapter 1**

**Speed
Techniques**

Click to backtrack   Choose a template   Preview the template
you will create

Figure 1-2:
Create
documents
from
templates
in the
Available
Templates
window.

Click Create (or double-click a template) to create a document

Constructing your blank default document

When you open a new, blank document by pressing Ctrl+N or choosing the Blank Document icon in the Available Templates window (refer to Figure 1-2), does the document meet your specifications? When you start typing, does the text appear in your favorite font? Are the margins just-so?

You can get a head start on creating documents by telling Word what you want new, blank documents to look like. To do that, open the Font dialog box (click the Font group button on the Home tab) followed by the Page Setup dialog box (click the Page Setup group button on the Page Layout tab), make your formatting choices in each dialog box, and click the Set As Default button. Changes you make this way are saved to the Blank Document template, the one used to create blank documents. (Chapter 3 of this mini-book explains what templates are).

Use these techniques in the Available Templates window to create a document:

✦ **Create a blank document.** Choose the Blank Document icon to create a bare-bones document with few styles. Blank Document is the default template for creating documents. (By pressing Ctrl+N, you can create a new, blank document without opening the Available Templates window.)

✦ **Create a brochure, form, invoice, or other specialty document.** Take your pick of these techniques to create a specialty document:

- *Use a template on your computer.* Choose Sample Templates. Templates that you loaded on your computer when you installed Office appear in the window.

- *Download a template from Microsoft.* Under Office.com Templates, do one of the following: (1) choose the type of template you want, or (2) make sure that your computer is connected to the Internet, enter a search term in the Search box, and click the Start Searching button (or press Enter). Choose a template and click the Download button to download it to your computer.

- *Use a template you created (or downloaded earlier from Microsoft or acquired from a third party).* Click the My Templates icon. The New dialog box appears so that you can choose a template.

✦ **Create a document from a template you recently used.** Click the Recent Templates icon and choose a template.

✦ **Create a document from another document.** If you can use another document as the starting point for creating a new document, click the New from Existing icon. In the New from Existing Document dialog box, select the document and click the Create New button.

If your search for the perfect template takes you too far afield, you can click the Home, Back, or Forward button in the Available Templates window to backtrack.

Book I, Chapter 1 explains how to save documents after you create them, as well as how to open the document you want to work on.

Getting a Better Look at Your Documents

A computer screen can be kind of confining. There you are, staring at the darn thing for hours at a stretch. Do you wish the view were better? The Word screen can't be made to look like the Riviera, but you can examine documents in different ways and work in two places at one time in the same document. Better read on.

**Book II
Chapter 1**

**Speed
Techniques**

Viewing documents in different ways

In word processing, you want to focus sometimes on the writing, sometimes on the layout, and sometimes on the organization of your work. To help you stay in focus, Word offers different ways of viewing a document. Figure 1-3 shows these views. These pages explain how to change views, the five different views, and why to select one over the other. (Be sure to visit Book I, Chapter 3 as well; it describes how to view a document through more than one window and how to open a second window on a document.)

Changing views

Use these techniques to change views:

+ Click one of the five View buttons on the right side of the status bar.

+ On the View tab, click one of the five buttons in the Document Views group.

Print Layout view

Switch to Print Layout view to see the big picture. In this view, you can see what your document will look like when you print it. You can see graphics, headers, footers, and even page borders in Print Layout view. You can also see clearly where page breaks occur (where one page ends and the next begins). In Print Layout view, you can click the One Page, Two Pages, or Page Width button on the View tab to display more or fewer pages on your screen.

Full Screen Reading view

Switch to Full Screen Reading view to focus on the text itself and proofread your documents. In this view, everything gets stripped away — the Ribbon, scroll bars, status bar, and all. All you see is the text and artwork in your documents. You can't enter or edit text (unless you open the View Options menu and choose Allow Typing).

Figure 1-3:
The different document views (top to bottom): Print Layout, Full Screen Reading, Web Layout, Outline, and Draft.

Click the View Options button to open a menu with options for improving your view. For example, you can increase or decrease the size of text, show one or two document pages at a time, and display page margins. To get from page to page, click buttons along the top of the window. Click the Close button to leave this view.

Web Layout view

Switch to Web Layout view to see what your document would look like as a Web page. Background colors appear (if you chose a theme or background color for your document). Text is wrapped to the window rather than around the artwork in the document. Book VIII, Chapter 2 explains how to save an Office file, a Word document included, as a Web page.

Outline view

Switch to Outline view to see how your work is organized. In this view, you can see only the headings in a document. You can get a sense of how your document unfolds and easily move sections of text backward and forward in a document. In other words, you can reorganize a document in Outline view. Chapter 6 of this mini-book explains outlines in torturous detail.

Draft view

Switch to Draft view when you're writing a document and you want to focus on the words. Clip-art images, shapes, and other objects don't appear in this view, nor do page breaks (although you can clearly see section breaks). Draft view is best for writing first drafts.

Splitting the screen

Besides opening a second window on a document (a subject of Book I, Chapter 3), you can be two places at one time in a Word document by splitting the screen. One reason you might do this: You are writing a long report and want the introduction to support the conclusion, and you also want the conclusion to fulfill all promises made by the introduction. That's difficult to do sometimes, but you can make it easier by splitting the screen so that you can be two places at one time as you write your introduction and conclusion.

Splitting a window means to divide it into north and south halves, as shown in Figure 1-4. In a split screen, two sets of scroll bars appear so that you can travel in one half of the screen without disturbing the other half. Word offers two ways to split the screen:

✦ Move the mouse pointer to the *split box* at the top of the scroll bar on the right. Move it just above the View Ruler button. When the pointer turns into double arrows, click and drag the gray line down the screen. When you release the mouse button, you have a split screen.

✦ On the View tab, click the Split button. A gray line appears on-screen. Roll the mouse down until the gray line is where you want the split to be, and click. You get two screens split down the middle.

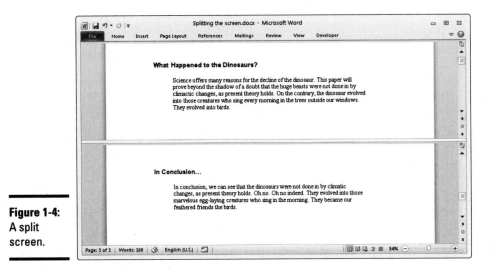

Figure 1-4:
A split
screen.

When you tire of this schizophrenic arrangement, click the Remove Split button on the View tab or drag the line to the top or bottom of the screen. You can also double-click the line that splits the screen in two.

In a split screen, you can choose a different view for the different halves. For example, click in the top half of the screen and choose Outline view to see your document in outline form, and click in the bottom half and choose Draft view to see the other half in Draft view. This way, you can see the headings in a document while you write the introduction.

Selecting Text in Speedy Ways

Book I, Chapter 2 explains how to enter text and change its appearance and size. After you enter text, you inevitably have to copy, move, or delete it, but you can't do those tasks until you select it first. Table 1-1 describes shortcuts for selecting text.

If a bunch of highlighted text is on-screen and you want it to go away but it won't (because you pressed F8), press the Esc key.

TIP

After you press F8, all the keyboard shortcuts for moving the cursor also work for selecting text. For example, press F8 and then press Ctrl+Home to select everything from the cursor to the top of the document. Later in this chapter, "Keys for getting around quickly" describes keyboard shortcuts for getting from place to place.

Table 1-1	Shortcuts for Selecting Text
To Select This	*Do This*
A word	Double-click the word.
A line	Click in the left margin next to the line.
Some lines	Drag the mouse pointer over the lines or drag it down the left margin.
A sentence	Ctrl+click the sentence.
A paragraph	Double-click in the left margin next to the paragraph.
A mess of text	Click at the start of the text, hold down the Shift key, and click at the end of the text.
A gob of text	Put the cursor where you want to start selecting, press F8, and press an arrow key, drag the mouse, or click at the end of the selection.
Text with the same formats	On the Home tab, click the Select button and choose Select Text with Similar Formatting (you may have to click the Editing button first).
A document	Hold down the Ctrl key and click in the left margin; triple-click in the left margin; press Ctrl+A; or go to the Home tab, click the Select button, and choose Select All (you may have to click the Editing button first).

**Book II
Chapter 1**

**Speed
Techniques**

Viewing the hidden format symbols

Sometimes it pays to see the hidden format symbols when you're editing and laying out a document. The symbols show lines breaks, tab spaces, paragraph breaks, and the space or spaces between words. To see the hidden format symbols, go to the Home tab and click the Show/Hide ¶ button. Click the button again to hide the symbols.

Here's what the hidden symbols look like on-screen.

Symbol	How to Enter
Line break (↵)	Press Shift+Enter
Optional hyphen -(¬)	Press Ctrl+hyphen
Paragraph (¶)	Press Enter
Space (·)	Press the spacebar
Tab (→)	Press tab

Moving Around Quickly in Documents

Besides sliding the scroll bar, Word offers a handful of very speedy tech-niques for jumping around in documents: pressing shortcut keys, browsing in the Select Browse Object menu, using the Go To command, and navigating with the Document Map or thumbnails. Read on to discover how to get there faster, faster, faster.

Keys for getting around quickly

One of the fastest ways to go from place to place is to press the keys and key combinations listed in Table 1-2.

Table 1-2	Keys for Moving Around Documents
Key to Press	*Where It Takes You*
PgUp	Up the length of one screen
PgDn	Down the length of one screen
Ctrl+PgUp	To the previous page in the document
Ctrl+PgDn	To the next page in the document
Ctrl+Home	To the top of the document
Ctrl+End	To the bottom of the document

If pressing Ctrl+PgUp or Ctrl+PgDn doesn't get you to the top or bottom of a page, you clicked the Select Browse Object button at the bottom of the verti-cal scroll bar, which makes Word go to the next bookmark, comment, head-ing, or whatever. Click the Select Browse Object button and choose Browse By Page to make these key combinations work again.

Here's a useful keystroke for getting from place to place: Shift+F5. Press it once to go to the location of your most recent edit. Press it two or three times to go back one or two edits before that. Pressing Shift+F5 is useful when you want to return to the place where you made an edit but can't quite remember where that place is.

Navigating from page to page or heading to heading

In lengthy documents such as the one in Figure 1-5, the best way to get from place to place is to make use of the Navigation pane. Click a heading or a page in the Navigation pane and Word takes you there in the twinkling of an eye.

Click a heading   Click a page thumbnail

Figure 1-5:
In the
Navigation
pane, click
a heading
or page
thumbnail
to go from
place to
place.

To display the Navigation pane, go to the View tab and click the Navigation Pane check box (you may have to click the Show button first). Then select a tab in the Navigation pane and go to it:

✦ **Going from heading to heading:** Select the Browse the Headings tab. Headings in your document appear (provided you assigned heading styles to headings). You can use the Navigation pane like a table of contents and click headings to get from place to place. Right-click a heading and choose a heading-level option on the shortcut menu to tell Word which headings to display. You can also right-click a heading and choose Expand All or Collapse All to see or hide lower-level headings.

✦ **Going from page to page:** Select the Browse the Pages tab. A thumbnail image of each page in the document appears. To quickly move from page to page, use the scroll bar in the Navigation pane or click a page thumbnail. Each thumbnail is numbered so that you always know which page you are viewing.

"Browsing" around a document

A really fast way to move around quickly is to click the Select Browse Object button in the lower-right corner of the screen. When you click this button (or press Ctrl+Alt+Home), Word presents 12 *Browse By* icons: Field, Endnote,

Footnote, Comment, Section, Page, Go To, Find, Edits, Heading, Graphic, and Table. Select the icon that represents the element you want to go to, and Word takes you there immediately. For example, click the Browse by Heading icon to get to the next heading in your document (provided that you assigned heading styles to headings).

After you have selected a Browse By icon, the navigator buttons — the double arrows directly above and below the Select Browse Object button — turn blue. Click a navigator button to get to the next example or the previous example of the element you chose. For example, if you selected the Browse by Heading icon, all you have to do is click the blue navigator buttons to get from heading to heading, backward or forward in your document.

Going there fast with the Go To command

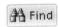

Another fast way to go from place to place in a document is to use the Go To command. On the Home tab, open the drop-down list on the Find button and choose Go To (you may have to click the Editing button first). You see the Go To tab of the Find and Replace dialog box, as shown in Figure 1-6. You can also open this dialog box by pressing Ctrl+G or F5.

Figure 1-6:
Using the
Go To
command.

The Go to What menu in this dialog box lists everything that can conceivably be numbered in a Word document, and other things, too. Everything that you can get to with the Select Browse Object button, as well as lines, equations, and objects, can be reached by way of the Go To tab. Click a menu item, enter a number, choose an item from the drop-down list, or click the Previous, Next, or Go To buttons to go elsewhere.

Bookmarks for hopping around

Rather than press PgUp or PgDn or click the scroll bar to thrash around in a long document, you can use *bookmarks*. All you do is put a bookmark in an important spot in your document that you'll return to many times. To return to that spot, open the Bookmark dialog box and select a bookmark name, as shown in Figure 1-7. True to the craft, the mystery writer whose bookmarks are shown in Figure 1-7 wrote the end of the story first and used bookmarks to jump back and forth between the beginning and end to make all the clues fit together.

Bookmark

Bookmark name:

Mystery_Solved

Clues
Dark_Alley
More_Mayhem
Mystery_Solved
Shady_Characters
Suspicious_Persons
The_Case
The_Crime

Add

Delete

Go To

Sort by: ◉ Name
         ○ Location

☐ Hidden bookmarks

Cancel

Figure 1-7:
The
Bookmark
dialog box.

Follow these instructions to handle bookmarks:

✦ **Adding a bookmark:** Click where you want the bookmark to go, visit the Insert tab, and click the Bookmark button (you may have to click the Links button first, depending on the size of your screen). Then, in the Bookmark dialog box, type a descriptive name in the Bookmark Name box, and click the Add button. Bookmarks can't start with numbers or include blank spaces. You can also open the Bookmark dialog box by pressing Ctrl+Shift+F5.

✦ **Going to a bookmark:** On the Insert tab, click the Bookmark button (you may have to click the Links button first), double-click the bookmark in the Bookmark dialog box, and click the Close button.

✦ **Deleting a bookmark:** Select the bookmark in the Bookmark dialog box and click the Delete button.

Word uses bookmarks for many purposes. For example, bookmarks indicate where cross-references are located in a document.

Inserting a Whole File into a Document

One of the beautiful things about word processing is that you can recycle documents. Say that you wrote an essay on the Scissor-Tailed Flycatcher that would fit very nicely in a broader report on North American birds. You can insert the Scissor-Tailed Flycatcher document into your report document:

1. **Place the cursor where you want to insert the document.**

2. **On the Insert tab, open the drop-down list on the Object button and choose Text from File.**

You see the Insert File dialog box.

3. **Find and select the file you want to insert.**

4. **Click the Insert button.**

Entering Information Quickly in a Computerized Form

A *form* is a means of soliciting and recording information. You can use forms like the one shown in Figure 1-8 to enter data faster and to reduce data-entry errors. Instead of entering all the information by hand, you or a data-entry clerk can choose entries from combo boxes, drop-down lists, and date pickers. You save time because you don't have to enter all the information by hand, and the information you enter is more likely to be accurate because you choose it from prescribed lists instead of entering it yourself.

Drop-down list

Combo box   Date picker

Figure 1-8:
A data-entry
form.

To create a form like the one shown in Figure 1-8, start by creating a template for your form and putting *data-entry controls* — the combo boxes, drop-down lists, and date pickers — in the form. To fill out a form, you create a document from the form template and go to it. These pages explain how to create a form and use forms to record information.

Creating a computerized form

The first step in creating a data-entry form is to create a template for holding the form. After that, you design the form itself by labeling the data fields and creating the data-entry controls. Better keep reading.

Creating a template to hold the form

Follow these steps to create a new template:

1. **On the File tab, choose New.**

   You see the Available Templates window.

2. **Click the My Templates icon.**

   The New dialog box appears. It lists Word templates that are on your computer.

3. **Click the Template option button.**

   You can find this button under Create New in the lower-right corner of the dialog box.

4. **Click OK.**

5. **Click the Save button (or press Ctrl+S) to open the Save As dialog box.**

6. **Enter a descriptive name for your template and click the Save button.**

   Chapter 3 of this mini-book explains templates in detail.

Book II
Chapter 1

Speed
Techniques

Creating the form and data-entry controls

Your next task is to create the form and data-entry controls for your template. Enter labels on the form where you will enter information. The form in Figure 1-8, for example, has five labels: Name, Phone, Fee Paid?, Association, and Date. After you enter the labels, follow these steps to create the data-entry controls:

1. **Display the Developer tab, if necessary.**

   If this tab isn't showing, go to the File tab, choose Options, and on the Customize Ribbon tab of the Word Options dialog box, select the Developer check box and click OK. (Book VIII, Chapter 1 explains in detail how to customize the Ribbon.)

2. **Click where you want to place a control, and then create the control by clicking a Controls button followed by the Properties button on the Developer tab.**

   Here are instructions for creating three types of controls:

   - *Drop-down list:* A *drop-down list* is a menu that "drops" when you open it to reveal different option choices (refer to Figure 1-8). Click the Drop-Down List Content Control button and then the Properties button. You see the Content Control Properties dialog box, as shown in Figure 1-9. For each option you want to place on the drop-down list, click the Add button, and in the Add Choice dialog box, enter the option's name in the Display Name text box and click OK, as shown in Figure 1-9.

- *Combo box:* Like a drop-down list, a *combo box* "drops" to reveal choices. However, as well as choosing an option on the drop-down list, data-entry clerks can enter information in the box (refer to Figure 1-8). Click the Combo Box Content Control button and then the Properties button. In the Content Control Properties dialog box, enter option names the same way you enter them in a drop-down list, as shown in Figure 1-9.

- *Date picker:* A *date picker* is a mini-calendar from which data-entry clerks can enter a date (refer to Figure 1-8). Click the Date Picker Content Control button and then the Properties button. In the Content Control Properties dialog box, choose a display format for dates and click OK.

3. **Click the Save button to save your template.**

   Now you're ready to use your newly made form to enter data.

Figure 1-9: Click the Add button to create options for a drop-down list or combo box.

Entering data in the form

Now that you have the template, you or someone else can enter data cleanly in easy-to-read forms:

1. **On the File tab, choose New.**

   You see the Available Templates window.

2. **Click the My Templates icon.**

   The New dialog box opens and shows you Word templates on your computer.

3. **Double-click the name of the template you created for entering data in your form.**

The form appears.

4. **Enter information in the input fields.**

Press the up or down arrow, or press Tab and Shift+Tab to move from field to field. You can also click input fields to move the cursor there.

5. **When you're done, print the document or save it.**

Chapter 2: Laying Out Text and Pages

In This Chapter

- Entering a section break
- Starting a new line and page
- Changing the margins
- Indenting text
- Numbering pages and handling headers and footers
- Adjusting the space between lines and paragraphs
- Handling numbered and bulleted lists
- Hyphenating the text

This chapter explains how to format text and pages. A well-laid-out document says a lot about how much time and thought was put into it. This chapter presents tips, tricks, and techniques for making pages look just right.

In this chapter, you find out what section breaks are and why they are so important to formatting. You discover how to establish the size of margins, indent text, number pages, construct headers and footers, determine how much space appears between lines of text, handle lists, and hyphenate text.

Paragraphs and Formatting

Back in English class, your teacher taught you that a paragraph is a part of a longer composition that presents one idea or, in the case of dialogue, presents the words of one speaker. Your teacher was right, too, but for word-processing purposes, a paragraph is a lot less than that. In word processing, a paragraph is simply what you put on-screen before you press the Enter key.

For instance, a heading is a paragraph. If you press Enter on a blank line to go to the next line, the blank line is considered a paragraph. If you type **Dear John** at the top of a letter and press Enter, "Dear John" is a paragraph.

It's important to know this because paragraphs have a lot to do with formatting. If you click the Paragraph group button on the Home tab and monkey around with the paragraph formatting in the Paragraph dialog box, your changes affect everything in the paragraph where the cursor is located. To make format changes to a whole paragraph, all you have to do is place the cursor there. You don't have to select the paragraph. And if you want to make format changes to several paragraphs, all you have to do is select those paragraphs first.

Inserting a Section Break for Formatting Purposes

When you want to change page numbering schemes, headers and footers, margin sizes, and page orientations in a document, you have to create a *section break* to start a new section. Word creates a new section for you when you create newspaper-style columns or change the size of margins.

Follow these steps to create a new section:

1. **Click where you want to insert a section break.**

2. **On the Page Layout tab, click the Breaks button.**

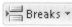

You open a drop-down list.

3. **Under Section Breaks on the drop-down list, select a section break.**

All four section break options create a new section, but they do so in different ways:

✦ **Next Page:** Inserts a page break as well as a section break so that the new section can start at the top of a new page (the next one). Select this option to start a new chapter, for example.

✦ **Continuous:** Inserts a section break in the middle of a page. Select this option if, for example, you want to introduce newspaper-style columns in the middle of a page.

✦ **Even Page:** Starts the new section on the next even page. This option is good for two-sided documents in which the headers on the left- and right-side pages are different.

✦ **Odd Page:** Starts the new section on the next odd page. You might choose this option if you have a book in which chapters start on odd pages. (By convention, that's where they start.)

To delete a section break, make sure that you are in Draft view so that you can see section breaks, click the dotted line, and press the Delete key.

WARNING!

In the same way that paragraph marks store formats for a paragraph, section breaks store formats for an entire section. When you delete a section break, you apply new formats, because the section is folded into the section that formerly followed it and the section you deleted adopts that next section's formats. Because it's easy to accidentally delete a section break and create havoc, I recommend working in Draft view when your document has many section breaks. In Draft view, you can tell where a section ends because `Section Break` and a double dotted line appear on-screen. The only way to tell where a section ends in Print Layout view is to click the Show/Hide¶ button on the Home tab. (You can make section information appear on the status bar. Right-click the status bar and choose Section on the pop-up menu.)

Seeing what the formats are

Sometimes seeing how text was formatted merely by looking is difficult. However, by pressing Shift+F1, you can see precisely how text and paragraphs were formatted in the Reveal Formatting task pane. It describes how the text, paragraph, and section where the cursor is located are formatted.

While the Reveal Formatting task pane is open, you can take advantage of these amenities:

✔ **Compare one part of a document to another:** Click the Compare to Another Section check box and then click another part of your document. The Reveal Formatting task pane describes how the two parts differ. Knowing how parts of a document differ can be invaluable when you're creating and modifying styles.

✔ **Find out which style was assigned:** Click the Distinguish Style Source check box. The task pane lists the style you assigned to the part of your document where the cursor is located.

✔ **See the formatting marks:** Click the Show All Formatting Marks check box. You can see where paragraphs end, where line breaks are, and where tab spaces were entered. Clicking this check box has the same results as clicking the Show/Hide¶ button on the Home tab.

Breaking a Line

To break a line of text before it reaches the right margin without starting a new paragraph, press Shift+Enter. Figure 2-1 shows how you can press Shift+Enter to make lines break better. The paragraphs are identical, but I broke lines in the right-side paragraph to make the text easier to read. Line breaks are marked with the ↵ symbol. To erase line breaks, click the Show/Hide¶ button to see these symbols and then backspace over them.

Figure 2-1:
Break lines
to make
reading
easier.

"A computer in every home and a chicken in every pot is our goal!" stated Rupert T. Verguenza, president and CEO of the New Technics Corporation International at the annual shareholder meeting yesterday.

"A computer in every home and a chicken in every pot is our goal!" stated Rupert T. Verguenza, president and CEO of the New Technics Corporation International at the annual shareholder meeting yesterday.

Starting a New Page

Word gives you another page so that you can keep going when you fill up one page. But what if you're impatient and want to start a new page right away? Whatever you do, *don't* press Enter again and again until you fill up the page. Instead, create a *hard page break* by doing one the following on the Insert tab:

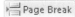

✦ Click the Page Break button (or press Ctrl+Enter). Word starts a new page at the cursor position. (You can also go to the Page Layout tab, click the Breaks button, choose Page on the drop-down list.)

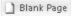

✦ Click the Blank Page button. Word enters two hard page breaks to create an empty, blank page at the cursor position.

In Draft view, you can click the Show/Hide¶ button on the Home tab and tell where you inserted a hard page break because you see the words `Page Break` and a dotted line on-screen. You can't tell where hard page breaks are in Print Layout view.

To delete a hard page break, switch to Draft view, click the Show/Hide¶ button on the Home tab, click the words `Page Break`, and press the Delete key.

Setting Up and Changing the Margins

Margins are the empty spaces along the left, right, top, and bottom of a page, as shown in Figure 2-2. Headers and footers fall, respectively, in the top and bottom margins. And you can put graphics, text boxes, and page numbers in the margins as well. Margins serve to frame the text and make it easier to read.

Outside margin   Inside margins   Outside margin

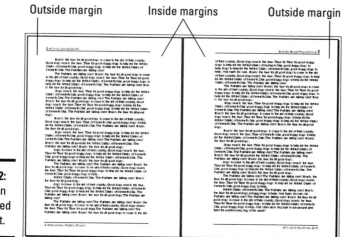

Figure 2-2:
Margins in
a two-sided
document.

When you start a new document, give a moment's thought to the margins. Changing the size of margins after you have entered the text, clip art, graphics, and whatnot can be disastrous. Text is indented from the left and right margins. Pages break on the bottom margin. If you change margin settings, indents and page breaks change for good or ill throughout your document. By setting the margins carefully from the beginning, you can rest assured that text will land on the page where you want it to land.

Don't confuse margins with indents. Text is indented from the margin, not from the edge of the page. If you want to change how far text falls from the page edge, indent it. To change margin settings in the middle of a document, you have to create a new section.

To set up or change the margins, go to the Page Layout tab and click the Margins button. You see a drop-down list with margin settings. Either choose a setting or select Custom Margins to open the Margins tab of the Page Setup dialog box and choose among these commands for handling margins:

✦ **Changing the size of the margins:** Enter measurements in the Top, Bottom, Left, and Right boxes to tell Word how much blank space to put along the sides of the page.

✦ **Making room for the gutter:** The *gutter* is the part of the paper that the binding eats into when you bind a document. Enter a measurement in the Gutter box to increase the left or inside margin and make room for the binding. Notice on the pages of this book, for example, that the margin closest to the binding is wider than the outside margin. Choose Top on the Gutter Position menu if you intend to bind your document from the top, not the left, or inside, of the page. Some legal documents are bound this way.

✦ **Using mirror margins (inside and outside margins) in two-sided documents:** In a bound document in which text is printed on both sides of the pages, the terms left margin and right margin are meaningless. What matters instead is in the *inside margin*, the margin in the middle of the page spread next to the bindings, and the *outside margin*, the margin on the outside of the page spread that isn't affected by the bindings (refer to Figure 2-2). Choose Mirror Margins on the Multiple Pages drop-down list and adjust the margins accordingly if you intend to print on both sides of the paper.

✦ **Applying margin changes:** On the Apply To drop-down list, choose Whole Document to apply your margin settings to the entire document; This Section to apply them to a section; or This Point Forward to change margins in the rest of a document. When you choose This Point Forward, Word creates a new section.

If you're in a hurry to change margins, you can change them on the ruler. Display the ruler and drag the Left Margin, Right Margin, or Top Margin marker. You can find these markers by moving the pointer onto a ruler and looking for the two-headed arrow near a margin boundary. It appears, along with a pop-up label, when the pointer is over a margin marker.

To get a good look at where margins are, go to the File tab and choose Options. In the Word Options dialog box, select the Advanced category, and click the Show Text Boundaries check box (you'll find it under "Show Document Content").

Indenting Paragraphs and First Lines

An *indent* is the distance between a margin and the text, not the edge of the page and the text. Word offers a handful of ways to change the indentation of paragraphs. You can change the indentation of first lines as well as entire paragraphs. To start, select all or part of the paragraphs you want to re-indent (just click in a paragraph if you want to re-indent only one paragraph). Then click an Indent button, fiddle with the indentation marks on the ruler, or go to the Paragraph dialog box. All three techniques are described here.

Clicking an Indent button (for left-indents)

On the Home tab, click the Increase Indent or Decrease Indent button (or press Ctrl+M or Ctrl+Shift+M) to move a paragraph a half inch farther away from or closer to the left margin. If you created tab stops, text is indented to the next or previous tab stop as well as to the next or previous half inch. This is the fastest way to indent text, although you can't indent first lines or indent from the right margin this way.

"Eye-balling it" with the ruler

You can also change indentations by using the ruler to "eyeball it." This technique requires some dexterity with the mouse, but it allows you to see precisely where paragraphs and the first lines of paragraphs are indented. If necessary, display the ruler by going to the View tab and clicking the Ruler check box. Then click in or select the paragraph or paragraphs that need indenting and use these techniques to re-indent them:

**Book II
Chapter 2**

**Laying Out Text
and Pages**

✦ **Indenting an entire paragraph from the left margin:** Drag the *left-indent marker* on the ruler to the right. Figure 2-3 shows where this marker is located. Dragging the left-indent marker moves the first-line indent marker as well.

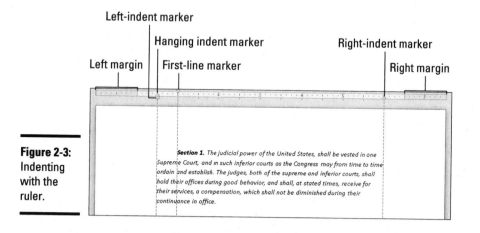

Left-indent marker

Hanging indent marker   Right-indent marker

Left margin   First-line marker   Right margin

Figure 2-3:
Indenting with the ruler.

Section 1. The judicial power of the United States, shall be vested in one Supreme Court, and in such inferior courts as the Congress may from time to time ordain and establish. The judges, both of the supreme and inferior courts, shall hold their offices during good behavior, and shall, at stated times, receive for their services, a compensation, which shall not be diminished during their continuance in office.

✦ **Indenting the first line of a paragraph:** Drag the *first-line indent marker* to the right (refer to Figure 2-3). This marker determines how far the first line of the paragraph is indented.

✦ **Making a hanging indent:** Drag the *hanging indent marker* to the right of the first-line indent marker (refer to Figure 2-3). A *hanging indent* is one in which the first line of a paragraph appears to "hang" into the margin because the second and subsequent lines are indented to the right of the start of the first line. Bulleted and numbered lists employ hanging indents.

✦ **Indenting an entire paragraph from the right margin:** Drag the *right-indent marker* to the left (refer to Figure 2-3).

Notice the shaded areas on the left and right side of the ruler. These areas represent the page margins.

Indenting in the Paragraph dialog box

Yet another way to indent a paragraph or first line is to visit the Paragraph dialog box. Click in or select the paragraph or paragraphs in question, go to the Home tab, and click the Paragraph group button. You see the Indents and Spacing tab of the Paragraph dialog box. Change the indentation settings. If you want to indent the first line or create a hanging indent, choose First Line or Hanging on the Special drop-down list and enter a measurement in the By box.

Numbering the Pages

How do you want to number the pages in your document? You can number them in sequence starting with the number 1, start numbering pages with a number other than 1, use Roman numerals or other number formats, and include chapter numbers in page numbers. What's more, you can number the pages differently in each section of your document as long as you divided your document into sections.

When it comes to numbering pages, you can proceed in two ways, as shown in Figure 2-4:

✦ Put a page number by itself on the pages of your document.

✦ Include the page number in the header or footer.

After you enter a page number, you can format it in different ways in the Page Number Format dialog box (see Figure 2-4) and (Header & Footer Tools) Design tab.

To handle page numbers (as well as headers and footers), you must be in Print Layout view. Click the Print Layout view button on the status bar or go to the View tab and click the Print Layout button.

Page number included in a header

Page number by itself | Choose page number format options

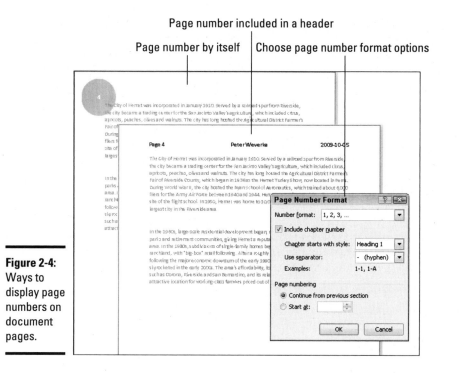

Figure 2-4:
Ways to
display page
numbers on
document
pages.

Numbering with page numbers only

Follow these steps to insert a page number by itself in the header, footer, or margin of the pages:

Page Number ▾

1. **On the Insert tab, click the Page Number button.**

2. **On the drop-down list, choose where on the page you want to put the page number (Top of Page, Bottom of Page, or Page Margins).**

3. **On the submenu that appears, choose a page number option.**

The farther you scroll on the submenu, the fancier the page number formats are.

If you change your mind about the page number format you chose, switch to Print Layout view and double-click in the header or footer where the page number is displayed. The (Header & Footer Tools) Design tab opens. Click the Page Number button and make a different choice, or choose Remove Page Numbers.

Including a page number in a header or footer

To put the page number part in a header or footer, click in the header or footer where you want the page number to appear (later in this chapter, "Putting Headers and Footers on Pages" explains headers and footers). Then follow these steps to insert the page number:

`📄 Page Number ▾`

1. **On the (Header & Footer Tools) Design tab, click the Page Number button.**

2. **Choose Current Position.**

   You see a submenu with page number choices.

3. **Scroll through the submenu and choose a page number format.**

   The "Page X of Y" option is for listing the total number of pages in a document as well as the page number. For example, page 2 of a 10-page document is numbered "Page 2 of 10."

Changing page number formats

Change page number formats in the Page Number Format dialog box (refer to Figure 2-4). To display this dialog box, make sure that you're in Print Layout view and double-click your header or footer. Then use one of the following methods to change page number formats:

`📄 Page Number ▾`

✦ On the Insert tab, click the Page Number button and choose Format Page Numbers.

✦ On the (Header & Footer Tools) Design tab, click the Page Number button and choose Format Page Numbers.

In the Page Number Format dialog box, make your page numbers just so:

✦ **Choosing a different number format:** Open the Number Format drop-down list and choose a page-numbering format. You can use numbers, letters, or roman numerals.

✦ **Including chapter numbers in page numbers:** If your document generates chapter numbers automatically from headings assigned the same style (a subject not covered in this book), you can include the chapter number in the page number. Click the Include Chapter Number check box, choose a style, and choose a separator to go between the chapter number and page number.

✦ **Numbering each section separately:** Click the Start At option button (not the Continue from Previous Section button) to begin counting pages anew at each section in your document. Earlier in this chapter, "Inserting a Section Break for Formatting Purposes" explains sections.

✦ **Start numbering pages at a number other than 1:** Click the Start At option button and enter a number other than 1.

TIP

To keep some pages in a document from being numbered, create a section for those pages, and then remove page numbers from the section. To paginate your document, Word skips the section you created and resumes numbering pages in the following section.

Putting Headers and Footers on Pages

A *header* is a little description that appears along the top of a page so that the reader knows what's what. Usually, headers include the page number and a title, and often the author's name appears in the header as well. A *footer* is the same thing as a header except that it appears along the bottom of the page, as befits its name.

Book II
Chapter 2

Laying Out Text and Pages

These pages explain everything a mere mortal needs to know about headers and footers. Meanwhile, here are the ground rules for managing them:

✦ **Switching to Print Layout view:** To enter, read, edit, or delete headers and footers, you must be in Print Layout view. You can't see headers and footers in the other views.

✦ **Displaying the (Header & Footer Tools) Design tab:** As shown in Figure 2-5, you manage headers and footers by way of buttons on the (Header & Footer Tools) Design tab. To display this tab after you create a header or footer, switch to Print Layout view and double-click a header or footer.

✦ **Closing the (Header & Footer Tools) Design tab:** Click the Close Header & Footer button or double-click outside the header or footer.

✦ **Placing different headers and footers in the same document:** To change headers or footers in the middle of a document, you have to create a new section. See "Inserting a Section Break for Formatting Purposes" earlier in this chapter.

Figure 2-5: Manage headers and footers on the (Header & Footer Tools) Design tab.

Creating, editing, and removing headers and footers

Follow these instructions to create, edit, and delete headers and footers:

✦ **Creating a header or footer:** On the Insert tab, click the Header or the Footer button, and choose a header or footer on the gallery. The gallery presents headers or footers with preformatted page numbers, dates, and places to enter a document title and author's name. Click More Headers (or Footers) from Office.com to download headers or footers from Microsoft. (Later in this chapter, "Fine-tuning a header or footer" explains how to insert the date and time and change headers and footers from section to section.)

✦ **Choosing a different header or footer:** Don't like the header or footer you chose? If necessary, double-click your header or footer to display the (Header & Footer Tools) Design tab. Then click the Header or Footer button and choose a new header or footer from the gallery.

✦ **Editing a header or footer:** Click the Header or the Footer button and choose Edit Header or Edit Footer on the drop-down list. The cursor moves into the header or footer so that you can enter or format text.

✦ **Changing the appearance of a header or footer:** Click a shape or text box in a header or footer and visit the (Drawing Tools) Format tab to change the shape or text box's color, background, or size. (Book I, Chapter 8 describes the drawing tools.)

✦ **Removing a header or footer:** Click the Header or Footer button and choose Remove Header or Remove Footer on the drop-down list.

To switch back and forth between the header and footer, click the Go to Header or Go to Footer button on the (Header & Footer Tools) Design tab.

As you work away on your header and footer, you can call on most of the text-formatting commands on the Home tab. You can change the text's font and font size, click an alignment button, and paste text from the Clipboard. Tabs are set up in most headers and footers to make it possible to center, left-align, and right-align text. You can click the Insert Alignment Tab button on the (Header & Footer Tools) Design tab to insert a new tab.

Fine-tuning a header or footer

Here is advice for making a perfect header on the (Header & Footer Tools) Design tab:

✦ **Inserting a page number:** See "Including a page number in a header or footer" and "Changing page number formats" earlier in this chapter.

✦ **Inserting the date and time:** Click the Date & Time button, choose a date format in the Date and Time dialog box, and click OK. Click the Update Automatically check box if you want the date to record when you print the document, not when you created your header or footer.

Creating your own header or footer for the gallery

When you click the Header or the Footer button on the Insert tab, a gallery appears with headers or footers. You can create your own header or footer and place it on this gallery. For example, create a header or footer with your company logo. After you design and create your header or footer, follow these instructions to wrangle with it:

✔ **Placing a header or footer in the gallery:** Select your header or footer by dragging over it or by clicking in the margin to its left. On the (Header & Footer Tools) Design tab, click the Quick Parts button and choose Save Selection to Quick Part Gallery. You see the Create New Building Block dialog box. Enter a descriptive name for the header or footer, choose Footers or Headers on the Gallery drop-down list, and click OK.

✔ **Inserting a header or footer you created:** On the Insert tab, click the Header or Footer button and choose your header or footer in the gallery. It is located in the Built-In or General category, depending on where you chose to put it.

✔ **Removing and editing headers or footers:** On the Insert tab, click the Quick Parts button and choose Building Blocks Organizer. The Building Blocks Organizer dialog box appears. Select your header or footer and click the Delete button to remove it from the gallery or the Edit Properties button to change its name, gallery assignment, or category assignment.

Create New Building Block		? ×
Name:	My Company Name with Logo	
Gallery:	Headers	▼
Category:	Built-In	▼
Description:		
Save in:	Building Blocks	▼
Options:	Insert content only	▼
	OK	Cancel

✦ **Changing headers and footers from section to section:** Use the Link to Previous button to determine whether headers and footers are different from section to section (you must divide the document into sections to have different headers and footers). Deselecting this button tells Word that you want your header or footer to be different from the header or footer in the previous section of the document; selecting this button (clicking it so that it looks selected) tells Word that you want your header or footer to be the same as the header or footer in the previous section of your document. To make a different header or footer, deselect the Link to Previous button and enter a different header or footer.

When the header or footer is the same as that of the previous section, the Header or Footer box reads `Same as Previous` (refer to Figure 2-5); when the header or footer is different from that of the previous section, the words `Same as Previous` don't appear. You can click the Previous or Next button to examine the header or footer in the previous or next section.

✦ **Different headers and footers for odd and even pages:** Click the Different Odd & Even Pages check box to create different headers and footers for odd and even pages. As "Setting Up and Changing the Margins" explains earlier in this chapter, documents in which text is printed on both sides of the page can have different headers and footers for the left and right side of the page spread. The Header or Footer box reads Odd or Even to tell you which side of the page spread you're dealing with as you enter your header or footer.

✦ **Removing headers and footers from the first page:** Click the Different First Page check box to remove a header or footer from the first page of a document or section. Typically, the first page of letters and reports are not numbered.

Adjusting the Space Between Lines

To change the spacing between lines, select the lines whose spacing you want to change, or simply put the cursor in a paragraph if you're changing the line spacing throughout a paragraph (if you're just starting a document, you're ready to go). Then, on the Home tab, click the Line and Paragraph Spacing button and choose an option on the drop-down list.

To take advantage of more line-spacing options, click the Paragraph group button on the Home tab or choose Line Spacing Options on the Line and Paragraph Spacing button drop-down list. You see the Paragraph dialog box. Select an option on the Line Spacing drop-down list:

✦ **At Least:** Choose this one if you want Word to adjust for tall symbols or other unusual text. Word adjusts the lines but makes sure that there is, at minimum, the number of points you enter in the At box between each line.

✦ **Exactly:** Choose this one and enter a number in the At box if you want a specific amount of space between lines.

✦ **Multiple:** Choose this one and put a number in the At box to get triple-spaced, quadruple-, quintuple-, or any other number of spaced lines.

To quickly single-space text, click the text or select it if you want to change more than one paragraph, and press Ctrl+1. To quickly double-space text, select the text and press Ctrl+2. Press Ctrl+5 to put one and a half lines between lines of text.

Adjusting the Space between Paragraphs

Rather than press Enter to put a blank line between paragraphs, you can open the Paragraph dialog box and enter a point-size measurement in the Before or After text box. The Before and After measurements place a specific amount of space before and after paragraphs.

Truth be told, the Before and After options are for use with styles (a subject of the next chapter). When you create a style, you can tell Word to always follow a paragraph in a certain style with a paragraph in another style. For example, a paragraph in the Chapter Title style might always be followed by a paragraph in the Chapter Intro style. In cases like these, when you know that paragraphs assigned to one type of style will always follow paragraphs assigned to another style, you can confidently put space before and after paragraphs. But if you use the Before and After styles indiscriminately, you can end up with large blank spaces between paragraphs.

Go to the Home tab and use one of these techniques to adjust the amount of space between paragraphs:

✦ Click the Line and Paragraph Spacing button and choose Add Space Before Paragraph or Add Space after Paragraph on the drop-down list. These commands place 10 points of blank space before or after the paragraph that the cursor is in.

✦ Click the Paragraph group button to open the Paragraph dialog box, and enter point-size measurements in the Before and After boxes (or choose Auto in these boxes to enter one blank line between paragraphs in whatever your line-spacing choice is). The Don't Add Space between Paragraphs of the Same Style check box tells Word to ignore Before and After measurements if the previous or next paragraph is assigned the same style as the paragraph that the cursor is in.

Creating Numbered and Bulleted Lists

What is a word-processed document without a list or two? It's like an emperor with no clothes. Numbered lists are invaluable in manuals and books like this one that present a lot of step-by-step procedures. Use bulleted lists when you want to present alternatives to the reader. A *bullet* is a black, filled-in circle or other character. These pages explained numbered lists, bulleted lists, and multilevel lists.

Simple numbered and bulleted lists

The fastest, cleanest, and most honest way to create a numbered or bulleted list is to enter the text without any concern for numbers or bullets. Just press Enter at the end of each step or bulleted entry. When you're done, select the list, go to the Home tab, and click the Numbering or Bullets button. You can also click the Numbering or Bullets button and start typing the list. Each time you press Enter, Word enters the next number or another bullet.

Meanwhile, here are some tricks for handling lists:

✦ **Ending a list:** Press the Enter key twice after typing the last entry in the list. You can also right-click the list, choose Bullets or Numbering, and choose None on the submenu.

✦ **Removing the numbers or bullets:** Select the list and click the Numbering or Bullets button.

✦ **Adjusting how far a list is indented:** Right-click anywhere in the list, choose Adjust List Indents, and enter a new measurement in the Text Indent box.

✦ **Resuming a numbered list:** Suppose that you want a numbered list to resume where a list you entered earlier ended. In other words, suppose that you left off writing a four-step list, put in a graphic or some paragraphs, and now you want to resume the list at Step 5. Click the Numbering button to start numbering again. The AutoCorrect Options button appears. Click it and choose Continue Numbering, or right-click and choose Continue Numbering on the shortcut menu.

✦ **Starting a new list:** Suppose that you want to start a brand-new list right away. Right-click the number Word entered and choose Restart at 1 on the shortcut menu.

Constructing lists of your own

If you are an individualist and you want numbered and bulleted lists to work your way, follow these instructions for choosing unusual bullet characters and number formats:

Automatic lists and what to do about them

Word creates automatic lists for you whether you like it or not. To see what I mean, type the number 1, type a period, and press the spacebar. Word immediately creates a numbered list. In the same manner, Word creates a bulleted list when you type an asterisk (*) and press the spacebar.

Some people find this kind of behind-the-scenes skulduggery annoying. If you are one such person, do one of the following to keep Word from making lists automatically:

✔ Click the AutoCorrect Options button — it appears automatically — and choose Stop Automatically Creating Lists.

✔ On the File tab, choose Options, select the Proofing category in the Word Options dialog box, and click the AutoCorrect Options button. On the AutoFormat As You Type tab in the AutoCorrect dialog box, uncheck the Automatic Numbered Lists and Automatic Bulleted Lists check boxes.

✦ **Choosing a different numbering scheme:** On the Home tab, open the drop-down list on the Numbering button and choose a numbering scheme. You can also choose Define New Number Format. As shown in Figure 2-6, you see the Define New Number Format dialog box, where you can choose a number format, choose a font for numbers, and toy with number alignments.

✦ **Choosing a different bullet character:** On the Home tab, open the drop-down list on the Bullets button and choose a different bullet character on the drop-down list. You can also choose Define New Bullet to open the Define New Bullet dialog box, shown in Figure 2-6, and click the Symbol button to choose a bullet character in the Symbol dialog box (Book I, Chapter 2 describes symbols). The dialog box also offers opportunities for indenting bullets and the text that follows them in unusual ways.

**Book II
Chapter 2**

**Laying Out Text
and Pages**

Figure 2-6:
Customizing
a numbered
or bulleted
list.

Managing a multilevel list

A *multilevel list,* also called a *nested list,* is a list with subordinate entries, as shown in Figure 2-7. To create a multilevel list, you declare what kind of list you want, and then, as you enter items for the list, you indent the items that you want to be subordinate. Follow these steps to create a multilevel list:

1. **On the Home tab, click the Multilevel List button and choose what kind of list you want.**

   If none of the lists suit you, you can choose Define New Multilevel List and create a new kind of list in the Define New Multilevel List dialog box.

2. **Enter the items for the list, pressing Enter as you complete each one.**

3. **Select a list item (or items) and click the Increase Indent button (or press Ctrl+M) to make the items subordinate in the list; click the Decrease Indent button (or press Ctrl+Shift+M) to raise their rank in the list.**

Repeat Step 3 until the list is just so.

Figure 2-7:
Examples
of multilevel
lists.

Working with Tabs

Tabs are a throwback to the days of the typewriter, when it was necessary to make tab stops in order to align text. Except for making leaders and aligning text in headers and footers, everything you can do with tabs can also be done by creating a table — and it can be done far faster. All you have to do is align the text inside the table and then remove the table borders. (Book I, Chapter 5 explains tables.)

A *tab stop* is a point around which or against which text is formatted. As shown in Figure 2-8, Word offers five tab types for aligning text: Left, Center, Right, Decimal, and Bar (a bar tab stop merely draws a vertical line on the page). When you press the Tab key, you advance the text cursor by one tab stop. Tab stops are shown on the ruler; symbols on the ruler tell you what type of tab you're dealing with.

By default, tabs are left-aligned and are set at half-inch intervals. Display the ruler (click the Ruler check box on the View tab) and follow these steps to change tabs or change where tabs appear on the ruler:

1. **Select the paragraphs that need different tab settings.**

2. **Click the Tab box on the left side of the ruler as many times as necessary to choose the kind of tab you want.**

Symbols on the tab box indicate which type of tab you're choosing.

3. **Click on the ruler where you want the tab to go.**

You can click as many times as you want and enter more than one kind of tab.

Click to choose a different tab stop   Decimal tab

Left tab   Center tab   Right tab   Bar tab

Last Name	Title	City	Rating
Macy	President	Stamford	10.8
Childs	CFO	Rock Springs	44.378
Ng	VP	Needles	107.1
Munoz	Controller	Santa Fe	13.95
DeSilva	Officer	New Orleans	92.134
Manigault	CEO	Fairfax	49.3
Church	VP	San Carlos	114.93
Lee	CN	Bryland	90.00

Figure 2-8:
Different
kinds of tab
stops.

All about tab leaders

In my opinion, the only reason to fool with tabs and tab stops is to create tab leaders like the ones shown here. A *leader* is a series of punctuation marks — periods in the illustration — that connect text across a page. Leaders are very elegant. For the figure, I used left-aligned tab stops for the characters' names and right-aligned tab stops for the players' names. I included leaders so that you can tell precisely who played whom.

Follow these steps to create tab leaders:

1. **Enter the text and, in each line, enter a tab space between the text on the left side and the text on the right side.**

2. **Select the text you entered.**

3. **On the Home tab, click the Paragraph group button, and in the Paragraph dialog box, click the Tabs button.**

   You see the Tabs dialog box.

4. **Enter a position for the first new tab in the Tab Stop Position box.**

5. **Under Leader in the dialog box, select the punctuation symbol you want for the leader.**

6. **Click OK, display the ruler, and drag tab markers to adjust the space between the text on the left and right.**

THE PLAYERS

Romeo...McGeorge Wright
Juliet..Gabriela Hernandez
Mercutio ....Chris Suzuki
Lady Capulet.........................Mimi Hornstein

To move a tab stop, drag it to a new location on the ruler. Text that is aligned with the tab stop moves as well. To remove a tab stop, drag it off the ruler. When you remove a tab stop, text to which it was aligned is aligned to the next remaining tab stop on the ruler or to the next default tab stop if you didn't create any tab stops of your own.

 Sometimes it's hard to tell where tabs were put in the text. To find out, click the Show/Hide¶ button on the Home tab to see the formatting characters, including the arrows that show where the Tab key was pressed.

Hyphenating Text

The first thing you should know about hyphenating words is that you may not need to do it. Text that hasn't been hyphenated is much easier to read, which is why the majority of text in this book, for example, isn't hyphenated. It has a *ragged right margin,* to borrow typesetter lingo. Hyphenate only when text is trapped in columns or in other narrow places, or when you want a very formal-looking document.

 Do not insert a hyphen simply by pressing the hyphen key, because the hyphen will stay there even if the word moves to the middle of a line and doesn't need to be broken in half. Instead, when a big gap appears in the right margin and a word is crying out to be hyphenated, put the cursor where the hyphen needs to go and press Ctrl+hyphen. This way, you enter what is called a *discretionary hyphen,* and the hyphen appears only if the word breaks at the end of a line. (To remove a manual hyphen, press the Show/Hide¶ button so that you can see it, and then backspace over it.)

Automatically and manually hyphenating a document

Select text if you want to hyphenate part of a document, not all of it, and use one of these techniques to hyphenate words that break on the end of a line of text:

✦ **Automatic hyphenation:** On the Page Layout tab, click the Hyphenation button and choose Automatic on the drop-down list. Word hyphenates your document (or a portion of your document, if you selected it first).

You can tell Word how to hyphenate automatically by clicking the Hyphenation button and choosing Hyphenation Options. You see the Hyphenation dialog box shown in Figure 2-9. Deselect the Hyphenate Words in CAPS check box if you don't care to hyphenate words in uppercase. Words that fall in the hyphenation zone are hyphenated, so enlarging the hyphenation zone means a less ragged right margin but more ugly hyphens, and a small zone means fewer ugly hyphens but a more ragged right margin. You can limit how many hyphens appear consecutively by entering a number in the Limit Consecutive Hyphens To box.

Figure 2-9:
Telling Word how to hyphenate (left) and deciding where a hyphen goes (right).

Book II Chapter 2

Laying Out Text and Pages

✦ **Manual hyphenation:** On the Page Layout tab, click the Hyphenation button and choose Manual on the drop-down list. Word displays a box with some hyphenation choices in it (refer to Figure 2-9). The cursor blinks on the spot where Word suggests putting a hyphen. Click Yes or No to accept or reject Word's suggestion. Keep accepting or rejecting Word's suggestions until the text is hyphenated.

Em and en dashes

Here is something about hyphens that editors and typesetters know, but the general public does not know: There is a difference between hyphens and dashes. Most people insert a hyphen where they ought to use an em dash or an en dash:

✔ An *em dash* looks like a hyphen but is wider—it's as wide as the letter *m*. The previous sentence has an em dash in it. Did you notice?

✔ An *en dash* is the width of the letter *n*. Use en dashes to show inclusive numbers or time periods, like so: pp. 45–50; Aug.–Sept. 1998; Exodus 16:11–16:18. An en dash is a little bit longer than a hyphen.

To place an em or en dash in a document and impress your local typesetter or editor, not to mention your readers, press Ctrl+Alt+– (the minus sign key on the Numeric keypad) to enter an em dash, or Ctrl+– (on the numeric keypad) to enter an en dash. You can also go to the Insert tab, click the Symbol button, choose More Symbols on the drop-down list, select the Special Characters tab in the Symbol dialog box, and choose Em Dash or En Dash.

Unhyphenating and other hyphenation tasks

More hyphenation esoterica:

✦ **Unhyphenating:** To "unhyphenate" a document or text you hyphenated automatically, go to the Page Layout tab, click the Hyphenation button, and choose Hyphenation Options. In the Hyphenation dialog box (refer to Figure 2-9), deselect the Automatically Hyphenate Document check box and click OK.

✦ **Preventing text from being hyphenated:** Select the text and, on the Home tab, click the Paragraph group button. In the Paragraph dialog box, select the Line and Page Breaks tab, and select the Don't Hyphenate check box. (If you can't hyphenate a paragraph, it's probably because this box was selected unintentionally.)

Chapter 3: Word Styles

In This Chapter

✔ Discovering how styles and templates work

✔ Applying a new style

✔ Creating your own styles

✔ Altering a style

✔ Creating a new template

*W*elcome to what may be the most important chapter of this book — the most important in Book II, anyway. Styles can save a ridiculous amount of time that you would otherwise spend formatting and wrestling with text. And many Word features rely on styles. You can't create a table of contents or use the Navigation pane unless each heading in your document has been assigned a heading style. Nor can you take advantage of Outline view and the commands for moving text around in that view. You can't cross-reference headings or number the headings in a document.

If you want to be stylish, at least where Word is concerned, you have to know about styles.

All about Styles

A *style* is a collection of formatting commands assembled under one name. When you apply a style, you give many formatting commands simultaneously, and you spare yourself the trouble of visiting numerous tabs and dialog boxes to format text. Styles save time and make documents look more professional. Headings assigned the same style — Heading1, for example — all look the same. When readers see that headings and paragraphs are consistent with one another across all the pages of a document, they get a warm, fuzzy feeling. They think the person who created the document really knew what he or she was doing.

Styles and templates

Every document comes with built-in styles that it inherits from the template with which it was created. You can create your own styles to supplement styles from the template. For that matter, you can create a template, populate it with styles you design, and use your new template to create distinctive letters or reports for your company.

A simple document created with the Blank Document template — a document that you create by pressing Ctrl+N — has only a few styles, but a document that was created with a sophisticated template comes with many styles. The Oriel Report template, for example, comes with styles for formatting titles, subtitles, headings, and quotations. Figure 3-1 illustrates how choosing styles from a template changes text formatting. Notice how choosing style options in the Styles pane reformats the text.

Figure 3-1:
Apply styles
to reformat
text.

Types of styles

In the Styles pane (refer to Figure 3-1), the symbol next to each style name tells you what type of style you're dealing with. Word offers four style types:

¶ ✦ **Paragraph styles:** Determine the formatting of entire paragraphs. A paragraph style can include these settings: font, paragraph, tab, border, language, bullets, numbering, and text effects. Paragraph styles are marked with the paragraph symbol (¶).

a ✦ **Character styles:** Apply to text, not to paragraphs. You select text before you apply a character style. Create a character style for text that is hard to lay out and for foreign-language text. A character style can include these settings: font, border, language, and text effects. When you apply a character style to text, the character-style settings override the paragraph-style settings. For example, if the paragraph style calls for 14-point Arial font but the character style calls for 12-point Times Roman font, the character style wins. Character styles are marked with the letter *a*.

✦ **Linked (paragraph and character):** Apply paragraph formats as well as text formats throughout a paragraph. These styles are marked with the paragraph symbol (¶) as well as the letter *a*.

Applying Styles to Text and Paragraphs

Word offers several ways to apply a style, and you are invited to choose the one that works best for you. These pages explain how to apply a style and tell Word how to present style names in the various places where style names are presented for your enjoyment and pleasure.

Applying a style

The first step in applying a style is to select the part of your document that needs a style change:

✦ **A paragraph or paragraphs:** Because paragraph styles apply to all the text in a paragraph, you need only click in a paragraph before applying a style to make a style apply throughout the paragraph. To apply a style to several paragraphs, select all or part of them.

✦ **Text:** To apply a character style, select the letters whose formatting you want to change.

Next, apply the style with one of these techniques:

✦ **Quick Style gallery:** On the Home tab, choose a style in the Quick Style gallery (depending on the size of your screen, you may have to click the Quick Styles button first). Figure 3-2 shows where the Quick Style gallery is located. The formatted letters above each style name in the gallery show you what your style choice will do to paragraphs or text. You can "live-preview" styles on the Quick Style gallery by moving the pointer over style names.

✦ **Styles pane:** On the Home tab, click the Styles group button to open the Styles pane, and select a style, as shown in Figure 3-2. Click the Show Preview check box at the bottom of the Styles pane to see formatted style names in the pane and get an idea of what the different styles are. You can drag the Styles pane to different locations on your screen. It remains on-screen after you leave the Home tab.

✦ **Apply Styles task pane:** Choose a style on the Apply Styles task pane, as shown in Figure 3-2. To display this task pane, go to the Home tab, open the Quick Style gallery, and choose Apply Styles (look for this option at the bottom of the gallery). You can drag the Apply Styles task pane to a corner of the screen. As does the Styles pane, the Apply Styles task pane remains on-screen after you leave the Home tab.

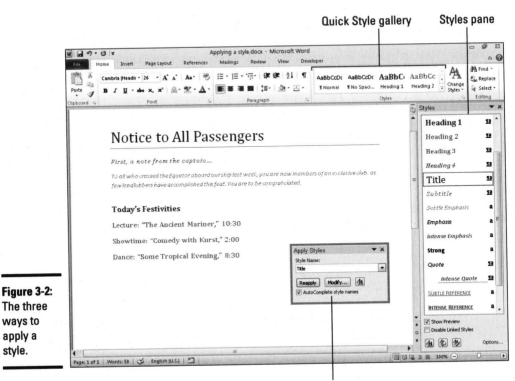

Figure 3-2: The three ways to apply a style.

Quick Style gallery   Styles pane

Apply Styles task pane

To strip a paragraph or text of its style and give it the generic Normal style, select it and choose Clear Formatting in the Quick Style gallery or Clear All at the top of the Styles pane.

Keyboard shortcuts for applying styles

A handful of keyboard shortcuts can be very handy when applying paragraph styles:

- ✓ Normal: Ctrl+Shift+N
- ✓ Heading 1: Ctrl+Alt+1
- ✓ Heading 2: Ctrl+Alt+2

- ✓ Heading 3: Ctrl+Alt+3
- ✓ Next higher heading: Alt+Shift+←
- ✓ Next lower heading: Alt+Shift+→

You can assign keyboard shortcuts to styles. Book VIII, Chapter 1 explains how.

Experimenting with style sets

A *style set* is a slight variation on the styles in the template you chose when you created your document. Style sets include Classic, Elegant, Fancy, and Modern. Choosing a style set imposes a slightly different look on your document — you make it classier, more elegant, fancier, or more modern. All templates, even those you create yourself, offer style sets. Style sets are a convenient way to experiment with the overall look of a document.

 To experiment with style sets, go to the Home tab, click the Change Styles button, choose Style Set on the drop-down list, and do one of the following:

✦ **Choose a new style set:** Select a style set on the submenu.

✦ **Use the original styles in the template:** Choose Reset to Quick Styles from Template on the submenu.

Choosing which style names appear on the Style menus

One of the challenges of applying styles is finding the right style to apply in the Quick Style gallery, Styles pane, or Apply Styles task pane (refer to Figure 3-2). All three can become crowded with style names. To make finding and choosing styles names easier, you can decide for yourself which names appear on the three style menus.

Quick Style gallery

In the Quick Style gallery, remove a style name by right-clicking it and choosing Remove from Quick Style gallery. If you regret removing style names, click the Change Styles button and choose Style Set⇨Reset to Quick Styles from Template.

Styles pane and Apply styles task pane

To decide for yourself which style names appear in the Styles pane and Apply Styles task pane, click the Styles group button, and in the Styles pane, click the Options link (you can find this link near the bottom of the pane). You see the Style Pane Options dialog box shown in Figure 3-3. Choose options to tell Word which style names appear in the Styles pane and Apply Styles task pane:

✦ **Select Styles to Show:** Choose All Styles to show all style names. The other options place a subset of names in the window and task pane. Recommended style names are those Microsoft thinks you need most often.

Figure 3-3:
Deciding
which
names to
put in the
Styles pane
and Apply
Styles task
pane.

> **Style Pane Options**
>
> Select styles to show:
> Recommended
>
> Select how list is sorted:
> As Recommended
>
> Select formatting to show as styles:
> ☐ Paragraph level formatting
> ☐ Font formatting
> ☐ Bullet and numbering formatting
>
> Select how built-in style names are shown
> ☑ Show next heading when previous level is used
> ☐ Hide built-in name when alternate name exists
>
> ⦿ Only in this document   ○ New documents based on this template
>
> OK   Cancel

✦ **Select How List Is Sorted:** Choose an option to describe how to list styles. Except for Based On, these options, I think, are self-explanatory. The Based On option lists styles in alphabetical order according to which style each style is based on (later in this chapter, "Creating a style from the ground up" explains how the Based On setting is used in constructing styles).

✦ **Select Formatting to Show As Styles:** Choose options to declare which styles to list — those that pertain to paragraph-level formatting, fonts, and bulleted and numbered lists.

Determining which style is in use

How can you tell which style has been applied to a paragraph or text? Sometimes you need to know which style is in play before you decide whether applying a different style is necessary.

Click the paragraph or text and use these techniques to find out which style was applied to it:

✔ **Glance at the Quick Style gallery and Styles pane to see which style is selected.** The selected style is the one that was applied to your paragraph or text.

✔ **Click the Style Inspector button at the bottom of the Styles pane.** The Style Inspector pane opens and lists the current style.

✔ **Press Shift+F1.** The Reveal Formatting task pane opens. It lists the style that was applied to the paragraph or text.

If you're especially keen to know about styles in your document, you can make style names appear to the left of the text in Outline and Draft view. On the Find tab, choose Options. In the Word Options dialog box, go to the Advanced tab and enter .5 or another measurement in the Style Area Pane Width in Draft and Outline Views box (look for this box under "Display"). You can drag the border of the Style Area pane to enlarge or shrink it.

✦ **Select How Built-In Style Names Are Shown:** Choose options to tell how to handle built-in styles, the obscure styles that Word applies on its own when you create tables of contents and other self-generating lists.

✦ **Apply to this document or to the template as well:** Click the Only in This Document option button to apply your choices only to the document you're working on; click the New Documents Based on This Template option button to apply your choices to your document and to all future documents you create with the template you're using.

Creating a New Style

You can create a new style by creating it from a paragraph or building it from the ground up. To do a thorough job, build it from the ground up because styles you create this way can be made part of the template you are currently working in and can be copied to other templates (later in this chapter, "Creating and Managing Templates" explains templates).

Creating a style from a paragraph

Follow these steps to create a new style from a paragraph:

1. **Click in a paragraph whose formatting you want to turn into a style.**

2. **Right-click and choose Styles⇨Save Selection As a New Quick Style.**

   You see the Create New Style from Formatting dialog box. You can also open this dialog box by opening the Quick Style gallery and choosing Save Selection As a New Quick Style.

3. **Enter a name for your new style.**

4. **Click OK.**

   A style you create this way becomes a part of the document you're working on; it isn't made part of the template from which you created your document.

Creating a style from the ground up

To make a style available in documents you will create in the future, make it part of a template and build it from the ground up. In the Styles pane, click the New Style button (you can find it at the bottom of the pane). You see the Create New Style from Formatting dialog box shown in Figure 3-4. Fill in the dialog box and click OK.

Create New Style from Formatting

Properties

Name: Intro

Style type: Paragraph

Style based on: ¶ Normal

Style for following paragraph: ¶ Normal

Formatting

Times New Roman | 10 | **B** *I* U | Automatic

Preview Paragraph Previous Paragraph Previous Paragraph Previous Paragraph Previous Paragraph Previous Paragraph Previous Paragraph Previous Paragraph Previous Paragraph Previous Paragraph

The white flies. The humid fetid jungle heat. The occasional river crossing which I came to dread after the second one, when I slipped on a flimsy log bridge and Jobo had to rescue me from the dangerous current. The incessant croaking of god knows what. I'

Following Paragraph Following Paragraph

Font: Italic, Do not check spelling or grammar, Indent:
 Left: 1", Style: Quick Style
Based on: Normal
Following style: Normal

☑ Add to Quick Style list ☐ Automatically update
◉ Only in this document ○ New documents based on this template

Format ▾ | OK | Cancel

Figure 3-4:
Creating
a brand-
spanking-
new style.

Here's a rundown of the options in the Create New Style from Formatting dialog box:

✦ **Name:** Enter a descriptive name for the style.

✦ **Style Type:** On the drop-down list, choose a style type ("Types of styles," earlier in this chapter, describes the style types).

✦ **Style Based On:** If your new style is similar to a style that is already part of the template with which you created your document, choose the style to get a head start on creating the new one. Be warned, however, that if you or someone else changes the Based On style, your new style will inherit those changes and be altered as well.

✦ **Style for Following Paragraph:** Choose a style from the drop-down list if the style you're creating is always followed by an existing style. For example, a new style called Chapter Title might always be followed by a style called Chapter Intro Paragraph. For convenience, someone who applies the style you're creating and presses Enter automatically applies the style you choose here on the next line of the document. Applying a style automatically to the following paragraph saves you the trouble of having to apply the style yourself.

✦ **Formatting:** Choose options from the menus or click buttons to fashion or refine your style (you can also click the Format button to do this).

✦ **Add to Quick Style List:** Select this check box to make the style's name appear in the Quick Style gallery, Styles pane, and Apply Styles task pane.

✦ **Automatically Update:** Normally, when you make a formatting change to a paragraph, the style assigned to the paragraph does not change at all, but the style does change if you check this box. Checking this box tells Word to alter the style itself each time you alter a paragraph to which you've assigned the style. With this box checked, all paragraphs in the document that were assigned the style are altered each time you change a single paragraph that was assigned the style.

✦ **Only in This Document/New Documents Based on This Template:** To make your style a part of the template from which you created your document as well as the document itself, click the New Documents Based on This Template option button. This way, new documents you create that are based on the template you are using can also make use of the new style.

✦ **Format:** This is the important one. Click the button and make a formatting choice. Word takes you to dialog boxes so that you can create or refine the style.

Modifying a Style

What if you decide at the end of an 80-page document that all 35 introductory paragraphs to which you assigned the Intro Para style look funny? If you clicked the Automatically Update check box in the New Style dialog box when you created the style, all you have to do is alter a paragraph to which you assigned the Intro Para style to alter all 35 introductory paragraphs. However, if you decided against updating styles automatically, you can still change the introductory paragraphs throughout your document.

Follow these steps to modify a style that isn't updated automatically:

1. **Click in any paragraph, table, or list to which you've assigned the style; if you want to modify a character style, select the characters to which you've assigned the style.**

2. **In the Styles pane or Apply Styles task pane, make sure that the name of the style you want to modify is selected.**

   If the right name isn't selected, select it now in the Styles pane or Apply Styles task pane.

3. **In the Styles pane, open the style's drop-down list and choose Modify; in the Apply Styles task pane, click the Modify button.**

   You see the Modify Style dialog box. Does the dialog box look familiar? It is nearly identical to the Create New Style from Formatting dialog box you used to create the style in the first place (refer to Figure 3-4). The only difference is that you can't choose a style type in the Modify Style dialog box.

4. **Change the settings in the Modify Styles dialog box and click OK.**

   The previous section in this chapter explains the settings.

After you modify a style, all paragraphs or text to which the style was assigned are instantly changed. You don't have to go back and reformat text and paragraphs throughout your document.

Creating and Managing Templates

As I explain at the start of this chapter, every document you create is fashioned from a *template*. The purpose of a template is to store styles for documents. In the act of creating a document, you choose a template, and the styles on the template become available to you when you work on your document (Chapter 1 of this mini-book explains how to choose a template when you create a new document).

For example, when you double-click the Blank Template icon in the Available Templates window or press Ctrl+N, you create a document with the Blank Document template, a relatively simple template with few styles. When you create a document with a template from Office.com or a template from the New dialog box, more styles are available to you because these templates are more sophisticated.

To save time formatting your documents, you are invited to create templates with styles that you know and love. You can create a new template from scratch, create a template from a document, or create a template by assembling styles from other templates and documents. Styles in templates, like styles in documents, can be modified, deleted, and renamed.

Creating a new template

How do you want to create a new template? You can do it from scratch, create a new template from a document, or assemble styles from other templates. Read on.

To create a document from a template you created yourself, open the Available Templates window (on the File tab, choose New) and click the My Templates icon. The New dialog box opens. Select your template and click the Open button.

Creating a template from scratch

Follow these steps to create a template from scratch:

1. **On the File tab, choose New.**

The Available Templates window opens.

2. **Click the My Templates icon to open the New dialog box.**

3. **Select the Blank Document icon.**

4. **Select the Template option button.**

   This option button is located in the lower-right corner of the dialog box.

5. **Click OK.**

   Your template appears in the Word window.

Create, modify, and delete styles as necessary (see "Creating a New Style" and "Modifying a Style," earlier in this chapter). Click the Save button to save your template, and in the Save As dialog box, enter a name for the template and click the Save button.

Creating a template from a document

If a document has all or most of the styles you want for a template, convert the document into a template so that you can use the styles in documents you create in the future. Follow these steps to create a Word template from a Word document:

1. **Open the Word document you will use to create a template.**

2. **On the File tab, choose Save As.**

   The Save As dialog box appears.

3. **Enter a name for your template.**

4. **Open the Save As Type menu and choose Word Template.**

5. **Under Favorite Links, click Templates to see the folder where templates are stored.**

6. **Click the Save button.**

Probably your new template includes text that it inherited from the document it was created from. Delete the text (unless you want it to appear in documents you create from your new template).

Assembling styles from other documents and templates

The third way to create a new template is to create a template from scratch and then gather styles from other documents and templates in your new template. Later in this chapter, "Copying styles from different documents and templates" explains how to assemble styles into a template.

Where templates are stored

Templates are stored in the Templates folder. To copy, move, or send templates, and to trade styles between templates, you have to know where the Templates folder is located on your computer. Where templates are stored by default depends on which version of Windows your computer runs:

- ✔ **Windows 7 and Windows Vista:** `C:\Users\` `Username\AppData\Roaming\` `Microsoft\Templates` folder.

- ✔ **Windows XP:** `C:\Documents and` `Settings\Username\` `Application Data\Microsoft\` `Templates` folder.

If you're having trouble finding the Templates folder, you can find out where it is located with these techniques:

- ✔ On the File tab, choose Options. In the Word Options dialog box, go to the Advanced Category and scroll to the File Locations button. Clicking this button opens the File Locations dialog box, where, under User Templates, you can see the name of the folder in which your templates are stored.

- ✔ On the File tab, choose New. In the Available Templates window, click the My Templates icon. The New dialog box appears. Right-click a template and choose Properties. The Properties dialog box lists the location of the folder where the templates are stored.

Opening a template so that you can modify it

Open a template the same way you open a document. On the File tab, choose Open. You see the Open dialog box. Under Favorite Links, click Templates and then double-click the name of the template. It opens in the Word window. Style modifications you make in the template become available to all documents that were fashioned from the template.

Copying styles from different documents and templates

Suppose that you like a style in one document and you want to copy it to another so that you can use it there. Or you want to copy it to a template to make it available to documents created with the template. Read on to find out how to copy styles between documents and between templates.

Copying a style from one document to another

Copy a style from one document to another when you need the style on a one-time basis. Follow these steps:

1. **Select a paragraph that was assigned the style you want to copy.**

Be sure to select the entire paragraph. If you want to copy a character style, select text to which you have assigned the character style.

2. **Press Ctrl+C or right-click and choose Copy to copy the paragraph to the Clipboard.**

3. **Switch to the document you want to copy the style to and press Ctrl+V or click the Paste button on the Home tab.**

4. **Delete the text you just copied to your document.**

   The style remains in the Styles pane and Quick Style gallery even though the text is deleted. You can call upon the style whenever you need it.

Copying styles to a template

Use the Organizer to copy styles from a document to a template or from one template to another. After making a style a part of a template, you can call upon the style in other documents. You can call upon it in each document you create or created with the template. Follow these steps to copy a style into a template:

1. **Open the document or template with the styles you want to copy.**

   Earlier in this chapter, "Opening a template so that you can modify it" explains how to open a template.

2. **In the Styles pane, click the Manage Styles button.**

   This button is located at the bottom of the window. The Manage Styles dialog box appears.

3. **Click the Import/Export button.**

   You see the Organizer dialog box shown in Figure 3-5. Styles in the document or template that you opened in Step 1 appear in the In list box on the left side.

Select the styles you want to copy

Figure 3-5:
Copying styles to a template.

Click to close one template and open another

4. **Click the Close File button on the right side of the dialog box.**

   The button changes names and becomes the Open File button.

5. **Click the Open File button and, in the Open dialog box, find and select the template to which you want to copy styles; then, click the Open button.**

   You can click the Templates button (under Favorite Links) to open the Templates folder where templates are located. See the sidebar "Where templates are stored," earlier in this chapter, if you have trouble finding the Templates folder.

   The names of styles in the template you chose appear on the right side of the Organizer dialog box.

6. **In the Organizer dialog box, Ctrl+click to select the names of styles on the left side of the dialog box that you want to copy to the template listed on the right side of the dialog box.**

   As you click the names, they become highlighted.

7. **Click the Copy button.**

   The names of styles that you copied appear on the right side of the Organizer dialog box.

8. **Click the Close button and click Save when Word asks whether you want to save the new styles in the template.**

Attaching a different template to a document

It happens in the best of families. You create or are given a document only to discover that the wrong template is attached to it. For times like those, Word gives you the opportunity to switch templates. Follow these steps:

1. **On the Developer tab, click the Document Template button.**

   You see the Templates and Add-Ins dialog box. If the Developer tab isn't displayed on your screen, go to the File tab, choose Options, visit the Customize Ribbon category in the Word Options dialog box, select the Developer check box, and click OK.

2. **Click the Attach button to open the Attach Template dialog box.**

3. **Find and select the template you want and click the Open button.**

   You return to the Templates and Add-ins dialog box, where the name of the template you chose appears in the Document Template box.

4. **Click the Automatically Update Document Styles check box.**

   Doing so tells Word to apply the styles from the new template to your document.

5. **Click OK.**

Modifying, deleting, and renaming styles in templates

Modify, delete, and rename styles in a template the same way you do those tasks to styles in a document (see "Modifying a Style," earlier in this chapter). However, in the Modify Style dialog box, select the New Documents Based on This Template option button before clicking OK.

Your style modifications will apply to all documents you create in the future with your template. For the style modifications to take effect in documents you already created with your template, tell Word to automatically update document styles in those documents. Follow these steps:

1. **Save and close your template if it is still open.**

   If any documents you fashioned from the template are open, close them.

2. **Open a document that you want to update with the style modifications you made to the template.**

3. **Go to the Developer tab.**

   To display this tab if necessary, open the File tab, choose Options, go to the Customize Ribbon category in the Word Options dialog box, select the Developer check box, and click OK.

4. **Click the Document Template button.**

   The Templates and Add-ins dialog box opens. It should list the path to the Templates folder and the template you modified. If the wrong template is listed, click the Attach button and select the correct template in the Attach Template dialog box.

5. **Select the Automatically Update Document Styles check box.**

6. **Click OK.**

Chapter 4: Desktop Publishing with Word

In This Chapter

✔ **Considering ways to desktop-publish in Word**

✔ **Fine-tuning tables**

✔ **Wrapping text around graphics and other objects**

✔ **Running text in newspaper-style columns**

✔ **Putting text boxes in documents**

✔ **Putting borders on pages**

✔ **Decorating pages with drop caps and watermarks**

✔ **Printing landscape documents and on varying sizes of paper**

*O*nce upon a time, word processors were nothing more than glorified typewriters. They were good for typing and basic formatting, and not much else. But over the years, Microsoft Word has become a desktop publishing program in its own right. This chapter explains a few desktop publishing features that can make your documents stand out in the crowd — columns, text boxes, page borders, watermarks, and drop caps, to name a few.

Making Use of Charts, Diagrams, Shapes, Clip Art, and Photos

Figure 4-1 shows a newsletter that includes a chart, diagram, shape, clip-art image, and photo. You are invited to include these items in your Word documents, and you'll be glad to know that including them isn't very much trouble.

✦ **Charts:** A chart is an excellent way to present data for comparison purposes. The pie slices, bars, columns, or lines tell readers right away which business is more productive, for example, or who received the most votes. Book I, Chapter 6 explains how to create charts.

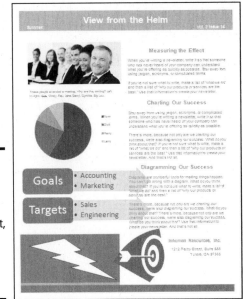

Figure 4-1:
This
newsletter
includes a
photo, chart,
diagram,
shape, and
clip-art
image.

♦ **Diagrams:** A diagram allows readers to quickly grasp an idea, relationship, or concept. Instead of explaining an abstract idea, you can portray it in a diagram. Book I, Chapter 7 explains diagrams.

♦ **Shapes and lines:** Shapes and lines can also illustrate ideas and concepts. You can also use them for decorative purposes in Word documents. Book I, Chapter 8 explains how to draw lines, arrows, and shapes.

♦ **Clip-art images:** Clip-art images make a document livelier. They add a little color to documents. Book VIII, Chapter 4 explains how to place clip-art images in documents.

♦ **Photos:** A well-placed photo or two can make a newsletter or brochure that much more attractive. Book VIII, Chapter 3 explains how to include photos in Word documents.

Constructing the Perfect Table

Create a table to present raw data to your readers or plead your case with numbers and facts. Provided the row labels and column headings are descriptive, looking up information in a table is the easiest way to find it. And tables impose order on chaos. What used to be a knotty lump of nondescript data can be turned into an orderly statement of fact if the data is presented in a table. No report is complete without one or two of them.

Fitting a table on the page

Ideally, a table should fit on a single page, because studying table data that is spread across two or more pages can be difficult. Here are some suggestions for fitting a table on a single page:

✔ **Present the table in landscape mode.** In Landscape mode, a page is turned on its ear so that it is wider than it is tall and you have room for more columns. To print in Landscape mode, however, you must create a new section for the pages in question. Later in this chapter, "Landscape Documents" explains how to switch from portrait to landscape mode.

✔ **Shrink the font size.** Sometimes shrinking the font size throughout a table shrinks the table just enough to fit it on a page. To shrink fonts throughout a table, go to the Home tab and click the Shrink Font button (or press Ctrl+[). Keep shrinking the font size until the table fits on one page.

✔ **Shrink the columns.** On the (Table Tools) Layout tab, click the AutoFit button, and choose AutoFit Contents on the drop-down list to make each column only wide enough to accommodate its widest entry.

✔ **Change the orientation of heading row text.** In a top-heavy table in which the heading row cells contain text and the cells below contain numbers, you can make the entire table narrower by changing the orientation of the text in the heading row. To turn text on its ear, select the cells whose text needs a turn, go to the (Table Tools) Layout tab, and click the Text Direction button. Keep clicking until the text turns the direction you want.

Chances are, if your table can't fit on one page, presenting the information in a table isn't the best option. Try presenting it in bulleted or numbered lists. Or present the information in short paragraphs under small fourth- or fifth-level headings.

	Yes	*No*	*Maybe*	*Often*	*Never*
Prof. Plum in the Library	3			3	
Miss Scarlet in the Drawing Room		3	3		3
Col. Mustard in the Dining Room	3			3	

Book II Chapter 4

Desktop Publishing with Word

Book I, Chapter 5 explains how to create a table, as well as how to include mathematical calculations in Word tables. These pages explain a few table techniques that pertain strictly to Word documents — repeating the heading rows, fitting a table on a single page, and turning a list into a table.

Repeating heading rows on subsequent pages

Making sure that the *heading row*, sometimes called the *header row*, appears on a new page if the table breaks across pages is essential. The heading row is the first row in the table, the one that usually describes what is in the columns below. Without a heading row, readers can't tell what the information in a table means. Follow these steps to make the heading row (or rows) repeat on the top of each new page that a table appears on:

1. **Place the cursor in the heading row or select the heading rows if your tables includes more than one heading row.**

2. **On the (Table Tools) Layout tab, click the Repeat Header Rows button (depending on the size of your screen, you may have to click the Data button first).**

    Heading rows appear only in Print Layout view, so don't worry if you can't see them in Draft view.

Turning a list into a table

In order to turn a list into a table, all components of the list — each name, address, city name, state, and zip code listing, for example — must be separated from the next component by a tab space or a comma. Word looks for tab spaces or commas when it turns a list into a table, and the program separates data into columns according to where the tab spaces or commas are located. You have to prepare your list carefully by entering tab spaces or commas in all the right places before you can turn a list into a table.

Follow these steps to turn a list into a table after you've done all the preliminary work:

1. **Select the list.**

2. **On the Insert tab, click the Table button and choose Convert Text To Table on the drop-down list.**

    You see the Convert Text to Table dialog box.

    Note the number in the Number of Columns box. It should list the number of components into which you separated your list. If the number doesn't match the number of components, you misplaced a tab entry or comma in your list. Click Cancel, return to your list, and examine it to make sure that each line has been divided into the same number of components.

3. **Under Separate Text At, choose the Tabs or Commas option, depending on which you used to separate the components on the list.**

4. **Click OK.**

You can turn a table into a list by clicking the Convert to Text button on the (Table Tools) Layout tab (you may have to click the Data button first, depending on the size of your screen).

Positioning and Wrapping Objects Relative to the Page and Text

"Object" is just Office's generic term for a shape, line, text box, clip-art image, photo, diagram, WordArt image, or chart that you insert in a document. Book I, Chapter 8 explains how to manipulate an object — how to change its size, shape, and other qualities. When you place an object in a Word document, you have to consider more than its size and shape. You also have to consider where to position it on the page and how to wrap text around it. In Word lingo, *wrap* refers to what text does when it butts heads with a shape, text box, photo, diagram, or other object. You must be in Print Layout view to wrap and position objects on a page.

WARNING!

When you insert an object, it lands *inline with text*. That means it lands against the left margin and text doesn't wrap around its side. Before you can change the position of an object, you must select it and choose a text-wrapping option apart from Inline with Text.

Wrapping text with precision

You can decide for yourself how close or far text is from an object when you wrap text. Select the object, and on the Format tab, click the Wrap Text button and choose Edit Wrap Points on the drop-down list. Small black squares called *wrap points* appear around the object. Click and drag the wrap points to push text away from or bring text closer to the object in question.

Statue of Liberty

The Statue of Liberty, officially titled Liberty Enlightening the World (*la Liberté éclairant le monde*), dedicated on October 28, 1886, is a monument that commemorates the centennial of the signing of the United States Declaration of Independence. It was given to the United States by the people of France to acknowledge the friendship between the two countries established during the American Revolution. The statue represents a woman wearing a stola, a radiant crown and sandals, trampling a broken chain, carrying a torch in her raised right hand and a tabula ansata tablet, where the date of the Declaration of Independence is inscribed, in her left arm.

Wrapping text around an object

Figure 4-2 shows the 15 different ways you can wrap text around an object. Select the object you want to wrap text around, go to the Format tab, and use one of these techniques to wrap text around the object:

✦ Click the Wrap Text button and choose an option on the drop-down list. (You may have to click the Arrange button first, depending on the size of your screen.)

✦ Click the Wrap Text button and choose More Layout Options on the drop-down list, or click the Size group button and select the Text Wrapping tab in the Layout dialog box. Then choose a wrapping style and side around which to wrap text. Figure 4-2 shows what the different combinations of Wrapping Style and Wrap Text options do.

Wrapped text looks best when it is justified and hyphenated. That way, text can get closer to the object that is being wrapped.

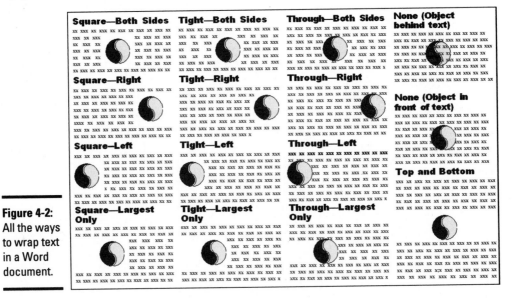

Figure 4-2:
All the ways to wrap text in a Word document.

Positioning an object on a page

To position an object in a Word page, you can drag it to a new location. As Book I, Chapter 8 explains in torturous detail, dragging means to select the object, move the pointer over its perimeter, click when you see the four-headed arrow, and slide the object to a new location.

To make positioning objects on a page a little easier, Word also offers Position commands for moving objects. Select your object, go to the Format tab, and use one of these techniques to move your object precisely into place:

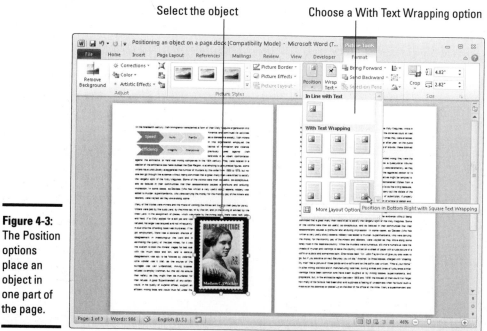

✦ Click the Position button and select a With Text Wrapping option on the drop-down list, as shown in Figure 4-3. (You may have to click the Arrange button first, depending on the size of your screen.) These options position an object squarely in a corner, a side, or the middle of the page.

✦ Click the Position button and choose More Layout Options on the drop-down list, or click the Size group button and select the Position tab in the Layout dialog box. Then choose position options. Go to the Layout dialog box when you want to place objects in the very same position on different pages.

Select the object   Choose a With Text Wrapping option

Figure 4-3:
The Position options place an object in one part of the page.

An object you position with an option on the Position drop-down list travels from page to page if you move the paragraph to which it's connected. This happens because, when you insert an object, Word attaches it to the paragraph where the cursor is located when you make the insertion. If you move that paragraph to another page or the paragraph gets moved as you edit text, the object moves right along with the paragraph. You can locate the paragraph to which an object is connected by clicking the Show/Hide¶ button on the Home tab and then clicking the object; the anchor symbol appears beside the paragraph that the object is connected to.

Working with the Drawing Canvas

As Book I, Chapter 8 explains, shapes and lines are a great way to illustrate ideas. You can in effect doodle on the page and give readers another insight into what you want to explain. In Word, however, drawing lines and shapes is problematic unless you draw them on the drawing canvas.

The *drawing canvas* works like a corral to hold lines and shapes. After you create a drawing canvas, you can draw inside it as though you were drawing on a little page, as shown in Figure 4-4. You can treat the drawing canvas as an object in its own right. You can move it, along with the things inside it, to new locations. You can also, by way of the (Drawing Tools) Format tab, give the drawing canvas an outline shape and fill color. The drawing canvas makes working with objects on a page, especially lines and shapes, that much easier.

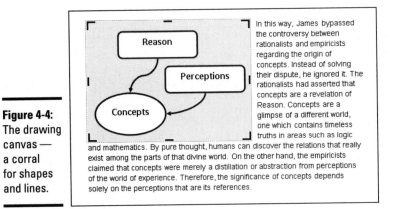

Figure 4-4:
The drawing
canvas —
a corral
for shapes
and lines.

Follow these steps to create a drawing canvas for holding lines and shapes:

1. **Place the cursor roughly where you want the drawing canvas to be.**

2. **Go to the Insert tab.**

3. **Click the Shapes button and choose New Drawing Canvas.**

You can find the New Drawing Canvas command at the bottom of the Shapes drop-down list. A drawing canvas appears on your screen.

The drawing canvas is an object in its own right. You can wrap text around it, give it an outline, and give it a color fill. You can drag it to a new location. To change its size, drag a handle on the side or corner.

Choosing a Theme for Your Document

When you installed Word on your computer, you also installed a dozen or more themes. A theme is a colorful, ready-made design for headings and text. Each theme imposes a slightly different look on a document. If you want to experiment with themes, more power to you, but be prepared to click the Undo button and backtrack as you rummage around for the right one.

Staring on the Page Layout tab, follow these instructions to experiment with themes:

✦ **Choosing a new theme:** Click the Themes button and choose a theme on the drop-down list.

✦ **Choosing a new set of colors for your theme:** Click the Theme Colors button, slide the pointer over the different color sets on the drop-down list, and see what effect they have on your document.

✦ **Changing the fonts:** Click the Theme Fonts button and choose a combination of fonts on the drop-down list for the headings and text in your document.

✦ **Changing theme effects:** Click the Theme Effects button and choose a theme effect on the drop-down list. A *theme effect* is a slight refinement to a theme.

Putting Newspaper-Style Columns in a Document

Columns look great in newsletters and similar documents. And you can pack a lot of words in columns. I should warn you, however, that the Columns command is only good for creating columns that appear on the same page. Running text to the next page with the Columns command can be problematic. If you're serious about running text in columns, I suggest either constructing the columns from text boxes or using Publisher, another Office program. Book VII explains Publisher.

Sometimes it is easier to create columns by creating a table or by using text boxes, especially when the columns refer to one another. In a two-column résumé, for example, the left-hand column often lists job titles ("Facsimile Engineer") whose descriptions are found directly across the page in the right-hand column ("I Xeroxed stuff all day long"). Creating a two-column résumé with Word's Columns command would be futile because making the columns line up is nearly impossible. Each time you add something to the left-hand column, everything *snakes* — it gets bumped down in the left-hand column and the right-hand column as well.

Doing the preliminary work

Before you put text in newspaper-style columns, write it. Take care of the spelling, grammar, and everything else first because making text changes to words after they've been arranged in columns is difficult. Columns appear only in Print Layout view.

Running text into columns

To "columnize" text, select it, go to the Page Layout tab, and click the Columns button. Then either choose how many columns you want on the drop-down list or choose More Columns to create columns of different widths.

You see the Columns dialog box shown in Figure 4-5 if you choose More Columns. Here are the options in the Columns dialog box:

✦ **Preset columns:** Select a Presets box to choose a preset number of columns. Notice that, in some of the boxes, the columns aren't of equal width.

Figure 4-5:
Running text
in columns.

✦ **Number of columns:** If a preset column doesn't do the trick, enter the number of columns you want in the Number of Columns box.

✦ **Line between columns:** A line between columns is mighty elegant and is difficult to do on your own. Select the Line Between check box to run lines between columns.

✦ **Columns width:** If you deselect the Equal Column Width check box, you can make columns of unequal width. Change the width of each column by using the Width boxes.

✦ **Space between columns:** Enter a measurement in the Spacing boxes to determine how much space appears between columns.

✦ **Start New Column:** This check box is for putting empty space in a column, perhaps to insert a text box or picture. Place the cursor where you want the empty space to begin, choose This Point Forward on the Apply To drop-down list, and select the Start New Column check box.

Word creates a new section if you selected text before you columnized it, and you see your columns in Print Layout view. Chapter 2 of this mini-book explains sections.

To "break" a column in the middle and move text to the next column, click where you want the column to break and press Ctrl+Shift+Enter or go to the Page Layout tab, click the Breaks button, and choose Column on the drop-down list.

Working with Text Boxes

Put text in a text box when you want a notice or announcement to stand out on the page. Like other objects, text boxes can be shaded, filled with color, and given borders, as the examples in Figure 4-6 demonstrate. You can also lay them over graphics to make for interesting effects. I removed the borders and the fill color from the text box on the right side of Figure 4-6, but rest assured, the text in this figure lies squarely in a text box. (Book I, Chapter 8 explains how to give borders, shading, and color to objects such as text boxes.)

Figure 4-6:
Examples of
text boxes.

> Announcing a
> **FROG JUMPING
> CONTEST**
> ~~Calaveras County~~
> *July 5-6*

Announcing a
**FROG JUMPING
CONTEST**
~~Calaveras County~~
July 5-6

You can move a text box around at will on the page until it lands in the right place. You can even use text boxes as columns and make text jump from one text box to the next in a document — a nice feature, for example, when you want a newsletter article on page 1 to be continued on page 2. Instead of cutting and pasting text from page 1 to page 2, Word moves the text for you as the column on page 1 fills up.

Inserting a text box

To create a text box, go to the Insert tab, click the Text Box button, and use one of these techniques:

✦ **Choose a ready-made text box**: Scroll in the drop-down list and choose a preformatted text box.

✦ **Draw a conventional text box:** Choose Draw Text Box on the drop-down list, and then click and drag to draw the text box. Lines show you how big it will be when you release the mouse button.

After you insert the text box, you can type text in it and call on all the formatting commands on the (Drawing) Format tab. These commands are explained in Book I, Chapter 8. It also describes how to turn a shape such as a circle or triangle into a text box (create the shape, right-click it, choose Add Text, and start typing).

Here's a neat trick: You can turn the text in a text box on its side so that it reads from top to bottom or bottom to top, not from left to right. Create a text box, enter the text, go to the (Drawing Tools) Format tab, click the Text Direction button, and choose a Rotate option on the drop-down list.

Making text flow from text box to text box

As I mention earlier, you can link text boxes so that the text in the first box is pushed into the next one when it fills up. To link text boxes, start by creating all the text boxes that you need. You cannot link one text box to another if the second text box already has text in it. Starting on the (Drawing Tools) Format tab, follow these directions to link text boxes:

 ✦ **Creating a forward link:** Click a text box and then click the Create Link button to create a forward link. The pointer changes into a very odd-looking pointer that is supposed to look like a pitcher. Move the odd-looking pointer to the next text box in the chain and click there to create a link.

✦ **Breaking a link:** To break a link, click the text box that is to be the last in the chain, and then click the Break Link button.

Sprucing Up Your Pages

You can play interior decorator with the pages of a document by putting a border around pages, splashing color on pages, and taking advantage of the predesigned cover pages that Word provides for you. Keep reading if making the pages of your document a little prettier interests you.

Decorating a page with a border

Word offers a means of decorating title pages, certificates, menus, and similar documents with a page border. Besides lines, you can decorate the sides of a page with stars, pieces of cake, and other artwork. If you want to place a border around a page in the middle of a document, you must create a section break where the page is.

Before you create your border, place the cursor on the page where the border is to appear. Place the cursor on the first page of a document if you want to put a border around only the first page. If your document is divided into sections and you want to put borders around certain pages in a section, place the cursor in the section — either in the first page if you want the borders to go around it, or in a subsequent page.

With the cursor in the right place, follow these steps to decorate your page or pages with a border:

☐ Page Borders

1. **Go to the Page Layout tab and click the Page Borders button.**

You see the Borders and Shading dialog box, as shown in Figure 4-7.

Figure 4-7:
Putting borders on pages.

2. **Under Setting, choose which kind of border you want.**

The Custom setting is for putting borders on one, two, or three sides of the page, not four. Use the None setting to remove borders.

3. **On the Apply To drop-down list, tell Word which page or pages in the document get borders.**

4. **Select options to construct the border you want and then click OK.**

The Page Border tab offers a bunch of tools for fashioning a border:

+ **Line for borders:** Under Style, scroll down the list and choose a line for the borders. You will find interesting choices at the bottom of the menu. Be sure to look in the Preview window to see what your choices in this dialog box add up to.

+ **Color for borders:** Open the Color drop-down list and choose a color for the border lines if you want a color border.

+ **Width of borders:** If you chose artwork for the borders, use the Width drop-down list to tell Word how wide the lines or artwork should be.

+ **Artwork for borders**: Open the Art drop-down list and choose a symbol, illustration, star, piece of cake, or other artwork, if that is what you want for the borders. You will find some amusing choices on this long list, including ice cream cones, bats, and umbrellas.

+ **Borders on different sides of the page:** Use the four buttons in the Preview window to tell Word on which sides of the page to draw borders. Click these buttons to remove or add borders, as you want.

+ **Distance from edge of page:** Click the Options button and fill in the Border and Shading Options dialog box if you want to get specific about how close the borders can come to the edge of the page or pages.

Putting a background color on pages

Especially if you intend to save your Word document as a Web page, you will be glad to know that putting a background color on pages is easy. You can't, however, pick and choose which pages get a background color. Putting background colors on the pages of a document is an all-or-nothing proposition.

To grace a page with a background color or gradient color mixture, go to the Page Layout tab, click the Page Color button, and choose a color on the drop-down list. Choose Fill Effects to open the Fill Effects dialog box and apply gradient color mixtures or patterns to the pages.

Getting Word's help with cover letters

Writing and designing a cover page for a letter or report is a chore. Word can't dictate a cover page for you, but it can provide a handsome preformatted cover page that looks nice at the front of a report or article. To place a cover page at the start of a document, go to the Insert tab, click the Cover Page button, and choose a cover page predesign.

Dropping In a Drop Cap

A *drop cap* is a large capital letter that "drops" into the text, as shown in Figure 4-8. Drop caps appear at the start of chapters in many books, this book included, and you can find other uses for them, too. In Figure 4-8, one drop cap marks the A side of a list of songs on a homemade music CD.

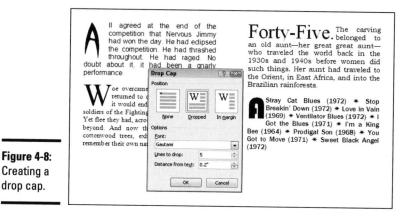

Figure 4-8: Creating a drop cap.

To create a drop cap, start by clicking anywhere in the paragraph whose first letter you want to "drop." If you want to "drop" more than one character at the start of the paragraph, select the characters. Then go to the Insert tab, click the Drop Cap button, and choose Dropped or Drop Cap Options. Choosing Drop Cap Options opens the Drop Cap dialog box shown in Figure 4-8, where you can experiment with these options:

✦ **Position:** Choose which kind of drop cap you want. In Margin places the drop cap to the left of the paragraph, in the margin, not in the paragraph itself.

✦ **Font:** Choose a font from the Font drop-down list. Choose a different font from the text in the paragraph.

✦ **Lines to Drop:** Enter the number of text lines to drop the letter.

✦ **Distance from Text:** Keep the 0 setting unless you're dropping an *I, 1,* or other skinny letter or number.

Click the Drop Cap button and choose None to remove a drop cap.

Watermarking for the Elegant Effect

A *watermark* is a pale image or set of words that appears behind text on each page in a document. True watermarks are made in the paper mold and can be seen only when the sheet of paper is held up to a light. You can't make true watermarks with Word, but you can make the closest thing to them that can be attained in the debased digital world in which we live. Figure 4-9 shows two pages of a letter in which the paper has been "watermarked." Watermarks are one of the easiest formatting tricks to accomplish in Word.

Figure 4-9:
Watermarks
showing
faintly on
the page.

[A] Watermark ▾

To create a watermark for every page of a document, go to the Page Layout tab and click the Watermark button. From the drop-down list, create your watermark:

✦ **Prefabricated text watermark**: Scroll down the list and choose an option. You will find "Confidential," "Urgent," and other text watermarks.

✦ **Picture watermark:** Choose Custom Watermark, and in the Printed Watermark dialog box, click the Picture Watermark option button. Then click the Select Picture button. In the Insert Picture dialog box, select a graphic file to use for the watermark and click the Insert button. Back in the Printed Watermark dialog box, choose or enter a size for the graphic on the Scale drop-down list. I don't recommend deselecting the Washout check box — do so and your image may be so dark that it obscures the text.

✦ **Text watermark:** Choose Custom Watermark and, in the Printed Watermark dialog box, click the Text Watermark option button. Type a word or two in the Text box (or choose an entry from the drop-down list). Choose a font, size, color, and layout for the words. If you deselect the Semitransparent check box, you do so at your peril because the watermark words may be too dark on the page.

To tinker with a watermark, reopen the Printed Watermark dialog box. To remove a watermark, click the Watermark button and choose Remove Watermark on the drop-down list.

Landscape Documents

A *landscape* document is one in which the page is wider than it is long, like a painting of a landscape, as shown on the right side of Figure 4-10. Most documents, like the pages of this book, are printed in *portrait* style, with the short sides of the page on the top and bottom. However, creating a landscape document is sometimes a good idea because a landscape document stands out from the usual crowd of portrait documents and sometimes printing in landscape mode is necessary to fit text, tables, and graphics on a single page.

Figure 4-10: A portrait document (left) and landscape document (right).

You're ready to go if you want to turn all the pages in your document into landscape pages. To turn some of the pages into landscape pages, create a section for the pages that need to appear in Landscape mode and click in the section (Chapter 2 of this mini-book explains sections). Starting on the Page Layout tab, use these techniques to change the page orientation:

✦ **Landscape pages:** Click the Orientation button and choose Landscape on the drop-down list.

✦ **Portrait pages:** Click the Orientation button and choose Portrait on the drop-down list.

Printing on Different Sizes of Paper

You don't have to print exclusively on standard 8.5-x-11 paper; you can print on legal-size paper and other sizes of paper as well. A newsletter with an unusual shape really stands out in a crowd and gets people's attention. Go to the Page Layout tab and use one of these techniques to change the size of the paper on which you intend to print a document:

✦ Click the Size button and choose an option on the drop-down list.

✦ Click the Page Setup group button, select the Paper tab in the Page Setup dialog box, and choose a setting on the Paper Size drop-down list. If none of the settings suits you, enter your own settings in the Width and Height text boxes.

Chapter 5: Getting Word's Help with Office Chores

This chapter is dedicated to the proposition that everyone should get their work done sooner. It explains how Word can be a help in the office, especially when it comes to working on team projects. This chapter explains comments, using revision marks to record edits, and mail merging, which is Microsoft's term for generating form letters, labels, and envelopes for mass mailings.

Highlighting Parts of a Document

In my work, I often use the Highlight command to mark paragraphs and text that need reviewing later. And on rainy days, I use it to splash color on my documents and keep myself amused. Whatever your reasons for highlighting text in a document, go to the Home tab and use one of these techniques to do it:

✦ **Select text and then choose a highlighter:** Select the text you want to highlight and then either click the Text Highlight Color button (if it's displaying your color choice) or open the drop-down list on the button and choose a color.

✦ **Choose a highlighter and then select text:** Either click the Text Highlight Color button (if it's already displaying your color choice) or open the drop-down list on the button and choose a color. The pointer changes into a crayon. Drag across the text you want to highlight. When you finish highlighting, click the Text Highlight Color button again or press Esc.

To remove highlights, select the highlighted text, open the drop-down list on the Text Highlight Color button, and choose No Color. Select the entire document (press Ctrl+A) and choose No Color to remove all highlights from a document.

Highlight marks are printed along with the text. To keep highlights from being printed, go to the File tab, choose Options, click the Display category in the Word Options dialog box, and deselect the Show Highlighter Marks check box.

Commenting on a Document

In the old days, comments were scribbled illegibly in the margins of books and documents, but in Word, comments are easy to read. To show where a comment has been made on the text, Word puts brackets around text and highlights the text. Each commenter is assigned a different highlighting color so that you can tell at a glance who made each comment. As shown in Figure 5-1, you can read comments in the Reviewing pane, in pop-up boxes (in Draft view and Outline view), and in balloons (in Print Layout view and Web Layout view).

Figure 5-1: Comments appear in (left to right) the Reviewing pane, pop-up boxes, and balloons.

Entering a comment

If you're putting together a proposal, you can pass it around the office and invite everyone to comment. If someone makes an especially good comment, you can include it in the main text merely by copying and pasting it. To write a comment:

1. **Select the word or sentence that you want to comment on.**

2. **On the Review tab, click the New Comment button.**

   In Draft and Outline view, the Reviewing pane opens on the left side or bottom of the screen so that you can enter a comment; in Print Layout and Web Layout view, a new balloon appears on the right side of the screen so that you can enter a comment. (On the Review tab, open the drop-down list on the Reviewing Pane button and choose an option to place the pane on the left side or bottom of the screen.)

3. **Type your comment in the space provided.**

In Draft and Outline view, commenters' names and initials appear beside each comment and comments are numbered. If the wrong name and initials appear beside your comments, open the drop-down list on the Track Changes button, choose Change User Name, and enter your correct name and initials in the Word Options dialog box.

Caring for and feeding comments

Starting on the Review tab, here is a handful of tasks that deserve comment (if you'll pardon my little pun):

✦ **Editing a comment:** Right-click between the brackets and choose Edit Comment or just click in the Reviewing pane in Print Layout view. Then rewrite the comment in the Reviewing pane or the balloon.

✦ **Going from comment to comment:** Click the Previous or Next button on the Review tab. In Draft and Outline view, the Reviewing pane opens, and you can read the comment you landed on at the top of the pane. In Print Layout and Web Layout view, balloons on the right side of the screen are highlighted as you go from comment to comment.

✦ **Seeing and hiding the Reviewing pane:** Click the Reviewing Pane button to display or hide the Reviewing pane. On the button's drop-down list, choose an option to put the pane on the left side or bottom of the screen.

✦ **Temporarily removing the comments:** Click the Show Markup button and deselect Comments on the drop-down list to wipe away the comments; select Comments to see them again.

✦ **Displaying comments by a particular reviewer:** Click the Show Markup button, choose Reviewers, and deselect All Reviewers on the submenu. Then click the button again, choose Reviewers, and choose the name of a reviewer. To see all comments again, click the Show Markup button and choose Reviewers➪All Reviewers.

✦ **Deleting a comment:** Click a comment in the Reviewing pane, click between brackets, or click a comment balloon and then click the Delete button. You can also right-click and choose Delete Comment.

✦ **Deleting all the comments in the document:** Open the drop-down list on the Delete button and choose Delete All Comments in Document.

✦ **Deleting comments made by one or two people:** First, isolate comments made by people whose comments you want to delete (see "Displaying comments by a particular reviewer" earlier in this list). Then open the drop-down list on the Delete button and choose Delete All Comments Shown.

Letting the air out of the balloons

In Print Layout and Web Layout view, comments and revisions appear in balloons on the right side of the screen. Sometimes seeing revisions and comments in balloons is helpful; sometimes it's hard to make sense of them when they're so far to the side of the page.

To hide or display balloons in Print Layout and Web Layout view, you can click the Show Markup button on the Review tab, choose Balloons, and choose an option on the submenu:

✔ Show Revisions in Balloons displays the balloons.

✔ Show All Revisions Inline moves comments and revisions onto the page and effectively lets all the air out of the balloons.

✔ Show Only Comments and Formatting in Balloons shows comments only, not revision marks.

Tracking Changes to Documents

When many hands go into revising a document, figuring out who made changes to what is impossible. What's more, it's impossible to tell what the first draft looked like. Sometimes it's hard to tell whether the changes were for good or ill. To help you keep track of changes to documents, Word offers the Track Changes command. When this command is in effect:

✦ All changes to a document are recorded in a different color, with one color for each reviewer.

✦ In Draft and Outline view, new text is underlined and deleted text is crossed out.

✦ In Print Layout and Web Layout view, new text is underlined, and deleted text appears in balloons on the right side of the window.

✦ In all views, a vertical line appears on the left side of the screen to indicate where changes were made.

By moving the pointer over a change, you can read the name of the person who made it as well as the words that were inserted or deleted. You can see changes as well in the Reviewing pane. As you review changes, you can accept or reject each change. You can also see the original document, a copy with revisions, or the final copy simply by making a choice from the Display for Review drop-down list on the Review tab.

To give you an idea of what tracking marks look like, Figure 5-2 shows the first two sentences of Vladimir Nabokov's autobiography *Speak, Memory* in Draft view, with marks showing where additions were made and deletions scratched out.

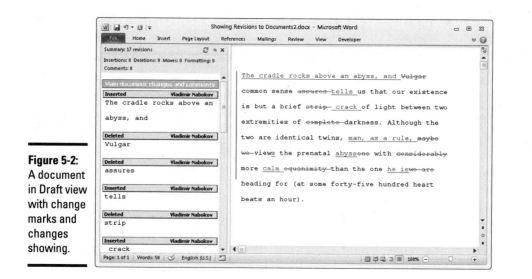

Figure 5-2:
A document in Draft view with change marks and changes showing.

Telling Word to start marking changes

To start tracking where editorial changes are made to a document, turn Track Changes on. You can do that with one of these techniques:

✦ On the Review tab, click the Track Changes button (or open its drop-down list and choose Track Changes).

✦ Press Ctrl+Shift+E.

✦ On the status bar, click the words *Track Changes* so that the status bar reads "Track Changes: On." If you don't see the words *Track Changes* on your status bar and you want to see them there, right-click the status bar and select Track Changes on the pop-up menu.

To stop tracking changes to a document, click the Track Changes button again, press Ctrl+Shift+E again, or click the words *Track Changes* on the status bar so that the words read "Track Changes: Off."

Telling Word how to mark changes

To tell Word precisely how to mark changes, open the drop-down list on the Track Changes button (you may have to click the Tracking button first) and choose Change Tracking Options. You see the colorful Track Changes Options dialog box. It offers these options:

✦ **Markup options:** Declare how you want to mark insertions and deletions, and with which color you want to mark them.

✦ **Moves options:** Declare how you want to mark text that has been cut and pasted.

✦ **Table Cell Highlighting options:** When editing tables, you can mark inserted, deleted, merged, and split cells in different colors.

✦ **Formatting options:** Choose an option to mark formatting changes as well as changes to text.

✦ **Balloons:** Choose Always if you prefer to mark deleted text with balloons to the right of the text in Print Layout and Web Layout view. If you prefer not to see balloons in Print Layout and Web Layout view, choose Never. You must display the balloons to examine revised documents in Final Showing Markup and Original Showing Markup view (see "Marking changes when you forgot to turn on change marks" later in this chapter). Earlier in this chapter, the sidebar "Letting the air out of the balloons" explains how you can quickly hide or display balloons in Print Layout and Web Layout view.

If your name doesn't appear with the change marks you make, go to the Review tab, open the drop-down list on the Track Changes button, choose Change User Name, and enter your name and initials in the Word Options dialog box.

Reading and reviewing a document with change marks

Reading and reviewing a document with change marks isn't easy. The marks can get in the way. Fortunately, Word offers the Display for Review menu on the Review tab for dealing with documents that have been scarred by change marks. Choose options on the Display for Review drop-down list to get a better idea of how your changes are taking shape:

✦ **See more clearly where text was deleted from the original document:** Choose Final: Show Markup. In Print Layout view, deleted material appears in balloons on the right side of the screen and insertions are underlined.

✦ **See what the document would look like if you accepted all changes:** Choose Final. All change marks are stripped away and you see what your document would look like if you accepted all changes made to it.

✦ **See more clearly where text was inserted in the document:** Choose Original: Show Markup. In Print Layout view, insertions appear in balloons on the right side of the screen and a line appears through text that has been deleted.

✦ **See what the document would look like if you rejected all changes:** Choose Original. You get the original, pristine document back.

Marking changes when you forgot to turn on change marks

Suppose that you write the first draft of a document and someone revises it but that someone doesn't track changes. How can you tell where changes were made? For that matter, suppose that you get hold of a document, you change it around without tracking changes, and now you want to see what your editorial changes did to the original copy. I have good news: You can compare documents to see the editorial changes that were made to them. Word offers a command for comparing the original document to a revised edition and another for comparing two different revised editions of the same document.

After you make the comparison, Word creates a third document similar to the one shown in Figure 5-3. In the Source Document pane on the right side of the window, you can see the documents you're comparing. The Compared Document pane, meanwhile, shows who made changes and what those changes are.

Follow these steps to compare an original document to its revised copy or two revised copies:

1. **On the Review tab, click the Compare button.**

   You see a drop-down list (depending on the size of your screen, you may have to choose Compare more than once to get to the drop-down list).

2. **On the drop-down list, choose Compare to compare the original document to its revised edition; choose Combine to compare two editions of the same document that were revised separately.**

   You see the Compare Documents dialog box or the Combine Documents dialog box, as shown in Figure 5-4. These dialog boxes work the same way.

Book II
Chapter 5

Getting Word's Help with Office Chores

Figure 5-3: Comparing documents to see editorial changes.

Figure 5-4:
Choosing
which
documents
to compare.

3. **On the Original Document drop-down list, choose the original or a revised edition of the document; if its name isn't there, click the Browse button and select it in the Open dialog box.**

4. **On the Revised Document drop-down list, choose a revised copy, or else click the Browse button and select it in the Open dialog box.**

5. **Click the More button.**

   You see more options for comparing or combining documents.

6. **If you so desire, deselect the Comparison Settings check boxes to tell Word what you want to compare.**

7. **Click OK.**

   Word creates a new document that shows where changes were made to the original copy or where the revised copies differ (refer to Figure 5-3). You can save this document if you want to.

To help with document comparisons, you can tell Word what to display in the Source Documents pane on the right side of the screen. On the Review tab, click the Compare button, choose Show Source Documents, and choose an option on the submenu. You can hide the source documents, show the original document, show the revised edition, or show both editions.

Accepting and rejecting changes to a document

Word gives you the chance to accept or reject changes one at a time, but in my considerable experience with changes (I am a sometime editor), I find that the best way to handle changes is to go through the document, reject the changes you don't care for, and when you have finished reviewing, accept all the remaining changes. That way, reviewing changes is only half as tedious.

Whatever your preference for accepting or rejecting changes, start by selecting a change. To do so, either click it or click the Previous or Next button on the Review tab to locate it in your document. With the change selected, do one of the following:

+ **Accept a change:** Click the Accept button or open the drop-down list on the Accept button and choose Accept Change or Accept and Move to Next. You can also right-click and choose Accept.

+ **Reject a change:** Click the Reject button or open the drop-down list on the Reject button and choose Reject Change or Reject and Move to Next. You can also right-click and choose Reject.

+ **Accept all changes:** Open the drop-down list on the Accept button and choose Accept All Changes in Document.

+ **Reject all changes:** Open the drop-down list on the Reject button and choose Reject All Changes in Document.

Book II
Chapter 5

Getting Word's Help with Office Chores

By way of the Accept and Reject buttons, you can also accept or reject all changes made by a single reviewer. First, isolate the reviewer's changes by clicking the Show Markup button, choosing Reviewers, and selecting a reviewer's name. Then open the drop-down list on the Accept or Reject button, and choose Accept All Changes Shown or Reject All Changes Shown.

Printing an Address on an Envelope

Printing addresses gives correspondence a formal, official look. It makes you look like a big shot. (Later in this chapter, "Churning Out Letters, Labels, and Envelopes for Mass Mailings" explains how to print more than one envelope at a time). Here's how to print an address and a return address on an envelope:

1. **To save a bit of time, open the document that holds the letter you want to send; then select the name and address of the person you want to send the letter to.**

By doing so, you save yourself from having to type the address. However, you don't have to open a document to start with.

2. **On the Mailings tab, click the Envelopes button (you may have to click the Create button first, depending on the size of your screen).**

The Envelopes tab of the Envelopes and Labels dialog box appears, as shown in Figure 5-5.

Figure 5-5:
Printing
on an
envelope.

3. **Enter a name and address in the Delivery Address box (the address is already there if you selected it in Step 1).**

4. **Enter your return address in the Return Address box, if you want.**

5. **Click the Omit check box if you don't want your return address to appear on the envelope.**

6. **Click the Options button, and in the Envelope Options dialog box, tell Word what size your envelopes are and how your printer handles envelopes.**

   Tell Word about your envelopes on the Envelope Options and Printing Options tabs, and click OK:

   • *Envelope Options tab:* Choose an envelope size, a font for printing the delivery and return address, and a position for the addresses. The sample envelope in the Preview shows you what your position settings do when the envelope is printed.

   • *Printing Options tab:* Choose a technique for feeding envelopes to your printer. Consult the manual that came with your printer, select one of the Feed Method boxes, click the Face Up or Face Down option button, and open the Feed From drop-down list to tell Word which printer tray the envelope is in or how you intend to stick the envelope in your printer.

7. **Click the Print button.**

   All that trouble just to print an address on an envelope!

Printing a Single Address Label (Or a Page of the Same Label)

If you need to print a single label or a sheet of labels that are all the same, you can do it. Before you start printing, however, take note of the label's Avery stock number, what size the label is, and its brand name. You are asked about label brands and sizes when you print labels. (Later in this chapter, "Churning Out Letters, Labels, and Envelopes for Mass Mailings" explains how to print multiple labels as part of a mass mailing.)

Follow these steps to print a single label or a sheet full of identical labels:

1. **On the Mailings tab, click the Labels button (you may have to click the Create button first, depending on the size of your screen).**

   You see the Labels tab of the Envelopes and Labels dialog box, as shown in Figure 5-6.

Book II
Chapter 5

Getting Word's Help
with Office Chores

Figure 5-6: Printing labels.

2. **Enter the label — the name and address — in the Address box.**

3. **Either click the Options button or click the label icon in the Label box to open the Label Options dialog box.**

4. **In the Printer Information area, select either Continuous-Feed Printers or Page Printers to declare which kind of printer you have; on the Tray drop-down list, choose the option that describes how you will feed labels to your printer.**

5. **Open the Label Vendors drop-down list and choose the brand or type of labels that you have.**

   If your brand is not on the list, click the Details button, and describe your labels in the extremely confusing Information dialog box. A better way, however, is to measure your labels and see whether you can find a label of the same size by experimenting with Product Number and Label Information combinations.

6. **In the Product Number menu, select the product number listed on the box that your labels came in.**

   Look in the Label Information box on the right to make sure that the Height, Width, and Page Size measurements match those of the labels you have.

7. **Click OK to return to the Envelopes and Labels dialog box.**

8. **Choose a Print option.**

   Tell Word to print a single label or a sheet full of labels:

   - *Full Page of the Same Label:* Select this option button if you want to print a pageful of the same label. Likely, you'd choose this option to print a pageful of your own return addresses. Click the New Document button after you make this choice. Word creates a new document with a pageful of labels. Save and print this document on a sheet of labels.

   - *Single Label:* Select this option button to print one label. Then enter the row and column where the label is located and click the Print button.

Churning Out Letters, Envelopes, and Labels for Mass Mailings

Thanks to the miracle of computing, you can churn out form letters, labels, and envelopes for a mass mailing in the privacy of your home or office, just as the big companies do. Churning out form letters, envelopes, and labels is easy, as long as you take the time to prepare the source file. The *source file* is the file that the names and addresses come from. A Word table, an Excel worksheet, a Microsoft Access database table or query, or an Outlook Contacts list or Address Book can serve as the source file. (Book III explains Outlook; Book V explains Excel; Book VI explains Access.)

To generate form letters, envelopes, or labels, you merge the form letter, envelope, or label document with a source file. Word calls this process *merging.* During the merge, names and addresses from the source file are plugged into the appropriate places in the form letter, envelope, or label document. When the merge is complete, you can either save the form letters, envelopes, or labels in a new file or start printing right away.

The following pages explain how to prepare the source file and merge addresses from the source file with a document to create form letters, labels, or envelopes. Then you discover how to print the form letters, labels, or envelopes after you have generated them.

Word offers a mail-merge wizard (*wizard* is Microsoft's name for a step-by-step procedure you can follow to accomplish a task). If you want to try your hand at using the wizard to complete a mail merge, go to the Mailings tab, click the Start Mail Merge button, and choose Step by Step Mail Merge Wizard on the drop-down list. Good luck to you!

Preparing the source file

If you intend to get addresses for your form letters, labels, or envelopes from an Outlook Contact List or Address Book on your computer, you're ready to go. However, if you haven't entered the addresses yet or you are keeping them in a Word table, Excel worksheet, Access database table, or Access query, make sure that the data is in good working order:

Book II
Chapter 5

Getting Word's Help with Office Chores

✦ **Word table:** Save the table in its own file and enter a descriptive heading at the top of each column. In the merge, when you tell Word where to plug in address and other data, you will do so by choosing a heading name from the top of a column. In Figure 5-7, for example, the column headings are Last Name, First Name, Street, and so on. (Book I, Chapter 5 explains how to construct a Word table.)

Figure 5-7: A Word source table for a mail merge.

Last Name	First Name	Street	City	State	ZIP	Birthday
Creed	Hank	443 Oak St.	Atherton	CA	93874	July 31
Daws	Leon	13 Spruce St.	Colma	CA	94044	April 1
Maves	Carlos	11 Guy St.	Reek	NV	89201	February 28
Ng	Winston	1444 Unger Ave.	Colma	CA	94404	November 12
Smith	Jane	121 First St.	Colma	CA	94044	January 10
Weiss	Shirley	441 Second St.	Poltroon	ID	49301	May 4

✦ **Excel worksheet:** Arrange the worksheet in table format with a descriptive heading atop each column and no blank cells in any columns. Word will plug in address and other data by choosing heading names.

✦ **Access database table or query:** Make sure that you know the field names in the database table or query where you keep the addresses. During the merge, you will be asked for field names. By the way, if you're comfortable in Access, query a database table for the records you will need. As you find out shortly, Word offers a technique for choosing only the records you want for your form letters, labels, or envelopes. However, by querying first in Access, you can start off with the records you need and spare yourself from having to choose records in Word.

A Word table, Excel worksheet, or Access table or query can include more than address information. Don't worry about deleting information that isn't required for your form letters, labels, and envelopes. As you find out soon, you get to decide which information to include from the Word table, Excel worksheet, or Access table or query.

Merging the document with the source file

After you prepare the source file, the next step in generating form letters, labels, or envelopes for a mass mailing is to merge the document with the source file. Follow these general steps to do so:

1. **Create or open a document.**

   - *Form letters:* Either create a new document and write your form letter, being careful to leave out the parts of the letter that differ from recipient to recipient, or open a letter you have already written and delete the addressee's name, the address, and other parts of the letter that are particular to each recipient.

   - *Envelopes:* Create a new document.

   - *Labels:* Create a new document.

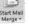

2. **On the Mailings tab, click the Start Mail Merge button.**

3. **Choose Letters, Envelopes, or Labels on the drop-down list.**

4. **Prepare the groundwork for creating form letters, envelopes, or labels for a mass mailing.**

   What you do next depends on what kind of mass mailing you want to attempt:

   - *Form letters:* You're ready to go. The text of your form letter already appears on-screen if you followed the directions for creating and writing it in Step 1.

   - *Envelopes:* You see the Envelope Options dialog box, where, on the Envelope Options and Printing Options tabs, you tell Word what size envelope you will print on. See "Printing an Address on an Envelope," earlier in this chapter, for instructions about filling out these tabs (see Step 6). A sample envelope appears on-screen.

   - *Labels:* You see the Label Options dialog box, where you tell Word what size labels to print on. See "Printing a Single Address Label (or a Page of the Same Label)" earlier in this chapter, if you need advice for filling out this dialog box (refer to Steps 4 through 7).

5. **Click the Select Recipients button and choose an option on the drop-down list to direct Word to your source file or the source of your address and data information.**

Earlier in this chapter, "Preparing the source file" explains what a source file is. Your options are as follows:

- *Addresses from a Word table, Excel worksheet, Access database table, or Access query:* Choose Use Existing List. You see the Select Data Source dialog box. Locate the Word file, the Excel worksheet, or the Access database, select it, and click Open.

  If you select an Excel worksheet or Access database, you see the Select Table dialog box. Select the worksheet, table, or query you want and click the OK button.

- *Addresses from Microsoft Outlook:* Choose Select from Outlook Contacts (Outlook must be your default e-mail program to get addresses from Outlook). Then, in the Select Contact dialog box, choose Contacts and click OK.

6. Click the Edit Recipient List button.

The Mail Merge Recipients dialog box appears, as shown in Figure 5-8.

7. In the Mail Merge Recipients dialog box, select the names of people to whom you will send mail; then click OK.

To select recipients' names, check or uncheck the boxes on the left side of the dialog box.

Mail Merge Recipients

This is the list of recipients that will be used in your merge. Use the options below to add to or change your list. Use the checkboxes to add or remove recipients from the merge. When your list is ready, click OK.

Data Source	☐	Last_Name	First_Name	City	State	Zip_Code
C:\Office 2010\Off...	☑	Creed	Hank	Atherton	CA	93874
C:\Office 2010\Off...	☐	Daws	Leon	Colma	CA	94044
C:\Office 2010\Off...	☑	Maves	Carlos	Reek	NV	89201
C:\Office 2010\Off...	☑	Ng	Winston	Colma	CA	94404
C:\Office 2010\Off...	☑	Smith	Jane	Colma	CA	94044
C:\Office 2010\Off...	☐	Weiss	Shirley	Poltroon	ID	49301

Data Source

C:\Office 2010\Office\Art - Off

Refine recipient list

- ↓ Sort....
- Filter....
- Find duplicates....
- Find recipient....
- Validate addresses....

Edit...   Refresh

OK

Figure 5-8:
Choosing who gets mail.

Choose the names of recipients

8. **Enter the address block on your form letters, envelopes, or labels.**

   The *address block* is the address, including the recipient's name, company, title, street address, city, and ZIP Code. If you're creating form letters, click in the sample letter where the address block will go. If you're printing on envelopes, click in the middle of the envelope where the delivery address will go. Then follow these steps to enter the address block:

   a. Click the Address Block button. The Insert Address Block dialog box appears, as shown in Figure 5-9.

Figure 5-9: Creating the address block (left) and linking it with address fields (right).

Address block

   b. Choose a format for entering the recipient's name in the address block. As you do so, watch the Preview window; it shows the actual names and addresses that you selected in Step 7.

   c. Click the Match Fields button. You see the Match Fields dialog box, shown in Figure 5-9.

   d. Using the drop-down lists on the right side of the dialog box, match the fields in your source file with the address block fields on the left side of the dialog box. In Figure 5-9, for example, the Street field is the equivalent of the Address 1 field on the left side of the dialog box, so Street is chosen from the drop-down list to match Address 1.

   e. Click OK in the Match Fields dialog box and the Insert Address Block dialog box. The <<AddressBlock>> field appears in the document where the address will go. Later, when you merge your document with the data source, real data will appear where the field is now. Think of a field as a kind of placeholder for data.

9. **Click the Preview Results button on the Mailings tab to see real data rather than fields.**

Now you can see clearly whether you entered the address block correctly. If you didn't enter it correctly, click the Match Fields button (it's in the Write & Insert Fields group) to open the Match Fields dialog box and make new choices.

10. **Put the finishing touches on your form letters, labels, or envelopes:**

- *Form letters:* Click where the salutation ("Dear John") will go and then click the Greeting Line button. You see the Insert Greeting Line dialog box, as shown in Figure 5-10. Make choices in this dialog box to determine how the letters' salutations will read.

Figure 5-10:
Entering the
greeting.

The body of your form letter may well include other variable information such as names and birthdays. To enter that stuff, click in your letter where variable information goes and then click the Insert Merge Field button. The Insert Merge Field dialog box appears and lists fields from the source file. Select a field, click the Insert button, and click the Close button. (You can also open the drop-down list on the Insert Merge Field button and choose a field from the source file.)

If you are editing your form letter and you need to see precisely where the variable information you entered is located, click the Highlight Merge Fields button. The variable information is highlighted in your document.

- *Envelopes:* To position the address block correctly, you may have to press the Enter key and tab key to move it to the center of envelope. If you don't like the fonts or font sizes on the envelope, select an address, go to the Home tab, and change fonts and font sizes there.

  To enter a return address, click in the upper-left corner of the envelope and enter it there.

- *Labels:* Click the Update Labels button to enter all recipients' labels in the sample document.

11. **Click the Next Record and Previous Record buttons on the Mailings tab to skip from recipient to recipient and make sure that you have entered information correctly.**

These buttons are located in the Preview Results group. The items you see on-screen are the same form letters, envelopes, or labels you will see when you have finished printing. (Click the Preview Results button if you see field names rather than people's names and addresses).

If an item is incorrect, open the source file and correct it there. When you save the source file, the correction is made in the sample document.

At last — you're ready to print the form letters, envelopes, or labels. Better keep reading.

Printing form letters, envelopes, and labels

After you have gone to the trouble to prepare the data file and merge it with the document, you're ready to print your form letters, envelopes, or labels. Start by loading paper, envelopes, or sheets of labels in your printer:

+ **Form letters:** Form letters are easiest to print. Just put the paper in the printer.

+ **Envelopes:** Not all printers are capable of printing envelopes one after the other. Sorry, but you probably have to consult the dreary manual that came with your printer to find out the correct way to load envelopes.

+ **Labels:** Load the label sheets in your printer.

Now, to print the form letters, envelopes, or labels, save the material in a new document or send it straight to the printer:

+ **Saving in a new document:** Click the Finish & Merge button and choose Edit Individual Documents (or press Alt+Shift+N). You see the Merge to New Document dialog box. Click OK. After Word creates the document, save it and print it. You can go into the document and make changes here and there before printing. In form letters, for example, you can write a sentence or two in different letters to personalize them.

+ **Printing right away:** Click the Finish & Merge button and choose Print Documents (or press Alt+Shift+M) to print the form letters, envelopes, or labels without saving them in a document. Click OK in the Merge to Printer dialog box and then negotiate the Print dialog box.

Save the form letters, labels, or envelopes in a new document if you intend to print them at a future date or ink is running low on your printer and you may have to print in two or more batches. Saving in a new document permits you to generate the mass mailing without having to start all over again with the merge process and all its tedium.

Chapter 6: Tools for Reports and Scholarly Papers

In This Chapter

✔ Putting a list in alphabetical order

✔ Working in Outline view

✔ Creating a table of contents

✔ Indexing and cross-referencing your work

✔ Managing footnotes and endnotes

✔ Putting together a bibliography

This chapter is hereby dedicated to everyone who has had to delve into the unknown and write a report about it. Writing reports, manuals, and scholarly papers is not easy. You have to explore uncharted territory. You have to contemplate the ineffable. And you have to write bibliographies and footnotes and maybe an index, too. Word cannot take you directly to uncharted territory, but it can take some of the sting out of it.

This chapter explains how to handle footnotes and endnotes, generate a table of contents, index a document, include cross-references in documents, and stitch together a bibliography.

Alphabetizing a List

Which comes first in an alphabetical list, "San Jose, California" or "San José, Costa Rica"? You could research the matter on your own, delving into various dictionaries and online references, or you could rely on the Sort button for the answer. Follow these steps to quickly alphabetize a list:

1. **Select the list.**

2. **On the Home page, click the Sort button.**

    You see the Sort Text dialog box. The Then By options are for sorting tables; they don't concern you, because you're sorting a list.

3. **Click OK.**

    That was easy.

Outlines for Organizing Your Work

Outline view is a great way to see at a glance how your document is organized and whether you need to organize it differently. To take advantage of this feature, you must have assigned heading styles to the headings in your document (Chapter 3 of this mini-book explains styles). In Outline view, you can see all the headings in your document. If a section is in the wrong place, you can move it by simply dragging an icon or by clicking one of the buttons on the Outlining tab. To change the rank of a heading, simply click a button to promote or demote it.

To switch to Outline view, click the Outline button on the status bar or go to the View tab and click the Outline button. You see the Outlining tab, as shown in Figure 6-1. Rather than see text, you see the headings in your document, as well as the first line underneath each heading. Now you get a sense of what is in your document and whether it is organized well. By choosing an option from the Show Level drop-down list, you can decide which headings to see on-screen.

To leave Outline view when you're done reorganizing your document, click the Close Outline View button or a view button apart from Outline on the status bar.

Choose which headings to see

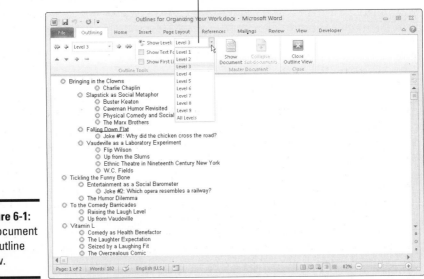

Figure 6-1:
A document in Outline view.

Viewing the outline in different ways

Before you start rearranging your document in Outline view, get a good look at it:

✦ **View some or all headings:** Choose an option from the Show Level drop-down list. To see only first-level headings, for example, choose Level 1. To see first-, second-, and third-level headings, choose Level 3. Choose All Levels to see all the headings.

✦ **View heading formats:** Click the Show Text Formatting check box. When this check box is selected, you can see how headings were formatted and get a better idea of their ranking in your document.

✦ **View or hide the subheadings in one section:** To see or hide the sub-headings and text in one section of a document, select that section by clicking the plus sign beside its heading; then, click the Expand button (or press Alt+Shift+plus sign) to see the subheadings, or click the Collapse button (or press Alt+Shift+minus sign) to hide the subheadings. You can also double-click the plus sign beside a heading to view or hide its subheadings.

✦ **View or hide paragraph text:** Click the Show First Line Only check box (or press Alt+Shift+L). When this check box is selected, you see only the first line in each paragraph. First lines are followed by an ellipsis (. . .) so that you know that more text follows.

Notice the plus and minus icons next to the headings and the text. A plus icon means that the item has subheadings and text under it. For example, headings almost always have plus icons because text comes after them. A minus icon means that nothing is found below the item in question. For example, body text usually has a minus icon because body text is lowest on the Outline totem pole.

Rearranging document sections in Outline view

Outline view is mighty convenient for moving sections in a document and for promoting and demoting sections. Use these techniques to rearrange and reorganize your document:

✦ **Move a section:** To move a section up or down in the document, select it and click the Move Up or Move Down button (or press Alt+Shift+↑ or Alt+Shift+↓). You can also drag the plus sign to a new location. If you want to move the subheadings and subordinate text along with the section, be sure to click the Collapse button to tuck all the subheadings and subtext into the heading before you move it.

✦ **Promote and demote headings:** Click the heading and then click the Promote button or Demote button (or press Alt+Shift+← or Alt+Shift+→). For example, you can promote a Level 3 heading to Level 2 by clicking the

Promote button. Click the Promote To Heading 1 button to promote any heading to a first-level heading; click the Demote To Body text button to turn a heading into prose.

✦ **Choose a new level for a heading:** Click the heading and choose a new heading level from the Outline Level drop-down list.

Generating a Table of Contents

A book-size document or long report isn't worth very much without a table of contents (TOC). How else can readers find what they're looking for? Generating a table of contents with Word is easy, as long as you give the headings in the document different styles — Heading 1, Heading 2, and so on. (Chapter 3 of this mini-book explains styles.) The beautiful thing about Word TOCs is the way they can be updated nearly instantly. If you add a new heading or erase a heading, you can update the TOC with a snap of your fingers. Moreover, you can quickly go from a TOC entry to its corresponding heading in a document by Ctrl+clicking the entry.

Before you create your TOC, create a new section in which to put it and number the pages in the new section with Roman numerals (Chapter 2 of this mini-book explains sections and how to number pages). TOCs, including the TOC in this book, are usually numbered in this way. The first entry in the TOC should cite page number 1. If you don't heed my advice and create a new section, the TOC will occupy the first few numbered pages of your document, and the numbering scheme will be thrown off.

Creating a TOC

To create a table of contents, place the cursor where you want the TOC to go, visit the References tab, and click the Table of Contents button. On the drop-down list, choose one of Word's automatic TOC options or choose Insert Table of Contents to fashion a TOC on your own in the Table of Contents dialog box. (See "Customizing a TOC," later in this chapter, for information about fashioning a TOC in the Table of Contents dialog box.)

Suppose that you want to copy a TOC to another document? To copy a TOC, drag the pointer down its left margin to select it, and then press Ctrl+Shift+F9. Next, use the Copy and Paste commands to copy the TOC to the other document. Because Word gives the text of TOCs the Hyperlink character style, you have to change the color of the text in the TOC (it's blue) and remove the underlines. As for the original TOC, you "disconnected" it from the headings in your document when you pressed Ctrl+Shift+F9. Press the Undo button to undo the effects of pressing Ctrl+Shift+F9 and "disconnecting" your TOC from the headers to which it refers.

Updating and removing a TOC

Follow these instructions to update and remove a TOC:

`Update Table`

✦ **Updating a TOC:** If you add, remove, or edit a heading in your document, your TOC needs updating. To update it, go to the References tab and click the Update Table button, or click in the TOC and press F9. A dialog box asks how to update the TOC. Either update the page numbers only or update the entire table, including all TOC entries and page numbers.

✦ **Removing a TOC:** On the References tab, click the Table of Contents button and choose Remove Table of Contents on the drop-down list.

Customizing a TOC

`Table of Contents ▾`

Want to tinker with your TOC? You can number the headings in different ways and tell Word to include or exclude certain headings.

To change around a TOC, click inside it, go to the References tab, click the Table of Contents button, and choose Insert Table of Contents on the drop-down list. You see the Table of Contents dialog box shown in Figure 6-2. Choose options to declare which headings you want for your TOC and how you want to format it:

✦ **Showing page numbers:** Deselect the Show Page Numbers box if you want your TOC to be a simple list that doesn't refer to headings by page.

✦ **Aligning the page numbers:** Select the Right Align Page Numbers check box if you want page numbers to line up along the right side of the TOC so that the ones and tens line up under each other.

✦ **Choosing a tab leader:** A *leader* is the punctuation mark that appears between the heading and the page number the heading is on. If you don't want periods as the leader, choose another leader or choose (None).

✦ **Choosing a format:** Choose a format from the Formats drop-down list if you don't care to use the one from the template. Just be sure to watch the Print Preview and Web Preview boxes to see the results of your choice.

✦ **Choosing a TOC depth:** The Show Levels box determines how many heading levels are included in the TOC. Unless your document is a legal contract or other formal paper, enter a **2** or **3** here. A TOC is supposed to help readers find information quickly. Including lots of headings that take a long time to read through defeats the purpose of having a TOC.

Figure 6-2:
You can decide for yourself which headings go in a TOC and how it's numbered.

Changing the structure of a TOC

Sometimes the conventional TOC that Word generates doesn't do the trick. Just because a heading has been given the Heading 1 style doesn't mean that it should receive first priority in the TOC. Suppose that you created another style called Chapter Title that should stand taller in the hierarchy than Heading 1. In that case, you need to rearrange the TOC so that Heading 1 headings rank second, not first, in the TOC hierarchy.

Use the Table of Contents Options and Style dialog boxes to tinker with a TOC. These dialog boxes are shown in Figure 6-3. To open them, click, respectively, the Options button or Modify button in the Table of Contents dialog box (refer to Figure 6-2).

✦ **Assigning TOC levels to paragraph styles:** The Table of Contents Options dialog box lists each paragraph style in the document you're working in. For headings you want to appear in the TOC, enter a number in the TOC Level text box to determine the headings' rank. If headings assigned the Heading 1 style are to rank second in the TOC, for example, enter a 2 in Heading 1's TOC Level text box. You can exclude headings from a TOC by deleting a number in a TOC Level box.

✦ **Including table entry fields:** To include text you marked for entry in the TOC, select the Table Entry Fields check box in the Table of Contents Options dialog box (later in this chapter, the sidebar "Marking oddball text for inclusion in the TOC" explains how TOC fields work).

✦ **Changing the look of TOC entries:** The Style dialog box you see when you click the Modify button gives you the chance to choose new fonts, character styles, and font sizes for TOC entries if you generated your TOC from a template. Click the Modify button. Then, in the Style dialog box, choose options to format the TOC style. For example, click the Bold button to boldface TOC entries. (Chapter 3 of this mini-book explains modifying styles.)

Figure 6-3:
Changing a TOC's structure and formatting.

Marking oddball text for inclusion in the TOC

Table of contents entries can refer to a particular place in a document, not just to headings that have been assigned heading styles. For example, you can include figure captions. Use one of these techniques to mark an entry in your document for inclusion in the TOC:

✔ Click in the heading, figure caption, or whatnot. Next, click the Add Text button on the References tab and choose a TOC level on the drop-down list (the Do Not Show in Table of Contents option keeps text from being included in the TOC). If you choose Level 2, for example, the entry appears with other second-level headings.

✔ Click in a heading or text and press Alt+Shift+O. Then, in the Mark Table of Contents Entry dialog box, make sure that the words you want to appear in the TOC appear in the Entry text box (edit or enter the words if need be), and make sure that C (for Contents) appears in the Table Identifier box. In the Level box, enter a number to tell Word how to treat the entry when you generate the table of contents. For example, entering **1** tells Word to treat the entry like a first-level heading and give it top priority. A **3** places the entry with the third-level headings. Finally, click the Mark button.

When you generate the table of contents, be sure to include the oddball entries. To do that, click the Options button in the Table of Contents dialog box and, in the Table of Contents Options dialog box (refer to Figure 6-3), select the Table Entry Fields check box.

Indexing a Document

A good index is a thing of beauty. User manuals, reference works of any length, and reports that readers will refer to all require indexes. Except for the table of contents, the only way to find information in a long document is to look in the index. An index at the end of a company report reflects well on the person who wrote the report. It gives the appearance that the author put in a fair amount of time to complete the work, even if he or she didn't really do that.

An index entry can be formatted in many ways. You can cross-reference index entries, list a page range in an index entry, and break out an index entry into subentries and sub-subentries. To help you with your index, Figure 6-4 explains indexing terminology.

Main entry

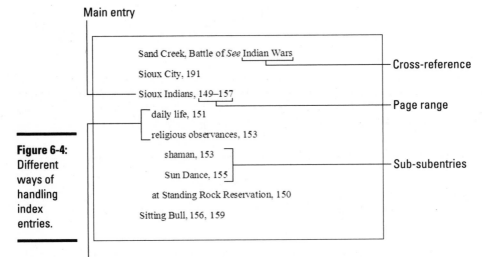

Sand Creek, Battle of *See* Indian Wars — Cross-reference

Sioux City, 191

Sioux Indians, 149–157 — Page range

daily life, 151

religious observances, 153

shaman, 153 — Sub-subentries

Sun Dance, 155

at Standing Rock Reservation, 150

Sitting Bull, 156, 159

Figure 6-4:
Different ways of handling index entries.

Subentries

Writing a good index entry is as hard as writing a good, descriptive heading. As you enter index entries in your document, ask yourself how you would look up information in the index, and enter your index entries accordingly.

Marking index items in the document

The first step in constructing an index is to mark index entries in your document. Marking index items yourself is easier than it seems. After you open the Mark Index Entry dialog box, it stays open so that you can scroll through your document and make entries.

1. **If you see a word or phrase in your document that you can use as a main, top-level entry, select it; otherwise, place the cursor in the paragraph or heading whose topic you want to include in the index.**

   You can save a little time by selecting a word, as I describe shortly.

2. **On the References tab, click the Mark Entry button (or press Alt+Shift+X).**

   The Mark Index Entry dialog box appears. If you selected a word or phrase, it appears in the Main Entry box.

3. **Choose how you want to handle this index entry (refer to Figure 6-4 to see the various ways to make index entries).**

   (refer to Figure 6-4)

   When you enter the text, don't put a comma or period after it. Word does that when it generates the index. The text that you enter appears in your index.

   - *Main Entry:* If you're entering a main, top-level entry, leave the text in the Main Entry box (if it's already there), type new text to describe this entry, or edit the text that's already there. Leave the Subentry box blank.

   - *Subentry:* To create a subentry, enter text in the Subentry box. The subentry text will appear in the index below the main entry text, so make sure that some text is in the Main Entry box and that the subentry text fits under the main entry.

   - *Sub-subentry:* A sub-subentry is the third level in the hierarchy. To create a sub-subentry, type the subentry in the Subentry box, enter a colon (:), and type the sub-subentry without entering a space, like so: **religious observances:shaman**.

4. **Decide how to handle the page reference in the entry.**

   Again, your choices are many:

   - *Cross-reference:* To go without a page reference and refer the reader to another index entry, click the Cross-Reference option button and type the other entry in the text box after the word *See*. What you type here appears in your index, so be sure that the topic you refer the reader to is really named in your index.

   - *Current Page:* Click this option to enter a single page number after the entry.

   - *Page Range:* Click this option if you're indexing a subject that covers several pages in your document. A page range index entry looks something like this: "Sioux Indians, 149–157." To make a page range entry, you must create a bookmark first. Leave the Mark Index Entry dialog box, select the text in the page range, and press Ctrl+Shift+F5 or click the Bookmark button on the Insert tab. In the Bookmark dialog box, enter a name in the Bookmark Name box, and click the Add button. (Chapter 1 of this mini-book explains bookmarks.)

5. **You can boldface or italicize a page number or page range by clicking a Page Number Format check box.**

   In some indexes, the page or page range where the topic is explained in the most depth is italicized or boldfaced so that readers can get to the juiciest parts first.

6. **If you selected a single word or phrase in Step 1, you can click the Mark All button to have Word go through the document and mark all words that are identical to the one in the Main Entry box; click Mark to put this single entry in the index.**

   Click outside the Mark Index Entry dialog box and find the next topic or word that you want to mark for the index. Then click the Mark Entry button on the References tab and make another entry.

A bunch of ugly field codes appear in your document after you mark an index entry. You can render them invisible by clicking the Show/Hide¶ button on the Home tab (or pressing Ctrl+Shift+8).

Generating the index

After you mark all the index entries, it's time to generate the index:

1. **Place the cursor where you want the index to go, most likely at the end of the document.**

   You might type the word **Index** at the top of the page and format the word in a decorative way.

2. **On the References tab, click the Insert Index button.**

   You see the Index dialog box shown in Figure 6-5.

Figure 6-5:
Generating an index.

3. **Choose options in the dialog box and click OK.**

   As you make your choices, watch the Print Preview box to see what happens.

Here are the options in the Index dialog box:

+ **Type:** Choose Run-in if you want subentries and sub-subentries to run together; choose Indented to indent subentries and sub-subentries below main entries (refer to Figure 6-4).

+ **Columns:** Stick with 2, unless you don't have subentries or sub-subentries and you can squeeze three columns on the page or you are working on a landscape document.

+ **Language:** Choose a language for the table, if necessary and if you have installed a foreign language dictionary. If you have installed the dictionary, you can run the spell checker over your index and make sure that the entries are spelled correctly. (Book I, Chapter 4 explains foreign language dictionaries.)

+ **Right Align Page Numbers:** Normally, page numbers appear right after entries and are separated from entries by a comma, but with this option you can right-align the entries so that they line up under one another.

+ **Tab Leader:** Some index formats place a *leader* between the entry and the page number. A leader is a series of dots or dashes. If you're working with a format that has a leader, you can choose a leader from the drop-down list.

+ **Formats:** Word offers a number of attractive index layouts. You can choose one from the list.

+ **Modify:** Click this button if you're adventurous and want to create an index style of your own (Chapter 3 of this mini-book explains styles).

To update an index after you create or delete entries, click it and then click the Update Index button or right-click the index and then choose Update Field on the shortcut menu.

Editing an index

After you generate an index, read it carefully to make sure that all entries are useful to readers. Inevitably, something doesn't come out right, but you can edit index entries as you would the text in a document. Index field markers are enclosed in curly brackets with the letters *XE* and the text of the index entry in quotation marks, like so: { XE: "Wovoka: Ghost Dance" }. To edit an index marker, click the Show/Hide¶ button on the Home tab (or press Ctrl+Shift+8) to see the field markers and find the one you need to edit. Then delete letters or type letters as you would do in normal text.

TIP

Here's a quick way to find index field markers: After clicking the Show/Hide¶ button, with the index fields showing, press Ctrl+G to open the Go To tab of the Find and Replace dialog box. In the Go to What menu, choose Field; type **XE** in the Enter Field Name box, and click the Next button until you find the marker you want to edit. You can also use the Find command on the Home tab to look for index entries. Word finds index entries as well as text provided that you click the Show/Hide¶ button to display index fields in your document.

Putting Cross-References in a Document

Cross-references are very handy indeed. They tell readers where to go to find more information on a topic. The problem with cross-references, however, is that the thing being cross-referenced really has to be there. If you tell readers to go to a heading called "The Cat's Pajamas" on page 93, and neither the heading nor the page is really there, readers curse and tell you where to go, rather than the other way around.

Fortunately for you, Word lets you know when you make errant cross-references. You can refer readers to headings, page numbers, footnotes, endnotes, and plain-old paragraphs. And as long you create captions for your cross-references with the Insert Caption button on the References tab, you can also make cross-references to equations, figures, graphs, listings, programs, and tables. If you delete the thing that a cross-reference refers to and render the cross-reference invalid, Word tells you about it the next time you update your cross-references. Best of all, if the page number, numbered item, or text that a cross-reference refers to changes, so does the cross-reference.

To create a cross-reference:

1. **Write the first part of the cross-reference text.**

For example, you could write **To learn more about these cowboys of the pampas, see page** and then type a blank space. The blank space separates the word *page* from the page number in the cross-reference. If you are referring to a heading, write something like **For more information, see "**. Don't type a blank space this time because the cross-reference heading text will appear right after the double quotation mark.

⌐⁺⌐ Cross-reference   *2.* **On the References tab, click the Cross-Reference button.**

The Cross-Reference dialog box appears, as shown in Figure 6-6.

3. **Choose what type of item you're referring to in the Reference Type drop-down list.**

If you're referring to a plain-old paragraph, choose Bookmark. Then click outside the dialog box, scroll to the paragraph you're referring to, and place a bookmark there (Chapter 1 of this mini-book explains bookmarks.)

Choose what the reference refers to

Choose how to refer to the item

Figure 6-6:
Entering
a cross-
reference.

**Tools for
Reports and
Scholarly Papers**

4. **Make a choice in the Insert Reference To box to refer to text, a page number, or a numbered item.**

   The options in this box are different, depending on what you chose in Step 3.

   - *Text:* Choose this option (Heading Text, Entire Caption, and so on) to include text in the cross-reference. For example, choose Heading Text if your cross-reference is to a heading.

   - *Number:* Choose this option to insert a page number or other kind of number, such as a table number, in the cross-reference.

   - *Include Above/Below:* Select this box to include the word *above* or *below* to tell readers where, in relation to the cross-reference, the thing being referred to is located in your document.

5. **If you want, leave the check mark in the Insert as Hyperlink check box to create a hyperlink as well as a cross-reference.**

   With a hyperlink, someone reading the document on-screen can Ctrl+click the cross-reference and go directly to what it refers to.

6. **In the For Which box, tell Word where the thing you're referring to is located.**

   To do so, select a heading, bookmark, footnote, endnote, equation, figure, graph, or whatnot. In long documents, you almost certainly have to click the scrollbar to find the one you want.

7. **Click the Insert button and then click the Close button.**

8. **Back in your document, enter the rest of the cross-reference text, if necessary.**

When you finish creating your document, update all the cross-references. To do that, press Ctrl+A to select the entire document. Then press F9 or right-click in the document and choose Update Field on the shortcut menu.

If the thing referred to in a cross-reference is no longer in your document, you see `Error! Reference source not found` where the cross-reference should be. To find cross-reference errors in long documents, look for the word *Error!* with the Find command (press Ctrl+F). Investigate what went wrong, and repair or delete errant cross-references.

Putting Footnotes and Endnotes in Documents

A *footnote* is a bit of explanation, a comment, or a reference that appears at the bottom of the page and is referred to by a number or symbol in the text. An *endnote* is the same thing, except that it appears at the end of the section, chapter, or document. If you've written a scholarly paper of any kind, you know what a drag footnotes and endnotes are.

You will be glad to know that Word takes some of the drudgery out of footnotes and endnotes. For example, if you delete or add a note, all notes after the one you added or deleted are renumbered. And you don't have to worry about long footnotes because Word adjusts the page layout to make room for them. You can change the numbering scheme of footnotes and endnotes at will. When you are reviewing a document, all you have to do is move the pointer over a footnote or endnote citation. The note icon appears, as does a pop-up box with the text of the note.

Entering a footnote or endnote

To enter a footnote or endnote in a document:

1. **Place the cursor in the text where you want the note's number or symbol to appear.**

2. **On the References tab, click the Insert Footnote button (or press Ctrl+Alt+F) or the Insert Endnote button (or press Ctrl+Alt+D).**

   If you are in Draft view, the Notes pane opens at the bottom of the screen with the cursor beside the number of the note you're about to enter. In Print Layout view, Word scrolls to the bottom of the page or the end of the document or section so that you can enter the note, as shown in Figure 6-7.

3. **Enter your footnote or endnote.**

4. **Click the Close button in the Notes pane if you're in Draft view; in Print Layout view, scroll upward to return to the main text.**

Figure 6-7:
Entering a
footnote in
Print Layout
view (left);
the Footnote
and Endnote
dialog box
(right).

Click the Show Notes button at any time to see your notes in the Notes pane, at the bottom of the page, or at the end of the section or document.

To quickly return from writing a note to the place in your document where the footnote or endnote number citation is located, double-click the number citation at the bottom of the page (in Print Layout view) or the Notes pane (in Draft view). For example, if you just finished entering footnote 3, double-click the number *3*.

Choosing the numbering scheme and position of notes

Choosing the numbering scheme and positioning of endnotes and footnotes is quite easy. On the References tab, click the Footnotes group button. The Footnote and Endnote dialog box appears (refer to Figure 6-7). Tell Word where to place your notes:

✦ **Footnotes:** Choose Bottom of Page to put footnotes at the bottom of the page no matter where the text ends; choose Below Text to put footnotes directly below the last line of text on the page.

✦ **Endnotes:** Choose End of Section if your document is divided into sections (such as chapters) and you want endnotes to appear at the back of sections; choose End of Document to put all endnotes at the very back of the document.

In the Format area, tell Word how to number the notes:

✦ **Number Format:** Choose A B C, i ii iii, or another numbering scheme, if you want. You can also enter symbols by choosing the last option on this drop-down list.

✦ **Custom Mark:** You can mark the note with a symbol by clicking the Symbol button and choosing a symbol in the Symbol dialog box. If you go this route, you have to enter a symbol each time you insert a note.

Not only that, you may have to enter two or three symbols for the second and third notes on each page or document because Word can't renumber symbols.

✦ **Start At:** To start numbering the notes at a place other than 1, A, or i, enter **2**, **B**, **ii**, or whatever in this box.

✦ **Numbering:** To number the notes continuously from the start of your document to the end, choose Continuous. Choose Restart Each Section to begin anew at each section of your document. For footnotes, you can begin anew on each page by choosing Restart Each Page.

By the way, the Convert button in the Footnote and Endnote dialog box is for fickle scholars who suddenly decide that their endnotes should be footnotes or vice versa. Click it and choose an option in the Convert Notes dialog box to turn footnotes into endnotes, turn endnotes into footnotes, or — in documents with both endnotes and footnotes — make the endnotes footnotes and the footnotes endnotes.

Deleting, moving, and editing notes

If a devious editor tells you that a footnote or endnote is in the wrong place, that you don't need a note, or that you need to change the text in a note, all is not lost:

✦ **Editing:** To edit a note, double-click its number or symbol in the text. You see the note on-screen. Edit the note at this point.

✦ **Moving:** To move a note, select its number or symbol in the text and drag it to a new location, or cut and paste it to a new location.

✦ **Deleting:** To delete a note, select its number or symbol and press the Delete key.

Footnotes and endnotes are renumbered when you move or delete one of them.

Compiling a Bibliography

A *bibliography* is a list, usually in alphabetical order by author name, of all the books, journal articles, Web sites, interviews, and other sources used in the writing of an article, report, or book. Writing a good bibliography is a chore. Besides keeping careful track of sources, you have to list them correctly. Does the author's name or work's name come first in the citation? How do you list a Web site or magazine article without an author's name?

Word's Bibliography feature is very nice in this regard: It solves the problem of how to enter citations for a bibliography. All you have to do is enter the bare facts about the citation — the author's name, title, publication date, publisher, and so on — and Word presents this information correctly in the bibliography. You can choose among several popular bibliographical styles (APA, Chicago, and others) from the Style drop-down list, as shown in Figure 6-8. After you make your choice, Word reformats all bibliography citations. You don't have to worry about whether titles should be underlined or italicized, or how authors' names should be listed in the bibliography.

Insert a citation   Choose a bibliography style

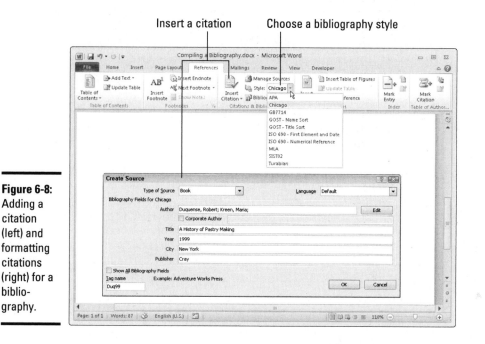

Figure 6-8:
Adding a citation (left) and formatting citations (right) for a bibliography.

Inserting a citation for your bibliography

Abbreviated citations appear in the text of your document in between parentheses where you enter citations; the complete citation appears in the bibliography. After you enter the information about a citation, entering it a second time is easy because Word keeps a master list of all citations you have used in your work, both in the document you are working on and in your other documents. To enter a citation, click in your document at the place that refers to the source, go to the References tab, and use one of these techniques to enter the citation:

✦ **Entering a citation you've already entered in your document:** Click the Insert Citation button and choose the citation on the drop-down list. The top of the drop-down list presents citations you've already entered.

✦ **Creating a new citation:** Click the Insert Citation button and choose Add New Source. You see the Create Source dialog box shown in Figure 6-8. Choose an option on the Type of Source drop-down list and enter particulars about the source. You can click the Show All Bibliography Fields check box to enlarge the dialog box and enter all kinds of information about the source. Whether clicking the check box is necessary depends on how detailed you want your bibliography to be.

✦ **Inserting a citation placeholder:** Click the Insert Citation button and choose Add New Placeholder if you're in a hurry and you don't currently have all the information you need to describe the source. The Placeholder Name dialog box appears. Enter a placeholder name for the source and click OK. Later, when you have the information for the source, either click the citation in the text and choose Edit Source on its drop-down list or click the Manage Sources button, and in the Source Manager dialog box, select the placeholder name (it has a question mark next to it) and click the Edit button. You see the Edit Source dialog box. Enter the information and click OK.

✦ **Inserting a citation you've entered in another document:** Click the Manage Sources button. You see the Source Manager dialog box. In the Master List, select the source you need and click the Copy button. Then click Close and enter the citation by clicking the Insert Citation button and choosing the name of the citation you copied.

Your citation appears in text in parentheses. Move the pointer over it and you see an inline drop-down list that you can open to edit the citation as it appears in-text as well as edit it in the bibliography, as shown in Figure 6-9.

Figure 6-9:
In-text citations have inline drop-down lists.

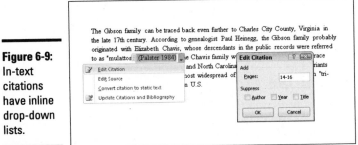

Editing a citation

Use one of these techniques to edit a citation:

✦ Open the citation's inline drop-down list (refer to Figure 6-9) and choose Edit Source. You see the Edit Source dialog box, where you can edit the citation.

✦ Click the Manage Sources button on the References tab. The Source Manager dialog box appears. Select the citation, click the Edit button, and change around the citation in the Edit Source dialog box.

Changing how citations appear in text

Citations appear in text enclosed in parentheses. Use one of these techniques to change how a citation appears in the text of your document:

✦ **Changing what's in parentheses:** Open the citation's drop-down list and choose Edit Citation (refer to Figure 6-9). You see the Edit Citation dialog box. To suppress the author's name, year, or title from appearing inside parentheses, click the Author, Year, or Title check box (whether the citation in parentheses lists the author, year, or title depends on which citation style you choose). To make page numbers appear with the citation, enter page numbers in the Pages box.

✦ **Removing the in-text citation:** Swipe over the citation to select it and press Delete. Removing an in-text citation this way does not prevent the citation from appearing in the bibliography.

Generating the bibliography

Go to the References tab and follow these steps to generate your bibliography:

1. **Click in your document where you want the bibliography to appear.**

Probably that place is toward the end of the document.

2. **On the References tab, open the Style drop-down list and choose a style.**

If you're generating your bibliography for a paper you will submit to a journal or institution, ask the editors which style they prefer for bibliographies and choose that style from the list.

3. **Click the Manage Sources button.**

You see the Source Manager dialog box. Citations in the Current List box will appear in your bibliography.

4. **If necessary, address citations in the Current List box.**

If you entered any citation placeholders, their names appear in the list next to question marks. Select these placeholders, click the Edit button, and enter information in the Edit Source dialog box.

To keep a citation from appearing in the bibliography, select it and click the Delete button.

5. **Click the Close button in the Source Manager dialog box.**

6. **Click the Bibliography button and choose a built-in bibliography or the Insert Bibliography command on the drop-down list.**

There it is — your bibliography.

Book III

Outlook

"Yeah, this should help me with my business. It's got 'FelonHelper,' 'Goonicator,' 'You Outlookin' at Me?'..."

Contents at a Glance

Chapter 1: Getting Acquainted with Outlook

In This Chapter

✔ Getting around in Outlook

✔ Viewing folders in different ways

✔ Categorizing items so that you can locate them easily

✔ Searching in folders

✔ Deleting items

✔ Backing up your Outlook file

✔ Importing e-mail and contact information from other software programs

✔ Archiving old-and-in-the-way items

*T*his chapter pulls back the curtain and gives you a first glimpse of *Outlook*, the e-mailer and personal organizer in the Office 2010 suit of programs. Read on to find out once and for all what Outlook does, how to get from folder to folder, and the different ways to view the stuff in folders. You can find advice about keeping folders well organized, deleting stuff, backing up an Outlook file, and cleaning out items in folders that you no longer need.

What Is Outlook, Anyway?

Outlook isn't in character with the rest of the Office programs. It's a little different in that what you see on-screen changes when you click a Navigation pane button on the left side of the window. Click a Navigation pane button — Mail, Calendar, Contacts, Tasks, Notes, Folder List, or Shortcuts — and you go to a different Outlook window altogether.

Outlook can be confusing because the program serves many different purposes. To wit, Outlook is all this:

✉ Mail

✦ **An e-mail program:** You can use it to send and receive e-mail messages and files, as well as organize e-mail messages in different folders so that you can keep track of them. (See Chapter 3 of this mini-book.)

♦ **An appointment scheduler:** Outlook is a calendar for scheduling appointments and meetings. You can tell at a glance when and where you're expected, as well as be alerted to upcoming appointments and meetings. (See Chapter 4 of this mini-book.)

♦ **An address book:** The program can store the addresses, phone numbers, and e-mail addresses of friends, foes, clients, and family members. Looking up this information in the Contacts List is easy. (See Chapter 2 of this mini-book.)

♦ **A task reminder:** Outlook is a means of planning projects. You can tell when deadlines fall and plan your workload accordingly. (See Chapter 5 of this mini-book.)

♦ **A notes receptacle:** This part of the program is a place to jot down notes and reminders. (See Chapter 5 of this mini-book.)

Outlook is a lot of different things all rolled into one. For that reason, the program can be daunting at first. But hang in there. Soon you'll be running roughshod over Outlook and making it suffer on your behalf.

Do you need Outlook?

Before you penetrate the mysteries of Outlook, ask yourself whether you need the program. If you don't receive volumes of e-mail, your calendar isn't crowded, and the office where you work doesn't require you to use Outlook, consider using an e-mail program that isn't as cumbersome as Outlook, or better yet, consider using a Web-based e-mail program.

Outlook is good at organizing e-mail so that you can find and reply to messages quickly. It is good at handling volumes of e-mail. Outlook can help you manage schedules and coordinate meetings with co-workers. It can help you keep track of where you're supposed to be and when you're supposed to be there.

On the minus side, however, Outlook is an example of what people in the computer industry call "bloatware." The program has many more features than most people need, and all these features clutter Outlook and make it hard to use. What's more, e-mail messages are kept on your computer. Unless you carry around a laptop, you have to be at your home or office computer to collect your e-mail. With a Web-based e-mail program, messages are stored on a server on the Internet, and all e-mail activity — composing, sending, and receiving messages — is accomplished through a Web browser. You can be in Timbuktu and still collect your e-mail if you can find a computer with an Internet connection. You don't have to be at home or at the office to read your e-mail.

If Web-based e-mailing appeals to you, ask your Internet service provider whether it offers a Web-based e-mail service. Or check out these Web-based e-mail programs, both of which are free and easy to use: Google Mail (www.gmail.com) and Yahoo! Mail (mail.yahoo.com). These programs offer a calendar and other amenities as well as e-mailing. If you want to keep it simple and you can manage to do that, steer clear of Outlook.

Navigating the Outlook Folders

The first thing you should know about Outlook is this: All items are kept in folders, as shown in Figure 1-1. E-mail messages when they arrive are kept in the Inbox folder. Calendar items are kept in the Calendar folder. Notes are kept in the Notes folder. When you want to undertake a new task, you go to a different folder.

Navigation pane

Selected folder

To-Do bar

Figure 1-1: Outlook with the Inbox folder selected.

Reading pane

Book III Chapter 1

Getting Acquainted with Outlook

Here are the ways to get from folder to folder in Outlook and undertake a new task:

✦ **Navigation pane:** Click a button in the Navigation pane — Mail, Calendar, Contacts, Tasks, or Notes — to go to a folder. The Navigation pane appears on the left side of the window (refer to Figure 1-1).

✦ **Folder List:** Click the Folder List button (or press Ctrl+6) and select a folder in the Navigation pane. For example, to read incoming e-mail messages, select the Inbox folder (refer to Figure 1-1). The Folder List button is located at the bottom of the Navigation pane.

You can open a folder in a new window. To do so, right-click a Navigation pane button or folder name and choose Open in New Window. To close a window you opened this way, click its Close button (the *X* in the upper-right corner).

Wrestling with the Navigation Pane and To-Do Bar

Outlook is designed for you to move from folder to folder with no trouble. All you have to do to open a new folder is click a button or folder icon in the Navigation pane. However, sometimes the Navigation pane gets in the way. You need the extra space for reading e-mail messages or rummaging in the Contacts folder. Here are instructions for wrestling with the Navigation pane, To-Do Bar, and Reading pane:

✦ **Hiding and displaying the Navigation pane:** As I explain earlier, the Navigation pane appears on the left side of the window and offers buttons and folder names that you can click to go to different folders (refer to Figure 1-1). Click the Expand or Maximize buttons in the Navigation pane (or press Alt+F1) to display or hide it. You can also go to the View tab, click the Navigation Pane button, and choose an option on the drop-down list.

✦ **Hiding and displaying the To-Do Bar:** The *To-Do Bar* appears on the right side of the screen and shows your calendar, upcoming appointments, and tasks arranged by due date (refer to Figure 1-1). Click a calendar day to open the Calendar on that day. Double-click an appointment to open an Appointment window, or a task to open a Task window. To display or hide the To-Do Bar, click its Expand or Minimize button (or press Alt+F2). You can also go the View tab, click the To-Do Bar button, and choose an option on the drop-down list.

✦ **Hiding and displaying Reading pane:** The *Reading pane* appears on the right side or bottom of the window and gives you a more detailed look at an item you selected. It comes in handy when you're reading e-mail because you can read a message and still view your message list (refer to Figure 1-1). To display or hide the Reading pane, go to the View tab, click the Reading Pane button, and choose Right, Bottom, or Off from the drop-down list. When the Reading pane is displayed, you can also hide it by dragging its border to the bottom or right side of the window.

Getting a Better View of Items in a Folder

Because you spend so much time gazing at folders, it pays to know the different ways to view items in folders. Each folder offers different ways of viewing its contents. Go to the Home tab and View tab to discover different techniques for viewing items. Figure 1-2 shows the Contacts folder in Business Cards view. You can see contacts in business card form by going to the Home tab and choosing Business Cards in the Current View gallery. I explain different ways of looking at items in folders throughout this mini-book.

Figure 1-2:
The Contacts folder in Business Cards view.

Categorizing Items

One of your biggest tasks in Outlook, if you choose to accept it, is to categorize items in folders so that you can find and deal with them. Finding items can be a chore in a folder with a lot of items, but by categorizing items, you can find the ones you're looking for. Categories are color-coded to make identifying them easier. After you assign a category to an item, you can arrange items in folders by category, and in so doing, find items. Categorizing is a great way to stay on top of all the chores you have to do.

Creating a category

Follow these steps to create a category for organizing folder items:

1. **Select an item in a folder to which you want to assign your new category.**

2. **On the Home tab, click the Categorize button and choose All Categories on the drop-down list.**

   You see the Color Categories dialog box, as shown in Figure 1-3. At this point, you can create a category from scratch or revamp one of Outlook's color-named categories:

   • *Creating your own category:* Click the New button to open the Add New Category dialog box, as shown in Figure 1-3. Then enter a name for your category and choose a color from the drop-down list. While you're at it, you can open the Shortcut Key drop-down list and choose a shortcut key combination for assigning your new category to items (refer to Figure 1-3). Click the OK button in the Color Categories dialog box.

- *Renaming a category:* In the Color Categories dialog box (refer to Figure 1-3), select a color category, and click the Rename button. Then enter a new name where the old one is now. You can choose a different color for your category by choosing a color in the Color drop-down list. To assign it a shortcut key, open the Shortcut Key drop-down list and choose a shortcut key combination.

Figure 1-3:
Click the New button or Rename button to create a new category.

To delete a category, return to the Color Categories dialog box, select the category's name, and click the Delete button. Although the category is deceased, items to which you assigned the category keep their category assignments.

Assigning items to categories

Follow these steps to assign a category to a folder item:

1. Select the item.

2. On the Home tab, click the Categorize button and choose a category on the drop-down list.

You can also right-click, choose Categorize, and select a category on the shortcut menu, or press a Ctrl+key combination if you assigned one to the category. An item can be assigned more than one category.

To remove a category assignment, select the item, click the Categorize button, and choose Clear All Categories.

Another way to quickly categorize an e-mail message is to click the Category column of the message in a mail folder window. To tell Outlook which category to assign when you click the Category column, click the Categorize button and choose Set Quick Click. You see the Set Quick Click dialog box.

Choose the category on the drop-down list that you want to assign by
"quick-clicking" in the Category column.

Arranging items by category in folders

To arrange items by category in a folder, select the folder in the Navigation
pane and use one of these techniques:

✦ On the View tab, choose Categories in the Arrange By gallery.

✦ In a list, click the Categories column heading to sort items by category.

You can also click the Categorized button on the (Search Tools) Search tab
to organize the results of a search by category.

Searching for Stray Folder Items

If you can't locate an item in a folder by scrolling, changing views, or any
other means, run a search. To start your search, go to the folder you want to
search and click in the Search box (or press Ctrl+E). You can find the Search
box below the Ribbon. As soon as you click in the Search box, Outlook opens
the (Search Tools) Search tab so that you can describe what you're seeking,
as shown in Figure 1-4.

**Book III
Chapter 1**

**Getting Acquainted
with Outlook**

Search box

Figure 1-4:
Describe
what you're
searching
for on the
(Search
Tools)
Search tab.

Search results (with keywords highlighted)

As the following pages explain, you can conduct an instant search, narrow your search by choosing Refine options, or conduct an advanced search starting from the (Search Tools) Search tab. Search results appear in the window below the Search box. To close the search and go back to seeing the contents of your folder, click the Close Search button (the *X* on the right side of the Search box).

Here's a fast way to run a search: Click the Recent Searches button on the (Search Tools) Search tab and choose a search on the drop-down list to rerun one of the last six searches you conducted.

Conducting an instant search

What Microsoft calls an "instant search" is a keyword search of the folder you're viewing. If a keyword you enter in the Search box is found in an e-mail message, calendar appointment, contact, or other item, the item appears in the search results and the keyword is highlighted (refer to Figure 1-4). Search results begin appearing as soon as you start to type. You don't have to press the Enter key to begin the search.

To change how instant searches are conducted, click the Search Tools button and choose Search Options on the drop-down list. You go to the Search category in the Outlook Options dialog box. From there, you can choose which folders are searched and how search results are displayed when you conduct an instant search.

Refining a search

Refine a search when an instant search brings up too many or too few search results. Starting on the (Search Tools) Search tab, refine your search by changing its scope and choosing Refine options.

Changing the scope of a search

How wide the scope of a search is determines how many results are found in the search. To narrow or widen a search, click a button in the Scope group on the (Search Tools) Search tab:

✦ **All Items:** Searches the folder you selected on the Navigation pane as well as its related folders. For example, clicking the All Mail Items button searches all folders that contain e-mail, including the Drafts and Sent Items folders. This button changes names, depending on which folder you selected. You can also press Ctrl+Alt+A.

✦ **Current Folder:** Searches the folder you selected on the Navigation pane. You can also press Ctrl+Alt+K.

✦ **All Subfolders:** Searches the folder you selected on the Navigation pane as well as its subfolders. You can also press Ctrl+Alt+Z.

✦ **All Outlook Items:** Searches all Outlook folders.

Choosing Refine options

To narrow a search, click buttons in the Refine group on the (Search Tools) Search tab. After you click a button, Outlook provides a place in the Search box for you to enter a keyword. Which buttons appear in the Refine group depends on which folder you search.

In a folder that contains e-mail, for example, you can click the From button and enter a sender name in the Search box to search for e-mails you received from a particular person. You can click the Subject button and enter a keyword to search the subject descriptions in e-mail you received.

Conducting an advanced search

If, woe is me, you can't find what you're looking for with an instant search or a refined search, you can try your luck with an advanced search. On the (Search Tools) Search tab, click the Search Tools button and choose Advanced Find on the drop-down list. You see the Advanced Find dialog box. In the Look For drop-down list, choose what you want to search for. Click the Browse button to open the Select Folder(s) dialog box, where you can select more than one folder to search in. Then choose options in the three tabs to formulate your search. Which options are available depends on which folder you're searching.

Deleting E-Mail Messages, Contacts, Tasks, and Other Items

Outlook folders are notorious for filling quickly. E-mail messages, contacts, and tasks soon clog the folders if you spend any time in Outlook. From time to time, go through the e-mail folders, Contacts window, Task window, and Calendar to delete items you no longer need. To delete items, select them and do one of the following:

✦ Click the Delete button.

✦ Press the Delete key.

✦ Right-click and choose Delete.

Deleted items — e-mail messages, calendar appointments, contacts, and tasks — land in the Deleted Items folder in case you want to recover them. To delete items once and for all, open the Deleted Items folder and start deleting like a madman.

To empty the Delete Items folder altogether, right-click the folder and choose Empty Folder. You can also visit the File tab, choose Info, click the

Cleanup Tools button, and choose Empty Deleted Items Folder on the drop-down list.

Be sure to check out "Running the Mailbox Cleanup command" at the end of this chapter. It explains a quick way to delete unwanted Inbox messages.

Finding and Backing Up Your Outlook File

All the data you keep in Outlook — e-mail messages, names and addresses, calendar appointments and meetings — is kept in a .pst file on your computer. Locating this file on your computer sometimes requires the services of Sherlock Holmes. The file isn't kept in a standard location. It can be any number of places, depending on the operating system on your computer and whether you upgraded from an earlier version of Office.

The all-important .pst file is hiding deep in your computer, but you need to find it. You need to know where this file is located so that you can back it up to a CD, flash drive, or other backup medium. It holds clients' names and the names of relatives and loved ones. It holds the e-mail messages you think are worth keeping. It would be a shame to lose this stuff if your computer failed.

Here's a quick way to find the .pst file on your computer and back it up:

File

1. **On the File tab, choose Info.**

   The Account Information window opens.

2. **Click the Account Settings button and choose Account Settings on the drop-down list.**

   You see the Account Settings dialog box.

3. **Go to the Data Files tab.**

   This tab is shown in Figure 1-5. It lists the location of your .pst file (or files).

4. **Select your .pst file and click the Open File Location button.**

   Windows Explorer opens, and you see the folder where your .pst file is kept.

5. **Close Outlook.**

   Sorry, but you can't back up a .pst file if Outlook is running.

6. **To back up the file, right-click it in Windows Explorer, choose Send To on the shortcut menu, and choose the option on the submenu that represents where you back up files.**

   If an accident befalls your computer, copy the backup .pst file that you made into the folder where the .pst file is stored on your computer.

Quick-steppin'

When you visit a folder that holds e-mail and go to the Home tab, you see the Quick Steps gallery. Choose a so-called *quick step* in this gallery to accomplish a task quickly. For example, choose Reply & Delete to open a message window, reply to a message, and delete the message automatically when you send your reply. You can save a bit of time by making use of the quick steps in the Quick Steps gallery.

If you're ambitious, you can add your own quick step to the gallery. Click Create New in the gallery, and in the Edit Quick Step dialog box, name and choose an action to add to the gallery. You can choose from filing actions, change status actions, and other types of actions. Click the Add Action button to place your new action in the Quick Steps gallery.

To feed and care for quick steps, open the Quick Steps gallery and choose Manage Quick Steps. In the Manage Quick Steps dialog box, you can edit quick steps, delete them, and rearrange them in the Quick Step gallery.

**Book III
Chapter 1**

Getting Acquainted with Outlook

Figure 1-5:
Click the Open File Location button to find out where your Outlook file is located.

Importing E-Mail and Addresses from Another Program

Suppose that you've been using Outlook Express, Lotus Organizer, or another e-mail program to handle your e-mail and contact addresses, but now you've become a convert to Outlook. What do you do with the e-mail messages and names and addresses in the other program? You can't let them just sit there or you can import them into Office and pick up where you left off.

File

To import e-mail and contact addresses from another program, go to the File tab, choose Open, and click the Import button. You see the Import and Export Wizard. What you do next depends on where you now do your e-mailing and address tracking:

✦ **Outlook Express:** Select Import Internet Mail and Addresses and click Next. In the Outlook Import Tool dialog box, select Outlook Express, select check boxes to decide what to import (Mail, Addresses, and/or Rules), and click the Finish button.

✦ **Eudora:** Select Import Internet Mail and Addresses and click Next. In the Outlook Import Tool dialog box, select Eudora, choose options to decide what to do about duplicate entries, and click the Finish button. In the Browser for Folder dialog box, select the file where the Eudora data is kept and click OK.

✦ **Lotus Organizer:** Select Import from Another Program or File, click Next, select a Lotus Organizer, and click Next again. Click Next while you go along. You're asked how to handle duplicate items, to locate the Lotus Organizer data file, and to select an Outlook folder to put the data in.

Before you import e-mail and addresses from another program, weed out the e-mail messages and addresses you no longer need. Why ferry this stuff into Outlook when you no longer need it?

Cleaning Out Your Folders

Getting rid of unneeded items in folders is essential for good mental health. All that clutter can be distressing. Earlier in this chapter, "Deleting E-Mail Messages, Contacts, Tasks, and Other Items" explains how to muck out folders by emptying them. These pages explain two more techniques for removing detritus from folders — archiving and the Mailbox Cleanup command.

Archiving the old stuff

In some cases, Outlook puts e-mail messages, tasks, and appointments older than six months in the *Archive folder,* a special folder for items that Outlook thinks are stale and not worth keeping anymore. Outlook calls sending these items to the Archive folder "autoarchiving." Items that have been archived aren't lost forever. You can visit them by opening the Archive Folders folder and its subfolders on the Folders List. These folders and subfolders are created automatically the first time you archive items.

Archiving is a way of stripping your mail folders, tasks lists, and calendar of items that don't matter anymore. How and when items are archived is up to you. To archive items, you establish a default set of archiving rules that apply to all folders, and if a folder needs individual attention and shouldn't be subject to the default archiving rules, you establish special rules for that folder. Each folder can have its own set of archiving rules or be subject to the default rules.

To tell Outlook how to archive old stuff:

> **File**

+ **Establishing default archiving rules:** On the File tab, choose Options to open the Outlook Options dialog box. Then, on the Advanced tab, click the AutoArchive Settings button. You see the AutoArchive dialog box shown in Figure 1-6. See "Default archiving rules."

> **AutoArchive Settings**

+ **Establishing rules for a specific folder:** Select the folder, go to the Folder tab, and click the AutoArchive Settings button. You see the AutoArchive tab of the Properties dialog box, as shown in Figure 1-6. See "Archiving rules for a folder."

Figure 1-6:
Making
the default
archiving
rules (left)
and rules
for a folder
(right).

Default archiving rules

Negotiate these options to establish default archiving rules (refer to Figure 1-6):

+ **Run AutoArchive Every:** Enter a number to tell Outlook how often to archive items.

✦ **Prompt Before Archive Runs:** If this check box is selected, you see a message box before archiving begins, and you can decline to archive if you want by selecting No in the message box.

✦ **Delete Expired Items (E-Mail Folders Only):** Select this check box to delete all e-mail messages when the time period has expired.

✦ **Archive or Delete Old Items:** Deselect this option if you *don't* want to archive items.

✦ **Show Archive Folder in Folder List:** Select this option if you want to keep the archived version of the folder in the Folder List. Archived items are kept in this folder so that you can review them.

✦ **Clean Out Items Older Than:** Choose a cutoff time period after which to archive items.

✦ **Move Old Items To:** Click the Browse button and select a folder if you want to store the Archive file in a certain location.

✦ **Permanently Delete Old Items:** Select this option if you want to delete, not archive, old items.

Archiving rules for a folder

Choose among these options to establish archiving rules for a specific folder (refer to Figure 1-6):

✦ **Do Not Archive Items in This Folder:** Select this option if items in the folder aren't worth archiving.

✦ **Archive Items in This Folder Using the Default Settings**: Select this option to defer to the default archiving rules for the folder.

✦ **Archive This Folder Using These Settings**: Select this option to establish archiving rules for the folder.

✦ **Clean Out Items Older Than:** Choose a cutoff time period after which to archive the items in the folder.

✦ **Move Old Items To:** Click the Browse button and select a folder if you want to store the archived items in a specific location.

✦ **Permanently Delete Old Items:** Select this option if you want to delete, not archive, items in this folder.

Besides archiving, another way to remove bric-a-brac automatically is to take advantage of the Rules Wizard to delete certain kinds of messages when they arrive. See Chapter 3 of this mini-book for more information.

Running the Mailbox Cleanup command

The Mailbox Cleanup command is an all-purpose command for finding e-mail messages, archiving items, deleting items, and deleting alternate versions of items. To use the command, go to the File tab, choose Info, click the Cleanup Tools button, and choose Mailbox Cleanup. You see the Mailbox Cleanup dialog box shown in Figure 1-7. The dialog box offers a speedy entrée into these different Outlook tasks:

✦ **Seeing how much hard drive space folders occupy:** Click the View Mailbox Size button and then take note of folder sizes in the Folder Size dialog box.

Figure 1-7: Mucking out the mailboxes.

✦ **Finding items:** Select an option button to find items older than a certain number of days or larger than a certain number of kilobytes, enter a days or kilobytes number, and click the Find button. You land in the Advanced Find dialog box. Earlier in this chapter, "Conducting an advanced search" explains this dialog box. Use it to select items and delete them.

✦ **Archiving items:** Click the AutoArchive button to archive items in your folders. See "Archiving the old stuff" in this chapter for details.

✦ **Emptying the deleted items folder:** Click the Empty button to empty the Deleted Items folder. See "Deleting E-Mail Messages, Contacts, Tasks, and Other Items," earlier in this chapter.

Chapter 2: Maintaining the Contacts Folder

In This Chapter

✔ Recording information about a new contact

✔ Creating a contact group

✔ Locating a contact in the Contacts folder

✔ Printing contact information in the Contacts folder

*I*n *pathology* (the study of diseases and how they're transmitted) a *contact* is a person who passes on a communicable disease, but in Outlook, a *contact* is someone about whom you keep information. Information about contacts is kept in the Contacts folder. This folder is a super-powered address book. It has places for storing people's names, addresses, phone numbers, e-mail addresses, Web pages, pager numbers, birthdays, anniversaries, nicknames, and other stuff besides. When you enter an e-mail address, you can get it straight from the Contacts folder to be sure that the address is entered correctly. As I explain in Book II, Chapter 5, you can also get addresses from the Contacts folder when you generate form letters, labels, and envelopes for mass mailings in Word.

This short but happy chapter explains how to maintain a tried-and-true Contacts folder, enter information about people in the folder, create contact groups to make sending the same message to many people easier, find a missing contact, and print the information in the Contacts folder.

Maintaining a Happy and Healthy Contacts Folder

A Contacts folder is only as good and as thorough as the information about contacts that you put into it. These pages explain how to enter information about a contact and update the information if it happens to change.

Don't despair if you have been using another software program to track addresses. Chapter 1 of this mini-book explains how to import those addresses into Outlook without having to reenter them.

Entering a new contact in the Contacts folder

To place someone in the Contacts List, open the Contacts folder and start by doing one of the following:

✦ Click the New Contact button.

✦ Press Ctrl+N (in the Contacts Folder window) or Ctrl+Shift+C (in another window).

You see the Contact form, as shown in Figure 2-1. In this form are places for entering just about everything there is to know about a person except his or her favorite color and secret vices. Enter all the information you care to record, keeping in mind these rules of the road as you go along:

Figure 2-1:
A Contact form.

✦ **Full names, addresses, and so on:** Although you may be tempted to simply enter addresses, phone numbers, names, and so on in the text boxes, don't do it! Click the Full Name button, for example, to enter a name (refer to Figure 2-1). Click the Business or Home button to enter an address in the Check Address dialog box (refer to Figure 2-1). By clicking these buttons and entering data in dialog boxes, you permit Outlook to separate the component parts of names, addresses, and phone numbers. As such, Outlook can use names and addresses as a source for mass mailings and mass e-mailings.

When entering information about a company, not a person, leave the Full Name field blank and enter the company's name in the Company field.

+ **Information that matters to you:** If the form doesn't appear to have a place for entering a certain kind of information, try clicking a triangle button and choosing a new information category from the pop-up menu. Click the triangle button next to the Business button and choose Home, for example, if you want to enter a home address rather than a business address.

+ **File As:** Open the File As drop-down list and choose an option for filing the contact in the Contacts folder. Contacts are filed alphabetically by last name, first name, company name, or combinations of the three. Choose the option that best describes how you expect to find the contact in the Contacts folder.

+ **Mailing addresses:** If you keep more than one address for a contact, display the address to which you want to send mail and select the This Is the Mailing Address check box. This way, in a mass mailing, letters are sent to the correct address.

+ **E-mail addresses:** You can enter up to three e-mail addresses for each contact. (Click the triangle button next to the E-mail button and choose E-mail 2 or E-mail 3 to enter a second or third address.) In the Display As text box, Outlook shows you what the To: line of e-mail messages looks like when you send e-mail to a contact. By default, the To: line shows the contact's name followed by his or her e-mail address in parentheses. However, you can enter whatever you want in the Display As text box, and if entering something different helps you distinguish between e-mail addresses, enter something different. For example, enter Lydia – Personal so that you can tell when you send e-mail to Lydia's personal address as opposed to her business address.

+ **Photos:** To put a digital photo in a Contact form, click the Add Contact Photo placeholder, and in the Add Contact Picture dialog box, select a picture and click OK.

+ **Details:** To keep a detailed dossier on a contact, click the Details button (you may have to click the Show button first, depending on the size of your Contact form) and enter information in the Details window. This window offers places for recording birthdays and other minutia.

**Book III
Chapter 2**

**Maintaining the
Contacts Folder**

Be sure to write a few words in the Notes box to describe how and where you met the contact. When the time comes to weed out contacts in the Contacts folder list, reading these descriptions helps you decide who gets weeded and who doesn't.

When you finish entering information, click the Save & Close button. If you're in a hurry to enter contacts, click the Save & New button. Doing so opens an empty form so that you can record information about another contact.

Here's a fast way to enter contact information for someone who has sent you an e-mail message: Open the message, right-click the sender's name in the From: line, and choose Add to Outlook Contacts on the shortcut menu. You see the Contact form. Enter more information about the sender if you can and then click the Save & Close button.

Changing a contact's information

All Fields

Changing a contact's information is a chore if you do it by going from field to field in the General or Details window of the Contact form. A faster way to update the information you have about a contact is to click the All Fields button and enter the information in the All Fields window, as shown in Figure 2-2. The All Fields window lists fields in a line-by-line fashion. Choose an option on the Select From drop-down list, scroll in the form, and update fields as necessary.

Figure 2-2: Editing data in the All Fields window.

Mapping out an address

To find your way to a contact's home or place of business, click the Map It button in the Contact form window (or click the More button and choose Map It). As long as your computer is connected to the Internet and an address is on file for the contact, your Web browser opens to the Bing.com Web site, where you find a map with the address at its center. You can get driving directions from this map. Good luck getting there!

Contact Groups for Sending Messages to Groups

The captain of the volleyball team and the secretary of the PTA are examples of people who have to send e-mail messages to the same group of people on a regular basis. You might be in the same boat. You might have to send e-mail messages to the same 10 or 12 people from time to time. Entering e-mail addresses for that many people each time you want to send e-mail is a drag. To keep from having to enter so many e-mail addresses, you can create a *contact group*, a list with multiple e-mail addresses. To address your e-mail message, you simply enter the name of the contact group, not the individual names, as shown in Figure 2-3.

Figure 2-3: Instead of entering many addresses (top), enter a contact group name (bottom).

Creating a contact group

Follow these steps to bundle e-mail addresses into a contact group:

1. **On the Home tab, click the New Contact Group button (or press Ctrl+Shift+L).**

You see the Contact Group window, as shown in Figure 2-4.

2. **Enter a descriptive name in the Name text box.**

Figure 2-4:
Entering
addresses
for a contact
group.

3. **Click the Add Members button and choose an option on the drop-down list to tell Outlook where you store the addresses of friends and colleagues.**

   If you're a loyal user of Outlook, you likely choose From Outlook Contacts. You see the Select Members dialog box.

4. **Hold down the Ctrl key and select the name of each person you want to include in the contact group.**

5. **Click the Members button and click OK.**

   You can find the Members button in the lower-left corner of the dialog box. The names you chose appear in the Contact Group window.

   You can add the names of people who aren't in your Contacts folder by clicking the Add Members button, choosing New E-Mail Contact on the drop-down list, and filling out the Add New Member dialog box.

6. **Click the Save & Close button in the Contact Group window.**

   In the Contacts folder, contact group names appear in boldface and are marked with the Contact group icon.

Addressing e-mail to a contact group

To address an e-mail message to a contact group, start in the Inbox folder and click the New E-Mail button. A Message window opens. Click the To button to open the Select Names dialog box and then select a contact group name. Contact group names appear in boldface and are marked with a Contact Group icon.

Editing a contact group

The names of contact groups appear in the Contacts folder, where they are boldfaced and marked with an icon showing two heads in profile. You can treat the groups like regular contacts. In the Contacts folder, double-click a contact group name to open the Contact Group window (refer to Figure 2-4). From there, you can add names to and remove names from the group.

Finding a Contact in the Contacts Folder

The Contacts folder can grow very large, so Outlook offers a number of ways to locate contacts. After you find the contact you're looking for, double-click the contact's name to open the Contact form window. Here are some techniques for locating a contact in the Contacts folder:

✦ **Use the scrollbar:** Click the arrows or drag the scroll box to move through the list.

✦ **Click a letter button:** Click a letter button on the right side of the window to move in the list to names beginning with a specific letter.

✦ **Change views:** On the Home tab, go to the Current View gallery and choose a view option: Business Card, Card, Phone, or List. Changing views often helps in a search.

✦ **Type a name in the Find a Contact text box:** On the Home tab, enter a name or e-mail address in this text box and press Enter.

✦ **Search Contacts text box:** Enter a keyword in the Search Contacts text box (see Chapter 1 of this mini-book for instructions about searching for items in folders).

✦ **Search by category:** Categorize contacts as you enter them and switch to By Category view to arrange contacts by category (see Chapter 1 of this mini-book for information about categories).

Printing the Contacts Folder

The paperless office hasn't arrived yet in spite of numerous predictions to the contrary, and sometimes it's necessary to print the Contacts folder on old-fashioned paper. For times like these, I hereby explain the different ways to print the Contacts folder and how to fiddle with the look of the printed pages.

To print information about a single contact, double-click his or her name to open the Contact window. Then press Ctrl+P, and in the Print window, click the Print button.

Different ways to print contact information

Follow these steps to print information about contacts in the Contacts folder:

1. **On the Home tab, open the Current View gallery and choose a view.**

Which printing options you get when you print information from the Contacts folder depends on which view of the Contacts folder is showing when you give the command to print:

- If you start in Business Card or Card view, you can print Contact information in these styles: card style, booklet style, memo style, or phone directory style (you find out what these styles are shortly).

- If you start in Phone or List view, your printing choices are narrower because you can print only in table style.

2. **Press Ctrl+P.**

You see the Print window, as shown in Figure 2-5.

3. **Under Settings, choose an option.**

Glance at the right side of the window to see what the option choices are and choose the option that suits you best.

4. **Click the Print Options button if you want to change the number of columns that are printed, change fonts, change headers and footers, or otherwise fiddle with the printed pages.**

The next section in this chapter explains these options.

5. **Click the Print button to start printing.**

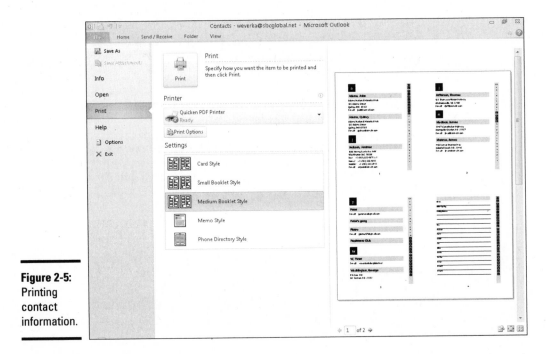

Figure 2-5:
Printing
contact
information.

Changing the look of printed pages

To determine what Contact folder information looks like when you print it, click the Print Options button in the Print window (refer to Figure 2-5). You see the Print dialog box. In this dialog box, click the Page Setup button and choose options on the Format tab of the Page Setup dialog box to change the look of the printed pages:

✦ **Where contact information is printed:** Contact information is printed alphabetically with a letter heading to mark where the As, Bs, Cs, and so on begin. To place contacts that begin with each letter on separate pages, select the Start on a New Page option button.

✦ **Number of columns:** Enter a number in the Number of Columns text box to tell Outlook how many columns you want.

✦ **Contact index:** Select the Contact Index on Side check box to print thumbnail letter headings on the sides of pages.

✦ **Letter headings:** To remove the letter headings that mark where contacts starting with a certain letter begin, deselect the Headings for Each letter check box.

✦ **Fonts and font sizes:** Click a Font button and choose a different font or font size for headings and body text.

✦ **Gray shades:** Gray shades appear behind contact names, but you can remove them by deselecting the Print Using Gray Shading check box.

In the Header/Footer tab, the three boxes are for deciding what appears on the left side, middle, and right side of headers and footers. Type whatever you please into these text boxes. You can also click buttons in the dialog box to enter fields — a page number, total page number, printing date, printing time, or your name — in headers or footers.

Chapter 3: Handling Your E-Mail

In This Chapter

- ✔ Addressing, sending, replying to, and forwarding e-mail messages
- ✔ Sending files and pictures with e-mail
- ✔ Understanding the HTML, plain text, and rich text format
- ✔ Receiving e-mail and files over the Internet
- ✔ Organizing and managing your e-mail
- ✔ Creating and using different folders to store e-mail
- ✔ Preventing junk e-mail

"**N**either snow nor rain nor heat nor gloom of night stays these couriers from the swift completion of their appointed rounds," reads the inscription on the Eighth Avenue New York Post Office Building. E-mailers face a different set of difficulties. Instead of snow, rain, or gloomy nights, they face the task of having to manage volumes of e-mail.

This chapter explains the basics of sending and receiving e-mail, but it also goes a step further to help you organize and manage your e-mail messages. It shows you how to send files and pictures with e-mail messages, and postpone sending a message. You can also find out how to be advised when someone has read your e-mail, reorganize e-mail in the Inbox window, and be alerted to incoming messages from certain people or from people writing about certain subjects. This chapter shows you how to create folders for storing e-mail and explains how to prevent junk e-mail from arriving on your digital doorstep.

Addressing and Sending E-Mail Messages

Sorry, you can't send chocolates or locks of hair by e-mail, but you can send digital pictures and computer files. These pages explain how to do it. You also discover how to send copies and blind copies of e-mail messages, reply to and forward e-mail, send e-mail from different accounts, and postpone sending a message. Better keep reading.

The basics: Sending an e-mail message

The first half of this chapter addresses everything you need to know about sending e-mail messages. Here are the basics:

1. **In the Inbox or Drafts folder, click the New E-Mail button or press Ctrl+N.**

   A Message window like the one in Figure 3-1 appears. You can open this window in a folder apart from the Inbox or Drafts folder by clicking the New Items button and choosing E-Mail Message on the drop-down list (or by pressing Ctrl+Shift+M). The New Items button is located on the Home tab.

2. **Enter the recipient's e-mail address in the To text box.**

   The next topic in this chapter, "Addressing an e-mail message," explains the numerous ways to address an e-mail message. You can address the same message to more than one person by entering more than one address in the To text box. For that matter, you can send copies of the message and blind copies of the message to others (see "Sending copies and blind copies of messages," later in this chapter).

3. **In the Subject text box, enter a descriptive title for the message.**

   When your message arrives on the other end, the recipient sees the subject first. Enter a descriptive subject that helps the recipient decide whether to read the message right away. After you enter the subject, it appears in the title bar of the Message window.

   Outlook offers different ways to get a recipient's attention. For example, you can give your message a priority rating. See the sidebar, "Prioritizing the messages you send," later in this chapter.

4. **Type the message.**

   Whatever you do, don't forget to enter the message itself! You can spell-check your message by pressing F7 or clicking the Spelling & Grammar button on the Review tab.

Figure 3-1:
Addressing and composing an e-mail message.

As long as you compose messages in HTML format and the person receiving your e-mail messages has software capable of reading HTML, you can decorate messages to your heart's content (later in this chapter, "All about Message Formats" explains the HTML issue). Experiment with fonts and font sizes. Boldface and underline text. Throw in a bulleted or numbered list. You can find many formatting commands in the Insert, Options, and Format Text tabs. These are the same formatting commands found in Word.

5. **Click the Send button (or press Alt+S).**

   As "Postponing sending a message" explains later in this chapter, you can put off sending a message. And if you have more than one e-mail account, you can choose which one to send the message with, as "Choosing which account to send messages with" explains. Messages remain in the Outbox folder if you postpone sending them or if Outlook can't send them right away because your computer isn't connected to the Internet.

> If you decide in the middle of writing a message to write the rest of it later, click the Save button on the Quick Access toolbar (or press Ctrl+S) and close the Message window. The message lands in the Drafts folder. When you're ready to finish writing the message, open the Drafts folder and double-click your unfinished message to resume writing it.

Copies of the e-mail messages you send are kept in the Sent Items folder. If you prefer not to keep copies of sent e-mail messages on hand, click the File tab and choose Options. On the Mail category of the Options dialog box, deselect the Save Copies of Messages in Sent Items Folder check box.

Making Outlook your default e-mail program

If you switched to Outlook from Outlook Express or another e-mail program and you like Outlook, you need to tell your computer that Outlook is henceforward the e-mail program you want to use by default. The default e-mail program is the one that opens when you click an e-mail hyperlink on a Web page or give the order to send an Office file from inside an Office program. Follow these steps to make Outlook the default e-mail program on your computer:

1. Go to the File tab and choose Options.

2. In the Outlook Options dialog box, visit the General category.

3. Select the Make Outlook the Default Program for E-Mail, Contacts, and Calendar check box.

4. Click OK.

Addressing an e-mail message

How do you address an e-mail message in the To text box of the Message window (refer to Figure 3-1)? Let me count the ways:

✦ **Get the address (or addresses) from the Contacts folder:** Click the To (or Cc) button to send a message to someone whose name is on file in your Contacts folder. You see the Select Names dialog box, as shown in Figure 3-2. Click or Ctrl+click to select the names of people to whom you want to send the message. Then click the To-> button (or the Cc-> or Bcc-> button) to enter addresses in the To text box (or the Cc or Bcc text boxes) of the Message window. Click OK to return to the Message window. This is the easiest way to address an e-mail message to several different people.

Figure 3-2:
Getting
addresses
from the
Contacts
folder.

✦ **Type a person's name from the Contacts folder:** Simply type a person's name. If the name is on file in the Contacts folder, a drop-down list with the name appears, and you can select the name on the drop-down list.

✦ **Type the address:** Type the address if you know it offhand. You can paste an address into the Message window by right-clicking and choosing the Paste command.

✦ **Reply to a message sent to you:** Select the message in the Inbox folder and click the Reply button. The Message window opens with the address of the person to whom you're replying already entered in the To text box. You can also click the Reply All button to reply to enter the e-mail addresses of all the people to whom the original message was sent.

Sending e-mail from inside another Office program

As long as Outlook is your default e-mail program (I explain how to make it the default program earlier in this chapter), you can send e-mail messages or file attachments from other Office programs without opening Outlook. If the Word document, Excel worksheet, PowerPoint presentation, or Publisher publication needs sending right away, save it and follow these steps to send it as a file attachment to an e-mail message:

1. **With the file you want to send on-screen, go to the File tab and choose Save & Send.**

2. **In the Save & Send window, choose Send Using E-Mail.**

3. **Choose a Send option.**

These options differ from program to program. For example, you can send the file as an attachment to an e-mail message or send it as a PDF file. The Message window appears after you choose a Send option.

4. **Enter the recipient's address in the To box and type a message in the Message box.**

5. **Click the Send button.**

That was fast! It was faster than opening Outlook and attaching the file to the e-mail message on your own. The message is sent right away if Outlook is running. Otherwise, the message is sent next time you open Outlook.

Book III
Chapter 3

Handling Your
E-Mail

You can create contact groups for sending the same e-mail message to a group of people without having to enter an address for each recipient. For information about contact groups, see Chapter 2 of this mini-book.

These days, many people have more than one e-mail address, and when you enter an e-mail address in the To text box of the Message window, it's hard to be sure whether the address you entered is the right one. To make sure that you send e-mail to the right address, go to the Message tab and click the Check Names button (or press Ctrl+K). You see the Check Names dialog box. Select the correct name and address in the dialog box and then click OK.

Sending copies and blind copies of messages

When you send a copy of a message, the person who receives the message knows that copies have been sent because the names of people to whom copies were sent appear at the top of the e-mail message. But when you send blind copies, the person who receives the message doesn't know that others received it.

Follow these instructions to send copies and blind copies of messages:

✦ **Send a copy of a message:** Enter e-mail addresses in the Cc text box of the Message window, or in the Select Names dialog box (refer to Figure 3-2), select names and then click the Cc-> button.

✦ **Send a blind copy of a message:** On the Options tab, click the Bcc button, or click the To or Cc button in the Message window to open the Select Names dialog box (refer to Figure 3-2), select names, and click the Bcc-> button or else enter addresses in the Bcc-> text box.

You may well ask why these buttons are called Cc and Bcc. Why the extra *C*? The Cc stands for "carbon copy" and the Bcc stands for "blind carbon copy." These terms originated in the Mesozoic era when letters were composed on the typewriter, and to make a copy of a letter, you inserted carbon paper between two paper sheets and typed away.

Replying to and forwarding e-mail messages

Replying to and forwarding messages is as easy as pie. For one thing, you don't need to know the recipient's e-mail address to reply to a message. In the Inbox, select or open the message you want to reply to or forward and do the following on the Home tab or Message tab:

✦ **Reply to author:** Click the Reply button (or press Ctrl+R). The Message window opens with the sender's name already entered in the To box and the original message in the text box below. Write a reply and click the Send button.

✦ **Reply to all parties who received the message:** Click the Reply All button (or press Ctrl+Shift+R). The Message window opens with the names of all parties who received the message in the To and Cc boxes and the original message in the text box. Type your reply and click the Send button.

✦ **Forward a message:** Click the Forward button (or press Ctrl+F). The Message window opens with the text of the original message. Either enter an e-mail address in the To text box or click the To button to open the Select Names dialog box and then select the names of the parties to whom the message will be forwarded. Add a word or two to the original message if you like; then click the Send button.

Forwarding a message to a third party without the permission of the original author is a breach of etiquette and very bad manners. I could tell you a story about an e-mail message of mine that an unwitting editor forwarded to a cantankerous publisher, but I'm saving that story for the soap opera edition of this book.

To add a sender's name to the Contacts folder, right-click the name in the Message window and choose Add to Outlook Contacts.

Sending a file along with a message

Sending a file along with an e-mail message is called *attaching* a file in Outlook lingo. Yes, it can be done. You can send a file or several files along with an e-mail message by following these steps:

1. **In the Message window open, go to the Message or Insert tab and click the Attach File button.**

You see the Insert File dialog box.

2. **Locate and select the file that you want to send along with your e-mail message.**

Ctrl+click filenames to select more than one file.

3. **Click the Insert button.**

The name of the file (or files) appears in the Attached text box in the Message window. Address the message and type a note to send along with the file. You can right-click a filename in the Attach text box and choose Open on the shortcut menu to open a file you're about to send. Or, if you change your mind about sending the file, you can click Remove.

TIP

Here's a fast way to attach a file to a message: Find the file in Windows Explorer and drag it into the Message window. The file's name appears in the Attach box as though you placed it there by clicking the Attach File button.

Prioritizing the messages you send

Every day, billions of e-mail messages arrive on people's computers, each one begging for the recipient's attention, each one crying out, "Read me first." With this kind of cutthroat competition, how can you give your e-mail messages a competitive advantage? How can you make yours stand out in the crowd?

The best way is to write a descriptive title in the Subject box of the Message window. The subject is the first thing people see in their Inbox. They decide whether to read a message now, later, or never on the basis of what they see on the Subject line.

Another way to (maybe) get other's attention is to assign a high priority rating to your message. If the recipient reads his or her e-mail with Outlook or Outlook Express, a red exclamation point appears beside the message in the Inbox folder. Conversely, you can assign a low priority to messages as well, in which case a downward-pointing arrow appears next to the message heading in the Inbox folder. However, prioritizing this way is only worthwhile if the recipient runs Outlook or Outlook Express because other e-mail programs don't know what to make of the exclamation point or the arrow.

To assign a priority to a message, go to the Message tab in the Message window and click the High Importance or Low Importance button. In the Inbox folder, click the Sort By Importance button, the leftmost sorting button, to arrange messages by their priority ratings.

Including a picture in an e-mail message

As shown in Figure 3-3, you can include a picture in the body of an e-mail message, but in order to see it, the recipient's e-mail software must display messages by using HTML. As "All about Message Formats" explains later in this chapter, not everyone has software that displays e-mail by using HTML. People who don't have HTML e-mail software get the picture anyhow, but it doesn't appear in the body of the e-mail message; it arrives as an attached file (see "Handling Files That Were Sent to You," later in this chapter, to find out about receiving files by e-mail). To view the attached file, the recipient has to open it with a graphics software program, such as Paint or Windows Picture and Fax Viewer.

Figure 3-3:
Inserting a
picture in
an e-mail
message.

Follow these steps to adorn an e-mail message with a picture:

1. **In the Message window, go to the Insert tab.**

2. **Click in the body of the e-mail message where you want the picture to go.**

3. **Click the Picture button.**

You see the Insert Picture dialog box.

4. **Locate and select the digital picture you want to send; then click the Insert button.**

The picture lands in the Message window. Select the picture, go to the (Picture Tools) Format tab, open the drop-down list on the Wrap Text button, and choose an option to decide how text should behave nearby the picture. Book VIII, Chapter 3 explains graphics in detail; Book I, Chapter 8 explains how to manipulate graphic images.

Want to remove a picture from an e-mail message? Select it and press the Delete key.

Choosing which account to send messages with

If you have more than one e-mail account, you can choose which one to send an e-mail message with. Follow these instructions to choose an account for sending e-mail messages:

+ **Choosing the default account for sending messages:** When you click the Send button in the Message window, the e-mail message is sent by way of the default e-mail account. To tell Outlook which account that is, go to the File tab, choose Info, click the Account Settings button, and choose Account Settings on the drop-down list. You see the Account Settings dialog box. Select the account that you want to be the default and click the Set As Default button.

+ **Sending an individual message:** To bypass the default e-mail account and send a message with a different account, click the Account button in the Message window, and choose an account name from the drop-down list. Then click the Send button.

Postponing sending a message

As you probably know, e-mail messages are sent immediately when you click the Send button in the Message window if your computer is connected to the Internet. If it isn't connected, the message lands in the Outbox folder, where it remains until you connect to the Internet.

But suppose you want to postpone sending a message? Outlook offers two techniques for putting off sending a message:

+ **Moving messages temporarily to the Drafts folder:** Compose your message, click the Save button in the Message window (or press Ctrl+S), and close the Message window. Your e-mail message goes to the Drafts folder. When you're ready to send it, open the Drafts folder, double-click your message to open it, and click the Send button in the Message window.

+ **Postponing the send date:** On the Options tab in the Message window, click the Delay Delivery button. You see the Properties dialog box, as shown in Figure 3-4. Select the Do Not Deliver Before check box, enter a date on the calendar, and if you so desire, select a time from the drop-down list. Then click the Close button. In the Message window, click the Send button. Your message goes to the Outbox folder, where it remains until the time arrives to send it and you open Outlook.

**Book III
Chapter 3**

**Handling Your
E-Mail**

Figure 3-4:
Putting off
sending
an e-mail
message.

Being Advised When Someone Has Read Your E-Mail

Outlook offers a command whereby you can be informed when someone
has received or read an e-mail message you sent. You can even send a mini-
ballot to someone else, solicit their vote, and have the vote sent to you by
e-mail. To perform this magic trick, start in the Message window and go to
the Options tab. In the Tracking group, select one or more of these options:

✦ **Use Voting Buttons:** Voting buttons are included on a drop-down list in
the e-mail message you send. Choose a set of buttons from the drop-
down list, as shown in Figure 3-5. The recipient clicks the Vote button,
chooses an option on a drop-down list, and the response is sent to you
in the form of an e-mail message with the word Approve, Reject, Yes, No,
or Maybe in the subject line.

✦ **Request a Delivery Receipt**: You're informed by e-mail after the message is delivered. Select the Request a Delivery Receipt check box. To be
informed, however, you and the recipient must use the same Exchange
Server, and the recipient must choose to inform you that the message
was delivered. Don't count on this one really working.

✦ **Request a Read Receipt:** The message box appears, as shown in Figure
3-5. If the recipient clicks the Yes button, a Message window appears
immediately so that he or she can send an e-mail informing you that the
message was read. The message, when it arrives on your end, lists the
date and time that the response message was sent. Select the Request a
Read Receipt check box.

The Receipt Read message box

Voting buttons

Figure 3-5:
Making sure
that you get
a response.

All about Message Formats

Outlook offers three formats for sending e-mail messages: HTML, plain text, and rich text. What are the pros and cons of the different formats? How do I choose a format for my e-mail messages? I'm so glad you asked.

The three message formats

Outlook offers these three formats for sending e-mail messages:

✦ **HTML format:** These days, almost all e-mail is transmitted in HTML (HyperText Markup Language) format, the same format with which Web pages are made. If HTML is the default format you use for creating messages in Outlook — and it is unless you tinkered with the default settings — the e-mail messages you send are, in effect, little Web pages. HTML gives you the most opportunities for formatting text and graphics. In HTML format, you can place pictures in the body of an e-mail message, use a background theme, and do any number of sophisticated formatting tricks.

✦ **Plain text format:** In plain text format, only letters and numbers are transmitted. The format doesn't permit you to format text or align paragraphs in any way, but you can rest assured that the person who receives the message can read it exactly as you wrote it.

✦ **Rich text format:** The third e-mail message format, rich text, is proprietary to Microsoft e-mailing software. Only people who use Outlook and Outlook Express can read messages in rich text format, and I don't recommend it for that reason.

When someone sends you an e-mail message, you can tell which format it was transmitted in by looking at the title bar, where *HTML, Plain Text,* or *Rich Text* appears in parentheses after the subject of the message. Outlook is smart enough to transmit messages in HTML, plain text, or rich text format when you reply to a message that was sent to you in that format.

Choosing a format for your e-mail messages

Follow these instructions if you need to change the format in which your e-mail messages are transmitted:

✦ **Changing the default format:** On the File tab, choose Options. In the Options dialog box, go to the Mail category. From the Compose Messages in This Format drop-down list, choose HTML, Rich Text, or Plain Text.

✦ **Changing the format for a single e-mail message:** In the Message window, go to the Format Text tab and click the HTML, Plain Text, or Rich Text button.

Receiving E-Mail Messages

Let's hope that all the e-mail messages you receive carry good news. These pages explain how to collect your e-mail and all the different ways that Outlook notifies you when e-mail has arrived. You can find several tried-and-true techniques for reading e-mail messages in the Inbox window. Outlook offers a bunch of different ways to rearrange the window as well as the messages inside it.

Getting your e-mail

Starting in the Inbox folder on the Send/Receive tab, here are all the different ways to collect e-mail messages that were sent to you:

✦ **Collect all e-mail:** Click the Send/Receive All Folders button (or press F9). Mail is sent from and delivered to all your e-mail accounts.

✦ **Collect mail for the Inbox folder only:** Click the Update Folder button (or press Shift+F9).

✦ **Send all unsent mail:** Click the Send All button.

✦ **Collect e-mail from a single account (if you have more than one):** Click the Send/Receive Groups button, and on the drop-down list, choose the name of a group or an e-mail account. (See the sidebar, "Groups for handling e-mail from different accounts," later in this chapter to find out what groups are.)

✦ **Collect e-mail automatically every few minutes:** Click the Send/Receive Groups button and choose Define Send/Receive Groups on the drop-down list. You see the Send/Receive Groups dialog box, as shown in Figure 3-6. Select a group (groups are explained in the sidebar, "Groups for handling e-mail from different accounts"), select the Schedule an Automatic Send/Receive Every check box, and enter a minutes setting. To temporarily suspend automatic e-mail collections, click the Send/Receive Groups button and choose Disable Scheduled Send/Receive.

Figure 3-6: Handling group settings.

Send/Receive Groups

A Send/Receive group contains a collection of Outlook accounts and folders. You can specify the tasks that will be performed on the group during a send/receive.

Group Name	Send/Receive when
All Accounts	Online and Offline
Main E-Mail Account	Offline Only

New...
Edit...
Copy...
Remove
Rename

Setting for group "All Accounts"

☑ Include this group in send/receive (F9).
☑ Schedule an automatic send/receive every 30 minutes.
☐ Perform an automatic send/receive when exiting.

When Outlook is Offline

☑ Include this group in send/receive (F9).
☐ Schedule an automatic send/receive every 30 minutes.

Close

Book III
Chapter 3

Handling Your
E-Mail

Being notified that e-mail has arrived

Take the e-mail arrival quiz. Winners get the displeasure of knowing that they understand far more than is healthy about Outlook. You can tell when e-mail has arrived in the Inbox folder because:

A) You hear this sound: *ding*.

B) The mouse cursor briefly changes to a little envelope.

C) A little envelope appears in the notification area to the left of the Windows clock. (You can double-click the envelope to open the Inbox folder.)

D) A pop-up *desktop alert* with the sender's name, the message's subject, and the text of the message appears briefly on your desktop.

E) All of the above.

The answer is E, "All of the above," but if four arrival notices strike you as excessive, you can eliminate one or two. On the File tab, choose Options, and on the Mail tab of the Options dialog box, go the Message Arrival area and change the settings.

Groups for handling e-mail from different accounts

Groups are meant to help people who have more than one e-mail account handle their e-mail. To begin with, all e-mail accounts belong to a group called All Accounts. Unless you change the default settings, all your e-mail accounts belong to the All Accounts group, and e-mail is sent by and received from all your e-mail accounts at the same time.

If you want to change these default settings, go to the Send/Receive tab, click the Send/Receive Groups button, and choose Define Send/Receive Groups on the drop-down list. You see the Send/Receive Groups dialog box (refer to Figure 3-6). Follow these instructions in the dialog box to change how you handle e-mail from different accounts:

✔ **Excluding an account from the All Accounts group**: Exclude an account if you don't want to collect its e-mail on a regular basis. Maybe you want to collect mail from this account sporadically. To exclude an account, select the All Accounts group and click the Edit button. You land in the Send/Receive Settings – All Accounts dialog box. In the Accounts list, select the account you want to exclude and deselect the Include the Selected Account in this Group check box.

✔ **Creating a new group:** Create a new group if you want to establish settings for a single e-mail account or group of accounts. Click the New button in the Send/Receive Groups dialog box, enter a name in the Send/Receive Group Name dialog box, and click OK. You see the Send/Receive Settings dialog box. For each account you want to include in your new group, select an account name and then select the Include the Select Account in This Group check box.

✔ **Choosing settings for a group:** In the Send/Receive Groups dialog box, select the group whose settings you want to establish. At the bottom of the dialog box (see Figure 3-6), select whether to send and receive e-mail when you press F9, whether to send and receive automatically every few minutes, and whether to send and receive when you exit Outlook.

Reading Your E-Mail in the Inbox Window

Messages arrive in the Inbox window, as shown in Figure 3-7. In the window, unread messages are shown in boldface type and have envelope icons next to their names; messages that you've read (or at least opened to view) are shown in Roman type and appear beside open envelope icons. In the Folder List, a number in parentheses beside the Inbox folder and Deleted Items folder tells you how many unread messages are in those folders. (The number in square brackets beside the Drafts and Junk E-Mail folders tells you how many items, read and unread, are in those folders).

To read a message, select it and look in the Reading pane, or to focus more closely on a message, double-click it to open it in a Message window, as shown in Figure 3-7.

Reading pane

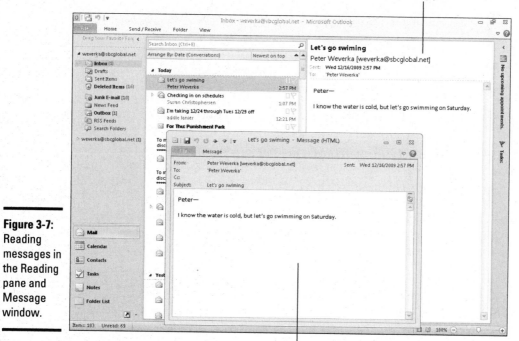

Figure 3-7:
Reading
messages in
the Reading
pane and
Message
window.

Message window

Later in this chapter, "Techniques for Organizing E-Mail Messages," explains
how to organize messages in the Inbox folder. Meanwhile, here are some
simple techniques you can use on the View tab to unclutter the Inbox folder
and make messages easier to read:

✦ **Changing your view of messages:** Click the Change View button and
choose Compact, Single, or Preview on the drop-down list. Compact and
Single display more messages on-screen. In Preview view, the first two
lines of unread messages appear so that you can read them.

✦ **Rearranging messages:** Open the Arrange By gallery and choose an
option. For example, choose Date to arrange messages according to the
date and time they were received. Choose From to arrange messages
by sender name in alphabetical order. Click the Reverse Sort button to
reverse the way the messages are arranged.

✦ **Arranging messages by group:** After you choose a means of arranging
messages, open the Arrange By gallery and select or deselect the Show in
Groups option. Grouped items appear under headings. For example, if you
choose From to arrange messages by sender, messages are displayed
under senders' names when you select the Show in Groups option.

You can expand and collapse groups by clicking the triangle buttons beside their names or by clicking the Expand/Collapse button and making a choice on the drop-down list.

✦ **Arranging messages by conversation:** If you arrange messages by date, you can also arrange messages by conversation, as shown in Figure 3-8. A *conversation* is a back-and-forth collection of e-mails between the same two people or group of people about the same subject. Click the Show As Conversations check box, click the Conversation Settings button, and choose options on the drop-down list to view e-mails in conversation groups.

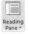

✦ **Hiding and displaying the Reading pane:** Click the Reading Pane button and choose Off, Right, or Bottom on the drop-down list to make the Reading pane appear or disappear. The Reading pane gives you an opportunity to read messages without opening them in a Message window.

✦ **Hiding and displaying the Navigation pane:** Click the Navigation Pane button and choose Normal or Minimized (or press Alt+F1). By hiding the Navigation pane, you get even more room to display messages.

Click to expand the conversation

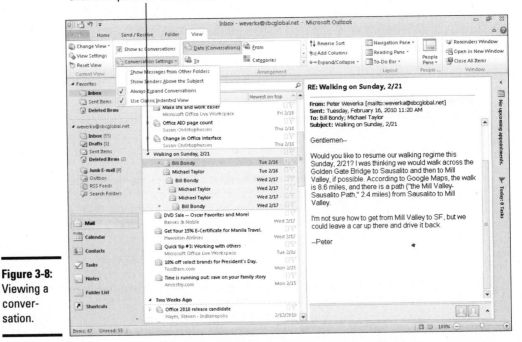

Figure 3-8: Viewing a conversation.

Suppose you open an e-mail message but you regret doing so because you want the unopened envelope icon to appear beside the message's name. In other words, you want to handle the message later on. To make a message in the Inbox window appear as if it has never been opened, right-click it and choose Mark As Unread.

Handling Files That Were Sent to You

You can tell when someone sends you files along with an e-mail message because the paper clip icon appears in the Attachment column of the Inbox window (if column headings are displayed), as shown in Figure 3-9. The name of the file that was sent to you appears in the Reading pane (if the Reading pane is open) and in the Message window as well if you open the message in a window.

Attached file

Click to save files

Figure 3-9:
Receiving a
file.

Right-click to handle incoming files

Files that are sent to you land deep inside your computer in a subfolder of the Temporary Internet Files folder where you will never find them. The best way to handle an incoming file is to save it right away to a folder where you can find it when you need it.

Saving a file you received

To save a file that was sent to you and stash it in a folder of your choice, do one of the following:

✦ Click to select the filename, and on the (Attachment Tools) Attachments tab, click the Save As button and save the file using the Save Attachment dialog box. Click the Save All Attachments button to save more than one file.

✦ Right-click the filename, choose Save As on the shortcut menu, and save the file in the Save Attachment dialog box. Right-click and choose Save All Attachments to save more than one file.

Opening a file you received

Use any of the following ways to open a file that was sent to you:

✦ Double-click the filename.

✦ Click to select the filename, and on the (Attachment Tools) Attachments tab, click the Open button.

✦ Right-click the filename and choose Open on the shortcut menu.

If the file you receive is a Word, PowerPoint, Excel, or Publisher file, you can preview it inside the Message window or Reading pane. To do so, right-click the filename and choose Preview on the shortcut menu.

Techniques for Organizing E-Mail Messages

If you're one of those unfortunate souls who receives 20, 30, 40 or more e-mail messages daily, you owe it to yourself and your sanity to figure out a way to organize e-mail messages such that you keep the ones you want, you can find e-mail messages easily, and you can quickly eradicate the e-mail messages that don't matter to you. Outlook offers numerous ways to manage and organize e-mail messages. Pick and choose the techniques that work for you.

In a nutshell, here are all the techniques for organizing e-mail messages:

✦ **Change views in the Inbox window:** On the View tab, click the Change View button and choose a view. Earlier in this chapter, "Reading Your E-Mail in the Inbox Window" explains all the ways to change views.

✦ **Delete the messages that you don't need:** Before they clutter the Inbox, delete messages that you're sure you don't need as soon as you get them. To delete a message, select it and click the Delete button on the Home tab, press the Delete key, or right-click and choose Delete.

✦ **Move messages to different folders:** Create a folder for each project you're involved with, and when an e-mail message about a project arrives, move it to a folder. See "All about E-Mail Folders," later in this chapter.

✦ **Move messages automatically to different folders as they arrive:** Instead of moving messages yourself after they arrive, you can tell

Outlook to move messages automatically to different folders. See "Rules for earmarking messages as they arrive," later in this chapter.

✦ **Destroy junk mail as it arrives:** You can delete junk mail automatically. See "Yes, You Can Prevent Junk Mail (Sort Of)," later in this chapter.

Ignore

✦ **Ignore messages from pesky senders:** On the Home tab, select a message and click the Ignore button to prevent messages from a sender from appearing in the Inbox. Ignored messages go straight to the Deleted Items folder.

✦ **Flag messages:** Flag a message with a color-coded flag to let you know to follow up on it. See "Flagging e-mail messages," the next section in this chapter.

✦ **Categorize messages:** Assign e-mail messages to categories; then, arrange e-mail messages by category in the Inbox window. See Chapter 1 of this mini-book for info about categorizing items in a folder.

✦ **Have Outlook remind you to reply to a message:** Instruct Outlook to make the Reminder message box appear at a date and time in the future so that you know to reply to a message. See "Being reminded to take care of e-mail messages," later in this chapter.

✦ **Make liberal use of the Search commands:** You can always find a stray message with the Search commands. (See Chapter 1 of this mini-book to know more about searching for items in folders.)

✦ **Archive messages you no longer need:** Archiving is a good way to strip the Inbox folder of items that you don't need. See Chapter 1 of this mini-book for more about archiving.

✦ **Use the Mailbox Cleanup command:** This handy command archives messages, deletes them, and deletes alternate versions of messages. See Chapter 1 of this mini-book for more about the Mailbox Cleanup command.

Flagging e-mail messages

One way to call attention to e-mail messages is to flag them with a color-coded flag. You can use red flags, for example, to mark urgent messages and green flags to mark not-so-important ones. After you flag a message, you can arrange messages by their flag status in the Inbox folder. Follow these instructions to flag an e-mail message:

Follow Up ▾

✦ **Starting in the Message window:** Click the Follow Up button and choose a flag on the drop-down list.

✦ **Starting in the Inbox folder:** Select the message, and on the Home tab, click the Follow Up button and choose a flag. You can also right-click, choose Follow Up, and choose a flag.

Book III
Chapter 3

Handling Your
E-Mail

To "unflag" a message, click the Follow Up button and choose Clear Flag, or right-click and choose Clear Flag. You can also choose Mark Complete to put a checkmark where the flag used to be and remind yourself that you're done with the message. Later in this chapter, "Rules for earmarking messages as they arrive" explains how you can flag messages automatically as they arrive.

Being reminded to take care of e-mail messages

If you know your way around the Calendar and Tasks windows, you know that the Reminder message box appears when an appointment or meeting is about to take place or a task deadline is about to arrive. What you probably don't know, however, is that you can put the Reminders dialog box to work in regard to e-mail messages by following these steps:

1. **Select the message.**

2. **Click the Follow Up button and choose Add Reminder.**

   You see the Custom dialog box, as shown in Figure 3-10. You can also right-click a message and choose Follow Up⇨Add Reminder to see the dialog box.

Figure 3-10: Reminding yourself to take care of an e-mail message.

Click to open the e-mail message

3. **On the Flag To drop-down list, choose an option that describes why the e-mail message needs your attention later, or if none of the options suits you, enter a description in the Flag To text box.**

   The description you choose or enter will appear above the message in the Reading pane and message window, as well in the Reminder message box (refer to Figure 3-10).

4. **In the Due Date drop-down list, choose when you want the Reminder message box to appear.**

As Chapter 5 of this mini-book explains in detail, the Reminder message box appears 15 minutes before the default due date time.

5. **Click OK.**

   When the reminder falls due, you see the Reminder message box (refer to Figure 3-10), where you can click the Open Item button to open the e-mail message. See Chapter 5 of this mini-book if you need to find out how the Reminder message box works.

Rules for earmarking messages as they arrive

To help you organize messages better, Outlook gives you the opportunity to mark messages in various ways and even move messages automatically as they arrive to folders apart from the Inbox folder. Being able to move messages immediately to a folder is a great way to keep e-mail concerning different projects separate. If you belong to a newsgroup that sends many messages per day, being able to move those messages instantly into their own folder is a real blessing because newsgroup messages have a habit of cluttering the Inbox folder.

To earmark messages for special treatment, Outlook has you create so-called rules. To create a rule, start by trying out the Create Rule command, and if that doesn't work, test-drive the more powerful Rules Wizard.

**Book III
Chapter 3**

Simple rules with the Create Rule command

Use the Create Rule command to be alerted when e-mail arrives from a certain person or the Subject line of a message includes a certain word. You can make the incoming message appear in the New Mail Alerts window (as shown at the top of Figure 3-11), play a sound when the message arrives, or move the message automatically to a certain folder.

Follow these steps to create a simple rule:

1. **Select an e-mail message from a person whose messages require a rule.**

2. **On the Home tab, click the Rules button.**

   You see the Create Rule dialog box (refer to Figure 3-11).

3. **Fill in the dialog box and click OK.**

   These commands are self-explanatory.

To change or delete a rule, click the Rules button and choose Manage Rules & Alerts. On the E-Mail Rules tab of the Rules and Alerts dialog box, select a rule and change, copy, or delete it.

Figure 3-11:
The New
Mail Alerts
window
(top) and
Create Rule
dialog box
(bottom).

Complex rules with the Rules Wizard

Use the Rules Wizard to create complex rules that earmark messages with words in the message body or earmark messages sent to contact groups. You can also create a rule to flag messages automatically or delete a conversation (the original message and all its replies).

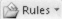

To run the Rules Wizard, go to the Home tab, click the Rules button, and choose Manage Rules & Alerts. You see the Rules and Alerts dialog box. On the E-Mail Rules tab, click the New Rule button and keep clicking Next in the Rules Wizard dialog boxes as you complete the two steps to create a rule:

✦ **Step 1:** Choose the rule you want to create or how you want to be alerted in the New Mail Alerts window (refer to Figure 3-11).

✦ **Step 2:** Click a hyperlink to open a dialog box and describe the rule. For example, click the Specific Words link to open the Search Text dialog box and enter the words that earmark a message. Click the Specified link to open the Rules and Alerts dialog box and choose a folder to move the messages to. You must click each link in the Step 2 box to describe the rule.

To edit a rule, double-click it in the Rules and Alerts dialog box and complete Steps 1 and 2 all over again.

All about E-Mail Folders

Where Outlook e-mail is concerned, everything has its place and everything has its folder. E-mail messages land in the Inbox folder when they arrive.

Messages you write go to the Outbox folder until you send them. Copies of e-mail messages you send are kept in the Sent Items folder. And you can create folders of your own for storing e-mail.

If you're one of those unlucky people who receive numerous e-mail messages each day, you owe it to yourself to create folders in which to organize e-mail messages. Create one folder for each project you're working on. That way, you know where to find e-mail messages when you want to reply to or delete them. These pages explain how to move e-mail messages between folders and create folders of your own for storing e-mail.

Moving e-mail messages to different folders

Open or select the message you want to move and use one of these techniques to move an e-mail message to a different folder:

✦ On the Home tab or Message tab, click the Move button and choose a folder name on the drop-down list. If the folder's name isn't on the list, choose Other Folder and select a folder in the Move Items dialog box.

✦ Right-click, choose Move, and select a folder name or choose Other Folder and select a folder in the Move Items dialog box.

✦ Display the folder you want to receive the message in the Navigation pane. Then drag the message from the Inbox to the folder in the Navigation pane.

Earlier in this chapter, "Rules for earmarking messages as they arrive" explains how to move e-mail messages automatically to folders as e-mail is sent to you.

Creating a new folder for storing e-mail

Follow these steps to create a new folder:

1. **On the Folder tab, click the New Folder button.**

You see the Create New Folder dialog box, as shown in Figure 3-12. You can also open this dialog box by pressing Ctrl+Shift+E or right-clicking a folder in the Folder list and choosing New Folder.

2. **Select the folder that the new folder will go inside.**

To create a first-level folder, select Personal Folders (or the name of the topmost folder in the hierarchy).

3. **Enter a name for the folder.**

4. **Click OK.**

To delete a folder you created, open it, go to the Folder tab, and click the Delete Folder button. Items in the folder are deleted along with the folder itself. To rename a folder, open it, go to the Folder tab, click the Rename Folder button, and enter a new name.

Figure 3-12:
Creating a
new folder.

Outlook maintains a folder called Junk E-Mail especially for storing junk e-mail, or *spam* as the digital variety is sometimes called. E-mail messages with certain words or phrases in the Subject line — *for free!*, *money-back guarantee*, *order now* — are routed automatically to the Junk E-Mail folder, where they needn't bother you. What's more, you can add senders' names to the Blocked Senders list and route mail from those senders straight into the Junk E-Mail folder.

As nice as it is, the Junk E-Mail folder has one fatal flaw — sometimes a legitimate e-mail message finds its way into the folder. From time to time, you have to look in the Junk E-Mail folder to see whether something of value is in there — and that sort of defeats the purpose of routing messages automatically to the Junk E-Mail folder. You still have to look through all that junk e-mail!

Realistically, the only way to prevent getting junk e-mail is to safeguard your e-mail address. These pages explain how to help stamp out junk mail in your lifetime by using features inside Outlook and taking preventive measures.

Defining what constitutes junk e-mail

Outlook maintains a *Safe Senders* and *Blocked Senders list* to help distinguish e-mail from junk e-mail. To help Outlook recognize junk e-mail and route it to the Junk E-Mail folder, you can take these measures to add addresses to the lists:

Yes, You Can Prevent Junk Mail (Sort Of)

✦ **Add a sender to the Safe Senders list:** Senders on this list are deemed legitimate, and their e-mail messages are always routed to the Inbox folder. In the Message window or Home tab of a mail folder, click the Junk button and choose Never Block Sender. Choose this option if you find a legitimate e-mail message in the Junk E-Mail folder.

✦ **Add an address to the Blocked Senders list:** E-mail from senders on the Blocked Senders list goes straight to the Junk E-Mail folder. In the Message window or Home tab of a mail folder, click the Junk button and choose Block Sender.

✦ **Edit the Safe Senders and Blocked Senders lists:** Click the Junk button and choose Junk E-Mail Options. The Junk E-Mail Options dialog box opens. On the Safe Senders and Blocked Senders tab, select e-mail addresses as necessary, and click the Remove button.

To quickly move an e-mail message from the Junk E-Mail folder to the Inbox folder, click the Junk button and choose Not Junk on the drop-down list. The Mark As Not Junk dialog box appears. Click the Always Trust E-Mail From check box and click OK.

Preventive medicine for junk e-mail

As zealous as Outlook is about preventing junk e-mail, the program can't really do the job. Junk e-mailers change addresses frequently. They are clever about putting words in the subject lines of their messages so that the messages aren't recognized as spam. The only foolproof way to keep your e-mail address free of junk e-mail is to follow these suggestions:

✦ **Use a secondary e-mail address:** Create a secondary e-mail account and give its e-mail address to businesses and merchants on the Internet who might sell your address to spammers or might themselves be spammers. The Internet offers many places to create free Web-based e-mail accounts. For example, check out Gmail (`http://gmail.google.com`) and Yahoo! Mail (`http://mail.yahoo.com`). Never give your primary e-mail address to strangers.

✦ **Don't reply to spam:** Don't reply to junk e-mail messages under any circumstances. By replying, all you do is alert the spammer to the fact that your e-mail address is legitimate, and that makes you a target of even more spam.

✦ **Don't unsubscribe to junk e-mail messages:** Some spam messages contain an Unsubscribe link that you can click to prevent more messages from coming. The links are a ruse. All you do by clicking them is make spammers aware that your e-mail address is live and therefore worth targeting with more spam.

✦ **Don't buy anything advertised by spam:** Even if the message is selling what looks to be a terrific bargain, resist the temptation. By buying, you expose yourself to all the risks of replying to junk e-mail.

**Book III
Chapter 3**

**Handling Your
E-Mail**

✦ **Be careful where (and how) you post your e-mail address:** Spammers gather e-mail addresses from the Internet. They get the addresses from Web pages, newsgroups, chat rooms, and message boards. Harvestware, a variety of spamware, can scour the Internet for the telltale "at" symbol (@) found in e-mail addresses and copy those addresses back to a spammer's computer. If you have to post your e-mail address on the Internet, get around the problem by putting blank spaces between the letters in your address, or spell out the address like so:

```
johndoe at earthlink dot net
```

Chapter 4: Managing Your Time and Schedule

In This Chapter

✔ **Understanding how the Calendar works**

✔ **Going to different dates in the Calendar**

✔ **Scheduling appointments and events**

✔ **Rescheduling an activity**

✔ **Getting different views of your schedule**

The purpose of the Outlook Calendar is to keep you from arriving a day late and a dollar short. Use the Calendar to schedule meetings and appointments. Use it to make the most of your time. This chapter explains how to go from day to day, week to week, and month to month in the Calendar window. It shows you how to schedule and reschedule appointments and meetings and look at your schedule in different ways.

Introducing the Calendar

Calendar

Use the Calendar to juggle appointments and meetings, remind yourself where you're supposed to be, and get there on time. Surveying your schedule in the Calendar window is easy. Merely by clicking a button, you can tell where you're supposed to be today, any given day, this week, this work week, this month, or any month.

Figure 4-1 shows, for example, someone's schedule during the work week of December 14–18 (a work week comprises Monday through Friday, not Monday through Sunday). All you have to do to find out how busy you are on a particular day, week, or month is gaze at the Calendar window. Whether someone invites you to a meeting or wants to schedule an appointment, you can open the Calendar and see right away if your schedule permits you to attend the meeting or make the appointment.

Click to change views   Date Navigator

Figure 4-1:
The
Calendar in
Work Week
view.

Outlook gives you opportunities to categorize meetings and appointments so that you can tell at a glance what they're all about. Moving a meeting or appointment is simply a matter of dragging it elsewhere in the Calendar window. By double-clicking a meeting or appointment in the Calendar window, you can open a window to find out where the meeting takes place or read notes you jotted down about the meeting. You can even make a bell ring and the Reminder message box appear when a meeting or appointment is forthcoming.

To make the Task List, an abbreviated Tasks window, appear below the Calendar window, go to the View tab, click the To-Do Bar button, and choose Task List on the drop-down list. Chapter 5 of this mini-book explains how to schedule tasks in the Tasks window.

The Different Kinds of Activities

For scheduling purposes, Outlook makes a distinction between appointments, events, and meetings. Meetings, however, aren't everybody's concern. If your computer is connected to a network and the network uses the Microsoft Exchange Server, you can use Outlook to invite colleagues on the network to come to meetings. But if your computer isn't on a network, don't bother with meetings. Schedule appointments and events instead. You can schedule the following activities:

✦ **Appointment:** An activity that occupies a certain time period on a certain day. For example, a meeting that takes place between 11 a.m. and 12 p.m. is an appointment.

✦ **Recurring appointment:** An appointment that takes place daily, weekly, or monthly on the same day and same time each day, week, or month. A weekly staff meeting is a recurring appointment. The beauty of recurring appointments is that Outlook enters them weeks and months in advance in the Calendar window. You don't have to reenter these appointments over and over.

✦ **Event:** An activity that lasts all day. A trade show, for example, is an event. A birthday is an event. A day spent on vacation is also an event (is it ever!). On the Calendar, events and recurring events appear first.

✦ **Recurring event:** An all-day activity that takes place each week, month, or year. Unromantic (or forgetful) users of Outlook are hereby advised to schedule these recurring events in the Calendar: Valentine's Day, their significant other's birthday, and first-date and wedding anniversaries. Thanks to Outlook, no one will ever accuse you again of being cold-hearted or indifferent.

✦ **Meeting:** Same as an appointment except that you can invite others to attend. Scheduling meetings isn't covered in this book. See your network administrator for details.

Seeing Your Schedule

Days on which meetings or appointments are scheduled appear in boldface in the Date Navigator, the calendar in the upper-right corner of the window (refer to Figure 4-1). Following are techniques for getting around in the Calendar window and viewing your schedule in different ways.

Going to a different day, week, or month

Use these techniques to go to different days, weeks, or months in the Calendar window:

✦ **To today:** On the Home tab, click the Today button. Clicking this button selects today's date on your calendar in whatever view you happen to be in.

✦ **To the next seven days:** On the Home tab, click the Next 7 Days button to see the next seven days starting with today's date.

✦ **To a specific day:** Click a day in the Date Navigator in the To-Do bar. You can also press Ctrl+G and select a day in the Go To Date dialog box. If you don't see the Date Navigator, go to the View tab, click the To-Do Bar button, and choose Date Navigator on the drop-down list.

✦ **To the previous or next day, work week, week, or month:** Click a Back or Forward arrow. These arrows are in the upper-left corner of the Calendar window and on either side of the month name in the Date Navigator.

Here's a quick way to go from month to month in the Date Navigator: Click the month name in the Date Navigator and hold down the mouse button. You see a list of month names. Drag the pointer to the name of the month you want to go to.

Use the scroll bar on the right side of the window to travel from hour to hour in Day view and Work Week view. In Week view and Month view, manipulating the scroll bar takes you from week to week.

Rearranging the Calendar window

To get a sense of what is expected of you and where you're supposed to be, go to the Home or View tab and click one of these buttons to rearrange your view of the Calendar window:

✦ **Day:** Shows today's date only.

✦ **Work Week:** Shows Monday through Friday of this week.

✦ **Week:** Shows the entire week, Sunday through Saturday.

✦ **Month:** Shows the entire month. In Month view, you can open the drop-down list on the Month button and choose a Detail option (Low, Medium, or High) to see increasing levels of information about the appointments and meetings you've scheduled.

Scheduling Appointments and Events

Now that you know how the Calendar window works, the next step is to fill the pages of the Calendar with all kinds of busywork. These pages explain how to schedule activities, schedule recurring activities, and magically transform an e-mail message into a Calendar item. You can find many intriguing shortcuts on these pages.

Scheduling an activity: The basics

Follow these basic steps to schedule an appointment, recurring appointment, event, or recurring event:

1. **Select the day in which you want to schedule the activity.**

If the activity occupies a certain time period, you can select the time period in Day or Week view and save yourself the trouble of entering a time period in the Appointment window. To select a time period, drag downward in the Calendar window. To create a half-hour appointment, simply double-click a half-hour slot in Day or Week view. The Appointment dialog box opens with the Start and End time entered already.

2. **Click the New Appointment button (or press Ctrl+N).**

   As shown in Figure 4-2, you see the Appointment window for naming the activity, stating its starting and ending time, and choosing whether you want to be alerted to its occurrence. In a folder apart from the Calendar, you can display this window by going to the Home tab, clicking the New Items button, and choosing Appointment on the drop-down list.

Click to schedule a recurring appointment or event

Figure 4-2: The window for scheduling activities.

Click to schedule an event

3. **Enter information in the Appointment tab.**

   Enter a subject, location (you can open the drop-down list and choose one you've entered before), start date and time, and end date and time. To enter a recurring event or appointment, click the Recurrence button. To enter an event rather than an appointment, click the All Day Event check box.

   If the appointment time you enter conflicts with an appointment you've already scheduled, the Appointment window tells you as much. You can click the Calendar button to view the calendar and look for open timeslots.

4. **Open the Reminder drop-down list and choose an option if you want to be reminded when the activity is imminent (or choose None if you don't care to be reminded).**

Choose an option from the drop-down list to make the Reminder message box appear before the activity begins. Chapter 5 of this mini-book explains how reminders work.

5. **Click the Save & Close button when you finish describing the appointment or event.**

The appointment or event is entered in the Calendar window.

Scheduling a recurring appointment or event

To enter a recurring appointment or event, click the Recurrence button in the Appointment window (refer to Figure 4-2). You see the Appointment Recurrence dialog box, as shown in Figure 4-3. Describe how persistent the activity is and click OK:

✦ **Appointment Time:** Enter the starting and ending time, if you didn't do so already in the Appointment form.

Figure 4-3:
My, this appointment is persistent!

Choose an option from the drop-down list... [Appointment Recurrence dialog box]

Appointment Recurrence

Appointment time

Start: 7:00 PM

End: 12:00 PM

Duration: 17 hours

Recurrence pattern

○ Daily   Recur every 1 week(s) on:
◉ Weekly   ☐ Sunday ☐ Monday ☐ Tuesday ☐ Wednesday
○ Monthly ☑ Thursday ☐ Friday ☐ Saturday
○ Yearly

Range of recurrence

Start: Thu 12/17/2009   ◉ No end date
                         ○ End after: 10 occurrences
                         ○ End by: Thu 2/18/2010

OK   Cancel   Remove Recurrence

✦ **Recurrence Pattern:** Use the options and drop-down lists to describe how often the activity recurs.

✦ **Range of Recurrence:** Describe when the recurring events will cease recurring. Choose the No End Date option button if the activity occurs *ad infinitum, ad nauseam* (that's Latin for "unto infinity, most nauseously").

In the Calendar window, recurring activities are shown in green and are marked by the arrow chasing its tail icon. To change a recurring activity into a one-time activity, select the activity in the calendar, go to the (Calendar Tools) Appointment Series tab, click the Recurrence button, and in the Appointment Recurrence dialog box, click the Remove Recurrence button.

Using an e-mail message to schedule an appointment

Here's a neat little trick that can save you time when e-mail correspondence has to do with scheduling an appointment. To get a head start on scheduling, drag the e-mail message from the Inbox folder to the Calendar folder in the Navigation pane. On the theory that you want to schedule an appointment around the information in the e-mail message, the Appointment window appears on-screen. For the subject of the appointment, Outlook enters the subject of the e-mail message. The text of the e-mail message appears in the window as well. Fiddle with the particulars of the appointment and click the Save & Close button.

Scheduling an event

Select the All Day Event check box in the Appointment window (refer to Figure 4-2) to schedule an event, not an appointment. As I explain earlier, an event is an activity that lasts all day. In the Calendar, events are listed at the start of the day before appointments and meetings.

Canceling, Rescheduling, and Altering Activities

Canceling, rescheduling, and altering appointments and events is pretty easy. You can always double-click an activity to open an Appointment or Event window and change the particulars there. And you can take advantage of these shortcuts:

✦ **Canceling:** Select an activity, go the (Calendar Tools) Appointment tab, and click the Delete button. When you click the Delete button to cancel a recurring activity, a drop-down list appears on the Delete button so that you can delete one occurrence of the activity or the entire series.

✦ **Rescheduling:** Drag the activity to a new location in the schedule. Release the mouse button when the activity is in the new timeslot.

✦ **Changing start and end times:** In Day, Work Week, or Week view, move the pointer over the top or bottom of the activity and start dragging when you see the double arrow.

✦ **Changing the description:** Click in the activity's box and start typing or editing.

Chapter 5: Tasks, Reminders, and Notes

In This Chapter

✔ **Creating, handling, and managing tasks**

✔ **Being reminded when deadlines and activities are forthcoming**

✔ **Jotting down digital notes**

This short chapter describes some Outlook goodies that were neglected in the other chapters of this mini-book. It explains how the Tasks window can help you meet your deadlines and how to be alerted when an activity is looming, a task deadline is arriving, an e-mail message needs your attention, or someone in your Contacts folder needs love and attention. Finally, it explain Outlook's digital stick 'em notes.

Tasks: Seeing What Needs to Get Done

☑ Tasks

As shown in Figure 5-1, use the Tasks window to see what needs to be done, when it's due, and whether it's overdue. On this list, due dates clearly show how smartly the whip is being cracked and how close you are to meeting or missing deadlines. A gray line appears across tasks that are done. Tasks that are overdue appear in red. Read on if you want to find out how to enter a task, attach a file to a task, and manage tasks in the Tasks window.

Select a task   Tasks on the To-Do bar

Examine it in the Reading pane

The best way to examine tasks is to display the Reading pane. This way,
you can select a task and read notes you've made about it (refer to Figure
5-1). To display the Reading pane, go to the View tab, click the Reading Pane
button, and choose Right or Bottom on the drop-down list.

Entering a task in the Tasks window

Outlook offers two ways to enter a task in the Tasks window:

✦ **The fast way:** Click at the top of the window where it says "Click here to
add a new Task," type a few words to describe the task, press the Tab
key to go to the Due Date box, and enter the due date there. To enter the
date, type it or open the drop-down calendar and choose a date there.

✦ **The slow but thorough way:** On the Home tab, click the New Task button
(or press Ctrl+N). You see the Task window, as shown in Figure 5-2. In this
window are places for describing the task, entering start and due dates,
describing the task's status, prioritizing the task, and jotting down notes
about it. Click the Save & Close button when you finish describing the task.

By clicking the Recurrence button in the Task window, you can enter a Sisyphean task that gets repeated over and over again. In the Task Recurrence dialog box, describe how often the task recurs. Recurring tasks are marked in the Tasks window with an unusual icon. What is that? Looks to me like a clipboard with a piece of toilet paper stuck to it.

Figure 5-2:
Describing
a task.

Click the Details button in the Task window to track the hours you worked on a project, the companies you worked for, and how many miles you logged going to and fro in your work.

Attaching a file to a task

Attaching a file to a task is a neat way to get down to work quickly. Instead of fumbling in your computer for a Word document, Excel worksheet, or other type of file to work on, you can open it merely by double-clicking its name in the Tasks window or Reading pane of the Tasks folder. To attach a file to a task:

✓ Go to the Insert tab in the Task window and click the Attach File button. Then, in the Insert File dialog box, select the file and click the Insert button.

✓ Drag and drop a file to the Task window.

Examining tasks in the Tasks window

Juggling many different tasks is a high art, and to help you get better at it, the Tasks window offers these techniques for examining tasks that need doing:

✦ **Choose To-Do List or Tasks in the Navigation pane:** Under My Tasks at the top of the Navigation pane, choose To-Do List to examine all tasks, including those you fashioned from e-mail messages and Calendar appointments; choose Tasks to see only the tasks you set for yourself in the Tasks folder.

✦ **Arrange tasks:** On the View tab, open the Arrange By gallery and choose an option to arrange tasks on the Tasks list by Due Date, Category, Importance, or one of the other options.

✦ **Change views:** On the Home or View tab, click the Change View button and choose a View option. For example, choose Overdue or Next 7 Days to focus on the tasks that *really* need doing.

To display tasks on the To-Do bar (refer to Figure 5-1), go to the View tab, click the To-Do Bar button, and choose Task List. No matter which folder you're viewing in Outlook, you can double-click a task on the To-Do bar and see it in a Task window.

Handling and managing tasks

When the time comes to manage the tasks in the Tasks window, I hope you are a stern taskmaster. Here's advice for handling and managing tasks:

✦ **Marking a task as complete:** Click the check box beside the task name in the Tasks window. Outlook draws a line through completed tasks.

✦ **Deleting a task:** Select the task and click the Delete button or press the Delete key.

✦ **Editing a task:** Double-click a task in the Tasks window to open the Task window and change the particulars there.

Reminders for Being Alerted to Activities and Tasks

Outlook offers the Reminder message box to alert you when an appointment or event from the Calendar is about to take place (see Chapter 4 of this minibook), when a task deadline is looming (see the preceding topic in this chapter), when an e-mail message needs a reply (see Chapter 3 of this minibook), or when someone whose name is in your Contacts folder needs attention (see Chapter 2 of this mini-book).

Figure 5-3 shows the Reminder message box. When Outlook is running and you least expect it, a Reminder message box similar to the one in the figure may appear to keep you on your toes. These pages explain how to handle reminder messages, schedule messages, and make the messages appear when you want them to appear.

Figure 5-3:
The
Reminder
message
box.

Handling reminder messages

Select a reminder in the Reminder message box and do the following to handle a reminder:

Book III
Chapter 5

Tasks, Reminders,
and Notes

✦ **Dismiss it:** Click the Dismiss button to shelve the reminder notice. If more than one notice appears in the Reminder message box and you want to erase them all, click the Dismiss All button.

✦ **Be reminded later:** Click the Snooze button. At the bottom of the dialog box, the Click Snooze to Be Reminded Again In text box tells you when the next reminder message will arrive. To change this setting, open the drop-down list and choose a different time period.

✦ **Open the item:** Click the Open Item button to examine the appointment, task, e-mail message, or contact to which the reminder pertains.

✦ **Procrastinate:** Click the Close button (the *X*) in the Reminder message box to make it disappear. To open the message box later, go to the View tab and click the Reminders Window button.

Reminders work only for items that are stored in these folders: Tasks, Calendar, Inbox, and Contacts. Store an item in another folder or a subfolder of one of the folders I just named, and you won't see the Reminder message box when the reminder is due. To make sure that you get reminded, store items in these folders: Tasks, Calendar, Inbox, or Contacts.

Scheduling a reminder message

Follow these instructions to schedule a reminder message:

✦ **Calendar appointment or event:** In the Appointment window, open the Reminder drop-down list and choose how many minutes, hours, or weeks in advance of the appointment or event to make the reminder appear.

✦ **Task deadline:** In the Task window (refer to Figure 5-2), select the Reminder check box and choose a day and time to be reminded in the drop-down lists.

✦ **E-mail message:** In the Message window or Inbox window, click the Follow Up button and choose Add Reminder on the drop-down list. You see the Custom dialog box. Select the Reminder check box and choose a date and time in the drop-down lists. If you enter a date but not a time, the Reminder message box appears at 5:00 p.m.

✦ **Contacts name:** In a Contact window or the Contacts window, click the Follow Up button and choose Add Reminder on the drop-down list. The Custom dialog box opens. Treat this dialog box the same way you treat the one for e-mail messages (see the preceding item in this list).

Making reminders work your way

You can do two or three things to make reminders work your way. On the File tab, choose Options to open the Options dialog box. Then follow these instructions to have your way with reminder notices:

✦ **Changing the reminder time for appointments and events:** By default, the Reminder message box appears 15 minutes before appointments and events start. To change this setting, go to the Calendar category, and enter a new setting in the Default Reminders drop-down list.

✦ **Changing the default time for task reminders:** When a task's deadline arrives, the Reminders dialog box lets you know at 8:00 a.m. (or when you start Outlook, if you start the program after 8:00 a.m.). To change this default setting, go to the Tasks category and choose a new time from the Default Reminder Time drop-down list.

✦ **Playing a different sound (or no sound):** By default, you hear a little chime when the Reminder message box appears on-screen. To hear a different sound or no sound at all, go to the Advanced category of the Options dialog box. To play no sound, deselect the Play Reminder Sound check box. To play a different sound, click the Browse button and then select a .wav sound file in the Reminder Sound File dialog box.

Making Notes to Yourself

Notes

As shown in Figure 5-4, notes resemble the yellow stick 'em notes that you often see affixed to manuscripts and refrigerator doors. Click the Notes button in the Navigation pane to go to the Notes window. Write a note to mark down a deadline, for example, or remind yourself to take out the cat. Here are instructions for doing all and sundry with notes:

Figure 5-4:
Notes, notes, and more notes.

**Book III
Chapter 5**

Tasks, Reminders, and Notes

✦ **Creating a note:** Click the New Note button (or press Ctrl+N) and type the note in the Note window. Then click outside the window. You can create a note when you're not in the Notes window by clicking the New Items button and choosing More Items➪Note on the drop-down list (or by pressing Ctrl+Shift+N).

✦ **Opening a note:** Double-click a note to read it in its Note window.

✦ **Forwarding a note:** To forward a note to someone in an e-mail message, right-click the note and choose Forward. A Message window opens so that you can address the message. The note arrives in the form of a file attachment, and the recipient must have Outlook in order to read it.

✦ **Deleting a note:** Select the note and click the Delete button or press the Delete key.

Book IV

PowerPoint

Contents at a Glance

Chapter 1: Getting Started in PowerPoint

In This Chapter

✔ **Introducing PowerPoint**

✔ **Finding your way around the screen**

✔ **Understanding what creating a presentation is all about**

✔ **Creating a presentation**

✔ **Inserting the slides**

✔ **Changing views of the screen**

✔ **Rearranging the Slides and Notes panes**

✔ **Manipulating slides**

✔ **Creating a photo album**

✔ **Hiding slides for use in a presentation**

*1*t's impossible to sit through a conference, seminar, or trade show without seeing at least one PowerPoint presentation. PowerPoint has found its way into nearly every office and boardroom. I've heard of a man (a very unromantic man) who proposed to his wife by way of a PowerPoint presentation.

As nice as PowerPoint can be, it has its detractors. If the software isn't used properly, it can come between the speaker and the audience. In a *New Yorker* article titled "Absolute PowerPoint: Can a Software Package Edit Our Thoughts?," Ian Parker argued that PowerPoint may actually be more of a hindrance than a help in communicating. PowerPoint, Parker wrote, is "a social instrument, turning middle managers into bullet-point dandies." The software, he added, "has a private, interior influence. It edits ideas. . . . It helps you make a case, but also makes its own case about how to organize information, how to look at the world."

To make sure that you use PowerPoint wisely, this chapter shows what creating a PowerPoint presentation entails. After a brief tour of PowerPoint, you find out how to create presentations, get a better view of your work, insert slides, put together a photo album, and hide slides.

Getting Acquainted with PowerPoint

Figure 1-1 (top) shows the PowerPoint window. That thing in the middle is a *slide,* the PowerPoint word for an image that you show your audience.

Surrounding the slide are many tools for entering text and decorating slides. When the time comes to show your slides to an audience, you dispense with the tools and make the slide fill the screen, as shown in Figure 1-1 (bottom).

Figure 1-1:
The PowerPoint window (top) and a slide as it looks in a presentation (bottom).

To make PowerPoint do your bidding, you need to know a little jargon:

✦ **Presentation:** All the slides, from start to finish, that you show your audience. Sometimes presentations are called "slide shows." Presentations are saved in presentation files (`.pptx` files).

✦ **Slides:** The images you create with PowerPoint. During a presentation, slides appear on-screen one after the other. Don't be put off by the word *slide* and dreary memories of sitting through your uncle's slide show vacation memories. You don't need a slide projector to show these slides. You can now plug a laptop or other computer into special monitors that display PowerPoint slides.

✦ **Notes:** Printed pages that you, the speaker, write and print so that you know what to say during a presentation. Only the speaker sees notes. Chapter 5 in this mini-book explains notes.

✦ **Handout:** Printed pages that you may give to the audience along with a presentation. A handout shows the slides in the presentation. Handouts are also known by the somewhat derogatory term *leave-behinds*. Chapter 5 of this mini-book explains handouts.

A Brief Geography Lesson

Figure 1-2 shows the different parts of the PowerPoint screen. I'd hate for you to get lost in PowerPoint Land. Fold down the corner of this page so that you can return here if screen terminology confuses you:

File

✦ **File tab:** The tab you visit to create, open, and save PowerPoint presentations, as well as do other file-management tasks.

✦ **Quick Access toolbar:** A toolbar with three buttons — Save, Undo, and Repeat. You see this toolbar wherever you go in PowerPoint.

✦ **Ribbon:** The place where the tabs are located. Click a tab — Home, Insert, Design, Transitions, Animations, Slide Show, Review, or View — to start a task.

✦ **Slides pane:** In Normal view, the place on the left side of the screen where you can see the slides or the text on the slides in your presentation. Scroll in the Slides pane to move backward and forward in a presentation.

✦ **Slide window:** Where a slide (in Normal view) or slides (in Slide Sorter view) are displayed. Scroll to move backward or forward in your presentation.

✦ **Notes pane:** Where you type notes (in Normal view) that you can refer to when giving your presentation. The audience can't see these notes — they're for you and you alone. See Chapter 5 of this mini-book for details.

**Book IV
Chapter 1**

**Getting Started
in PowerPoint**

File tab

Quick Access toolbar

Slides pane

Slide

The Ribbon

Figure 1-2:
The different
parts of the
PowerPoint
screen.

Notes pane

View buttons

Zoom controls

✦ **View buttons:** Buttons you can click to switch to (from left to right) Normal, Slide Sorter, Slide Show, and Reading view. See "Getting a Better View of Your Work," later in this chapter.

✦ **Zoom controls:** Tools for enlarging or shrinking a slide (in Normal and Slide Sorter view).

A Whirlwind Tour of PowerPoint

To help you understand what you're getting into, you're invited on a whirlwind tour of PowerPoint. Creating a PowerPoint presentation entails completing these basic tasks:

✦ **Creating the slides:** After you create a new presentation, your next task is to create the slides. PowerPoint offers many preformatted slide layouts, each designed for presenting information a certain way.

✦ **Notes:** As you create slides, you can jot down notes in the Notes pane. You can use these notes later to formulate your presentation and decide what you're going to say to your audience while each slide is on-screen (see Chapter 5 of this mini-book).

✦ **Designing your presentation**: After you create a presentation, the next step is to think about its appearance. You can change slides' colors and backgrounds, as well as choose a *theme* for your presentation, an all-encompassing design that applies to all (or most of) the slides (see Chapter 2 of this mini-book).

✦ **Inserting tables, charts, diagrams, and shapes:** A PowerPoint presentation should be more than a loose collection of bulleted lists. Starting on the Insert tab, you can place tables, charts, and diagrams on slides, as well as adorn your slides with text boxes, WordArt images, and shapes (see Chapter 4 of this mini-book).

✦ **"Animating" your slides:** PowerPoint slides can play video and sound, as well as be "animated" (see Chapter 4 of this mini-book). You can make the items on a slide move on the screen. As a slide arrives, you can make it spin or flash.

✦ **Delivering your presentation:** During a presentation, you can draw on the slides. You can also blank the screen and show slides out of order. In case you can't be there in person, PowerPoint gives you the opportunity to create self-running presentations and presentations that others can run on their own. You can also distribute presentations on CDs and as videos (see Chapter 5 of this mini-book).

Creating a New Presentation

When you start PowerPoint, the program creates a new, blank presentation just for you. You can make this bare-bones presentation the starting point for constructing your presentation, or you can get a more sophisticated, fully realized layout and design by starting with a template. Templates are a mixed blessing. They're designed by artists and they look very good. Some templates come with *boilerplate text* — already written material that you can recycle into your presentation. However, presentations made from templates are harder to modify. Sometimes the design gets in the way. As well, a loud or intricate background may overwhelm a diagram or chart you want to put on a slide.

| File |

No matter what kind of presentation you want to create, start creating it by going to the File tab and choosing New. You see the Available Templates and Themes window shown in Figure 1-3. This window offers templates for creating many types of presentations. Click a template to preview it on the right side of the window. Double-click a template (or select it and click the Create button) to create a presentation. Use one of these techniques to create a presentation:

✦ **Blank presentation:** Double-click the Blank Presentation icon. A new presentation appears. Try visiting the Design tab and choosing a theme or background style to get a taste of all the things you can do to decorate a presentation. (By pressing Ctrl+N, you can create a new, blank presentation without opening the Available Templates and Themes window.)

Figure 1-3:
The Available Templates and Themes window is the starting point for creating a presentation.

✦ **Recently used template:** Click the Recent Templates icon to use a template listed there.

✦ **Template on your computer:** Click the Sample Templates icon. Templates that you loaded on your computer when you installed PowerPoint appear.

✦ **Template you created (or downloaded earlier from Microsoft):** Click the My Templates icon. The New Presentation dialog box appears. Select a template and click OK.

✦ **Template available online at Office.com:** Enter a search term in the Search box, make sure that your computer is connected to the Internet, and click the Start Searching button. Templates appear in the window. Double-click a template to download and use it to create a presentation.

✦ **Recycle another presentation:** If you can use another presentation as the starting point for creating a new presentation, nab slides from the other presentation. Click the New from Existing icon. In the New from Existing Presentation dialog box, select the presentation and click the Open button.

You can click the Home, Back, or Forward button in the Available Templates and Themes window to backtrack as you search for a template.

If you intend to create a presentation from photos you took of a vacation or family reunion, consider creating a photo album. See "Putting Together a Photo Album" later in this chapter.

Advice for Building Persuasive Presentations

Before you create any slides, think about what you want to communicate to your audience. Your goal isn't to dazzle the audience with your PowerPoint skills, but communicate something — a company policy, the merits of a product, the virtues of a strategic plan. Your goal is to bring the audience around to your side. To that end, here is some practical advice for building persuasive presentations:

✦ **Start by writing the text in Word.** Start in Microsoft Word, not PowerPoint, so that you can focus on the words. In Word, you can clearly see how a presentation develops. You can make sure that your presentation builds to its rightful conclusion. PowerPoint has a special command for getting headings from a Word file. (See "Conjuring slides from Word document headings," later in this chapter.)

✦ **When choosing a design, consider the audience.** A presentation to the American Casketmakers Association calls for a mute, quiet design; a presentation to the Cheerleaders of Tomorrow calls for something bright and splashy. Select a slide design that sets the tone for your presentation and wins the sympathy of the audience.

✦ **Keep it simple.** To make sure that PowerPoint doesn't upstage you, keep it simple. Make use of the PowerPoint features, but do so judiciously. An animation in the right place at the right time can serve a valuable purpose. It can highlight an important part of a presentation and grab the audience's attention. But stuffing a presentation with too many gizmos turns a presentation into a carnival sideshow and distracts from your message.

✦ **Follow the one-slide-per-minute rule.** At the very minimum, a slide should stay on-screen for at least one minute. If you have 15 minutes to speak, you're allotted no more than 15 slides for your presentation, according to the rule.

✦ **Beware the bullet point.** Terse bullet points have their place in a presentation, but if you put them there strictly to remind yourself what to say next, you're doing your audience a disfavor. Bullet points can cause drowsiness. They can be a distraction. The audience skims the bullets when it should be attending to your voice and the argument you're making. When you're tempted to use a bulleted list, consider using a table, chart, or diagram instead. Figure 1-4 demonstrates how a bulleted list can be presented instead in a table, chart, or diagram.

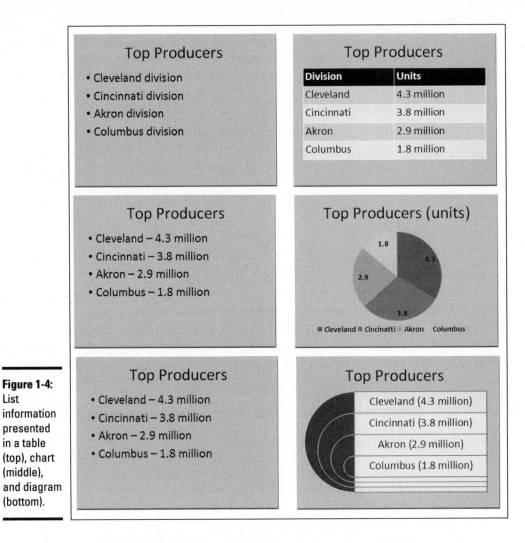

Figure 1-4:
List information presented in a table (top), chart (middle), and diagram (bottom).

♦ **Take control from the start.** Spend the first minute introducing yourself to the audience without running PowerPoint (or, if you do run PowerPoint, put a simple slide with your company name or logo on-screen). Make eye contact with the audience. This way, you establish your credibility. You give the audience a chance to get to know you.

♦ **Make clear what you're about.** In the early going, state very clearly what your presentation is about and what you intend to prove with your presentation. In other words, state the conclusion at the beginning as well as the end. This way, your audience knows exactly what you're driving at and can judge your presentation according to how well you build your case.

✦ **Personalize the presentation.** Make the presentation a personal one. Tell the audience what *your* personal reason for being there is or why *you* work for the company you work for. Knowing that you have a personal stake in the presentation, the audience is more likely to trust you. The audience understands that you're not a spokesperson, but a *speaker* — someone who has come before them to make a case for something that you believe in.

✦ **Tell a story.** Include an anecdote in the presentation. Everybody loves a pertinent and well-delivered story. This piece of advice is akin to the previous one about personalizing your presentation. Typically, a story illustrates a problem for *people* and how *people* solve the problem. Even if your presentation concerns technology or an abstract subject, make it about people. "The people in Shaker Heights needed faster Internet access," not "the data switches in Shaker Heights just weren't performing fast enough."

✦ **Rehearse and then rehearse some more.** The better you know your material, the less nervous you will be. To keep from getting nervous, rehearse your presentation until you know it backward and forward. Rehearse it out loud. Rehearse it while imagining you're in the presence of an audience.

✦ **Use visuals, not only words, to make your point.** You really owe it to your audience to take advantage of the table, chart, diagram, and picture capabilities of PowerPoint. People understand more from words and pictures than they do from words alone. It's up to you — not the slides — as the speaker to describe topics in detail with words.

Want to see just how PowerPoint can suck the life and drama out of a dramatic presentation? Try visiting the Gettysburg PowerPoint Presentation, a rendering of Lincoln's Gettysburg Address in PowerPoint. Yikes! You can find it here: `http://.norvig.com/Gettysburg`.

Creating New Slides for Your Presentation

After you create a presentation, your next step on the path to glory is to start adding the slides. To create a new slide, you start by choosing a slide layout. *Slide layouts* are the preformatted slide designs that help you enter text, graphics, and other things. Some slide layouts have *text placeholder frames* for entering titles and text; some come with *content placeholder frames* designed especially for inserting a table, chart, diagram, picture, clip-art image, or media clip.

When you add a slide, select the slide layout that best approximates the slide you have in mind for your presentation. Figure 1-5 shows the slide layouts that are available when you create a presentation with the Blank Presentation template. These pages explain how to insert slides and harvest them from Word document headings.

Book IV Chapter 1

Getting Started in PowerPoint

Figure 1-5:
The first step in creating a slide is to choose a slide layout. The left side of this figure shows the slide layouts on the New Slide drop-down list.

Figure 1-5:
continued

Inserting a new slide

Follow these steps to insert a new slide in your presentation:

1. **Select the slide that you want the new slide to go after.**

   In Normal view, select the slide on the Slides pane. In Slide Sorter view, select the slide in the main window.

2. **On the Home tab, click the bottom half of the New Slide button.**

   You see a drop-down list of slide layouts. (If you click the top half of the New Slide button, you insert a slide with the same layout as the one you selected in Step 1.) Figure 1-5 shows what the slide layouts look like (left), what a slide looks like right after you insert it (middle), and finished slides (right).

3. **Select the slide layout that best approximates the slide you want to create.**

   Don't worry too much about selecting the right layout. You can change slide layouts later on, as "Selecting a different layout for a slide" explains later in this chapter.

**Book IV
Chapter 1**

**Getting Started
in PowerPoint**

Speed techniques for inserting slides

When you're in a hurry, use these techniques to insert a slide:

✦ **Creating a duplicate slide:** Select the slide or slides you want to dupli-cate, and on the Home tab, open the drop-down list on the New Slide button and choose Duplicate Selected Slides. You can also open the drop-down list on the Copy button and choose Duplicate.

✦ **Copying and pasting slides:** Click the slide you want to copy (or Ctrl+click to select more than one slide) and then click the Copy button on the Home tab (or press Ctrl+C). Next, click to select the slide that you want the copied slide (or slides) to appear after and click the Paste button (or press Ctrl+V).

✦ **Recycling slides from other presentations:** Select the slide that you want the recycled slides to follow in your presentation, and on the Home tab, open the drop-down list on the New Slide button and choose Reuse Slides. The Reuse Slides task pane opens. Open the drop-down list on the Browse button, choose Browse File, and select a presentation in the Browse dialog box. The Reuse Slides task pane shows thumbnail versions of slides in the presentation you selected. One at a time, click slides to add them to your presentation. You can right-click a slide and choose Insert All Slides to grab all the slides in the presentation.

Conjuring slides from Word document headings

If you think about it, Word headings are similar to slide titles. Headings, like slide titles, introduce a new topic. If you know your way around Word and you want to get a head start creating a PowerPoint presentation, you can borrow the headings in a Word document for your PowerPoint slides. After you import the headings from Word, you get one slide for each Level 1 heading (headings given the Heading 1 style). Level 1 headings form the title of the slides, Level 2 head-ings form first-level bullets, Level 3 headings form second-level bullets, and so on. Paragraph text isn't imported. Figure 1-6 shows what headings from a Word document look like after they land in a PowerPoint presentation.

Follow these steps to use headings in a Word document to create slides in a PowerPoint presentation:

> Outline

1. **In Normal view, click the Outline tab in the Slides pane.**

   The Outline tab displays slide text (see Figure 1-6). You get a better sense of how headings from the Word document land in your presenta-tion by viewing your presentation from the Outline tab.

2. **Select the slide that the new slides from the Word document will follow.**

Each level-1 heading in the Word document becomes a slide title in PowerPoint

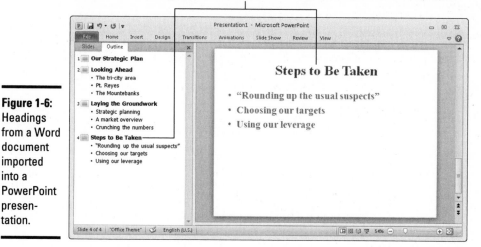

Figure 1-6:
Headings
from a Word
document
imported
into a
PowerPoint
presen-
tation.

 3. **On the Home tab, open the drop-down list on the New Slide button and choose Slides from Outline.**

You see the Insert Outline dialog box.

4. **Select the Word document with the headings you want for your presentation and click the Insert button.**

Depending on how many first-level headings are in the Word document, you get a certain number of new slides. These slides probably need work. The Word text may need tweaking to make it suitable for a PowerPoint presentation.

Selecting a different layout for a slide

If you mistakenly choose the wrong layout for a slide, all is not lost. You can start all over. You can graft a new layout onto your slide with one of these techniques:

 ✦ On the Home tab, click the Layout button and choose a layout on the drop-down list.

✦ Right-click the slide (being careful not to right-click a frame or object), choose Layout, and choose a layout on the submenu.

 PowerPoint also offers the Reset command for giving a slide its original layout after you've fiddled with it. If you push a slide all out of shape and you regret doing so, select your slide, go to the Home tab, and click the Reset button.

Book IV
Chapter 1

Getting Started
in PowerPoint

Getting a Better View of Your Work

Depending on the task at hand, some views are better than others. These pages explain how to change views and the relative merits of Normal, Slide Sorter, Notes Page, Slide Show, Slide Master, Reading View, Handout Master, and Notes Master view.

Changing views

PowerPoint offers two places to change views:

✦ **View buttons on the status bar:** Click a View button — Normal, Slide Sorter, Slide Show, or Reading View — on the status bar to change views, as shown in Figure 1-7.

✦ **View tab:** On the View tab, click a button on the Presentation Views or Master Views group, as shown in Figure 1-7.

Click a View button on the View tab. . .

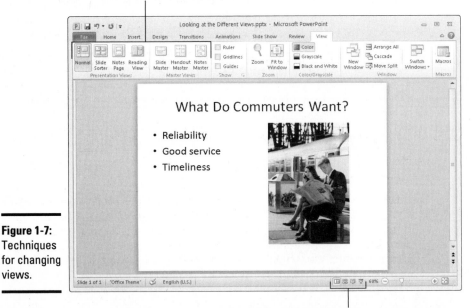

Figure 1-7: Techniques for changing views.

or click a View button on the status bar

Looking at the different views

Here is a survey of the different views with suggestions about using each one:

Slides

✦ **Normal/Slides view for examining slides:** Switch to Normal view, move the pointer to the Slides pane, and select the Slides tab when you want to examine a slide. In this view, thumbnail slides appear in the Slides pane, and you can see your slide in all its glory in the middle of the screen.

Outline

✦ **Normal/Outline view for fiddling with text:** Switch to Normal view, move the pointer to the Slides pane, and select the Outline tab to enter or read text (refer to Figure 1-6). You can find the Outline tab at the top of the Slides pane. The words appear in outline form. Normal/Outline view is ideal for focusing on the words in a presentation.

✦ **Slide Sorter view for moving and deleting slides:** In Slide Sorter view, you see thumbnails of all the slides in the presentation (use the Zoom Slider to change the size of thumbnails). From here, moving slides around is easy, and seeing many slides simultaneously gives you a sense of whether the different slides are consistent with one another and how the whole presentation is shaping up. The slides are numbered so that you can see where they appear in a presentation.

✦ **Notes Page view for reading your speaker notes:** In Notes Page view, you see notes you've written to aid you in your presentation, if you've written any. You can write notes in this view as well as in the Notes pane in Normal view. Chapter 5 of this mini-book explains notes pages.

✦ **Reading View view for focusing on slides' appearance:** In Reading View view, you also see a single slide, but it appears on-screen with the View buttons and with buttons for moving quickly from slide to slide. Switch to Reading View view to proofread slides and put the final touches on a presentation.

✦ **Slide Show view for giving a presentation:** In Slide Show view, you see a single slide. Not only that, but the slide fills the entire screen. This is what your presentation looks like when you show it to an audience.

✦ **The Master views for a consistent presentation:** The master views — Slide Master, Handout Master, and Notes Master — are for handling *master styles,* the formatting commands that pertain to all the slides in a presentation, handouts, and notes. To switch to these views, go to the View tab and click the appropriate button. Chapter 2 of this mini-book looks into master slides and master styles.

 PowerPoint offers a button called Fit Slide to Current Window that you can click while you're in Normal view to make the slide fill the window. This little button is located in the lower-right corner of the screen, to the right of the Zoom controls.

**Book IV
Chapter 1**

**Getting Started
in PowerPoint**

Hiding and Displaying the Slides Pane and Notes Pane

In Normal view, the Slides pane with its slide thumbnails appears on the left side of the screen, and the Notes pane appears on the bottom of the screen so that you can scribble notes about slides. Sometimes these panes just take up valuable space. They clutter the screen and occupy real estate that could be better used for formatting slides. Follow these instructions to temporarily close the Slides and Notes pane:

✦ **Closing the Notes pane:** Move the pointer over the border between the pane and the rest of the screen, and after the pointer changes to a two-headed arrow, drag the border to the bottom of the screen.

✦ **Closing the Slides pane (and the Notes pane):** Click the Close button on the Slides pane. This button is located to the right of the Outline tab. Clicking it closes the Notes pane as well as the Slides pane.

✦ **Restoring the Slides and Notes pane:** Click the Normal button (on the status bar or View tab). You can also move the pointer to the left side or bottom of the screen and, when you see the double-headed arrow, click and start dragging toward the center of the screen.

You can change the size of either pane by moving the pointer over its border and then clicking and dragging.

Selecting, Moving, and Deleting Slides

As a presentation takes shape, you have to move slides forward and backward. Sometimes you have to delete a slide. And you can't move or delete slides until you select them first. Herewith are instructions for selecting, moving, and deleting slides.

Selecting slides

The best place to select slides is Slide Sorter view (if you want to select several at a time). Use one of these techniques to select slides:

✦ **Select one slide:** Click the slide.

✦ **Select several different slides:** Hold down the Ctrl key and click each slide in the Slides pane or in Slide Sorter view.

✦ **Select several slides in succession:** Hold down the Shift key and click the first slide and then the last one.

✦ **Select a block of slides:** In Slide Sorter view, drag across the slides you want to select. Be sure when you click and start dragging that you don't click a slide.

✦ **Select all the slides:** On the Home tab, click the Select button and choose Select All on the drop-down list.

Moving slides

To move or rearrange slides, you're advised to go to Slide Sorter view. Select the slide or slides that you want to move and use one of these techniques to move slides:

✦ **Dragging and dropping:** Click the slides you selected and drag them to a new location. You see the drag pointer, and in Slide Sorter view, a vertical line shows you where the slide or slides will land when you release the mouse button. On the Slides pane, a horizontal line appears between slides to show you where the slide or slides will land when you release the mouse button.

✦ **Cutting and pasting:** On the Home tab, cut the slide or slides to the Windows Clipboard (click the Cut button, press Ctrl+X, or right-click and choose Cut). Then select the slide that you want the slide or slides to appear after and give the Paste command (click the Paste button, press Ctrl+V, or right-click and choose Paste). You can right-click between slides to paste with precision.

Deleting slides

Before you delete a slide, think twice about deleting. Short of using the Undo command, you can't resuscitate a deleted slide. Select the slide or slides you want to delete and use one of these techniques to delete slides:

✦ Press the Delete key.

✦ Right-click and choose Delete Slide on the shortcut menu.

Putting Together a Photo Album

Photo album is just PowerPoint's term for inserting many photographs into a presentation all at once. You don't necessarily have to stuff the photo album with travel or baby pictures for it to be a proper photo album. The Photo Album is a wonderful feature because you can use it to dump a bunch of photos in a PowerPoint presentation without having to create slides one at a time, insert the photos, and endure the rest of the rigmarole. Create a photo album to quickly place a bunch of photos on PowerPoint slides.

**Book IV
Chapter 1**

**Getting Started
in PowerPoint**

Creating your photo album

PowerPoint creates a new presentation for you when you create a photo album. To start, take note of where on your computer the photos you want for the album are. Then go to the Insert tab and click the Photo Album button. You see the Photo Album dialog box, as shown in Figure 1-8. For such a little thing, the Photo Album dialog box offers many opportunities for constructing a PowerPoint presentation. Your first task is to decide which pictures you want for your album. Then you choose a slide layout for the pictures.

Insert photos   Change the order of slides

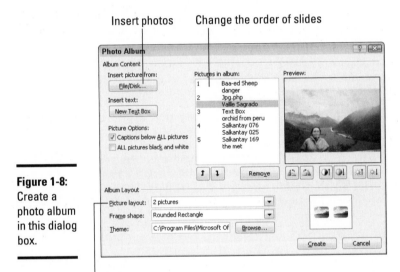

Figure 1-8:
Create a photo album in this dialog box.

Choose a layout

Inserting pictures and creating slides

Here is the lowdown on choosing pictures for a photo album:

✦ **Inserting photos:** Click the File/Disk button and choose photos in the Insert New Pictures dialog box. You can select more than one photo at a time by Ctrl+clicking. The filenames of photos you selected appear in the Pictures in Album box. Slide numbers appear as well so that you know which photos are on which slides.

✦ **Deciding how photos are framed:** Open the Frame Shape drop-down list and choose an option for placing borders or rounded corners on your photos. (This option isn't available if you choose Fit to Slide on the Picture Layout drop-down list.)

✦ **Inserting a text box:** Insert a text box if you want to enter commentary in your photo album. In the Pictures in Album box, select the picture or text box that you want your new text box to go after and then click the New Text Box button. Later, you can go into your presentation and edit the placeholder text, which PowerPoint aptly enters as *Text Box*.

✦ **Providing captions for all pictures:** To place a caption below all the pictures in your photo album, select the Captions Below ALL Pictures check box. PowerPoint initially places the picture filename in the caption, but you can delete this caption and enter one of your own. (To select this option, you must choose a picture layout option besides Fit to Slide.)

✦ **Changing the order of pictures:** Select a picture in the Pictures in Album box and then click an arrow button to move it forward or backward in the presentation.

✦ **Changing the order of slides:** Ctrl+click to select each picture on a slide. Then click an arrow as many times as necessary to move the slide forward or backward in the presentation.

✦ **Removing a picture:** Select a picture in the Pictures in Album box and click the Remove button to remove it from your photo album. You can Ctrl+click pictures to select more than one.

Choosing a layout for slides

Your next task is to go to the bottom of the Photo Album dialog box (refer to Figure 1-8) and choose a layout for the slides in the presentation. Open the Picture Layout drop-down list to choose one of the seven picture layouts:

✦ Choose Fit to Slide for a presentation in which each picture occupies an entire slide.

✦ Choose a "pictures" option to fit 1, 2, or 4 pictures on each slide.

✦ Choose a "pictures with" option to fit 1, 2, or 4 pictures as well as a text title frame on each slide.

Changing the look of pictures

The Photo Album dialog box (refer to Figure 1-8) offers a handful of tools for changing the look of the pictures. When you use these tools, keep your eye on the Preview box — it shows you what you're doing to your picture.

✦ **Making all photos black and white:** Select the ALL Pictures Black and White check box.

✦ **Rotating pictures:** Click a Rotate button to rotate a picture clockwise or counterclockwise.

✦ **Changing the contrast:** Click a Contrast button to sharpen or mute the light and dark colors or shades in the picture.

✦ **Changing the brightness**: Click a Brightness button to make a picture brighter or more somber.

✦ **Choosing a frame shape for pictures:** If you opted for a "picture" or "picture with" slide layout, you can choose a shape — Beveled, Oval, or others — for your pictures on the Frame Shape drop-down list.

✦ **Choosing a theme for your photo album:** If you selected a "picture" or "picture with" slide layout, you can choose a theme for your slide presentation. Click the Browse button and choose a theme in the Choose Theme dialog box.

At last, click the Create button when you're ready to create the photo album. PowerPoint attaches a title slide to the start of the album that says, *Photo Album* with your name below.

Putting on the final touches

Depending on the options you chose for your photo album, it needs all or some of these final touches:

✦ **Fix the title slide:** Your title slide should probably say more than the words *Photo Album* and your name.

✦ **Fill in the text boxes:** If you asked for text boxes with your photo album, by all means, replace PowerPoint's generic text with meaningful words of your own.

✦ **Write the captions:** If you asked for photo captions, PowerPoint entered photo filenames below photos. Replace those filenames with something more descriptive.

Editing a photo album

To go back into the Photo Album dialog box and rearrange the photos in your album, go to the Insert tab, open the drop-down list on the Photo Album button, and choose Edit Photo Album on the drop-down list. You see the Edit Photo Album dialog box. It looks and works exactly like the Photo Album dialog box (refer to Figure 1-8). Of course, you can also edit your photo album by treating it like any other PowerPoint presentation. Change the theme, fiddle with the slides, and do what you will to torture your photo album into shape.

Hidden Slides for All Contingencies

Hide a slide when you want to keep it on hand "just in case" during a presentation. Hidden slides don't appear in slide shows unless you shout *Ollie ollie oxen free!* and bring them out of hiding. Although you, the presenter, can see hidden slides in Normal view and Slide Sorter view, where their slide numbers are crossed through, the audience doesn't see them in the course of a presentation unless you decide to show them. Create hidden slides if you anticipate having to steer your presentation in a different direction — to answer a question from the audience, prove your point more thoroughly, or revisit a topic in more depth. Merely by right-clicking and choosing a couple of commands, you can display a hidden slide in the course of a slide show.

Hiding a slide

The best place to put hidden slides is the end of a presentation where you know you can find them. Follow these steps to hide slides:

1. **Select the slide or slides that you want to hide.**

2. **On the Slide Show tab, click the Hide Slide button.**

   You can also right-click a slide in the Slides pane or Slide Sorter view and choose Hide Slide. Hidden slides' numbers are boxed and crossed through in the Slides pane and the Slide Sorter window.

To unhide a slide, click the Hide Slide button again or right-click the slide and choose Hide Slide.

Showing a hidden slide during a presentation

Hidden slides don't appear during the course of a presentation, but suppose that the need arises to show one. Before showing a hidden slide, take careful note of which slide you're viewing now. You have to return to this slide after viewing the hidden slide. Follow these steps to view a hidden slide during a presentation:

1. **Right-click the screen and choose Go to Slide.**

   You see a submenu with the titles of slides in your presentation.

2. **Select a hidden slide so that the audience can view it.**

   You can tell which slides are hidden because their slide numbers are enclosed in parentheses.

How do you resume your presentation after viewing a hidden slide? If you look at only one hidden slide, you can right-click and choose Last Viewed on the shortcut menu to return to the slide you saw before the hidden slide. If you've viewed several hidden slides, right-click the screen, choose Go to Slide, and select a slide to pick up where you left off.

Chapter 2: Fashioning a Look for Your Presentation

In This Chapter

✔ Introducing themes and background styles

✔ Selecting and tweaking slide themes

✔ Creating a solid color, gradient, clip-art, picture, and texture slide background

✔ Selecting a theme or background for specific slides

✔ Redesigning your presentation with master slides

From the audience's point of view, this chapter is the most important in this mini-book. What your presentation looks like — which theme and background style you select for the slides in your presentation — sets the tone. From the very first slide, the audience judges your presentation on its appearance. When you create a look for your presentation, what you're really doing is declaring what you want to communicate to your audience.

This chapter explains how to handle slide backgrounds. It examines what you need to consider when you select colors and designs for backgrounds. You also discover how to select and customize a theme, and how to create your own slide backgrounds. This chapter looks into how to change the background of some but not all of the slides in a presentation. It also explains how to use master slides and master styles to make sure that slides throughout your presentation are consistent with one another.

Looking at Themes and Background Styles

What a presentation looks like is mostly a matter of slide backgrounds, and when you select a background for slides, you start by selecting a theme. A *theme* is a "canned" slide design. Themes are designed by graphic artists. Most themes include sophisticated background patterns and colors. For each theme, PowerPoint offers several alternative theme colors, fonts, and background styles. As well, you can create a background of your own from a single color, a gradient mixture of two colors, or a picture.

Figure 2-1 shows examples of themes. Themes range from the fairly simple to the quite complex. When you installed PowerPoint on your computer, you also installed a dozen or more themes, and you can acquire more themes online from Office.com and other places. After you select a theme for your presentation, you can tweak it a little bit. You can do that by choosing a background style or by creating an entirely new background of your own.

Figure 2-1:
Examples of themes.

Figure 2-2 shows examples of backgrounds you can create yourself. Self-made backgrounds are not as intrusive as themes. The risk of the background overwhelming the lists, tables, charts, and other items in the forefront of slides is less when you fashion a background style yourself.

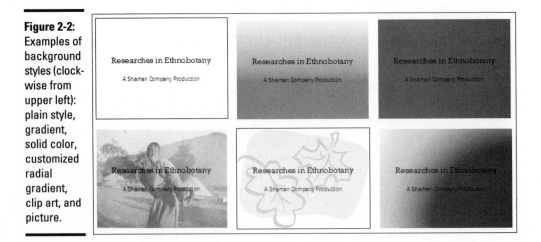

Figure 2-2:
Examples of background styles (clockwise from upper left): plain style, gradient, solid color, customized radial gradient, clip art, and picture.

More than any other design decision, what sets the tone for a presentation are the colors you select for slide backgrounds. If the purpose of your presentation is to show photographs you took on a vacation to Arizona's Painted Desert, select light-tone, hot colors for the slide backgrounds. If your presentation is an aggressive sales pitch, consider a black background. There is no universal color theory for selecting the right colors in a design because everyone is different. Follow your intuition. It will guide you to the right background color choices.

Choosing a Theme for Your Presentation

After you initially select a theme, you can do one or two things to customize it. These pages explain how to find and select a theme for your presentation and diddle with a theme after you select it. By the way, the name of the theme that is currently in use is listed on the left side of the status bar, in case you're curious about a theme you want to replace.

Selecting a theme

Use one of these techniques to select a new theme for your presentation:

✦ **Selecting a theme in the Themes gallery:** On the Design tab, open the Themes gallery and move the pointer over different themes to "live-preview" them. Click a theme to select it.

✦ **Borrowing a theme from another presentation:** On the Design tab, open the Themes gallery, and click Browse for Themes. You see the Choose Theme or Themed Document dialog box. Locate and select a presentation with a theme you can commandeer for your presentation and click the Apply button.

Tweaking a theme

Starting on the Design tab, you can customize a theme with these techniques and in so doing alter all the slides in your presentation:

[Colors ▾] ✦ **Choosing a new set of colors:** The easiest and best way to experiment with customizing a theme is to select a different color set. Click the Colors button, slide the pointer over the different color sets on the drop-down list, and see what effect they have on your slides.

[A Fonts ▾] ✦ **Change the fonts:** Click the Fonts button and choose a font combination on the drop-down list. The first font in each pair applies to slide titles and the second to slide text. You can also choose Create New Theme Fonts on the list and select theme fonts of your own.

◆ **Change theme effects:** Click the Effects button and choose a theme effect on the drop-down list. A *theme effect* is a slight refinement to a theme.

◆ **Choosing background style variation:** Most themes offer background style variations. Click the Background Styles button to open the Background Styles gallery and select a style. The next topic in this chapter, "Creating Slide Backgrounds on Your Own," explains how you can create backgrounds similar to these, as well as how to create a single-color, gradient, clip-art, picture, and texture background.

 Suppose you regret customizing a theme. To get the original theme back, select it again. Make like you were selecting a theme for the first time and select it in the Themes gallery.

Creating Slide Backgrounds on Your Own

Besides a theme or background style, your other option for creating slide backgrounds is to do it on your own. For a background, you can have a solid color, a transparent color, a gradient blend of colors, a picture, or a clip-art image.

◆ **Solid color:** A single, uniform color. You can adjust a color's transparency and in effect "bleach out" the color to push it farther into the background.

◆ **Gradient:** A mixture of different colors with the colors blending into one another.

◆ **Clip art:** A clip-art image from the Microsoft Clip Organizer.

◆ **Picture:** A photograph or graphic.

◆ **Texture:** A uniform pattern that gives the impression that the slide is displayed on a material such as cloth or stone.

How to create these kinds of slide backgrounds on your own is the subject of the next several pages.

Using a solid (or transparent) color for the slide background

Using a solid or transparent color for the background gives your slides a straightforward, honest look. Because all the slides are the same color or transparent color, the audience can focus better on the presentation itself rather than the razzle-dazzle. Follow these steps to use a solid or transparent color as the background for slides:

Background Styles ▾ **1. On the Design tab, click the Background Styles button and choose Format Background on the drop-down list.**

You see the Fill category of the Format Background dialog box.

2. Select the Solid Fill option button.

3. Click the Color button and choose a color on the drop-down list.

The muted theme colors are recommended because they look better in the background, but you can select a standard color or click the More Colors button and select a color in the Colors dialog box.

4. Drag the Transparency slider if you want a "bleached out" color rather than a slide color.

At 0% transparency, you get a solid color; at 100%, you get no color at all.

5. Click the Apply to All button and then the Close button.

I sincerely hope you like your choice of colors, but if you don't, try, try, try again.

Creating a gradient color blend for slide backgrounds

Gradient refers to how and where two or more colors grade, or blend, into one another on a slide. As well as the standard linear gradient direction, you can opt for a radial, rectangular, or path gradient direction. Figure 2-3 shows examples of gradient fill backgrounds. These backgrounds look terribly elegant. Using a gradient is an excellent way to create an original background that looks different from all the other presenter's slide backgrounds.

Follow these steps to create a gradient background for slides:

Background Styles ▾ **1. On the Design tab, click the Background Styles button, and choose Format Background on the drop-down list.**

You see the Fill category of the Format Background dialog box. Drag this dialog box to the left side of the screen so that you can get a better view of your slide.

2. Click the Gradient Fill option button.

Before you experiment with gradients, try opening the Preset Colors drop-down list to see whether one of the ready-made gradient options does the job for you.

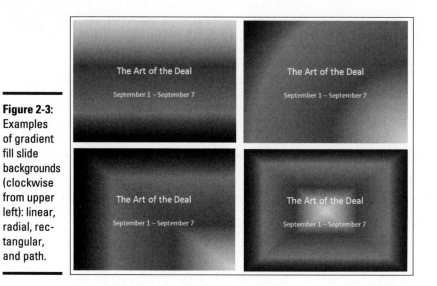

Figure 2-3: Examples of gradient fill slide backgrounds (clockwise from upper left): linear, radial, rectangular, and path.

3. **On the Type drop-down list, choose what type of gradient you want — Linear, Radial, Rectangular, Path, or Shade from Title (see Figure 2-3).**

   If you choose Linear, you can enter a degree measurement in the Angle box to change the angle at which the colors blend. At 90 degrees, for example, colors blend horizontally across the slide; at 180 degrees, they blend vertically.

4. **Create a gradient stop for each color transition you want on your slides.**

   Gradient stops determine where colors are, how colors transition from one to the next, and which colors are used. You can create as many gradient stops as you want. Here are techniques for handling gradient stops:

   - *Adding a gradient stop:* Click the Add Gradient Stop button. A new gradient stop appears on the slider. Drag it to where you want the color blend to occur.

   - *Removing a gradient stop:* Select a gradient stop on the slider and click the Remove Gradient Stop button.

   - *Choosing a color for a gradient stop:* Select a gradient stop on the slider, click the Color button, and choose a color on the drop-down list.

   - *Positioning a gradient stop:* Drag a gradient stop on the slider or use the Position box to move it to a different location.

5. **Drag the Brightness slider to make the colors dimmer or brighter.**

6. **Drag the Transparency slider to make the colors on the slides more or less transparent.**

   At 0% transparency, you get solid colors; at 100%, you get no color at all.

7. **Click the Apply to All button.**

   Very likely, you have to experiment with stop colors and stop positions until you blend the colors to your satisfaction. Good luck.

Placing a clip-art image in the slide background

As long as they're on the pale side or you've made them semitransparent, clip-art images do fine for slide backgrounds. They look especially good in title slides. Figure 2-4 shows examples of clip-art images as backgrounds. As Book VIII, Chapter 4 explains, PowerPoint comes with numerous clip-art images. You're invited to place one in the background of your slides by following these steps:

Background Styles ▾

1. **On the Design tab, click the Background Styles button and choose Format Background on the drop-down list.**

   The Fill category of the Format Background dialog box appears.

Figure 2-4: For backgrounds, clip art usually has to be at least somewhat transparent. These slides are (from left to right) 0%, 40%, 65%, and 85% transparent.

2. **Click the Picture or Texture Fill option button.**

3. **Click the Clip Art button.**

   You see the Select Picture dialog box.

4. **Find and select a clip-art image that you can use in the background of your slides.**

   You can scroll through the clip-art images until you find a good one, enter a search term in the Search Text box and click the Go button (click the Include Content from Office Online check box to search online at Microsoft for a clip-art image), or click the Import button to get an image from your computer.

5. **In the Format Background dialog box, enter a Transparency measurement.**

   Drag the Transparency slider or enter a measurement in the box. The higher the measurement, the more transparent the image is (see Figure 2-4).

6. **Enter measurements in the Offsets boxes to make your clip-art image fill the slide.**

7. **Click the Apply to All button and then click Close.**

   There you have it. The clip-art image you selected lands in the slides' backgrounds.

Using a picture for a slide background

Figure 2-5 shows examples of pictures being used as slide backgrounds. Select your picture carefully. A picture with too many colors — and that includes the majority of color photographs — obscures the text and makes it difficult to read. You can get around this problem by "recoloring" a picture to give it a uniform color tint, selecting a grayscale photograph, selecting a photo with colors of a similar hue, or making the picture semi-transparent, but all in all, the best way to solve the problem of a picture that obscures the text is to start with a quiet, subdued picture. (Book VIII, Chapter 3 explains all the ins and outs of using pictures in Office 2010.)

One more thing: Select a landscape-style picture that is wider than it is tall. PowerPoint expands pictures to make them fill the entire slide background. If you select a skinny, portrait-style picture, PowerPoint has to do a lot of expanding to make it fit on the slide, and you end up with a distorted background image.

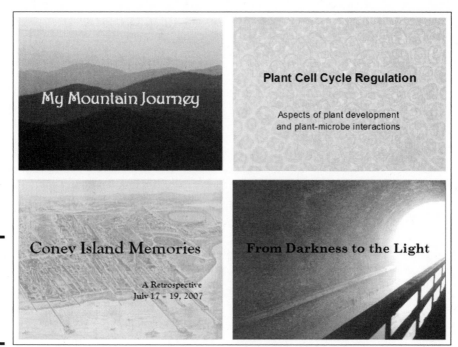

Figure 2-5: Examples of pictures used as slide backgrounds.

Follow these steps to use a picture as a slide background:

1. **On the Design tab, click the Background Styles button and choose Format Background on the drop-down list.**

You see the Fill category of the Format Background dialog box.

2. **Click the Picture or Texture Fill option button.**

3. **Click the File tab.**

The Insert Picture dialog box appears.

4. **Locate the picture you want, select it, and click the Insert button.**

The picture lands on your slide.

5. **Enter a Transparency measurement to make the picture fade a bit into the background.**

Drag the slider or enter a measurement in the Transparency box. The higher percentage measurement you enter, the more "bleached out" the picture is.

Book IV Chapter 2

Fashioning a Look for Your Presentation

6. **Using the Offsets text boxes, enter measurements to make your picture fit on the slides.**

7. **Click the Apply to All button.**

   How do you like your slide background? You may have to open the Format Background dialog box again and play with the transparency setting. Only the very lucky and the permanently blessed get it right the first time.

Using a texture for a slide background

Yet another option for slide backgrounds is to use a texture. As shown in Figure 2-6, a *texture* gives the impression that the slide is displayed on a material such as marble or parchment. A texture can make for a very elegant slide background. Follow these steps to use a texture as a slide background:

1. **On the Design tab, click the Background Styles button and choose Format Background on the drop-down list.**

   The Fill category of the Format Background dialog box appears.

Figure 2-6: Different textures (clockwise from upper left): Papyrus, Canvas, Newsprint, and Cork.

2. **Click the Picture or Texture Fill option button.**

3. **Click the Texture button and choose a texture on the drop-down list.**

4. **Enter a Transparency measurement to make the texture less imposing.**

   Drag the slider or enter a measurement in the Transparency box.

5. **Click the Apply to All button and then click Close.**

Changing the Background of a Single or Handful of Slides

To make a single slide (or a handful of slides) stand out in a presentation, change their background style or theme. A different background tells your audience that the slide being presented is a little different from the one before it. Maybe it imparts important information. Maybe it introduces another segment of the presentation. Use a different background style or theme to mark a transition, indicate that your presentation has shifted gears, or mark a milestone in your presentation.

Follow these steps to change the background of one or several slides in your presentation:

1. **In Slide Sorter view, select the slides that need a different look.**

   You can select more than one slide by Ctrl+clicking slides.

2. **On the Design tab, choose a different theme or background for the slides you selected.**

   How you do this depends on whether you're working with a theme or a slide background:

   - *Theme:* In the Themes Gallery, right-click a theme and choose Apply To Selected Slides. The same goes for theme colors, fonts, and effects: To apply a theme color, font, or effect, right-click it on the drop-down list and choose Apply to Selected Slides. (See "Choosing a Theme for Your Presentation" earlier in this chapter for details.)

   - *Slide background:* Make like you're creating a background style for all the slides (see "Creating Slide Backgrounds on Your Own" earlier in this chapter) but right-click a choice on the Background Styles drop-down list and choose Apply to Selected Slides. If you're creating a background in the Format Background dialog box, click the Close button, not the Apply to All button.

**Book IV
Chapter 2**

**Fashioning a
Look for Your
Presentation**

When you assign a different theme to some of the slides in a presentation, PowerPoint creates another Slide Master. You may be surprised to discover that when you add a new slide to your presentation, a second, third, or fourth set of slide layouts appears on the New Slide drop-down list. These extra layouts appear because your presentation has more than one Slide Master. The next topic in this chapter, "Using Master Slides and Master Styles for a Consistent Design," explains what Slide Masters are.

Using Master Slides and Master Styles for a Consistent Design

Consistency is everything in a PowerPoint design. Consistency of design is a sign of professionalism and care. In a consistent design, the fonts and font sizes on slides are consistent from one slide to the next, the placeholder text frames are in the same positions, and the text is aligned the same way across different slides. In the bulleted lists, each entry is marked with the same bullet character. If the corner of each slide shows a company logo, the logo appears in the same position.

It would be torture to have to examine every slide to make sure that it is consistent with the others. In the interest of consistency, PowerPoint offers master styles and master slides. A *master slide* is a model slide from which the slides in a presentation inherit their formats. A *master style* is a format that applies to many different slides. Starting from a master slide, you can change a master style and in so doing, reformat many slides the same way. These pages explain how master slides can help you quickly redesign a presentation.

Switching to Slide Master view

To work with master slides, switch to *Slide Master view,* as shown in Figure 2-7. From this view, you can start working with master slides:

1. **Go to the View tab.**

2. **Click the Slide Master button.**

In Slide Master view, you can select a master slide in the Slides pane, format styles on a master slide, and in this way reformat many different slides. (Click the Close Master View button or a view button such as Normal or Slide Sorter to leave Slide Master view.)

Select the Slide Master. . .

or a layout   Change a master style

Figure 2-7:
In Slide
Master view,
you can
reformat
many
different
slides simul-
taneously.

Understanding master slides and master styles

Master slides are special, high-powered slides. Use master slides to deliver the same formatting commands to many different slides. Whether the commands affect all the slides in your presentation or merely a handful of slides depends on whether you format the Slide Master (the topmost slide in Slide Master view) or a layout (one of the other slides):

✦ **The Slide Master:** The *Slide Master* is the first slide in the Slides pane in Slide Master view (refer to Figure 2-7). It's a little bigger than the master slides, as befits its status as Emperor of All Slides. Formatting changes you make to the Slide Master affect all the slides in your presentation. When you select a theme for your presentation, what you're really doing is assigning a theme to the Slide Master. Because formatting commands given to the Slide Master apply throughout a presentation, the theme design and colors are applied to all slides. If you want a company logo to appear on all your slides, place the logo on the Slide Master.

✦ **Layouts:** As you know, you choose a slide layout — Title and Content, for example — on the New Slide drop-down list to create a new slide.

In Slide Master view, PowerPoint provides one *layout* for each type of slide layout in your presentation. By selecting and reformatting a layout in Slide Master view, you can reformat all slides in your presentation that were created with the same slide layout. For example, to change fonts, alignments, and other formats on all slides that you created with the Title layout, select the Title layout in Slide Master view and change master styles on the Title layout. Each layout controls its own little fiefdom in a PowerPoint presentation — a fiefdom comprised of slides created with the same slide layout.

✦ **Master styles:** Each master slide — the Slide Master and each layout — offers you the opportunity to click to edit master styles (refer to Figure 2-7). The master style governs how text is formatted on slides. By changing a master style on a master slide, you can change the look of slides throughout a presentation. For example, by changing the Master Title Style font, you can change fonts in all the slide titles in your presentation.

PowerPoint's Slide Master–layouts–slides system is designed on the "trickle down" theory. When you format a master style on the Slide Master, formats trickle down to layouts and then to slides. When you format a master style on a layout, the formats trickle down to slides you created using the same slide layout. This chain-of-command relationship is designed to work from the top down, with the master slide and layouts barking orders to the slides below. In the interest of design consistency, slides take orders from layouts, and layouts take orders from the Slide Master.

In Slide Master view, you can move the pointer over a layout thumbnail in the Slides pane to see a pop-up box that tells you the layout's name and which slides in your presentation "use" the layout. For example, a pop-up box that reads "Title and Content Layout: used by slide(s) 2-3, 8" tells you that slides 2 through 3 and 8 in your presentation are governed by the Title and Content layout.

Editing a master slide

Now that you know the relationship among the Slide Master, layouts, and slides, you're ready to start editing master slides. To edit a master slide, switch to Slide Master view, select a master slide, and change a master style. To insert a picture on a master slide, visit the Insert tab.

Changing a master slide layout

Changing the layout of a master slide entails changing the position and size of text frames and content frames as well as removing these frames:

✦ **Changing size of frames:** Select the frame you want to change, and then move the pointer over a frame handle on the corner, side, top or bottom of the frame and drag when you see the double-headed arrow.

✦ **Moving frames:** Move the pointer over the perimeter of a frame, click when you see the four-headed arrow, and drag.

✦ **Removing a frame from the Slide Master:** Click the perimeter of the frame to select it and then press Delete.

✦ **Adding a frame to the Slide Master:** Select the slide master, and on the Slide Master tab, click the Master Layout button. You see the Master Layout dialog box. Select the check box beside the name of each frame you want to add and click OK.

Chapter 3: Entering the Text

This chapter explains how to change the appearance of text, create text boxes, and create text box shapes. I solve the riddle of what to do when text doesn't fit in a text box or text placeholder frame. You also discover how to align text, handle bulleted and numbered lists, and put a footer on all or some of the slides in your presentation.

By the time you finish reading this chapter, if you read it all the way through, you will be one of those people others turn to when they have a PowerPoint question about entering text on slides. You'll become a little guru in your own right.

Entering Text

No presentation is complete without a word or two, which is why the first thing you see when you add a new slide to a presentation are the words "Click to add text." As soon as you "click," those words of instruction disappear, and you're free to enter a title or text of your own. Most slides include a text placeholder frame at the top for entering a slide title; many slides also have another, larger text placeholder frame for entering a bulleted list.

As shown in Figure 3-1, the easiest way to enter text on slides is to click in a text placeholder frame and start typing. The other way is to switch to Normal view, select the Outline tab in the Slides pane (see Figure 3-1), and enter text there.

On the Slides pane in Normal/Outline view   In a text placeholder frame

Figure 3-1:
Ways of
entering
text.

Enter text on slides the same way you enter text in a Word document — by wiggling your fingers over the keyboard. While you're at it, you can change fonts, the font size of text, and the color of text, as the following pages explain. (Chapter 1 of this mini-book describes how to get the text for slides from the headings in a Word document; Book I, Chapter 2 explains everything a sane person needs to know about handling fonts.)

Choosing fonts for text

If you aren't happy with the fonts in your presentation, you have three ways to remedy the problem:

✦ **Dig in and choose new fonts on a slide-by-slide basis.** Select the text, go to the Home tab, and choose a font from the Font drop-down list or the Font dialog box.

✦ **Select new theme fonts for your presentation.** Theme fonts are combinations of fonts that the designers of PowerPoint themes deem appropriate for the theme you're working in. To change theme fonts, go to the Design tab, click the Fonts button, and select a new font combination.

✦ **Choose a new font on a master slide to change fonts throughout your presentation.** Chapter 2 of this mini-book explains master slides and how you can use them to change formats simultaneously on many slides. In Slide Master view, select a master slide and change its fonts on the Home tab.

Changing the font size of text

For someone in the back row of an audience to be able to read text in a PowerPoint presentation, the text should be no smaller than 28 points. Try this simple test to see whether text in your presentation is large enough to read: Stand 5 or so feet from your computer and see whether you can read the text. If you can't read it, make it larger.

Go to the Home tab and select the text whose size you want to change. Then use one of these techniques to change font sizes:

✦ **Font Size drop-down list:** Open this list and choose a point size. To choose a point size that isn't on the list, click in the Font Size text box, enter a point size, and press Enter.

✦ **Font dialog box:** Click the Font group button to open the Font dialog box. Then either choose a point size from the Size drop-down list or enter a point size in the Size text box and click OK.

✦ **Increase Font Size and Decrease Font Size buttons:** Click these buttons (or press Ctrl+> or Ctrl+<) to increase or decrease the point size by the next interval on the Font Size drop-down list. Watch the Font Size list or your text and note how the text changes size. This is an excellent technique when you want to "eyeball it" and you don't care to fool with the Font Size list or Font dialog box.

Changing the color of text

Before you change the color of text, peer into your computer screen and examine the background theme or color you selected for your slides. Unless the color of the text is different from the theme or color, the audience can't read the text. Besides choosing a color that contributes to the overall tone of the presentation, select a color that's easy to read.

Select the text that needs touching up and then use one of these techniques to change the color of text:

✦ On the mini-toolbar, open the drop-down list on the Font Color button and choose a color.

✦ On the Home tab, open the drop-down list on the Font Color button and choose a color.

✦ On the Home tab, click the Font group button to open the Font dialog box, click the Font Color button in the dialog box, and choose a color on the drop-down list.

The Font Color drop-down list offers theme colors and standard colors. You are well advised to choose a theme color. These colors jive with the theme you choose for your presentation.

**Book IV
Chapter 3**

Entering the Text

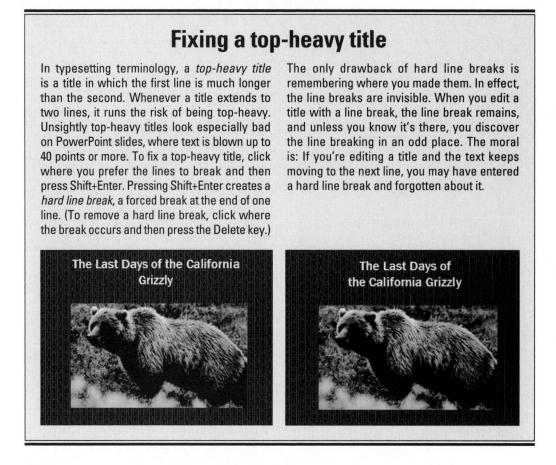

Fixing a top-heavy title

In typesetting terminology, a *top-heavy title* is a title in which the first line is much longer than the second. Whenever a title extends to two lines, it runs the risk of being top-heavy. Unsightly top-heavy titles look especially bad on PowerPoint slides, where text is blown up to 40 points or more. To fix a top-heavy title, click where you prefer the lines to break and then press Shift+Enter. Pressing Shift+Enter creates a *hard line break,* a forced break at the end of one line. (To remove a hard line break, click where the break occurs and then press the Delete key.)

The only drawback of hard line breaks is remembering where you made them. In effect, the line breaks are invisible. When you edit a title with a line break, the line break remains, and unless you know it's there, you discover the line breaking in an odd place. The moral is: If you're editing a title and the text keeps moving to the next line, you may have entered a hard line break and forgotten about it.

The Last Days of the California Grizzly

The Last Days of the California Grizzly

Fun with Text Boxes and Text Box Shapes

Text boxes give you an opportunity to exercise your creativity. They add another element to slides. Use them to position text wherever you want, annotate a chart or equation, or place an announcement on a slide. You can even create a vertical text box in which the text reads from top to bottom instead of left to right, or turn a text box into a circle, arrow, or other shape. Figure 3-2 shows examples of text boxes and text box shapes.

In Office terminology, a PowerPoint text box is an object. Book I, Chapter 8 explains all the different techniques for handling objects, including how to make them overlap and change their sizes. Here are the basics of handling text boxes in PowerPoint:

✦ **Creating a text box:** On the Insert tab, click the Text Box button and move the pointer to a part of the slide where you can see the *text box pointer,* a downward-pointing arrow. Then click and start dragging to create your text box, and enter the text.

✦ **Filling a text box with a color style:** On the (Drawing Tools) Format tab, choose a style on the Shape Styles gallery.

✦ **Rotating a text box (text included):** Use one of these techniques to rotate a text box along with the text inside it:

   • Drag the rotation handle, the green circle above the text box.

   • On the (Drawing Tools) Format tab, click the Rotate button and choose a Rotate or Flip command on the drop-down list.

   • On the (Drawing Tools) Format tab, click the Size group button (you may have to click the Size button first) and, in the Size category of the Format Shape dialog box, enter a measurement in the Rotation box.

✦ **Turning a shape into a text box:** Create the shape, and then click in the shape and start typing. (Book I, Chapter 8 explains how to create a shape.)

✦ **Turning a text box into a shape:** Right-click the text box and choose Format Shape. In the Format Shape dialog box, click the Text Box category and, under AutoFit, click the Do Not AutoFit option button. Then close the dialog box, go to the (Drawing Tools) Format tab, click the Edit Shape button, choose Change Shape on the drop-down list, and choose a shape on the Change Shape submenu.

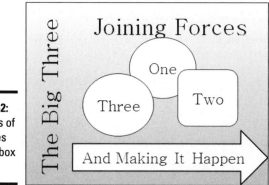

Figure 3-2:
Examples of text boxes and text box shapes.

Book IV
Chapter 3

Entering the Text

Many people object to the small text boxes that appear initially when you create a text box. If you prefer to establish the size of text boxes when you create them, not when you enter text, change the AutoFit setting and then create a default text box with the new setting. The next section in this chapter explains how to change the AutoFit settings.

Controlling How Text Fits in Text Frames and Text Boxes

When text doesn't fit in a text placeholder frame or text box, PowerPoint takes measures to make it fit. In a text placeholder frame, PowerPoint shrinks the amount of space between lines and then it shrinks the text itself. When text doesn't fit in a text box, PowerPoint enlarges the text box to fit more text. PowerPoint handles overflow text as part of its AutoFit mechanism.

How AutoFit works is up to you. If, like me, you don't care for how PowerPoint enlarges text boxes when you enter the text, you can tell PowerPoint not to "AutoFit" text, but instead to make text boxes large from the get-go. And if you don't care for how PowerPoint shrinks text in text placeholder frames, you can tell PowerPoint not to shrink text. These pages explain how to choose AutoFit options for overflow text in your text frames and text boxes.

Choosing how PowerPoint "AutoFits" text in text frames

When text doesn't fit in a text placeholder frame and PowerPoint has to "AutoFit" the text, you see the AutoFit Options button. Click this button to open a drop-down list with options for handling overflow text, as shown in Figure 3-3. The AutoFit options — along with a couple of other techniques, as I explain shortly — represent the "one at a time" way of handling overflow text. You can also change the default AutoFit options for handling overflow text, as I also explain if you'll bear with me a while longer and quit your yawning.

The AutoFit Options button appears when text doesn't fit in a text frame.

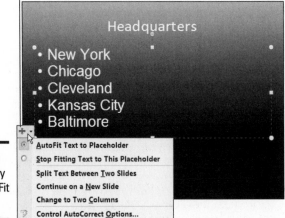

Figure 3-3: The laundry list of AutoFit options.

"AutoFitting" the text one frame at a time

When text doesn't fit in a text placeholder frame, especially a title frame, the first question to ask is, "Do I want to fool with the integrity of the slide design?" Making the text fit usually means shrinking the text, enlarging the text frame, or compromising the slide design in some way, but audiences notice design inconsistencies. Slides are shown on large screens where design flaws are easy to see.

Making text fit in a text frame usually means making a compromise. Here are different ways to handle the problem of text not fitting in a text frame. Be prepared to click the Undo button when you experiment with these techniques:

- ✦ **Edit the text:** Usually when text doesn't fit in a frame, the text needs editing. It needs to be made shorter. A slide is not a place for a treatise. Editing the text is the only way to make it fit in the frame without compromising the design.

- ✦ **Enlarge the frame:** Click the AutoFit Options button and choose Stop Fitting Text to This Placeholder on the shortcut menu (refer to Figure 3-3). Then select the frame and drag the bottom or top selection handle to enlarge it.

- ✦ **Decrease the font size:** Select the text, go to the Home tab, and choose a smaller Font Size measurement. You can also click the Decrease Font Size button (or press Ctrl+<) to decrease the font size.

- ✦ **Decrease the amount of spacing between lines:** On the Home tab, click the Paragraph group button to open the Paragraph dialog box and decrease the After measurement under Spacing.

- ✦ **Change the frame's internal margins:** Similar to a page, text frames have internal margins to keep text from getting too close to a frame border. By shrinking these margins, you can make more room for text. Right-click the text frame and choose Format Shape. Then, in the Text Box category of the Format Shape dialog box, enter smaller measurements for the Internal Margin boxes.

- ✦ **Create a new slide for the text:** If you're dealing with a list or paragraph text in a body text frame, the AutoFit Options drop-down list offers two ways to create a new slide (refer to Figure 3-3). Choose Continue on a New Slide to run the text onto another slide; choose Split Text Between Two Slides to divide the text evenly between two slides. I don't recommend either option, though. If you need to make a new slide, do it on your own and then rethink how to present the material. Inserting a new slide to accommodate a long list throws a presentation off-track.

Choosing default AutoFit options for text frames

Unless you change the default AutoFit options, PowerPoint shrinks the amount of space between lines and then shrinks the text itself to make text fit in text placeholder frames. Follow these steps if you want to decide for yourself whether PowerPoint "auto-fits" text in text frames:

1. **Open the AutoFormat As You Type tab in the AutoCorrect dialog box.**

   Here are the two ways to get there:

   - Click the AutoFit Options button (refer to Figure 3-3) and choose Control AutoCorrect Options on the drop-down list.

   - On the File tab, choose Options to open the PowerPoint Options dialog box. In the Proofing category, click the AutoCorrect Options button.

2. **Deselect the AutoFit Title Text to Placeholder check box to prevent auto-fitting in title text placeholder frames.**

3. **Deselect the AutoFit Body Text to Placeholder check box to prevent auto-fitting in text placeholder frames apart from title frames.**

4. **Click OK.**

Choosing how PowerPoint "AutoFits" text in text boxes

PowerPoint offers three options for handling overflow text in text boxes:

+ **Do Not AutoFit:** Doesn't fit text in the text box but lets text spill out

+ **Shrink Text on Overflow**: Shrinks the text to make it fit in the text box

+ **Resize Shape to Fit Text:** Enlarges the text box to make the text fit inside it

Follow these steps to tell PowerPoint how or whether to fit text in text boxes:

1. **Select the text box.**

2. **Right-click the text box and choose Format Shape.**

   You see the Format Shape dialog box.

3. **Go to the Text Box category.**

4. **Choose an AutoFit option: Do Not AutoFit, Shrink Text on Overflow, or Resize Shape to Fit Text.**

5. **Click the Close button.**

Some people find it easier to dispense with "auto-fitting." If you're one of those people, go to the Text Box category of the Format Shape dialog box, and under AutoFit, choose the Do Not AutoFit option or the Shrink Text on Overflow option. To make your AutoFit setting applicable to all the text boxes you create in your presentation, right-click the text box and choose Set As Default Text Box on the shortcut menu.

Positioning Text in Frames and Text Boxes

How text is positioned in text frames and text boxes is governed by two sets of commands: the Align Text commands and the Align commands. By choosing combinations of Align and Align Text commands, you can land text where you want it in a text frame or text box. Just wrestle with these two commands until you land your text where you want it to be in a text frame or box:

✦ **Align commands** control horizontal (left-to-right) alignments. On the Home tab, click the Align Left (press Ctrl+L), Center (press Ctrl+E), Align Right (press Ctrl+R), or Justify button.

✦ **Align Text commands** control vertical (up-and-down) alignments. On the Home tab, click the Align Text button and choose Top, Middle, or Bottom on the drop-down list, as shown in Figure 3-4.

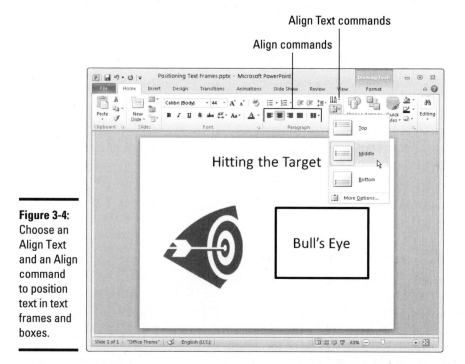

Figure 3-4: Choose an Align Text and an Align command to position text in text frames and boxes.

Handling Bulleted and Numbered Lists

What is a PowerPoint presentation without a list or two? It's like an emperor without any clothes on. This part of the chapter explains everything there is to know about bulleted and numbered lists.

These lists can be as simple or complex as you want them to be. PowerPoint offers a bunch of different ways to format these lists, but if you're in a hurry or you don't care whether your lists look like everyone else's, you can take advantage of the Numbering and Bullets buttons and go with standard lists. Nonconformists and people with nothing else to do, however, can try their hand at making fancy lists. The following pages cover that topic, too.

Creating a standard bulleted or numbered list

In typesetting terms, a *bullet* is a black, filled-in circle or other character that marks an item on a list. Many slide layouts include text frames that are already formatted for bulleted lists. All you have to do in these text frames is "click to add text" and keep pressing the Enter key while you enter items for your bulleted list. Each time you press Enter, PowerPoint adds another bullet to the list. Bulleted lists are useful when you want to present the audience with alternatives or present a list in which the items aren't ranked in any order. Use a numbered list to rank items in a list or present step-by-step instructions.

Follow these instructions to create a standard bulleted or numbered list:

✦ **Creating a bulleted list:** Select the list if you've already entered the list items, go to the Home tab, and click the Bullets button. You can also right-click, choose Bullets on the shortcut menu, and choose a bullet character on the submenu if you don't care for the standard, black, filled-in circle.

✦ **Creating a numbered list:** Select the list if you've already entered the list items, go to the Home tab, and click the Numbering button. You can also right-click, choose Numbering on the shortcut menu, and select a numbering style on the submenu.

✦ **Converting a numbered to a bulleted list (or vice versa):** Drag over the list to select it, go to the Home tab, and then click the Bullets or Numbering button.

To remove the bullets or numbers from a list, select the list, open the drop-down list on the Bullets or Numbering button, and choose None.

Choosing a different bullet character, size, and color

As Figure 3-5 demonstrates, the black filled-in circle isn't the only character you can use to mark items in a bulleted list. You can also opt for what PowerPoint calls *pictures* (colorful bullets of many sizes and shapes) or symbols from the Symbol dialog box. While you're at it, you can change the bullets' color and size.

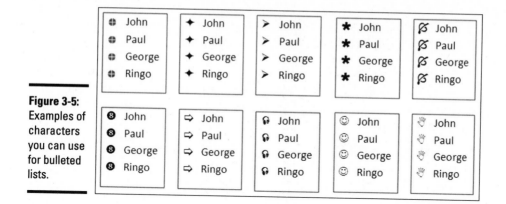

Figure 3-5: Examples of characters you can use for bulleted lists.

If you decide to change the bullet character in your lists, be consistent from slide to slide. Unless you want to be goofy, select the same bullet character throughout the lists in your presentation for the sake of consistency. You don't want to turn your slide presentation into a showcase for bullets, do you?

To use pictures or unusual symbols for bullets, start by selecting your bulleted list, going to the Home tab, and opening the drop-down list on the Bullets button. Do any of the bullets on the drop-down list tickle your fancy? If one does, select it; otherwise, click the Bullets and Numbering option at the bottom of the drop-down list. You see the Bulleted tab of the Bullets and Numbering dialog box. Starting there, you can customize your bullets:

+ **Using a picture for bullets:** Click the Picture button and select a bullet in the Picture Bullet dialog box.

+ **Using a symbol for bullets:** Click the Customize button and select a symbol in the Symbol dialog box. By opening the Font drop-down list and choosing a Wingdings font, you can choose an oddball character for bullets.

+ **Changing bullets' size:** Enter a percentage figure in the Size % of Text box. For example, if you enter **200**, the bullets are twice as large as the font size you choose for the items in your bulleted list.

+ **Changing bullets' color:** Click the Color button in the Bullets and Numbering dialog box and choose an option on the drop-down list. Theme colors are considered most compatible with the theme design you chose for your presentation.

**Book IV
Chapter 3**

Entering the Text

Choosing a different list-numbering style, size, and color

PowerPoint offers seven different ways of numbering lists. As well as choosing a different numbering style, you can change the size of numbers relative to the text and change the color of numbers. To select a different list-numbering style, size, or color, begin by selecting your list, going to the Home tab, and opening the drop-down list on the Numbering button. If you like one of the numbering-scheme choices, select it; otherwise, choose Bullets and Numbering to open the Numbered tab of the Bullets and Numbering dialog box. In this dialog box, you can customize list numbers:

✦ **Choosing a numbering scheme:** Select a numbering scheme and click OK.

✦ **Changing the numbers' size:** Enter a percentage figure in the Size % of Text box. For example, if you enter 50, the numbers are half as big as the font size you choose for the items in your numbered list.

✦ **Changing the numbers' color:** Click the Color button and choose a color on the drop-down list. Theme colors are more compatible with the theme design you chose than the other colors are.

Putting Footers (and Headers) on Slides

A *footer* is a line of text that appears at the foot, or bottom, of a slide. Figure 3-6 shows a footer. Typically, a footer includes the date, a company name, and/or a slide number, and footers appear on every slide in a presentation if they appear at all. That doesn't mean you can't exclude a footer from a slide or put footers on some slides, as I explain shortly. For that matter, you can move slide numbers, company names, and dates to the top of slides, in which case they become *headers*. When I was a kid, "header" meant crashing your bike and falling headfirst over the handlebars. How times change.

Figure 3-6:
An example
of a footer.

5/17/2009   What's Underfoot?   3

These pages explain everything a body needs to know about footers and headers — how to enter them, make them appear on all or some slides, and exclude them from slides.

Some background on footers and headers

PowerPoint provides the Header & Footer command to enter the date, a word or two, and a slide number on the bottom of all slides in your presentation. This command is really just a convenient way to enter a footer on the Slide Master without having to switch to Slide Master view. As Chapter 2 in this mini-book explains, the Slide Master governs the formatting and layout of all slides in your presentation. The Slide Master includes text placeholder frames for a date, some text, and a slide number. Anything you enter on the Slide Master, including a footer, appears on all your slides.

If a date, some text, and a slide number along the bottom of all the slides in your presentation is precisely what you want, you've got it made. You can enter a footer on every slide in your presentation with no trouble at all by using the Header & Footer command. However, if you're a maverick and you want your footers and headers to be a little different from the next guy's — if you want the date, for example, to be in the upper-right corner of slides or you want footers to appear on some slides but not others — you have some tweaking to do. You may have to create a nonstandard footer or remove the footer from some of the slides.

Putting a standard footer on all your slides

A standard footer includes the date, some text, and the page number. To put a standard footer on all the slides in your presentation, go to the Insert tab and then click the Header & Footer button. You see the Header and Footer dialog box. Choose some or all of these options and click the Apply to All button:

✦ **Date and Time:** Select this check box to make the date appear in the lower-left corner of all your slides. Then tell PowerPoint whether you want a current or fixed date:

- *Update Automatically:* Select this option button to make the day's date (or date and time) appear in the footer, and then open the drop-down list to choose a date (or date and time) format. With this option, the date you give your presentation always appears on slides.

- *Fixed:* Select this option button and enter a date in the text box. For example, enter the date you created the presentation. With this option, the date remains fixed no matter when or where you give the presentation.

✦ **Slide Number:** Select this check box to make slide numbers appear in the lower-right corner of all slides.

✦ **Footer:** Select this check box, and in the text box, enter the words that you want to appear in the bottom, middle of all the slides.

Creating a nonstandard footer

As "Some background on footers and headers" explains earlier in this chapter, you have to look elsewhere than the Header and Footer dialog box if you want to create something besides the standard footer. Suppose you want to move the slide number from the lower-right corner of slides to another position? Or you want to fool with the fonts in headers and footers?

Follow these steps to create a nonstandard footer:

1. **Create a standard footer if you want your nonstandard footer to include today's date and/or a slide number.**

   If you want to move the slide number into the upper-right corner of slides, for example, create a standard footer first (see the preceding section in this chapter). Later, you can move the slide number text frame into the upper-right corner of slides.

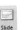

2. **On the View tab, click the Slide Master button.**

   You switch to Slide Master view. Chapter 2 of this mini-book explains this view and how to format many slides at one time with master slides.

3. **Select the Slide Master, the topmost slide in the Slides pane.**

4. **Adjust and format the footer text boxes to taste (as they say in cookbooks).**

   For example, move the slide number text frame into the upper-right corner to put slide numbers there. Or change the font in the footer text boxes. Or place a company logo on the Slide Master to make the logo appear on all your slides.

5. **Click the Close Master View button to leave Slide Master view.**

   You can always return to Slide Master view and adjust your footer.

Removing a footer from a single slide

On a crowded slide, the date, footer text, page number, and other items in the footer can get in the way or be a distraction. Fortunately, removing one or all of the footer text frames from a slide is easy:

1. **Switch to Normal view and display the slide with the footer that needs removing.**

2. **On the Insert tab, click the Header & Footer button.**

   The Header and Footer dialog box appears.

3. **Deselect check boxes — Date and Time, Slide Number, and Footer — to tell PowerPoint which parts of the footer you want to remove.**

4. **Click the Apply button.**

   Be careful not to click the Apply to All button. Clicking this button removes footers throughout your slide presentation.

Chapter 4: Making Your Presentations Livelier

In This Chapter

✔ Looking at ways to make a presentation livelier

✔ Slapping a transition or animation on a slide

✔ Making sound a part of your presentation

✔ Playing video during a presentation

The purpose of this chapter is to make your presentation stand out in a crowd. It suggests ways to enliven your presentation with pictures, charts, slides, and tables. It shows how transitions and animations can make a presentation livelier. Finally, you discover how to play sound and video during a presentation.

Suggestions for Enlivening Your Presentation

Starting on the Insert tab, you can do a lot to make a presentation livelier. The Insert tab offers buttons for putting pictures, tables, charts, diagrams, shapes, and clip-art images on slides:

✦ **Photos:** Everyone likes a good photo, but more than that, audiences understand more from words and pictures than they do from words alone. A well-chosen photo reinforces the ideas that you're trying to put across in your presentation. (See Book VIII, Chapter 3.)

✦ **Tables:** A table is a great way to plead your case or defend your position. Raw table data is irrefutable — well, most of the time, anyway. Create a table when you want to demonstrate how the numbers back you up. (See Book I, Chapter 5.)

✦ **Charts:** Nothing is more persuasive than a chart. The bars, pie slices, or columns show the audience instantaneously that production is up or down, or that sector A is outperforming sector B. The audience can compare the data and see what's what. (See Book I, Chapter 6.)

✦ **Diagrams:** A diagram is an excellent marriage of images and words. Diagrams allow an audience to literally visualize a concept, idea, or relationship. You can present an abstract idea such that the audience understands it better. (See Book I, Chapter 7.)

+ **Shapes:** Lines and shapes can also illustrate ideas and concepts. You can also use them as slide decorations. (See Book I, Chapter 8.)

+ **Clip-art images:** Clip-art images bring a little more color to presentations. They make presentations friendlier and easier to look at. (See Book VIII, Chapter 4.)

The grid and drawing guides

The *grid* is an invisible set of horizontal and vertical lines to which objects — clip-art images, pictures, and shapes — cling when you move them on a slide. The grid is meant to help objects line up squarely with one another. When you drag an object, it sticks to the nearest point on the grid.

PowerPoint also offers the *drawing guides* for aligning objects. You can drag these vertical and horizontal lines on-screen and use them to align objects with precision.

To display the grid and the drawing guides:

✔ **Displaying (and hiding) the grid:** Press Shift+F9 or go to the View tab and select the Gridlines check box.

✔ **Displaying (and hiding) the drawing guides**: Press Alt+F9 or go to the View tab and select the Guides check box.

By default, objects when you move them "snap to the grid." That means the objects stick to the nearest grid line when you move them across a slide. To control whether objects snap to the grid, right-click (but not on an object or frame), choose Grid and Guides, and in the Grid and Guides dialog box, deselect the Snap Objects to Grid check box.

Even if the Snap Objects to Grid check box in the Grid and Guides dialog box is selected, you can move objects without them snapping to a gridline by holding down the Alt key while you drag.

Select the Snap Objects to Other Objects check box if you want shapes to abut each other or fall along a common axis.

Exploring Transitions and Animations

In PowerPoint-speak, a *transition* is a little bit of excitement that occurs as one slide leaves the screen and the next slide climbs aboard. An *animation* is movement on the slide. For example, you can animate bulleted lists such that the bullet points appear on a slide one at a time when you click the mouse, rather than all at one time.

Before you know anything about transitions and animations, you should know that they can be distracting. The purpose of a presentation is to communicate with the audience, not display the latest, busiest, most dazzling presentation technology. For user-run, kiosk-style presentations, however, eye-catching transitions and animations can be useful because they draw an audience. (A user-run presentation plays on its own, as I explain in Chapter 5 of this mini-book.) For audiences that enjoy high-tech wizardry, transitions and animations can be a lot of fun and add to a presentation.

Showing transitions between slides

Transitions include the Switch, Fade, and Push. Figure 4-1 shows how a transition works. For the figure, I chose the Clock transition. This slide doesn't so much arrive on-screen as it does sweep onto the screen in a clockwise manner. Don't worry; you get a chance to test-drive these transitions before you attach them to slides.

Figure 4-1:
The Clock
transition in
action.

Assigning transitions to slides

To show transitions between slides, go to the Transitions tab, select the slide or slides that need transitions, and select a transition in the Transition to This Slide gallery. (To apply the same transition to all the slides in a presentation, click the Apply To All button after you select a transition.) The names and images in the gallery give you an idea of what the transitions are, and you can click the Preview button at any time to watch a transition you chose.

The Transitions tab offers these tools for tweaking a transition:

✦ **Effect Options:** Click the Effect Options button and choose an effect on the drop-down list. For example, choose From Top or From Bottom to make a transition arrive from the top or bottom of the screen. Not all transitions offer effect options.

✦ **Sound:** Open the Sound drop-down list and choose a sound to accompany the transition. The Loop Until Next Sound option at the bottom of the drop-down list plays a sound continuously until the next slide in the presentation appears.

✦ **Duration:** Enter a time period in the Duration box to declare how quickly or slowly you want the transition to occur.

As I mention earlier, you can click the Apply To All button to assign the same transition to all the slides in your presentation.

Altering and removing slide transitions

In the Slides pane and Slide Sorter view, the transition symbol, a flying star, appears next to slides that have been assigned a transition. Select the slides that need a transition change, go to the Transitions tab, and follow these instructions to alter or remove transitions:

✦ **Altering a transition:** Choose a different transition in the Transition to This Slide gallery. You can also choose different effect options and sounds, and change the duration of the transition.

✦ **Removing a transition:** Choose None in the Transition to This Slide gallery.

Animating parts of a slide

When it comes to animations, you can choose between *animation schemes,* the prebuilt special effects made by the elves of Microsoft, or customized animations that you build on your own. Only fans of animation and people with a lot of time on their hands go the second route.

Choosing a ready-made animation scheme

Follow these steps to preview and choose an animation scheme for slides:

1. **Go to the Animations tab.**

2. **Click to select the element on the slide that you want to animate.**

   For example, select a text frame with a bulleted list. You can tell when you've selected an element because a selection box appears around it.

3. **In the Animation Styles gallery, choose an animation effect, as shown in Figure 4-2.**

You can choose Entrance, Emphasis, and Exit animation effects. As soon as you make your choice, the animation springs to life, and you can click the Preview button at any time to see your animation in all its glory.

4. **Click the Effect Options button and experiment with choices on the drop-down list to tweak your animation.**

   Which options are available depends on the animation you chose.

5. **If you choose a text-box or text-frame element with more than one paragraph in Step 2, click the Effect Options button and tell PowerPoint whether to animate all the text or animate each paragraph separately from the others.**

   - *All at Once:* All the text is animated at the same time.

   - *By Paragraph:* Each paragraph is treated separately and is animated on its own. For example, each item in a bulleted list is treated as a separate element — each item fades, wipes, or flies in after the one before it, not at the same time as the one before it.

   Very briefly, you see a preview of the animation choice you made. To get a good look at the animation you just chose for your slide, click the Preview button on the Animations tab.

Choose an animation   How elements are animated

Figure 4-2:
Apply effects in the Animation gallery.

**Book IV
Chapter 4**

Making Your Presentations Livelier

To remove an animation, return to the Animation Styles gallery and choose None.

Fashioning your own animation schemes

To fashion your own animation scheme, go to the Animations tab and click the Animation Pane button. You see the Animation pane (refer to Figure 4-2). It lists, in order, each animation that occurs on your slide (if animations occur). Select an element on the slide and follow these general instructions to animate it:

✦ Click the Add Animation button and choose an animation.

✦ On the Start drop-down list, declare whether the animation begins when you click your slide (On Click), at the same time as the previous animation (With Previous), or after the previous animation (After Previous).

✦ In the Duration box, enter how long you want the animation to last.

✦ In the Delay box, enter a time period to declare how soon after the previous animation in the Animation pane you want your animation to occur.

✦ Select an animation in the task pane and click a Re-Order button to change the order in which animations occur, if more than one element is animated on your slide.

Making Audio Part of Your Presentation

Especially in user-run, kiosk-style presentations, audio can be a welcome addition. Audio gives presentations an extra dimension. It attracts an audience. PowerPoint offers two ways to make audio part of a presentation:

✦ **As part of slide transitions:** A sound is heard as a new slide arrives on-screen. On the Transitions tab, open the Sound drop-down list and choose a sound. (See "Showing transitions between slides," earlier in this chapter.)

✦ **On the slide itself:** The means of playing audio appears on the slide in the form of an Audio icon, as shown in Figure 4-3. By moving the mouse over this icon, you can display audio controls, and you can use these controls to play audio. You can also make audio play as soon as the slide arrives on-screen.

Table 4-1 describes the audio files you can use in PowerPoint presentations and whether each file type is a wave or MIDI sound. To find out what kind of audio file you're dealing with, note the file's three-letter extension; or open Windows Explorer or Computer, find the sound file, right-click it, and choose Properties.

Figure 4-3:
Making
audio
part of a
presentation.

File Type	Extension	Wave/MIDI
Table 4-1	**Sound File Formats**	
AIFF audio	`.aif,.aiff`	Wave
AU Audio	`.au`	Wave
Quick Time Audio	`.3g2,.aac,mp4`	Wave
MIDI Sequence	`.midi,.mid`	MIDI
MP3 audio file	`.mp3`	Wave
Wave audio	`.wav`	Wave
Windows Media Audio File	`.wma`	Wave

Inserting an audio file on a slide

Follow these steps to insert an audio file in a slide:

1. **Go to the Insert tab.**

2. **Click the Audio button.**

   You see the Insert Audio dialog box.

3. **Locate and select a sound file and then click Insert.**

   Earlier in this chapter, Table 4-1 lists the type of sound files that you can play in presentations.

An Audio icon appears on the slide to remind you that audio is supposed to play when your slide is on-screen. You can change the size of this icon by selecting it and dragging a corner handle or going to the (Audio Tools) Format tab and entering new Height and Width measurements. You can also drag the icon into an out-of-the-way corner of your slide.

To quit playing a sound file on a slide, select its Audio icon and then press the Delete key.

Telling PowerPoint when and how to play an audio file

To tell PowerPoint when and how to play an audio file, start by selecting the Audio icon and going to the (Audio Tools) Playback tab, as shown in Figure 4-4. From there, you can control when and how audio files play:

✦ **Controlling the volume:** Click the Volume button and choose an option on the drop-down list to control how loud the audio plays.

✦ **Deciding when to start playing audio:** On the Start drop-down list, choose Automatically to make the audio play as soon as the slide appears; choose On Click to play the audio when you click the Audio icon on your slide. The Play Across Slides option plays the audio file throughout a presentation.

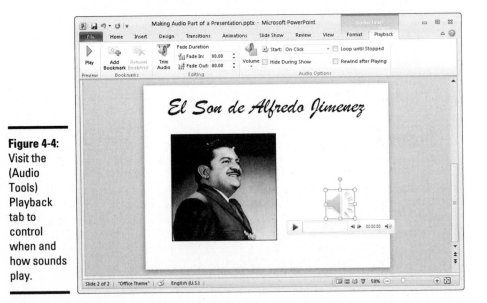

Figure 4-4: Visit the (Audio Tools) Playback tab to control when and how sounds play.

✦ **Hiding and unhiding the Audio icon:** Select the Hide During Show check box. If you hide the Audio icon, the file must play automatically; otherwise, you won't see the icon and be able to click it and view the audio controls.

✦ **Continuously playing audio:** Select the Loop Until Stopped check box to play the audio file over and over again or until you move to the next slide.

Click the Play button on the (Audio Tools) Playback tab to play an audio file.

Playing audio during a presentation

While an audio file is playing during a presentation, controls for starting, pausing, and controlling the volume appear on-screen (refer to Figure 4-3). They appear on-screen, I should say, if the Audio icon appears on your slide. (If you've hidden the Audio icon, you're out of luck because you can't see the Audio icon or use its audio controls.)

Follow these instructions to start, pause, and control the volume of an audio recording during a presentation:

✦ **Starting an audio file:** Move the pointer over the Audio icon, and when you see the Audio controls, click the Play/Pause button (or press Alt+P).

✦ **Pausing an audio file:** Click the Play/Pause button (or press Alt+P). Click the button again to resume playing the audio file.

✦ **Muting the volume:** Click the Mute/Unmute icon (or press Alt+U).

✦ **Controlling the volume:** Move the pointer over the Mute/Unmute icon to display the volume slider and then drag the volume control on the slider.

Playing Video on Slides

If a picture is worth a thousand words, what is a moving picture worth? Ten thousand? To give your presentation more cachet, you can play video on slides and in so doing, turn your presentation into a mini-movie theater.

To play video, PowerPoint relies on *Windows Media Player,* the media player that comes with Windows. Therefore, to play video on a slide, stick to formats that Windows Media Player can handle: ASF (Advanced Systems Format), AVI (Audio Visual Interleaved), MPEG (Motion Picture Experts Group), MPG (Media Planning Group), WMV (Windows Media Video), MOV (QuickTime Video), and .SWF (Adobe Flash).

Inserting a video on a slide

Follow these steps to insert a video on a slide:

1. Open the Insert Video dialog box.

You can open the dialog box with one of these techniques:

- Click the Media icon in a content placeholder frame.

- On the Insert tab, click the Video button.

2. Select a video file in the Insert Video dialog box and click Insert.

The video appears on your slide. If I were you, I would find out how (or whether) the video plays. To do that, click the Play/Pause button (or press Alt+P) or click the Play button on the (Video Tools) Playback or (Video Tools) Format tab.

Fine-tuning a video presentation

As shown in Figure 4-5, select the video and go to the (Video Tools) Playback tab to fine-tune a video presentation. The Playback tab offers all kinds of commands for making a video play the way you want it to play. Here are different ways to fine-tune a video presentation:

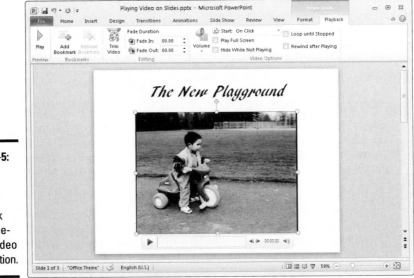

Figure 4-5: Visit the (Video Tools) Playback tab to fine-tune a video presentation.

✦ **Controlling the volume:** Click the Volume button and choose Low, Medium, High, or Mute to control how loud the video sound is.

✦ **Playing the video automatically or when you click the Play/Pause button:** Open the Start drop-down list and choose Automatically or On Click to tell PowerPoint when to start playing the video.

✦ **Playing the video at full screen:** Make a video fill the entire screen by selecting the Play Full Screen check box. Be careful of this one. Videos can look terribly grainy when they appear on the big screen.

✦ **Hiding the video when it isn't playing:** You can hide the video until you start playing it by selecting the Hide While Not Playing check box. Be sure to choose Automatically on the Start drop-down list if you select this check box.

✦ **Continuously playing, or looping, the video:** Play a video continuously or until you go to the next slide by selecting the Loop Until Stopped check box.

✦ **Rewinding the video when it's finished playing:** Rewind a video if you want to see the first frame, not the last, when the video finishes playing. Select the Rewind After Playing check box to make the start of the video appear after the video plays; deselect this option to freeze-frame on the end of the video when it finishes playing.

Chapter 5: Delivering a Presentation

In This Chapter

✔ Writing, editing, and printing speaker notes

✔ Rehearsing a presentation to see how long it is

✔ Going from slide to slide in a live presentation

✔ Drawing on slides during a presentation

✔ Delivering a presentation when you can't be there in person

At last, the big day has arrived. It's time to give the presentation. "Break a leg," as actors say before they go onstage. This chapter explains how to rehearse your presentation to find out how long it is and show your presentation. You discover some techniques to make your presentation livelier, including how to draw on slides with a pen or highlighter and blank out the screen to get the audience's full attention. The chapter describes how to handle the speaker notes and print handouts for your audience. In case you can't be there in person to deliver your presentation, this chapter shows you how to create a user-run presentation, a self-running presentation, a presentation designed to be viewed from a CD, and video of a presentation.

All about Notes

Notes are strictly for the speaker. They aren't for the unwashed masses. Don't hesitate to write notes to yourself when you put together your presentation. The notes will come in handy when you're rehearsing and giving your presentation. They give you ideas for what to say and help you communicate better. Here are instructions for entering, editing, and printing notes:

 ✦ **Entering a note:** To enter a note, start in Normal view, click in the Notes pane, and start typing. Treat the Notes pane like a page in a word processor. For example, press Enter to start a new paragraph and press the Tab key to indent text. You can drag the border above the Notes pane up or down to make the pane larger or smaller.

✦ **Editing notes in Notes Page view:** After you've jotted down a bunch of notes, switch to Notes Page view and edit them. To switch to Notes Page view, visit the View tab and click the Notes Page button. Notes appear in a text frame below a picture of the slide to which they refer. You may have to zoom in to read them.

✦ **Printing your notes:** On the File tab, choose Print (or press Ctrl+P). You see the Print window. Under Settings, open the second drop-down list and choose Note Pages. Then click the Print button.

Rehearsing and Timing Your Presentation

Slide presentations and theatrical presentations have this in common: They are as good as the number of times you rehearse them. Be sure to rehearse your presentation many times over. The more you rehearse, the more comfortable you are giving a presentation. Follow these steps to rehearse a presentation, record its length, and record how long each slide is displayed:

1. **Select the first slide in your presentation.**

2. **Go to the Slide Show tab.**

3. **Click the Rehearse Timings button.**

The Recording toolbar, shown in Figure 5-1, appears, and you switch to Slide Show view.

Advance to the next slide   Note how long your presentation is

Figure 5-1:
Timing the
rehearsal.

4. **Give your presentation one slide at a time and click the Next button on the Recording toolbar to go from slide to slide.**

When each slide appears, imagine that you're presenting it to an audience. Say what you intend to say during the real presentation. If you anticipate audience members asking questions, allot time for questions.

The Recording toolbar tells you how long each slide has been displayed and how long your presentation is so far. You can do these tasks from the Recording toolbar:

• *Go to the next slide:* Click the Next button.

• *Pause recording:* Click the Pause Recording button to temporarily stop the recording so that you can feed the dog or take a phone call. Click the Resume Recording button to resume recording.

• *Repeat a slide:* Click the Repeat button if you get befuddled and want to start over with a slide. The slide timing returns to 0:00:00.

5. **In the dialog box that asks whether you want to keep the slide timings, note how long your presentation is (refer to Figure 5-1).**

Is your presentation too long or too short? I hope, like baby bear's porridge, your presentation is "just right." But if it's too long or short, you have some work to do. You have to figure out how to shorten or lengthen it.

6. **In the dialog box that asks whether you want to keep the new slide timings, click Yes if you want to see how long each slide stayed on-screen during the rehearsal.**

By clicking Yes, you can go to Slide Sorter view and see how long each slide remained on-screen.

WARNING!

If you save the slide timings, PowerPoint assumes that, during a presentation, you want to advance to the next slide manually or after the recorded time, whichever comes first. For example, suppose the first slide in your presentation remained on-screen for a minute during the rehearsal. During your presentation, the first slide will remain on-screen for a minute and automatically yield to the second slide unless you click to advance to the second slide before the minute has passed. If you recorded slide timings strictly to find out how long your presentation is, you need to tell PowerPoint not to advance automatically to the next slide during a presentation after the recorded time period elapses. On the Slide Show tab, deselect the Use Timings check box.

Showing Your Presentation

Compared to the preliminary work, giving a presentation can seem kind of anticlimactic. All you have to do is go from slide to slide and woo your audience with your smooth-as-silk voice and powerful oratory skills. Well, at least the move-from-slide-to-slide part is pretty easy. These pages explain how to start and end a presentation, all the different ways to advance or retreat from slide to slide, and how to jump to different slides.

Starting and ending a presentation

Here are the different ways to start a presentation from the beginning:

✦ On the Slide Show tab, click the From Beginning button.

✦ Select the first slide and then click the Slide Show view button.

You can start a presentation in the middle by selecting a slide in the middle and then clicking the Slide Show view button or going to the Slide Show tab and clicking the From Current Slide button.

Here are the different ways to end a presentation prematurely:

✦ Press Esc, Ctrl+Break, or – (the Hyphen key).

✦ Click the Slide button and choose End Show on the pop-up menu. The Slide button is located in the lower-left corner of the screen.

✦ Right-click and choose End Show in the shortcut menu.

Going from slide to slide

In a nutshell, PowerPoint offers four ways to move from slide to slide in a presentation. Table 5-1 describes techniques for navigating a presentation, using the four different ways:

✦ **Use the slide control buttons:** Click a slide control button — Previous, Next — in the lower-left corner of the screen, as shown in Figure 5-2. If you don't see the slide control buttons, jiggle the mouse.

✦ **Click the Slide button:** Click this button and make a choice on the pop-up menu (refer to Figure 5-2).

✦ **Right-click on-screen:** Right-click and choose a navigation option on the shortcut menu.

✦ **Press a keyboard shortcut:** Press one of the numerous keyboard shortcuts that PowerPoint offers for going from slide to slide (see Table 5-1).

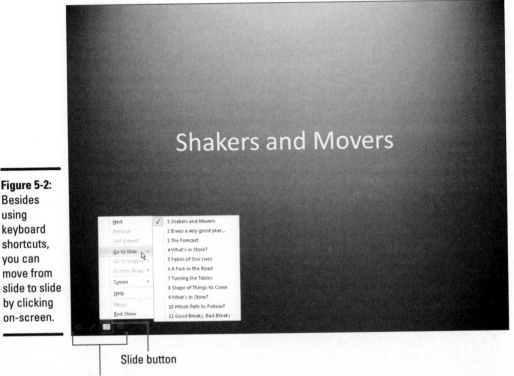

Figure 5-2: Besides using keyboard shortcuts, you can move from slide to slide by clicking on-screen.

Slide button

Slide controls

Table 5-1			Techniques for Getting from Slide to Slide	
To go here	*Slide control button*	*Click the Slide button and choose...*	*Right-click and choose...*	*Keyboard shortcut*
Next slide*	Next	Next	Next	Enter, spacebar, N, PgDn, ↓, or →
Previous slide	Previous	Previous	Previous	Backspace, P, PgUp, ↑, or ←
Specific slide		Go To Slide⇨ *Slide number and title*	Go to Slide⇨ *Slide number and title*	*Slide number+* Enter; Ctrl+S and then select *Slide number and title*
Last viewed slide		Last Viewed	Last Viewed	
Section		Go To Section⇨ *Section name*	Go To Section⇨ *Section name*	
First slide		Go To Slide⇨ *Slide 1*	Go To Slide⇨ *Slide 1*	Home
Last slide		Go To Slide⇨ *Slide (number of last slide)*	Go To Slide⇨ *Slide (number of last slide)*	End

If animations are on a slide, commands for going to the next slide instead make animations play in sequence. To bypass animations and go to the next slide, use a command for going forward across several slides. (See "Jumping forward or backward to a specific slide.")

Going forward (or backward) from slide to slide

To go forward from one slide to the following slide in a presentation, click on-screen. After you click, the next slide appears. If all goes well, clicking is the only technique you need to know when giving a presentation to go from slide to slide, but Table 5-1 lists other ways to go to the next slide in a presentation as well as techniques for going backward to the previous slide.

To go to the first slide in a presentation, press Home; to go to the last slide, press End.

Jumping forward or backward to a specific slide

If you find it necessary to jump forward or backward across several slides in your presentation to get to the slide you want to show, it can be done with these techniques:

✦ Either click the Slide button or right-click, choose Go to Slide, and then choose a slide in your presentation on the submenu (refer to Figure 5-2). If you created sections for your presentation, you can choose Go To Section and then choose a section name on the submenu.

✦ Press Ctrl+S. You see the All Slides dialog box. It lists all slides in your presentation. Select the slide you want to show and click the Go To button.

✦ Press the slide number you want on your keyboard (if you can remember the slide's number) and then press the Enter key. For example, to show the third slide in your presentation, press 3 and then press Enter.

If you need to return to where you started after you make the jump to a different slide, you can do so by right-clicking and choosing Last Viewed on the shortcut menu. You can also click the Slide button and choose Last Viewed (refer to Figure 5-2). The Last Viewed command takes you to the last slide you showed, wherever it is in your presentation.

Tricks for Making Presentations a Little Livelier

To make presentations a little livelier, whip out a pen and draw on a slide or blank the screen. Draw to underline words or draw check marks as you hit the key points, as shown in Figure 5-3. Drawing on slides is an excellent way to add a little something to a presentation. Blank the screen when you want the audience's undivided attention.

Wielding a pen or highlighter in a presentation

Follow these instructions so that you can draw on a slide:

✦ **Selecting a pen or highlighter:** PowerPoint offers the Pen for writing on slides and the Highlighter for highlighting text on slides. To select the Pen or Highlighter, click the Pen button and choose Pen or Highlighter (refer to Figure 5-3). You can also right-click, choose Pointer Options, and make a selection on the submenu.

✦ **Choosing a color for drawing:** After you select the Pen or Highlighter, click the Pen button, choose Ink Color, and select a color on the submenu (refer to Figure 5-3).

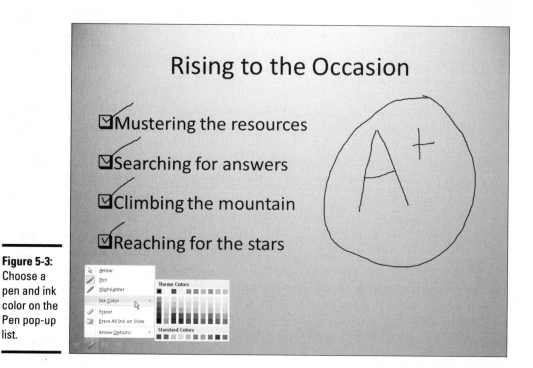

Figure 5-3:
Choose a
pen and ink
color on the
Pen pop-up
list.

Press Esc when you're finished using the pen. (Just be careful not to press Esc twice because the second press tells PowerPoint to end the presentation.)

Hiding and erasing pen and highlighter markings

Follow these instructions to hide and erase pen and highlighter markings:

✦ **Temporarily showing or hiding markings:** Right-click and choose Screen➪Show/Hide Ink Markup.

✦ **Permanently erasing markings one at a time:** Click the Pen button and choose Eraser (or right-click and choose Pointer Options➪Eraser). The Eraser appears. Click a line to erase it. Press Esc after you're finished using the Eraser.

✦ **Permanently erasing all the markings on a slide:** Press E or click the Pen button and choose Erase All Ink on Slide (refer to Figure 5-3).

✦ **Erasing markings you told PowerPoint to keep:** As I explain shortly, PowerPoint asks at the end of a presentation that you drew on or highlighted whether you want to keep the markings. If you elect to keep them, the markings become part of your presentation, and you can't delete them

**Book IV
Chapter 5**

**Delivering a
Presentation**

by clicking with the Eraser or by choosing the Erase All Ink on Slide command. To discard these markings later, go to the Review tab, open the drop-down list on the Delete button, and choose one of these options:

- *Delete All Markup on the Current Slide:* Deletes markings you made on a slide you selected

- *Delete All Markup in This Presentation:* Deletes markings you made on all the slides in your presentation

Markings aren't permanent, although you can keep them. At the end of a presentation in which you have marked on slides, a dialog box asks whether you want to keep or discard your markings. Click the Keep or Discard button. (If you prefer not to see this dialog box because you intend never to keep your markings, go to the File tab and choose Options. In the PowerPoint Options dialog box, select the Advanced category and deselect the Prompt to Keep Ink Annotations When Exiting check box.)

Blanking the screen

Here's a technique for adding a little drama to a presentation: When you want the audience to focus on you, not the PowerPoint screen, blank the screen. Make an all-black or all-white screen appear where a PowerPoint slide used to be. Every head in the audience will turn your way and listen keenly to what you have to say next. I sure hope that you have something important to say.

Follow these instructions to blank out the screen during a presentation:

- **Black screen:** Press B, the period key, or right-click and choose Screen⇨Black Screen.

- **White screen:** Press W, the comma key, or right-click and choose Screen⇨White Screen.

To see a PowerPoint slide again, click on-screen or press any key on the keyboard.

Delivering a Presentation When You Can't Be There in Person

PowerPoint offers numerous ways to deliver a presentation when you can't be there in person. You can deliver your presentation in the form of a *handout,* a printed version of the presentation with thumbnail slides; create a self-running presentation; or create a user-run presentation with action buttons that others can click to get from slide to slide. The rest of this chapter explains how to do all that as well as package your presentation so that people who don't have PowerPoint can view it and make a video of your presentation.

Book VIII, Chapter 2 describes two more ways to distribute PowerPoint presentations — by saving them as PDF files and publishing them on the Internet.

Providing handouts for your audience

Handouts are thumbnail versions of slides that you print and distribute to the audience. Figure 5-4 shows examples of handouts. Handouts come in one, two, three, four, six, or nine slides per page. If you select three slides per page, the handout includes lines that your audience can take notes on (see Figure 5-4); the other sizes don't offer these lines.

Figure 5-4:
Examples
of handouts
(from left
to right) at
one, three,
six, and nine
slides per
page.

To tell PowerPoint how to construct handouts, go to the View tab and click the Handout Master button. In Handout Master view, on the Handout Master tab, you can do a number of things to make your handouts more useful and attractive. As you make your choices, keep your eye on the sample handout page; it shows what your choices mean in real terms.

✦ **Handout Orientation:** Select Portrait or Landscape. In landscape mode, the page is turned on its side and is longer than it is tall.

✦ **Slide Orientation:** Select Portrait or Landscape, although I can't think of a good reason to choose Portrait.

✦ **Slides-Per-Page:** Open the drop-down list and choose how many slides appear on each page. Figure 5-4 shows what some of the choices are.

✦ **Header:** Select the Header check box and enter a header in the text frame to make a header appear in the upper-left corner of all handout pages. Candidates for headers include your name, your company name, and the location of a conference or seminar. The point is to help your audience identify the handout.

✦ **Footer:** Select the Footer check box and enter a footer in the text frame in the lower-left corner of handout pages. Candidates for footers are the same as candidates for headers.

+ **Date:** Select this check box if you want the date you print the handout to appear on the handout pages.

+ **Page Number:** Select this check box if you want page numbers to appear on the handout pages.

+ **Background Styles:** Open the Background Styles drop-down list and select a gradient or color, if you're so inclined. Chapter 2 of this mini-book explains background styles. Make sure that the background doesn't obscure the slide thumbnails or put too much of a burden on your printer.

To print handouts, go to the File tab and choose Print (or press Ctrl+P). You see the Print window. Under Settings, open the second drop-down list, and under Handouts, choose how many slides to print on each page. Then click the Print button.

Creating a self-running, kiosk-style presentation

A self-running, kiosk-style presentation is one that plays on its own. You can make it play from a kiosk or simply send it to co-workers so that they can play it. In a self-running presentation, slides appear on-screen one after the other without you or anyone else having to advance the presentation from slide to slide. When the presentation finishes, it starts all over again from Slide 1.

Telling PowerPoint how long to keep slides on-screen

PowerPoint offers two ways to indicate how long you want each slide to stay on-screen:

+ **Entering the time periods yourself:** Switch to Slide Sorter view and go to the Transitions tab. Then deselect the On Mouse Click check box and select the After check box, as shown in Figure 5-5. Next, tell PowerPoint to keep all slides on-screen the same amount of time or choose a different time period for each slide:

  • *All slides at the same time:* Enter a time period in the After text box and click the Apply to All button.

  • *Each slide at a different time:* One by one, select each slide and enter a time period in the After text box.

+ **Rehearsing the presentation:** Rehearse the presentation and save the timings. (See "Rehearsing and Timing Your Presentation," earlier in this chapter.) Be sure to save the slide timings after you're finished rehearsing. In Slide Sorter view, you can see how long each slide will stay on-screen (refer to Figure 5-5).

Enter a time period

Figure 5-5:
Enter how long you want each slide or all the slides to remain on-screen.

Telling PowerPoint that your presentation is self-running

Before you can "self-run" a presentation, you have to tell PowerPoint that you want it to do that. Self-running presentations don't have the control buttons in the lower-left corner. You can't click the screen or press a key to move forward or backward to the next or previous slide. The only control you have over a self-running presentation is pressing the Esc key (pressing Esc ends the presentation).

Follow these steps to make yours a kiosk-style, self-running presentation:

1. **Go to the Slide Show tab.**

2. **Click the Set Up Slide Show button.**

   You see the Set Up Slide Show dialog box.

3. **Under Show Type, select the Browsed at a Kiosk (Full Screen) option.**

   When you select this option, PowerPoint automatically selects the Loop Continuously Until 'Esc' check box.

4. **Make sure that the Using Timings, If Present option button is selected.**

5. **Click OK.**

   That's all there is to it.

Creating a user-run presentation

A *user-run*, or *interactive*, presentation is one that the viewer gets to control. The viewer decides which slide appears next and how long each slide remains on-screen. User-run presentations are similar to Web sites. Users can browse from slide to slide at their own speed. They can pick and choose what they want to investigate. They can backtrack and view slides they saw previously or return to the first slide and start anew.

Self-run presentations are shown in Reading view (click the Reading View view button on the status bar to see what self-run presentations looks like). A taskbar appears along the bottom of the screen. On the right side of the taskbar, viewers can click the Previous button or Next button to go from slide to slide. They can also click the Menu button to open a pop-up menu with commands for navigating slides.

Another way to help readers get from slide to slide is to create action buttons. An *action button* is a button that you can click to go to another slide in your presentation or the previous slide you viewed, whatever that slide was. PowerPoint provides 11 action buttons in the Shapes gallery. Figure 5-6 shows some action buttons and the dialog box you use to create them.

Figure 5-6: Action buttons.

Drawing an action button

After you draw an action button from the Shapes gallery, the Action Settings dialog box (refer to Figure 5-6) appears so that you can tell PowerPoint which slide to go to when the button is clicked. Select the slide (or master slide) that needs action and follow these steps to adorn it with an action button:

1. **On the Home or Insert tab, open the Shapes gallery and scroll to the Action Buttons category at the bottom.**

2. **Click an action button to select it.**

Choose the button that best illustrates which slide will appear when the button is clicked.

3. Draw the button on the slide.

To do so, drag the pointer in a diagonal fashion. (As far as drawing them is concerned, action buttons work the same as all other shapes and other objects. Book I, Chapter 8 explains how to manipulate objects.) The Action Settings dialog box (refer to Figure 5-6) appears after you finish drawing your button.

4. Go to the Mouse Over tab if you want users to activate the button by moving the mouse pointer over it, not clicking it.

5. Select the Hyperlink To option button.

6. On the Hyperlink To drop-down list, choose an action for the button.

You can go to the next slide, the previous slide, the first or last slide in a presentation, the last slide you viewed, or a specific slide.

To make clicking the action button take users to a specific slide, choose Slide on the list. You see the Hyperlink to Slide dialog box, which lists each slide in your presentation. Select a slide and click OK.

7. To play a sound when your action button is activated, select the Play Sound check box and select a sound on the drop-down list.

"Mouse-over" hyperlinks can do with sound accompaniment so that users understand when they've activated an action button.

8. Click OK in the Actions Settings dialog box.

To test your button, you can right-click it and choose Open Hyperlink.

 To change a button's action, select it and then click the Action button on the Insert tab, or right-click your action button and choose Edit Hyperlink. In the Action Settings dialog box, choose a new action and click OK.

Making yours a user-run presentation

Follow these steps to declare yours a user-run presentation:

1. Go to the Slide Show tab.

2. Click the Set Up Slide Show button.

You see the Set Up Show dialog box.

3. Select the Browsed by an Individual (Window) option button.

4. Click OK.

Your presentation is no longer quite yours. It also belongs to all the people who view it in your absence.

Packaging your presentation on a CD

The Package for CD command copies a presentation to a CD so that you can take a presentation on the road or distribute it to others on CDs. By using the Package for CD command, you can even distribute a presentation to people who don't have PowerPoint. Someone who doesn't have PowerPoint can download the *PowerPoint Viewer,* an abridged version of PowerPoint with all the PowerPoint slide-show commands (but none of the slide-creation commands). With the Package for CD command, you don't have to be concerned whether someone to whom you give your presentation has PowerPoint or whether PowerPoint is installed on the computer where you will give your presentation.

These pages explain the ins and outs of the Package for CD command. You find out how to copy a presentation to a CD or folder and play a presentation in PowerPoint Viewer.

Packaging a presentation on a CD

Follow these steps to copy your presentation and the PowerPoint Viewer to a CD or a folder:

1. **Open the presentation you want to package.**

2. **On the File tab, choose Save & Send.**

File

3. **Choose Package Presentation for CD, and click the Package for CD button.**

You see the Package for CD dialog box shown in Figure 5-7.

Figure 5-7: Packaging a CD to distribute to others.

4. **Enter a name for the CD or folder in the Name the CD text box.**

The name you enter will appear as the name of the CD if you view the CD in Windows Explorer or Computer; if you're copying your presentation to a folder, the name you enter will be given to the folder PowerPoint creates when it creates the packaged presentation file.

5. Create the packaged presentation and copy it to a CD or to a folder on your computer.

Copy the presentation to a folder if you want to send the presentation by e-mail rather than distribute it by CD.

- *Copying to a CD:* Click the Copy to CD button.

- *Copying to a folder:* Click the Copy to Folder button. In the Copy to Folder dialog box, click the Browse button, and in the Choose Location dialog box, select a folder for storing the folder where you will keep your packaged presentation. Then click the Select button and click OK in the Copy to Folder dialog box.

6. Click Yes in the message box that asks if you want to include linked content in the presentation.

It can take PowerPoint several minutes to assemble the files and copy them to the CD or folder.

If you're copying your presentation to a CD, PowerPoint asks whether you want to copy the same presentation to another CD. Either insert a fresh CD and click Yes, or click the No button.

Distributing a presentation to people who don't have PowerPoint

Not everyone has PowerPoint. Not everyone is so blessed. Some people live along in ignorant bliss without knowing anything about PowerPoint and its slide-show capabilities.

Don't be discouraged if you want to send your PowerPoint presentation to someone who doesn't have or may not have PowerPoint. Someone who doesn't have PowerPoint on his or her computer can still play a PowerPoint presentation by way of *PowerPoint Viewer,* a software program you can download for free from Microsoft starting at this Web page (enter **PowerPoint Viewer** in the Search text box and click the Go button):

www.microsoft.com/downloads

Here are instructions for running a presentation in PowerPoint Viewer:

- ✔ **Getting from slide to slide:** Click on-screen or right-click and choose Next on the shortcut menu.

- ✔ **Retreating:** Right-click and choose Previous or Last Viewed.

- ✔ **Going to a specific slide:** Right-click, choose Go to Slide, and select a slide on the submenu.

- ✔ **Ending the show:** Press Esc or right-click and choose End Show.

Book IV Chapter 5

Delivering a Presentation

Playing a packaged presentation

As shown in Figure 5-8, the AutoPlay dialog box appears when you put a CD-packaged PowerPoint presentation in the computer's CD drive. Tell the people to whom you distribute your CD that they can play the presentation starting in this dialog box whether or not PowerPoint is installed on their computers:

✦ **PowerPoint (or PowerPoint Viewer) is installed:** Click the Open Folder to View Files button in the AutoPlay dialog box. The Computer application opens to show the files on the CD. Double-click the PowerPoint presentation to play it.

✦ **PowerPoint isn't installed:** Click the Run Presentation Package button in the AutoPlay dialog box. A Web browser opens. Click the Download Viewer button to go to a Web page at Microsoft.com and download the PowerPoint Viewer. After downloading and installing PowerPoint Viewer, you can use it to play the PowerPoint presentation.

Figure 5-8:
Playing
a CD-
packaged
presentation.

Creating a presentation video

Yet another way to distribute a video is to record it in a WMV (Windows Media Video) file and distribute the file on a CD, distribute it by e-mail, or post it on the Internet. PowerPoint offers a command for creating a WMV-file version of a presentation. Every aspect of a PowerPoint presentation, including transitions, animations, sound, video itself, and voice narrations, is recorded in the presentation video.

Figure 5-9 shows a WMV-file version of a PowerPoint presentation being played in Windows Media Player. This utility comes with the Windows operating system. Everyone with a computer that runs Windows can play WMV-file versions of your presentations by playing them in Windows Media Player.

Figure 5-9:
Viewing a WMV-file version of a PowerPoint presentation in Windows Media Player.

Before creating your presentation video, consider how long you want each slide to appear on-screen. You can make each slide appear for a specific length of time or make all slides appear for the same length of time. To decide for yourself how long each slide appears, switch to Slide Sorter view, go to the Transitions tab, and for each slide, select the After check box and enter a measurement in the After text box. (Earlier in this chapter, "Creating a self-running, kiosk-style presentation" explains in detail how to establish how long each slide stays on-screen.)

Follow these steps to create a WMV-file version of a PowerPoint presentation:

1. **On the File tab, choose Save & Send.**

2. **Choose Create a Video.**

   You see the Create a Video window.

3. **Open the first drop-down list and choose a display resolution for your video.**

4. **Open the second drop-down list and choose whether to use recorded timings and narrations.**

   Your choices are twofold. If you recorded a voice narration for your PowerPoint presentation (a topic not covered in this book), choose the second option if you want to preserve the voice narration in the video.

- *Don't Use Recorded Timings and Narrations:* Each slide stays on-screen for the same amount of time. Enter a time period in the Seconds to Spend on Each Slide box to declare how long each slide stays on-screen.

- *Use Recorded Timings and Narrations:* Each slide stays on-screen for the time period listed on the Transition tab (see the Tip at the start of this section to find out how to list slide times on the Transition tab).

5. **Open the second drop-down list and choose Preview Timings and Narrations.**

   Your presentation video plays. How do you like it? This is what your video will look and sound like after you save it in a WMV file.

6. **Click the Create Video button.**

   The Save As dialog box opens.

7. **Choose a folder for storing the WMV file, enter a name for the file, and click the Save button.**

   The status bar along the bottom of the PowerPoint screen shows the progress of the video as it is being created. Creating a video can take several minutes, depending on how large your PowerPoint presentation is and how many fancy gizmos, such as sound and animation, it contains.

Book V

Excel

"No, that's not the icon for Excel, it's the icon for Excuse, the database of reasons why you haven't learned the other programs in Office."

Contents at a Glance

Chapter 1: Up and Running with Excel

In This Chapter

✔ Creating an Excel workbook

✔ Understanding what a worksheet is

✔ Entering text, as well as numeric, date, and time data

✔ Using the AutoFill command to enter lists and serial data

✔ Establishing conditional formats for text

✔ Setting up data-validation rules

This chapter introduces *Excel,* the official number cruncher of Office 2010. The purpose of Excel is to track, analyze, and tabulate numbers. Use the program to project profits and losses, formulate a budget, or analyze Elvis sightings in North America. Doing the setup work takes time, but after you enter the numbers and tell Excel how to tabulate them, you're on Easy Street. Excel does the math for you. All you have to do is kick off your shoes, sit back, and see how the numbers stack up.

This chapter explains what a workbook and a worksheet are and how rows and columns on a worksheet determine where cell addresses are. You also discover tips and tricks for quickly entering data in a worksheet, and how to construct data-validation rules to make sure that data is entered accurately.

Creating a New Excel Workbook

When you start Excel, the program greets you with a brand-new workbook with the generic name "Book1" on the title bar. *Workbook* is just the Excel term for the files you create with the program. You can start working right away on the generic workbook or you can take advantage of one of Excel's templates.

A *template* is a preformatted workbook designed for a specific purpose, such as budgeting, tracking inventories, or tracking purchase orders. Creating a workbook from a template is mighty convenient if you happen to find a template that suits your purposes, but in my experience, you almost always have to start from a generic, blank workbook because your data is your own. You need a workbook you create yourself, not one created from a template by someone else.

File

Whether you want to create a new workbook from a template or from scratch, start by going to the File tab and choosing New. You see the Available Templates window shown in Figure 1-1. This window offers templates for creating many kinds of workbooks. Click a template to see, on the right side of the window, a preview of the workbook you will create. Double-click a template (or select it and click the Create button) to create a new workbook.

Figure 1-1: Create a workbook by starting in the Available Templates window.

Use one of these techniques in the Available Templates window to create a workbook:

✦ **Create a blank workbook:** Double-click the Blank Workbook icon. (By pressing Ctrl+N, you can create a new, blank workbook without opening the Available Templates window.)

✦ **Create a workbook from a template:** Take your pick from these techniques to create a workbook from a template:

• *Use a template on your computer:* Click Sample Templates. Templates that you loaded on your computer when you installed Office appear in the window.

- *Download a template from Office.com:* Under Office.com Templates, either choose the type of template you want or make sure that your computer is connected to the Internet, enter a search term in the Search box, and click the Start Searching button (or press Enter). Choose a template and click the Download button to download it to your computer.

- *Use a template you created (or downloaded earlier from Microsoft):* Click the My Templates icon. The New dialog box appears. Select a template and click OK. (Chapter 4 of this mini-book describes how to create your own template; after you create a template, its name appears in this dialog box.)

- *Select a recently used template:* Click the Recent Templates icon and double-click a template name.

✦ **Recycle another workbook:** If you can use another workbook as the starting point for creating a new one, click the New from Existing icon. In the New from Existing Workbook dialog box, select the workbook and click the Create New button.

Book I, Chapter 1 explains how to save a workbook after you create it as well as how to open a workbook that you want to work on.

Getting Acquainted with Excel

If you've spent any time in an Office program, much of the Excel screen may look familiar to you. The buttons on the Home tab — the Bold and the Align buttons, for example — work the same in Excel as they do in Word. The Font and Font Size drop-down lists work the same as well. Any command in Excel that has to do with formatting text and numbers works the same in Excel and Word.

As I mention earlier, an Excel file is a *workbook.* Each workbook comprises one or more worksheets. A *worksheet,* also known as a *spreadsheet,* is a table where you enter data and data labels. Figure 1-2 shows a worksheet with data about rainfall in different counties.

A worksheet works like an accountant's ledger — only it's much easier to use. Notice how the worksheet is divided by gridlines into columns (A, B, C, and so on) and rows (1, 2, 3, and so on). The rectangles where columns and rows intersect are *cells,* and each cell can hold one data item, a formula for calculating data, or nothing at all. At the bottom of the worksheet are tabs — Sheet1, Sheet2, and Sheet3 — for visiting the other worksheets in the workbook.

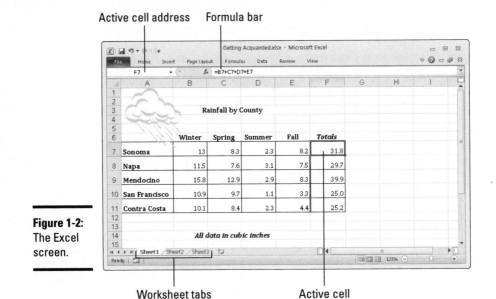

Active cell address   Formula bar

Figure 1-2:
The Excel
screen.

Worksheet tabs   Active cell

Each cell has a different cell address. In Figure 1-2, cell B7 holds 13, the amount of rain that fell in Sonoma County in the winter. Meanwhile, as the Formula bar at the top of the screen shows, cell F7, the *active cell,* holds the formula =B7+C7+D7+E7, the sum of the numbers in cells — you guessed it — B7, C7, D7, and E7.

The beauty of Excel is that the program does all the calculations and recalculations for you after you enter the data. If I were to change the number in cell B7, Excel would instantly recalculate the total amount of rainfall in Sonoma County in cell F7. People like myself who struggled in math class will be glad to know that you don't have to worry about the math because Excel does it for you. All you have to do is make sure that the data and the formulas are entered correctly.

After you enter and label the data, enter the formulas, and turn your worksheet into a little masterpiece, you can start analyzing the data. You can also generate charts like the one in Figure 1-3. Do you notice any similarities between the worksheet in Figure 1-2 and the chart in Figure 1-3? The chart is fashioned from data in the worksheet, and it took me about a half minute to create that chart. (Book I, Chapter 6 explains how to create charts in Excel, Word, and PowerPoint.)

Figure 1-3:
A chart
generated
from the
data in
Figure 1-2.

Rows, columns, and cell addresses

Not that anyone except an Enron accountant needs all of them, but an Excel worksheet has numerous columns and over 1 million rows. The rows are numbered, and columns are labeled A to Z; then AA to AZ; then BA to BZ, and so on. The important thing to remember is that each cell has an address whose name comes from a column letter and a row number. The first cell in row 1 is A1, the second is B1, and so on. You need to enter cell addresses in formulas to tell Excel which numbers to compute.

To find a cell's address, either make note of which column and row it lies in, or click the cell and glance at the Formula bar (refer to Figure 1-2). The left side of the Formula bar lists the address of the *active cell,* the cell that is selected in the worksheet. In Figure 1-2, cell F7 is the active cell.

Workbooks and worksheets

When you create a new Excel file, you open a *workbook,* a file with three worksheets in it. The worksheets are called Sheet1, Sheet2, and Sheet3 (you can change their names and add more worksheets). To get from worksheet to worksheet, click tabs along the bottom of the Excel window. Why three worksheets? Because you might need more than one worksheet for a single project. Think of a workbook as a stack of worksheets. Besides calculating the numbers in cells across the rows or down the columns of a worksheet, you can make calculations throughout a workbook by using numbers from different worksheets in a calculation.

Entering Data in a Worksheet

Entering data in a worksheet is an irksome activity. Fortunately, Excel offers a few shortcuts to take the sting out of it. These pages explain how to enter data in a worksheet, the different types of data, and how to enter text labels, numbers, dates, and times.

The basics of entering data

What you can enter in a worksheet cell falls in four categories:

+ Text

+ A value (numeric, date, or time)

+ A logical value (True or False)

+ A formula that returns a value, logical value, or text

Still, no matter what type of data you're entering, the basic steps are the same:

1. **Click the cell where you want to enter the data or text label.**

As shown in Figure 1-4, a square appears around the cell to tell you that the cell you clicked is now the active cell. Glance at the left side of the Formula bar if you're not sure of the address of the cell you're about to enter data in. The Formula bar lists the cell address.

Enter the data here. . .   or here

Figure 1-4: Entering data.

2. **Type the data in the cell.**

If you find typing in the Formula bar easier, click and start typing there. As soon as you type the first character, the Cancel button (an *X*) and Enter button (a check mark) appear beside the Insert Function button (labeled *fx*) on the Formula bar.

3. Press the Enter key to enter the number or label.

Besides pressing the Enter key, you can also press an arrow key (←, ↑, →, ↓), press Tab, or click the Enter button (the check mark) on the Formula bar.

If you change your mind about entering data, click the Cancel button or press Esc to delete what you entered and start over.

Chapter 3 of this mini-book explains how to enter logical values and formulas. The next several pages describe how to enter text labels, numeric values, date values, and time values.

The Paste Special command can come in very handy with worksheet data. As numbers are updated in the source file, they can be updated automatically in an Excel worksheet as well. Consider linking worksheets if your adventures in Excel enable you to keep source data in one place. Book VIII, Chapter 7 explains linking files.

Entering text labels

Sometimes a text entry is too long to fit in a cell. How Excel accommodates text entries that are too wide depends on whether data is in the cell to the right of the one you entered the text in:

✦ If the cell to the right is empty, Excel lets the text spill into the next cell.

✦ If the cell to the right contains data, the entry gets cut off. Nevertheless, the text you entered is in the cell. Nothing gets lost when it can't be displayed on-screen. You just can't see the text or numbers except by glancing at the Formula bar, where the contents of the active cell can be seen in its entirety.

To solve the problem of text that doesn't fit in a cell, widen the column, shorten the text entry, reorient the text (Chapter 4 of this mini-book explains aligning numbers and text in columns and rows), or wrap the contents of the cell. *Wrapping* means to run the text down to the next line, much the way the text in a paragraph runs to the next line when it reaches the right margin. Excel makes rows taller to accommodate wrapped text in a cell. To wrap text in cells, select the cells, go to the Home tab, and click the Wrap Text button (you can find it in the Alignment group).

Entering numeric values

When a number is too large to fit in a cell, Excel displays pound signs (###) rather than a number, or it displays the number in scientific notation. You can always glance at the Formula bar, however, to find out the number in the active cell. As well, you can always widen the column to display the entire number.

To enter a fraction in a cell, enter a 0 or a whole number, a blank space, and the fraction. For example, to enter ⅜, type a **0**, press the spacebar, and type **3/8**. To enter 5⅜, type the **5**, press the spacebar, and type **3/8**. For its purposes, Excel converts fractions to decimal numbers, as you can see by looking in the Formula bar after you enter a fraction. For example, 5⅜ displays as 5.375 in the Formula bar.

Here's a little trick for quickly entering numbers with decimals in all the Excel files you work on. To spare yourself the trouble of pressing the period key (.), you can tell Excel to enter the period automatically. Instead of entering 12.45, for example, you can simply enter 1245. Excel enters the period for you: 12.45. To perform this trick, go to the File tab, choose Options, visit the Advanced category in the Excel Options dialog box, click the Automatically Insert a Decimal Point check box, and in the Places text box, enter the number of decimal places you want for numbers. Deselect this option when you want to go back to entering numbers the normal way.

Entering date and time values

Dates and times can be used in calculations, but entering a date or time value in a cell can be problematic because these values must be entered in such a way that Excel can recognize them as dates or times, not text.

Not that you need to know it especially, but Excel converts dates and times to serial values for the purpose of being able to use dates and times in calculations. For example, July 31, 2004, is the number 38199. July 31, 2004, at noon is 38199.5. These serial values represent the number of whole days since January 1, 1900. The portion of the serial value to the right of the decimal point is the time, represented as a portion of a full day.

Entering date values

You can enter a date value in a cell in just about any format you choose, and Excel understands that you're entering a date. For example, enter a date in any of the following formats and you'll be all right:

m/d/yy	7/31/10
m-d-yyyy	7-31-2010
d-mmm-yy	31-Jul-10

Here are some basic things to remember about entering dates:

✦ **Date formats**: You can quickly apply a format to dates by selecting cells and using one of these techniques:

  • On the Home tab, open the Number Format drop-down list and choose Short Date (*m/d/yyyy*; 7/31/2010) or Long Date (*day-of-the-week, month, day, year*; Saturday, July 31, 2010), as shown in Figure 1-5.

- On the Home tab, click the Number group button to open the Number tab of the Format Cells dialog box. As shown in Figure 1-5, choose the Date category and then choose a date format.

✦ **Current date:** Press Ctrl+; (semicolon) and press Enter to enter the current date.

✦ **Current year's date:** If you don't enter the year as part of the date, Excel assumes that the date you entered is in the current year. For example, if you enter a date in the *m/d* (7/31) format during the year 2010, Excel enters the date as 7/31/10. As long as the date you want to enter is the current year, you can save a little time when entering dates by not entering the year, as Excel enters it for you.

✦ **Dates on the Formula bar:** No matter which format you use for dates, dates are displayed in the Formula bar in the format that Excel prefers for dates: *m/d/yyyy* (7/31/2010). How dates are displayed in the worksheet is up to you.

✦ **20th and 21st century two-digit years:** When it comes to entering two-digit years in dates, the digits 30 through 99 belong to the 20th century (1930–1999), but the digits 00 through 29 belong to the 21st century (2000–2029). For example, 7/31/10 refers to July 31, 2010, not July 31, 1910. To enter a date in 1929 or earlier, enter four digits rather than two to describe the year: **7-31-1929**. To enter a date in 2030 or later, enter four digits rather than two: **7-31-2030**.

Figure 1-5:
Format dates and numbers on the Number Format drop-down list or Format Cells dialog box.

+ **Dates in formulas:** To enter a date directly in a formula, enclose the date in quotation marks. (Make sure that the cell where the formula is entered has been given the Number format, not the Date format.) For example, the formula =TODAY()-"1/1/2010" calculates the number of days that have elapsed since January 1, 2010. Formulas are the subject of Chapter 3 of this mini-book.

Entering time values

Excel recognizes time values that you enter in the following ways:

h:mm AM/PM	3:31 AM
h:mm:ss AM/PM	3:31:45 PM

Here are some things to remember when entering time values:

+ **Use colons:** Separate hours, minutes, and seconds with a colon (:).

+ **Time formats:** To change to the *h:mm:ss* AM/PM time format, select the cells, go to the Home tab, open the Number Format drop-down list, and choose Time (refer to Figure 1-5). You can also change time formats by clicking the Number group button on the Home tab and selecting a time format on the Number tab of the Format Cells dialog box.

+ **AM or PM time designations:** Unless you enter AM or PM with the time, Excel assumes that you're operating on military time. For example, 3:30 is considered 3:30 a.m.; 15:30 is 3:30 p.m. Don't enter periods after the letters *am* or *pm* (don't enter a.m. or p.m.).

+ **Current time:** Press Ctrl+Shift+; (semicolon) to enter the current time.

+ **Times on the Formula bar:** On the Formula bar, times are displayed in this format: *hours:minutes:seconds,* followed by the letters AM or PM. However, the time format used in cells is up to you.

Combining date and time values

You can combine dates and time values by entering the date, a blank space, and the time:

+ 7/31/10 3:31 am

+ 7-31-10 3:31:45 pm

Quickly Entering Lists and Serial Data with the AutoFill Command

Data that falls in the "serial" category — month names, days of the week, and consecutive numbers and dates, for example — can be entered quickly with the AutoFill command. Believe it or not, Excel recognizes certain kinds of serial data and enters it for you as part of the AutoFill feature. Instead of laboriously entering this data one piece at a time, you can enter it all at one time by dragging the mouse. Follow these steps to "autofill" cells:

1. **Click the cell that is to be first in the series.**

For example, if you intend to list the days of the week in consecutive cells, click where the first day is to go.

2. **Enter the first number, date, or list item in the series.**

3. **Move to the adjacent cell and enter the second number, date, or list item in the series.**

If you want to enter the same number or piece of text in adjacent cells, it isn't necessary to take this step, but Excel needs the first and second items in the case of serial dates and numbers so that it can tell how much to increase or decrease the given amount or time period in each cell. For example, entering **5** and **10** tells Excel to increase the number by 5 each time so that the next serial entry is 15.

4. **Select the cell or cells you just entered data in.**

To select a single cell, click it; to select two, drag over the cells. Chapter 2 of this mini-book describes all the ways to select cells in a worksheet.

5. **Click the AutoFill handle and start dragging in the direction in which you want the data series to appear on your worksheet.**

The *AutoFill handle* is the little black square in the lower-right corner of the cell or block of cells you selected. Finding it can be difficult. Carefully move the mouse pointer over the lower-right corner of the cell, and when you see the mouse pointer change into a black cross, click and start dragging. As you drag, the serial data appears in a pop-up box, as shown in Figure 1-6.

Drag the AutoFill handle

Q1	Q2	Q3		
			Q4	
Monday	Tuesday	Wednesday		
			Thursday	
Jan	Feb	March		
			April	
1999	2000	2001		
			2002	
5	10	15		
			20	

Figure 1-6:
Entering
serial data
and text.

Creating your own AutoFill list

As you probably know, Excel is capable of completing lists on its own with the AutoFill feature. You can enter the days of the week or month names simply by entering one day or month and dragging the AutoFill handle to enter the others. Here's some good news: The AutoFill command can also reproduce the names of your co-workers, the roster of a softball team, street names, or any other list that you care to enter quickly and repeatedly in a worksheet.

Follow these steps to enter items for a list so that you can enter them in the future by dragging the AutoFill handle:

1. **If you've already entered items for the list on your worksheet, select the items.**

    If you haven't entered the items yet, skip to Step 2.

2. **On the File tab, choose Options to open the Excel Options dialog box.**

3. **Select the Advanced category.**

4. **Click the Edit Custom Lists button (you have to scroll down to find it).**

    You see the Custom Lists dialog box.

5. **In the List Entries box, do one of the following:**

    If you selected the items in Step 1, click the Import button. The items you selected appear in the List Entries box.

    If you need to enter items for the list, enter them in the List Entries box, with one item on each line.

6. **Click the Add button.**

7. **Click OK.**

Custom Lists   [?][✕]

Custom Lists

Custom lists: List entries:

NEW LIST	Groucho, Chico, Harpo, Zeppo	**Add**
Sun, Mon, Tue, Wed, Thu, Fri, S		
Sunday, Monday, Tuesday, Wed		Delete
Jan, Feb, Mar, Apr, May, Jun, J		
January, February, March, April		
Tom, Dick, Harry		
San Francisco, Daly City, Colma		

Press Enter to separate list entries.
Import list from cells: [▦]   **Import**

OK   Cancel

The AutoFill Options button appears after you enter the serial data. Click it and choose an option if you want to copy cells or fill the cells without carrying along their formats.

TIP

To enter the same number or text in several empty cells, drag over the cells to select them or select each cell by holding down the Ctrl key as you click. Then type a number or some text and press Ctrl+Enter.

Formatting Numbers, Dates, and Time Values

When you enter a number that Excel recognizes as belonging to one of its formats, Excel assigns the number format automatically. Enter **45%**, for example, and Excel assigns the Percentage Style format. Enter **$4.25**, and Excel assigns the Currency Style format. Besides assigning formats by hand, however, you can assign them to cells from the get-go and spare yourself the trouble of entering dollar signs, commas, percent signs, and other extraneous punctuation. All you have to do is enter the raw numbers. Excel does the window dressing for you.

Excel offers five number-formatting buttons on the Home tab — Accounting Number Format, Percent Style, Comma Style, Increase Decimal, and Decrease Decimal. Select cells with numbers in them and click one of these buttons to change how numbers are formatted:

+ **Accounting Number Format:** Places a dollar sign before the number and gives it two decimal places. You can open the drop-down list on this button and choose a currency symbol apart from the dollar sign.

+ **Percent Style:** Places a percent sign after the number and converts the number to a percentage.

+ **Comma Style:** Places commas in the number.

+ **Increase Decimal:** Increases the number of decimal places by one.

+ **Decrease Decimal:** Decreases the number of decimal places by one.

To choose among many formats and to format dates and time values as well as numbers, go to the Home tab, click the Number group button, and make selections on the Number tab of the Format Cells dialog box. Figure 1-7 shows this dialog box. Choose a category and select options to describe how you want numbers or text to appear.

To strip formats from the data in cells, select the cells, go to the Home tab, click the Clear button, and choose Clear Formats.

Figure 1-7:
The Number
category of
the Format
Cells dialog
box.

Entering ZIP Codes can be problematic because Excel strips the initial zero from the number if it begins with a zero. To get around that problem, visit the Number tab of the Format Cells dialog box (see Figure 1-7), choose Special in the Category list, and select a ZIP Code option.

Conditional Formats for Calling Attention to Data

A *conditional format* is one that applies when data meets certain conditions. To call attention to numbers greater than 10,000, for example, you can tell Excel to highlight those numbers automatically. To highlight negative numbers, you can tell Excel to display them in bright red. Conditional formats help you analyze and understand data better.

Select the cells that are candidates for conditional formatting and follow these steps to tell Excel when and how to format the cells:

1. **On the Home tab, click the Conditional Formatting button (you may have to click the Styles button first, depending on the size of your screen).**

2. **Choose Highlight Cells Rules or Top/Bottom Rules on the drop-down list.**

You see a submenu with choices about establishing the rule for whether values in the cells are highlighted or otherwise made more prominent:

- *Highlight Cells Rules:* These rules are for calling attention to data if it falls in a numerical or date range, or it's greater or lesser than a specific value. For example, you can highlight cells that are greater than 400.

- *Top/Bottom Rules:* These rules are for calling attention to data if it falls within a percentage range relative to all the cells you selected. For example, you can highlight cells with data that falls in the bottom 10 percent range.

3. Choose an option on the submenu.

You see a dialog box similar to the ones in Figure 1-8.

Figure 1-8:
Establishing a condition format for data.

4. On the left side of the dialog box, establish the rule for flagging data.

5. On the With drop-down list, choose how you want to call attention to the data.

For example, you can display the data in red or yellow. You can choose Custom Format on the drop-down list to open the Format Cells dialog box and choose a font style or color for the text.

6. Click OK.

To remove conditional formats, select the cells with the formats, go to the Home tab, click the Conditional Formatting button, and choose Clear Rules⇨ Clear Rules from Selected Cells.

Establishing Data-Validation Rules

By nature, people are prone to enter data incorrectly because the task of entering data is so dull. This is why data-validation rules are invaluable. A *data-validation rule* is a rule concerning what kind of data can be entered in a cell. When you select a cell that has been given a rule, an input message tells you what to enter, as shown in Figure 1-9. And if you enter the data incorrectly, an error alert tells you as much, also shown in Figure 1-9.

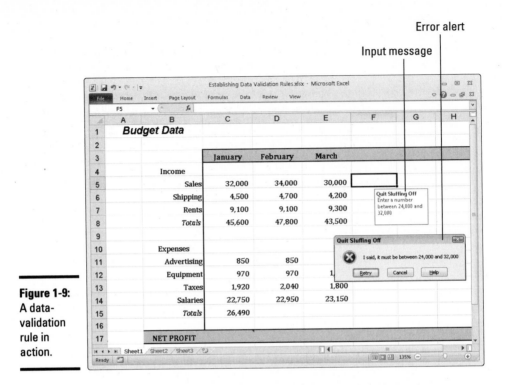

Figure 1-9:
A data-
validation
rule in
action.

Data-validation rules are an excellent defense against sloppy data entry and that itchy feeling you get when you're in the middle of an irksome task. In a cell that records date entries, you can require dates to fall in a certain time frame. In a cell that records text entries, you can choose an item from a list instead of typing it yourself. In a cell that records numeric entries, you can require the number to fall within a certain range. Table 1-1 describes the different categories of data-validation rules.

Table 1-1	Data-Validation Rule Categories
Rule	*What Can Be Entered*
Any Value	Anything whatsoever. This is the default setting.
Whole Number	Whole numbers (no decimal points allowed). Choose an operator from the Data drop-down list and values to describe the range of numbers that can be entered.
Decimal	Same as the Whole Number rule except numbers with decimal points are permitted.

Rule	What Can Be Entered
List	Items from a list. Enter the list items in cells on a worksheet, either the one you're working in or another. Then reopen the Data Validation dialog box, click the Range Selector button (you can find it on the right side of the Source text box), and select the cells that hold the list. The list items appear in a drop-down list on the worksheet.
Date	Date values. Choose an operator from the Data drop-down list and values to describe the date range. Earlier in this chapter, "Entering date and time values" describes the correct way to enter date values.
Time	Time values. Choose an operator from the Data drop-down list and values to describe the date and time range. Earlier in this chapter, "Entering date and time values" describes the correct way to enter a combination of date and time values.
Text Length	A certain number of characters. Choose an operator from the Data drop-down list and values to describe how many characters can be entered.
Custom	A logical value (True or False). Enter a formula that describes what constitutes a true or false data entry.

Follow these steps to establish a data-validation rule:

1. Select the cell or cells that need a rule.

2. On the Data tab, click the Data Validation button.

As shown in Figure 1-10, you see the Settings tab of the Data Validation dialog box.

3. On the Allow drop-down list, choose the category of rule you want.

Table 1-1, earlier in this chapter, describes these categories.

Figure 1-10:
Creating a data-validation rule.

4. **Enter the criteria for the rule.**

   What the criteria is depends on what rule category you're working in. Table 1-1 describes how to enter the criteria for rules in each category. You can refer to cells in the worksheet by selecting them. To do that, either select them directly or click the Range Selector button and then select them.

5. **On the Input Message tab, enter a title and input message.**

   You can see a title ("Quit Sluffing Off") and input message ("Enter a number between 24,000 and 32,000") in Figure 1-9. The title appears in boldface. Briefly describe what kind of data belongs in the cell or cells you selected.

6. **On the Error Alert tab, choose a style for the symbol in the Message Alert dialog box, enter a title for the dialog box, and enter a warning message.**

   In the error message in Figure 1-9, the Stop symbol was chosen. The title you enter appears across the top of the dialog box, and the message appears beside the symbol.

7. **Click OK.**

   To remove data-validation rules from cells, select the cells, go to the Data tab, click the Data Validation button, and on the Settings tab of the Data Validation dialog box, click the Clear All button, and click OK.

Chapter 2: Refining Your Worksheet

In This Chapter

✔ Changing worksheet data

✔ Going here and there in a worksheet

✔ Freezing and splitting columns and rows to make data entry easier

✔ Documenting a worksheet with comments

✔ Selecting cells

✔ Copying and moving data

✔ Moving among, deleting, and renaming worksheets

✔ Hiding and protecting worksheets so that they can't be altered

This chapter delves into the workaday world of worksheets (say that three times fast). It explains how to edit worksheet data and move quickly here and there in a worksheet. You also discover a couple of techniques for entering data quickly, how to select cells, and how to copy and move data in cells. This chapter describes how to move, delete, and rename worksheets, as well as protect them from being edited or altered.

Editing Worksheet Data

Not everyone enters data correctly the first time. To edit data you entered in a cell, do one of the following:

✦ **Double-click the cell.** Doing so places the cursor squarely in the cell, where you can start deleting or entering numbers and text.

✦ **Click the cell and press F2.** This technique also lands the cursor in the cell.

✦ **Click the cell you want to edit.** With this technique, you edit the data on the Formula bar.

If nothing happens when you double-click, or if pressing F2 lands the cursor in the Formula bar, not a cell, somebody has been fooling with the Options settings. On the File tab, choose Options, select the Advanced category in the Excel Options dialog box, and click the Allow Editing Directly in Cells check box.

Moving Around in a Worksheet

Going from place to place gets progressively more difficult as a worksheet gets larger. Luckily for you, Excel offers keyboard shortcuts for jumping around. Table 2-1 describes these keyboard shortcuts.

Table 2-1	Keyboard Shortcuts for Getting Around in Worksheets
Press. . .	**To Move the Selection. . .**
Home	To column A
Ctrl+Home	To cell A1, the first cell in the worksheet
Ctrl+End	To the last cell in the last row with data in it
←, →, ↑, ↓	To the next cell
Ctrl+←, →, ↑, ↓	In one direction toward the nearest cell with data in it or to the first or last cell in the column or row
PgUp *or* PgDn	Up or down one screen's worth of rows
Ctrl+PgUp *or* Ctrl+PgDn	Backward or forward through the workbook, from worksheet to worksheet

In addition to pressing keys, you can use these techniques to get from place to place in a worksheet:

✦ **Scroll bars:** Use the vertical and horizontal scroll bars to move to different areas. Drag the scroll box to cover long distances. To cover long distances very quickly, hold down the Shift key as you drag the scroll box on the vertical scroll bar.

✦ **Scroll wheel on the mouse:** If your mouse is equipped with a scroll wheel, turn the wheel to quickly scroll up and down.

✦ **Name box:** Enter a cell address in the Name box and press Enter to go to the cell. The Name box is found to the left of the Formula bar.

✦ **The Go To command:** On the Home tab, click the Find & Select button, and choose Go To on the drop-down list (or press Ctrl+G or F5). You see the Go To dialog box. Enter a cell address in the Reference box and click OK. Cell addresses you've already visited with the Go To command are already listed in the dialog box. Click the Special button to open the Go To Special dialog box and visit a formula, comment, or other esoteric item.

✦ **The Find command:** On the Home tab, click the Find & Select button, and choose Find on the drop-down list (or press Ctrl+F). Enter the data you seek in the Find What box and click the Find Next button. Click the

Find All button to find all instances of the item you're looking for. A list of the items appears at the bottom of the dialog box; click an item to go to it.

To scroll to the active cell if you no longer see it on-screen, press Ctrl+Backspace.

Getting a Better Look at the Worksheet

Especially when you're entering data, it pays to get a good look at the worksheet. You need to know which column and row you're entering data in. These pages explain techniques for changing your view of a worksheet so that you always know where you are. Read on to discover how to freeze, split, and hide columns and rows. (On the subject of changing views, Book I, Chapter 3 explains an essential technique for changing views: zooming in and zooming out.)

Freezing and splitting columns and rows

Sometimes your adventures in a worksheet take you to a faraway cell address, such as X31 or C39. Out there in the wilderness, it's hard to tell where to enter data because you can't see the data labels in the first column or first row that tell you where to enter data on the worksheet.

To see one part of a worksheet no matter how far you stray from it, you can *split* the worksheet or *freeze* columns and rows on-screen. In Figure 2-1, I split the worksheet so that column A (Property) always appears on-screen, no matter how far I scroll to the right; similarly, row 1 (Property, Rent, Management Fees, and so on) also appears at the top of the worksheet no matter how far I scroll down. Notice how the row numbers and column letters are interrupted in Figure 2-1. Because I split the screen, I always know what data to enter in a cell because I can clearly see property names in the first column and the column headings along the top of the worksheet.

Freezing columns or rows on a worksheet works much like splitting except that lines instead of gray bars appear on-screen to show which columns and rows are frozen, and you can't adjust where the split occurs by dragging the boundary where the worksheet is split.

Splitting the worksheet is superior to freezing columns or rows because, for one, you can drag the split lines to new locations when you split the worksheet, and moreover, you can remove a horizontal or vertical split simply by double-clicking it. However, if your goal is simply to freeze the topmost row or leftmost column in your worksheet, use a Freeze Panes command because all you have to do is go to the View tab, click the Freeze Panes button, and choose Freeze Top Row or Freeze First Column.

Drag to adjust the split   Double-click to remove a split line   Split bar

Figure 2-1:
Splitting a
worksheet.

Giving the Split or Freeze Panes command

Follow these steps to split or freeze columns and rows on-screen:

1. **Click the cell directly below the row you want to freeze or split, and click in the column to the right of the column that you want to freeze or split.**

   In other words, click where you want the split to occur.

2. **On the View tab, split or freeze the columns and rows.**

   Go to the View tab and use one of these techniques:

   - *Splitting:* Click the Split button and then click and drag the split bars to split the screen horizontally or vertically. The other way to split a worksheet is to grab hold of a *split bar,* the little division markers directly above the vertical scroll bar and directly to the right of the horizontal scroll bar (in the lower-right corner of your screen). You can tell where split bars are because the pointer turns into a double arrow when it's over a split bar.

   - *Freezing:* Click the Freeze Panes button and choose one of three Freeze options on the drop-down list. The second and third options, respectively, freeze the top row or first column. The first option, Freeze Panes, freezes the column(s) to the left and the row(s) above the cell you selected in Step 1.

   Bars or lines appear on-screen to show which row(s) and column(s) have been frozen or split. Move where you will in the worksheet. The column(s) and row(s) you froze or split stay on-screen.

Your own customized views

After you go to the trouble of freezing the screen or zooming in to a position you're comfortable with, you may as well save your view of the screen as a customized view. That way, you can call upon the customized view whenever you need it. View settings, the window size, the position of the grid on-screen, and cells that are selected can all be saved in a customized view.

Follow these steps to create a customized view:

1. **On the View tab, click the Custom Views button.**

    You see the Custom Views dialog box. It lists views you've already created, if you've created any.

2. **Click the Add button.**

    The Add View dialog box appears.

3. **Enter a name for the view and click OK.**

To switch to a customized view, click the Custom Views button, select a view in the Custom Views dialog box, and click the Show button.

Unsplitting and unfreezing

Use one of these techniques to keep your worksheet from splitting or freezing to death:

✦ **Unsplitting:** Click the Split button again; double-click one of the split bars to remove it; or drag a split bar into the top or left side of the worksheet window.

✦ **Unfreezing:** On the View tab, click the Freeze Panes button and choose Unfreeze Panes on the drop-down list.

Hiding columns and rows

Another way to take the clutter out of a worksheet is to temporarily hide columns and rows:

✦ **Hiding columns or rows:** Drag over the column letters or row numbers of the columns or rows that you want to hide. Dragging this way selects entire columns or rows. Then go to the Home tab, click the Format button, choose Hide & Unhide, and choose Hide Columns or Hide Rows.

✦ **Unhiding columns and rows:** Select columns to the right and left of the hidden columns, or select rows above and below the hidden rows. To select columns or rows, drag over their letters or numbers. Then go to the Home tab, click the Format button, choose Hide & Unhide, and choose Unhide Columns or Unhide Rows.

It's easy to forget where you hid columns or rows. To make sure that all columns and rows in your worksheet are displayed, click the Select All button (or press Ctrl+A) to select your entire worksheet. Then go to the Home tab, click the Format button and choose Hide & Unhide⇨Unhide Columns; click the Format button again and choose Hide & Unhide⇨Unhide Rows.

Comments for Documenting Your Worksheet

It may happen that you return to your worksheet days or months from now and discover to your dismay that you don't know why certain numbers or formulas are there. For that matter, someone else may inherit your worksheet and be mystified as to what the heck is going on. To take the mystery out of a worksheet, document it by entering comments here and there.

A *comment* is a note that describes part of a worksheet. Each comment is connected to a cell. You can tell where a comment is because a small red triangle appears in the upper-right corner of cells that have been commented on. Move the pointer over one of these triangles and you see the pop-up box, a comment, and the name of the person who entered the comment, as shown in Figure 2-2. Click the Show All Comments button on the Review tab to see every comment in a worksheet.

Here's everything a mere mortal needs to know about comments:

✦ **Entering a comment:** Click the cell that deserves the comment, go to the Review tab, and click the New Comment button. Enter your comment in the pop-up box. Click in a different cell when you finish entering your comment.

✦ **Reading a comment:** Move the pointer over the small red triangle and read the comment in the pop-up box (refer to Figure 2-2).

✦ **Finding comments:** On the Review tab, click the Previous or Next button to go from comment to comment.

✦ **Editing a comment:** On the Review tab, select the cell with the comment, click the Edit Comment button, and edit the comment in the pop-up box. You can also right-click the cell and choose Edit Comment.

Figure 2-2:
Comments
explain
what's
what in a
worksheet.

✦ **Deleting comments:** On the Review tab, click a cell with a comment, and then click the Delete button, or right-click the cell and choose Delete Comment. To delete several comments, select them by Ctrl+clicking and then click the Delete button.

✦ **Deleting all comments in a worksheet:** Select all comments and then, on the Review tab, click the Delete button. You can select all comments by clicking the Find & Select button on the Home tab, choosing Go To, and in the Go To dialog box, clicking the Special button and choosing Comments in the Go To Special dialog box.

TIP If your name doesn't appear in the pop-up box after you enter a comment and you want it to appear there, go to the File tab, choose Options, select the General category in the Excel Options dialog box, and enter your name in the User Name text box.

You can print the comments in a worksheet. On the Page Layout tab, click the Page Setup group button, and on the Sheet tab of the Page Setup dialog box, open the Comments drop-down list and choose At End of Sheet or As Displayed on Sheet.

Selecting Cells in a Worksheet

To format, copy, move, delete, and format numbers and words in a worksheet, you have to select the cells in which the numbers and words are found. Here are ways to select cells and the data inside them:

✦ **A block of cells:** Drag diagonally across the worksheet from one corner of the block of cells to the opposite corner. You can also click in one corner and Shift+click the opposite corner.

✦ **Adjacent cells in a row or column:** Drag across the cells.

✦ **Cells in various places:** While holding down the Ctrl key, click different cells.

✦ **A row or rows:** Click a row number to select an entire row. Click and drag down the row numbers to select several adjacent rows.

✦ **A column or columns:** Click a column letter to select an entire column. Click and drag across letters to select adjacent columns.

✦ **Entire worksheet:** Click the Select All button, the square to the left of the column letters and above the row numbers; press Ctrl+A; or press Ctrl+Shift+Spacebar.

Press Ctrl+Spacebar to select the column that the active cell is in; press Shift+Spacebar to select the row where the active cell is.

You can enter the same data item in several different cells by selecting cells and then entering the data in one cell and pressing Ctrl+Enter. This technique comes in very handy, for example, when you want to enter a place-holder zero (0) in several different cells.

Deleting, Copying, and Moving Data

In the course of putting together a worksheet, it is sometimes necessary to delete, copy, and move cell contents. Here are instructions for doing these chores:

✦ **Deleting cell contents:** Select the cells and then press the Delete key; on the Home tab, click the Clear button and choose Clear Contents; or right-click and choose Clear Contents. (Avoid the Delete button on the Home tab for deleting cell contents. Clicking that button deletes cells as well as their contents.)

✦ **Copying and moving cell contents:** Select the cells and use one of these techniques:

• *Cut or Copy and Paste commands:* When you paste the data, click where you want the first cell of the block of cells you're copying or moving to go. (Book I, Chapter 2 explains copying and moving data in detail.) Be careful not to overwrite cells with data in them when you copy or move data. After you paste data, you see the Paste Options button. Click this button and choose an option from the drop-down list to format the data in different ways.

• *Drag and drop:* Move the pointer to the edge of the cell block, click when you see the four-headed arrow, and start dragging. Hold down the Ctrl key to copy the data.

Handling the Worksheets in a Workbook

As a glance at the bottom of the worksheet tells you, each workbook comes with three worksheets named (not very creatively) Sheet1, Sheet2, and Sheet3. Follow these instructions to move among, add, delete, rename, and change the order of worksheets:

✦ **Moving among worksheets:** To go from one worksheet to another, click a worksheet tab along the bottom of the screen. If you can't see a tab, click one of the scroll arrows to the left of the worksheet tabs.

✦ **Renaming a worksheet:** Right-click the worksheet tab, choose Rename on the shortcut menu, type a new name, and press Enter. You can also go to the Home tab, click the Format button, choose Rename Sheet on the drop-down list, and enter a new name. Spaces are allowed in names, and names can be 31 characters long. Brackets ([]) are allowed in names, but you can't use these symbols: / \ : ? and *.

✦ **Selecting worksheets:** Click the worksheet's tab to select it. To select several worksheets, Ctrl+click their tabs or click the first tab and then Shift+click the last tab in the set. To select all the worksheets, right-click a tab and choose Select All Sheets on the shortcut menu.

✦ **Rearranging worksheets:** Drag the worksheet tab to a new location. As you drag, a tiny black arrow and a page icon appear to show you where the worksheet will land after you release the mouse button. You can also select a sheet, go to the Home tab, click the Format button, and choose Move or Copy Sheet on the drop-down list. The Move or Copy dialog box appears, as shown in Figure 2-3. Select the sheet in the Before Sheet list where you want the worksheet to go and click OK.

✦ **Inserting a new worksheet:** Click the Insert Sheet button (you can find it to the right of the worksheet tabs); press Shift+F11; or on the Home tab, open the drop-down list on the Insert button and choose Insert Sheet.

Figure 2-3:
Besides dragging it, you can move a worksheet in this dialog box.

Delete ✦ **Deleting a worksheet:** Select the sheet, and on the Home tab, open the drop-down list on the Delete button and choose Delete Sheet. You can also right-click a worksheet tab and choose Delete. Be careful because you can't restore your deleted worksheet by pressing the Undo button.

✦ **Copying a worksheet:** Select the sheet, hold down the Ctrl key, and drag the worksheet tab to a new location.

✦ **Color-coding a worksheet:** Right-click a worksheet tab and choose Tab Color. Then select a color in the submenu, or choose More Colors and select a color in the Colors dialog box. You can also select a worksheet tab, go to the Home tab, click the Format button, choose Tab Color on the drop-down list, and choose a color on the submenu.

 You can change the size of columns or apply numeric formats to the same addresses in different worksheets by selecting all the sheets first and then formatting one worksheet. The formats apply to all the worksheets that you select. Being able to format several different worksheets simultaneously comes in handy, for example, when your workbook tracks monthly data and each worksheet pertains to one month. Another way to handle worksheets with similar data is to create the first worksheet and copy it to the second, third, and fourth worksheets with the Copy and Paste commands.

Keeping Others from Tampering with Worksheets

People with savvy and foresight sometimes set up workbooks so that one worksheet holds raw data and the other worksheets hold formulas that calculate the raw data. This technique prevents others from tampering with the raw data. Furthermore, if the worksheet with raw data is hidden, the chance it will be tampered with is lower; and if the worksheet is protected, no one can tamper with it unless they have a password. These pages explain how to hide a worksheet so that others are less likely to find it and how to protect a worksheet from being edited.

Hiding a worksheet

Follow these instructions to hide and unhide worksheets:

Hide ✦ **Hiding a worksheet:** Select the worksheet you want to hide, go to the View tab, and click the Hide button. You can also right-click the worksheet's tab and choose Hide on the shortcut menu. And you can also display the worksheet, go to the Home tab, click the Format button, and choose Hide &Unhide⇨Hide Sheet.

Unhide ✦ **Unhiding a worksheet:** On the View tab, click the Unhide button, select the name of the worksheet you want to unhide in the Unhide dialog box, and click OK. To open the Unhide dialog box, you can also right-click any worksheet tab and choose Unhide; or go to the Home tab, click the Format button, and choose Hide & Unhide⇨Unhide Sheet.

Protecting a worksheet

Protecting a worksheet means to restrict others from changing it — from formatting it, inserting new rows and columns, or deleting rows and columns, among other tasks. You can also prevent any editorial changes whatsoever from being made to a worksheet. Follow these steps to protect a worksheet from tampering by others:

1. **Select the worksheet that needs protection.**

2. **On the Review tab, click the Protect Sheet button.**

   You see the Protect Sheet dialog box shown in Figure 2-4. You can also open this dialog box by going to the Home tab, clicking the Format button, and choosing Protect Sheet.

3. **Enter a password in the Password to Unprotect Sheet box if you want only people with the password to be able to unprotect the worksheet after you protect it.**

4. **On the Allow All Users of This Worksheet To list, select the check box next to the name of each task that you want to permit others to do.**

   For example, click the Format Cells check box if you want others to be able to format cells.

   Deselect the Select Locked Cells check box to prevent any changes from being made to the worksheet. By default, all worksheet cells are locked, and by preventing others from selecting locked cells, you effectively prevent them from editing any cells.

5. **Click OK.**

   If you entered a password in Step 3, you must enter it again in the Confirm Password dialog box and click OK.

Figure 2-4:
Select what you want others to be able to do.

To unprotect a worksheet that you protected, go to the Review tab and click the Unprotect Sheet button. You must enter a password if you elected to require others to have a password before they can unprotect a worksheet.

Chapter 3: Formulas and Functions for Crunching Numbers

In This Chapter

✔ Constructing a formula

✔ Using cell ranges in formulas

✔ Naming cell ranges

✔ Referring to cells in other worksheets

✔ Copying formulas to other columns and rows

✔ Preventing errors in formulas

✔ Using functions in formulas

*F*ormulas are where it's at as far as Excel is concerned. After you know how to construct formulas, and constructing them is pretty easy, you can put Excel to work. You can make the numbers speak to you. You can turn a bunch of unruly numbers into meaningful figures and statistics.

This chapter explains what a formula is, how to enter a formula, and how to enter a formula quickly. You also discover how to copy formulas from cell to cell and how to keep formula errors from creeping into your workbooks. Finally, this chapter explains how to make use of the hundred or so functions that Excel offers.

How Formulas Work

A *formula,* you may recall from the sleepy hours you spent in math class, is a way to calculate numbers. For example, 2+3=5 is a formula. When you enter a formula in a cell, Excel computes the formula and displays its results in the cell. Click in cell A3 and enter **=2+3**, for example, and Excel displays the number 5 in cell A3.

Referring to cells in formulas

As well as numbers, Excel formulas can refer to the contents of different cells. When a formula refers to a cell, the number in the cell is used to compute the formula. In Figure 3-1, for example, cell A1 contains the number 2; cell A2 contains the number 3; and cell A3 contains the formula =A1+A2. As shown in cell A3, the result of the formula is 5. If I change the number in cell A1 from 2 to 3, the result of the formula in cell A3 (=A1+A2) becomes 6, not 5. When a formula refers to a cell and the number in the cell changes, the result of the formula changes as well.

Formula in the formula bar

Figure 3-1:
A simple
formula.

Results of the formula

To see the value of using cell references in formulas, consider the worksheet shown in Figure 3-2. The purpose of this worksheet is to track the budget of a school's Parent Teacher Association (PTA):

		Actual Income	Projected Income	Over/Under Budget	
Income					
	Book Fair	4,876.40	5,500.00	-623.60	
	Dances	1,476.95	1,800.00	-323.05	
	Fundraising	13,175.00	5,000.00	8,175.00	
	Merchandise Sales	5,888.50	7,000.00	-1,111.50	
	Membership Fees	3,918.00	3,000.00	918.00	
Total Income		$29,334.85	$22,300.00	$7,034.85	

Figure 3-2:
Using
formulas
in a
worksheet.

◆ Column C, Actual Income, lists income from different sources.

◆ Column D, Projected Income, shows what the PTA members thought income from these sources would be.

◆ Column E, Over/Under Budget, shows how actual income compares to projected income from the different sources.

As the figures in the Actual Income column (column C) are updated, figures in the Over/Under Budget column (column E) and the Total Income row (row 8) change instantaneously. These figures change instantaneously because the formulas refer to the numbers in cells, not to unchanging numbers (known as *constants*).

Figure 3-3 shows the formulas used to calculate the data in the worksheet in Figure 3-2. In column E, formulas deduct the numbers in column D from the numbers in column C to show where the PTA over- or underbudgeted for the different sources of income. In row 8, you can see how the SUM function is used to total cells in rows 3 through 7. The end of this chapter explains how to use functions in formulas.

Figure 3-3:
The formulas used to generate the numbers in Figure 3-2.

Excel is remarkably good about updating cell references in formulas when you move cells. To see how good Excel is, consider what happens to cell addresses in formulas when you delete a row in a worksheet. If a formula refers to cell C1 but you delete row B, row C becomes row B, and the value in cell C1 changes addresses from C1 to B1. You would think that references in formulas to cell C1 would be out of date, but you would be wrong. Excel automatically adjusts all formulas that refer to cell C1. Those formulas now refer to cell B1 instead.

In case you want to know, you can display formulas in worksheet cells instead of the results of formulas, as was done in Figure 3-3, by pressing Ctrl+' or clicking the Show Formulas button on the Formulas tab (you may have to click the Formula Auditing button first, depending on the size of your screen). Click the Show Formulas button a second time to see formula results again.

Referring to formula results in formulas

Besides referring to cells with numbers in them, you can refer to formula results in a cell. Consider the worksheet shown in Figure 3-4. The purpose of this worksheet is to track scoring by the players on a basketball team over three games:

Figure 3-4:
Using
formula
results
as other
formulas.

◆ The Totals column (column E) shows the total points each player scored in the three games.

◆ The Average column (column F), using the formula results in the Totals column, determines how much each player has scored on average. The Average column does that by dividing the results in column E by 3, the number of games played.

In this case, Excel uses the results of the total-calculation formulas in column E to compute average points per game in column F.

Operators in formulas

Addition, subtraction, and division aren't the only operators you can use in formulas. Table 3-1 explains the arithmetic operators you can use and the key you press to enter each operator. In the table, operators are listed in the order of precedence.

Table 3-1   **Arithmetic Operators for Use in Formulas**

Precedence	Operator	Example Formula	Returns
1	% (Percent)	=50%	50 percent, or 0.5.
2	^ (Exponentiation)	=50^2	50 to the second power, or 2500.
3	* (Multiplication)	=E2*4	The value in cell E2 multiplied by 4.
3	/ (Division)	=E2/3	The value in cell E2 divided by 3.
4	+ (Addition)	=F1+F2 +F3	The sum of the values in those cells.
4	− (Subtraction)	=G5−8	The value in cell G5 minus 8.
5	& (Concatenation)	="Part No. "&D4	The text *Part No.* and the value in cell D4.
6	= (Equal to)	=C5=4	If the value in cell C5 is equal to 4, returns TRUE; returns FALSE otherwise.
6	<> (Not equal to)	=F3<>9	If the value in cell F3 is *not* equal to 9, returns TRUE; returns FALSE otherwise.
6	< (Less than)	=B9<E11	If the value in cell B9 is less than the value in cell E11; returns TRUE; returns FALSE otherwise.
6	<= (Less than or equal to)	=A4<=9	If the value in cell A4 is less than or equal to 9, returns TRUE; returns FALSE otherwise.
6	> (Greater than)	=E8>14	If the value in cell E8 is greater than 14, returns TRUE; returns FALSE otherwise
6	>= (Greater than or equal to)	=C3>=D3	If the value in cell C3 is less than or equal to the value in cell D3; returns TRUE; returns FALSE otherwise.

The order of precedence

When a formula includes more than one operator, the order in which the operators appear in the formula matters a lot. Consider this formula:

=2+3*4

Does this formula result in 14 (2+[3*4]) or 20 ([2+3]*4)? The answer is 14 because Excel performs multiplication before addition in formulas. In other words, multiplication takes precedence over addition. The order in which calculations are made in a formula that includes different operators is called the *order of precedence*. Be sure to remember the order of precedence when you construct complex formulas with more than one operator:

1. Percent (%)

2. Exponentiation (^)

3. Multiplication (*) and division (/); leftmost operations are calculated first

4. Addition (+) and subtraction (-); leftmost operations are calculated first

5. Concatenation (&)

6. Comparison (<, <=, >,>=, and <>)

To get around the order of precedence problem, enclose parts of formulas in parentheses. Operations in parentheses are calculated before all other parts of a formula. For example, the formula =2+3*4 equals 20 when it is written this way: =(2+3)*4.

Another way to compute a formula is to make use of a function. As "Working with Functions" explains later in this chapter, a function is a built-in formula that comes with Excel. SUM, for example, adds the numbers in cells. AVG finds the average of different numbers.

The Basics of Entering a Formula

No matter what kind of formula you enter, no matter how complex the formula is, follow these basic steps to enter it:

1. **Click the cell where you want to enter the formula.**

2. **Click in the Formula bar if you want to enter the data there rather than in the cell.**

3. **Enter the equals sign (=).**

You must be sure to enter the equals sign before you enter a formula. Without it, Excel thinks you're entering text or a number, not a formula.

4. **Enter the formula.**

For example, enter **=B1*.06**. Make sure that you enter all cell addresses correctly. By the way, you can enter lowercase letters in cell references. Excel changes them to uppercase after you finish entering the formula. The next section in this chapter explains how to quickly enter cell addresses in formulas.

5. **Press Enter or click the Enter button (the check mark on the Formula bar).**

The result of the formula appears in the cell.

Speed Techniques for Entering Formulas

Entering formulas and making sure that all cell references are correct is a tedious activity, but fortunately for you, Excel offers a few techniques to make entering formulas easier. Read on to find out how ranges make entering cell references easier and how you can enter cell references in formulas by pointing and clicking. You also find instructions here for copying formulas.

Clicking cells to enter cell references

The hardest part about entering a formula is entering the cell references correctly. You have to squint to see which row and column the cell you want to refer to is in. You have to carefully type the right column letter and row number. However, instead of typing a cell reference, you can click the cell you want to refer to in a formula.

In the course of entering a formula, simply click the cell on your worksheet that you want to reference. As shown in Figure 3-5, shimmering marquee lights appear around the cell that you clicked so that you can clearly see which cell you're referring to. The cell's reference address, meanwhile, appears in the Formula bar. In Figure 3-5, I clicked cell F3 instead of entering its reference address on the Formula bar. The reference F3 appears on the Formula bar, and the marquee lights appear around cell F3.

Get in the habit of pointing and clicking cells to enter cell references in formulas. Clicking cells is easier than typing cell addresses, and the cell references are entered more accurately.

Click a cell to enter its cell reference address in a formula

	A	B	C	D	E	F	G	H
						=C3+D3+E3+F3		
1			Sales by Quarter					
2			Jan	Feb	Mar	Apr	Totals	
3		North	23,456	41,281	63,421	42,379	=C3+D3+E3+F3	
4		East	4,881	8,907	4,897	6,891		
5		West	42,571	37,191	50,178	47,098		
6		South	5,719	6,781	5,397	4,575		
7								

Figure 3-5:
Clicking to enter a cell reference.

Entering a cell range

A *cell range* is a line or block of cells in a worksheet. Instead of typing cell reference addresses one at a time, you can simply select cells on your worksheet. In Figure 3-6, I selected cells C3, D3, E3, and F3 to form cell range C3:F3. This spares me the trouble of entering the cell addresses one at a time: C3, D3, E3, and F3. The formula in Figure 3-6 uses the SUM function to total the numeric values in cell range C3:F3. Notice the marquee lights around the range C3:F3. The lights show precisely which range you're selecting. Cell ranges come in especially handy where functions are concerned (see "Working with Functions" later in this chapter).

Figure 3-6:
Using a cell range in a formula.

To identify a cell range, Excel lists the outermost cells in the range and places a colon (:) between cell addresses:

+ A cell range comprising cells A1, A2, A3, and A4 is listed this way: A1:A4.

+ A cell range comprising a block of cells from A1 to D4 is listed this way: A1:D4.

You can enter cell ranges on your own without selecting cells. To do so, type the first cell in the range, enter a colon, and type the last cell.

Naming cell ranges so that you can use them in formulas

Whether you type cell addresses yourself or drag across cells to enter a cell range, entering cell address references is a chore. Entering =C1+C2+C3+C4, for example, can cause a finger cramp; entering =SUM(C1:C4) is no piece of cake, either. To take the tedium out of entering cell ranges in formulas, you can name cell ranges. Then, to enter a cell range in a formula, all you have to do is select a name in the Paste Name dialog box or click the Use in Formula button on the Formulas tab, as shown in Figure 3-7. Naming cell ranges has an added benefit: You can choose a name from the Name Box drop-down list and go directly to the cell range whose name you choose, as shown in Figure 3-7.

Choose a name to move there   Enter a named cell range in a formula

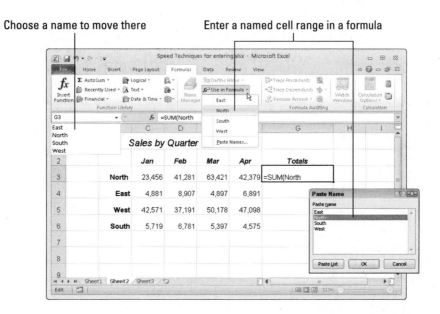

Figure 3-7:
Choosing a
named cell
range.

Naming cell ranges has one disadvantage, and it's a big one. Excel doesn't adjust cell references when you copy a formula with a range name from one cell to another. A range name always refers to the same set of cells. Later in this chapter, "Copying Formulas from Cell to Cell" explains how to copy formulas.

Creating a cell range name

Follow these steps to create a cell range name:

1. Select the cells that you want to name.

2. On the Formulas tab, click the Define Name button.

You see the New Name dialog box.

3. Enter a descriptive name in the Name box.

Names can't begin with a number or include blank spaces.

4. On the Scope drop-down list, choose Workbook or a worksheet name.

Choose a worksheet name if you intend to use the range name you're creating only in formulas that you construct in a single worksheet. If your formulas will refer to cell range addresses in different worksheets, choose Workbook so that you can use the range name wherever you go in your workbook.

5. Enter a comment to describe the range name, if you want.

Enter a comment if doing so will help you remember where the cells you're naming are located or what type of information they hold. As I explain shortly, you can read comments in the Name Manager dialog box, the place where you go to edit and delete range names.

6. Click OK.

In case you're in a hurry, here's a fast way to enter a cell range name: Select the cells for the range, click in the Name Box (which you find to the left of the Formula bar; refer to Figure 3-7), enter a name for the range, and press the Enter key.

Entering a range name as part of a formula

To include a cell range name in a formula, click in the Formula bar where you want to enter the range name and then use one of these techniques to enter the name:

    ✦ On the Formulas tab, click the Use in Formula button and choose a cell range name on the drop-down list (refer to Figure 3-7).

   ✦ Press F3 or click the Use in Formula button and choose Paste Names on the drop-down list. You see the Paste Name dialog box (refer to Figure 3-7). Select a cell range name and click OK.

Quickly traveling to a cell range that you named

To go quickly to a cell range you named, open the drop-down list on the Name Box and choose a name (refer to Figure 3-7). The Name Box drop-down list is located to the left of the Formula bar.

To make this trick work, the cursor can't be in the Formula bar. The Name Box drop-down list isn't available when you're constructing a formula.

Managing cell range names

To rename, edit, or delete cell range names, go to the Formulas tab and click the Name Manager button. You see the Name Manager dialog box, as shown in Figure 3-8. This dialog box lists names, cell values in names, the worksheet on which the range name is found, and whether the range name can be applied throughout a workbook or only in one worksheet. To rename, edit, or delete a cell range name, select it in the dialog box and use these techniques:

✦ **Renaming:** Click the Edit button and enter a new name in the Edit Name dialog box.

✦ **Reassigning cells:** To assign different cells to a range name, click the Edit button. You see the Edit Name dialog box. To enter a new range of cells, either enter the cells' addresses in the Refers To text box or click the Range Selector button (it's to the right of the text box), drag across the cells on your worksheet that you want for the cell range, and click the Cell Selector button again to return to the Edit Name dialog box.

✦ **Deleting:** Click the Delete button and click OK in the confirmation box.

Figure 3-8:
The Name
Manager
dialog box.

Referring to cells in different worksheets

Excel gives you the opportunity to use data from different worksheets in a formula. If one worksheet lists sales figures from January and the next lists sales figures from February, you can construct a "grand total" formula in either worksheet to tabulate sales in the two-month period. A reference to a cell on a different worksheet is called a *3D reference*.

Construct the formula as you normally would, but when you want to refer to a cell or cell range in a different worksheet, click a worksheet tab to move to the other worksheet and select the cell or range of cells there. Without returning to the original worksheet, complete your formula in the Formula bar and press Enter. Excel returns you to the original worksheet, where you can see the results of your formula.

The only thing odd about constructing formulas across worksheets are the cell references. As a glance at the Formula bar tells you, cell addresses in cross-worksheet formulas list the sheet name and an exclamation point (!) as well as the cell address itself. For example, this formula in Worksheet 1 adds the number in cell A4 to the numbers in cells D5 and E5 in Worksheet 2:

`=A4+Sheet2!D5+Sheet2!E5`

This formula in Sheet 2 multiplies the number in cell E18 by the number in cell C15 in Worksheet 1:

`=E18*Sheet1!C15`

This formula in Worksheet 2 finds the average of the numbers in the cell range C7:F7 in Worksheet 1:

`=AVERAGE(Sheet1!C7:F7)`

Copying Formulas from Cell to Cell

Often in worksheets, the same formula but with different cell references is used across a row or down a column. For example, in the worksheet shown in Figure 3-9, column F totals the rainfall figures in rows 7 through 11. To enter formulas for totaling the rainfall figures in column F, you could laboriously enter formulas in cells F7, F8, F9, F10, and F11. But a faster way is to enter the formula once in cell F7 and then copy the formula in F7 down the column to cells F8, F9, F10, and F11.

When you copy a formula to a new cell, Excel adjusts the cell references in the formula so that the formula works in the cells to which it has been copied. Astounding! Opportunities to copy formulas abound on most worksheets. And copying formulas is the fastest and safest way to enter formulas in a worksheet.

Follow these steps to copy a formula:

1. **Select the cell with the formula you want to copy down a column or across a row.**

2. **Drag the AutoFill handle across the cells to which you want to copy the formula.**

This is the same AutoFill handle you drag to enter serial data (see Chapter 1 of this mini-book about entering lists and serial data with the AutoFill command). The AutoFill handle is the small black square in the lower-right corner of the cell. When you move the mouse pointer over it, it changes to a black cross. Figure 3-9 shows a formula being copied.

3. Release the mouse button.

If I were you, I would click in the cells to which you copied the formula and glance at the Formula bar to make sure that the formula was copied correctly. I'd bet you it was.

You can also copy formulas with the Copy and Paste commands. Just make sure that cell references refer correctly to the surrounding cells.

Drag the AutoFill handle

F7		fx	=B7+C7+D7+E7			
	A	B	C	D	E	F	G
6		Winter	Spring	Summer	Fall	Totals	
7	Sonoma	13	8.3	2.3	8.2	31.8	
8	Napa	11.5	7.6	3.1	7.5		
9	Mendocino	15.8	12.9	2.9	8.3		
10	San Francisco	10.9	9.7	1.1	3.3		
11	Contra Costa	10.1	8.4	2.3	4.4		
12							

Sheet1 Sheet2 Sheet3

Drag outside selection to extend series or fill; drag inside to clear   175%

F7		fx	=B7+C7+D7+E7			
	A	B	C	D	E	F	G
6		Winter	Spring	Summer	Fall	Totals	
7	Sonoma	13	8.3	2.3	8.2	31.8	
8	Napa	11.5	7.6	3.1	7.5	29.7	
9	Mendocino	15.8	12.9	2.9	8.3	39.9	
10	San Francisco	10.9	9.7	1.1	3.3	25	
11	Contra Costa	10.1	8.4	2.3	4.4	25.2	
12							

Sheet1 Sheet2 Sheet3

Drag outside selection to extend series or fill; drag inside to clear   175%

Figure 3-9:
Copying a
formula.

Detecting and Correcting Errors in Formulas

It happens. Everyone makes an error from time to time when entering formulas in cells. Especially in a worksheet in which formula results are calculated into other formulas, a single error in one formula can spread like a virus and cause miscalculations throughout a worksheet. To prevent that from happening, Excel offers several ways to correct errors in formulas. You can correct them one at a time, run the error checker, and trace cell references, as the following pages explain.

[icon] Show Formulas   By the way, if you want to see formulas in cells rather than formula results, go to the Formulas tab and click the Show Formulas button (or press Ctrl+'). Sometimes seeing formulas this way helps to detect formula errors.

Correcting errors one at a time

When Excel detects what it thinks is a formula that has been entered incorrectly, a small green triangle appears in the upper-left corner of the cell where you entered the formula. And if the error is especially egregious, an *error message,* a cryptic three or four letters preceded by a pound sign (#), appears in the cell. Table 3-2 explains common error messages.

Table 3-2	Common Formula Error Messages
Message	*What Went Wrong*
#DIV/0!	You tried to divide a number by a zero (0) or an empty cell.
#NAME	You used a cell range name in the formula, but the name isn't defined. Sometimes this error occurs because you type the name incorrectly. (Earlier in this chapter, "Naming cell ranges so that you can use them in formulas" explains how to name cell ranges.)
#N/A	The formula refers to an empty cell, so no data is available for computing the formula. Sometimes people enter N/A in a cell as a placeholder to signal the fact that data isn't entered yet. Revise the formula or enter a number or formula in the empty cells.
#NULL	The formula refers to a cell range that Excel can't understand. Make sure that the range is entered correctly.
#NUM	An argument you use in your formula is invalid.
#REF	The cell or range of cells that the formula refers to aren't there.
#VALUE	The formula includes a function that was used incorrectly, takes an invalid argument, or is misspelled. Make sure that the function uses the right argument and is spelled correctly.

To find out more about a formula error and perhaps correct it, select the cell with the green triangle and click the Error button. This small button appears beside a cell with a formula error after you click the cell. The drop-down list on the Error button offers opportunities for correcting formula errors and finding out more about them.

Running the error checker

Error Checking ▾

Another way to tackle formula errors is to run the error checker. When the checker encounters what it thinks is an error, the Error Checking dialog box tells you what the error is, as shown in Figure 3-10. To run the error checker, go to the Formulas tab and click the Error Checking button (you may have to click the Formula Auditing button first, depending on the size of your screen).

If you see clearly what the error is, click the Edit in Formula Bar button, repair the error in the Formula bar, and click the Resume button in the dialog box (you find this button at the top of the dialog box). If the error isn't one that really needs correcting, either click the Ignore Error button or click the Next button to send the error checker in search of the next error in your worksheet.

Figure 3-10: Running the error checker.

Tracing cell references

In a complex worksheet in which formulas are piled on top of one another and the results of some formulas are computed into other formulas, it helps to be able to trace cell references. By tracing cell references, you can see how the data in a cell figures into a formula in another cell. Also, if the cell contains a formula, you can tell which cells the formula is gathering its data from to make its computation. You can get a better idea of how your worksheet is constructed, and in so doing, find structural errors more easily.

Figure 3-11 shows how cell tracers describe the relationships between cells. A *cell tracer* is a blue arrow that shows the relationships between cells used in formulas. You can trace two types of relationships:

Figure 3-11: Tracing the relationships between cells.

Trace Precedents

✦ **Tracing precedents:** Select a cell with a formula in it and trace the formula's *precedents* to find out which cells are computed to produce the results of the formula. Trace precedents when you want to find out where a formula gets its computation data. Cell tracer arrows point from the referenced cells to the cell with the formula results in it.

To trace precedents, go to the Formulas tab and click the Trace Precedents button (you may have to click the Formula Auditing button first, depending on the size of your screen).

Trace Dependents

✦ **Tracing dependents:** Select a cell and trace its *dependents* to find out which cells contain formulas that use data from the cell you selected. Cell tracer arrows point from the cell you selected to cells with formula results in them. Trace dependents when you want to find out how the data in a cell contributes to formulas elsewhere in the worksheet. The cell you select can contain a constant value or a formula in its own right (and contribute its results to another formula).

To trace dependents, go to the Formulas tab and click the Trace Dependents button (you may have to click the Formula Auditing button first, depending on the size of your screen).

Remove Arrows To remove the cell tracer arrows from a worksheet, go to the Formulas tab and click the Remove Arrows button. You can open the drop-down list on this button and choose Remove Precedent Arrows or Remove Dependent Arrows to remove only cell-precedent or cell-dependent tracer arrows.

Working with Functions

A *function* is a canned formula that comes with Excel. Excel offers hundreds of functions, some of which are very obscure and fit only for use by rocket scientists or securities analysts. Other functions are very practical. For example, you can use the SUM function to quickly total the numbers in a range of cells. Instead of entering =C2+C3+C4+C5 on the Formula bar, you can enter =SUM(C2:C5), which tells Excel to total the numbers in cell C2, C3, C4, and C5. To obtain the product of the number in cell G4 and .06, you can use the PRODUCT function and enter =PRODUCT(G4,.06) on the Formula bar.

 Table 3-3 lists the most common functions. To get an idea of the numerous functions that Excel offers, go to the Formulas tab and click the Insert Function button. You see the Insert Function dialog box shown in Figure 3-12. (Later in this chapter, I show you how you this dialog box helps you use functions in formulas.) Choose a function category in the dialog box, choose a function name, and read the description. You can click the Help on This Function link to open the Excel Help window and get a thorough description of the function and how it's used.

Table 3-3	Common Functions and Their Use
Function	*Returns*
AVERAGE(*number1,number2,...*)	The average of the numbers in the cells listed in the arguments
COUNT(*value1,value2,...*)	The number of cells that contain the numbers listed in the arguments
MAX(*number1,number2,...*)	The largest value in the cells listed in the arguments
MIN(*number1,number2,...*)	The smallest value in the cells listed in the arguments
PRODUCT(*number1,number2,...*)	The product of multiplying the cells listed in the arguments
STDEV(*number1,number2,...*)	An estimate of standard deviation based on the sample cells listed in the argument
STDEVP(*number1,number2,...*)	An estimate of standard deviation based on the entire sample cells listed in the arguments
SUM(*number1,number2,...*)	The total of the numbers in the arguments
VAR(*number1,number2,...*)	An estimate of the variance based on the sample cells listed in the arguments
VARP(*number1,number2,...*)	A variance calculation based on all cells listed in the arguments

Using arguments in functions

Every function takes one or more *arguments*. Arguments are the cell references or numbers, enclosed in parentheses, that the function acts upon. For example, =AVERAGE(B1:B4) returns the average of the numbers in the cell range B1 through B4; =PRODUCT(6.5,C4) returns the product of multiplying the number 6.5 by the number in cell C4. When a function requires more than one argument, enter a comma between the arguments (enter a comma without a space).

Choose a category

Choose a function name

Figure 3-12:
The Insert
Function
dialog box.

Click to learn more

Entering a function in a formula

To enter a function in a formula, you can enter the function name by typing it in the Formula bar, or you can rely on Excel to enter it for you. Enter function names yourself if you're well acquainted with a function and comfortable using it.

No matter how you want to enter a function as part of a formula, start this way:

1. **Select the cell where you want to enter the formula.**

2. **In the Formula bar, type an equals sign (=).**

Please, please, please be sure to start every formula by entering an equals sign (=). Without it, Excel thinks you're entering text or a number in the cell.

3. **Start constructing your formula, and when you come to the place where you want to enter the function, type the function's name or call upon Excel to help you enter the function and its arguments.**

Later in this chapter, "Manually entering a function" shows you how to type in the function yourself; "Getting Excel's help to enter a function" shows you how to get Excel to do the work.

If you enter the function on your own, it's up to you to type the arguments correctly; if you get Excel's help, you also get help with entering the cell references for the arguments.

Quickly entering a function and its arguments

To quickly total the numbers in cells, click on your worksheet where you want the total to appear, and then click the AutoSum button on the Home or Formulas tab. Excel takes an educated guess as to which cells need totaling, and the program highlights those cells. If Excel guesses correctly and highlights the cells you want to total, click the Enter button (or press Enter) and be done with it. Otherwise, select the cells you want to add up and then press Enter.

Similarly, you can use the drop-down list on the AutoSum button to quickly obtain the average, count of, maximum amount, or minimum amount of cells by clicking in a nearby cell, opening the drop-down list on the AutoSum button, and choosing Average, Count Numbers, Max, or Min.

	B	C	D	E	F	G
6	*1 Qtr*	*2 Qtr*	*3 Qtr*	*4 Qtr*	*Totals*	
7 **Sonoma**	13	8.3	2.3	8.2	31.8	
8 **Napa**	11.5	7.6	3.1	7.5	29.7	
9 **Mendocino**	15.8	12.9	2.9	8.3	39.9	
10 **San Francisco**	10.9	9.7	1.1	3.3	25	
11 **Contra Costa**	10.1	8.4	2.3	4.4	25.2	
12 *Totals*					=SUM(F7:F11)	

Manually entering a function

Be sure to enclose the function's argument or arguments in parentheses. Don't enter a space between the function's name and the first parenthesis. Likewise, don't enter a comma and a space between arguments; enter a comma, nothing more:

=SUM(F11,F14,23)

You can enter function names in lowercase. Excel converts function names to uppercase after you click the Enter button or press Enter to complete the formula. Entering function names in lowercase is recommended because doing so gives you a chance to find out whether you entered a function name correctly. If Excel doesn't convert your function name to uppercase, you made a typing error when you entered the function name.

Getting Excel's help to enter a function

Besides entering a function by typing it, you can do it by way of the Function Arguments dialog box, as shown in Figure 3-13. The beauty of using this dialog box is that it warns you if you enter arguments incorrectly, and it spares you the trouble of typing the function name without making an error. What's more, the Function Arguments dialog box shows you the results of the formula as you construct it so that you get an idea whether you're using the function correctly.

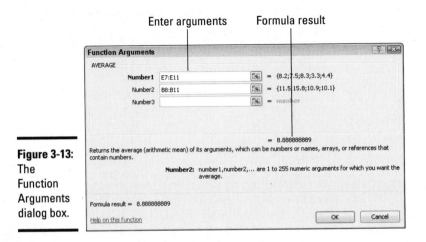

Figure 3-13: The Function Arguments dialog box.

Follow these steps to get Excel's help with entering a function as part of a formula:

1. **On the Formulas tab, tell Excel which function you want to use.**

You can do that with one of these techniques:

- *Click a Function Library button:* Click the button whose name describes what kind of function you want and choose the function's name on the drop-down list. You can click the Financial, Logical, Text, Date & Time, Lookup & Reference, Math & Trig, or More Functions buttons.

- *Click the Recently Used button:* Click this button and choose the name of a function you used recently.

- *Click the Insert Function button:* Clicking this button opens the Insert Function dialog box (refer to Figure 3-12). Find and choose the name of a function. You can search for functions or choose a category and then scroll the names until you find the function you want.

You see the Function Arguments dialog box (refer to Figure 3-13). It offers boxes for entering arguments for the function to compute.

2. **Enter arguments in the spaces provided by the Function Arguments dialog box.**

   To enter cell references or ranges, you can click or select cells in your worksheet. If necessary, click the Range Selector button (you can find it to the right of an argument text box) to shrink the Function Arguments dialog box and get a better look at your worksheet.

3. **Click OK when you finish entering arguments for your function.**

   I hope you didn't have to argue too strenuously with the Function Arguments dialog box.

Chapter 4: Making a Worksheet Easier to Read and Understand

In This Chapter

✔ **Aligning numbers and text**

✔ **Changing column and row sizes**

✔ **Applying cell styles to data in cells**

✔ **Splashing color on a worksheet**

✔ **Drawing borders between cells and titles**

✔ **Making worksheets fit well on the page**

✔ **Preparing a worksheet before you print it**

*T*his chapter explains how to dress a worksheet in its Sunday best in case you want to print and present it to others. It explains how to align numbers and text, insert rows and columns, as well as change the size of rows and columns. You find out how to decorate a worksheet with colors and borders, as well as create and apply styles to make formatting tasks go more quickly. Finally, this chapter describes everything you need to know before you print a worksheet, including how to make it fit on one page and repeat row labels and column names on all pages.

Laying Out a Worksheet

Especially if you intend to print your worksheet, you may as well dress it in its Sunday best. And you can do a number of things to make worksheets easier to read and understand. You can change character fonts. You can draw borders around or shade important cells. You can also format the numbers so that readers know, for example, whether they're staring at dollar figures or percentages. This part of Chapter 4 is dedicated to the proposition that a worksheet doesn't have to look drab and solemn.

Aligning numbers and text in columns and rows

To start with, numbers in worksheets are right-aligned in cells, and text is left-aligned. Numbers and text sit squarely on the bottom of cells. You can, however, change the way that data is aligned. For example, you can make data float at the top of cells rather than rest at the bottom, and you can center or justify data in cells. Figure 4-1 illustrates different ways to align text and numbers. How text is aligned helps people make sense of your worksheets. In Figure 4-1, for example, Income and Expenses are left-aligned so that they stand out and make it clearer what the right-aligned column labels below are all about.

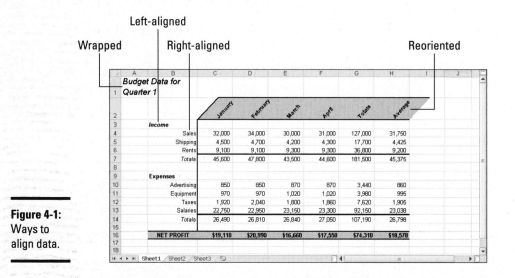

Figure 4-1:
Ways to
align data.

Select the cells whose alignment needs changing and follow these instructions to realign data in the cells:

✦ **Changing the horizontal (side-to-side) alignment:** On the Home tab, click the Align Text Left, Center, or Align Text Right button. You can also click the Alignment group button, and on the Alignment tab of the Format Cells dialog box, choose an option on the Horizontal drop-down list. Figure 4-2 shows the Format Cells dialog box.

✦ **Changing the vertical (top-to-bottom) alignment:** On the Home tab, click the Top Align, Middle Align, or Bottom Align button. You can also click the Alignment group button to open the Format Cells dialog box (refer to Figure 4-2) and choose an option on the Vertical drop-down list. The Justify option makes all the letters or numbers fit in a cell, even if it means wrapping text to two or more lines.

✦ **Reorienting the cells:** On the Home tab, click the Orientation button and choose an option on the drop-down list. (For Figure 4-2, I chose the Angle Counterclockwise option.) You can also click the Alignment group button, and on the Alignment tab of the Format Cells dialog box (refer to Figure 4-2), drag the diamond in the Orientation box or enter a number in the Degrees text box.

Merging and centering text across several cells

In the illustration shown here, "Sales Totals by Regional Office" is centered across four different cells. Normally, text is left-aligned, but if you want to center it across several cells, drag across the cells to select them, go to the Home tab, and click the Merge & Center button. Merging and centering allows you to display text across several columns.

To "unmerge and uncenter" cells, select the text that you merged and centered, open the drop-down list on the Merge & Center button, and choose Unmerge Cells. You can also deselect the Merge Cells check box in the Format Cells dialog box (refer to Figure 4-2).

B	C	D	E	F	G
	Sales Totals by Regional Office				
	North	**West**	**East**	**South**	

Figure 4-2:
The Alignment tab of the Format Cells dialog box.

Changing the orientation of text in cells is an elegant solution to the problem of keeping a worksheet from getting too wide. Numbers are usually a few characters wide, but heading labels can be much wider than that. By changing the orientation of a heading label, you make columns narrower and keep worksheets from growing too fat to fit on the screen or page.

Inserting and deleting rows and columns

At some point, everybody has to insert new columns and rows and delete ones that are no longer needed. Make sure before you delete a row or column that you don't delete data that you really need. Do the following to insert and delete rows and columns:

✦ **Deleting rows or columns:** Drag across the row numbers or column letters of the rows or columns you want to delete; then right-click and choose Delete, or, on the Home tab, open the drop-down list on the Delete button and select Delete Sheet Rows or Delete Sheet Columns.

✦ **Inserting rows:** Select the row below the row you want to insert; then, on the Home tab, open the drop-down list on the Insert button and choose Insert Sheet Rows, or right-click the row you selected and choose Insert on the shortcut menu. For example, to insert a new row above row 11, select the current row 11 before choosing Insert Sheet Rows. You can insert more than one row at a time by selecting more than one row before giving the Insert Sheet Rows command.

✦ **Inserting columns:** Select the column to the right of where you want the new column to be; then, on the Home tab, open the drop-down list on the Insert button and choose Insert Sheet Columns, or right-click the column you selected and choose Insert on the shortcut menu. You can insert more than one column this way by selecting more than one column before giving the Insert command.

> **TIP**
>
> A fast way to insert several rows or columns is to insert one and keep pressing F4 (the Repeat command) until you insert all the rows or columns you need.

After you insert rows or columns, the Insert Options button appears. Click it and choose an option from the drop-down list if you want your new row or column to have the same or different formats as the row or column you selected to start the Insert operation.

> **REMEMBER**
>
> To insert more than one row or column at a time, select more than one row number or column letter before giving the Insert command.

Changing the size of columns and rows

By default, columns are 8.43 characters wide. To make columns wider, you have to widen them yourself. Rows are 12.75 points high, but Excel makes them higher when you enter letters or numbers that are taller than 12.75 points (72 points equals 1 inch). Excel offers a bunch of different ways to change the size of columns and rows. You can start on the Home tab and choose options on the Format button drop-down list, shown in Figure 4-3, or you can rely on your wits and change sizes manually by dragging or double-clicking the boundaries between row numbers or column letters.

Laying Out a Worksheet **497**

Book V
Chapter 4

Making a Worksheet
Easier to Read and
Understand

Before you change the size of columns or rows, select them (Chapter 2 of this mini-book explains how). Click or drag across row numbers to select rows; click or drag across column letters to select columns.

Drag a boundary   Or choose a Format option

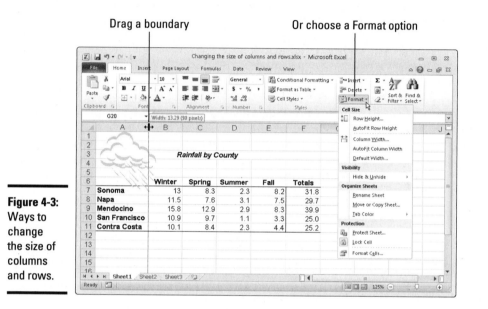

Figure 4-3:
Ways to
change
the size of
columns
and rows.

Adjusting the height of rows

Here are ways to change the height of rows:

✦ **One at a time:** Move the mouse pointer onto the boundary between row numbers and, when the pointer changes to a cross, drag the boundary between rows up or down. A pop-up box tells you how tall the row will be after you release the mouse button.

✦ **Several at a time:** Select several rows and drag the boundary between one of the rows; all rows change height. You can also go to the Home tab, click the Format button, choose Row Height, and enter a measurement in the Row Height dialog box.

✦ **Tall as the tallest entry:** To make a row as tall as its tallest cell entry, double-click the border below a row number (after you've selected a row), or go to the Home tab, click the Format button, and choose AutoFit Row Height.

Adjusting the width of columns

Here are ways to make columns wider or narrower:

+ **One at a time:** Move the mouse pointer onto the boundary between column letters, and when the pointer changes to a cross, drag the border between the columns. A pop-up box tells you what size the column is.

+ **Several at a time:** Select several columns and drag the boundary between one of the columns; all columns adjust to the same width. You can also go to the Home tab, click the Format button, choose Column Width, and enter a measurement in the Column Width dialog box.

+ **As wide as their entries:** To make columns as wide as their widest entries, select the columns, go to the Home tab, click the Format button, and choose AutoFit Column Width on the drop-down list. You can also double-click the right border of a column letter. By "auto-fitting" columns, you can be certain that the data in each cell in a column appears on-screen.

To change the 8.43-character standard width for columns in a worksheet, go to the Home tab, click the Format button, choose Default Width on the drop-down list, and enter a new measurement in the Standard Width dialog box.

Decorating a Worksheet with Borders and Colors

The job of gridlines is simply to help you line up numbers and letters in cells. By default, gridlines aren't printed, and because gridlines aren't printed, drawing borders on worksheets is absolutely necessary if you intend to print your worksheet. Use borders to steer the reader's eye to the most important parts of your worksheet — the totals, column labels, and heading labels. You can also decorate worksheets with colors. This part of the chapter explains how to put borders and colors on worksheets.

Cell styles for quickly formatting a worksheet

A *style* is a collection of formats — boldface text, a background color, or a border around cells — that can be applied all at one time to cells without having to visit a bunch of different dialog boxes or give a bunch of different commands. Styles save time. If you find yourself choosing the same formatting commands time and time again, consider creating a style. That way, you can apply all the formats simultaneously and go to lunch earlier. Excel comes with many built-in styles, and you can create styles of your own, as the following pages explain.

Applying a built-in cell style

By way of the Cell Styles gallery, you can choose from any number of attractive styles for cells in a worksheet. Excel offers styles for titles and headings, styles for calling attention to what kind of data is in cells, and styles to accent cells. Follow these steps to reformat cells by choosing a cell style:

1. **Select the cells that need a new look.**

2. **On the Home tab, click the Cell Styles button.**

As shown in Figure 4-4, the Cell Styles gallery opens. (Depending on the size of your screen, you may have to click the Styles button and then click the More button to open the Cell Styles gallery.)

Figure 4-4:
Choosing a
new style
from the
Cell Styles
gallery.

3. **Select a cell style.**

The Cell Styles gallery is divided into categories. Scroll through the categories until you find a style that suits your purposes.

To remove a style from cells, select the cells, open the Cell Styles gallery, and choose Normal. (You find Normal in the "Good, Bad, and Neutral" category.)

Creating your own cell style

The names of cell styles you create on your own are placed at the top of the Cell Styles gallery under the Custom heading. Create a cell style if you're the creative type or if no built-in style meets your high standards. Follow these steps to create a cell style:

1. **Apply the formatting commands you want for your style to a single cell.**

For example, left-align cell data. Or apply a fill color to the cells (see "Decorating worksheets with colors," later in this chapter). Or change fonts and font sizes. Knock yourself out. Choose all the formatting commands you want for your new style.

2. **On the Home tab, click the Cell Styles button to open the Cell Styles gallery.**

Depending on the size of your screen, you may have to click the Styles button and then click the More button first.

3. **Choose New Cell Style at the bottom of the gallery.**

You see the Style dialog box shown in Figure 4-5. It lists formatting specifications you chose for the cell you selected in Step 1. If these specifications aren't what you're after, or if you want to change a specification, you can click the Format button and describe your new style in the Format Cells dialog box.

Figure 4-5:
Creating a
new style
for the
Cell Styles
gallery.

4. **Enter a descriptive name for your style in the Style Name text box.**

5. **Click OK.**

Next time you open the Cell Styles gallery, you see the name of your style at the top under Custom.

To remove a style you created from the Cell Styles gallery, right-click its name in the gallery and choose Delete on the shortcut menu.

Formatting cells with table styles

Especially if your worksheet data is arranged neatly into columns and rows so that it looks like a conventional table, one of the easiest ways to decorate cells is to take advantage of table styles. Excel offers many preformatted table styles that you can apply to columns and rows on a worksheet.

Follow these steps to experiment with table styles:

1. **Select the cells you want to format as a table.**

2. **On the Home tab, click the Format As Table button and move your pointer over the table styles in the gallery to "live-preview" them.**

3. **Select a table style.**

The Format As Table dialog box appears.

4. **If the cells you want to format include headers, the labels at the top of column rows that describe the data in the columns below, select the My Table Has Headers check box.**

   If you didn't select cells in Step 1, click outside the Format As Table dialog box and select cells on your worksheet to tell Excel which cells to format.

5. **Click OK in the Format As Table dialog box.**

   You can go to the (Table Tools) Design tab to refine your table. Book I, Chapter 5 (about tables) describes the tools on this tab.

To remove a table style from cells, select the cells, go to the (Table Tools) Design tab, and choose None in the Table Styles gallery.

Slapping borders on worksheet cells

Put borders on worksheet cells to box in cells, draw lines beneath cells, or draw lines along the side of cells. Borders can direct people who review your worksheet to its important parts. Typically, for example, a line appears above the Totals row of a worksheet to separate the Totals row from the rows above and help readers locate cumulative totals.

To draw borders on a worksheet, start by selecting the cells around which or through which you want to place borders. Then do one of the following to draw the borders:

✦ **Borders button:** On the Home tab, open the drop-down list on the Borders button (it's in the Font group) and choose a border, as shown in Figure 4-6.

Figure 4-6:
Drawing a border with the Borders button.

[Format ▾]

✦ **Format Cells dialog box:** On the Home tab, click the Format button and choose Format Cells, or choose More Borders on the Borders button drop-down list. The Format Cells dialog box opens, as shown in Figure 4-7. On the Border tab, select a border style and either click in the Border box to tell Excel where to draw the border or click a Presets button. The Border tab offers different lines for borders and colors for borderlines as well.

Figure 4-7:
Go to the
Format Cells
dialog box
to apply
color (left)
or draw
borders
(right).

To remove the border from cells, select the cells, open the drop-down list on the Borders button, and choose No Border.

Decorating worksheets with colors

Apply background colors to cells to make them stand out or help the people who review your worksheets understand how they are laid out. Select the cells that need a background color and use one of these techniques to splash color on your worksheet:

[Format ▾]

✦ On the Home tab, click the Format button and choose Format Cells on the drop-down list. You see the Format Cells dialog box. On the Fill tab, select a color and click OK. Figure 4-7 shows what the Fill tab looks like.

✦ On the Home tab, open the drop-down list on the Fill Color button and select a color.

To remove colors from cells, select them, go to the Home tab, open the drop-down list on the Fill Color button, and choose No Fill.

Saving your formats in a template

If you go to the trouble to lay out a very fine workbook, you may as well save it as a template. That way, you (or your co-workers) can call upon your newfangled workbook next time you want to create a new Excel workbook. Any workbook that could be of use to someone else is a candidate for becoming a template.

Follow these steps to save a workbook as a template and be able to call upon its formats later on:

1. **On the File tab, choose Save As.**

   You see the Save As dialog box.

2. **Enter a descriptive name for your template in the File Name text box.**

3. **In the Save As Type drop-down list, choose Excel Template.**

4. **Click the Save button.**

5. **Back in your worksheet, delete the data that you don't need when you create a file from your template and then click the Save button to save the template again.**

To call upon the template you made to create a new Excel workbook, go to the File tab, choose New, click the My Templates icon in the Available Templates window, and in the New dialog box, select your template and click OK.

Getting Ready to Print a Worksheet

Printing a worksheet isn't simply a matter of giving the Print command. A worksheet is a vast piece of computerized sprawl. Most worksheets don't fit neatly on a single page. If you simply click the Print button to print your worksheet, you wind up with page breaks in unexpected places, both on the right side of the page and the bottom. Read on to discover how to set up a worksheet so that the people you hand it to can read and understand it.

Making a worksheet fit on a page

Unless you tell it otherwise, Excel prints everything from cell A1 to the last cell with data in it in the southeast corner of the worksheet. Usually, it isn't necessary to print all those cells because some of them are blank. And printing an entire worksheet often means breaking the page up in all kinds of awkward places. To keep that from happening, following are some techniques for making a worksheet fit tidily on one or two pages.

 As you experiment with the techniques described here, switch occasionally to Page Layout view. In this view, you get a better idea of what your worksheet will look like when you print it. To switch to Page Layout view, click the Page Layout button on the status bar or View tab.

Printing part of a worksheet

To print part of a worksheet, select the cells you want to print, go to the Page Layout tab, click the Print Area button, and choose Set Print Area on the drop-down list. This command tells Excel to print only the cells you selected. On the worksheet, a dotted line appears around cells in the print area. To remove the dotted lines from your worksheet, click the Print Area button and choose Clear Print Area on the drop-down list.

Printing a landscape worksheet

If your worksheet is too wide to fit on one page, try turning the page on its side and printing in landscape mode. In landscape mode, pages are wider than they are tall. Landscape mode is often the easiest way to fit a worksheet on a page.

To make yours a landscape worksheet rather than a portrait worksheet, go to the Page Layout tab, click the Orientation button, and choose Landscape on the drop-down list.

Seeing and adjusting the page breaks

Reading a worksheet is extremely difficult when it's broken awkwardly across pages. Where one page ends and the next begins is a *page break*. Use these techniques to see where page breaks occur, adjust the position of page breaks, and insert and remove page breaks:

✦ **Viewing where pages break occur:** Click the Page Break Preview button on the status bar or View tab. As shown in Figure 4-8, you switch to Page Break Preview view. In this view, page numbers appear clearly on the worksheet and dashed lines show you where Excel wants to break the pages.

✦ **Adjusting page break positions:** In Page Break Preview view, drag a dashed line to adjust the position of a page break. After you drag a dashed line, it ceases being a default page break and becomes a manual page break. Manual page breaks are marked by solid lines, not dashed lines (refer to Figure 4-8). You can drag them, too. Excel shrinks the numbers and letters on your worksheet if you try to squeeze too much data on a worksheet by dragging a page break.

✦ **Inserting a page break:** Select the cell directly below where you want the horizontal break to occur and directly to the right of where you want the vertical break to be, go to the Page Layout tab, click the Breaks button, and choose Insert Page Break (refer to Figure 4-8). Drag a page break to adjust its position.

✦ **Removing a page break:** Select a cell directly below or directly to the right of the page break, go to the Page Layout tab, click the Breaks button, and choose Remove Page Break (refer to Figure 4-8).

Insert and remove page breaks

Figure 4-8:
Deciding
where
pages
break.

Manual page break   Default page break

✦ **Removing all manual page breaks:** To remove all manual page breaks
   you inserted, go to the Page Layout tab, click the Breaks button, and
   choose Reset All Page Breaks.

Switch to Page Layout or Normal view after you're done fooling with page
breaks. You can clearly see page breaks in Page Layout view. In Normal view,
page breaks are marked by a dotted line.

"Scaling to fit" a worksheet

To scale the numbers and letters in a worksheet and make them a bit smaller
so that they fit on a page, you can experiment with the Scale to Fit options.
These options are located on the Page Layout tab. Starting in Page Layout
view, go to the Page Layout tab and test-drive these options to make your
worksheet fit on a single page or a certain number of pages:

✦ **Scaling by width:** Open the Width drop-down list and choose an option
   to make your worksheet fit across one or more pages. Choose the 1 Page
   option, for example, to squeeze a worksheet horizontally so that it fits
   on one page.

✦ **Scaling by height:** Open the Height drop-down list and choose an option
   to make your worksheet fit across on a select number of pages. For
   example, choose the 2 Pages option to shrink a worksheet vertically so
   that it fits on two pages.

✦ **Scaling by percentage:** Enter a percentage measurement in the Scale box to shrink a worksheet vertically and horizontally. In order to scale this way, you must choose Automatic in the Width and Height drop-down lists.

You can also fit a worksheet on a select number of pages by going to the Page Setup dialog box shown in Figure 4-9. With this technique, you get a chance to "print-preview" your worksheet and get a better look at it after you change the scale. On the Page Layout tab, click the Page Setup group button to open the Page Setup dialog box. On the Page tab, select the Fit To option button and enter the ideal number of pages you want for your worksheet in the Page(s) Wide By and Tall text boxes. Excel shrinks the data as much as is necessary to make it fit on the number of pages you asked for. Click the Print Preview button to preview your worksheet in the Print window and find out whether shrinking your worksheet this way helps.

Adjusting the margins

Another way to stuff all the data onto one page is to narrow the margins a bit. Go to the Page Layout tab and use either of these techniques to adjust the size of the margins:

✦ Click the Margins button and choose Narrow on the drop-down list.

✦ Click the Page Setup group button, and on the Margins tab of the Page Setup dialog box, change the size of the margins (refer to Figure 4-9). By clicking the Print Preview button, you can preview your worksheet in the Print window and adjust margins there by dragging them. Select the Show Margins button to display the margins. (This little button is in the lower-right corner of the Print window.)

Figure 4-9:
The Page (left) and Margins tab (right) of the Page Setup dialog box.

Making a worksheet more presentable

Before you print a worksheet, visit the Page Setup dialog box and see what you can do to make your worksheet easier for others to read and understand. To open the Page Setup dialog box, go to the Page Layout tab and click the Page Setup group button. Here are your options:

✦ **Including page numbers on worksheets:** On the Page tab of the Page Setup dialog box (refer to Figure 4-9), enter **1** in the First Page Number text box. Then, on the Header/Footer tab, open the Header or Footer drop-down list and choose an option that includes a page number. Choosing the Page 1 of ? option, for example, enters the page number and the total number of pages in the worksheet in your header or footer.

✦ **Putting headers and footers on pages:** On the Header/Footer tab of the Page Setup dialog box, choose options from the Header and Footer drop-down lists. You can find options for listing the file name, page numbers, the date, and your name. By clicking the Custom Header or Custom Footer button, you can open the Header or Footer dialog box and construct a header or footer there. Figure 4-10 shows the Header dialog box.

Figure 4-10: Constructing a fancy header.

✦ **Centering worksheet data on the page:** On the Margins tab, select Horizontally or Vertically to center the worksheet relative to the top or bottom or sides of the page. You can select both check boxes. The preview screen shows what your choices mean in real terms.

✦ **Printing gridlines, column letters, and row numbers:** By default, the gridlines, column letters, and row numbers that you know and love in a worksheet aren't printed, but you can print them by going to the Sheet tab of the Page Setup dialog box and selecting the Gridlines check box as well as the Row and Column Headings check box.

Repeating row and column headings on each page

If your worksheet is a big one that stretches beyond one page, you owe it to the people who view your worksheet to repeat row and column headings from page to page. Without these headings, no one can tell what the data in the worksheet means. Follow these steps to repeat row and column headings from page to page:

1. **On the Page Layout tab, click the Print Titles button.**

   You see the Sheet tab of the Page Setup dialog box.

2. **Select the Row and Column Headings check box.**

   You can find this check box under Print.

3. **To repeat rows, click the Range Selector button next to the Rows to Repeat at Top text box; to repeat columns, click the Range Selector button next to the Columns to Repeat at Left text box.**

   These buttons are located on the right side of the dialog box. The dialog box shrinks so that you can get a better look at your worksheet.

4. **Select the row or column with the labels or names you need.**

   As long as they're next to each other, you can select more than one row or column by dragging over the row numbers or column letters.

5. **Click the Range Selector button to enlarge the dialog box and see it again.**

   The text box now lists a cell range address.

6. **Repeat Steps 3 through 5 to select column or row headings.**

7. **Click OK to close the Page Setup dialog box.**

   If I were you, I would click the Print Preview button in the Page Setup dialog box first to make sure that row and column headings are indeed repeating from page to page.

To remove row and column headings, return to the Sheet tab of the Page Setup dialog box and delete the cell references in the Rows to Repeat at Top text box and the Columns to Repeat at Left text box. You can also press Ctrl+F3 and delete Print_Titles in the Name Manager dialog box.

Chapter 5: Analyzing Data

In This Chapter

✔ Sorting information in a worksheet list

✔ Filtering a list to find the information you need

✔ Using the Goal Seek command to produce formula results

✔ Performing what-if analyses with data tables

*T*his chapter offers a handful of tricks for analyzing the data that you so carefully and lovingly enter in a worksheet. Delve into this chapter to find out how to manage, sort, and filter worksheet lists. You also discover how the Goal Seek command can help you target values in different kinds of analysis, and how you can map out different scenarios with data by using one- and two-input data tables.

Managing Information in Lists

Although Excel is a spreadsheet program, many people use it to keep and maintain lists — address lists, product lists, employee lists, and inventory lists, among other types of lists. These pages deal with all the different things you can do with a worksheet list. They explain the difference between a conventional worksheet and a list, constructing a list, sorting a list, and filtering a list.

Constructing a list

To sort and filter data in a worksheet, your worksheet must be constructed like a list. Make sure that your worksheet has these characteristics:

✦ **Column labels:** Enter column labels along the top row, as shown in Figure 5-1. Excel needs these labels to identify and be able to filter the data in the rows below. Each label must have a different name. The row along the top of the worksheet where the column labels are is called the *header row.*

✦ **No empty rows or columns:** Sorry, but you can't put an empty row or column in the middle of the worksheet list.

✦ **No blank columns on the left:** Don't allow any empty columns to appear to the left of the list.

 ✦ **A single worksheet:** The list must occupy a single worksheet. You can't keep more than one list on the same worksheet.

Product ID	Product Name	Production Cost	Packaging	Ship Cost	Sale per Unit	Profit	Warehouse	Supervisor
11100	Widget	1.19	0.14	0.45	4.11	2.33	Trenton	Munoz
11101	Gasket	2.24	0.29	0.89	4.14	0.72	Pickford	Salazaar
11102	Tappet	4.13	1.11	0.18	7.12	1.70	Trenton	Munoz
11103	Widget	8.19	3.40	0.45	14.80	2.76	LaRue	Smith
11104	Pludget	6.41	0.29	0.32	7.89	0.87	Massy	Yee
11105	Placker	7.39	0.98	1.11	12.14	2.66	Pickford	Salazaar
11106	Stacker	11.00	1.14	0.89	14.89	1.86	LaRue	Smith
11107	Knacker	14.31	3.14	0.45	20.98	3.08	Massy	Yee
11108	Tipplet	2.11	0.14	0.32	5.81	3.24	Trenton	Munoz
11109	Culet	4.16	0.17	0.32	6.01	1.36	Trenton	Munoz
11110	Ropper	13.44	2.89	0.79	21.43	4.31	LaRue	Smith
11111	Knocker	23.08	2.10	0.89	32.89	6.82	Trenton	Munoz
11112	Topper	1.14	0.09	0.11	4.02	2.68	Pickford	Salazaar
11113	Rammer	2.15	0.16	0.32	5.10	2.47	Massy	Yee
11114	Cricker	3.34	0.27	0.33	6.12	2.18	LaRue	Smity
11115	Knicker	8.78	1.01	0.89	10.79	0.11	Trenton	Munoz
11116	Stamler	2.14	0.53	0.20	6.78	3.91	LaRue	Smith
11117	Doublet	9.46	1.01	0.99	14.33	2.87	Pickford	Salazaar

Figure 5-1:
A worksheet as a list.

If you know anything about databases, the rules for constructing a worksheet list no doubt sound familiar. These are the same rules that apply to constructing a database table. You might consider managing your list as a database if it's a long and complex one. Book VI explains how to use Access, the database program in Office 2010.

Sorting a list

Sorting means to rearrange the rows in a list on the basis of data in one or more columns. Sort a list on the Last Name column, for example, to arrange the list in alphabetical order by last name. Sort a list on the ZIP Code column to arrange the rows in numerical order by ZIP code. Sort a list on the Birthday column to arrange it chronologically from earliest born to latest born.

Starting on the Data tab, here are all the ways to sort a list:

 ✦ **Sorting on a single column:** Click any cell in the column you want to use as the basis for the sort, and then click the Sort Smallest to Largest or Sort Largest to Smallest button. (On the Home tab, you can get to these buttons by clicking the Sort & Filter button first.) For example, to sort item numbers from smallest to largest, click in the Item Number column and then click the Sort Smallest to Largest button.

 ✦ **Sort on more than one column:** Click the Sort button on the Data tab. You see the Sort dialog box, as shown in Figure 5-2. Choose which columns you want to sort with and the order in which you want to sort. To add a second or third column for sorting, click the Add Level button.

Figure 5-2:
Sort to
arrange the
list data in
different
ways.

Filtering a list

Filtering means to scour a worksheet list for certain kinds of data. To filter,
you tell Excel what kind of data you're looking for, and the program assembles rows with that data to the exclusion of rows that don't have the data.
You end up with a shorter list with only the rows that match your filter criteria. Filtering is similar to using the Find command except that you get more
than one row in the results of the filtering operation. For example, in a list of
addresses, you can filter for only addresses in California. In a price list, you
can filter for items that fall within a certain price range.

To filter a list, start by going to the Data tab and clicking the Filter button. As
shown in Figure 5-3, a drop-down list appears beside each column header.

Click the Filter button

Figure 5-3:
Filter a
worksheet
to isolate
data.

Your next task is to open a drop-down list in the column that holds the criteria you want to use to filter the list. For example, if you want to filter the list to items that cost more than $100, open the Cost column drop-down list; if you want to filter the list so that only the names of employees who make less than $30,000 annually appears, open the Salary drop-down list.

After you open the correct column drop-down list, tell Excel how you want to filter the list:

✦ **Filter by exclusion:** On the drop-down list, deselect the Select All check box and then select the check box next to each item you *don't* want to filter out. For example, to filter an Address list to addresses in Boston, Chicago, and Miami, deselect the Select All check box and then select the check boxes next to Boston, Chicago, and Miami on the drop-down list. Your filter operation turns up only addresses in these three cities.

✦ **Filter with criteria:** On the drop-down list, choose Number Filters, and then choose a filter operation on the submenu (or simply choose Custom Filter). You see the Custom AutoFilter dialog box.

Choose an operator (equals, is greater than, or another) from the drop-down list, and either enter or choose a target criterion from the list on the right side of the dialog box. You can search by more than one criterion. Select the And option button if a row must meet both criteria to be selected, or select the Or option button if a row can meet either criterion to be selected.

Click the OK button on the column's drop-down list or the Custom AutoFilter dialog box to filter your list.

K Clear   To see all the data in the list again — to *unfilter* the list — click the Clear button on the Data tab.

Forecasting with the Goal Seek Command

In a conventional formula, you provide the raw data, and Excel produces the results. With the Goal Seek command, you declare what you want the results to be, and Excel tells you the raw data you need to produce those results. The Goal Seek command is useful in analyses when you want the outcome to be a certain way and you need to know which raw numbers will produce the outcome that you want.

Figure 5-4 shows a worksheet designed to find out the monthly payment on a mortgage. With the PMT function, the worksheet determines that the monthly payment on a $250,000 loan with an interest rate of 6.5 percent and to be paid over a 30-year period is $1,580.17. Suppose, however, that the person who calculated this monthly payment determined that he or she could pay more than $1,580.17 per month? Suppose the person could pay $1,750 or $2,000 per month. Instead of an outcome of $1,580.17, the person wants to know how much he or she could borrow if monthly payments — the outcome of the formula — were increased to $1,750 or $2,000.

Figure 5-4:
Experiment-
ing with the
Goal Seek
command.

To make determinations such as these, you can use the Goal Seek command. This command lets you experiment with the arguments in a formula to achieve the results you want. In the case of the worksheet in Figure 5-4, you can use the Goal Seek command to change the argument in cell C3, the total amount you can borrow, given the outcome you want in cell C6, $1,750 or $2,000, the monthly payment on the total amount.

Follow these steps to use the Goal Seek command to change the inputs in a formula to achieve the results you want:

1. **Select the cell with the formula whose arguments you want to experiment with.**

2. **On the Data tab, click the What-If Analysis button and choose Goal Seek on the drop-down list.**

   You see the Goal Seek dialog box (refer to Figure 5-4). The address of the cell you selected in Step 1 appears in the Set Cell box.

3. **In the To Value text box, enter the target results you want from the formula.**

   In the example in Figure 5-4, you enter 1750 or 2000, the monthly payment you can afford for the 30-year mortgage.

4. **In the By Changing Cell text box, enter the address of the cell whose value is unknown.**

   To enter a cell address, select a cell on your worksheet. In Figure 5-4, you select the address of the cell that shows the total amount you want to borrow.

5. **Click OK.**

   The Goal Seek Status dialog box appears (refer to Figure 5-4). It lists the target value that you entered in Step 3.

6. **Click OK.**

   On your worksheet, the cell with the argument you wanted to alter now shows the target you're seeking. In the case of the example worksheet in Figure 5-4, you can borrow $316,422 at 6.5 percent, not $250,000, by raising your monthly mortgage payments from $1,580.17 to $2,000.

Performing What-If Analyses with Data Tables

For something a little more sophisticated than the Goal Seek command (which I describe in the preceding section), try performing what-if analyses with data tables. With this technique, you change the data in input cells and observe what effect changing the data has on the results of a formula. The difference between the Goal Seek command and a data table is that, with a data table, you can experiment simultaneously with many different input cells and in so doing experiment with many different scenarios.

Using a one-input table for analysis

In a *one-input table,* you find out what the different results of a formula would be if you change one *input cell* in the formula. In Figure 5-5, that input cell is the interest rate on a loan. The purpose of this data table is to find out how monthly payments on a $250,000, 30-year mortgage are different, given different interest rates. The interest rate in cell B4 is the input cell.

Follow these steps to create a one-input table:

1. **On your worksheet, enter values that you want to substitute for the value in the input cell.**

   To make the input table work, you have to enter the substitute values in the right location:

   - *In a column:* Enter the values in the column starting one cell below and one cell to the left of the cell where the formula is located. In Figure 5-5, for example, the formula is in cell E4 and the values are in the cell range D5:D15.

   - *In a row:* Enter the values in the row starting one cell above and one cell to the right of the cell where the formula is.

Substitute values

Input cell

Formula cell

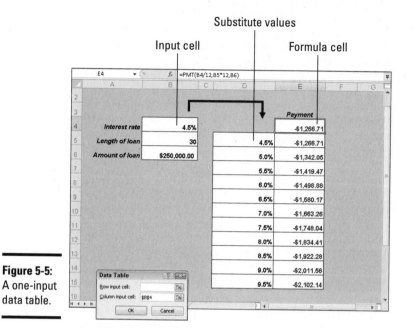

Figure 5-5:
A one-input
data table.

2. Select the block of cells with the formula and substitute values.

Select a rectangle of cells that encompasses the formula cell, the cell beside it, all the substitute values, and the empty cells where the new calculations will soon appear. In the case of a column, you select the formula cell, the cell to its left, as well as all the substitute-value cells and the cells below the formula cell. In the case of a row, select the formula cell, the cell above it, as well as the substitute values in the cells directly to the right and the now-empty cells where the new calculations will appear.

3. On the Data tab, click the What-If Analysis button and choose Data Table on the drop-down list.

You see the Data Table dialog box.

4. In the Row Input Cell or Column Input Cell text box, enter the address of the cell where the input value is located.

The input value is the value you're experimenting with in your analysis. In the case of Figure 5-5, the input value is located in cell B4, the cell that holds the interest rate.

If the new calculations appear in rows, enter the address of the input cell in the Row Input Cell text box; if the calculations appear in columns (refer to Figure 5-5), enter the input cell address in the Column Input Cell text box.

5. **Click OK.**

   Excel performs the calculations and fills in the table.

To generate the one-input table, Excel constructs an array formula with the TABLE function. If you change the cell references in the first row or plug in different values in the first column, Excel updates the one-input table automatically.

Using a two-input table for analysis

In a two-input table, you can experiment with two input cells rather than one. Getting back to the example of the loan payment in Figure 5-5, you can calculate not only how loan payments change as interest rates change, but how payments change if the life of the loan changes. Figure 5-6 shows a two-input table for examining monthly loan payments given different interest rates and two different terms for the loan, 15 years (180 months) and 30 years (360 months).

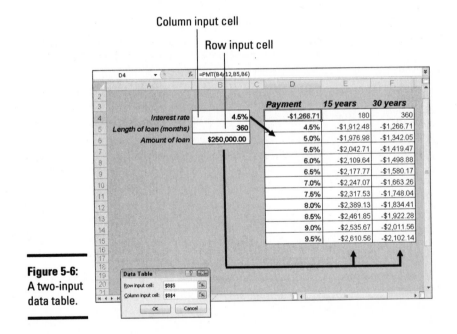

Figure 5-6: A two-input data table.

Follow these steps to create a two-input data table:

1. **Enter one set of substitute values below the formula in the same column as the formula.**

In Figure 5-6, different interest rates are entered in the cell range D5:D15.

2. **Enter the second set of substitute values in the row to the right of the formula.**

In Figure 5-6, 180 and 360 are entered. These numbers represent the number of months of the life of the loan.

3. **Select the formula and all substitute values.**

Do this correctly and you select three columns, including the formula, the substitute values below it, and the two columns to the right of the formula. You select a big block of cells (the range D4:F15, in this example).

4. **On the Data tab, click the What-If Analysis button and choose Data Table on the drop-down list.**

The Data Table dialog box appears (refer to Figure 5-6).

5. **In the Row Input Cell text box, enter the address of the cell referred to in the original formula where substitute values to the right of the formula can be plugged in.**

In Figure 5-6, for example, the rows to the right of the formula are for length of loan substitute values. Therefore, I select cell B5, the cell referred to in the original formula where the length of the loan is listed.

6. **In the Column Input Cell text box, enter the address of the cell referred to in the original formula where substitute values below the formula are.**

In Figure 5-6, the substitute values below the formula cell are interest rates. Therefore, I select cell B4, the cell referred to in the original formula where the interest rate is entered.

7. **Click OK.**

Excel performs the calculations and fills in the table.

Book VI

Access

The 5th Wave   By Rich Tennant

"Once I told Mona that Access was an 'argument' based program, she seemed to warm up to it."

Contents at a Glance

Chapter 1: Introducing Access

In This Chapter

✔ Understanding how databases work

✔ Looking at tables, queries, forms, and other database objects

✔ Creating a database

✔ Opening and closing tables

✔ Designing the tables, queries, forms, and the other parts of a database

The word *database* is prone to making most people feel kind of queasy. Can you blame them? Database terminology — record, field, and filter — is the worst of the worst. It even puts other computer terminology to shame. Databases intimidate most people. Even brave souls with a considerable amount of experience in Word and Excel shy away from *Access,* the Office 2010 database program. However, Access can be invaluable for storing and organizing customer lists, inventories, addresses, payment histories, donor lists, and volunteer lists. What's more, Access is easy to use, after you get the hang of it. No kidding!

This chapter starts you down the road to the Land of Oz. In truth, it introduces databases and the concepts behind databases. It shows you how to create a database and database tables for storing information. The second half of this chapter explains how to design databases. Sorry, but you have to know about database design before you can start fooling with databases. You can't jump right in as you can with the other Office programs.

Access offers a practice database called Northwind Traders that you can experiment with as you get to know your way around databases. To open this database, start Access and select Sample Templates in the Available Templates window. Then scroll in the list of sample templates, select Northwind, and click the Create button.

What Is a Database, Anyway?

Whether you know it or not, you're no stranger to databases. The address book on your computer is a database. The telephone directory in the desk drawer is, too. A recipe book is also a database in that recipes are categorized under different headings. If you ever arranged a CD collection in a certain way — in alphabetical order or by musical genre, for example — you created a database of CDs, one that makes finding a particular CD easier. Any place where information is stored in a systematic way can be considered a *database*. The only difference between a computerized database and a conventional database, such as a telephone directory, is that storing, finding, and manipulating data is much easier in a computerized database.

Imagine how long it would take to find all the New York addresses in an address list with 10,000 entries. In Access, you can query a 10,000-entry database and find all New York addresses in a matter of seconds. For that matter, you can query to find all the addresses in a certain ZIP Code. You can put the list in alphabetical order by last name or in numerical order by ZIP Code. Doing these chores without a computer requires many hours of dreary, monotonous labor.

Tables, Queries, Forms, and Other Objects

One problem with getting to know a database program — and the primary reason that people are intimidated by databases — is that you can't jump right in. You have to know how data is stored in a database and how it is extracted, to use programmer terminology. You have to know about *objects,* Access's bland word for database tables, queries, forms, and all else that makes a database a database. To help you get going, these pages offer a crash course in databases. They explain the different *objects* — tables, queries, forms, and reports — that make up a database. Fasten your seat belt. If you complete the crash course without crashing, you're ready to create your first database.

Database tables for storing information

Information in databases is stored in *database tables* like the one in Figure 1-1. In a database table, you include one field for each category of information you want to keep on hand. *Fields* are the equivalent of columns in a table. Your first duty when you create a database table is to name the fields and tell Access what kind of information you propose to store in each field. The database table in Figure 1-1 is for storing employee information. It has seven fields: ID, First Name, Last Name, E-mail Address, Business Phone, Company, and Job Title.

A database can comprise one database table or many different tables that are linked together. If you're dealing with a lot of information, storing data in more than one table is to your advantage. Later in this chapter, "Separating information into different database tables" explains why storing data across several database tables is advantageous.

A record   A field   Cells

Figure 1-1:
A database
table.

Book 6
Chapter 1

Introducing Access

Access database terminology

Stumbling over database terminology is easy. To keep yourself from stumbling, fold back the corner of this page and return here if one of these database terms puzzles you:

✔ **Cell:** In a database table, a place for entering one piece of data. Cells appear in a database table where a field and record intersect.

✔ **Database:** A systematic way of organizing information so that it can be retrieved and manipulated easily.

✔ **Database table:** A collection of data records arranged into well-defined categories, or fields. Most relational databases have more than one table.

✔ **Dynaset:** The results of a search for data in a database. (This term is short for dynamic set.) A dynaset is not to be confused with a dinosaur.

✔ **Field:** One category of information in a database table. Fields are the equivalent of columns in a conventional table.

✔ **Filtering:** Finding the records in a database table that have the same or nearly the same field value. Filtering is a more convenient but not as sophisticated means of querying a database.

✔ **Foreign field:** In a relationship between two database tables, the field that is on the "many" side of a one-to-many relationship. The primary key field is on the "one" side.

✔ **Form:** Similar to a dialog box, a place with text boxes and drop-down lists for entering records in a database table.

✔ **Module:** A Visual Basic procedure whose job is to perform a certain task in Access.

(continued)

(continued)

- **Object:** The catchall term for the tables, queries, forms, and reports that you create and open starting in the Navigation pane.

- **Primary key field:** The field in a database table where unique, one-of-a-kind data is stored. To query more than one database table at a time, the tables must have primary key fields.

- **Query:** A question asked of a database that yields information. Queries can be made of a single database table, several tables, or even other queries.

- **Record:** In a database table, all the data that's recorded about one person or thing. A record is the equivalent of a row in a conventional table.

- **Relational database:** A database program in which data is kept in more than one database table, relationships are established between tables, and queries can be conducted and reports made by assembling data from different tables. Access is a relational database. A database that permits only one table is a *flat-file database.*

- **Report:** Information gathered from a database and laid out in such a way that it's easy to read and understand. Reports are meant to be printed and distributed.

- **Sort:** To rearrange records in a database table so that the records appear in alphabetical, numerical, or date order in one field.

Forms for entering data

After you create the fields in the database table, you can start entering the records. A *record* describes all the data concerning one person or thing. In Figure 1-1, eight records are entered in the database table. Each record comprises a person's ID, first name, last name, e-mail address, business phone, company, and job title. Records are the meat of the database. Information is stored in records.

Although you can enter records straight into a database table, the easiest way to enter a record is with a *form.* Similar to a dialog box, a form has convenient text boxes and drop-down lists for entering information. Figure 1-2 shows the form for entering a record in the database table shown in Figure 1-1. Notice that the form has one place for entering data in each field in the database table — First Name, Last Name, and so on. On a form, you can see clearly what kind of information needs entering in each field.

Queries for getting the data out

Figure 1-3 shows a simple query for finding out which employees in the database table shown in Figure 1-1 are Sales Representatives. A *query* is a question you ask of a database. The question here is, "Who is a Sales Representative?" Notice the criterion "Sales Representative" in the Job Title field on the Query grid.

Fields

Figure 1-2:
A form for
entering
data.

Table being queried

Query criteria

Figure 1-3:
Querying a
database.

Results of the query

In an address database, you can use a query to find all the people in a particular ZIP Code or state. If information about contributions is stored in the database, you can find out who contributed more than $500 last year. Queries can get very complex. For example, you can find all the people in a particular city who contributed between $50 and $500 and volunteered more than eight hours in the past year. You can construct the query so that it produces each person's name and telephone number, or you can construct it so that all the information you have concerning each person appears in the query results.

When you get junk mail, it likely comes to your mailbox as the result of a database query. Companies routinely buy and sell customer databases. They query these databases to gather the names of people who they believe are well-disposed to purchasing the products they sell. Next time you get junk mail solicitation, study the letter and ask yourself, "How did I get in this database, and which database query produced my name?" The junk mailer is probably targeting extraordinarily beautiful, intelligent people.

After you create a query, you can save it and run it again. You can use it as the basis for constructing new queries. The information in database tables usually changes over time. Customers change addresses. New products come online, and others are discontinued. But no matter how much the data changes, you can find out exactly what you want to know from a database by running a well-crafted query.

Reports for presenting and examining data

Figure 1-4 shows a *report*. Reports can be made from database tables or from the results of queries. Reports are usually read by managers and others who don't get their hands dirty in databases. They're meant to be printed and distributed so that the information can be scrutinized and analyzed. Access offers many attractive reports. Don't worry — the program does most of the layout work for you, and exporting reports to a Word file is easy.

Macros and modules

Macros and modules aren't covered in this mini-book, but they are also database objects. A *macro* is a series of commands. You can store macros for running queries and doing other Access tasks. (Book VIII, Chapter 6 explains macros.) A *module* is a collection of Visual Basic procedures and declarations for performing tasks in Access.

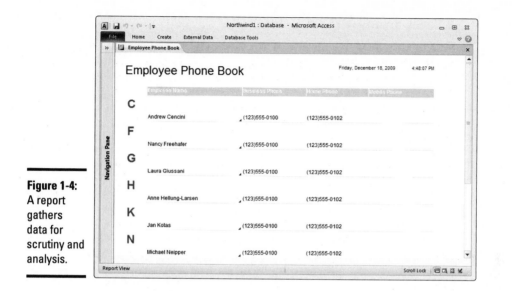

Figure 1-4:
A report
gathers
data for
scrutiny and
analysis.

Creating a Database File

Creating a database is a lot of work, at least in the beginning. You have to design the database (a subject that I explain shortly). You have to enter the raw information into the tables. You have to construct queries that allow yourself and others to read meaning into the data (see Chapter 4 of this mini-book). By contrast, creating a database file for storing the information is the easy part.

Access offers two ways to create a new database file. You can do it from scratch or get the help of a template. With a template, some of the work is done already for you. The template comes with prefabricated queries, forms, and reports. However, templates are for people who already know their way around Access databases. To make use of a template, you have to know how to modify a preexisting database.

Before you create a database file, start by deciding where in your computer to store it. Unlike other Office programs, Access requires you to save and name a new file as soon as you create it.

Creating a blank database file

Follow these instructions to create a blank database file:

1. **Start Access (if it isn't already running), or go to the File tab and choose New.**

The Available Templates window appears.

2. **Click the Blank Database icon.**

3. **Click the folder icon (it's in the lower-right corner of the window beside the File Name text box), and in the File New Database dialog box, select the folder where you want to keep the database file, enter a name in the File Name text box, and click OK.**

4. **Click the Create button.**

   The Navigation pane and a blank table appear. Later in this chapter, "Finding Your Way Around the Navigation Pane" explains what this pane is all about. I suggest you go there without delay or deferral.

Getting the help of a template

As I explain earlier, templates are wonderful if you have the wherewithal to modify them. Access offers prefabricated databases for tracking assets, keeping inventory, scheduling resources, and doing other things. Unfortunately, the only way to find out whether one of the templates is worthwhile is to go to the trouble to create a database from a template, open up the database file, and look around.

Follow these steps to create a database file from a template:

1. **Start Access or go to the File tab and choose New.**

   The Available Template window opens.

2. **Click the Sample Templates icon.**

3. **Select a template.**

   The template name appears on the right side of the window.

4. **Click the folder icon (it's in the lower-right corner of the window beside the File Name text box), and in the File New Database dialog box, select the folder where you want to keep the database file, enter a name in the File Name text box, and click OK.**

5. **Click the Create button.**

Finding Your Way Around the Navigation Pane

The first thing you see when you open most database files is a Navigation pane like the one in Figure 1-5. This is the starting point for doing all your work in Access. From here, you can select an object — that horrible word again! — and begin working. Tables, queries, and other objects you create are added to the Navigation pane when you create them.

Object Type drop-down list

Figure 1-5:
Finding and
selecting
objects
with the
Navigation
pane.

Groups   Objects in this group

Here are shorthand instructions for doing this, that, and the other thing in the Navigation pane:

✦ **Choosing an object type:** Select a group (Tables, Queries, Forms, Reports, and so on) from the Object Type drop-down list at the top of the Navigation pane, or select All Access Objects to see all the groups, as shown in Figure 1-5.

✦ **Creating a new object:** Go to the Create tab and choose what type of object you want to create. When creating new forms and reports, click a table or query in the Navigation pane to base the new form or report on a table or query.

✦ **Opening an object:** To open a database table, query, form, or report, double-click it, select it and press Enter, or right-click it and choose Open on the shortcut menu.

✦ **Opening an object in Design view:** The task of formulating database tables, forms, and queries is done in Design view. If an object needs reformulating, right-click it and choose Design View on the shortcut menu.

✦ **Finding objects:** Use the Search bar (located at the top of the Navigation pane) to search for objects.

✦ **Opening and closing the Navigation pane:** Click the Shutter Bar Open/Close button on the upper-right corner of the Navigation pane (or press F11) when you want to shrink it and get it out of the way. You can also resize this pane by clicking the far-right edge and dragging it left or right.

Designing a Database

Being a database designer isn't nearly as glamorous as being a fashion designer, but it has its rewards. If you design your database carefully and correctly, it can be very useful to you and others. You can enter information accurately. When the time comes to draw information from the database, you get precisely the information you need. These pages explain everything you need to consider when designing a database. Pay close attention to "Separating information into different database tables," later in this chapter, because the hardest part about designing a database is deciding how to distribute information across database tables and how many database tables to have.

Deciding what information you need

The first question to ask yourself is about the kind of information you want to get out of the database. Customer names and addresses? Sales information? Information for inventory tracking? Interview your co-workers to find out what information could be helpful to them. Give this matter some serious thought. Your goal is to set up the database so that every tidbit of information your organization needs can be recorded.

A good way to find out what kind of information matters to an organization is to examine the paper forms that the organization uses to solicit or record information. These forms show precisely what the organization deems worthy of tracking in a database. Figure 1-6, for example, shows the paper form that players fill out to sign up for a baseball league whose database tables appear in Figure 1-7. Compare Figure 1-6 with Figure 1-7, and you can see that the Players, Teams, and Divisions database tables all have fields for entering information from this form.

Separating information into different database tables

After you know the information you want to record in the database, think about how to separate the information into database tables. Many are tempted to put all the information into a single database table, but because Access is a *relational database,* you can query more than one table at a time, and in so doing, assemble information from different tables.

Figure 1-6:
Paper forms
also have
fields.

Figure 1-7:
Plans for
database
tables and
field names.

To see how it works, consider the simple database shown in Figure 1-7. The purpose of this little database and its four tables is to store information about the players, coaches, and teams in a baseball league. The Team Name field appears in three tables. It serves as the link between the tables and permits more than one to be queried. By querying individual tables or combinations of tables in this database, I can assemble team rosters, make a list of coaches and their contact information, list teams by division, put together a mailing list of all players, find out which players have paid their fee, and list players by age group, among other things. This database comprises four tables:

✦ **Players:** Includes fields for tracking players' names, addresses, birthdays, which teams they're on, and whether they paid their fees.

✦ **Coaches:** Includes fields for tracking coaches' names, addresses, and the names of the teams they coach.

✦ **Teams:** Includes fields for tracking team names and which division each team is in.

✦ **Divisions:** Includes fields for tracking division numbers and names.

Deciding how many database tables you need and how to separate data across the different tables is the hardest part of designing a database. To make the task a little easier, do it the old-fashioned way with a pencil and eraser. Here are the basic rules for separating data into different tables:

✦ **Restrict a table to one subject only:** Each database table should hold information about one subject only — customers, employees, products, and so on. This way, you can maintain data in one table independently from data in another table. Consider what would happen in the little league database (refer to Figure 1-7) if coach and team data were kept in a single table, and one team's coach was replaced by someone new. You would have to delete the old coach's record, delete information about the team, enter information about the new coach, and reenter information about the team that you just deleted. But by keeping team information separate from coach information, you can update coach information and still maintain the team information.

✦ **Avoid duplicate information:** Try not to keep duplicate information in the same database table or duplicate information across different tables. By keeping the information in one place, you have to enter it only once, and if you have to update it, you can do so in one database table, not several.

Entire books have been written about database design, and this book can't do the subject justice. You can, however, store all your data in a single table if the data you want to store isn't very complex. The time you lose entering all the data in a single table is made up by the time you save not having to design a complex database with more than one table.

Choosing fields for database tables

As I explain earlier, *fields* are categories of information. Each database table needs at least one field. If the table itself is a subject, you could say that its fields are facts about the subject. An Address database table needs fields for recording street addresses, cities, states, and ZIP codes. A Products database table needs fields for product ID numbers, product names, and unit prices. Just the facts, ma'am. Within the confines of the subject, the database table needs one field for each piece of information that is useful to your organization.

When you're planning which fields to include in a database table, follow these guidelines:

✦ Break up the information into small elements. For example, rather than a Name field, create a First Name field and a Last Name field. This way, you can sort database tables by last name more easily.

✦ Give descriptive names to fields so that you know what they are later. A more descriptive name, such as *Serial Number,* is clearer than *SN.*

✦ Think ahead and include a field for each piece of information your organization needs. Adding a field to a database table late in the game is a
chore. You have to return to each record, look up the information, and
enter it.

✦ Don't include information that can be derived from a calculation. As I
explain in Chapter 4 of this mini-book, calculations can be performed as
part of a query or be made part of a table. For example, you can total the
numbers in two fields in the same record or perform mathematical calculations on values in fields.

Deciding on a primary key field for each database table

REMEMBER

Each database table must have a *primary key field.* This field, also known
as the *primary key,* is the field in the database table where unique, one-of-a-
kind data is stored. Data entered in this field — an employee ID number, a
part number, a bid number — must be different in each record. If you try to
enter the same data in the primary key field of two different records, a dialog
box warns you not to do that. Primary key fields prevent you from entering
duplicate records. They also make queries more efficient. In a query, you
tell Access what to look for in database tables, Access searches through
the tables, and the program assembles information that meets the criteria.
Primary key fields help Access recognize records and not collect the same
information more than once in a query.

Social security numbers make good primary key fields because no two
people have the same social security number. Invoice numbers and serial
numbers also make excellent primary key fields. Returning to the sample
baseball league database (refer to Figure 1-7), which fields in the little league
database tables are primary key fields? In the Teams table, Team Name can
be the primary key field because no two teams have the same name. Division
Number can also be a primary key field because divisions in the league are
numbered and no two divisions have the same number.

The Players and Coaches database tables, however, present a problem when
it comes to choosing a primary key field. Two players might have the same
last name, which rules out Last Name as a primary key field. A brother and
sister might have the same telephone number, which rules out a Telephone
No. field. Because no field holds values that are certain to be different
from record to record, I introduce fields called Player Number and Coach
Number. For the purpose of this database, players and coaches are assigned
numbers. (Chapter 2 in this mini-book explains how Access can assign
sequential numbers for you in a database table.)

Mapping the relationships between tables

If your database includes more than one table, you have to map how the tables relate to one another. Usually, relationships are formed between the primary key field in one table and the corresponding field in another, called the *foreign key*. Figure 1-8 shows the relationships between the tables in the little league database. Because these tables are linked by common fields, I can gather information from more than one table in a query or report. Chapter 2 in this mini-book takes up the subject of linking tables in more detail. For now, when you design your database, consider how to connect the various tables with common fields.

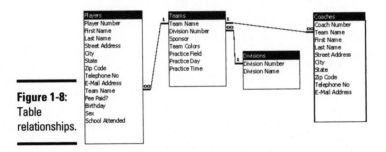

Figure 1-8:
Table
relationships.

Chapter 2: Building Your Database Tables

In This Chapter

✔ Creating database tables

✔ Creating fields for a database table

✔ Choosing a primary key field

✔ Using field properties to make data entries more accurate

✔ Indexing fields in a table

✔ Forming relationships between tables

Database tables are the building blocks of a database. They hold the raw data. Relationships between the tables permit you to query and generate reports from several different tables. How well your database tables are put together and how accurately data is entered in the tables determine whether your database is a thing of beauty or a wilted flower.

This chapter explains how to create database tables and fields for the tables. It explains what primary key fields are and how primary key fields and indexed fields make it easier for Access to sort, search, and query a database. This chapter describes how to forge relationships between tables. Fasten your seat belts. In this chapter, you find numerous tips and tricks for making sure that data is entered accurately in your database tables.

Creating a Database Table

Raw data is stored in database tables (or in a single table if you decide to keep all the data in one place). The first and most important part of setting up a database is creating the tables and entering the data. After you enter the data, you can harass your database for information about the things and people your database keeps track of. If you haven't done so already, read the sections in Chapter 1 of this mini-book that pertain to storing information and designing a database before you create a database table. Chapter 1 of this mini-book explains what database tables are and how to fashion a splendid one.

The business of creating a database table starts on the Create tab. As I explain in detail in the next pages, Access offers three ways to create a database table:

+ **Create the database table from scratch:** Enter and format the fields one at a time on your own.

+ **Get the help of a template:** Get prefabricated fields assembled in a table. This is the way to go if you know Access well, and you can modify database tables and table fields.

+ **Import the database table from another database:** This technique can be an enormous timesaver if you can recycle data that has already been entered in a database table in another Access database.

Creating a database table from scratch

Creating a table from scratch entails creating the table and then entering the fields one by one. After you open a database file, follow these steps to create a database table from scratch:

1. **Go to the Create tab.**

2. **Click the Table Design button.**

The Design window appears. From here, you enter fields for your database table. I hate to be like a City Hall bureaucrat who gives everybody the runaround, but I can't help myself. Turn to "Entering and Altering Table Fields," later in this chapter, to find out how to enter fields in a database table.

3. **Click the Save button on the Quick Access toolbar.**

The Save As dialog box appears.

4. **Enter a descriptive name for your table and click OK.**

Return to the Navigation pane and you see the name of the table you created. If you don't believe me, click the Tables group to see the names of tables in your database.

Creating a database table from a template

If you know your way around Access and know how to modify database tables, you can do worse than create a database table with a template. Access offers four table templates: Contacts (for storing contact addresses and phone numbers), Issues (for prioritizing issues), Tasks (for tracking projects, their status, and when they are due), and Users (for storing e-mail addresses). As well as creating a table, Access creates ready-made queries, forms, and reports to go along with the table. After you create a table with a template, you can remove fields that you don't want. It's always easier to delete fields than it is to add new ones.

Follow these steps to use a template to create a table (and accompanying queries, forms, and reports):

1. **Close all objects if any objects are open.**

To close an object, click its Close button.

2. **On the Create tab, click the Application Parts button.**

A drop-down list with options for creating forms and tables appears. (The tables are listed under "Quick Start.")

3. **Choose Contacts, Issues, Tasks, or Users.**

If there are other tables in your database, a dialog box asks whether you want to create a relationship between the table you're creating and another table.

**Book VI
Chapter 2**

**Building Your
Database Tables**

4. **Select the There Is No Relationship option button and click Create.**

Later in this chapter, "Establishing Relationships between Database Tables" explains how to create relationships on your own. If you want to create these relationships now and you have the wherewithal to do it, select an option besides There Is No Relationship, choose a table on the drop-down list, and click the Next button to choose which field to forge the relationship with.

5. **On the Navigation pane, right-click the name of the table you created and choose Design View.**

In Design view, you can see the names of the fields in the table. If the table contains fields you don't want or you want to change the names of the fields, turn to "Entering and Altering Table Fields," later in this chapter.

Importing a table from another database

Few things are more tedious than entering records in a database table. If the records you need were already entered elsewhere, more power to you. Follow these steps to get a database table from another Access database:

1. **Go to the External Data tab.**

2. **Click the Access button.**

The Get External Data – Access Database dialog box opens.

3. **Click the Browse button, and in the File Open dialog box, select the Access database with the table you need and click Open.**

You return to the Get External Data – Access Database dialog box.

4. **Select the first option button (Import Tables, Queries, Forms, Reports, Macros, and Modules into the Current Database) and click OK.**

You see the Import Objects dialog box, as shown in Figure 2-1.

Figure 2-1:
Fetching a
table from
another
database.

5. On the Tables tab, select the database table you want.

You can import more than one database table by clicking several table names or clicking the Select All button.

You can import a table structure — its field names and formats — without importing the data in the table. To do so, click the Options button in the Import Objects dialog box, and under Import Tables, select the Definition Only option button.

6. Click OK.

If the table you want to import includes lookup fields, import the tables or queries that the lookup fields refer to as well as the table itself. Without those tables or queries, the lookup fields won't be able to obtain any values. Later in this chapter, "Creating a lookup data-entry list" explains what lookup fields are.

Opening and Viewing Tables

To open a table, start in the Navigation pane and select the Tables group to view the names of database tables you created. How you open a table depends on whether you want to open it in Datasheet view or Design view. Figure 2-2 illustrates the difference between these views. Datasheet view is for entering and examining data in a table; Design view is for creating fields and describing their parameters.

**Book VI
Chapter 2**

**Building Your
Database Tables**

Figure 2-2:
A table in
Design view
(top) and
Datasheet
view
(bottom).

Select a table on the Navigation pane and use one of these techniques to
open and view it:

✦ **Opening in Design view:** Right-click the table's name in the Navigation
pane and choose Design View on the shortcut menu.

✦ **Opening in Datasheet view:** On the Navigation pane, double-click the
table's name or right-click its name and choose Open on the shortcut
menu.

✦ **Switching between views with the View button:** On the Home tab, click
the View button. This button changes appearance, depending on
whether you're in Design view or Datasheet view.

✦ **Switching between views on the status bar:** Click the Datasheet View or
Design View button on the right side of the status bar.

✦ **Switching between views by right-clicking:** Right-click the table's title
bar and choose Datasheet View or Design View.

Entering and Altering Table Fields

After you create a database table, the next task is to enter the fields, or if
Access created the table for you, alter the fields to your liking. As Chapter
1 of this mini-book explains, fields represent categories of information in a

database table. They are the equivalent of columns in a conventional table. Fields determine what kind of information is stored in a database table.

These pages explain how to create a field, choose the right data type, display data in fields, and designate the primary key field in a table. While I'm on the subject of fields, W.C. Fields said, "Horse sense is the thing a horse has which keeps it from betting on people."

Creating a field

Create a field on your own or get Access's help and create a ready-made field. Both techniques are described here. Ready-made fields include fields designed especially for storing currency data, hyperlinks, and date information.

Creating a field on your own

To create a field on your own, open the table that needs a new field and follow these steps on the (Table Tools) Design tab:

1. **Switch to Design view if you aren't already there.**

   To switch to Design view, click the View button on the Home tab and choose Design View on the drop-down list.

2. **If necessary, insert a new row for the field.**

   ⌹ Insert Rows

   To do so, click in the field that is to go after the new field and then click the Insert Rows button.

3. **Enter a name in the Field Name column.**

   Names can't include periods or be longer than 64 letters, but you don't want to enter a long name anyway because it won't fit very well along the top of the table.

   Some database programs don't permit spaces in field names. If you intend to export Access data to other database programs, don't include spaces in field names. Instead, run the words together or separate words with an underscore character, like this: underscore_character.

4. **Press the Tab key or click in the Data Type column, and choose a data type from the drop-down list, as shown in Figure 2-3.**

   Data types classify what kind of information is kept in the field. The next topic in this chapter, "All about data types," explains data types.

5. **If you want, enter a description in the Description column.**

   These descriptions can be very helpful when you need to reacquaint yourself with a field and find out what it's meant to do.

Choose a data type   Define field properties

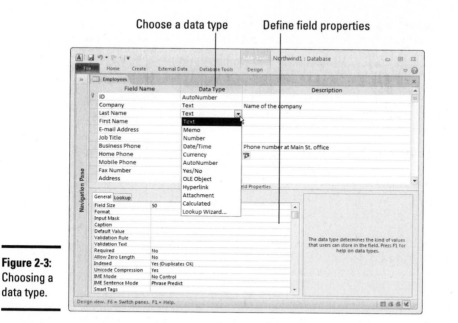

Figure 2-3:
Choosing a
data type.

In case the name you choose for your field isn't descriptive enough, you can give the field a second name. The name appears in Datasheet view, on forms, and on reports. To enter a second, descriptive field name, enter the name in the Caption field on the General tab of the Design view window.

Later in this chapter, "Field Properties for Making Sure That Data Entries Are Accurate" demonstrates how to define field properties in the Design view window to make it easier for data-entry clerks to enter the data.

Taking advantage of ready-made fields

You can get a head start creating a field by using a ready-made field and then modifying it, if necessary. To create a ready-made field, switch to Datasheet view and select the field that you want your new field to go after. Then, on the (Table Tools) Fields tab, click a field button or click the More Fields button and choose the name of a field on the drop-down list.

Look for field buttons in the Add & Delete group. Field buttons include Text, Number, and Currency. After you create your new field, switch to Design view and examine its field properties. Some of these properties may need modifying. See "Field Properties for Making Sure That Data Entries Are Accurate" for information about field properties.

All about data types

To choose a data type for a field, open the Data Type drop-down list in the Design view window and choose a data type (refer to Figure 2-3). Data types are the first line of defense in making sure that data is entered correctly in a table. Try to enter text in a field assigned the Currency or Number data type, and Access tells you that your entry is invalid. You get the chance to fix your mistake as soon as you make it.

Table 2-1 explains the options on the Data Type drop-down list. Choose data types carefully because how you classify the data that is entered in a field determines how you can query the field for information. Querying for a number range is impossible, for example, if the field you're querying isn't classified as a Number or Currency field on the Data Type drop-down list.

Table 2-1	**Data Types for Fields**
Data Type	*What It's For*
Text	For storing text (city names, for example), combinations of text and numbers (street addresses, for example), and numbers that won't be calculated or used in expressions (telephone numbers, ZIP Codes, and social security numbers, for example). By default, a Text field is 50 characters long but Text fields can be 255 characters if you need that many. If you need that many characters, however, you probably need the Memo data type, not the Text data type.
Memo	For storing long descriptions. Fields assigned this data type can hold 65,535 characters (not that anyone needs that many).
Number	For storing numbers to be used in calculations or sorting. (If you're dealing with monetary figures, choose the Currency data type.)
Date/Time	For storing dates and times and being able to sort data chronologically or use dates and times in calculations.
Currency	For storing monetary figures for use in calculations and sorting.
AutoNumber	For entering numbers in sequence that will be different from record to record. Use the AutoNumber data type for the primary key field if no other field stores unique, one-of-a-kind data. (See "Designating the primary key field," later in this chapter.)
Yes/No	For storing True/False, Yes/No, On/Off type data. Choose this data type to enter data with a check box in the field. When the box is selected, the data in the field is True, Yes, or On, for example.

Data Type	What It's For
OLE Object	For embedding an OLE link in your Access table to another object — an Excel worksheet or Word document. (Consider using the Attachment data type as well.)
Hyperlink	For storing hyperlinks to other locations on the Internet or on the company intranet.
Attachment	For storing an image, spreadsheet, document, chart, or other file. Attaching a file to a database table is similar to attaching a file to an e-mail message. Attachments do not require as much hard drive space as OLE objects because they don't require Access to store a bitmap image of the original file.
Calculated	For entering a mathematical expression that uses data from other fields in the database table.
Lookup Wizard	For creating a drop-down list with choices that a data-entry clerk can choose from when entering data. See "Creating a lookup data-entry list," later in this chapter.

**Book VI
Chapter 2**

Building Your
Database Tables

Designating the primary key field

As I explain in Chapter 1 of this mini-book, no database table is complete without a primary key field. The *primary key field* identifies which field in the table is unique and contains data that differs from record to record. Duplicate values and null values can't be entered in the primary key field. (A *null value* indicates a missing or unknown value.) Choosing a primary key field is so important that Access doesn't let you close a table unless you choose one.

If no field in your table holds one-of-a-kind data that is different from record to record, get around the problem with one of these techniques:

✦ **The AutoNumber data type:** Create a new field, give it a name, choose AutoNumber from the Data Type drop-down list (refer to Figure 2-3), and make your new field the primary key field. This way, when you enter data, Access enters a unique number to identify each record in the field. (To generate random numbers rather than sequential numbers in an AutoNumber field, go to the General tab of the Design view window, open the New Values drop-down list, and choose Random rather than Increment.)

Deciding how the data in fields is displayed

To decide how numbers, times, dates, currency values, and Yes/No data are displayed in fields, go to the General tab in the Field Properties part of the Design view and choose an option on the Format drop-down list. The display options are useful indeed. Choose the Currency format, for example, and you don't have to enter the dollar signs or commas when you enter a dollar figure in the field because the dollar sign and commas are entered for you.

Moreover, you can create a format of your own by entering these placeholder symbols in the Format text box:

✔ **@ (at symbol):** A character or space is required. For example, @@@@-@@ inserts a hyphen between the first set of numbers and the second. You don't have to enter the hyphen, only the text or numbers.

✔ **& (ampersand):** A character or space is optional. For example, @@@@@-&&&& in a ZIP Code field tells Access that either

entry is correct, a five-character ZIP Code or a five-character plus the four extra characters ZIP Code.

✔ **> (right bracket):** Displays all characters in the field as uppercase. Merely by entering this symbol in the Format text box, you can display all entries in the field as uppercase without the data-entry clerk having to hold down the Shift or Caps Lock key.

✔ **< (left bracket):** Displays all characters in the field as lowercase.

General	Lookup	
Field Size	Long Integer	
Format		▼
Decimal Places	General Number	3456.789
Input Mask	Currency	$3,456.79
Caption	Euro	€3,456.79
Default Value	Fixed	3456.79
Validation Rule	Standard	3,456.79
Validation Text	Percent	123.00%
Required	Scientific	3.46E+03
Indexed	Yes (Duplicates OK)	
Smart Tags		
Text Align	General	

◆ **A multiple-field primary key:** Combine two or more fields and designate them as the primary key. For example, if you're absolutely certain that no two people whose names will be entered in your database table have the same name, you can make the First Name and Last Name fields the primary key. The problem with multiple-field primary keys, however, is that it takes Access longer to process them, and you run the risk of entering duplicate records.

Follow these steps on the (Table Tools) Design tab to designate a field in a database table as the primary key field:

1. **In Design view, select the field or fields you want to be the primary key.**

To select a field, click its *row selector,* the small box to its left; Ctrl+click row selectors to select more than one field.

2. **Click the Primary Key button.**

A small key symbol appears on the row selector to let you know which field or fields is the primary key field.

To remove a primary key, click its row selector and then click the Primary Key button all over again.

Moving, renaming, and deleting fields

Suppose that you need to move, rename, or delete a field. To do so, switch to Design view and follow these instructions:

✦ **Moving a field:** Select the field's row selector (the box to its left) and release the mouse button. Then click again and drag the selector up or down to a new location.

✦ **Renaming a field:** Click in the Field Name box where the name is, delete the name that's there, and type a new name.

✦ **Deleting a field:** Click in the Field Name box, go to the (Table Tools) Design tab, and click the Delete Rows button. You can also right-click the field and choose Delete Rows on the shortcut menu.

Field Properties for Making Sure That Data Entries Are Accurate

Unfortunately, entering the data in a database table is one of the most tedious activities known to humankind. And because the activity is so dull, people are prone to make mistakes when they enter data in a database table. One way to cut down on mistakes is to take advantage of the Field Properties settings on the General tab in the Design view window. Figure 2-4 shows the General tab.

Field properties   Description of the property

Figure 2-4: Establishing field properties.

These properties determine what can and can't be entered in the different fields of a database table. Some of the settings are invaluable. The Field Size property, for example, determines how many characters can be entered in a field. In a State field where two-letter state abbreviations are to be entered, make the Field Size property 2 to be certain that no one enters more than two characters. If the majority of people you're tracking in an address database live in New York, enter NY in the Default Value property. That way, you spare data-entry clerks from having to enter NY the majority of the time. They won't have to enter it because NY is already there.

The Lookup tab in the Field Properties part of the Design view window is for creating a data-entry drop-down list. It, too, is invaluable. If you happen to know that only four items can be entered in a field, create a drop-down list with the four items. That way, data-entry clerks can choose from a list of four valid items instead of having to enter the data themselves and perhaps enter it incorrectly. (See "Creating a lookup data-entry list," later in this chapter.)

A look at the Field Properties settings

Especially if yours is a large database, you're encouraged to study the field properties carefully and make liberal use of them. The Field Properties settings safeguard data from being entered incorrectly. Following is a description of the different properties (listed here in the order in which they appear in the Design view window) and instructions for using them wisely. Which properties you can assign to a field depends on which data type the field was assigned.

Field Size

In the Field Size box for Text fields, enter the maximum number of characters that can be entered in the field. Suppose that the field you're dealing with is ZIP Code, and you want to enter five-number ZIP Codes. By entering **5** in the Field Size text box, only five characters can be entered in the field. A sleepy data-entry clerk couldn't enter a six-character ZIP Code by accident.

For Number fields, select a value for the field size from the drop-down list. Table 2-2 describes these field sizes.

Table 2-2	Numeric Field Sizes
Field Size	*Description*
Byte	An integer that holds values from 0–255.
Integer	An integer that holds values from -32,768–+32,767.
Long Integer	An integer that holds values from -2,147,483,648–+2,147,483,647.
Single	A floating point number that holds large values up to 7 significant digits.

Field Size	Description
Double	A floating point number that holds large values up to 15 significant digits.
Replication ID*	A globally unique identifier (GUID) required for replication; this number is generated randomly.
Decimal	A number with defined decimal precision. The default precision is 0, but you can set the scale up to 28.

Not supported by the ACCDB file format.

The Single, Double, and Decimal field size options hold different ranges of numbers. For now, if you need to store numbers after the decimal point, choose the Double field size so that you cover most situations.

Format

Earlier in this chapter, the "Deciding how the data in fields is displayed" sidebar explains the Format property. Click the drop-down list and choose the format in which text, numbers, and dates and times are displayed.

Decimal Places

For a field that holds numbers, open the Decimal Places drop-down list and choose how many numbers can appear to the right of the decimal point. This property affects how numbers and currency values are displayed, not their real value. Numbers are rounded to the nearest decimal point. The Auto option displays the number of decimal places that the format you choose on the Format drop-down list permits.

Input Mask

For Text and Date field types, this feature provides a template with punctuation marks to make entering the data easier. Telephone numbers, social security numbers, and other numbers that typically are entered along with dashes and parentheses are ideal candidates for an input mask (another ridiculous database term!). On the datasheet, blank spaces appear where the numbers go, and the punctuation marks stand at the ready to receive numbers, as shown in Figure 2-5.

Figure 2-5:
Input masks.

Address Book				_ □ X
ID ▾	First Name ▾	Last Name ▾	Home Phone ▾	Social Security Number ▾
1 Bob	Smith		(555) 555-1234	123-45-6789
2 Jane	Doe		(555) 555-4321	▌ -__-____
* (New)				

Record: ◄ ◄ 2 of 2 ► ►I ►* 🚫 No Filter Search ◄ ▭ ►

In the Input Mask text box, enter a **0** where numbers go, and enter the punctuation marks where they go. For example, enter (000) 000-0000 or 000/000-0000 to enter an input mask for a telephone number like the one shown in Figure 2-5. You can also create input masks by clicking the three dots beside the Input Mask text box. Doing so opens the Input Mask Wizard dialog box, where you can fashion a very sophisticated input mask.

Caption

If the field you're working on has a cryptic or hard-to-understand name, enter a more descriptive name in the Caption text box. The value in the Caption property appears as the column heading in Datasheet view, as a label on forms, and on reports in place of the field name. People entering data understand what to enter after reading the descriptive caption.

Default Value

When you know that the majority of records require a certain value, number, or abbreviation, enter it in the Default Value text box. That way, you save yourself the trouble of entering the value, number, or abbreviation most of the time because the default value appears already in each record when you enter it. You can always override the default value by entering something different.

Validation Rule

As long as you know your way around operators and Boolean expressions, you can establish a rule for entering data in a field. For example, you can enter an expression that requires dates to be entered in a certain time frame. Or you can require currency figures to be above or below a certain value. To establish a validation rule, enter an expression in the Validation Rule text box. To use dates in an expression, the dates must be enclosed by number signs (#). Here are some examples of validation rules:

>1000	The value you enter must be over 1000.
<1000	The value you enter must be under 1000.
>=10	The value you enter must be greater than or equal to ten.
<>0	The value you enter cannot be zero.
>=#1/1/2009#	The date you enter must be January 1, 2009, or later.
>=#1/1/2007# And <#1/1/2008#	The date you enter must be in the year 2007.

To get help forming expressions, click the three dots beside the Validation Rule text box to open the Expression Builder, shown in Figure 2-6, and build an expression there. Try clicking the Help button in the Expression Builder dialog box. Doing so opens the Access Help program, where you can get advice about building expressions.

Figure 2-6: Creating a validation rule.

Validation Text

If someone enters data that violates a validation rule that you enter in the Validation Rule text box, Access displays a standard error message. The message reads, "One or more values are prohibited by the validation rule set for [this field]. Enter a value that the expression for this field can accept." If this message is too cold and impersonal for you, you can create a message of your own for the error message dialog box. Enter your friendly message in the Validation Text text box.

Required

By default, no entry has to be made in a field, but if you choose Yes instead of No in the Required box and you fail to make an entry in the field, a message box tells you to be sure to make an entry.

Allow Zero Length

This property allows you to enter zero-length strings in a field. A *zero-length string* — two quotation marks with no text or spaces between them ("") — indicates that no value exists for a field. To see how zero-length strings work, suppose that your database table calls for entering e-mail addresses. If you didn't know whether one person has an e-mail address, you would leave the E-Mail Address field blank. If, however, you knew that the person didn't have an e-mail address, you could indicate as much by entering a zero-length string. Choose Yes on the drop-down list to permit zero-length strings to be entered in the field.

Indexed

Indicates that the field has been indexed. As "Indexing for Faster Sorts, Searches, and Queries" explains later in this chapter, indexes make sorting a field and searching through a field go faster. The word *No* appears in this text box if the field has not been indexed.

Unicode Expression

Choose Yes from the Unicode Expression drop-down list if you want to compress data that is now stored in Unicode format. Storing data this way saves on hard drive space, and you probably don't want to change this property.

Smart Tags

If you intend to enter Smart Tags in the field, indicate which kind you enter by clicking the three dots next to the Smart Tags box and choosing an option in the Action Tags dialog box.

Text Align

This property determines how the text is aligned in a column or on a form or report. Select General to let Access determine the alignment, or select Left, Right, Center, or Distribute.

Text Format

Available on Memo fields, this drop-down list lets you choose to allow rich text in the field. With this property set to Rich Text, you can make different words bold, italic, underline, and change font sizes and colors. Set it to Plain Text for plain, boring text with no formatting. I wonder why that isn't the setting's name.

Append Only

Available on Memo fields, this lets you add data only to a Memo field to collect a history of comments.

Show Date Picker

Available on Date/Time fields, choosing For Dates places a button next to the column that data-entry clerks can click to open a calendar and select a date instead of typing numbers.

Creating a lookup data-entry list

Perhaps the best way to make sure that data is entered correctly is to create a data-entry drop-down list. Whoever enters the data in your database table has only to choose an item from the list, as shown in Figure 2-7. This saves time and prevents invalid data from being entered. Access offers two ways to create the drop-down list:

Figure 2-7: A so-called lookup list.

✦ **Create the list by entering the items yourself:** Go this route when you're dealing with a finite list of items that never change.

✦ **Get the items from another database table:** Go this route to get items from a column in another database table. This way, you can choose from an ever-expanding list of items. When the number of items in the other database table changes, so does the number of items in the drop-down list because the items come from the other database table. This is a great way to get items from a primary key field in another table.

Creating a drop-down list on your own

Follow these steps to create a drop-down, or *lookup,* list with entries you type:

1. **In Design view, click the field that needs a drop-down list.**

2. **Open the Data Type drop-down list and choose Lookup Wizard, the last option in the list.**

   The Lookup Wizard dialog box appears.

3. **Select the second option, I Will Type in the Values That I Want, and click the Next button.**

4. **Under Col1 in the next dialog box, enter each item you want to appear in the drop-down list; then click the Next button.**

 You can create a multicolumn list by entering a number in the Number of Columns text box and then entering items for the list.

5. **Enter a name for the field, if necessary, and click the Finish button.**

 Switch to Datasheet view and open the drop-down list in the field to make sure that it displays properly.

To remove a lookup list from a field, select the field, go to the Lookup tab in the Design view window, and choose Text Box on the Display Control drop-down list.

TIP

To see what's on a drop-down list, select the field for which you created the list, switch to Design view, and select the Lookup tab in the Field Properties pane. As shown in Figure 2-8, you can edit the list by editing or removing items in the Row Source text box. Be sure that a semicolon (;) appears between each item.

Figure 2-8:
Lookup field
properties.

General	Lookup	
Display Control	Combo Box	
Row Source Type	Value List	
Row Source	"King";"Queen";"Jack";"Knave";"Jongler"	
Bound Column	1	
Column Count	1	
Column Heads	No	
Column Widths	1"	
List Rows	16	
List Width	1"	
Limit To List	No	
Allow Multiple Values	No	
Allow Value List Edits	No	
List Items Edit Form		
Show Only Row Source Values	No	

The data type determines the kind of values that users can store in the field. Press F1 for help on data types.

Getting list items from a database table

Before you can get list items from another database table, you might want to define a relationship between the tables; it's not required, but it's recommended. Later in this chapter, "Establishing Relationships between Database Tables" explains how to do that. Follow these steps to get items in a drop-down list from another database table:

1. **In Design view, click the field that needs a list, open the Data Type drop-down list, and choose Lookup Wizard.**

 The Lookup Wizard dialog box appears.

2. **Select the first option, I Want the Lookup Field to Get the Values from Another Table or Query, and click Next.**

 You see a list of tables in your database.

3. **Select the table with the data you need and click the Next button.**

   The dialog box shows you a list of available fields in the table.

4. **Select the field where the data for your list is stored.**

5. **Click the > button.**

   The name of the list appears on the right side of the dialog box, under Selected Fields.

6. **Click the Next button.**

   Normally, lists are displayed in ascending order, but you can select a field and click the Ascending button to reverse the order of the list. (Note that the button turns into the Descending button.)

7. **Click the Finish button.**

   If you're so inclined, you can change the width of the list before clicking Finish, but you can always do that on the datasheet, as Chapter 3 of this mini-book explains.

 Suppose that you obtain the items from the wrong field or wrong database table? To fix that problem, select the field for which you created the list, and in Design view, select the Lookup tab (refer to Figure 2-8). Choose Text Box rather than Combo Box on the Display Control drop-down list and start all over.

Indexing for Faster Sorts, Searches, and Queries

Indexing means to instruct Access to keep information about the data in a field or combination of fields. Because Access keeps this information on hand, it doesn't have to actually search through every record in a database table to sort data, search for data, or run a query. In a large database table, indexes make sorting, searching, and querying go considerably faster because Access looks through its own data rather than the data in tables. The performance difference between querying a database table that has and has not been indexed is astonishing. That's the good news. The bad news is that indexes inflate the size of Access files.

By default, the field you choose as the primary key field is indexed. I recommend choosing other fields for indexing if you often conduct queries and searches. When you choose a field to index, choose one with data that varies from record to record and is likely to be the subject of searches, sorts, and queries. That way, the index means something. However, a field with data that is mostly the same from record to record is a waste of a good index, not to mention hard drive space. By the way, Access automatically indexes fields whose names include the words *ID, Code, Num,* and *Key,* the idea being that these fields are likely to store essential information worthy of indexing.

Indexing a field

To index a field, switch to Design view, select the field you want to index, and on the General tab of the Field Properties part of the Design window, open the Indexed drop-down list and choose one of these options:

✦ **Yes (Duplicates OK):** Indexes the field and allows duplicate values to be entered in the field.

✦ **Yes (No Duplicates):** Indexes the field and disallows duplicate values. If you choose this option, the field works something like a primary key field in that Access does not permit you to enter the same value in two different records.

Indexing based on more than one field

An index created on more than one field is called a *multifield index*. Multifield indexes make sorting, querying, and searching the database table go faster. They are especially valuable in sorting operations where records in one field are usually the same but records in a companion field are different. In a large database table that stores names and addresses, for example, many names in the Last Name field are the same, so indexing on the Last Name field isn't worthwhile, but indexing the First Name and Last Name fields helps Access distinguish records from one another.

Follow these steps to generate a multifield index:

1. Switch to Design view, and on the (Table Tools) Design tab, click the Indexes button.

You see the Indexes dialog box, as shown in Figure 2-9. The dialog box lists the primary key field already because it's indexed by default. You also see any fields to which you set the Indexed property to Yes.

Single field indexes

Figure 2-9:
The Indexes
dialog box.

Multifield index

2. **On a blank line in the dialog box, enter a name for the index in the Index Name column.**

3. **In the Field Name column, open the drop-down list and choose the first field you want for the multifield index.**

   Access sorts the records first on this field and then on the second field you choose.

4. **In the next row, leave the Index Name blank and choose another field name from the drop-down list.**

   This field is the second field in the index. You can use as many as ten different fields in a multifield index. In Figure 2-9, two fields are in a multifield index: First Name and Last Name.

5. **Choose Descending in the Sort Order column if you want the field sorted in descending order.**

   Most of the time, you want leave the Sort Order set to Ascending because most people read from A to Z.

6. **Click the Close button.**

   Click the Indexes button in Design view if you need to return to the Indexes dialog box and change how fields are indexed.

Establishing Relationships between Database Tables

As Chapter 1 of this mini-book explains, you have to establish relationships between tables if you want to query or generate reports with data from more than one database table. Relationships define the field that two different tables have in common. To understand why relationships between tables are necessary, consider the query shown in Figure 2-10. The purpose of this query is to list all companies that ordered items in 2009, list the companies by name, and list the city and country where each company is located.

Consider what Access does to run this query:

✦ Access deals with two database tables, Customers and Orders.

✦ In the Orders table, Access looks in the Order Date field to isolate all records that describe orders made in the year 2009. The expression for finding these records is shown on the Criteria line in Figure 2-10: `Between #1/1/2009# And #12/31/2009#`.

✦ Because there is a relationship between the ID field in the Customers table and the Customer ID field in the Orders table — because the two fields hold the same type of information — Access can match the 2009 records it finds in the Orders table with corresponding records in the Customers table. Where the Customer ID of a 2009 record in the Orders table and an ID in the Customers table match, Access assembles a new record and places it in the query results.

✦ Data for determining which records appear in the query results is found in the Order Date field in the Orders table. But the information compiled in the query results — customer IDs, company names, cities, and countries — comes from fields in the Customers table. Thanks to the relationship between the ID and Customer ID fields in these tables, Access can draw upon information from both tables.

Table relationship

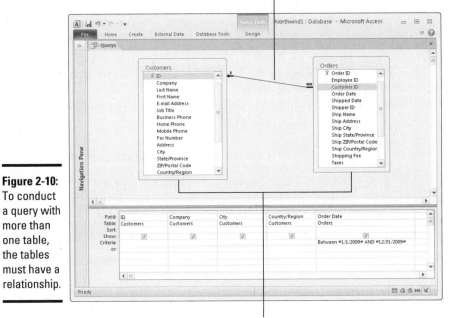

Figure 2-10:
To conduct
a query with
more than
one table,
the tables
must have a
relationship.

Tables being queried

Types of relationships

The vast majority of relationships between tables are *one-to-many relationships* between the primary key field in one database table and a field in another. Table relationships fall in these categories:

✦ **One-to-many relationship:** Each record in one table is linked to many records in another table. The relationship in Figure 2-10 is a one-to-many relationship. Each ID number appears only once in the ID field of the Customers table, but in the Orders table, the same Customer ID number can appear in many records because the same customer can order many different products. When you link tables, Access creates a one-to-many relationship when one of the fields being linked is either a primary key field or an indexed field assigned the No (No Duplicates) setting. (See "Indexing for Faster Sorts, Searches, and Queries," earlier in this chapter.)

✦ **One-to-one relationship:** Two fields are linked. This relationship is rare and is sometimes used for security purposes.

✦ **Many-to-many relationship:** This complex relationship actually describes crisscrossing relationships in which the linking field is not the primary key field in either table. To create a many-to-many relationship, an intermediary table called a *junction table* is needed. This relationship is rare.

Sometimes, fields in separate tables that hold the same data also have the same name, but that isn't necessary. For example, a field called ZIP Code in one table might be called Postal Code in another. What matters is that fields that are linked have the same data type. For example, you can't create a relationship between a text field and a number field.

Handling tables in the Relationships window

To display the tables in a database and link tables to one another or see how they're related to each other, go to the Database Tools tab and click the Relationships button. You see the Relationships window, as shown in Figure 2-11. Notice the field names in each table. The primary key field is shown with a picture of a key next to it. Lines in the window show how relationships have been established between tables.

Placing tables in the Relationships window

The first time you open the Relationships window, you see the Show Table dialog box. Use this dialog box to tell Access which tables to put in the Relationships window. Ctrl+click to select tables and then click the Add button.

If you create a new database table and want to place it in the Relationships window, click the Relationships button to display the Relationships window; then click the Show Table button on the (Relationship Tools) Design tab. The Show Table dialog box appears. Select your new table and click the Add button.

Right-click a line to edit or delete a relationship

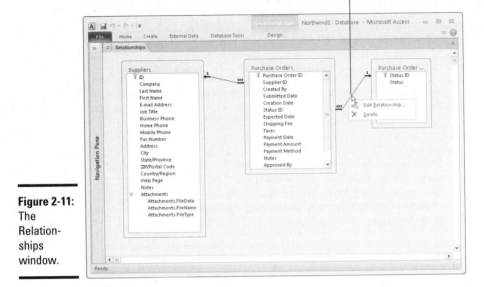

Figure 2-11:
The
Relation-
ships
window.

Apart from linking tables in the Relationships window (a subject I explain shortly), use these techniques on the (Relationship Tools) Design tab to handle tables:

✦ **Repositioning and resizing the tables:** Each table appears in its own window. Drag tables from place to place, drag a border to change a window's size, and scroll to see field names.

✦ **Removing a table from the window:** Select the table and click the Hide Table button.

✦ **Removing all tables from the window:** Click the Clear Layout button and choose Yes in the confirmation box.

✦ **Placing tables back on the window:** Click the Show Table button, and in the Show Table dialog box, select the tables and click the Add button.

✦ **Placing all tables back in the window:** To put all the tables with relationships back in the window, click the All Relationships button.

✦ **Studying a table's relationships:** Click the Clear Layout button to remove all tables from the window; then place the table back in the window, select it, and click the Direct Relationships button. All tables that are related to the selected table are added to the layout.

To generate and print an Access report that shows how tables in your database are linked, go to the (Relationship Tools) Design tab and click the Relationship Report button. Then save the report and print it. Chapter 5 of this mini-book explains reports.

Forging relationships between tables

On the (Relationship Tools) Design tab (refer to Figure 2-11), make sure that both tables are on display and then follow these steps to forge a relationship between them:

1. **Click to select the field in one table; then hold down the mouse button, drag the pointer to the field in the other table where you want to forge the link, and release the mouse button.**

You see the Edit Relationships dialog box, as shown in Figure 2-12. This dragging between table fields is probably the most awkward thing you undertake in Office 2010! If you do it right, a bar appears where the pointer is while you move it over the second table, and the names of the two fields appear in the Edit Relationships dialog box.

Book VI
Chapter 2

Building Your
Database Tables

Figure 2-12:
Creating
a table
relationship.

Notice the Relationship Type at the bottom of the dialog box. If you accidentally create a link to the wrong field, choose the correct field from the drop-down list in the dialog box.

2. **Select the Enforce Referential Integrity check box.**

If you don't select this box, the relationship between the tables is indeterminate, instead of being a one-to-many relationship. *Referential integrity* (another hideous database term!) has to do with whether values in the two different fields corroborate each other.

3. **Select Cascade options if you so choose.**

   One of these options is excellent, and the other is dangerous:

   - *Cascade Update Related Fields:* If you change a value on the "one" side of the relationship, a matching value on the "many" side changes as well to preserve referential integrity. For example, if you create a multifield primary key of First Name and Last Name and then change the name of someone, the related fields in the other table change automatically to preserve referential integrity. This is a great way to make sure that information is up-to-date.

   - *Cascade Delete Related Records:* If you delete a record in the "one" table, all records in the "many" table to which the deleted record is linked are also deleted. For example, if you delete an employee from the "one" table, all records in the "many" table that include that employee are deleted! Access warns you before making the deletion, but still! This option is dangerous, and I don't recommend selecting it.

4. **Click the Create button to forge the relationship.**

   In the Relationships window (refer to Figure 2-11), a line is drawn between the table fields. The number 1 appears on the "one" side of the relationship and the infinity symbol (∞) appears on the "many" side.

After you create a one-to-many relationship between tables with the Enforce Referential Integrity check box selected, you can't enter a value in the "many" table unless it's already in the "one" table. For example, suppose that the "one" table includes a primary key field called Employee Number, and this field is linked to a field in the "many" table that is also called Employee Number. If you enter an Employee Number in the "many" table that isn't in the "one" table, Access warns you that it can't be done without violating referential integrity. The best way to solve this problem is to create a lookup data-entry list in the "many" table with values from the primary key field in the "one" table. See "Creating a lookup data-entry list," earlier in this chapter.

Editing table relationships

In the Relationships window (refer to Figure 2-11), select the line that represents the relationship between two database tables and follow these instructions to edit or remove the relationship:

✦ **Editing the relationship:** Click the Edit Relationships button or right-click and choose Edit Relationship. You see the Edit Relationships dialog box, where you can overhaul the relationship (the previous topic in this chapter explains how).

✦ **Deleting the relationship:** Press the Delete key or right-click and choose Delete. Then select Yes in the confirmation box.

Subdatasheets

In Datasheet view, Access gives you the opportunity to view the "many" records that are linked to a field when a relationship is established between tables. The records appear on a *subdatasheet*. In the database shown in this illustration, the Orders and Order Details tables are linked on the Order ID field — the primary key of the Orders table and the "one" side of the relationship. In the Order Details table, I can click the plus sign (+) in a record to see the "many" records that are linked to Order ID, the primary key field. For this illustration, I clicked the plus sign to see the details for Order 31. The information on the subdatasheet comes from the Order Details table. Click the minus sign (–) to hide a subdatasheet.

Book VI Chapter 2

Building Your Database Tables

Chapter 3: Entering the Data

In This Chapter

✔ **Entering data on a datasheet**

✔ **Changing the look of a datasheet**

✔ **Creating a form for entering data**

✔ **Finding records in a field or database table**

✔ **Finding and replacing your data**

A t last — you can start entering the data. If you set up your database tables, named the fields, and established relationships between the tables, you're ready to go. This short chapter explains how to enter the data in a database table. It shows you how to enter data on a datasheet or enter data by way of a form. This chapter also describes how to find missing records in case one goes astray.

There's no getting around it: Entering data is truly a tedious activity. But if you set up the fields well and take advantage of input masks and other field properties, it isn't so bad. It's better than stepping on a shovel blade, anyway.

The Two Ways to Enter Data

When it comes to entering data in a database table, you can take your pick between Datasheet view and a form. Figure 3-1 compares and contrasts the two. Here are the advantages of entering data in Datasheet view:

✦ Many records appear simultaneously.

✦ You can compare data easily between records.

✦ You can sort by column with the commands in the Sort and Filter group on the Home tab (as discussed in Chapter 4 of this mini-book).

✦ You can scroll up or down to locate records.

Here are the advantages of entering the data in a form:

✦ You don't have to scroll left or right to see all the fields.

✦ Getting from field to field is easier.

✦ Fields are clearly labeled so that you always know what to enter.

Figure 3-1:
Entering
records in
Datasheet
view (left)
and in a
form (right).

Entering the Data in Datasheet View

Entering data in Datasheet view is like entering data in a conventional table. As with a table, a datasheet has columns and rows. Records are entered in rows, and each column represents a field. Fans of Datasheet view like being able to look at a dozen records simultaneously. They like being able to open subdatasheets. (Chapter 2 of this mini-book explains what those are.) For fans of Datasheet view, these pages explain how to enter data in a datasheet and change a datasheet's appearance.

Database tables open in Datasheet view when you double-click their names in the Navigation pane. But if you happen to be gazing at a table in Design view, click the View command on the Home tab or the Datasheet View button on the status bar.

Entering data

In Datasheet view, the bottom of the window tells you how many records are entered in the database table and which record the cursor is in. To enter a new record, move to a new, empty row and start entering the data. To create a new row, do one of the following:

- ✦ On the Home tab, click the New button.

- ✦ Click the New (Blank) Record button in the Datasheet navigation buttons. These buttons are located at the bottom of the Datasheet view window.

- ✦ Scroll to the bottom of the Datasheet view window and begin typing in the row with an asterisk (*) next to it.

- ✦ Press Ctrl++ (the plus key).

A pencil icon appears on the row selector to let you know which record you're dealing with. To get from field to field, click in a field, press the Tab key, or press Enter. Table 3-1 lists keyboard shortcuts for getting around in a datasheet.

**Book VI
Chapter 3**

Entering the Data

Table 3-1	Datasheet Shortcuts
Press. . .	*To Move. . .*
↑	To the previous record. You can also press the Previous button on the Navigation buttons.
↓	To the next record. You can also press the Next button.
Tab or Enter	To the next field in the record.
Shift+Tab	To the previous field in the record.
Home	To the first field in the record.
End	To the last field in the record.
Ctrl+Home	To the first field in the first record. You can also press the First button.
Ctrl+End	To the last field in the last record. You can also press the Last button.
Page Up	Up one screen.
Page Down	Down one screen.

To delete a record, click its row selector and press the Delete key or the Delete button (located on the Home tab). You can also click in a record, go to the (Table Tools) Fields tab, and click the Delete button there.

Two tricks for entering data quicker

In a database table with many fields, it's sometimes hard to tell what data to enter. When the pointer is in the sixth or seventh field, for example, you can lose sight of the first field, the one on the left side of the datasheet that usually identifies the person or item whose record you're entering.

Entering data in the Zoom box

To make putting a long entry in a field a little easier, Access offers the Zoom box. Instead of having to stay within the narrow confines of a datasheet field, you can press Shift+F2 to open the Zoom box and enter the data there. After you click OK, the data is entered in the field. The Zoom box is especially convenient for entering data in a Memo field. As Chapter 2 in this mini-book explains, Memo fields can hold a whopping 65,535 characters. Move the cursor into a field and press Shift+F2 to open the Zoom box and read all the text in the field.

> **Zoom**
>
> Entering data in the Zoom box is much easier than entering data in a measly little cell.
>
> OK
> Cancel
> Font...

To freeze a field so that it appears on-screen no matter how far you travel toward the right side of the datasheet, right-click the column's heading and choose Freeze Fields on the shortcut menu. To unfreeze the fields, right-click the column heading and choose Unfreeze All Fields on the shortcut menu. You can freeze more than one field by dragging across field names at the top of the datasheet before choosing to freeze the columns. Is it getting cold in here?

Another way to handle the problem of not being able to identify where data is supposed to be entered is to hide columns in the datasheet. To perform this trick, select the columns you want to hide by dragging the pointer across their names; then right-click the column heading and choose Hide Fields on the shortcut menu. To see the columns again, right-click any column heading and choose Unhide Fields on the shortcut menu. You see the Unhide Columns dialog box. Select the fields that you want to see on the datasheet.

The fastest way to hide a column is to drag the border between it and the next column to the left until the column disappears.

Changing the appearance of the datasheet

To make the datasheet a little less cluttered and unwieldy, try experimenting with its appearance. Access offers a few handy shortcuts for doing just that:

✦ **Rearranging columns:** To move a column to a different location, click its name at the top of the datasheet and drag it to the left or right.

✦ **Resizing columns:** Move the pointer between column names at the top of the datasheet, and when you see the double-headed arrow, click and start dragging. To make a column just large enough to fit its widest entry, move the pointer between column names and double-click when you see the double-headed arrow.

✦ **Changing fonts:** The default font for a datasheet is Calibri 11-point, but the Home tab offers commands for changing fonts and font sizes. Look for these commands in the Text Formatting group.

✦ **Changing the look of gridlines:** On the Home tab, open the drop-down list on the Gridlines button and choose options to change the number and thickness of gridlines.

✦ **Alternate row colors:** Open the drop-down list on the Alternate Row Color button and choose a color for alternating rows on the datasheet.

To experiment all at one time with the many options for changing a datasheet's appearance, go to the Home tab and click the Text Formatting group button. You see the Datasheet Formatting dialog box, as shown in Figure 3-2. If you want a customized look for all the datasheets you work on, click the File tab and select Options. Then go to the Datasheet category in the Options dialog box and go to town.

**Book VI
Chapter 3**

Entering the Data

Figure 3-2:
The
Datasheet
Formatting
dialog box.

Entering the Data in a Form

Forms like the one shown in Figure 3-3 are very convenient for entering data. The labels tell you exactly what to enter. Personally, I prefer entering data in a form to entering data on a datasheet. On a form, you take it one step — make that one record — at a time. Not looking at a dozen records makes the task of entering data a little easier. These pages explain how to create a form for entering information in a database table. You also get tried-and-true advice for moving around with the Navigation buttons.

Figure 3-3:
A form.

Creating a form

Form Wizard

Fortunately, the Form Wizard makes it very simple to create a form for entering information in a database table. All you have to do is start the wizard, choose the table, and make a couple of design decisions. To create a form, go to the Create tab and click the Form Wizard button. You see the first of several Form Wizard dialog boxes. Answer these questions and keep clicking the Next button until the time comes to click Finish:

✦ **Tables/Queries:** From the drop-down list, choose the name of the database table you need to enter data in.

✦ **Selected Fields:** Click the >> button to enter all the field names in the Select Fields box.

✦ **Layout:** Select the Columnar option button. The other layouts aren't much good for entering data in a table. If you choose Tabular or Datasheet, you may as well enter data straight into the datasheet rather than rely on a form.

✦ **Title:** Name your form after the table you created it for so that you can identify the form easily in the Navigation pane.

To delete a form, right-click its name in the Navigation pane and choose Delete on the shortcut menu.

Entering the data

To open a form and begin entering data in its database table, display the form's name in the Navigation pane and then double-click the form's name. You can also right-click the name of the form and choose Open.

To enter data in a form, click the New (Blank) Record button. This button is located with the Navigation buttons at the bottom of the form window. A new, empty form appears. Start typing. Press the Tab key, press the Enter key, or click to move from field to field. You can move backward through the fields by pressing Shift+Tab. If you enter half a record and want to start over, press the Esc key to empty the current field. Press Esc again to empty all the fields.

The Navigation buttons at the bottom of the form window tell you how many records are in the database table and which record you're looking at. From left to right, the Navigation buttons take you to the first record, previous record, next record, and last record.

**Book VI
Chapter 3**

Entering the Data

Finding a Missing Record

Sometimes data goes astray. You scroll through a datasheet but simply can't find the item or record you need so bad. For times like those, Access offers the Find command. Use the command to scour a database for errant information.

Open the database table with the data that needs finding. If you know in which field the data is located, click in the field. You can save a little time that way. Then, on the Home tab, click the Find button (or press Ctrl+F). You see the Find and Replace dialog box, as shown in Figure 3-4. Fill in the dialog box as follows:

Figure 3-4:
Finding
data.

> **Find and Replace**
>
> Find | Replace
>
> Find What: Smith | Find Next
>
> Cancel
>
> Look In: Current field
> Match: Whole Field
> Search: All
> ☐ Match Case ☐ Search Fields As Formatted

✦ **Find What:** Enter the item you're looking for. If you're looking for a null value, enter **null** in this text box. Enter "" (two double-quotation marks) to find zero-length strings. Table 3-2 describes the wildcard characters you can use in searches.

✦ **Look In:** If you clicked in a field before choosing the Find command, Current Field is selected in this box. To search the entire database table, choose Current Document on the drop-down list.

✦ **Match:** Choose the option that describes what you know about the item. Choosing the Any Part of Field option can make for a long search. For example, a search for the letters *chin* finds, among others, China, Ching, and itching — any word with the consecutive letters *chin*.

✦ **Search:** Choose an option — All, Up, or Down — that describes which direction to start searching.

✦ **Match Case:** If you know the combination of upper- and lowercase letters you're after and you enter the combination in the Find What text box, select this check box.

✦ **Search Fields As Formatted:** If you're searching for a field that has been formatted a certain way, select this check box and make sure that the text or numbers you enter in the Find What text box are formatted correctly. For example, if you're searching for a record with the date July 31, 1958, and you choose the *mm/dd/yyyy* format, enter the date as 07/31/1958.

Click the Find Next button to conduct the search. The item might be found in more than one location. Keep clicking Find Next (or pressing Alt+F) until you find the item or you die of thirst on the hot sands of the digital desert.

Table 3-2	Wildcard Characters for Searches	
Character	*Description*	*Example*
?	A single character	**b?t** finds *bat, bet, bit,* and *but.*
#	A single numeric digit	**9411#** finds *94111, 94112, 94113,* and so on.
*	Any group of consecutive characters	**t*o** finds *to, two,* and *tattoo.*
[xyz]	Any character in the brackets	**t[aio]pper** finds *tapper, tipper,* and *topper,* but not *tupper.*
[!xy]	Any character not in the brackets	**p[!io]t** finds *pat* and *pet,* but not *pit* and *pot.*
x–z	Any character in a range of characters	**[1–4]000** finds *1000, 2000, 3000,* and *4000,* but not *5000.* The range must be in ascending order.

To quickly find the first value of a search term, start typing in the Search box in the form window or in Datasheet view. As soon as you start typing, the cursor moves to the first instance of the data you enter.

Finding and Replacing Data

Finding and replacing data is remarkably similar to finding data. The difference is that you enter data in the Replace With text box as well as the familiar Find What text box and other option boxes. Figure 3-5 shows the Replace tab of the Find and Replace dialog box. Does it look familiar? If it doesn't, read the preceding topic in this chapter.

Find and Replace

| Find | Replace |

Find What:	Sm?th		Find Next
Replace With:	Smith		Cancel
Look In:	Current field		
Match:	Whole Field		Replace
Search:	All		Replace All
☑ Match Case	☐ Search Fields As Formatted		

Figure 3-5: Replacing data.

To find and replace data, go to the Home tab and click the Replace button (or press Ctrl+H). You see the Replace tab of the Find and Replace dialog box. After you enter the replacement data in the Replace With text box, make sure that Whole Field is selected in the Match drop-down list. Conducting a find-and-replace operation with Any Part of Field or Start of Field selected in the Match drop-down list can have unintended consequences. For example, a search for *Brook* also finds *Brooklyn, Middlebrook,* and other words that include *brook*. Blindly replacing the *brook* text string with *stream* produces, for example, *Streamlyn* and *Middlestream.*

Unless you're as confident as a gambler with four aces, don't click the Replace All button to replace all instances of the text or numbers in the database table or field you're searching in. Instead, click the Replace button to find and replace text or numbers one instance at a time.

You can also find and replace data with an update query. Chapter 4 of this mini-book covers update queries.

Chapter 4: Sorting, Querying, and Filtering for Data

In This Chapter

✔ Sorting, or rearranging, records in a database table

✔ Filtering records in a table to see only the records you need

✔ Querying to collect and examine information stored in a database

✔ Looking at different kinds of queries

*N*ow that you've laid the groundwork, you can put your database through its paces and make it do what databases are meant to do — provide information of one kind or another. This chapter explains how to pester a database for names, addresses, dates, statistical averages, and what not. It shows how to sort records and filter a database table to see records of a certain kind. You also find out how to query a database to get it to yield its dirty little secrets and invaluable information.

Sorting Records in a Database Table

Sorting rearranges records in a database table (or subdatasheet) so that the records appear in alphabetical, numerical, or date order in one field. By sorting the records in a database, you can locate records faster. What's more, being able to sort data means that you don't have to bother about the order in which you enter records because you can always sort them later to put them in a particular order.

Ascending versus descending sorts

Records can be sorted in ascending or descending order:

✦ **Ascending order:** Arranges records in alphabetical order from A to Z, numbers from smallest to largest, and dates chronologically from earliest to latest.

✦ **Descending order:** Arranges text from Z to A, numbers from largest to smallest, and dates chronologically from latest to earliest.

Sorting records

Follow these steps to sort the records in a database table:

1. **In Datasheet view, click anywhere in the field by which you want to sort the records.**

2. **On the Home tab, click the Ascending or Descending button.**

You can also right-click a field name at the top of a column and choose Sort A to Z or Sort Z to A on the shortcut menu. The menu choices change based on the type of data. For Number fields, you can sort smallest to largest and vice versa; for Date fields, choose to sort oldest to newest, or vice versa.

You can sort on more than one field by clicking a field and sorting it, and then clicking a second field and sorting it. Just make sure that you sort the fields in reverse order. For example, to sort the database by the Employee, Customer, and Order ID fields, click in Order ID and sort it in ascending order; click in Customer and sort it in ascending order; click in Employee and sort it in ascending order. If you mess up and forget how the table is sorted, click the Remove Sort button. This button is located on the Home tab underneath the Sort A to Z and Sort Z to A buttons.

Filtering to Find Information

Filtering isolates all the records in a database table that have the same field values or nearly the same field values. Instead of all the records in the table appearing on the datasheet, only records that meet the filtering criteria appear, as shown in Figure 4-1.

Figure 4-1:
Results of
a filtering
operation.

Filter indicators

The difference between a filter and a query

The biggest difference between filtering and querying is that you can save a query and call upon it more than once. Queries are kept at the ready in the Navigation pane. A filter, on the other hand, is as good as the first time you use it, although you can save and run it as a query. Filters apply to a single database table, whereas you can query to assemble information from more than one table. In the results of a query, you can include as many fields as you want, but the results of a filtering operation show all the fields in the database table, whether you want them or not.

When it comes to examining data, a query is more sophisticated than a filter. Although you can use standard comparison operators to find records by filtering, querying gives you the opportunity to use complex expressions as well as comparison operators. You can filter, for example, to find people whose income is greater than or less than a certain amount. However, because you can write expressions in queries, you can query to find people whose income falls within a certain range.

The basic idea behind filtering is to choose a field value in the database table and use it as the standard for finding or excluding records. For example, you can find all the orders for a particular customer, all orders taken in the month of April, or all the orders that a particular customer placed in April. For that matter, you can filter by exclusion and see the records of all the orders in a database table *not* taken in April and *not* for a particular customer. Filtering is useful when you need to find records with specific information in a single database table.

Different ways to filter a database table

Here are shorthand descriptions of the four ways to filter a database table. All filtering operations begin in Datasheet view on the Home tab. These techniques are described in detail in the upcoming pages.

✦ **Filter by Selection:** Select all or part of a field in the database table, click the Selection button, and choose a filtering option. Access isolates all records with the data you select. This method works best when you can't quite decide what you're looking for. It's the only filtering method that permits you to look for data found in a whole field or part of a field. You can also filter data that doesn't match the selection.

✦ **Filter for Input:** Select the field you want to filter with and click the Filter button. A dialog box appears so that you can choose values in the field or enter comparison operators to describe the numeric or date values you are filtering for. With this technique, you can filter for data ranges.

✦ **Filter by Form:** Click the Advanced button and choose Filter by Form. You see a form with one drop-down list for each field in your table. From the drop-down lists, make choices to describe the records you're looking for and then click the Toggle Filter button. This method is more flexible than the others because you can conduct OR as well as AND filtering operations. For example, you can isolate the records of people named Smith who also live in California, or the people who live in California or New York.

✦ **Advanced Filter/Sort:** Click the Advanced button and choose Advanced Filter/Sort. The Filter window opens. Drag the name of the field you want to filter onto the grid. Then choose a Sort option and enter a search criterion. This filtering technique has more in common with queries than filters. Truth be told, the Advanced Filter/Sort command is merely a way to query a single table.

After you filter a database table, you can run a second (or third or fourth) filter operation to filter the data even more and further isolate the data you are looking for.

"Unfiltering" a database table

You can tell when you're looking at a database table that has been filtered instead of a database table with all its records because the word *Filtered* appears at the bottom of the window next to the Navigation buttons (refer to Figure 4-1). Moreover, the filter icon appears in the field names of columns used in the filter operation and the Toggle Filter button on the Ribbon is highlighted.

When you have finished filtering a database table, use one of these techniques to "unfilter" it and see all the records in the table again:

✦ Click the word *Filtered* at the bottom of the window. You can click this word again or click the Toggle Filter button to repeat the filter operation.

✦ On the Home tab, click the Toggle Filter button. You can click this button again to repeat the filter operation.

✦ On the Home tab, click the Advanced button and choose Clear All Filters on the drop-down list. Choosing this option kills the filter operation; you can't repeat it except by reconstructing it in the Datasheet window.

Filtering by selection

Filtering by selection is the fastest way to filter a database table. It's also the best way when you're not sure what you're looking for, because you can search for partial words and phrases. Follow these steps to filter by selection:

1. **Display the database table that needs filtering in Datasheet view.**

2. **Tell Access how to filter the records.**

To find all records with the same value or text in a particular field, simply click in a field with the value or text. If you aren't quite sure what to look for, select part of a field. For example, to find all names that start with the letters *St,* select St in one of the name fields.

3. **On the Home tab, click the Selection button and choose a filtering option.**

The options you see are specific to the cell you clicked or the data you selected in Step 2. For example, if you click a Last Name field that contains the name *Smith*, your options include Equals "Smith" and Does Not Contain "Smith." Select an option to include or exclude records in the filter operation.

Filtering for input

Filtering for input gives you the advantage of being able to filter for data ranges. Use this technique to isolate records that fall within a numerical or date range. Follow these steps to filter for input:

1. **Display the database table that you want to filter in Datasheet view.**

2. **Select the field with the data you want to use for the filter operation.**

3. **On the Home tab, click the Filter button.**

As shown in Figure 4-2, a dialog box appears so that you can describe the records you want to filter for. You can also open this dialog box by clicking the button to the right of a field name.

Book VI
Chapter 4

Sorting, Querying, and
Filtering for Data

Figure 4-2:
Filtering by input for numeric data values.

4. **Tell Access how to filter the database table.**

You can choose values or describe a data range:

- *Choose values in the field:* The dialog box lists all values in the field. Deselect the Select All check box and then click to select the values you want to filter with.

- *Describe a numeric or date range:* Choose Number Filters or Date Filters and select a comparison operator on the submenu (refer to Figure 4-2). The Custom Filter dialog box appears. Enter a comparison value and click OK.

You can repeat Steps 2 through 4 to filter the database table even further.

Filtering by form

Filtering by form is a sophisticated filtering method. It permits you to filter in more than one field using an *OR search*. For example, you can tell Access to look in the Last Name field for people named *Martinez,* as well as look in the City field for *Martinez*es who live in Los Angeles *or* San Francisco. Moreover, you can use comparison operators in the filter operation. Follow these steps to filter by form:

1. **In Datasheet view, go to the Home tab, click the Advanced button, and choose Filter by Form on the drop-down list.**

Only field names appear on the datasheet, as shown in Figure 4-3.

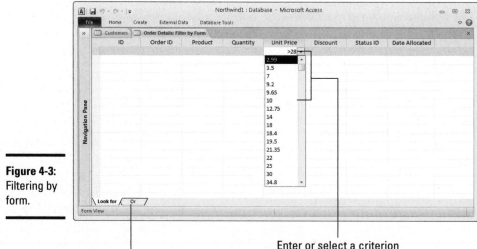

Figure 4-3:
Filtering by form.

Enter or select a criterion

Click to filter more than once in the same field

2. Click in a field, open its drop-down list, and enter a comparison value or select a value on the drop-down list.

You can select a value on the drop-down list or, in Number and Currency fields, enter a comparison operator and a value. Table 4-1 explains the comparison operators.

3. If you want, enter more criteria for the filtering operation.

You can enter values in other fields as well as filter more than once in the same field.

- *Enter values in other fields:* Open the drop-down list in a field and enter a comparison value or select a value on the drop-down list.

- *Filter more than once in the same field:* Select a field in which you already entered a search criterion. Then click the Or tab and either enter a comparison value or select a value from the drop-down list.

When you click the Or tab, the search choices you made previously disappear from the screen. Don't worry — Access remembers them on the Look For tab. You can click the Or tab again if you want to enter more criteria for Or searching.

▼ Toggle Filter **4. Click the Toggle Filter button.**

The results of the filtering operation appear in the datasheet.

Table 4-1   Comparison Operators for Filtering and Querying

Operator	Name	Example
<	Less than	<10, any number smaller than ten
<=	Less than or equal to	<=10, ten as well as any number smaller than ten
>	Greater than	>10, any number larger than ten
>=	Greater than or equal to	>=10, ten as well as any number equal to or larger than ten
=	Equal to	=10, ten — not any other number
<>	Not equal to	<>10; all numbers except ten (rather than <>, you can enter the word *not*)
Between . . . And . . .	Between	Between 10 And 15, a number between 10 and 15 or equal to 10 or 15

Querying: The Basics

Querying means to ask a question of a database and get an answer in the form of records that meet the query criteria. Query when you want to ask a detailed question of a database. "Who lives in Los Angeles and donated more than $500 last year?" is an example of a query. So is "Which orders were purchased by people who live in California and therefore, have to pay sales tax, and how much sales tax was charged with these orders?" A query can search for information in more than one database table. For that matter, you can query other queries for information. A query can be as sophisticated or as simple as you need it to be. In the results of the query, you can show all the fields in a database table or only a few necessary fields.

Access offers several different ways to query a database (the different techniques are described later in this chapter in "Six Kinds of Queries"). Still, no matter which kind of query you're dealing with, the basics of creating and running a query are the same. You start on the Create tab to build new queries. To open a query you already created, double-click its name on the Navigation pane. The following pages introduce you to queries, how to create them, and how to modify them.

Creating a new query

To create a new query, start on the Create tab and click the Query Design or Query Wizard button.

+ **Create the query in Design view:** Click the Query Design button to see the Query Design window, shown in Figure 4-4, as well as the Show Table dialog box for telling Access which database tables to query. Construct your query in the Design window (the following pages explain how).

+ **Create the query with a wizard:** Click the Query Wizard button to display the New Query dialog box and then choose a wizard option (four possible Query Wizards are available) and answer the questions that the Query Wizard asks. You're asked which table or tables to query, which fields to include in the query, and which fields to include in the query results (the following pages explain these issues).

To run a query, open the query in the Query window, go to the (Query Tools) Design tab, and click the Run button. The results of the query appear in Datasheet view.

Table pane

Figure 4-4:
The Query
Design
window.

Design grid

Viewing queries in Datasheet and Design view

Select a query on the Navigation pane and use these techniques to view it
in Datasheet or Design view. Datasheet view shows the results of running a
query. Create and modify queries in Design view.

✦ **Opening in Design view:** Right-click the query's name in the Navigation
pane and choose Design View on the shortcut menu.

✦ **Opening in Datasheet view:** On the Navigation pane, double-click the
query's name or right-click its name and choose Open on the shortcut
menu.

✦ **Switching between views with the View button:** On the Home tab, click
the View button. This button changes appearance, depending on
whether you're in Design view or Datasheet view.

✦ **Switching between views on the status bar:** Click the Datasheet View or
Design View button on the right side of the status bar.

✦ **Switching between views by right-clicking:** Right-click the query's title
bar and choose Datasheet View or Design View.

Finding your way around the Query Design window

The Query Design window (refer to Figure 4-4) is where you construct a query or retool a query you constructed already. Switch to Design view to see the Query Design window. You see this window straightaway after you click the Query Design button to construct a new query. The Query Design window is divided into halves:

✦ **Table pane:** Lists the database tables you're querying as well as the fields in each table. You can drag the tables to new locations or drag a table border to change its size and view more fields.

✦ **Design grid:** Lists which fields to query from the tables, how to sort the query results, which fields to show in the query results, and criteria for locating records in fields.

Choosing which database tables to query

To choose which database tables (and queries as well) to get information from, go to the (Query Tools) Design tab and click the Show Table button. You see the Show Table dialog box (refer to Figure 4-4). The Tables tab lists all the database tables you created for your database. Ctrl+click to select the tables you want to query and then click the Add button. To query a query, go to the Queries tab and select the query.

The tables and queries you choose appear in the Table pane of the Query Design window (refer to Figure 4-4). To remove a table from a query, right-click it in the Table pane and choose Remove Table on the shortcut menu.

In order to query more than one table, you need to establish relationships between tables. (Chapter 2 of this mini-book has information about establishing relationships between database tables.) So-called *join lines* in the Query Design window show how the tables are related to one another.

If you haven't defined relationships between the tables, you can still join them together by dragging a field from one table onto a field in another table. This is the same method used to create relationships between tables. Joining tables in a query doesn't create an actual relationship; it's just a temporary join for the sake of the query.

Choosing which fields to query

After you choose which tables to query, the next step is to choose which fields to query from the tables you selected. The object is to list fields from the Table pane in the first row of the Design grid. Fields whose names you enter in the first row of the Design grid are the fields that produce query results, as demonstrated by Figure 4-5.

Figure 4-5: How query fields translate into query results.

Access offers these techniques for listing field names in the first row of the Design grid:

- ✦ **Dragging a field name:** Drag a field name into a column on the Design grid. The field name appears on the grid, as does the name of the table that you drag the field name from.

- ✦ **Double-clicking a field name:** Double-click a field name to place it in the next available column in the Design grid.

- ✦ **Choosing a table and field name:** Click in the Table row, open the drop-down list, and choose the name of a table. Then, in the Field box directly above, open the drop-down list and choose a field name.

- ✦ **Selecting all the fields in a table:** In the unlikely event that you want all the fields from a table to appear in the query results, either double-click the asterisk (*) at the top of the list of field names or drag the asterisk into the Design grid. Access places the name of the table followed by an asterisk in the Field text box. The asterisk signifies that all the fields from the table are included in the query.

To remove a field name from the Design grid, select it and press the Delete key or go to the (Query Tools) Design tab and click the Delete Columns button.

Sorting the query results

At the start of this chapter, "Sorting Records in a Database Table" explains what sorting is. The Sort row of the Design grid — directly underneath the Table name — contains a drop-down list. To sort the query, click the drop-down list in a field and choose Ascending or Descending to sort the results of a query on a particular field. To sort the results on more than one field, make sure that the first field to be sorted appears to the left of the other fields. Access reads the sort order from left to right.

Moving field columns on the Query grid

The order in which field names appear in the Query grid is also the order in which they appear in the query results (refer to Figure 4-5). Follow these steps to put field columns in the right order in the Query grid:

1. **Click a column's selector button to select a column.**

This button is the narrow gray box directly above the field name. The pointer turns into a downward-pointing arrow when you move it over the selector button.

2. **Click the selector button again and drag the column to the left or right.**

Choosing which fields appear in query results

Although a field is part of a query and is listed in the Query grid, it isn't always necessary to display information from the field in the query results. Consider the Query grid shown in Figure 4-6. The object of this query is to get a list of customers by ZIP Code that ordered products in the year 2009. To that end, the query criteria cell in the Order Date field is `Between #1/1/2009# And #12/31/2009#`. However, when the query results are generated, listing the precise dates when the orders shipped isn't necessary because the object of the query is to get a list of customers by ZIP code who ordered products in 2009.

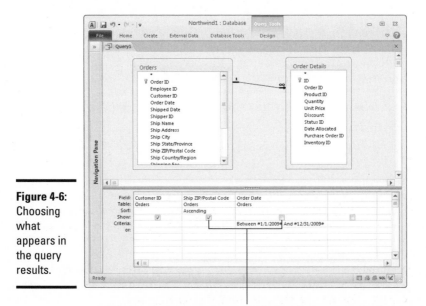

Figure 4-6: Choosing what appears in the query results.

Select or deselect to show a field's data in the query results

Whether a field's Show check box is selected in the Query grid determines if its results are part of the query results. Deselect the Show box if a field is necessary for producing records in a query but not necessary in the query results. By the way, after you save and reopen a query, Access moves deselected Show fields to the right side of the Query grid, where you usually have to scroll to see them.

Entering criteria for a query

What separates a run-of-the-mill query from a supercharged query is a *criterion,* an expression or value you enter on the Criteria line under a field. Enter criteria on the Criteria line of the Query grid. By entering criteria, you can pinpoint records in the database with great accuracy. In Figure 4-7, the Query grid instructs Access to retrieve orders with invoices due before January 1, 2009, that charged more than $2000 and were shipped to Massachusetts (MA), Connecticut (CT), or New York (NY).

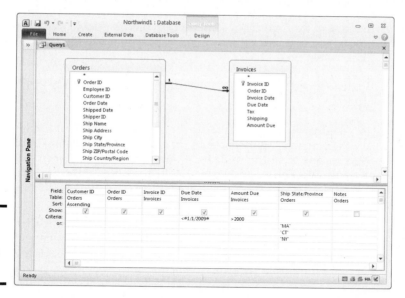

Figure 4-7:
Including
criteria in a
query.

 As Figure 4-7 shows, Access places double quotation marks ("") around text criteria and number signs (#) around date criteria. When you enter text or date criteria, don't enter the double quotation marks or number signs. Access enters them for you.

Builder When you need help writing an expression for a query, try clicking the Builder button to construct your query in the Expression Builder dialog box. This button is located on the (Query Tools) Design tab.

Entering numeric criteria

Enter numeric criteria in Number and Currency fields when you want to isolate records with specific values. Earlier in this chapter, Table 4-1 describes comparison operators you can use for querying and filtering. These operators are invaluable when it comes to mining a database for information. Use the greater than (>) and less than (<) operators to find values higher or lower than a target value. Use the Between operator to find values between two numbers. For example, *Between 62 And 55* in a Currency field isolates records with all items that sell for between $62.00 and $55.00.

Do not include commas in numbers when you enter them as criteria. For example, enter 3200, not 3,200. Enter a comma and you get a `The expression you entered contains invalid syntax. . .` error message.

Entering text criteria

To enter a text criterion, type it in the Criteria text box. For example, to find students who attended Ohio State University, enter Ohio State in the Criteria text box of the University field. Access places double quotation marks ("") around the text you enter as soon when you move the pointer out of the Criteria text box.

Wildcards and the Not operator can come in very handy when entering text criteria:

✦ **Wildcards:** Wildcards make it possible to query for data whose spelling you aren't quite sure of. (In Chapter 3 of this mini-book, Table 3-2 explains what the wildcard characters are and how to use them.) For example, entering Sm?th in the Criteria box of the Last Name field finds all Smiths and Smyths. Entering E* in the Company field finds all company names that begin with the letter *E*.

✦ **Not operator:** Use the Not operator to exclude records from query results. For example, to exclude records with Belgium in the Shipped To field, enter Not Belgium in the Criteria text box. This is a great way to strip unneeded records from a query.

Entering date criteria

All the operators that work for numeric data (refer to Table 4-1, earlier in this chapter) also work for data entered in a Date field. For example, enter >7/31/1958 in a Birth Date field to find all people born after (greater than) July 31, 1958. Enter Between 1/1/1920 And 12/31/1929 to retrieve data about people born in the Roaring Twenties.

Access places number signs (#) around date criteria after you enter it. You can enter dates in these formats:

✦ 11/22/10

✦ 11/22/2010

✦ 22-Nov-10

✦ November 22, 2010

For the purpose of entering two-digit years in dates, the digits 30 through 99 belong to the 20th Century (1930–1999), but the digits 00 through 29 belong to the 21st Century (2000–2029). For example, >4/1/24 refers to April 1, 2024, not April 1, 1924. To enter a date in 1929 or earlier, enter four digits rather than two to describe the year: >4/1/1929. To enter a date in 2030, or later, enter four digits rather than two: >4/1/2038. To avoid any confusion, enter four-digit years all the time.

The Date() function can come in very handy when you want to retrieve data relative to today's date, whatever it happens to be. For example, to retrieve purchase orders made between January 1, 2007, and today's date, enter this expression: **Between 1/1/2007 And Date()**.

At last — saving and running a query

To save a query and inscribe its name forever in the Navigation pane, click the Save button on the Quick Access toolbar and enter a descriptive name in the Save As dialog box. The name you enter appears in the Queries group in the Navigation pane.

After you laboriously construct your query, take it for a test drive. To run a query:

✦ **Starting from the Query Design window:** Click the Run button on the (Query Tools) Design tab.

✦ **Starting from the Navigation pane:** Double-click an existing query's name, or right-click its name and choose Open on the shortcut menu.

Six Kinds of Queries

For your pleasure and entertainment, the rest of this chapter describes six useful types of queries. Access offers a handful of other queries, but I won't go there. Those queries are pretty complicated. If you become adept at querying, however, you're invited to look into the Help system for advice about running the query types that aren't explained here.

Select query

A *select query* is the standard kind of query, which I explain earlier in this chapter. A select query gathers information from one or more database tables and displays the information in a datasheet. A select query is the most common query, the primal query, the starting point for most other queries.

Top-value query

A *top-value query* is an easy way to find out, in a Number or Currency field, the highest or lowest values. On the Query grid, enter the name of the Number or Currency field you want to know more about; then choose Ascending in the Sort drop-down list to rank values from lowest to highest or Descending in the Sort drop-down list to rank values from highest to lowest. Finally, on the (Query Tools) Design tab, enter a value in the Return text box or choose a value on the Return drop-down list:

✦ **Highest or lowest by percentage:** Enter or choose a percentage to find, for example, the highest or lowest 25 percent of the values. To enter a percentage, type a percent sign (%) after your entry and press the Enter key.

✦ **Highest or lowest by ranking number:** Enter or choose a number to find, for example, the top-ten or lowest-ten values. Press the Enter key after you enter a number.

This may seem counterintuitive, but to see the top values, you have to sort the field you're ranking in descending order. For example, if you sort employees by number of sales in descending order, the employees with the top sales appear at the top. To see the bottom values, sort in ascending order.

Summary query

Similar to a top-value query, a *summary query* is a way of getting cumulative information about all the data in a field. In a field that stores data about sales in Kentucky, for example, you can find the average amount of each sale, the total amount of all the sales, the total number of all the sales, and other data.

To run a summary query, go to the (Query Tools) Design tab and click the Totals button. A new row called Total appears on the Query grid. Open the Total drop-down list in the field whose contents you want to summarize and choose a function. Table 4-2 describes the functions.

Table 4-2	Summary Query Functions
Function	*Returns*
Sum	The total of all values in the field
Avg	The average of all values
Min	The lowest value
Max	The highest value
Count	The number of values
StDev	The standard deviation of the values
Var	The variance of the values
First	The first value
Last	The last value

The Group By, Expression, and Where choices in the Totals drop-down list are for including fields you're not performing a function on:

✦ **Group By:** For choosing which fields to show totals for.

✦ **Expression:** For creating a calculated field.

✦ **Where:** For setting criteria (you can't include the field in the query).

Calculation query

A *calculation query* is one in which calculations are performed as part of the query. For example, you can calculate the sales tax on items sold or total the numbers in two fields in the same record. The beauty of a calculation query is that the data is recomputed each time you run the query. If the data used to make a calculation changes, so does the result of the calculation. If you were to include the calculation in a database table, you would have to recalculate the data yourself each time one of the values changed. With a calculation query, Access does the math for you.

To construct a calculation query, create a new field in the Query grid for storing the results of the calculation; then enter a name for the field and a formula for the calculation. Follow these steps to create a calculation query:

1. **Create a query as you normally would and be sure to include the fields you want to use for calculation purposes in the Query grid.**

2. **In the Field box of a blank field, enter a name for the Calculation field and follow it with a colon.**

In Figure 4-8, I entered **Subtotal:**. The purpose of the new Subtotal field is to calculate the Unit Price × the Quantity.

New field's name

Fields used in calculation

Query results

Figure 4-8:
A calculation
query.

3. **After the colon, in square brackets ([ ]), enter the name of a field whose data you use for the calculation.**

   In Figure 4-8, data from the Unit Price and Quantity fields are used in the calculation, so their names appear in square brackets: [Unit Price] and [Quantity]. Be sure to spell field names correctly so that Access can recognize them.

4. **Complete the calculation.**

   How you do this depends on what kind of calculation you're making. In Figure 4-8, I entered an asterisk (*) to multiply two fields together. The equation multiplies the values in the Unit Price and Quantity fields. You can add the data from two different fields — including calculated fields — by putting their names in brackets and joining them with a plus sign, like so: [SubTotal]+[Shipping Cost].

Sometimes the results of the query aren't formatted correctly on the datasheet. To assign a new format to a field you create for the purposes of making a calculation query, right-click the field on the Query grid and choose Properties. The Property Sheet appears. On the General tab, click the Format drop-down list and choose the correct format for your new, hand-crafted field.

Delete query

Be careful about running delete queries. A *delete query* deletes records and doesn't give you the opportunity to get the records back if you change your mind about deleting them. If used skillfully, however, a delete query is a great way to purge records from more than one database table at once. Back up your database file before running a delete query. Edith Piaf didn't regret her delete query, but you might regret yours.

To run a delete query, start a new query, and on the (Query Tools) Design tab, click the Delete button. Then make as though you were running a select query but target the records you want to delete. Finally, click the Run button to run the query.

You can delete records from more than one table as long as the tables are related and you chose the Cascade Delete Related Records option in the Edit Relationships dialog box when you linked the tables. (See Chapter 2 of this mini-book for advice about forging relationships between tables.)

To preview the records that will be deleted before you run the delete query, switch to Datasheet view (click the View button). Those records you see? The delete query will delete them if you click the Run button.

Update query

An *update query* is a way to reach into a database and update records in several different tables all at one time. Update queries can be invaluable, but as with delete queries, they can have untoward consequences. Back up your database before you run an update query; then follow these steps to run it:

1. **Starting in Design view, go to the (Query Tools) Design tab and click the Update button.**

2. **In the field with the data that needs updating, enter text or a value in the Update To line. You can even enter another field name in square brackets ([ ]).**

   What you enter in the Update To line replaces what's in the field of the records you collect.

3. **Click the Run button.**

To update records in more than one table, you must have chosen the Cascade Update Related Fields option in the Edit Relationships dialog box when you linked the tables. (See the section in Chapter 2 of this mini-book about forging relationships between tables.)

Chapter 5: Presenting Data in a Report

In This Chapter

✔ Creating a new report

✔ Opening a report

✔ Changing the look of a report

The prettiest way to present data in a database table or query is to present it in a report. Even people who are allergic to databases can put up with database material in a report. Reports are easy to read and understand. They succinctly present the data so that you and others can interpret it. This brief chapter explains how to create reports, open them, and edit them.

Creating a Report

Access comes with all kinds of complicated tools for fashioning your own report — for laying out the pages in different ways and making data fields show up in different parts of the page. If ever a task called for relying on a wizard, creating a report is it. You can save yourself a lot of trouble, and fashion sophisticated-looking reports as well, by dispensing with the fancy report-making tools and letting the wizard do the job.

What's more, the easiest and best way to make a report is to base your report on a query. As part of fashioning a report with a wizard, you can tell Access which database tables and which fields to get the data from — in other words, you can query your database from inside the Report Wizard. However, doing that requires turning somersaults and cartwheels. It's far easier to run a query to produce the results you want in your report, save your query, and then fashion a report from the query results. Chapter 4 in this mini-book explains how to create a query.

`Report Wizard` To create a report with the Report Wizard, go to the Create tab and click the Report Wizard button. You see the first of several Report Wizard dialog boxes. Negotiate the dialog boxes as follows, clicking the Next button as you go along:

✦ **Tables/Queries:** Open this drop-down list and choose the query where the information in the report will come from. A list of fields in the query appears in the Available Fields box.

✦ **Available Fields and Selected Fields:** Select the fields whose data you want in the report by selecting the fields one at a time and clicking the > button. Doing so moves field names from the Available Fields box to the Selected Fields box. Add all the fields by clicking the >> button.

✦ **How Do You Want to View Your Data?:** Choose a field to define the grouping level. A *grouping level* is like a report subheading. For example, if you make Last Name the grouping level, information in the report is presented under people's last names.

✦ **Do You Want to Add Any Grouping Levels?:** Include subheadings in your report by selecting a field name and clicking the > button to make it a subheading. If you're building your report on a query that includes related tables, the Report Wizard automatically adds subheadings.

✦ **What Sort Order and Summary Information Do You Want?:** Select up to four fields to sort the data in your report. Even if you sort the fields in a query, the report handles sorting on its own. If you include grouping levels, the report already sorts on these fields.

✦ **How Would You Like to Lay Out Your Report?:** Experiment with the options, and watch the Preview box, to choose a layout for your report. If your report has a lot of fields, you may want to print it in Landscape view.

✦ **What Title Do You Want for Your Report?:** Enter a descriptive title. The name you choose appears in the Reports group in the Navigation pane. From there, you double-click the name when you want to see the report.

✦ **Preview the Report:** Select this option button and click Finish.

The report appears in the Preview window, as shown in Figure 5-1. How do you like it? Later in this chapter, "Tweaking a Report" offers some tips for making a report look spiffier.

		Q1	Q2	Q3	Q4	Total
Northwind Traders Coffee		$14,720.00	$230.00	$0.00	$0.00	$14,950.00
Northwind Traders Beer		$1,400.00	$5,418.00	$0.00	$0.00	$6,818.00
Northwind Traders Marmalade		$0.00	$3,240.00	$0.00	$0.00	$3,240.00
Northwind Traders Mozzarella		$0.00	$3,132.00	$0.00	$0.00	$3,132.00
Northwind Traders Clam Chowder		$1,930.00	$868.50	$0.00	$0.00	$2,798.50
Northwind Traders Curry Sauce		$680.00	$1,920.00	$0.00	$0.00	$2,600.00
Northwind Traders Chocolate		$1,402.50	$1,147.50	$0.00	$0.00	$2,550.00
Northwind Traders Boysenberry Spread		$250.00	$2,250.00	$0.00	$0.00	$2,500.00
Northwind Traders Crab Meat		$0.00	$2,208.00	$0.00	$0.00	$2,208.00
Northwind Traders Dried Apples		$530.00	$1,590.00	$0.00	$0.00	$2,120.00
Northwind Traders Ravioli		$0.00	$1,950.00	$0.00	$0.00	$1,950.00
Northwind Traders Fruit Cocktail		$0.00	$1,560.00	$0.00	$0.00	$1,560.00
Northwind Traders Dried Pears		$300.00	$900.00	$0.00	$0.00	$1,200.00
Northwind Traders Cajun Seasoning		$220.00	$660.00	$0.00	$0.00	$880.00
Northwind Traders Chocolate Biscuits N		$552.00	$230.00	$0.00	$0.00	$782.00
Northwind Traders Green Tea		$598.00	$0.00	$0.00	$0.00	$598.00
Northwind Traders Olive Oil		$0.00	$533.75	$0.00	$0.00	$533.75
Northwind Traders Syrup		$0.00	$500.00	$0.00	$0.00	$500.00

Figure 5-1:
An example
of a report.

**Book VI
Chapter 5**

Presenting Data
in a Report

Opening and Viewing Reports

If you've spent any time whatsoever in Access, you know the drill for opening a so-called object. Follow these steps to open a report:

1. **In the Navigation pane, select the Reports group.**

You see the names of reports you created.

2. **Double-click a report name or right-click a name and choose Open
from the shortcut menu.**

The report appears in Report view.

To update a report so that it includes recently added data, go to the Home
tab and click the Refresh All button.

Tweaking a Report

As I mention at the start of this chapter, Access offers a bunch of complex
tools for changing the layout and appearance of a report. If you're coura-
geous and have lots of time on your hands, you're invited to take these tools
in hand and go to it. In the Reports group of the Navigation pane, right-click
a report and choose Layout View on the shortcut menu. Your report appears
in Layout view, as shown in Figure 5-2. In this view, using tools on the Report
Layout Tools tabs, you can tweak your report's appearance.

Figure 5-2:
The report
in Figure 5-1
in Layout
view.

I tell you how to create a report with the Report Wizard in order to avoid your having to visit this imposing window. However, you can change a report's appearance in Layout view without going to very much trouble if you follow these instructions:

✦ **Choosing a new layout:** On the (Report Design Tools) Arrange tab, click the Stacked or Tubular button, or click the Gridlines button and choose an option on the drop-down list, to change your report's layout.

✦ **Including page numbers:** To include page numbers on the report, go the (Report Design Tools) Design tab and click the Page Numbers button. You see the Page Numbers dialog box shown in Figure 5-3. Choose the Page N option button to display a page number only, or select the Page N of M option button to display a page number as well as the total number of pages in the report (as in "Page 2 of 4"). Choose Alignment and Position options to describe where on the page to put the page number.

✦ **Changing the margins:** On the (Report Design Tools) Page Setup tab, click the Margins button and select Normal, Wide, or Narrow on the drop-down list.

Figure 5-3:
Putting on
the page
numbers.

An easier way to tweak a report — in Word

An easier way to tweak a report is to transfer your report to Microsoft Word and edit it there. Follow these steps to turn an Access report into a Word document:

1. **On the External Data tab, click the More button and choose Word on the drop-down list.**

   You see the Export - RTF File dialog box.

2. **Click the Browse button, and in the File Save dialog box, choose a folder for storing the Word document, and click the Save button.**

3. **In the Export - RTF File dialog box, choose Open the Destination File After the Export Operation Is Complete.**

4. **Click the OK button.**

In a moment, your Access report appears in Word. The file is an RTF (rich text format) file. To save it as a Word file, go to the File tab, choose Save As, and in the Save As dialog box, open the Save As Type drop-down list and choose Word Document. Books I and II describe how to work with files in Word.

Book VII

Publisher

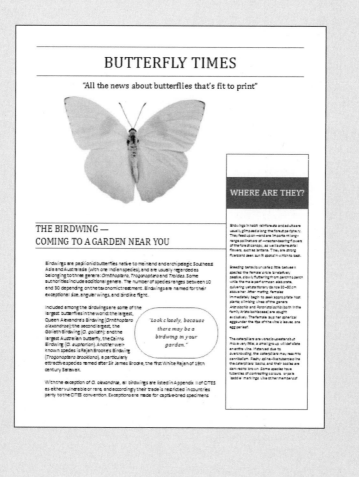

BUTTERFLY TIMES

"All the news about butterflies that's fit to print"

THE BIRDWING — COMING TO A GARDEN NEAR YOU

Birdwings are papilionid butterflies native to mainland and archipelagic Southeast Asia and Australasia (with one Indian species), and are usually regarded as belonging to three genera: *Ornithoptera, Trogonoptera* and *Troides*. Some authorities include additional genera. The number of species ranges between 10 and 30 depending on the taxonomic treatment. Birdwings are named for their exceptional size, angular wings, and birdlike flight.

Included among the birdwings are some of the largest butterflies in the world: the largest, Queen Alexandra's Birdwing (*Ornithoptera alexandrae*); the second largest, the Goliath Birdwing (*O. goliath*); and the largest Australian butterfly, the Cairns Birdwing (*O. euphorion*). Another well-known species is Rajah Brooke's Birdwing (*Trogonoptera brookiana*), a particularly attractive species named after Sir James Brooke, the first White Rajah of 19th century Sarawak.

With the exception of *O. alexandrae*, all birdwings are listed in Appendix II of CITES as either vulnerable or rare, and accordingly their trade is restricted in countries party to the CITES convention. Exceptions are made for captive-bred specimens

"Look closely, because there may be a birdwing in your garden."

WHERE ARE THEY?

Birdwings inhabit rainforests and adults are usually glimpsed along the forest periphery. They feed up on—and are important long-range pollinators of—nectar-bearing flowers of the forest canopy, as well as terrestrial flowers, such as lantana. They are strong flyers and seek sunlit spots in which to bask.

Breeding behaviour varies little between species: the female are relatively passive, slowly fluttering from perch to perch while the males perform an aerial dance, quivering vertabationary to rise 30–50 cm above her. After mating, females immediately begin to seek appropriate host plants climbing vines of the genera *Aristolochia* and *Pararistolochia* (both in the family Aristolochiaceae) are sought exclusively. The female lays her spherical eggs under the tip of the vine's leaves, one egg per leaf.

The caterpillars are voracious eaters but move very little, a small group will cannibalise another vine. If starved due to overcrowding, the caterpillars may ress the cannibalism. Fleshy spine-like tubercles line the caterpillars' backs, and their bodies are dark red to brown. Some species have tubercles of contrasting colours, or pale 'saddle' markings. Like other members of

Contents at a Glance

Chapter 1: Introducing Publisher

*W*elcome to Publisher 2010. Not long ago, creating professional publications like the kind you can create with Publisher required sophisticated printing equipment and a background in graphic design. However, even a novice can now create professional-looking publications with Publisher. As long as you rely on a publication design — a template that comes with Publisher — most of the layout work is done for you. All you have to do is enter the text and the other particulars.

"A Print Shop in a Can"

Publisher has been called "a print shop in a can" because the program is great for creating prefabricated brochures, business cards, calendars, newsletters, résumés, posters, and the like. To make these publications without going to a great deal of trouble, however, you have to stick to the template. Each *template* provides you with a ready-made brochure, calendar, and so on.

Chances are you can find a suitable template for whatever kind of publication you want to create. Figure 1-1 shows examples of advertising templates. Templates include placeholders for graphics and text. To create a publication, you choose a template, choose a design, enter graphics and text in the publication where the placeholders are, and tweak the publication to your liking.

Choose a template   Customize the design

Figure 1-1:
Creating a
publication
in the
Available
Templates
window.

Striking out on your own and designing publications like those in Figure 1-1 can be done, but you need a thorough knowledge of Publisher and a full head of hair. You need the hair because much of it will have been pulled out in frustration by the time you finish your design. I venture to say that the people who invented Publisher expect everyone to work from ready-made templates. Designing publications from scratch is simply too difficult. Don't be discouraged, however, because you can almost always find a publication design for whatever you want to communicate.

Introducing Frames

The publications that you make with Publisher are composed of frames. A *frame* is a placeholder for text, a graphic, or a table. Complex publications have dozens of frames; simple publications have only a few. Frames keep text and graphics from overlapping. They make sure that everything stays on the page where it should be. As you create a publication, you enter text or graphics in frames.

The publication in Figure 1-2 is made up of several frames that were stitched together to form a poster. On the left side of the figure, I selected the frames, and you can see the frame boundaries; the right side of the figure shows what the poster looks like after it is printed. Frames make laying out publications easier. When you want to move text, a picture, a table, or an image, you simply drag its frame to a new location. After you select a frame, the commands you give apply to the text or graphic in the frame. Frames do not appear in the finished product — they are meant strictly to help with the laying out of text and graphics.

Figure 1-2:
A poster with frames showing (left); the poster as it looks when printed (right).

 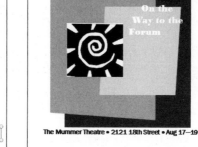

Book VII
Chapter 1

Introducing Publisher

Creating a Publication

File

To create a new publication, go to the File tab and choose New (or press Ctrl+N). You see the Available Templates window (refer to Figure 1-1). Starting here, you create a publication by selecting a template name and then clicking the Create button (if the template is stored on your computer) or the Download button (if you need to download the template from Office.com). As you search for a template, remember that you can click the Back, Forward, or Home button to retrace your search in the Available Templates window.

Use one of these techniques in the Available Templates window to create a publication:

✦ **Start from a template category:** Select the icon representing a category (Brochures, Business Cards, and so on). You see a dozen or more templates. Scroll through the list and select a template.

✦ **Search for a template:** In the Search for Templates text box, enter the name of a publication type and click the Search button (or press Enter). Then select a template.

✦ **Use a template you created:** Click the My Templates icon and then select your template.

After you select a template in the Available Templates window, you can choose a color scheme, font scheme for your publication, and other options on the right side of the Available Templates window. But I suggest waiting until you've created your publication before choosing colors and fonts. You can study your publication more closely after you create it. You can look through it and decide what you want it to look like. What's more, choosing new colors and fonts for a publication is as easy as pie, as I explain very shortly.

Redesigning a Publication

Make your design choices carefully. In theory, you can change publication designs, color schemes, and design options when you are well along in a project, but in practice, changing these designs can have unforeseen consequences. If you change the color of a headline, for example, and then choose a new color scheme, the headline might be swallowed or rendered invisible by a background color in the new scheme. If you enter a bunch of text, change the size of a few frames, and then choose a new template for your publication, you may turn your publication into corned-beef hash and have to start over.

To redesign a publication, go to the Page Design tab. As shown in Figure 1-3, this tab offers opportunities for changing templates, the orientation and size of pages, color schemes, and font schemes. If your publication has more than one page, click page thumbnails in the Page Navigation pane to visit different pages and see what they look like. (If you don't see the Page Navigation pane, go to the View tab and select the Page Navigation check box.)

Choosing a different template

Not happy with the template you chose when you created your publication? To exchange it for a new one, go to the Page Design tab and click the Change Template button. You return to the Available Templates window, where you can select a different template (refer to Figure 1-1).

Choosing a font scheme

You will be glad to know that most of the text formats that are available in Word are also available in Publisher on the Home tab. To boldface text, select it and click the Bold button. To change font sizes, choose an option on the Font Size drop-down list.

Change templates

Choose page options

Change the color scheme

Change the font scheme

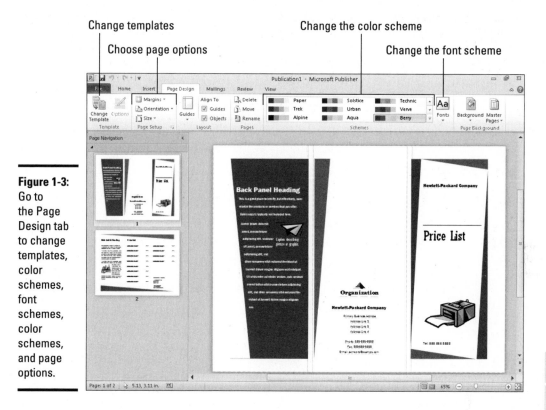

Figure 1-3:
Go to
the Page
Design tab
to change
templates,
color
schemes,
font
schemes,
color
schemes,
and page
options.

To avoid going to the trouble of formatting text, you can choose a *font scheme,*
a pair of fonts for the headings and body text in a publication. Font schemes
spare you the trouble of having to format the text on your own. The schemes
were designed by people who know what they're doing. They look good.

To choose a font scheme, go to the Page Design tab, click the Fonts button,
and select a scheme on the drop-down list. If you really know what you're
doing, you can choose Create New Font Scheme on the drop-down list and
select fonts for heading text and body text in the dialog box that appears.

Choosing a color scheme

To choose a different color scheme for your publication, go to the Page Design
tab and select a scheme in the Schemes gallery (refer to Figure 1-3). If you're
daring, choose Create New Color Scheme at the bottom of the gallery and
fashion your own color scheme in the Create New Color Scheme dialog box.

Entering business information

Brochures, newsletters, letterheads, envelopes, and a handful of other publication types include what Publisher calls "business information." Publisher plugs this information — an individual name, title, company name, address, phone number, motto, and even a logo — into the publication. The information comes from the Business Information dialog box. As long as the information in this dialog box is up-to-date, you needn't be concerned whether the information appears in the right places in a publication or whether it's accurate. And you don't have to enter the information directly into the publication you're working on.

To enter business information, go to the Insert tab, click the Business Information button, and choose Edit Business Information on the drop-down list. You see the Create New Business Information dialog box (if you entered business information previously, click the Edit button in the Business Information dialog box). Enter information in the dialog box, choose a name for the information, and click the Save button. The information you enter will be plugged into all publications you create in the future, as well

as the publication you're working on (if you click the Update Publication button).

If you need to edit the business information you entered or create secondary information about another business, click the Business Information button, choose Edit Business Information, and in the Business Information dialog box, click the Edit button. You see the Edit Business Information Set dialog box, where you can enter information about another business and save it under a different name.

Notice the Select a Business Information Set drop-down list in the Business Information dialog box. Open this drop-down list to select which business information set you need for the publication you're working on.

Publisher offers an unwieldy command for quickly entering business information one tidbit at a time: Select the frame where you want information to appear, click the Business Information button, and choose an information tidbit on the drop-down list. Then adjust the frame in which the information appears (Chapter 2 of this mini-book explains how).

Create New Business Information Set

Business Information for this set

Individual name:
Robert Smith

Job position or title:
Vice President

Organization name:
The Do-It Company

Address:
444 Main St.
Colma, CA 94044

Phone, fax, and e-mail:
Phone: 415-555-1234
Fax: 415-555-4321
E-mail: Robert@remain.com

Tagline or motto:
Let's do this thing!

Logo:

Change...   Remove

Business Information set name: Set01

Save   Cancel

Setting up your pages

On the Page Design tab, visit the Page Setup group to determine the margin size, orientation, and page size of your publication:

Margins ▾ ✦ **Margins:** Click the Margins button and choose an option on the drop-down list or click Custom Margins to enter margin measurements in the Layout Guides dialog box.

Orientation ▾ ✦ **Orientation:** Click the Orientation button and choose Portrait or Landscape on the drop-down list to stand your publication upright or turn it on its side.

Size ▾ ✦ **Size:** Click the Size button and select a page size on the drop-down list. You can choose Create New Page Size on the menu to declare a page size of your own for your publication in the Create New Page Size dialog box. Decide right away which page size to use for your publication. How large or small the page is determines how the headings, graphics, and text fit on the pages.

Getting a Better View of Your Work

Because seeing the little details as well as the big picture matters so much in a publication, Publisher offers many tools for changing views of your work. Figure 1-4 shows what these tools are. They are described in the following pages.

Zooming in and out

Apart from the standard Zoom controls found in most Office programs (Book I, Chapter 3 describes the Zoom controls in the lower-right corner of the screen), Publisher offers a handful of other commands for zooming in or out. Go to the View tab and take advantage of these techniques as you refine your publication:

Whole Page ✦ **Make the page fit squarely in the window:** Click the Whole Page button (or press Ctrl+Shift+L) to make the entire page fit in the window. The lower-right corner of the window also offers a Whole Page button; you can click it when you're not working in the View tab.

Page Width ✦ **Make the width of the page fit in the window:** Click the Page Width button.

Selected Objects ✦ **Focus on objects:** Select an object (a text frame or graphic, for example) or a handful of objects and click the Selected Objects button to zoom in on what you selected. Being able to focus this way is very helpful when you're working on a publication that is crowded with words and images.

100% ✦ **View your publication at its actual size:** Click the 100% button.

Choose a layout

Go from page to page

Zoom in or out

Figure 1-4:
Go to the
View tab
to change
views of
your work.

Viewing single pages and two-page spreads

On the View tab, click the Two-Page Spread button to see facing pages in newsletters, brochures, and other publications with more than one page (refer to Figure 1-4). Choose this command early and often. It permits you to see what readers of your publication will see when they view facing pages. Click the Single Page button to see a single page in the window.

Going from page to page

Use these techniques to get from page to page in a publication:

✦ **Page Navigation pane:** In a publication with more than one page, go from page to page by clicking thumbnail pages in the Page Navigation pane (refer to Figure 1-4). To display this pane, visit the View tab and click the Page Navigation check box.

✦ **The Go To Page dialog box:** On the Home tab, click the Find button (or press Ctrl+G) and enter a page number in the Go To Page dialog box.

To help you identify pages, you can name them. When you move the pointer over a page thumbnail in the Page Navigation pane, the name appears in a pop-up box. To name a page, right-click its thumbnail in the Page Navigation pane and choose Rename on the shortcut menu. In the Rename Page dialog box, enter a descriptive name.

Understanding and Using the Layout Guides

Making frames, graphics, and lines of text line up squarely on the page is essential if your publication is to look smart and snappy. Readers tend to go cockeyed when they see side-by-side columns with the text in one column slightly askew of the text in the column beside it. A graphic or text frame that spills into the margin is a breach of etiquette punishable by death. A row of graphics has to be just that — a row, not a crooked line. To keep pages neat and tidy, Publisher offers several types of layout guides, as the following pages explain.

Making use of layout guides

As shown in Figure 1-5, Publisher offers margin guides, grid guides, ruler guides, and baselines to help you lay out frames, graphics, and other objects on the pages of your publications. Use these layout guides early and often.

To see margin guides, grid guides, and ruler guides on your publication, you must go to the View tab and select the Guides check box.

Figure 1-5:
Layout guides (left to right): margin guides, grid guides, ruler guides, and baselines.

Margin guides

Margin guides are blue lines that clearly show where page margins begin and end (refer to Figure 1-5). Use the margin guides to make sure that objects don't stray too far into the margin.

Margin guides appear on the page as long as the Guides check box on the View tab is selected. Where the margin guides appear depends on the Margin setting you chose for your publication. (On the Page Design tab, click the Margins button and choose a setting.)

Grid guides

Grid guides are blue lines that appear in grid form across the page (refer to Figure 1-5). Frames and objects can be made to "snap to the grid" (see "Snapping objects to ruler and grid lines," later in this chapter). Because the objects snap, you're spared the trouble of aligning them because they line up on grid guides.

To determine where gridlines are and display them on pages, go to the Page Design tab, click the Guides button, and choose Grid and Baseline Guides on the drop-down list. You see the Grid Guides tab of the Layout Guides dialog box, as shown in Figure 1-6. Do the following and click OK.

✦ Enter numbers to determine how many rows and columns form the gird.

✦ Enter Spacing measurements to determine how close objects can come to grid guides. Think carefully about entering a number less than .2 in the Spacing boxes. If you enter 0, for example, objects and frames will touch each other when they snap to the grid.

✦ Select the Add Center Guide between Columns and Rows check box if you want to draw a line between the lines formed by columns and rows in the grid.

To remove grid guides, return to the Grid Guides tab of the Layout Guides dialog box and enter **1** in the Columns text box and **1** in the Rows text box. You can also go to the View tab and deselect the Guides check box to temporarily remove grid guides.

Figure 1-6:
Creating grid guides and baselines in the Layout Guides dialog box.

Ruler guides

Ruler guides are green horizontal and vertical lines that you can place on the page for assistance in aligning frames and objects (refer to Figure 1-5). You can draw ruler guides where you need them and remove the guides very easily when they get in the way. Whereas grid guides appear on every page in a publication, ruler guides appear on one page. You can, however, place the same ruler guides on every page by drawing the ruler guides on the master page (Chapter 3 of this mini-book describes master pages).

Go to the Page Design tab and use one of these techniques to place ruler guides on a page:

✦ **Built-in ruler guides:** Click the Guides button and choose a built-in ruler guide option on the drop-down list to place many ruler guides on a page.

✦ **Drawn ruler guides:** Click the Guides button and choose Add Horizontal Ruler Guide or Add Vertical Ruler Guide. A ruler guide appears horizontally or vertically across the center of the page. Click and drag the ruler guide across the page to a new location.

✦ **Ruler Guides dialog box:** Click the Guides button and choose Ruler Guides. You see the Ruler Guides dialog box. Enter horizontal or vertical measurements for the guides and click OK.

You can also place a ruler guide on a page by copying a ruler guide that is already there. Hold down the Ctrl key and drag an existing ruler guide to create a new guide.

To remove ruler guides from a page, go to the Page Design tab, click the Guides button, and choose No Ruler Guides on the drop-down list. You can temporarily remove ruler guides by deselecting the Guides check box on the View tab.

Book VII
Chapter 1

Introducing
Publisher

Baselines

Baselines are brown, dotted, horizontal lines that appear on the page to help with aligning frames, objects, and lines of text (refer to Figure 1-5). To make baselines appear, go to the View tab and select the Baselines check box.

To decide the frequency of baselines, go to the Page Design tab, click the Guides button, and choose Grid and Baseline Guides on the drop-down list. The Layout Guides dialog box appears. On the Baseline Guides tab, enter Spacing measurements to determine how tight or loose the lines are, and Offset measurements to determine how far off the margin settings the lines are. Figure 1-6 shows the Baseline Guides tab of the Layout Guides dialog box.

Snapping objects to ruler and grid lines

On the Page Design tab, the commands in the Layout group make frames and objects snap to ruler guides or grid guides. Snapping helps to make objects line up squarely. On the Page Design tab, select the Guides check box (or press Ctrl+Shift+W) to make objects snap to the guides; select the Objects check box to make objects snap to other objects on the page.

Handling the rulers

Rulers, when they aren't coming in very handy, get in the way. To display or hide rulers, go to the View tab and select or deselect the Rulers check box.

For precision work, you can drag a ruler into the middle of the window and use it as an aid for lining up frames and other objects. Hold down the Shift key, click on a ruler, and drag it into the middle of the window. To move it back where it came from, Shift+drag all over again.

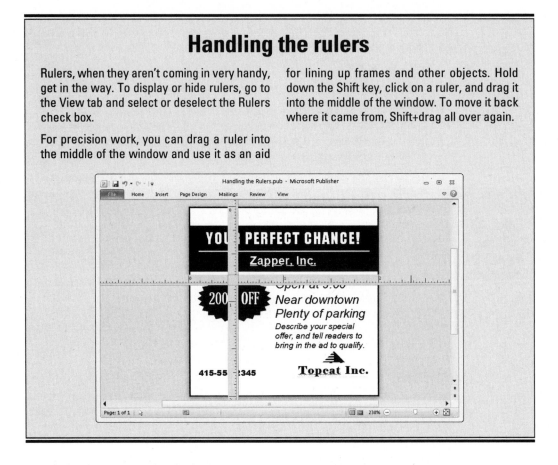

Chapter 2: Refining a Publication

In This Chapter

✓ **Entering and editing text**

✓ **Making text fit in frames**

✓ **"Flowing" text from frame to frame**

✓ **Wrapping text around frames and graphics**

✓ **Putting graphics in a publication**

✓ **Manipulating frames**

This chapter picks up where the previous chapter left off. In Chapter 1 of this mini-book, you discover how to create a publication, find your way around the screen, and use the different guides. In this chapter, you explore how to make a publication your own. This chapter offers speed techniques for entering and editing text. It explains how to handle frames, make text "flow" from frame to frame, and put graphics and other kinds of art in a publication. *Bon voyage!*

Entering Text on the Pages

The placeholder text that appears in publication designs has to go, of course. One of your first tasks is to replace the placeholder text with your own words. In the case of a story, you have a lot of writing and replacing to do (*story* is Publisher's term for an article that reaches across several text frames). If you're putting together a sign or greeting card, you have only a handful of words to write.

If you have to replace more than two dozen words, follow these steps to replace the placeholder text in a text frame with text of your own:

1. **Read the first paragraph of the placeholder text to see how many words can fit in the text frames that hold the story.**

    Each placeholder story starts with a sentence describing roughly how many words are in the story. You can spare yourself a lot of time and trouble by making the replacement text roughly as many words as the placeholder text.

2. In Word, write the text and save the text in a file.

You can call on all the Word commands to edit the text. You can also copy text from elsewhere into the Word document. Later you will copy this file into Publisher. The status bar in Word tells you how many words are in a file. See if you can keep to the number of words that are in the placeholder text.

3. In Publisher, click in the placeholder text, go to the Home tab, click the Styles button, and note on the Styles drop-down list which style has been assigned to the placeholder text.

You can tell which style has been assigned to the text because it is selected on the Styles drop-down list. In Step 6, you will assign the style that is currently applied to the text to the replacement text you insert into the text frame.

4. If necessary, press Ctrl+A to select the text in the story, and with the text selected, right-click and choose Change Text⇨Text File.

You see the Insert Text dialog box. You can also open this dialog box by going to the Insert tab and clicking the Insert File button.

5. Select the Word file with the replacement text and click the OK button.

Replacement text from the Word file "flows" into the text frame or frames. If the replacement text doesn't fit in the text frames allotted to the story, you see the Autoflow dialog box. You can click the Yes button to tell Publisher to flow the text into different text frames in the publication, but I recommend clicking No in the Autoflow dialog box. Later in this chapter, "Making text flow from frame to frame" explains how to decide on your own where to put overflow text from a story.

The replacement text maintains the styles assigned to it in the Word document. In the next step, you reassign a style to the text.

6. Press Ctrl+A to select the text in the story, go to the Home tab, click the Styles button, and choose the style that was assigned to the placeholder text.

In Step 2, you noted which style this was. Later in this chapter, "Formatting Text" explains how to format text with styles.

Making Text Fit in Text Frames

When text doesn't fit in a text frame, red selection handles appear around the frame, and if the text frame holds a story, the Text In Overflow icon appears in the lower-right corner of the text frame, as shown in Figure 2-1.

When you see this icon and the red selection handles, it means that you must make decisions about how to fit stray text into text frames. You can either fit the text into an existing frame, or, if you're dealing with a story, flow the text to other frames. These pages explain strategies for handling text that doesn't fit in text frames.

Buttons for managing text flow

Go to Previous Text Box icon

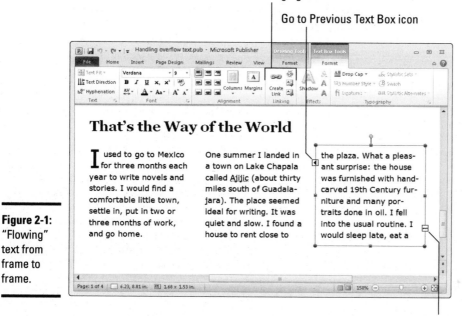

Figure 2-1: "Flowing" text from frame to frame.

Text in Overflow icon

Fitting overflow text in a single frame

To fit a heading or paragraph into a single text frame, try one of these techniques:

✦ **Shrink the text automatically:** On the (Text Box Tools) Format tab, click the Text Fit button and choose Shrink Text On Overflow on the drop-down list. This command shrinks the point size of text so that all text fits in the frame. Sometimes, however, shrinking the text this way makes the heading or paragraph hard to read.

✦ **Edit the text:** Snip out a word or sentence here and there to make the text fit. Have you ever wondered why magazine articles always fill the page and never end in the middle? That's because skillful editors and typesetters remove and add words here and there to make the story fit the page.

✦ **Make the text frame larger:** See "Changing the size and position of frames," later in this chapter.

✦ **Make the text frame margins smaller:** Like a page, text frames have internal margins to keep text from getting too close to the frame border. To shrink these margins and make more room for text, go to the (Text Box Tools) Format tab, click the Margins button, and choose Narrow on the drop-down list. You can also choose Custom Margins, and on the Text Box tab of the Format Text Box dialog box, enter smaller measurements for the text box margins.

Making text flow from frame to frame

As shown in Figure 2-1, the Text In Overflow icon and red selection handles appear when story text overflows a text frame. How do you flow story text from frame to frame and handle a story that is spread across several frames? Better keep reading.

Flowing text to another frame

If necessary, create a new text box for the overflow text and follow these steps to direct text from one frame to another in your publication:

1. **Select the text frame with overflowing text.**

You can tell when text is overflowing because the Text in Overflow icon appears in the lower-right corner of the frame (refer to Figure 2-1).

2. **On the (Text Box) Formatting tab, click the Create Link button.**

The pointer turns into an overflowing pitcher (or is that a beer stein?) after you click the button.

3. **Move the pointer over the box that you want the text to flow into.**

You may have to click a page navigation button to go to another page. See "Inserting Frames on the Pages," later in this chapter, if you need help creating a new text frame.

4. **Click in the target text box to make the text flow there.**

Continuation slugs

A *continuation slug* is a notice that tells the reader where to turn to continue reading an article or where an article is continued from. Publisher offers a nifty command for entering continuation slugs at the bottom or top of text frames:

1. **Right-click the text frame that needs a slug and choose Format Text Box.**

2. **On the Text Box tab of the Format Text Box dialog box, select the Include "Continued on Page" or Include "Continued from Page" check box and click OK.**

Handling text frames in a story

As I mention earlier, text frames that are linked are known as a story in Publisher-speak. Here are techniques for handling text frames that are linked in a story:

✦ **Going from text frame to text frame:** On the (Text Box) Formatting tab, click the Next or Previous button to go from frame to frame. You can also select a text frame and click its Go to Next Text Box or Go to Previous Text Box icon (refer to Figure 2-1).

✦ **Selecting the text in all the text frames:** Press Ctrl+A; or go to the Home tab, click the Select button, and choose Select All Text in Text Box on the drop-down list.

✦ **Breaking the link between frames:** Select the frame that you want to be the last one in the chain, and on the (Text Box Tools) Format tab, click the Break button.

In a crowded publication, it's easy to overlook a text frame with overflowing text. To find these text frames, go to the File tab, and on the Information page, click the Run Design Checker button. Then, in the Design Checker task pane, look for "Story with Text in Overflow Area."

Filling out a text frame

The opposite of an overflow problem is a text frame with too much blank space. Here are some techniques for handling semi-vacant text frames:

✦ **Use the Best Fit option:** On the (Text Box Tools) Format tab, click the Text Fit button and choose Best Fit on the drop-down list. This command enlarges the text so that it fills the frame. Sometimes, however, the command makes text too big.

✦ **Edit the text:** Add a word or sentence here or there. In the case of headings, write a subheading as well.

✦ **Insert a graphic, page part, or advertisement:** Placing a small graphic, page part, or advertisement on the page makes the page livelier and fills the dead space. Chapter 3 of this mini-book explains techniques for decorating dead space on pages.

Formatting Text

Use these techniques to format the text in a publication:

✦ **Home tab font and paragraph commands:** The commands on the Home tab for changing the look of text and paragraphs are nearly identical to the Home tab commands in Word and PowerPoint. Book I, Chapter 2 explains these commands.

✦ **Styles:** Select text, and on the Home tab, click the Styles button and choose a style on the drop-down list to format text. Each template comes with many different styles. Beware, however, because you can get lost on the Style drop-down list. Be prepared to click the Undo button often as you experiment with styles.

Making Text Wrap around a Frame or Graphic

Wrap text around a frame, clip-art image, picture, or WordArt image and you get a very elegant layout. Figure 2-2 shows text that has been wrapped around a clip-art image. Looks nice, doesn't it? Wrapping text may be the easiest way to impress innocent bystanders with your layout prowess. As Figure 2-2 shows, text wrapped tightly follows the contours of the picture, whereas text wrapped squarely runs flush with the picture's frame.

Figure 2-2: Text wrapped tightly (left) and squarely (right).

The ship is leaving soon. All aboard for the fun-filled adventure!

The ship is leaving soon. All aboard for the fun-filled adventure!

Here are shorthand instructions for wrapping text:

1. **Select the item that text is to wrap around.**

   In Figure 2-2, you would select the clip-art image.

2. **On the Format tab, click the Wrap Text button and choose a wrapping option on the drop-down list.**

   For Figure 2-2, I chose Tight for the picture on the left and Square for the picture on the right.

The Wrap Text commands are identical in Word and Publisher. Book II, Chapter 4 (about wrapping objects in Word) explains the wrapping commands in detail.

Replacing the Placeholder Pictures

As you must have noticed by now, publication designs are littered with generic clip-art images and graphics. Besides writing your own words where the placeholder ones are, replace the generic pictures with pictures of your own. Well, do it if you please. You are welcome to pass off the generic pictures as your own. I won't tell anybody.

Follow these steps to put a picture of your own where a placeholder picture is now:

1. **Click the placeholder picture to select it.**

   You can also select a picture by clicking its name in the Graphics Manager. To use the Graphics Manger, go to the View tab and click the Graphics Manager check box. The Graphics Manger opens on the right side of the screen.

2. **On the (Picture Tools) Format tab, click the Change Picture button and choose Change Picture on the drop-down list.**

   The Insert Picture dialog box appears. In the Graphics Manager, open the drop-down list on a picture name and choose Replace This Picture to open the Insert Picture dialog box.

3. **Select a picture and click the Insert button.**

   Your replacement picture may require cropping or recoloring. Book VIII, Chapter 3 describes how to handle graphics in all the Office programs. You'll be delighted to discover that graphics are handled the same way, no matter which program you're toiling in.

You can postpone choosing a picture to replace a placeholder picture. Right-click the picture in question and choose Change Picture⇨Remove Picture on the drop-down list. Publisher places a picture icon in the frame to remind you to insert a picture later on. You can click this picture icon to open the Insert Picture dialog box.

The next topic in this chapter is how to put a graphic on the page without the benefit of a placeholder graphic.

Inserting Frames on the Pages

Publications are made of frames — text box frames, table frames, picture frames, or clip-art frames. Nothing appears on the pages of a publication unless it appears within the confines of a frame. These pages explain everything you need to know about frames. You can find out how to insert a new frame, adjust the size of a frame, align frames, and place borders around frames. You can also see how to make frames and the words or images inside them overlap.

Inserting a new frame

How you insert a new frame depends on what you want to insert: a text box, table, picture, clip-art image, or WordArt image. Start by clicking on the page roughly where you want the frame to go. Then insert the new frame by using the techniques described here. (See "Making Text Wrap around a Frame or Graphic," earlier in this chapter, for information about wrapping text around a frame. See "Changing the size and position of frames," later in this chapter, to find out how to change a frame's shape.)

To delete a frame, all you have to do is select it and press the Delete key or right-click and choose Delete Object. You can tell when a frame is selected because selection handles appear on the corners and sides.

Inserting a text box frame

To insert a text-box frame, go to the Insert or Home tab and click the Draw Text Box button. Then click on the page and drag to create the text box. Book I, Chapter 8 explains how to change the background color and border of a text box.

Inserting a table

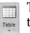
To insert a table, go to the Insert or Home tab and use one of these techniques:

✦ Click the Table button and move the pointer in the drop-down list to the number of columns and rows you want, click, and let go of the mouse button.

✦ Click the Table button and choose Insert Table on the drop-down list. The Create Table dialog box appears. Enter the number of rows and columns you want and click OK.

Book I, Chapter 5 explains everything a mortal needs to know about tables in Publisher.

Inserting a picture or clip-art image

Follow these steps to insert a picture, clip-art image, or WordArt image:

🖼 Picture Placeholder   **1. On the Insert tab, click the Picture Placeholder button.**

A picture placeholder frame appears.

2. **As best you can, make the frame the size you want your picture or image to be.**

   The next section in this chapter, "Changing the size and position of frames," describes how to do this.

3. **Insert a picture or clip-art image.**

   On the Insert tab, use one of these techniques to insert the item:

   Picture: Click the picture icon in the placeholder frame or the Picture button. You see the Insert Picture dialog box. Select a picture and click the Insert button.

   Clip-art image: Click the Clip Art button. The Clip Art task pane opens. Search for an image, select it, and open its drop-down list and choose Insert. Book VIII, Chapter 4 explains all the details of inserting clip-art images.

4. **On the (Picture Tools) Format tab, Click the Fill button to make a picture that is too large for the frame fit inside the frame, or Click the Fill button to make a picture that is too small for the frame fill the frame.**

   Book VIII, Chapter 3 explains all the doodads on the (Picture Tools) Format tab, in case you're curious.

Changing the size and position of frames

After you click a frame and see the selection handles, you're ready to change the size of the frame or adjust its position on the page. Use these standard techniques for resizing and moving frames:

✦ **Changing the size of a frame:** Move the pointer over a selection handle and start dragging. If you're dealing with anything but a text frame, be careful about dragging a selection handle on the side of the frame. Dragging a side handle changes the frame's size as well as its proportions. Images can blur or become distorted when you change their proportions.

✦ **Changing the position of a frame:** Move the pointer onto the frame (or the perimeter of a frame if you're dealing with a text box), and click and drag when you see the four-headed arrow. To move more than one frame simultaneously, Ctrl+click the frames you want to move.

As I explain in Chapter 1 of this mini-book, frames snap to the grid as you move them, but you can hold down the Alt key as you drag to adjust frames with precision. You can also press an arrow key to move them ever so slightly.

Making Frames Overlap

When frames overlap, you have to tell Publisher which frame goes in front of the other. And you are hereby invited to overlap frames because overlapping frames are artful and look good on the page. Figure 2-3 shows a portion of a newsletter. If you look closely, you can see where frames overlap in the figure. Overlapping frames like these make for a sophisticated layout.

Figure 2-3:
Examples of
overlapping
frames.

Making frames overlap like the ones in Figure 2-3 requires a delicate balancing act, using these commands:

✦ **Text wrapping:** On the Format tab, click the Wrap Text button and choose None on the drop-down list.

✦ **Fill Color:** For frames and objects on the bottom of the stack to show through, the frames and objects above them cannot have a fill color that would obscure other objects. To remove the fill color, select the object, and on the Format tab, open the drop-down list on the Shape Fill button and choose No Fill.

✦ **Object and frame order:** To tell Publisher which object goes where in the stack, go to the Format tab and click the Bring Forward or Send Backward button as necessary. Book I, Chapter 8 explains all the techniques for handling overlapping objects.

Inserting, Removing, and Moving Pages

Suppose that you have too many pages or you need to add a page or two. On the Page Navigation pane (select the Page Navigation check box on the View tab), click a thumbnail to select the page where you want to insert, remove, or move pages. Then follow these instructions:

✦ **Inserting a new page:** On the Insert tab, click the Page button and choose an option on the drop-down list:

• *Insert Blank Page:* Inserts an empty page.

- *Insert Duplicate Page:* Inserts a page identical to the thumbnail page you selected.

- *Insert Page:* Opens the Insert Page dialog box, where you can enter the number of pages you want to insert and click an option button to put the new pages before or after the page you selected. You can also tell Publisher what to put on the new page or pages.

✦ **Removing a page:** On the Page Design tab, click the Delete button. You can also right-click a page thumbnail and choose Delete.

✦ **Moving a page:** On the Page Design tab, click the Move button. Give instructions for moving the page in the Move Page dialog box and click OK.

Chapter 3: Putting on the Finishing Touches

In This Chapter

✔ Using horizontal rules and drop caps

✔ Decorating frames with borders and color backgrounds

✔ Putting a background on a page

✔ Putting objects and frames on the master page

✔ Preparing publications so that they can be printed commercially

This final chapter in Book VII is devoted to the Project to Beautify Publications, a joint effort of the Dummies Press and the author to try to make publications less bland and more original. The author has noticed, on the bulletin boards and lampposts in his neighborhood, that the rummage sale and lost pet notices look a little rough around the edges. The neighbors are using sophisticated software to produce their notices, but they're not using it well. They are relying solely on templates, which make the publications look alike. These pages explain a few simple tricks for making publications more sophisticated.

This chapter explores drop caps and horizontal rules, page backgrounds and borders, borders and backgrounds for frames, and how to place a logo in the same place on each page in a publication. It shows you Publisher's excellent Design Checker. Finally, this chapter offers advice for printing publications at a commercial print shop.

Decorating the Text

Herewith are a couple of tricks to amaze your friends and intimidate your enemies. These pages explain how horizontal rules and drop caps can make a publication a little livelier. Don't worry — horizontal rules have nothing to do with which side of the bed to sleep on, and drop caps don't explode when you unroll them on the sidewalk and strike them with a hammer.

Drawing a horizontal rule on a frame

A *horizontal rule* is a horizontal line that divides one part of a page from another and directs the reader's eye on the page. There are four horizontal rules in Figure 3-1. By varying the width of the lines — the width is known as the *weight* — and placing lines in strategic places, you can make a publication look more elegant and graceful.

Figure 3-1:
Examples of horizontal rules.

MODERN LIBRARIAN

Volume 3 Issue 2   Building happy healthy libraries

What's on the Horizon

Usually where horizontal rules come in pairs, the bottommost rule is thicker than its twin. The thicker bottom line encourages the reader's eye to move down the page and find an article to read.

Select the frame and follow these steps to draw a horizontal rule on a frame:

1. **On the Format tab, click the Text or Size group button.**

   You can also select the frame, right-click it, and choose Format (the Format command has different names depending on what type of frame or object you're working with). You see the Format dialog box.

2. **Select the Color and Lines tab.**

3. **In the Preview box, click the top of the box to draw a rule above the frame or the bottom of the box to draw a rule below.**

   By clicking part of the Preview box, you tell Publisher where you want to draw the rule.

4. **On the Color menu, choose a line color for the horizontal rule.**

5. **On the Style menu, choose the kind of line you want.**

   If you want a dashed line, select it from the Dashed drop-down list. You can adjust the thickness of the line in the Weight text box.

6. **To draw a second rule on the frame, click again in the Preview box and repeat steps 4 and 5.**

7. Click OK.

To remove a horizontal rule from a frame, select the frame, open the Format dialog box, open the Color drop-down list, and choose No Line.

Dropping in a drop cap

A *drop cap* is a large capital letter that "drops" into the text. Drop caps are usually found in the first paragraph of an article or chapter. Pound for pound, considering how little effort is required, a drop cap yields the most reward for the least amount of work. Follow these steps to place a drop cap in a publication:

1. **Click the paragraph that is to receive the drop cap.**

2. **On the (Text Box Tools) Format tab, click the Drop Cap button and choose a drop cap on the drop-down list or choose Custom Drop cap to open the Drop Cap dialog box.**

Figure 3-2 shows the Drop Cap dialog box. From here, you can choose how far to drop the capital letter or select a font and color for the letter.

To remove a drop cap, click the Drop Cap button and choose No Drop Cap (the first option on the drop-down list).

Figure 3-2: Fashioning a drop cap.

Techniques for Decorating Pages

No one likes a dull publication. Following are some simple techniques to make pages a little bit livelier. Read on to find out how to put borders and color backgrounds on frames, and how to take advantage of page parts, borders, accents, and advertisements. You will also find instructions for painting an entire page with a background color or gray shade.

Putting borders and color backgrounds on frames

As shown in Figure 3-3, putting borders and background colors on text frames makes the frames stand out. Everybody knows what a border is. A background color is a color or gray shade that fills a frame. Borders and background colors are ideal for calling readers' attention to important notices and items in publications. To really get readers' attention, for example, try using black for the background and white for the font color.

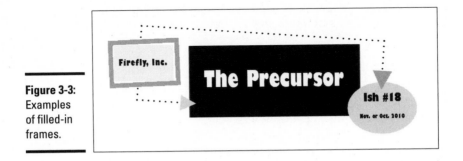

Figure 3-3:
Examples
of filled-in
frames.

How to put borders and colors on frames and other objects is a topic in Book I, Chapter 8, but to spare you a trip to that part of the book, here are shorthand instructions for giving a background color or a border to a frame. Select the frame, go to the (Drawing Tools) Format tab, and follow these instructions:

✦ **Shape Style:** Choose a style on the Shape Styles gallery. You can "live-preview" these styles, and assigning a style from the gallery is the easiest way to decorate a frame.

✦ **Background color:** Open the drop-down list on the Shape Fill button and select a color. Choose No Fill to remove the background color or to create no background color so that frames below the frame you're dealing with can show through.

✦ **Color and size of the border:** Open the drop-down list on the Shape Outline button and choose a color. On the shortcut menu, you can also choose Weight and a point size for the line that forms the border of the frame.

Instead of clicking buttons on the (Drawing Tools) Format tab, you can handle borders and backgrounds in the Format dialog box. Click the Shape Styles group button or right-click a frame and choose Format on the shortcut menu. In the Format dialog box, go to the Colors and Lines tab. It offers all kinds of commands for borders and backgrounds.

Plugging in a page part

"Page part" is Publisher's word for a page element that you can quickly plug into a page. Use a page part to fill in empty space on a page or get a head start in formatting part of a page. As shown in Figure 3-4, page parts include the following:

✦ **Headings:** A ready-made title for a page or story. Headings often include a subheading.

✦ **Pull quotes:** A preformatted text box frame for displaying a quotation from a story.

✦ **Sidebars:** A preformatted text-box frame for a companion story. Sidebars usually appear on a side of the page in a smaller font.

✦ **Stories:** A preformatted story, including a heading and a subheading.

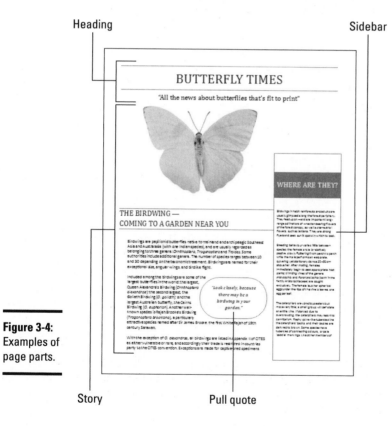

Heading   Sidebar

Figure 3-4:
Examples of page parts.

Story   Pull quote

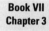

**Book VII
Chapter 3**

**Putting on the
Finishing Touches**

Follow these steps to put a page part on a page:

1. **On the Insert tab, click the Page Parts button.**

2. **Choose a heading, pull quote, sidebar, or story on the drop-down list.**

   Choose More Page Parts to open the Building Block Library and choose from many more page parts.

After the element lands on the page, you can change its size or shift its position by using the same techniques you use with other objects. (Book I, Chapter 8 explains how to manipulate objects.) If the story or sidebar you inserted includes a picture, right-click the picture and choose Change Picture⇨Change Picture to replace the picture with one of your own.

Experimenting with borders and accents

Publisher offers what it calls "borders and accents" to make pages a little livelier. Borders and accents are page decorations that also serve a purpose:

- ✦ **Bars:** Decorative patterns for filling empty page space
- ✦ **Emphasis:** Two-sided text-box frames to make text boxes stand out on the page
- ✦ **Frames:** Four-sided text-box frames to make text boxes stand out
- ✦ **Lines:** Unusual lines
- ✦ **Patterns:** Checkerboard and other patterns for filling empty page space

Follow these steps to place a border or accent on a publication page:

1. **On the Insert tab, click the Borders & Accents button.**

2. **Choose a border or accent on the drop-down list.**

   Choose More Borders and Accents and make a selection in the Building Block Library if you want to place a line or pattern on a page.

The border or accent lands on the page. (Book I, Chapter 8 explains how to manipulate objects such as borders and accents.)

Taking advantage of attention getters

If your goal in Publisher is to create an advertisement, you can get a head start on the task by sprinkling an "attention getter" or advertisement in your publication. Figure 3-5 shows examples of attention getters.

To use an attention getter or advertisement in your publication, go to the Insert tab, click the Advertisements button, and choose an ad or attention getter on the drop-down list. (Book I, Chapter 8 explains how to change the size and position of objects such as advertisements and attention getters.)

Figure 3-5:
Examples of "attention getters."

Backgrounds for pages

Yet another nifty trick is to put a color, gray-shade, or other type of background on the page. Be sure to choose a background that doesn't get in the way of your publication or render it impossible to read. Shrink the publication to 40 percent so that you can see what backgrounds really look like; then follow these steps to give a page or all the pages in your publication a background:

1. **On the Page Design tab, click the Background button.**

A drop-down list opens, as shown in Figure 3-6.

Figure 3-6:
Choosing a background for a page or all pages.

2. **Move the pointer over the options on the drop-down list to "live-preview" the choices.**

   You can choose More Backgrounds on the drop-down list to open the Fill Effects dialog box and choose or create a page background there. The dialog box gives you the opportunity to use a gradient, texture, pattern, picture, or tint for a page background.

3. **Apply your choice to a single page or all pages in your publication.**

   You have the option of changing the page background on one page or all the pages:

   - *One page:* On the Background button drop-down list, right-click your choice and choose Apply to Current Page.

   - *All pages:* On the Background button drop-down list, right-click your choice and choose Apply to All Pages.

To remove the background from a page, click the Background button and choose No Background on the drop-down list.

 To apply a page background from the Fill Effects dialog box to all the pages in a publication, switch to Master Page view, go to the Page Design tab, click the Background button, and create or choose a page background in the Fill Effects dialog box. Because it is on the master page, your page background choice applies to all pages. Master pages is the next topic in this chapter.

Master Pages for Handling Page Backgrounds

In a publication with many pages, the same object sometimes goes on every page. A company logo on the corner of each page looks mighty elegant. Page numbers and copyright information are also found on all the pages of some publications. The good news is that you don't have to place the objects on each page individually. Instead, you can place the objects on the *master page*. Whatever is on the master page appears on all pages in a publication (unless you decide that the master page shouldn't apply to a particular page). Forthwith are instructions for handling master pages.

Switching to Master Page view

To change the appearance of the master page, place an object on the master page, or see precisely what is on the master page, start by switching to Master Page view:

+ On the View tab, click the Master Page button.

+ On the Page Design tab, click the Master Pages button and choose Edit Master Pages on the drop-down list.

You can tell when you're looking at a master page because you see the Master Page tab on the Ribbon and the page thumbnails in the Page Navigation pane show letters rather than numbers.

To leave Master Page view, go to the Master Page tab and click the Close Master Page button.

Changing the look of a master page

All commands for changing the look of run-of-the-mill pages also apply to master pages. Place objects and frames on the master page as if you were putting them on run-of-the-mill pages. Change the page background as if you were changing the background of a normal page.

To edit a master page, switch to Master Page, select the master page you want to work with in the Page Navigation tab (if you've created more than one master page), and get to work.

Creating another master page

Sometimes creating more than one master page is necessary. In a publication with facing pages, creating two master pages, one for the left-facing pages and another for the right-facing pages, is convenient. Follow these steps to create another master page:

1. **In Master Page view, go to the View tab and select the Page Navigation check box (if it isn't already selected).**

You need to be able to see your new master page in the Page Navigation tab.

2. **On the Master Page tab, click the Add Master Page button.**

The New Master Page dialog box appears.

3. **Select the Two-Page Master check box if you're creating a master page for a publication with pages that will be folded.**

4. **If you want, enter a Page ID and description of your new master page.**

You can read page IDs and a description of master pages by moving the pointer over master page thumbnails in the Page Navigation pane.

5. **Click OK.**

Your new master page appears in the Page Navigation pane.

To turn a single master page into a two-page master (or vice versa), select the master page in the Page Navigation pane and click the Two Page Master button.

Applying (or unapplying) a master page to publication pages

By default, the master page applies to all pages, but sometimes unapplying a master page is necessary because objects on the master page get in the way. And if you created more than one master page, you have to tell Publisher which master page to apply to which publication page.

Follow these instructions to unapply or apply master pages to pages in a publication:

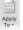

✦ **Unapplying a master page:** In Normal view, go to the Page Design tab, display the page you want to unattach from the master page, click the Master Pages button, and choose None on the drop-down list.

✦ **Applying a different master page:** Use one of these techniques to apply a different master page to pages in your publication:

- In Normal view, display a page, go to the Page Design tab, click the Master Pages button, and choose a different master page on the drop-down list.

- In Master Page view, go to the Master Page tab, select a master page in the Navigation pane, and click the Apply To button. On the Apply To drop-down list, choose Apply to All Pages to apply a different master page to all the pages in your publication. Choose Apply Master Page on the drop-down list and enter page-range numbers in the Apply Master Page dialog box to apply the master page to a select group of pages.

Running the Design Checker

When at last your publication is ready for printing, be sure to run the Design Checker. This helpful tool can alert you to frames that fall on nonprinting parts of the page, stories that "overflow" without finding a text frame to go to, invisible objects, and a host of other problems.

On the File tab, choose Info, and click the Run Design Checker button to run the Design Checker. As shown in Figure 3-7, the Design Checker task pane opens and lists items that need your attention. Open an item's drop-down list and choose Go to This Item to locate it in your publication. Sometimes the drop-down list offers a quick fix as well.

To see which design flaws the Design Checker looks for, click the Design Checker Options hyperlink in the Design Checker task pane. Then, in the Design Checker Options dialog box, select the Checks tab and read the list.

Figure 3-7:
Running
the Design
Checker.

Commercially Printing a Publication

You know the routine for printing a publication on your computer: Go to the
File tab, choose Print, negotiate the Print window, and click the Print button.
Sending a publication to a commercial printer is a different story. Publisher
offers a number of commands for preparing a publication for printing in a
print shop and packing up your publication before sending it to a printer.

Changing the commercial print settings

Commercial printers either print with process colors (also known as CMYK)
or spot colors. To put it simply, process colors are made by mixing cyan,
magenta, yellow, and black to make colors, whereas spot colors are premixed
before printing begins. Before you hand over your publication to a commercial printer, find out which color system the printer prefers. It costs more to
print with process colors than spot colors because process-color printing
requires each color to be created on a different color plate. Process colors,
however, produce color photographs much better than spot colors do.

Consult with the print shop where you intend to take your publication to
find out which color model it prefers and take these steps before handing
over your publication to the printer:

✦ **Choose a color model:** On the File tab, choose Info to go to the Information window. Then click the Commercial Print Settings button and choose Color Model. You see the Color Model dialog box. Choose a color definition setting and click OK.

✦ **Manage embedded fonts:** On the File tab, choose Info to open the Information window. Then click the Commercial Print Settings button and choose Manage Embedded Fonts. You see the Fonts dialog box. Click the Embed TrueType Fonts When Saving Publication check box to embed fonts. Whereas normally Publisher calls upon instructions from the computer to display fonts, embedding fonts make those instructions part of the file itself. These fonts display the same on all computers, including the computer your printer uses. Embedding fonts, however, makes files grow larger if your publication includes unusual fonts that the printer doesn't have.

Preparing your file for a commercial printer

Publisher offers the Pack and Go command for copying large files onto CDs and embedding fonts in a file. To use the Pack and Go command, go to the File tab, choose Save & Send, and choose Save for a Commercial Printer. Then, on the first drop-down list, choose Commercial Press, and on the second, choose Both PDF and Publisher .pub Files. Finally, click the Pack and Go Wizard button to burn your publication file to a CD or copy it to a removable storage device for use by the printer.

Book VIII

Office 2010:
One Step Beyond

The 5th Wave   By Rich Tennant

"I hate when you bring 'Office' with you on camping trips."

Contents at a Glance

Chapter 1: Customizing an Office Program

In This Chapter

✔ **Personalizing the Ribbon**

✔ **Changing around the Quick Access toolbar**

✔ **Choosing what appears on the status bar**

✔ **Choosing a new color scheme**

✔ **Devising keyboard shortcuts in Word**

This chapter describes a handful of things you can do to customize Office 2010 programs. Don't be afraid to make like a software developer and change a program to your liking. Many people are wary of retooling Office programs, but you can always reverse the changes you make if you don't like them, as I explain throughout this chapter.

This chapter shows how to put your favorite button commands on the Ribbon and Quick Access toolbar. Instead of fishing around for your favorite commands, you can assemble them on the Ribbon or Quick Access toolbar and locate them right away. You also discover how to change around the status bar, dress up an Office program in a new set of clothes, and designate your own keyboard shortcuts in Word.

Customizing the Ribbon

As you surely know by now, the Ribbon is the stretch of ground across the top of all Office programs. The Ribbon is composed of tabs. On each tab, commands are arranged by group. To undertake a task, you visit a tab on the Ribbon, find the group with the command you want, and choose the command. If you are so inclined, you can customize the Ribbon. You can place the tabs and commands you know and love where you want to find them on the Ribbon. And you can remove tabs and commands that aren't useful to you.

To customize the Ribbon, open the Customize Ribbon tab of the Options dialog box with one of these techniques:

File

✦ On the File tab, choose Options, and select the Customize Ribbon category in the Options dialog box.

✦ Right-click a tab or button and choose Customize the Ribbon.

You see commands for customizing the Ribbon, as shown in Figure 1-1. The right side of the dialog box ("Customize the Ribbon") lists the names of tabs, groups within tabs, and commands within groups that are currently on the Ribbon. To customize the Ribbon, you arrange the right side of the dialog box to your liking. You list the tabs, groups, and commands that you want for the Ribbon on the right side of the dialog box.

Figure 1-1: Starting in the Customize Ribbon category of the Options dialog box, you can customize the Ribbon.

The left side of the dialog box ("Choose Commands From") presents every tab, group, and command in your Office program. To customize the Ribbon, you select a tab, group, or command on the left side of the dialog box and move it to the right side.

Keep reading to find out how to display tabs, groups, and commands in the Options dialog box and how to do all else that pertains to customizing the Ribbon. In case you make a hash of the Ribbon, you also find instructions for restoring the Ribbon to its original state.

Displaying and selecting tab, group, and command names

To customize the Ribbon, you need to display and select tab names, group names, and command names in the Options dialog box (refer to Figure 1-1). Start by opening the drop-down lists and choosing a display option:

✦ **Choose Commands From:** Choose an option to locate the tab, group, or command you want to add to the Ribbon. For example, choose All Commands to see an alphabetical list of all the commands in the Office program you're working in; choose Main Tabs to see a list of tabs.

✦ **Customize the Ribbon:** Choose an option to display the names of all tabs, main tabs, or tool tabs. Tool tabs are the context-sensitive tabs that appear after you insert or click something. For example, the Table Tools tabs appear when you construct tables.

After you choose display options on the drop-down lists, display the names of groups and commands (refer to Figure 1-1):

✦ **Displaying group names:** Click a plus sign icon next to a tab name to see the names of its groups. You can click the minus sign icon to fold group names back into a tab name.

✦ **Displaying command names in groups**: Click the plus sign icon next to a group name to see the names of its commands. You can click the minus sign icon to collapse command names.

After you display the tab, group, or command name, click to select it.

Moving tabs and groups on the Ribbon

To change the order of tabs on the Ribbon or groups on a tab, go to the Customize Ribbon category of the Options dialog box (refer to Figure 1-1) and select the name of a tab or group on the right side of the dialog box. Then click the Move Up or Move Down button. Click these buttons as necessary until tabs or groups are in the order that you see fit.

Be careful about moving groups by clicking the Move Up or Move Down button. Clicking these buttons too many times can move a group to a different tab on the Ribbon.

Adding, removing, and renaming tabs, groups, and commands

In the Options dialog box (refer to Figure 1-1), display and select the tab, group, or command you want to add, remove, or rename. Then proceed to add, remove, or rename it. (Earlier in this chapter, "Displaying and selecting tab, group, and command names" explains how to display items in the Options dialog box.)

Adding items to the Ribbon

Follow these steps to add a tab, group, or command to the Ribbon:

1. **On the left side of the Customize Ribbon tab of the Options dialog box, select the tab, group, or command you want to add.**

   For example, to add the Tables group to the Home tab, select the Tables group.

2. **On the right side of the dialog box, select the tab or group where you want to place the item.**

   If you're adding a tab to the Ribbon, select a tab. The tab you add will go after the tab you select.

3. **Click the Add button.**

Removing items from the Ribbon

Follow these steps to remove a tab, group, or command from the Ribbon:

1. **On the right side of the Customize Ribbon tab of the Options dialog box, select the tab, group, or command you want to remove.**

2. **Click the Remove button.**

   Except for tabs you create yourself, you can't remove tabs from the Ribbon. And you can't remove a command unless you remove it from a group you created yourself.

Renaming tabs and groups

Sorry, you can't rename a command. As for tabs and groups, you can rename them, but only if you created them yourself. Tabs and groups that came with Office can't be renamed. Follow these steps to rename a tab or group:

1. **On the right side of the Customize Ribbon tab of the Options dialog box, select the tab or group you want to rename.**

2. **Click the Rename button.**

   You see the Rename dialog box.

3. **Enter a new name and click OK.**

Creating new tabs and groups

Create new tabs and groups on the Ribbon for commands that are especially useful to you. Follow these steps on the Customize Ribbon tab of the Options dialog box (refer to Figure 1-1) to create a new tab or group:

1. **On the right side of the dialog box, display and select the name of a tab or group.**

   Earlier in this chapter, "Displaying and selecting tab, group, and command names" explains how to select items in the Options dialog box.

   • *Tab:* If you're creating a tab, select a tab name. The tab you create will appear after the tab you select.

   • *Group:* If you're creating a group, select a group name. The group you create will appear after the group you select.

2. **Click the New Tab or New Group button.**

   Your Office program creates a new tab or group called "New Tab (Custom)" or "New Group (Custom)." If you created a tab, Office also creates a new group inside your new tab.

3. **Click the Rename button to give the tab, group, or both a name.**

   In the Rename dialog box, enter a descriptive name and click OK. If you're naming a group, the Rename dialog box gives you the opportunity to select an icon to help identify the group.

4. **Add groups, commands, or both to your newly made tab or group.**

   For instructions, see "Adding items to the Ribbon," earlier in this chapter.

Resetting your Ribbon customizations

If you make a hash of the Ribbon, all is not lost because you can restore the original settings. In the Options dialog box, click the Reset button (refer to Figure 1-1) and choose one of these commands on the drop-down list:

✦ **Reset Only Selected Ribbon Tab:** Select a tab name on the right side of the Options dialog box and choose this command to restore a tab to its original state.

✦ **Reset All Customizations:** Choose this command to restore the Ribbon in its entirety. All changes you made are reversed.

You can also remove tabs and groups you created if you discover you don't need them. See "Removing items from the Ribbon," earlier in this chapter.

Exporting and importing program customizations

You can preserve your Ribbon and Quick Access toolbar customizations for posterity in a special file called an Import Customization file; these files have the `.exportedUI` file extension. Keep the file on hand for when you need it, or distribute the file to co-workers. For that matter, a co-worker who is proud of his or her customizations can send them to you in a file and you can load the customizations into your Office program.

To save your Ribbon and Quick Access toolbar customization settings in a file, go to the File tab, choose Options, and visit the Customize

Ribbon or Quick Access Toolbar category of the Options dialog box. Then click the Import/Export button and choose Export All Customizations on the drop-down list. The File Save dialog box opens. Give the customizations file a name and click the Save button.

To load customizations from a file into your Office program, return to the Customize Ribbon or Quick Access Toolbar category of the Options dialog box, click the Import/Export button, and choose Import Customization File. You see the File Open dialog box. Select the file and click the Open button.

Customizing the Quick Access Toolbar

No matter where you go in Office, you see the Quick Access toolbar in the upper-left corner of the screen. This toolbar offers the Save, Undo, and Repeat buttons. However, which buttons appear on the Quick Access toolbar is entirely up to you. You can put your favorite buttons on the toolbar to keep them within reach. And if the Quick Access toolbar gets too big, you can move it below the Ribbon, as shown in Figure 1-2. Adding buttons to and removing buttons from the Quick Access toolbar is, I'm happy to report, a piece of cake. And moving the toolbar below the Ribbon is as easy as pie.

Right-click a button to add it to the toolbar

Figure 1-2:
Merely by right-clicking, you can add a button to the Quick Access toolbar.

The Quick Access toolbar below the Ribbon

Adding buttons to the Quick Access toolbar

Use one of these techniques to add buttons to the Quick Access toolbar:

✦ Right-click a button you want to see on the toolbar and choose Add to Quick Access Toolbar on the shortcut menu (refer to Figure 1-2). You can add all the commands in a group to the Quick Access toolbar by right-clicking the group name and choosing Add to Quick Access Toolbar.

✦ Click the Customize Quick Access Toolbar button (this button is located to the right of the Quick Access toolbar) and choose a button on the drop-down list. The list offers buttons deemed most likely to be placed on the Quick Access toolbar by the makers of Office.

✦ On the File tab, choose Options, and select the Quick Access Toolbar category in the Options dialog box (or right-click any button or tab and choose Customize Quick Access Toolbar on the shortcut menu). You see the Quick Access Toolbar category of the Options dialog box, as shown in Figure 1-3. On the Choose Commands From drop-down list, select the name of the tab with the button you want to add to the Quick Access toolbar. Then select the button's name and click the Add button.

Select a tab   Select a button and click Add

Figure 1-3: Add, remove, and reorder Quick Access toolbar buttons in the Options dialog box.

Book VIII Chapter 1

Customizing an Office Program

To restore the Quick Access toolbar to its original buttons, click the Reset button in the Options dialog box (refer to Figure 1-3) and choose Reset Only Quick Access Toolbar on the drop-down list. Choosing Reset All Customizations resets Ribbon customizations as well as Quick Access toolbar customizations.

Changing the order of buttons on the Quick Access toolbar

Follow these steps to change the order of buttons on the Quick Access toolbar:

1. **Click the Customize Quick Access Toolbar button and choose More Commands on the drop-down list.**

   The Quick Access Toolbar category of the Options dialog box appears (refer to Figure 1-3). You can also open this dialog box by right-clicking any button or tab and choosing Customize Quick Access Toolbar.

2. **Select the name of a button on the right side of the dialog box and click the Move Up or Move Down button.**

3. **Repeat Step 2 until the buttons are in the right order.**

4. **Click OK.**

Removing buttons from the Quick Access toolbar

Use one of these techniques to remove buttons from the Quick Access toolbar:

✦ Right-click a button and choose Remove from Quick Access Toolbar on the shortcut menu.

✦ Right-click any button or tab and choose Customize Quick Access Toolbar. You see the Quick Access Toolbar category of the Options dialog box (refer to Figure 1-3). Select the button you want to remove on the right side of the dialog box and click the Remove button.

You can click the Reset button in the Options dialog box (refer to Figure 1-3) to remove all the buttons you placed on the Quick Access toolbar.

Placing the Quick Access toolbar above or below the Ribbon

The Ribbon is the stretch of ground along the top of the screen where the tabs and buttons are found. If your Quick Access toolbar contains many buttons, consider placing it below the Ribbon, not above it (refer to Figure 1-3). Follow these instructions to place the Quick Access toolbar above or below the Ribbon:

✦ **Quick Access toolbar below the Ribbon:** Right-click the toolbar, and on the shortcut menu, choose Show Quick Access Toolbar Below the Ribbon.

✦ **Quick Access toolbar above the Ribbon:** Right-click the toolbar, and on the shortcut menu, choose Show Quick Access Toolbar Above the Ribbon.

The Options dialog box offers a check box called Show Quick Access Toolbar Below the Ribbon (refer to Figure 1-3). You can select this check box as well to move the toolbar below the Ribbon.

Customizing the Status Bar

The status bar along the bottom of the window gives you information about the file you're working on. The Word status bar, for example, tells you which page you're on, how many pages are in your document, and several other things. In PowerPoint, the status bar tells you which slide you're looking at and the theme you chose for your presentation. The status bar also presents the view buttons and Zoom controls.

To choose what appears on the status bar, right-click the status bar. You see a drop-down list similar to the one in Figure 1-4. By selecting and deselecting items in this list, you can decide what appears on the status bar.

Figure 1-4:
Right-click the status bar to customize it.

Changing the Color Scheme

Figure 1-5 shows three color schemes with which you can dress up Excel, Outlook, Access, Word, Publisher, and PowerPoint: Blue, Silver, and Black. Which do you prefer? Follow these steps to choose a color scheme:

Figure 1-5:
Take your choice of these color schemes: Blue (top), Silver (middle), or Black (bottom).

File

1. **On the File tab, choose Options.**

You see the Options dialog box.

2. **Select the General category.**

3. **Open the Color Scheme drop-down list and choose Blue, Silver, or Black.**

4. **Click OK.**

How do you like your new get-up?

Customizing Keyboard Shortcuts in Word

In Microsoft Word, you can change the keyboard shortcuts. A *keyboard shortcut* is a combination of keys that you press to give a command. For example, pressing Ctrl+P opens the Print window; pressing Ctrl+S gives the Save command. If you don't like a keyboard shortcut in Word, you can change it and invent a keyboard shortcut of your own. You can also assign keyboard shortcuts to symbols, macros, fonts, AutoText entries, and styles.

Follow these steps to choose keyboard shortcuts of your own in Microsoft Word:

File

1. **On the File tab, choose Options.**

   You see the Word Options dialog box.

2. **Select the Customize Ribbon category.**

3. **Click the Customize button (you can find it at the bottom of the dialog box next to the words "Keyboard Shortcuts").**

   You see the Customize Keyboard dialog box, as shown in Figure 1-6.

Figure 1-6:
Assigning keyboard shortcuts to Word commands.

Enter the shortcut   Select a command

4. **In the Categories list, choose the category with the command to which you want to assign the keyboard shortcut.**

   At the bottom of the list are the Macros, Fonts, AutoText, Styles, and Common Symbols categories.

5. **Choose the command name, macro, font, AutoText entry, style, or symbol name in the Commands list.**

6. **In the Press New Shortcut Key box, type the keyboard shortcut.**

   Press the actual keys. For example, if the shortcut is Ctrl+8, press the Ctrl key and the 8 key — don't type out C-t-r-l+8.

   If you try to assign a shortcut that has already been assigned, the words "Currently assigned to" and a command name appear below the Current Keys box. You can override the preassigned keyboard assignment by entering a keyboard assignment of your own.

**Book VIII
Chapter 1**

**Customizing an
Office Program**

7. If you want the keyboard shortcut changes you make to apply to the document you're working on, not to all documents created with the template you're working with, open the Save Changes In drop-down list and choose your document's name.

8. Click the Assign button.

9. When you finish assigning keyboard shortcuts, close the Customize Keyboard dialog box.

To delete a keyboard shortcut, display it in the Current Keys box, select it, and click the Remove button.

You can always get the old keyboard shortcuts back by clicking the Reset All button in the Customize Keyboard dialog box.

Chapter 2: Ways of Distributing Your Work

In This Chapter

✔ **Printing files**

✔ **Saving files so that others can read them in Adobe Acrobat Reader**

✔ **Sending a file by e-mail**

✔ **Saving a file so that it can be viewed in a Web browser**

✔ **Writing and keeping a blog from inside Word**

This chapter explains how to distribute your work to co-workers and friends. You'll be glad to know that people who don't have Office 2010 can still read and review an Office 2010 file you created. You can print it for them, save it so that it can be read in Adobe Acrobat Reader, or save it as a Web page. This chapter explains all that as well as how to send a file right away by e-mail and write and post blog entries from inside Word.

By the way, Book IV, Chapter 5 describes other ways to distribute PowerPoint presentations. You can provide audience handouts, ship presentations on CDs, and save presentations as video files.

Printing — the Old Standby

In spite of predictions to the contrary, the paperless office is still a pipe dream. The day when Johnny at his computer is completely digitized and communicating with his colleagues without having to print anything on paper has yet to materialize. As for Jane, she can hardly go a day without printing reports, spreadsheets, and brochures. The office is still awash in paper, and all Jane and Johnny can do for consolation is try their best to recycle.

File

To print a file, preview a file before you print it, and do all else that pertains to printing, go to the File tab and choose Print (or press Ctrl+P). You land in the Print window, as shown in Figure 2-1. From here, you can choose how many copies to print, choose a part of a file to print, and get a look at your file before you print it. Notice that the Print window offers buttons for Zoom controls and buttons for going from page to page (or slide to slide).

Figure 2-1: Starting in the Print window, you can preview and print files.

Distributing a File in PDF Format

As shown in Figure 2-2, you can save and distribute a file in the PDF (Portable Document File) format if the person to whom you want to give the file doesn't have the program with which it was created. For example, someone who doesn't have Excel can still view your Excel file in PDF format. Moreover, you can post PDF files on the Internet so that others can view them there.

About PDF files

PDF files are designed to be viewed and printed in a program called Adobe Reader. This program is very good at acquiring data from other programs and presenting it so that it can be read and printed easily. Nearly every computer has Adobe Reader. If someone to whom you sent a PDF file doesn't have the program, they can download it for free at this Web page:

```
http://get.adobe.com/reader/
```

Figure 2-2:
A Word document as seen through the eyes of Adobe Acrobat Reader.

Saving an Office file as a PDF

Follow these steps to save an Office file as a PDF file:

File

1. **Go to the File tab and choose Save & Send to open the Save & Send window.**

2. **Choose Create PDF/XPS Document.**

3. **Click the Create PDF/XPS button.**

   The Publish as PDF or XPS dialog box appears. If your goal is to create an XPS file, not a PDF file, open the Save As Type drop-down list and choose XPS Document (*.xps). Microsoft created the XPS format to compete with the PDF format. As are PDF files, XPS files are meant to present data from different programs, in this case in Internet Explorer. However, the XPS format is not nearly as well known or frequently used as the PDF format.

4. **Select a folder for storing your PDF (or XPS) file, give it a name, and click the Publish button.**

   The Adobe Reader program opens and you see your file. (If you created an XPS file, Internet Explorer opens.)

Later in this chapter, "Saving an Office File as a Web Page" explains another way to distribute Office files to people who don't have Office — by saving the files as Web pages.

**Book VIII
Chapter 2**

Ways of Distributing Your Work

Sending Your File in an E-Mail Message

As long as you handle your e-mail with Outlook 2010, you can send the file you're working on to a friend or co-worker without having to open Outlook 2010. Moreover, you can send a PDF or XPS version of the file. You simply choose a command and send the thing over the Internet. Follow these steps to send an open file you're working on to a friend or co-worker:

File

1. **Go to the File tab and choose Save & Send.**

   The Save & Send window opens.

2. **Choose Send Using E-Mail.**

3. **Choose a Send Using E-Mail option on the right side of the window.**

   How do you want to send your file? Click one of these buttons:

   - *Send as Attachment:* Send the file as an attachment to an e-mail message.

   - *Send a Link:* Send an e-mail link with a hyperlink to the file on a shared workspace.

   - *Send as PDF:* Send a PDF version of the file as an attachment to an e-mail message.

   - *Send as XPS:* Send an XPS version of the file as an attachment to an e-mail message.

   - *Send as Internet Fax:* Send the file as an Internet fax (you must have signed up with an Internet fax service provider).

   An Outlook 2010 message window appears with the name of your file on the subject line and the file itself in the Attach box. Your presentation is ready to send along with the e-mail message.

4. **Enter the recipient's address in the To box and a message in the Message box.**

   Book III, Chapter 3 explains how to address, compose, and send e-mail messages with Outlook.

5. **Click the Send button.**

   That was fast! It was faster than opening Outlook and attaching the file to the e-mail message on your own.

Saving an Office File as a Web Page

Figure 2-3 shows what a Word document looks like after it is saved as a Web page and displayed in a Web browser. Looks like a normal Word document, doesn't it? Anyone with a Web browser can view a Word document or other Office file after it's saved as a Web page. Save an Office file as a Web page and post it on the Internet so that people who don't have Office can view it.

These pages explain the different ways to save an Office file as a Web page, as well as how to save your Office file as a Web page and open a Web page you created in a Web browser.

Choosing how to save the component parts

When you save an Office file as a Web page, you have the choice of saving it as a Single File Web Page (`.mht`, `.mhtml`) or Web Page (`.htm`, `.html`).

✦ **Single File Web Page (`.mht`, `.mhtml`):** All component parts of the file — graphics, separate pages, and sounds, for example — are bundled into a single file. Keeping all the component parts in one file makes moving, copying, and sending the file easier. However, only the Internet Explorer browser can open and read `.mht` and `.mhtml` files. The popular Mozilla Firefox and Opera browsers can't handle them.

✦ **Web Page (`.htm`, `.html`):** All the component parts of the file are kept in separate files and are saved in the same folder. Keeping the component parts in separate files is the standard way to present pages on the Internet. Handling the half dozen or more files that are needed to display the Web page can be troublesome, but you can be certain that the Web page displays properly in all browsers.

Turning a file into a Web page

Before you save your file as a Web page, create a folder on your computer or computer network for storing the page if you intend to save it in several files in the .htm format. Unless you create a folder for storing all the files, you'll have a hard time locating them later, and you must be able to locate them to transfer them to a Web server for display on the Internet or to send them to someone else.

Follow these steps to save an Office file as a Web page:

1. **Go to the File tab and choose Save & Send.**

   The Save & Send window opens.

2. **Choose Change File Type.**

   Change File Type options appear on the right side of the window.

3. **Save your file as a single file Web page or Web page.**

   The previous topic in this chapter, "Choosing how to save the component parts," explains the difference between the two.

   - *Single file Web page:* Choose the Single File Web Page (*.mht, *.mhtml) option. The Save As dialog box opens.

   - *Web page:* Choose the Save as Another File Type option, and when the Save As dialog box appears, open the Save as Type drop-down list and choose Web Page (*.htm; *.html).

4. **In the Save As dialog box, click the Change Title button, enter a descriptive title in the Enter Text dialog box, and click OK.**

   The title you enter will appear in the title bar along the top of the Web browser window.

5. **Choose a folder for storing your new Web page.**

   If you followed my advice about creating a Web page, choose the folder you recently created for storing the page and its attendant files.

6. **Click the Save button.**

   If your file includes features that can't be displayed in a Web browser, the Compatibility Checker dialog box tells you what those features are. Click the Continue button to create your Web page.

Opening a Web page in your browser

To open a Web page you fashioned from an Office file, open the folder where you stored the Web page in Computer or Windows Explorer and double-click the .htm or .mht file. For example, if your file is called Sales Projections, double-click the Sales Projections.htm or Sales Projections.mht file to open the Web page.

Blogging from inside Word

The word *blog* is shorthand for *Web log*. A typical blog is a hodgepodge of commentary and links to online news sources and often other blogs where topics of concern to the blogger are discussed. Many blogs are online diaries. You get a daily picture of what the blogger is interested in — dating, technology, politics, and just about anything else under the sun.

To make it easier to keep a blog, Word offers special commands for writing blog entries and posting them immediately with a blogging service. Figure 2-4 shows the blogging feature in action. The title and the blog entry in the Word document are transported *in toto* to the blog without your having to enter a password or even visit a blogging service. What's more, Word offers a special Blog Post tab for posting blog entries and managing accounts with your blogging service. To take advantage of Word's blogging feature, you must already have an account with a blogging service.

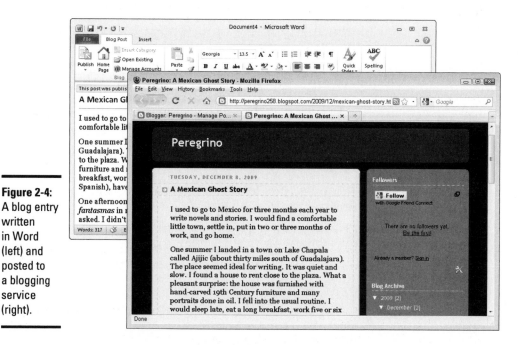

Figure 2-4:
A blog entry written in Word (left) and posted to a blogging service (right).

Describing a blog account to Word

Word can't post entries to a blog unless you tell it where the blog is located, what your password is, and some other juicy tidbits. As of this writing, Word is compatible with these blogging services: Blogger, Community Server, Sharepoint Blog, TypePad, and WordPress.

Follow these steps to register your blogging account with Word so that Word can upload blog entries:

1. **Go to the File tab and choose Save & Send.**

   The Save & Send window opens.

2. **Choose Publish as Blog Post.**

3. **Click the Publish as Blog Post button.**

   You see the Register a Blog Account dialog box.

4. **Click the Register Now button and answer questions in the dialog box to describe the blogging service you use.**

   Which questions you are asked depends on which blogging service you use. You're asked for a username and password, and also perhaps an http or ftp address for publishing pictures on your blog.

After you finish describing your blogging service, you will be pleased to discover a new tab in Word — the Blog Post tab (refer to Figure 2-4). You can use this tab to post blog entries and manage your blog accounts.

Posting an entry to your blog

When you're ready to share your thoughts with the world, follow these steps to write and post an entry to your blog from inside Word:

1. **In Word, write the entry from scratch or open a document you've already written.**

   You can start from a new document, or if you've written the entry, open the Word document with the entry.

2. **Go to the File tab, choose Save & Send, choose Publish as Blog Post, and click the Publish as Blog Post button.**

   You land in the Blog Post tab (refer to Figure 2-4). It offers all the character styles and proofing tools that you find in Word. Go to the Insert tab to enter a hyperlink. (Book I, Chapter 2 explains hyperlinks.)

3. **Enter a title for your blog entry in the space provided.**

4. **When you finish writing and preparing your blog entry, click the Publish button on the Blog Post tab.**

   If all goes well, Word informs you that your post has been published on your blogging service, and it lists the time and date it was published. This information appears in the Word document itself.

Instead of publishing your blog entry right away, you can open the drop-down list on the Publish button and choose Publish as Draft. Doing so uploads the blog entry to your blogging service without posting it. The entry lands on the Editing page, where you can select it, click the Editing button, and edit it online before publishing it.

Taking advantage of the Blog Post tab

By clicking buttons on the Blog Post tab, you can manage blog entries:

✦ **Go to your blog page:** Click the Home Page button to open your browser and display the home page of your blog.

✦ **Edit a blog entry:** Click the Open Existing button, and in the Open Existing Post dialog box, select a blog entry and click OK. The entry appears in Word. Edit it and click the Publish button to post it on your blog.

✦ **Manage accounts:** Click the Manage Accounts button to describe a new account to Word, change a blog account, or remove a blog account. Word provides the Blog Accounts dialog box for doing these activities.

Chapter 3: Handling Graphics

In This Chapter

- ✔ Understanding the different graphic file formats
- ✔ Placing a graphic in a Word document, PowerPoint slide, Excel worksheet, or Publisher publication
- ✔ Recoloring, cropping, and otherwise altering a picture
- ✔ Compressing graphics
- ✔ Handling graphics with Office Picture Manager

A picture, so they say, is worth a thousand words. Whether it's worth a thousand words or merely 950 is debatable. What is certain is that visuals help people remember things. A carefully chosen image in a PowerPoint presentation, Word document, Excel worksheet, or Publisher publication helps others understand you better. The image reinforces the ideas or information that you're trying to put across.

This chapter explains how you can make pictures — photographs and graphics — part of your Word documents, PowerPoint presentations, Excel worksheets, and Publisher publications. It looks into graphic file formats, copyrights, and other issues pertaining to graphics as well as how to touch up graphics in an Office program and in an auxiliary program called Office Picture Manager.

By the way, the next chapter looks at another way to decorate your work with images. It looks at using clip art.

All about Picture File Formats

Graphics and photographs come in many different file formats, and as far as Office 2010 is concerned, some are better than others. These pages explain what you need to know about graphic files to use them wisely in Office files. Here, you find out what bitmap and vector graphics are, what resolution and color depth are, and how graphic files are compressed.

Bitmap and vector graphics

All graphic images fall in the bitmap or vector category:

✦ A *bitmap graphic* is composed of thousands upon thousands of tiny dots called *pixels* that, taken together, form an image (the term pixel comes from "picture element").

✦ A *vector graphic* is drawn with the aid of computer instructions that describe the shape and dimension of each line, curve, circle, and so on.

The major difference between the two formats is that vector graphics do not distort when you enlarge or shrink them, whereas bitmap graphics lose resolution when their size is changed. Furthermore, vector images do not require nearly as much hard drive space as bitmap graphics. Drop a few bitmap graphics in a file and soon you're dealing with a file that is close to 750K in size.

Table 3-1 describes popular bitmap graphic formats; Table 3-2 lists popular vector graphic formats.

Table 3-1	Bitmap Graphic File Formats	
Extension	*File Type*	*Compression*
BMP, BMZ, DIB	Microsoft Windows Bitmap	None
FPX	FlashPix	Lossy
GFA, GIF	Graphics Interchange Format	Lossy
JPEG, JPG, JFIF, JPE	JPEG File Interchange Format	Lossy
PCD	Kodak Photo CD	Lossy
PICT	Macintosh PICT	None
PCX	PC Paintbrush	Lossless
PNG	Portable Network Graphics	Lossless
RLE	Bitmap File in RLE Compression Scheme	None
TIF, TIFF	Tagged Image File Format	Lossless

Table 3-2	Vector Graphic File Formats
Extension	*File Type*
CDR	CorelDRAW
CGM	Computer Graphics Metafile

Extension	File Type
DXF	AutoCAD Format 2-D
EMF	Enhanced Windows Metafile
EMZ	Windows Enhanced Metafile
EPS	Encapsulated PostScript
PCT	Macintosh PICT
WMF	Windows Metafile
WPG	WordPerfect Graphics

Resolution

Resolution refers to how many pixels comprise a bitmap image. The higher the resolution, the clearer the image is. Resolution is measured in *dots per inch* (dpi), sometimes called *pixels per inch* (ppi). Images with more dots (or pixels) per inch are clearer and display more fineness of detail. When you scan an image, your scanner permits you to choose a dots-per-inch setting.

High-resolution images look better but require more hard drive space than low-resolution images. Figure 3-1 illustrates the difference between a high- and low-resolution photograph.

Figure 3-1: A high-resolution photo (left) and the same photo at low resolution (right).

Compression

Compression refers to a mathematical algorithm by which bitmap graphic files can be made smaller. In effect, compression enables your computer to store a bitmap graphic with less hard drive space. Some bitmap graphic types can't be compressed; the other bitmap graphic types are compressed using either lossless or lossy compression:

✦ **Lossless compression:** To maintain the picture's integrity, the same number of pixels is stored in the compressed file as in the original. Because the pixels remain intact, you can change the size of a file that has undergone lossless compression without losing picture quality.

✦ **Lossy compression:** Without regard for the picture's integrity, pixel data in the original picture is lost during compression. Therefore, if you try to enlarge a picture that has undergone lossy compression, the picture loses quality.

Choosing file formats for graphics

One of the challenges of using graphics and photographs in Office files is keeping file sizes to a minimum. A file that is loaded down with many photographs can take a long time to load and send over the Internet because graphics and photographs make files that much larger. The trick is to find a balance between high-quality, high-resolution graphics and the need to keep files sizes low. Here are some tips for choosing graphic file formats:

✦ Consider sticking with vector graphics if you're including graphics in your file strictly for decoration purposes. As Chapter 4 of this minibook explains, Office provides vector clip-art images. These images are easy to come by, don't require very much hard drive space, and can be edited inside Word, PowerPoint, Excel, and Publisher.

✦ For photographs, make JPEG your first choice for graphics. JPEG images have a fairly high resolution. If you intend to post your file on the Internet, you can't go wrong with JPEGs; they are the de facto photograph standard on the Internet.

✦ If you're dealing with black-and-white photos or resolution doesn't matter, use GIF files. These files eat up the least amount of hard drive space.

The All-Important Copyright Issue

To save any image on the Internet to your computer, all you have to do is right-click it and choose Save Picture As. By starting from Google Image Search (www.images.google.com), you can scour the Internet for any image you need. Never before has it been easier to obtain images for your own use.

Still, obtaining images and using them legally are two different matters. Would it surprise you to know that the vast majority of graphics can't be used without the owner's permission? The copyright laws have a "fair use" provision for borrowing written words. You can quote others' words as long as you cite the author and work and you don't quote passages longer than 250 to a thousand words (the "fair use" provision is vague on this point).

The copyright law regarding graphics is quite straightforward. Unless you have the owner's permission, you can't legally use a graphic.

Sometimes it's hard to tell who owns a graphic. The artist or photographer (or his or her estate) doesn't necessarily own the copyright because artists sometimes relinquish their copyrights when they create works for hire. The only way to get permission to use a graphic is to ask. Contact the owner of the Web site with the image you want, the publisher if the image is in a book, or the museum if the work is owned by a museum. You will be asked to write a letter describing precisely how you intend to use the image, reproduce it, and distribute it. Your letter should also say how long you intend to use it and at what size you intend to reproduce it.

Inserting a Picture in an Office File

After you've weighed the merits of different kinds of graphics and decided which one is best for you, you can insert it. Inserting a picture is as simple as choosing it in the Insert Picture dialog box. Follow these steps to insert a picture on a PowerPoint slide, Word document, Excel worksheet, or Publisher page:

1. **Go to the Insert tab.**

2. **Click the Picture button.**

   You see the Insert Picture dialog box, as shown in Figure 3-2. In PowerPoint, you can also open this dialog box by clicking the picture icon in a content placeholder frame.

Choose a Views option   Select a picture file

Figure 3-2: You can preview a picture file before you insert it.

3. **Select a file in the Insert Picture dialog box.**

   As Figure 3-2 shows, you can open the drop-down list on the Views button and choose an option to see what a graphic looks like.

   You can click the File Types button to open a drop-down list and choose a file type to locate files of a certain type in the dialog box. Move the pointer over a picture in the dialog box to get information about its file type, dimensions, and size.

4. **Click the Insert button.**

   Select the (Picture Tools) Format tab to see all the different ways you can manipulate a picture after you insert it.

   After a picture lands on a file, it becomes an object. Book I, Chapter 8 explains how to manipulate objects — how to move them, change their size, and change their borders. Later in this chapter, "Touching Up a Picture" looks into various ways to change the appearance of graphics.

   If you chose the wrong picture, don't fret because you can exchange one picture for another. On the (Picture Tools) Format tab, click the Change Picture button and select a different picture in the Insert Picture dialog box.

Shooting a screenshot

Word, PowerPoint, Excel, and Outlook make it easier than ever to take a picture of a screen on your computer and insert it in a document, slide, worksheet, or e-mail message. Follow these steps to take a picture of a screen:

1. **If you want to capture a portion of one screen, open the screen.**

2. **On the Insert tab, click the Screenshot button.**

   A drop-down list shows you thumbnail images of each screen that is open on your computer.

3. **Choose a thumbnail image to shoot an entire screen, or choose Screen Clipping and drag on-screen to shoot a portion of a screen.**

A picture of the screen or a portion of the screen lands in your document, slide, worksheet, or e-mail message.

Here are a couple of other tried-and-true techniques for capturing screens:

- ✔ Press PrtScn (that is, the Print Screen key to the right of F12) to capture an entire screen to the Clipboard.

- ✔ Press Alt+PrtScn to capture the active part of the screen to the Clipboard. For example, to capture a dialog box, select the dialog box and press Alt+PrtScn.

After the screen capture is on the Clipboard, you can paste it where you will.

Touching Up a Picture

Every picture can be a collaboration. You can do the following to make a picture your own as well as the work of the original artist:

✦ **Softening and sharpening:** Mute or polish a picture. See "Softening and sharpening pictures," later in this chapter.

✦ **Changing the brightness and contrast**: Adjust a picture's tone. See "Correcting a picture's brightness and contrast."

✦ **Recoloring:** Give your picture a brand-new set of colors or gray shades. See "Recoloring a picture."

✦ **Choosing an artistic effect:** Take your picture for a walk on the wild side. See "Choosing an artistic effect."

✦ **Choosing a picture style:** Present your picture in an oval fame, soft-edged frame, or other type of frame. See "Selecting a picture style."

✦ **Cropping:** Cut out the parts of a picture that you don't want. See "Cropping off part of a picture."

✦ **Removing picture areas:** Keep the essentials of a picture and remove the rest. See "Removing the background."

To touch up a picture, visit the (Picture Tools) Format tab. As shown in Figure 3-3, you can also open the Format Picture dialog box and choose settings in these categories: Picture Corrections, Picture Color, Artistic Effects, and Crop. To open the Format Picture dialog box, right-click a picture and choose Format Picture on the shortcut menu.

Figure 3-3:
Touching up
a photo in
the Format
Picture
dialog box.

**Book VIII
Chapter 3**

Handling Graphics

If you regret experimenting with your picture and you want to start all over, go to the (Picture Tools) Format tab and click the Reset Picture button. Clicking this button restores a picture to its original condition.

 PowerPoint, Word, Excel, and Publisher offer only a handful of tools for changing a picture's appearance. If you have the time and the inclination, alter a graphic's appearance in a program designed especially for that purpose. You can find many more options for editing graphics in Photoshop, Paint Shop Pro, and Corel Photo-Paint, for example. Later in this chapter, "Using Microsoft Office Picture Manager" describes a nifty program that comes with Office for editing pictures.

Softening and sharpening pictures

Figure 3-4 shows the effects of the softening/sharpening settings. These settings mute a picture or make it look more succinct. To soften or sharpen a picture, select it and use one of these techniques:

✦ On the (Picture Tools) Format tab, click the Corrections button and choose a Sharpen and Soften option on the drop-down list.

✦ Open the Format Picture dialog box to the Picture Corrections category and drag the Soften-Sharpen slider or enter a negative or positive number in the text box. Negative numbers soften the picture; positive numbers sharpen it. To open the Format Picture dialog box, right-click your picture and choose Format Picture.

Figure 3-4:
Effects
of the
softening/
sharpening
settings.

Correcting a picture's brightness and contrast

Figure 3-5 shows a picture that has been made over several times with the Brightness and Contrast settings. Brightness settings govern the overall brightness of a picture; contrast settings determine how distinguishable the different parts of the picture are from one another. Change a picture's brightness and contrast to make it fit better on a page or slide. Select your picture and use one of these techniques:

Corrections ▾

✦ On the (Picture Tools) Format tab, click the Corrections button and choose a Brightness and Contrast option on the drop-down list.

✦ Open the Format Picture dialog box to the Picture Corrections category and change the Brightness and Contrast settings. Negative Brightness settings make a picture darker; positive settings make it brighter. Negative Contrast settings mute the differences between the parts of a picture; positive settings heighten the differences. To open the Format Picture dialog box, right-click your picture and choose Format Picture.

Figure 3-5:
Effects
of the
Brightness
and
Contrast
settings.

Recoloring a picture

Recolor a picture to give it a makeover. Figure 3-6 shows examples of Recolor options. As well as recoloring a picture, you can change its color saturation and color tone settings. *Color saturation* refers to the purity and intensity of the colors; *color tone* determines the degree of lightness and darkness. Recoloring is useful for giving a picture a uniform appearance. Select your picture and use these techniques to recolor it:

Color ▾

✦ On the (Picture Tools) Format tab, click the Color button and choose a Color Saturation, Color Tone, or Recolor option on the drop-down list. You can choose More Variations at the bottom of the list and choose a color on the sublist.

✦ Open the Format Picture dialog box to the Picture Color category and change the Color Saturation and Color Tone settings. Change the Saturation setting to mute or bring out the colors; change the Temperature setting to make the color tones darker or lighter. To open the Format Picture dialog box, right-click your picture and choose Format Picture.

Book VIII
Chapter 3

Handling Graphics

Figure 3-6:
Examples
of Recolor
options.

Making a color transparent

The (Picture Tools) Format tab offers the Set Transparent Color command for making one color in a picture transparent and thereby allowing the background to show through in certain parts of a picture. The Set Transparent Color command works by making all the pixels in a picture that are the same color transparent. In a picture in which one color predominates, you can make this color transparent and get some interesting effects.

To experiment with the Set Transparent Color command:

1. **Select the picture.**

2. **On the (Picture Tools) Format tab, click the Color button and choose Set Transparent Color on the drop-down list.**

3. **Click in your picture on the color that you want to be transparent.**

You can choose the Set Transparent Color command again and make another color in your picture transparent.

 Live-previewing really comes in handy when you're recoloring a graphic. Move the Format Picture dialog box to the side of your picture and watch what happens when you change the Picture Color settings.

Choosing an artistic effect

Figure 3-7 demonstrates four of the 23 artistic effects that you can apply to a picture: Pencil Sketch, Glow Diffused, Glass, and Glow Edges. To experiment with the artistic effects and maybe find one to your liking, select your picture and use one of these techniques:

🔲 Artistic Effects ▾

+ Go to the (Picture Tools) Format tab, click the Artistic Effects button, and choose an effect on the drop-down list.

+ Open the Format Picture dialog box to the Artistic Effects category and choose an artistic effect. To open the Format Picture dialog box, right-click your picture and choose Format Picture.

Figure 3-7:
Examples
of artistic
effects.

Selecting a picture style

A *picture style* is way of presenting or framing a picture. Figure 3-8 shows examples of picture styles. Picture styles include Simple Frame, Soft Edge Rectangle, Perspective Shadow, and Reflected Bevel. To choose a picture style for a picture, select it, go to the (Picture Tools) Format tab, open the Picture Styles gallery, and choose a style.

Figure 3-8:
Examples
of picture
styles.

If you don't like the picture style you chose (or you don't care for any change you made to a picture), click the Reset Picture button to reverse all your format changes and start over.

If you like the picture styles, you may be enamored as well with the picture effects. On the (Picture Tools) Format tab, click the Picture Effects button and experiment with the options on the drop-down list and sublists.

Cropping off part of a picture

Cropping means to cut off part of a picture. I'm afraid you can't use the Office cropping tool like a pair of scissors or an Xacto knife to zigzag cut around the edges of a picture or cut a hole in the middle. You can, however, cut strips from the side, top, or bottom. In Figure 3-9, the cropping tool is being used to cut off extraneous parts of a picture.

Figure 3-9: Cropping off parts of a picture.

Select your picture, go to the (Picture Tools) Format tab, and use one of these techniques to crop it:

+ **Crop manually:** Crop the picture by dragging its cropping handles. Click the Crop button. Cropping handles appear around the picture, as in Figure 3-9. Drag cropping handles to lop off a part or parts of the picture. Click the Crop button again or press Esc after you finish cropping.

+ **Crop to a shape:** Crop the picture to a rectangle, circle, or other shape. Open the drop-down list on the Crop button, choose Crop to Shape, and select a shape in the Shapes gallery.

+ **Crop to proportions:** Crop the picture to a proportional size setting. Open the drop-down list on the Crop button, choose Aspect Ratio, and choose a ratio. For example, choose 1:1 to crop to a perfect square with the width and height the same size.

+ **Crop by filling:** For placing an image in a picture placeholder, crop the image to make it fit in the placeholder box.

+ **Crop by fitting:** For placing an image in a picture placeholder, shrink the picture to make it fit.

With the cropping handles showing, you can drag the picture left, right, up, or down to determine where it is cropped.

Another way to crop pictures is to click the Size group button on the (Picture Tools) Format tab and enter measurements in the Crop category of the Format Picture dialog box. Use this method if you need to crop several different pictures in the same manner.

When you crop a picture, you don't cut off a part of it — not as far as your computer is concerned. All you do is tell Office not to display part of a graphic. The graphic is still whole. You can, however, compress a graphic after you crop it, and in so doing truly shave off a part of the graphic and thereby decrease the size of the file you're working with, as "Compressing Pictures to Save Hard Drive Space" explains later in this chapter.

Removing the background

Yet another way to diddle with pictures is to use the Remove Background command. This command endeavors to locate the unessential parts of a picture so that you can remove them, which sometimes means removing the foreground or the background, as shown in Figure 3-10. Select a picture and follow these steps to test-drive the Remove Background command:

1. **On the (Picture Tools) Format tab, click the Remove Background button.**

   The Background Removal tab opens and the parts of your picture that Office wants to remove turn a lurid shade of magenta, which you could see in the middle of Figure 3-10 if this book were in color.

Figure 3-10:
Removing parts of a picture (in this case the sky).

2. **On the Background Removal tab, indicate what you want to keep and remove.**

Keep your eye on what's magenta and what's not as you use these techniques, and consider zooming to 200 percent or more so that you can get a good look at your picture:

- *Changing the size of the box:* Drag the side and corner handles of the box to capture what you want to keep or remove.

- *Marking what you want to keep:* Click the Mark Areas to Keep button. The pointer changes into a pencil. Click your picture to indicate what you want to keep. Each time you click, a keep mark (a plus sign icon) appears on your picture.

- *Marking what you want to remove:* Click the Mark Areas to Remove button. The pointer changes to a pencil. Click your picture to indicate what you want to remove. When you click, a remove mark (a minus sign) appears.

- *Deleting keep and remove marks:* Click the Delete Mark button and then click a keep or remove mark to remove a mark and change what is and isn't removed from the picture.

Of course, you can click the Undo button to backtrack as you work. If you get thoroughly lost on the Background Removal tab, click the Discard All Changes button and start all over.

3. Click the Keep Changes button when you finish marking what you want to keep and remove.

How do you like your picture now? If it needs more work, click the Remove Background button again and diddle some more on the Background Removal tab. Click the Discard All Changes button if you want your original picture without the background removed.

Compressing Pictures to Save Hard Drive Space

By compressing pictures, you reduce their file size and consequently the size of the file you're working on. Not all pictures can be compressed, as "Compression" explains earlier in this chapter, and some types of graphics lose their integrity when they're compressed. You can't resize lossy-compressed graphics without their looking odd.

Compress pictures to make files load faster and make e-mail messages with file attachments travel faster over the Internet. Compressing a picture file reduces its pixels per inch (ppi) setting. Follow these steps to compress pictures:

1. **Optionally, select the picture or pictures you want to compress if you want to compress only one or two.**

The Compress Pictures command compresses all the graphics in a file unless you select graphics first.

2. Go to the (Picture Tools) Format tab.

3. Click the Compress Pictures button.

You see the Compress Pictures dialog box.

4. Select the Apply to Selected Pictures Only check box if you selected graphics in Step 1 and you want to compress only a couple of graphics.

5. Click the Delete Cropped Areas of Pictures check box if you want to delete the unused portions of pictures you cropped.

As "Cropping off part of a picture" explains earlier in this chapter, Office crops graphics in name only. It retains the cropped part of the graphic in case you want it back, but you can remove the cropped part as well by selecting this check box.

6. Choose a target output for the pictures.

These options tell Office which pixels per inch (ppi) setting to use when compressing graphics. Which setting you choose depends on where you intend to show your graphics. Graphics to be shown on a computer monitor need be no more than 72 ppi. If you intend to print your graphics, choose a setting in the 600–3000 ppi range. To print for an offset publication, choose an even higher setting.

7. Click OK.

Using Microsoft Office Picture Manager

You may not know it, but you installed a program for managing and editing pictures when you installed Office. The program is called Microsoft Office Picture Manager, and you can use it to organize graphics and touch up graphics before inserting them in a PowerPoint, Word, Excel, or Publisher file. As shown in Figure 3-11, Picture Manager displays graphics so that you can see precisely what your editorial changes do to them. The program makes it easy to find and organize graphic files on your computer. It also provides tools for editing graphics.

To open Picture Manager, click the Start button and choose All Programs⇨Microsoft Office⇨Microsoft Office 2010 Tools⇨Microsoft Office Picture Manager. You see the window shown in Figure 3-11. Starting there, you can display a graphic on your computer and change its appearance in several different ways.

Edit a graphic

Select a folder   Change views   Zoom in or out

Figure 3-11:
The Picture
Manager
window in
Filmstrip
view.

Mapping the graphic files on your computer

The first step in using the Picture Manager is to point to the folders on your computer where important graphic files are located. After you tell Picture Manager which folders graphic files are kept in, shortcuts to the folders appear in the Picture Shortcuts pane on the left side of the window (refer to Figure 3-11). By clicking one of these shortcuts, you can open a folder, view its contents, and edit a graphic file.

Follow these steps to create shortcuts to folders in the Picture Shortcuts pane:

1. **Choose File⇨Add Picture Shortcut or click the Add Picture Shortcut link in the Picture Shortcuts pane (click the Shortcuts button to see this pane).**

The Add Picture Shortcut dialog box opens.

2. **Select a folder where you store graphics that you want to work with.**

3. **Click the Add button.**

Repeat these steps until you've created shortcuts to folders where you store important graphics.

Instead of pointing to folders one at a time, you can choose File⇨Locate Pictures and have Picture Manager scour your computer or network for the graphic file types you select in the File Types dialog box. Shortcuts to folders with those file types appear in the Picture Shortcuts task pane. If you go this route, however, you'll likely discover many, many folders on your computer where graphic files are kept, and shortcuts to these folders will crowd the Picture Shortcuts task pane.

Click the Shortcuts button (or choose View⇨Shortcuts) to display the Picture Shortcuts task pane. To remove a shortcut from the task pane, right-click it and choose Remove Shortcut.

Displaying the graphic file you want to work with

After you've created shortcuts to the folders where you keep graphic files, you can display a graphic file by following these steps:

1. **Click the Shortcuts button, if necessary, to display the Picture Shortcuts task pane.**

2. **Click a shortcut to a folder.**

   Graphic files in the folder appear in the middle window (refer to Figure 3-11).

3. **Scroll to or choose a different view to pinpoint the file.**

   Picture Manager offers three views: Thumbnails, Filmstrip, and Single Picture. Choose an option on the View menu or click a View button to change views (refer to Figure 3-11).

Double-click a thumbnail image to see a graphic in Single Picture view. To zoom in and out, drag the Zoom Slider.

Editing a picture

With the graphic you want to edit on display, you're ready to start editing. Your next task is to display the editing tools you need on the right side of the window. Picture Manager offers two ways to get the editing tools you need:

✦ Click the Edit Pictures button to display the Edit Pictures task pane. It lists the names of editing tools. Click the link that represents the kind of editing you want to do. For example, to crop a graphic, click the Crop link.

✦ Open the Picture menu and choose Brightness and Contrast, Color, Crop, Rotate and Flip, Red Eye Removal, Resize, or Compress Pictures. For example, choose Picture⇨Crop to cut off part of a graphic.

To let Picture Manager try its hand at improving your graphic, click the AutoCorrect button (or choose Picture➪AutoCorrect).

If you regret making changes to a graphic, choose Edit➪Discard Changes. All changes you made are reversed and you get your original graphic back.

Click the Save button (or press Ctrl+S) to save your graphic after you finish editing it. For that matter, choose File➪Save As before you start editing and save the file under a new name so that you have the original in reserve.

If you edit one picture and go to another without saving the first one, Picture Manager takes notice. Copies of unsaved files are kept in the Unsaved Edits folder. To see the contents of this folder, click Unsaved Edits in the Picture Shortcuts task pane. Unsaved graphics appear on-screen so that you can select and save them, if you so choose.

Adjusting the brightness and contrast

Select a graphic and choose Picture➪Brightness and Contrast or click the Brightness and Contrast hyperlink in the Edit Pictures task pane to adjust a graphic's tonal intensity. You see a Brightness, Contrast, and Midtone slider on the Brightness and Contrast task pane. Without going into too much detail, here is what these sliders do:

✦ **Brightness:** Adjusts the inherent brightness value in each pixel. Increasing the brightness makes the image lighter; decreasing it makes the image darker.

✦ **Contrast:** Increasing the contrast, in the words of a laundry detergent manufacturer, "makes your whites whiter and your darks darker," whereas decreasing the contrast making the tones more similar.

✦ **Midtone:** Redefines the *midtones,* or tonal values between light and shadow, of an image. Dragging the slider to the right brightens the image.

If dragging the sliders doesn't provide the results you want, say the heck with it and just click the Auto Brightness button to let Picture Manager adjust the brightness and contrast for you.

Balancing the colors

Select a graphic and choose Picture➪Color or click the Color hyperlink in the Edit Pictures task pane to fine-tune a graphic's colors.

You can have Picture Manager do the fine-tuning for you. Click the Enhance Color button and then click a part of the graphic that is supposed to be white. If you don't like the results, try balancing the colors in the graphic yourself by dragging these three sliders:

✦ **Amount:** Increasing this value magnifies the hue and saturation settings; decreasing this value minimizes them.

✦ **Hue:** Increasing this value further distinguishes the colors from one another; decreasing this value makes the colors blend.

✦ **Saturation:** Increasing it makes colors more luminous; decreasing this value makes colors grayer.

Cropping a graphic

Select a graphic and choose Picture⇨Crop or click the Crop hyperlink in the Edit Pictures task pane to cut off parts of a graphic. Picture Manager shows precisely how much of the graphic you will crop when you click OK. The Crop task pane is especially useful if you want your graphic to be a certain size. Under Picture Dimensions, you can see exactly how many pixels high and wide your graphic is. By dragging the selected part of the graphic — the part that isn't grayed out — you can be very precise about what part of the graphic remains after you crop.

The Crop task pane offers two ways to crop a graphic:

✦ **Crop at will:** In the Aspect Ratio drop-down list, choose None and then drag a corner or side cropping handle.

✦ **Maintain symmetry when you crop:** Choose an option from the Aspect Ratio drop-down list and select the Landscape or Portrait option button before you drag a corner or side cropping handle. *Aspect ratio* proportionally describes the relationship between a graphic's width and height. For example, at the 4 x 6 aspect ratio, the graphic in Portrait mode is a third taller than it is wide ($\frac{2}{3}$); in Landscape mode, the graphic is a third wider than it is tall. Choose an aspect ratio setting when you want your graphic to have symmetry.

Cropping a graphic doesn't reduce its file size. To reduce a graphic's file size after you've cropped it, compress the graphic. See "Compressing a graphic," later in this chapter.

Book VIII
Chapter 3

Handling Graphics

Rotating and flipping graphics

Select a graphic and choose Picture⇨Rotate and Flip, or click the Rotate and Flip hyperlink in the Edit Pictures task pane to rotate or flip graphics. The Rotate commands turn the graphic on its side; the Flip commands provide mirror images of the original graphic. You can rotate a graphic by degrees by entering a value in the By Degree text box. The Formatting toolbar also offers Rotate buttons for rotating graphics.

Removing "red eyes" from a graphic

Sometimes the subject of a photo appears to have *red eyes,* not because the subject didn't get enough sleep, but because the camera flash made the subject's irises turn red. Follow these steps to remove red eye from a digital flash photograph:

1. **Choose Picture⇨Red Eye Removal or click the Red Eye Removal hyperlink in the Edit Pictures task pane.**

2. **Drag the Zoom slider to the right so that you get a good look at the red eyes in the photo.**

3. **Click each red eye to select it.**

4. **Click the OK button.**

   You can click the Reset Selected Eyes button to start all over, if you need to do that.

Resizing a graphic

To change the size of a graphic, select it and choose Picture⇨Resize or click the Resize hyperlink in the Edit Pictures task pane. You land in the Resize task pane. It offers three ways to change the size of a graphic:

✦ **Predefined Width x Height:** Select this option button, and on the drop-down list, choose the setting that best describes the graphic's size. For example, if you intend to post the graphic on a Web page, choose Web - Large or Web - Small.

✦ **Custom Width x Height:** Select this option button and enter pixel measurements for the width and height of the graphic. Be careful with this option because the graphic doesn't maintain its original proportions unless you calculate the proportions yourself, and when a resized graphic loses its original proportions, it can be skewed or blurred.

✦ **Percentage of Original Width x Height:** Select this option button and enter the percentage by which you want to enlarge or shrink the graphic.

The bottom of the task pane tells you how many pixels wide and high your graphic was to start with and how wide and high it is after resizing.

Compressing a graphic

Near the beginning of this chapter, "Compression" explains what compressing a graphic entails. Compress a graphic to reduce its file size. Compressing a graphic file reduces its pixels per inch (ppi) setting. Some graphic types, however, can't be compressed.

To compress a graphic, select it and choose Picture⇨Compress Pictures or click the Compress Pictures hyperlink in the Edit Pictures task pane. You see the Compress Pictures task pane. The bottom of the task pane tells you how much the graphic shrinks in size after you compress it. Choose a Compress For option button and click OK.

Before you compress a graphic, save a copy. After you compress graphics, you can't get the high-resolution originals back.

Chapter 4: Decorating Files with Clip Art

In This Chapter

✔ Understanding what clip art is

✔ Placing a clip-art image on a page, slide, or worksheet

✔ Changing the look of a clip-art image

✔ Using the Clip Organizer to store, organize, and insert clip art

This chapter explains how you can use clip art to decorate Word documents, PowerPoint slides, Excel worksheets, and Publisher publications. You also find a treatise on how to use the *Microsoft Clip Organizer,* an auxiliary program for storing clip art and other kinds of media files so that you can find the files in a hurry. If you often use media files in your work, you owe it to yourself to look into the Clip Organizer.

What Is Clip Art?

In the old days, long before the invention of computers, people would buy clip-art books. They would literally cut, or clip, images from these books and paste them into posters, letters, and advertisements. Today's clip art is the digital equivalent of old-fashioned clip art. You can paste clip art into computer programs such as Word, PowerPoint, Excel, and Publisher. You can resize clip-art images without the images losing their integrity. The clip art that comes with Office 2010 isn't encumbered by licensing restrictions; it's in the public domain, and you can use it as you please.

Figure 4-1 shows examples of some clip-art images that come with Office. Use images like these to decorate your files. Use them to help illustrate an idea or simply to add a little liveliness to your work. In my experience, the hardest task where clip art is concerned is finding the right image. You can choose from so many images that finding the right one is a chore.

Figure 4-1:
Examples
of clip-art
images.

Inserting a Clip-Art Image

To insert a clip-art image, you open the Clip Art task pane, search in the Clip Organizer for the image you want, and insert the image. The trick to finding the right image is knowing your way around the Clip Organizer. The majority of this chapter explains how to organize the art on your computer so that you can get it by way of the Clip Organizer. For now, you can follow these basic steps to insert a clip-art image in a page, slide, or worksheet:

1. **Go to the Insert tab.**

2. **Click the Clip Art button.**

You see the Clip Art task pane, as shown in Figure 4-2. In PowerPoint, you can also click the Clip-Art icon to insert a clip-art image in a content placeholder frame.

The Clip Art task pane is actually an entrée into the *Clip Organizer,* the Microsoft program for organizing and quickly inserting clip art. (The Clip Organizer is explained in more detail later in "Handling Media Files with the Clip Organizer.")

3. **In the Search For text box, enter a keyword that describes the clip-art image you need.**

Later in this chapter, "Searching for a media file in the Search pane" explains how keywords work.

4. **Select the Include Office.com content check box (and make sure that your computer is connected to the Internet) to search for images online as well as on your computer.**

5. **In the Results Should Be drop-down list, choose Illustrations, and if you want to search for photos as well, choose Photographs (refer to Figure 4-2).**

Enter a keyword　　　　　　Choose what to search for

Figure 4-2:
Inserting
a clip-art
image by
way of the
Clip Art task
pane.

6. **Click the Go button.**

   The bottom of the task pane shows the clip-art images found in your
   search. You may have to scroll through the task pane to see all the images.

7. **Double-click an image or open its drop-down list and choose Insert to
   place it in your Word document, PowerPoint slide, Excel worksheet,
   or Publisher publication.**

   Your next task is to move the image into position and perhaps change
   its size. Book I, Chapter 8 explains how to manipulate clip-art images
   and other objects.

Tinkering with a Clip-Art Image's Appearance

Sometimes a clip-art image doesn't sit well with the rest of the page, slide,
or worksheet. The image is too bright or too dark. It clashes with the other
images. When an image clashes, you don't have to abandon it in favor of
another image. As Figure 4-3 shows, you can alter a clip-art image's appearance
in different ways.

**Book VIII
Chapter 4**

**Decorating Files
with Clip Art**

Select your image, go to the (Picture Tools) Format tab, and change the image's appearance. Chapter 3 of this mini-book describes the different ways to touch up a picture or clip-art image.

Figure 4-3:
You can
change
the look of
a clip-art
image.

Handling Media Files with the Clip Organizer

As computers get faster and better, media files — clip art, graphics, video clips, and audio files — will play a bigger role in computing. Dropping a clip-art image in a Word document or PowerPoint slide won't be a big deal. Playing video clips on PowerPoint slides will be commonplace.

Well aware that the future is closing in on us, Microsoft created the Clip Organizer to help you manage the media files on your computer. By using the Clip Organizer, you can place graphics, video clips, and audio files in Word documents, PowerPoint presentations, Excel worksheets, and Publisher publications. More important, the Clip Organizer is the place to organize media files in your computer so that you can find them and make good use of them. These pages explain how to manage the Clip Organizer.

To open the Clip Organizer, click the Start button and choose All Programs⇨ Microsoft Office⇨Microsoft Office 2010 Tools⇨Microsoft Clip Organizer.

Knowing your way around the Clip Organizer

As shown in Figure 4-4, the Clip Organizer is divided in two parts, with a pane on the left and a window for displaying files on the right. The Clip Organizer offers two panes: Collection List and Search.

✦ **Collection List task pane:** Use the Collection List task pane to organize your media files and to quickly locate and insert a media file. To display the Collection List task pane, click the Collection List button or choose View⇨Collection List.

✦ **Search task pane:** Use the Search task pane to locate a media file on your computer. Notice that this task pane is similar to the Clip Art task pane in Office programs (refer to Figure 4-2). To display the Search task pane, click the Search button or choose View⇨Search.

Click to display a different task pane   Search results

Figure 4-4:
The Clip
Organizer
window
with the
Search
pane
displayed
(left) and
Collection
List pane
displayed
(right).

Locating the media file you need

The Clip Organizer presents two ways to find a media file you need. Starting
from the Search pane, you can conduct a keyword search; starting from the
Collection List pane, you can select folders and subfolders to display clip art
and other media files on the right side of the window.

Searching for a media file in the Search pane

By entering a keyword in the Search For text box, telling the Clip Organizer
where to look, and telling it what kind of files to look for, you can pinpoint
the clip-art image you need:

✦ **Search For text box:** Enter a keyword that describes what kind of
clip-art image you want. As Figure 4-5 shows, each clip-art image has
been assigned descriptive keywords. If the keyword you enter matches
a keyword assigned to a clip-art image, the image appears in the search
results. (To view an image's keywords, open its drop-down list and
choose Preview/Properties.)

✦ **Results Should Be:** Choose which type of media you're seeking —
illustrations, photographs, videos, or audio.

**Book VIII
Chapter 4**

**Decorating Files
with Clip Art**

✦ **Include Office.com Content:** Select this check box (and make sure that your computer is connected to the Internet) to search for images online as well as on your computer.

Click the Go button when you're ready to conduct the search. The results of the search appear on the right side of the window (see to Figure 4-5).

Figure 4-5: For searching purposes, each clip-art image has been assigned keywords.

Locating a media file in the Collection List

If you know that the media file you want is stored on your computer, you can find it by starting with the Collection List.

The folders in the Collection List pane work just the same as folders in Windows Explorer or Computer. Click a folder name to display its contents on the right side of the screen. Display or hide subfolders by clicking the plus sign (+) or minus sign (–) next to folder names.

When you select a folder (or subfolder) in the Collection List pane, its contents appear on the right side of the Clip Organizer window (refer to Figure 4-4). These are the top-level folders in the Collection List pane:

✦ **My Collections:** Includes the Favorites subfolder (where you can store media files you use most often), subfolders you create yourself for different projects, and the Downloaded Clips subfolder (where clip art you downloaded from Office.com is stored). How to store a file in the Favorites folder or a folder you create yourself is explained later in this chapter in "Creating your own My Collections subfolder for the Clip Organizer."

✦ **Office Collections:** Includes many subfolders, each named for a clip-art category. Select a subfolder to view clip art in a category. You installed these clip-art images when you installed Office. The clip-art images are located on your computer.

✦ **Web Collections:** Includes many subfolders, each named for a clip-art category. To see these clip-art images, your computer must be connected to the Internet.

Inserting a media file

After you've found the media file you want, either by searching in the Search pane or browsing among the folders in the Collection List pane, you can insert it by following these instructions:

✦ **Clip Organizer:** Open the file's drop-down list and choose Copy. Then click in your file, go to the Home tab, and click the Paste button (or right-click and choose Paste).

✦ **Clip Art task pane in an Office program:** Either double-click the image or open its drop-down list and choose Insert.

Getting clip art from Microsoft

Microsoft permits users of Office to get clip art, photos, audio files, and video clips from a Microsoft Web site. To see what kind of media Microsoft offers online, connect your computer to the Internet and click the Clips Online button (you can find it on the right side of the Standard toolbar in the Microsoft Clip Organizer.). You come to a Microsoft Web site where you can download collections of clip art and other media files to your computer.

When you find a file you like, move your pointer over the file and choose Add to Collection. To download the files to your computer, click the Unsaved Collection link (you can find this link on the upper-right corner of the window) and choose Download. In the Clip Organizer, you can find files you downloaded from Microsoft in the `My Collections\Downloaded Clips` subfolder.

Storing your own files in the My Collections folders

The Collection List pane in the Clip Organizer is a convenient place to go when you need a media file. Wouldn't it be nice if you could go to the Clip Organizer when you want a file of a family photo, graphics that pertain to your work, or a video you're involved with?

It so happens that you can use the Clip Organizer for your own media files, not just the media files that come from Office. You can arrange it so that the media files you need are available to you simply by selecting the Favorites subfolder in the Collection List pane. For that matter, you can create a subfolder of your own in the Collection List and keep your media files there.

Adding your own media files to the Clip Organizer

If you're a fan of the Clip Organizer — if you think it's a convenient place to store and get media files — place your own files in the Clip Organizer. This way, you can open the Clip Organizer and get right to work making graphics or videos for a project you're working on.

Follow these steps to put your own media files in the Clip Organizer:

1. **Click the Collection List button, if necessary, to see the Collection List.**

2. **Choose File⇨Add Clips to Organizer⇨On My Own.**

The Add Clips to Organizer dialog box appears, as shown in Figure 4-6.

Select files   Select a subfolder

Figure 4-6:
Making your
favorite
media files
available
in the Clip
Organizer.

3. **Select the file or files whose names you want to store in the Clip Organizer.**

   For example, open your My Pictures folder and select the graphic files that you often work with. You can select more than one file by Ctrl+clicking.

4. **Click the Add To button.**

   The Import to Collection dialog box appears, as shown in Figure 4-6. It lists subfolders of the My Collections folder.

5. **Select the subfolder where you want to store your file or files and click OK.**

6. **Click the Add button in the Add Clips to Organizer dialog box.**

When you add media files to the Clip Organizer, you don't move the files to a new location on your computer, although it may appear that way. Truth be told, the folders in the Clip Organizer don't really exist on your computer. The folders actually represent categories. Inside each category are shortcuts similar to the shortcuts on the Windows desktop that tell your computer where the files are located on your computer. When you place a file in the Clip Organizer, what you're really doing is placing a shortcut to a file located somewhere on your computer or network.

Organizing media files in the My Collections subfolders

The My Collections subfolders in the Collection List pane — Favorites and the others — are excellent places for storing the media files you use often. All you have to do to get them is select the Favorites subfolder or another subfolder in the Collection List. Follow these steps to copy or move a media file to the Favorites subfolder or another subfolder in the Clip Organizer (the next section in this chapter explains how to make subfolders of your own):

1. **Find the media file or files you want to store in a subfolder.**

   Earlier in this chapter, "Locating the media file you need" explains how to locate a media file.

2. **Select the file or files on the right side of the Clip Organizer window.**

   To select more than one file, Ctrl+click the files; choose Edit⇨Select All to select them all.

3. **Give the Copy to Collection or Move to Collection command.**

   You can give these commands two different ways:

   • Open the file's drop-down list and choose Copy to Collection or Move to Collection.

   • Open the Edit menu and choose Copy to Collection or Move to Collection.

Book VIII
Chapter 4

Decorating Files with Clip Art

You see the Copy to Collection or Move to Collection dialog box.

4. **Select a folder in the dialog box.**

   If necessary, click a plus sign (+) beside a folder to display its subfolders.

5. **Click OK.**

To remove a file from a subfolder, select it and then press the Delete key, or open its drop-down list and then choose Delete from Clip Organizer. Deleting a file this way doesn't remove it from your computer; it just takes its name out of the Clip Organizer.

Creating your own My Collections subfolder for the Clip Organizer

If you work with a number of media files, organize them into My Collections subfolders. Put photographs in a Photographs subfolder. Put audio files in a Music subfolder. That way, you can find media files simply by going to the subfolder where you placed them. Follow these steps to create a new subfolder in the Clip Organizer:

1. **Click the Collection List button, if necessary, to display the Collection List task pane.**

2. **Choose File⇨New Collection.**

   The New Collection dialog box appears.

3. **Select the folder in which to place your new subfolder.**

   Selecting My Collections is probably the best choice, but place your new subfolder wherever you want.

4. **Enter a name for the subfolder in the Name box.**

5. **Click OK.**

If you need to rename a folder, select it in the Collection List, choose Edit⇨ Rename Collection, and enter a new name. To remove it, choose Edit⇨Delete.

Chapter 5: Note Taking with OneNote

In This Chapter

✔ Getting acquainted with OneNote

✔ Creating notebooks, sections, pages, and subpages for storing notes

✔ Writing and drawing notes

✔ Navigating in OneNote

✔ Organizing and finding stray notes

✔ Selecting, moving, and deleting notes, sections, and pages

✔ Using OneNote in conjunction with other Office programs

Microsoft OneNote is designed for taking notes — at meetings, at conferences, or when talking on the telephone. Rather than scribble notes indiscriminately in a Word document, you can enter them in OneNote and be able to retrieve them later. You can use your notes as building blocks for reports and white papers. You can copy them to Excel, PowerPoint, Word, or another Office 2010 program. OneNote comes with all sorts of amenities for finding and filing notes. OneNote can help you brainstorm and organize your ideas.

This chapter explains what OneNote is, how you can use it to write notes, and how to organize and find notes. Finally, it explains a couple of tricks for recycling notes into other Office programs.

Running OneNote

Do one of the following to run OneNote:

✦ Click the Start button and choose All Programs⇨Microsoft Office⇨ Microsoft Office OneNote 2010.

✦ Right-click the OneNote icon in the Notification area (it's located in the lower-right corner of the screen next to the clock) and choose Open OneNote. If you don't see the icon in the Notification area and you want to see it there, go to the File tab in OneNote, choose Options on the drop-down list, visit the Display category in the Options dialog box, and select the Place OneNote Icon in the Notification area of the Taskbar check box.

OneNote opens to the notebook, section, and page that was open the last time you closed the program.

OneNote is unusual among Office programs in that it doesn't have a Save button or Save command. Every 30 seconds, OneNote saves all the notes for you. You needn't concern yourself with whether notes are being saved.

Introducing OneNote

Figure 5-1 shows the OneNote screen. The purpose of OneNote is to help you enter notes, keep track of notes, find notes when you need them, and organize your notes. Read on to discover how to find your way around OneNote and how OneNote organizes notes into notebooks, sections, and pages.

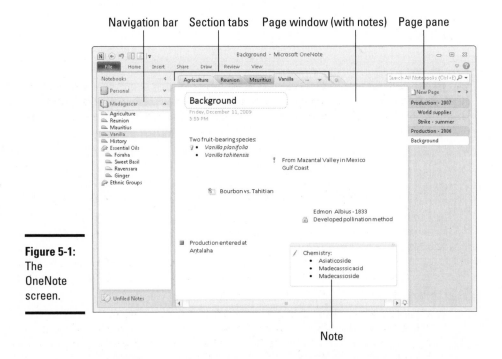

Figure 5-1: The OneNote screen.

Finding your way around the OneNote screen

Apart from the Ribbon along the top of the screen, these are the four main areas of OneNote (refer to Figure 5-1):

✦ **Navigation bar:** On the left side of the screen, the Navigation bar lists the names of notebooks you created, and within each notebook, section and section groups. Click the Collapse Navigation Bar or Expand Navigation Bar button to hide or display the Navigation bar. In the bar itself, you can click buttons to expand and collapse notebooks and section groups. Click a section name to open a section.

✦ **Section (and section group) tabs:** Section and section group names appear in tabs above the page. Click the name of a section to see its pages. (You can also click a section name in the Navigation bar.) Click the name of a section group to make its sections appear on the tabs.

✦ **Page window:** After you select a page in the Page pane, it appears in the Page window, and you can read notes you wrote on the page. The title of the page appears at the top of the window in the Title text box.

✦ **Page pane:** The names of pages and subpages in the section you selected appear on tabs in the Page pane.

Units for organizing notes

From largest to smallest, the program offers these units for organizing notes:

✦ **Notebook:** Create a *notebook* for each important project you're involved in. OneNote places one button on the Navigation bar for each notebook you create. The Navigation bar is located on the left side of the window (see Figure 5-1).

✦ **Sections:** A *section* is a subcategory of a notebook; it is used to store pages. Each notebook can have many different sections, and each section, in turn, can have many pages. In Figure 5-1, there are five sections in the Madagascar notebook: Agriculture, Reunion, Mauritius, Vanilla, and History.

✦ **Section groups:** A *section group* is a means of organizing and quickly finding sections. Although sections do not have to be stored in a section group, you can use section groups to store sections. The names of section groups appear below the names of sections on the Navigation bar and to the right of sections in the section tabs.

✦ **Pages and subpages:** A *page* is for writing and storing notes. Pages are stored in sections. Refer to Figure 5-1 to see how the names of pages appear on the Page pane (on the right side of the screen) on *page tabs*. Within a page, you can also create a *subpage*.

✦ **Notes:** Write your notes on pages and subpages. To write a note, all you have to do is click a page and start typing.

**Book VIII
Chapter 5**

Note Taking with
OneNote

Creating Storage Units for Notes

Before you write your first note, give a moment's thought to organizing notes in the notebook-section-pages hierarchy. Think of descriptive names for your notebook, sections, section groups, and pages. Then get to work creating the storage units you need for your notes. These pages explain how to do it.

Creating a notebook

OneNote creates a new notebook for you automatically the first time you start the program. This notebook is called Personal. Follow these steps to create a new notebook:

File

1. **On to the File tab, choose New.**

   The New Notebook window opens. You can also right-click the Notebooks pane and choose New Notebook.

2. **Choose Web, Network, or My Computer to tell OneNote where you intend to store the notebook you are about to create.**

3. **Enter a name for the notebook.**

4. **Select the folder in which you will store the notebook.**

   To do so, click the Browse button and select a folder in the Select Folder dialog box.

5. **Click the Create Notebook button.**

   The new notebook opens on-screen. OneNote creates a section (called New Section 1) and a page (called Untitled Page) in your notebook.

6. **Change the name of the section and page.**

   Follow these instructions to change section and page names:

   - *Changing the section name:* Right-click the section name, choose Rename on the shortcut menu, and enter a descriptive name. You can also double-click a name and enter a new one.

   - *Changing the page name:* Enter a name in the Title text box at the top of the page provided for names. After you enter the name, the new name appears as well on the Page pane on the right side of the screen.

To delete a notebook, close OneNote, open Windows Explorer or Computer, go to the folder where the notebook is stored, and delete the folder. To find out where notebooks are stored by default on your computer, go to the File tab, choose Options, go to the Save & Backup category of the OneNote Options dialog box, and look for the Default Notebook Location.

Creating sections, section groups, and pages

Create sections, section groups, and pages to organize your notes:

✦ **Creating a new section:** Click the Create a New Section button (which is located to the right of the section tabs) or right-click the Navigation bar or a section tab and choose New Section. A new section tab appears. Enter the section name on the tab and press Enter. (After you create a new section, OneNote automatically creates a new page to go with it. This page is called "Untitled Page." To rename this page, enter a name in the Title text box at the top of the page.

You can color-code sections to distinguish one section from the next. To change a section's color, right-click its tab, choose Section Color, and choose a color on the submenu. To rename a section, right-click its name, choose Rename, and enter a new name.

✦ **Creating a new section group:** Right-click the Navigation bar or a section tab and choose New Section Group. A section group tab appears. Enter a name and press the Enter key.

To move or copy a section you already created into a section group, right-click its name and choose Move or Copy. In the Move or Copy Section dialog box, select the name of a section group and click the Move or Copy button. You can also drag a section name in the Navigation bar into a section group.

✦ **Creating a new page:** Click the New Page button (it's located at the top of the Page pane), press Ctrl+N, or right-click the Page pane and choose New Page. A new page appears. Enter a page name in the Title text box. The name you enter appears on a page tab.

✦ **Creating a new subpage:** Display the page under which you will create a subpage, open the drop-down list on the New Page button, and choose New Subpage. Then enter a name in the Title text box.

You can rearrange pages and subpages in the Page pane by dragging their names.

Renaming and deleting groups, section groups, and pages

Think the words "right-click" when you want to rename or delete a group, section group, or page. To rename or delete one of these items, right-click it and choose Rename or Delete on the shortcut menu. After you choose Rename, enter a new name for your group, section group, or page.

**Book VIII
Chapter 5**

Note Taking with OneNote

Writing Notes

Although the program is called OneNote, you can enter three kinds of notes. You can enter typed notes, drawings, and screen clippings. Moreover, if you're using a Tablet PC to scribble your notes, OneNote can (at least in theory) recognize whether you're writing by hand or drawing. These pages explain how to type notes, draw notes, and take screen captures in notes.

Notes appear in what are called *containers,* as shown in Figure 5-2. Move the pointer over the top of a container and you see the four-headed arrow. At that point, you can click and drag a note elsewhere. Drag the right side of a note container to change its width.

Figure 5-2:
A typed note (left) and a drawn note (right).

There is only one way to escape from bloodhounds who are chasing you: find water. By wading in the shallows of a creek or river you can make the dogs lose your scent.

Typing a note

To type a note, simply click and start typing. Press the Enter key to begin a new paragraph in a note. You can draw upon the commands on the Home tab — do you recognize them from Microsoft Word? — to format the text or change its color.

To get more room on a page for notes, try collapsing the Navigation bar and page tabs. To do so, press F11 or go to the View tab and click the Full Page View button.

Drawing with a pen or highlighter

Follow these steps to draw a note with a pen or highlighter:

1. **On the Draw tab, click the Select & Type button.**

2. **Open the Pens gallery and choose a pen or highlighter.**

3. **Start drawing.**

   Click the Eraser button and click a line if you need to erase something you wrote or drew. Choose a shape from the Insert Shape gallery if that improves your drawing skills.

4. **Press Esc or click the Select & Type button again when you finish drawing or highlighting.**

Want proof that computers are getting smarter? Click the Select & Type button and write something on the page in your best handwriting. Then click the Ink to Text button on the Draw tab. OneNote converts your handwritten note to typewritten text.

Taking a screen-clipping note

In OneNote lingo, a *screen clipping* is a note with a screen shot inside it, as shown in Figure 5-3. OneNote makes it remarkably easy to take screen clippings like these. Go to the Web page, Word document, or other item that you need a picture of, and use one of these techniques to take a screen clipping:

✦ **Starting in OneNote:** Switch to OneNote, go to the Insert tab, and click the Screen Clipping button. You return to the program you were in previously. Drag the pointer to capture the portion of the screen you want for the clipping. When you finish dragging, you return to OneNote, and the screen clipping you took appears in a note.

Jotting down a side note

Suppose you're brainstorming and you come up with an idea that cries out to be preserved in a note. To quickly jot down your note, write a "side note" in the small but convenient Side Note window. This window works in cahoots with OneNote to help you record ideas before you forget them. When you enter a note in the window, it's entered as well in OneNote in the Unfiled Notes folder. Next time you open OneNote, you can go to the Unfiled Notes folder, locate your note, and copy or move it to another folder.

To open the Side Note window, click the OneNote icon in the Notification area or press Windows key+N. Enter your note and then click the Close button in the Side Note window.

To find your note the next time you open OneNote, click the Unfiled Notes button. You can find this button near the bottom of the Navigation bar. Your note is filed away on a page named after the note you entered. Later in this chapter, "Some Housekeeping Chores" explains how to move notes.

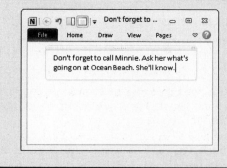

✦ **Starting in the Notification tray:** Right-click the OneNote icon in the Notification tray and choose Create Screen Clipping (or press Windows key+S). Then drag the pointer on your screen to capture the part of the screen you want for the clipping. The Select Location in OneNote dialog box appears. Do one of the following:

- Select a section in the dialog box and click the Send to Selected Location button. OneNote creates a new page in the section you chose for the clipping and places the clipping on the page.

- Click the Copy to Clipboard button. Back in OneNote, right-click a page and choose Paste to paste the clipping into OneNote.

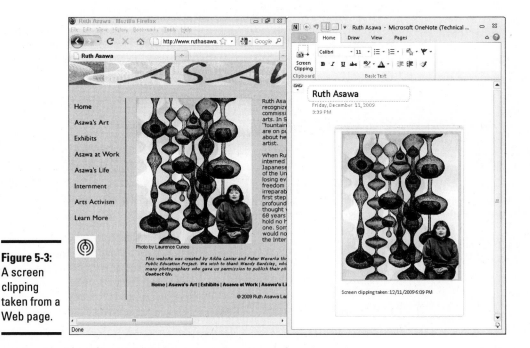

Figure 5-3:
A screen clipping taken from a Web page.

Getting from Place to Place in OneNote

As you fill up a notebook with sections, section groups, pages, subpages, and notes, finding the place you need to be to enter or read a note gets more difficult. Here are ways to get from section to section or page to page in the OneNote window:

✦ **Going to a different notebook:** Click a notebook button on the Navigation bar. Use one of these techniques to find out where clicking a notebook button takes you:

- Move the pointer over a button. You see a notebook's name and the folder where it is stored in a ScreenTip box.

- If the Navigation bar is collapsed, click the Expand Navigation Bar button. Now you can see the names of notebooks as well as the names of notebook sections on the Navigation bar. The Expand Navigation Bar button is located at the top of the Navigation bar.

✦ **Going to a different section or section group:** Click the name of a section or section group in the Navigation bar or along the top of the window. Section group names are listed at the bottom of the Navigation bar and to the right of section names. You can expand and collapse section groups in the Navigation bar by clicking the plus or minus sign on a section group symbol.

✦ **Go to a different page:** Click a page or subpage tab on the right side of the window. To make more room for page and subpage names, click the Expand Page Tabs button. You can find it to the right of the New Page button.

Finding and Keeping Track of Notes

If you're an habitual note taker, you may find yourself drowning in notes. You won't be able to find the note you're looking for. The great idea you had may be lost forever. To keep notes from getting lost, these pages explain how to find stray notes and how to organize notes so that they don't get lost in the first place.

Finding a stray note

To find a lost note, you must be able to remember a word or two in the note. Follow these steps to chase down a lost note:

1. **Click in the Search box.**

   This box is located to the right of the Section tabs, above the Page pane. As soon as you click in the Search box, a menu opens for telling OneNote where you want to search.

2. **To declare where you want to search for the note, click the Change Search Scope button (it's on the right side of the Search box) and choose This Section, This Notebook, or another option on the drop-down list.**

   You can also open this drop-down list by clicking the Type to Search In hyperlink.

3. **Enter the word or phrase you're looking for in the Search box.**

4. **Click the Find button.**

   OneNote lists all notes with the text you entered.

5. **Click a note to go to the page where it is located.**

Tagging notes for follow-up

The best way to keep notes from getting lost is to carefully place them in notebooks, sections, and pages. Short of that, you can tag notes to make it easier to follow up on them. OneNote offers numerous ways to tag notes. After you tag a note, you can search for it by opening the Tags Summary task pane, arranging notes according to how they were tagged, and pinpointing the note you want, as shown in Figure 5-4.

Choose how to arrange tagged notes

Tags Summary

Search completed

Group tags by:

Section

Show only unchecked items

▲ **Foraha**

  Foraha oil

▲ **Vanilla**

  Bourbon vs. Tahitian
  Developed pollination method
  From Mazantal Valley in Mexico Gulf Coast
  Production entered at Antalaha
  Vanilla planifolia

Search:

This notebook

This page group
This section
This section group
This notebook
All notebooks
Today's notes
Yesterday's notes
This week's notes
Last week's notes
Older notes

Figure 5-4:
Tag notes
so that you
can track
them better.

Choose where to look for notes

Tagging a note

Follow these steps to tag a note:

1. Select the note.

2. On the Home tab, open the Tags gallery and choose a tag.

All options except Remember for Later and Definition place an icon on the note. The aforementioned options highlight the note text, respectively, in yellow or green.

To remove a tag, open the Tags gallery and choose Remove Tag.

Arranging tagged notes in the task pane

Follow these steps to arrange notes that you tagged in the Tags Summary task pane:

1. **On the Home tab, click the Find Tags button.**

   You see the Tags Summary task pane (refer to Figure 5-4).

2. **Open the Group Tags By drop-down list and choose an option.**

   These options determine the order in which tagged notes appear in the task pane. Tag Name, for example, arranges notes according to which icon they're tagged with; Section arranges notes under section names; Note Text arranges notes in alphabetical order.

3. **Open the Search drop-down list and choose an option.**

   These options determine which notes appear in the task pane. This Section, for example, assembles only flagged notes from the section that appears on-screen; This Notebook gathers flagged notes from all sections in the notebook you're viewing.

   A list of notes appears in the task pane.

4. **Click the name of a note you want to visit.**

   OneNote opens the page with the note whose name you clicked and selects the note.

> **TIP**
>
> To remove tags from notes, select the notes and press Ctrl+0 (zero), or open the drop-down list on the Tags gallery and choose Remove Tag.

Some Housekeeping Chores

Unless you play loud soul music while you're doing it, housekeeping can be a tedious and irksome activity. Here are methods for handling a few housekeeping chores:

+ **Selecting notes:** Click the bar along the top of a note to select it. Ctrl+click to select several notes.

+ **Moving notes to another page:** Use the tried-and-true cut-and-paste method. Select the note, right-click, choose Cut, right-click the page where you want to move the note, and choose Paste.

+ **Moving a page to another section**: Right-click the page's tab and choose Move or Copy (or press Ctrl+Alt+M). You see the Move or Copy Pages dialog box. Select a section name and click the Move or Copy button.

✦ **Removing a notebook from the Navigation bar:** To remove a note-book's name from the Navigation bar and keep the bar from getting too crowded, right-click the notebook's button and choose Close This Notebook. To reopen a notebook, go to the File tab, choose Open, click the Open Notebook button, and select the notebook's name in the Open Notebook dialog box.

✦ **Deleting notes:** Select the notes you want to delete and press the Delete key or right-click and choose Delete.

✦ **Deleting a section:** Right-click the section tab and choose Delete. Because each section is actually a file, you can recover a section you deleted accidentally by retrieving it from the Recycle Bin.

✦ **Deleting a page or subpage:** Right-click the page tab and choose Delete. You can't recover a page of notes that you delete this way.

OneNote maintains a Recycle Bin of its own. If you mistakenly delete a section or page, you can recover it by going to the Share tab and clicking the Notebook Recycle Bin button. Sections and pages you deleted appear (deleted pages appear on the Deleted Pages tab). To restore a section or page, right-click it, choose Move or Copy, select the section you want to restore in the Move or Copy dialog box, and click the Move button.

OneNote and Other Office Programs

OneNote works hand in hand with its brothers and sisters in the Office suite. These pages describe how to recycle material from OneNote into other Office programs and recycle material from other Office programs into OneNote.

Using data from OneNote in other Office programs

To make use of OneNote data in other Office programs, you can copy the data, link it to a Word or PowerPoint file, send it by e-mail, or turn it into an Outlook task. Better keep reading.

Copying a note into another Office program

To copy a note into another program, use the copy-and-paste command. Select the note, right-click, and choose Copy. Then go to the other program, right-click, and choose Paste. Typed notes land in the other program in the form of text. Drawn notes land as Portable Network Graphics (.png) files.

Linking a Word or PowerPoint file to OneNote

By linking a Word or PowerPoint file to a OneNote section or page, you can open OneNote from inside Word or PowerPoint and refer right away to notes you took. Link a file to OneNote so that you can refer to notes you keep in OneNote while you're working on a Word or PowerPoint file.

Follow these steps to link a Word or PowerPoint file to a section or page in OneNote:

1. **Open the Word or PowerPoint file you want to link to notes you keep in OneNote.**

2. **On the Review tab, click the Linked Notes button.**

   OneNote opens (if it wasn't already open), and you see the Select Location in OneNote dialog box.

3. **In the dialog box, select the section or page with the notes that refer to your Word or PowerPoint file, and click OK.**

   The Linked Note icon appears in OneNote. This icon tells you that the section or page is linked to a Word or PowerPoint file.

To refer to the OneNote notes while you're working on your Word or PowerPoint file, go to the Review tab and click the Linked Notes button. OneNote opens in Dock to Desktop view. In this view, Word or PowerPoint appears on the left side of your screen, and OneNote appears on the right side. This arrangement makes it easy to work from your notes.

Sending notes by e-mail

As long as Outlook is installed on your computer, you can send the notes on a page by e-mail to someone else. Follow these steps to send notes by e-mail:

1. **Open the page with the notes you want to send.**

   Unfortunately, you can't send a single note unless it's the only one on the page.

2. **On the Home or Share tab, click the E-Mail Page button (or press Ctrl+Shift+E).**

   You see a message window with the OneNote page in the message area.

3. **Address the message and enter some words to accompany the notes.**

4. **Click the Send button.**

   The page of notes is sent by way of Outlook.

Turning a note into an Outlook task

As Book III, Chapter 5 explains, an Outlook task is a reminder to do something. You can make a note into an Outlook task and place the task in the Outlook Tasks window by following these steps:

1. **Select the note.**

2. **On the Home tab, open the drop-down list on the Outlook Task button and choose the option that describes a due date for the task.**

For example, choose Tomorrow if you want the note to be filed in the Outlook Tasks window under Due Date: Tomorrow.

In Outlook, you can go to the Home tab and click the OneNote button to open OneNote and read notes.

Using data from other Office programs in OneNote

To commandeer data from other Office programs for OneNote, you can attach files to notes and copy Office files into OneNote. These tasks are described forthwith.

Attaching an Office file to a note

Attach an Office file to a note so that you can quickly open the file from inside OneNote. When you attach a file, what you really do is create a short-cut from your note to the Office file. You can click the shortcut and open the attached file right away. Follow these steps to attach an Office file to a note:

1. **Select the note.**

2. **On the Insert tab, click the Attach File button.**

You see the Choose a File or Set of Files to Insert dialog box.

3. **Select the file or files.**

4. **Click the Insert button.**

As shown in Figure 5-5, filenames and icons appear on notes. The icons indicate what kind of file is attached to the note.

☆ Review the files in question:

[W] Check It

[X] Budget data

Figure 5-5:
Files
attached to
a note.

Copying an Office file into OneNote

Follow these steps to copy a file from Word, PowerPoint, Excel, or Publisher onto a OneNote page:

1. **On the Insert tab, click the File Printout button.**

The Choose Document to Insert dialog box opens.

2. **Select a file and click the Insert button.**

Starting in Word or PowerPoint, you can copy a file to OneNote by going to the File tab and choosing Print. In the Print window, open the Printer drop-down list, choose Send to OneNote 2010, and click the Print button. Then switch to OneNote, and in the Select Location in One Note dialog box, choose a section or page and click OK. If you select a section, OneNote creates a new page in the section for the material from Word or PowerPoint; if you select a page, the material lands on the page you selected.

Chapter 6: Automating Tasks with Macros

In This Chapter

✔ Understanding what a macro is

✔ Displaying and hiding the Developer tab

✔ Examining macro security issues

✔ Recording, running, and editing a macro

✔ Placing a macro button on the Quick Access toolbar

This brief chapter explains how macros can make your work a little easier. I describe how to display the Developer tab on the Ribbon, record a macro, run a macro, and edit a macro. I also look into macro security issues and show you how to place a macro button on the Quick Access toolbar.

What Is a Macro?

A *macro* is a set of command instructions recorded under a name. When you activate a macro, the program you're working in carries out the instructions in the macro. Macros help automate repetitive and complex tasks. Instead of entering commands yourself, the macro does it for you — and it enters the commands faster and more efficiently. Instead of reaching into several dialog boxes to get a task done, you can run a macro and let it do the work.

Not that you necessarily need to know it, but playing a macro involves running command sequences in *Visual Basic for Applications* (VBA), a programming language built into all the major Office 2010 applications. Behind the scenes, the application you're working in executes VBA code when you run a macro.

Displaying the Developer Tab

Before you can run a macro or do anything in the wonderful world of macros, you must display the Developer tab. Figure 6-1 shows the Developer tab in PowerPoint. Follow these steps to display or remove this tab:

Figure 6-1:
The Developer tab (in PowerPoint).

1. **On the File tab, choose Options.**

You see the Options dialog box.

2. **Go to the Customize Ribbon category.**

3. **On the right side of the dialog box, select the Developer check box.**

4. **Click OK.**

Managing the Macro Security Problem

A macro is a little (and sometimes not so little) computer program in its own right. As such, macros can contain computer viruses. When you run a macro in a PowerPoint presentation, Word document, Excel workbook, or any other file, you run the risk of infecting your computer with a virus.

To help protect you against macro viruses, Office gives you the opportunity to decide how you want to handle files that contain macros. You can disable all macros, disable some macros, or enable all macros. (If you're working in an office on a network, the network administrator may have decided for you whether you can run macro files on your computer. Network administrators can disable all files that contain macros.)

Follow these steps to tell Office how you want to handle macros:

1. **On the Developer tab, click the Macro Security button.**

You see the Macro Settings category of the Trust Center dialog box, as shown in Figure 6-2.

2. **Under Macro Settings, declare how you want to handle Office files that contain macros.**

Your choices are as follows:

 • *Disable All Macros without Notification:* You can't run macros, and moreover, you're not alerted to the fact that your file contains macros or given the opportunity to enable the macros.

- *Disable All Macros with Notification:* When you open a file with macros, you see the panel shown in Figure 6-3. It tells you that macros have been disabled, but gives you the opportunity to enable the macros by clicking the Enable Content button.

- *Disable All Macros Except Digitally Signed Macros:* You can run only macros that have been certified with a digital signature. Developers can apply for digital signatures that deem their macros safe to run. When you open a file with digitally signed macros, a dialog box tells you who developed the macros and gives you the opportunity to decide whether you want to allow them. However, you can't run macros that don't have a digital signature.

- *Enable All Macros:* You can run all macros, no matter where they came from and who made them. Choosing this option is a risky proposition. Choose it only if you get Office files from people or parties you know and trust.

3. **Click OK.**

Figure 6-2:
Choosing how to handle macro security.

Figure 6-3:
Choose whether to run macros.

Book VIII
Chapter 6

Automating Tasks
with Macros

Excel, PowerPoint, and Word files that contain macros have a file extension that ends in the letter *m* (the *m* stands for "macro"). Excel files have the extension .xlsm, PowerPoint files the extension .pptm, and Word files the extension .docm. Even if you disable macros, you can glance at a file's extension letters to tell whether it includes macros.

Recording a Macro

Recording a macro in an Office application is a matter of turning on the Macro Recorder and giving commands. The Macro Recorder is modeled after a tape recorder. You turn on the recorder, choose commands, and turn the thing off. Following are ground rules and instructions for recording macros.

Unless you want to construct them on your own using VBA code, you can't record your own macros in PowerPoint, Outlook, or Publisher. (You can record macros in Word, Excel, and Access.) To make use of macros in PowerPoint, Outlook, or Publisher, you have to obtain them from a developer or have them already in your files.

Enabling your files for macros

To record macros, you must make sure that the file in which you record them is *macro enabled*. Macro-enabled files have file extensions that end in *m* (the *m* stands for "macro"). Excel files have the extension .xlsm, PowerPoint files the extension .pptm, and Word files the extension .docm.

Follow these steps to macro-enable a file so that you can record and run macros in it:

| File |

1. **On the File tab, choose Save As.**

2. **In the Save As dialog box, open the Save As Type drop-down list and choose the macro-enable option.**

For example, to macro-enable a Word document, choose Word Macro-Enabled Document (*.docm).

3. **Click the Save button.**

Ground rules for recording macros

Before you record a macro, observe these ground rules:

✦ Plan ahead. If the actions you intend to record in the macro are complex, write them down beforehand so that you can execute the commands without making any mistakes.

✦ Set up the program the way it will be when you play back the macro. Before creating a macro that manipulates information in a worksheet, for example, open a worksheet that is typical of the kind of worksheet on which you'll run the macro. Unless you prepare yourself this way, you may have to pause the Macro Recorder (you can do that in Word) as you record, or you may have to edit the macro in the Visual Basic Editor later.

✦ Toggle commands that you can switch on and off have no place in macros because when the macro starts running, the Macro Recorder can't tell whether the command is on or off.

✦ Close open files that might get in the way. For example, before creating a macro that copies information from one file to another, close any open files that might confuse the issue.

✦ If you intend to include a Find or a Find-and-Replace operation in a Word macro, open the Find dialog box in Word before you start recording the macro, click the More button, and then click Cancel. This way, you can get to all the find-and-replace options when you open the dialog box as part of recording the macro.

✦ In Excel, click the Use Relative References button on the Developer tab if you want to record cell references as relative, not absolute, references.

Recording the macro

Having read and followed the ground rules, follow these steps to record a macro in Word or Excel:

Record Macro

1. **On the Developer tab, click the Record Macro button.**

The Record Macro dialog box, shown in Figure 6-4, opens.

Figure 6-4: The Macro Recorder dialog box in Word (left) and Excel (right).

If you can't find the Record Macro button, chances are an administrator removed it to prevent you from using or recording macros. Depending on which version of Windows you have, administrators can remove all macro and VBA functionality from Office by not installing the VBA component, or they can install the component but prevent individuals from accessing macros and VBA.

2. **In the Macro Name text box, enter a name for your macro.**

Macro names can be 80 characters long, must begin with a letter, and can include numbers and underscores. Blank spaces, symbols, and punctuation are not allowed in macro names.

3. **If you so desire, assign a toolbar button or keyboard shortcut to the macro.**

   In Word, you can click the Button or the Keyboard icon and assign a button or keyboard shortcut for activating the macro. Later in this chapter, "Running a Macro from a Button on the Quick Access Toolbar" explains how to put a macro on the Quick Access toolbar. Chapter 1 of this mini-book explains how to assign a keyboard shortcut to a Word macro.

   In Excel, you can assign a Ctrl+key combination to a macro by entering a key in the Ctrl+ text box.

4. **In the Store Macro In drop-down list, decide where to store the macro you're about to record.**

   In Word, you can store macros in the document you're working on, the template the document is attached to, or the Normal template (the global template that's always loaded). Store a macro with a template if you'd like to be able to run the macro in all documents you create with your template.

   In Excel, you can store macros in the workbook you're working on (choose the This Workbook menu item), a new workbook, or the Personal.Macro Workbook. The Personal.Macro Workbook is designed expressly for storing macros. It is created automatically the first time you choose Personal.Macro Workbook. The workbook is called `Personal.xlsb`, and it's stored in this folder if your machine runs Windows 7 or Windows Vista:

   ```
   C:\Users\Your Name\AppData\Roaming\Microsoft\Excel\XLStart
   ```

   The `Personal.xlsb` workbook is stored in this folder if your machine runs Windows XP:

   ```
   C:\Documents and Settings\Your Name\Application Data\Microsoft\Excel\
      XLSTART
   ```

5. **In the Description text box, enter a concise description of what the macro does.**

6. **Click OK.**

   The Record Macro dialog box closes.

7. **Perform the actions you want to record in the macro.**

   The Macro Recorder records every action you take, but it doesn't record actions in real time. Take your time when recording a macro. Concentrate on taking the actions in the right order so that you don't need to adjust the code afterward.

   Word offers the Pause Recording button. You can click it to suspend recording. Click it again to resume recording.

Avoid using the mouse as you record a macro (although you can use it to open menus and select menu commands). The Macro Recorder interprets some mouse actions ambiguously. Select data by using key presses. (In Excel, you can select cells with the mouse because the Macro Recorder is able to recognize cell addresses.)

When you visit a dialog box as part of recording your macro, take into account all the dialog box settings. For example, if you visit the Font dialog box and choose 12 points on the Font Size drop-down list, the Macro Recorder duly records the 12-point font size, but it also records the Times Roman font in the macro if Times Roman happens to be the font that is chosen in the Font dialog box. The moral: Take account of all the settings in a dialog box when you visit it while recording a macro.

In dialog boxes with tabs, you can't click tabs to switch from tab to tab and choose commands. Instead, click OK to close the dialog box, reopen it, click a different tab, choose a command on the tab, and close the dialog box again.

🔲 Stop Recording **8. Click the Stop Recording button.**

That's all she wrote — your macro is recorded. I suggest you test it to see how well it runs.

To delete a macro, click the Macros button on the Developer or View tab, and in the Macros dialog box, select the macro you want to delete and then click the Delete button.

Running a Macro

Before you run a macro, take note of where the cursor is located. The macro may require the cursor to be in a certain place to run properly. Follow these steps to run a macro:

1. On the Developer or View tab, click the Macros button (or press Alt+F8).

The Macro dialog box, shown in Figure 6-5, appears.

2. Select the macro that you want to run.

Macros have cryptic names, but you can usually tell what they do by glancing at their descriptions.

If you don't see the macro you want, make a new selection in the Macro In drop-down list.

3. Click the Run button.

If your macro is a long one and you need to stop it from running, press Ctrl+Break. (On most keyboards, the Break key is located along with the Pause key on the right side of the keyboard, to the right of the F12 key.)

Figure 6-5:
The Macro
dialog box.

Editing a Macro

Editing a macro entails opening the Visual Basic Editor and editing Visual Basic codes, which is not for the faint of heart. If your macro is an uncomplicated one, you're better off re-recording it. This book isn't a developer's guide, so it can't go into the details of using the Visual Basic Editor. However, the following pages explain the basics of reading a macro in the Visual Basic Editor, deleting parts of a macro, and editing the text in a macro.

Follow these steps to view a macro in the Visual Basic Editor:

1. **On the Developer tab, click the Macros button (or press Alt+F8).**

You see the Macro dialog box (refer to Figure 6-5).

2. **Select the name of the macro that needs editing.**

3. **Click the Edit button.**

You see the Visual Basic window, as shown in Figure 6-6.

4. **Choose File⇨Save (or press Ctrl+S) after you finish editing your macro.**

Macro names appear in the Procedure box on the right side of the window. Those computer codes in the Code window are scary, aren't they? You can find one line of code for each command in your macro. Edit computer codes the same way that you edit text in a Word document. For example, click to the left of a line to select it and then press Delete to delete a line. Or type in the Code window to add commands or change the text that the macro enters in documents.

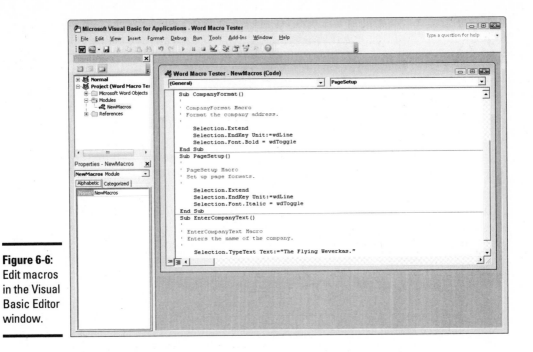

Figure 6-6:
Edit macros
in the Visual
Basic Editor
window.

Reading a macro in the Code window

Before you can do any editing in the Visual Basic Editor, you have to know
how to read the codes in the Code window. Observe these attributes of the
Code window:

✦ **Sub and End Sub line:** A macro begins with the Sub line and ends with
   the End Sub line.

✦ **Apostrophes (') at the beginning of lines:** Lines that begin with an
   apostrophe (') are descriptive comments and aren't part of the macro
   except insofar as they help you understand what it does. Notice, for
   example, that the description line (the one you wrote before recording
   the macro) near the top of the macro appears after an apostrophe. Enter
   blank lines and lines of commentary to make macros easier to read and
   understand.

✦ **Text enclosed in double quotation marks ("):** Text that is typed in as
   part of the macro is enclosed in double quotation marks ("). If you need
   to edit the text in your macro, edit the text inside double quotation
   marks.

✦ **With and End With lines:** Codes that pertain to choices made in a dialog
   box begin with the With line and end with the End With line.

✦ **All dialog box options are recorded:** Even if you select only a single option in a dialog box, the macro records all the options in the dialog box. A visit to the Font dialog box, for example, adds more than 20 lines to a macro, one for every option in the dialog box. However, you can edit out lines that your macro does not require.

Editing the text that a macro enters

As I mention earlier, text that is typed during a macro procedure is enclosed in double quotation marks (") in the Code window. To edit the text in a macro, you can edit the text between double quotation marks in the Code window. Edit this text as though you were editing it in Word.

Deleting parts of a macro

Delete part of a macro when you want to remove a command or command sequence. For that matter, you may delete parts of a macro if they are unnecessary. Deleting unnecessary lines makes a macro easier to read and run faster. As I mention in the preceding section of this chapter, a visit to a dialog box, such as the Font dialog box, adds many lines to a macro, most of which are unnecessary. Your macro requires only the lines that pertain to changing settings.

To delete part of a macro, delete the lines as though they were text in a Word document: Click or click and drag in the left margin and then press the Delete key.

Running a Macro from a Button on the Quick Access Toolbar

Any macro that you run often is a candidate for the Quick Access toolbar. As Chapter 1 of this mini-book explains, you can place your own buttons on the Quick Access toolbar and move the toolbar below the Ribbon as well. Follow these steps to assign a macro to a button and place the button on the Quick Access toolbar:

1. **Right-click any button or tab and choose Customize Quick Access Toolbar on the shortcut menu.**

   You see the Quick Access Toolbar category of the Options dialog box.

2. **In the Choose Commands From drop-down list, choose Macros (you can find it near the top of the list).**

   The cryptic names of macros in your file appear in the dialog box.

3. **Select the macro you want to assign to a button and click the Add button.**

   The macro's name appears in the right side of the dialog box alongside the names of buttons already on the Quick Access toolbar.

4. **Make sure that your macro is still selected and click the Modify button.**

   The Modify Button dialog box appears. It offers symbols you can place on your macro button.

5. **Select a symbol and click OK.**

6. **Click OK in the Options dialog box.**

   A button representing your macro appears on the Quick Access toolbar. You can click this button to run your macro. If you want to remove the button, right-click it and choose Remove from Quick Access Toolbar.

Chapter 7: Linking and Embedding in Compound Files

In This Chapter

✔ Understanding what object linking and embedding (OLE) is

✔ Linking to foreign data in another file

✔ Embedding foreign data in a file

A *compound file* is a computer file that brings together data created in different programs. A year-end report is a classic example of a compound file. Typically, a year-end report includes word-processed text, worksheet tables, and graphics. Thanks to object linking and embedding (OLE), you can create compound files. They can include data from different sources — Excel worksheets, Word text, or Paint graphic files. What's better, you can copy and continuously update material from other programs without leaving the Office 2010 program you're working in.

All this magic is accomplished with something called object linking and embedding (OLE). This chapter explains OLE, tells you how to embed data from another file, and explains how to link data from another file so that your files are updated automatically.

By the way, OLE is pronounced the same as *olé* ("oh-lay"), which is the word that the bullfighting audience shouts when the bull passes under the matador's cape. *¿Loco, verdad?*

What Is OLE, Anyway?

Object linking and embedding (OLE) is a means of putting more than one program to work on the same file. You can think of OLE as a high-powered version of the standby Copy and Paste commands. As you probably know, the Copy and Paste commands are for copying material from one place or program to another. For example, with the Copy and Paste commands, you can copy text from an Excel worksheet into a Word document. You can copy columns and rows from a Word table and paste them straight into a PowerPoint table.

Linking and embedding

Object linking takes the copy-and-paste concept a step further. When you copy text from a Word document to a PowerPoint slide, you can *link* the Word file and PowerPoint slide so that changes made to the Word text are made as well to the same text on your PowerPoint slide. In effect, linking means that you can run the Copy and Paste commands in the background without having to actually choose Copy or Paste. Linking establishes a connection between the two objects, in this case the text in the Word document and the text in the PowerPoint slide, so that the one automatically updates the other.

Similarly, *embedding* enables you to keep, or embed, foreign data from another program in the file you're working on. The program you're working in understands that the data is foreign. When you click the data, the program's tabs and buttons disappear to be replaced by tabs and buttons belonging to the program designed to handle the data. For example, when you click an Excel worksheet embedded in a Word document, you see Excel tabs and buttons for handling the worksheet data. In effect, you can open a second program inside the first program and use the second program to create data without having to copy the data from the second program. The object — the Word document or Excel worksheet — isn't connected to another file but is contained within the file.

Figure 7-1 shows an Excel worksheet embedded in a PowerPoint slide. Notice the Excel tabs and buttons in the window. The tabs and buttons are at the ready. After you finish using them, you can click outside the embedded object — you can click outside the Excel worksheet — and go back to using the PowerPoint tabs and buttons. Although the table data was made in Excel, it looks like a PowerPoint table. Embedding an object spares you from having to open a different program, construct material there, and copy it into the file you're working on.

A *linked object* is a little bit different from an embedded object. In the linked relationship, the program you're currently using shouts out to the program where the material was created to find out whether the material was edited or altered in any way. If the material was updated, you can tell Office to gather the updated material and incorporate it into your current file. Linking is an opportunity for you to keep your files up-to-date. You can fold the work that you or a co-worker did to the original file into your file without having to go outside the program you're using, and then copying and pasting it.

Uses for linking

Linking was designed to let files dynamically share information. The object — the Excel worksheet or Word file, for example — remains connected to its source. As the source file is updated, the files to which it is linked can be updated, too.

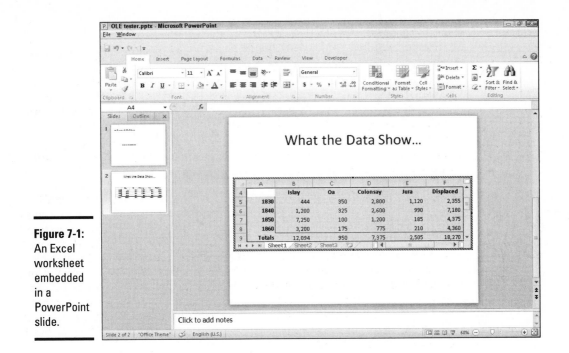

Figure 7-1:
An Excel worksheet embedded in a PowerPoint slide.

Linking saves you the trouble of updating files that often change. Co-workers can maintain a library of source files and use them to update the files to which the source files are linked. Here are some examples of object linking coming in handy:

✦ Your PowerPoint presentation contains sales data, and you want the data to be up-to-date. You create a link to the Excel worksheet where the sales data is stored so that your PowerPoint slide remains up-to-date as sales data changes.

✦ A co-worker has created an Excel worksheet with demographic data that often changes. In your Word report, you create a link to your co-worker's worksheet so that demographic data appears in your report and is always up-to-date.

✦ Your company maintains a Word file with a list of branch office addresses and telephone numbers, and you want this list to be available to employees. You link your Word file to the company's Word file. Your address and telephone list document stays up-to-date as addresses and telephone numbers change.

**Book VIII
Chapter 7**

Linking and Embedding in Compound Files

Uses for embedding

Embedding enables you to work inside an Office program on data that the program isn't equipped to handle or display. Embed an Excel worksheet in a Word document if you want to have a table with complex mathematical formulas. Embed a Word document in an Excel worksheet if you want to write paragraphs of explanatory text and be able to call upon Word formatting commands. Consider embedding an object if you want to attempt something that you can't normally do in the program you're working in.

Pitfalls of linking and embedding

Linking and embedding aren't for everybody. Here are some OLE pitfalls:

✦ **File size:** Including embedded objects in a file makes the file grow in size — and I mean really grow. A large file can be unwieldy and hard to store. It takes longer to load on-screen. By linking, you solve the file-size problem because the item has to be stored only once — in its original location.

✦ **Carrying charges:** Links are broken if you move your file or you or someone else moves a file to which your file is linked. A file with links can't be sent over the Internet or copied to a laptop without the links being broken. Linking is out of the question in the case of files that travel to other computers. If you link to files over a network, establish a scheme for storing files with your co-workers so that files aren't moved inadvertently.

✦ **Formatting embedded and linked objects:** Unfortunately, linked and embedded objects are often hard to format. Selecting the same fonts and colors as the fonts and colors in your file can be difficult because you have to rely on the commands in the source file to do the formatting. The end result is that linked and embedded objects sometimes look out of place.

Before you undertake any activity regarding object linking and embedding, save the file you're working on. The program with which you're working needs to know precisely where OLE objects go in order to execute OLE commands. Therefore, your file must be completely up-to-date for OLE commands to work.

Linking to Data in a Source File

Link a slide, document, or worksheet to another file so that changes made to the other file are made automatically to your slide, document, or worksheet. Earlier in this chapter, "Uses for linking" explains the benefits of linking to another file. These pages explain how to establish the link between your files, how to update the link, how to break a link, and how to mend broken links.

Links are broken when files are renamed or moved to different folders. Linking files is more trouble than it's worth if you often move or rename files. Very carefully create or choose folders for storing linked files so that you don't have to move them.

 Before you link one file to another, save the file you're working on. Your program needs to know precisely where OLE objects go in order to execute OLE commands. Therefore, your file must be completely up-to-date — and saved — for OLE commands to work.

Establishing the link

For the purposes of linking, the original file with the data you will link to is the *source.* Follow these steps to establish a link between your file and the source file so that your file can be updated whenever the source file is changed:

1. **Open the source file with the data that you'll link to your file.**

2. **Select the data you need and copy it to the Windows Clipboard.**

   You can do that by right-clicking and choosing Copy or pressing Ctrl+C.

3. **Click in the file where you want the linked data to appear.**

4. **Click the Save button.**

   As I explain earlier, all files must be saved and up-to-date for links to be successfully made.

5. **On the Home tab, establish the link between the source file and your file.**

   How you do this depends on the Office program you are working in. Do one of the following:

   - *Link and use styles:* Open the drop-down list on the Paste button and choose Link & Use Destination Styles on the drop-down list. You can also choose Link & Keep Source Formatting in the unlikely event that you want the text formatting in the source file to be retained in your file.

   - *Paste Special dialog box:* Open the drop-down list on the Paste button and choose Paste Special. You see the Paste Special dialog box.

     If you're pasting data between different programs as well as different files, the Paste Special dialog box has an As list that shows what kind of data is being transferred. Make sure that the correct option is chosen in the As list and click OK in the Paste Special dialog box.

     If you're pasting data between files created in the same program, the Paste Special dialog box offers options for choosing whether to copy formats and other things. For example, to copy data between Excel worksheets, you can copy the formulas or values only. Choose options and click the Paste Link button.

6. **Save your file by clicking the Save button.**

Congratulations. The link is established.

In some Office programs, you can open the source file from inside your file by right-clicking the linked data and choosing Linked Object⇨Open (or Open Link). The Linked Object command is named for the kind of data being linked. For example, if the link is to an Excel worksheet, the command is called Linked Worksheet Object.

To change the size of a linked object, click it, move the pointer over a selection handle, and drag. To move a linked object, move the pointer over the object and drag when you see a four-headed arrow. (To be able to move an object in Word, go to the Page Layout tab, click the Wrap Text button, and choose an option other than In Line with Text on the drop-down list.)

Updating a link

Each time you open a file with data linked to a source file, the program you're working in asks whether you want to update your file from the source file, as shown in Figure 7-2. Click the Yes, Update, or Update Links button in the dialog box to get new, up-to-the-minute data from the source file.

In some Office programs, you can update a link after you open a file. To do so, right-click the linked data and choose Update Link on the shortcut menu.

Figure 7-2:
Click Yes, Update, or Update Links to update your file from the source file.

Editing data in the source file

Suppose, while staring at the linked data in your file, you notice something wrong. The numbers in the table aren't accurate. There's a misspelling in the list. In some Office programs, you can open the source file and edit the data:

1. **Right-click the linked data and choose Linked Object⇨Edit (if the linked data is in an Office program) or Linked Object⇨Open (if the linked data is not in an Office program).**

   The program in which the source file was created and the source file itself open.

2. **Edit the data in the source file.**

   Changes you make are transferred immediately from the source file to your file.

3. **Click the Save button in the source file to save the editorial changes you made there.**

   When you return to your file, you see the changes you made.

Converting a linked object to an embedded object

As the start of this chapter explains in torturous detail, "embedded object" is Microsoft's term for data in a file that you create and manipulate with a program other than the one you are working in. In a Word document, for example, you can embed Excel data in a file and be able to edit the Excel data without leaving Word.

Suppose that the linked data in a file would serve you better if it were embedded. Rather than go to the source file to edit the data, you can put the data in your file by embedding it. For these occasions, convert your linked object into an embedded object by following these steps:

1. **Right-click the linked data and choose Linked Object⇨Convert.**

   The Convert dialog box, shown in Figure 7-3, appears.

2. **Select the Convert To option.**

3. **If necessary, select what type of data you are dealing with in the list.**

4. **Click OK.**

   There is a drawback to converting a linked object to an embedded object. The link to the source is broken, and you can no longer update the data from its original source.

Figure 7-3:
Converting a
linked to an
embedded
object.

Embedding Data from Other Programs

By embedding data, you can enter and edit foreign data without leaving the program you're working in. An Excel worksheet, for example, can be embedded on a PowerPoint slide (refer to Figure 7-1) When you double-click the embedded object, the computer program with which it was created opens so that you can start editing.

Embedding foreign data

How you embed data that is foreign to the program you're working in depends on whether the data has already been created. You can get a head start embedding data if you or someone else has already created it. Following are instructions for embedding an object so that you can enter the data on your own and embedding data that has already been created.

Creating an embedded object from scratch

Create an embedded object from scratch if the data you need hasn't been created yet. Follow these steps:

1. **Go to the Insert tab.**

   If your aim is to create an Excel table, click the Table button, choose Excel Spreadsheet, and be done with it.

2. **Click the Object button.**

   You see the Object (or Insert Object) dialog box, as shown on the left side of Figure 7-4.

3. **Click the Create New option tab (or option button).**

4. **In the Object Type list, choose the name of the program that handles the kind of data you want to embed.**

   For example, to insert a space for Word text, choose Microsoft Word Document.

Figure 7-4:
Creating
space for
embedding
data
(left) and
embedding
an entire file
(right).

5. Click OK.

Where your program's tabs and buttons used to be, you see different tabs and buttons. Use them to create and edit data.

Click outside the data when you finish working on it.

Embedding data that has already been created

If the data you want to embed has been created already in another program, you can embed the data in your file by following these steps:

1. Open the file with the data you want to embed.

Open the file in the program with which it was created.

2. Copy the portion of the file you want to embed with the Copy command.

Select the data, right-click, and choose Copy in the shortcut menu.

3. Return to the program where you want to embed the data.

4. Go to the Home tab.

5. Open the drop-down list on the Paste button and choose Paste Special.

You see the Paste Special dialog box, as shown in Figure 7-5.

6. Select the Paste option button.

7. In the As list, choose an option with the word *Object* in its name.

Which options appear in the list depends on which type of object you're embedding. The options without Object in their names are for pasting the data in picture format.

8. Click OK.

The data lands in your file.

**Book VIII
Chapter 7**

**Linking and
Embedding in
Compound Files**

Figure 7-5:
Choose the
program
where the
embedded
data comes
from.

> **Paste Special**
>
> Source: Microsoft Excel Worksheet
>   Sheet1!R4C1:R9C6
>
> As:
> ○ Paste   Microsoft Excel Worksheet Object
> ○ Paste link   HTML Format
>   Device Independent Bitmap
>   Bitmap
>   Picture (Enhanced Metafile)
>   Picture (Windows Metafile)
>
> [OK]   [Cancel]   ☐ Display as icon
>
> Result
>   Pastes the contents of the Clipboard into your
>   presentation so that you can activate it using Microsoft
>   Excel 12.

Embedding an entire file

You can embed an entire file in the file you're working on by following these
steps:

1. **In the Insert tab, click the Object button.**

   You see the Object (or Insert Object) dialog box.

2. **Select the Create from File tab (or option button).**

   You see the version of the Object (or Insert Object) dialog box, as shown
   on the right side of Figure 7-4 (shown previously).

3. **Click the Browse button.**

   The Browse dialog box opens.

4. **Select the file you want to embed in your file and click OK (or Insert).**

5. **Click OK in the Object (or Insert Object) dialog box.**

   That's all there is to it.

Editing embedded data

To edit an embedded object, double-click it. Where your program's tabs and
buttons used to be, you see a new set of tab and buttons — ones belonging
to the program normally used to edit the type of object you're editing. When
you finish editing the foreign data, click outside it.

To change the look of embedded data, right-click it and choose Format
Object. Then choose formatting commands in the Format Object dialog box.

The techniques for changing the size and position of embedded objects are
the same as the techniques for resizing and repositioning shapes, graphics,
clip-art images, and other objects (Book I, Chapter 8 enumerates these
techniques). To reposition an embedded object, move the pointer onto its
perimeter and drag. To resize an embedded object, move the pointer over a
selection handle and then drag.

Chapter 8: Office Web Apps

In This Chapter

✔ **Understanding how online applications work**

✔ **Understanding how the Office Web Apps work**

✔ **Signing up with Windows Live**

✔ **Going to the SkyDrive window**

✔ **Handling SkyDrive folders and files**

✔ **Working on Office Web App files**

✔ **Collaborating on and sharing files with others**

*T*his chapter looks into Office Web Apps, the online versions of Word, Excel, PowerPoint, and OneNote. Respectively, these applications are called Word Web App, Excel Web App, PowerPoint Web App, and OneNote Web App. Anyone can use these applications. You don't have to install Office 2010 or pay a fee of any kind. All you need is an Internet connection and an account with Windows Live. Moreover, users of the Office Web Apps can collaborate online with one another to create Word documents, Excel worksheets, PowerPoint presentations, and OneNote notebooks. As long as both of you are connected to the Internet, you and a colleague can work together on the same file simultaneously, even if one of you is in the Bugunda Kingdom and the other is in Uzbekistan.

Introducing Online Applications

The notion of using online applications takes some getting used to, but like it or not, you'll have to get used to it because soon the majority of applications will be online applications. These pages explain how online applications work and the advantages and disadvantages of using Office Web Apps and other online applications.

A new concept

Here's a computing concept that's in your future: In the years ahead, the personal computer as we know it will become obsolete and most computing activity will take place over the Internet. Rather than store files on the hard drive of your computer, you will store files on a Web server on the Internet. Rather than install and run programs on your computer, you will run programs that someone else installed for you on a Web server. To work on a file, you'll take these steps:

1. **Open your Web browser.**

For example, open Internet Explorer or Firefox.

2. **Go to the Web site where your files are stored.**

3. **Submit your password to the Web site.**

As a security measure, you submit a password to identify yourself and prevent others from seeing or editing your files.

4. **Open an online application on the Web site.**

Online applications look and work like the applications you use today on your personal computer. The difference is that online application software is installed on and run from a server on a Web site, not from a hard drive on a computer.

5. **Locate the folder where you store the file you want to work on.**

On the Web site, files are kept in folders. The folders look and work just like the folders on a personal computer.

6. **Open the file and get to work using the commands you see in your browser window.**

Does computing online and running online applications seem like science fiction? If it does, have a look at Figure 8-1. This figure shows an Excel worksheet called "Project01" inside a Web browser window. Notice the Ribbon and the familiar commands on the Home tab. What you're looking at is the Excel Web App, the online version of Excel. The Office Web Apps are online applications that you run by way of your browser from a Web site, working with files that you keep on the Web site.

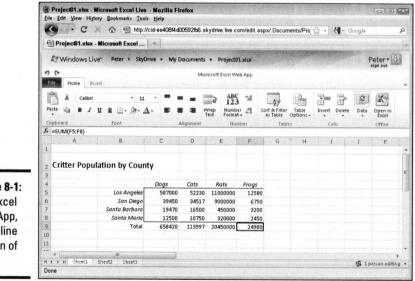

Figure 8-1:
The Excel
Web App,
the online
version of
Excel.

Advantages and disadvantages of online applications

Online applications are the wave of the future because the advantages of online applications are too good to pass up. Online applications are easier to install and maintain than traditional software. If you work in an office, you've had the experience of having to leave your desk while a technician installs new software or upgrades software on your computer. A technician doesn't have to visit computers throughout an office to install or upgrade an online application because online applications are installed in a single location — a Web server. As soon as a technician installs or upgrades an online application on the server, it becomes available to all the people who connect to the server to do their computing.

Online applications also make computing possible wherever you can find an Internet connection. You don't have to be in your office or your home or even carry your laptop with you. From a hotel room or friend's house, you can open a Web browser, connect to the Web site where your files are stored, and get to work. And because your files are kept in one place, not on one or more computers, you don't have to copy files between computers or wonder whether you're working on the most current file.

Storing files on a server frees you from having to back up files. Technicians back up files on the Web server, and if a file is corrupted and needs restoring, they can restore the file. Most people are not very good about backing up their files. Giving this onerous task to a technician is very nice indeed.

Another advantage of online applications, at least in the case of the Office Web Apps, is being able to work collaboratively. Because files are stored online where everyone who has permission can access them, more than one person can work on the same file simultaneously. For example, co-workers in various cities can go online and make last-minute changes to a PowerPoint presentation without having to endure a frantic conference call or pass the presentation around by e-mail.

With so many advantages to online applications, why would anyone not use them? In a word, the answer is *privacy*. Breaking into files stored on a Web server on the Internet is easier than breaking into files stored on a hard drive behind a firewall. Keeping files on a Web server — especially a server owned and maintained by a company that isn't your own — makes many people nervous.

Compared to Office 2010, the Office Web Apps present another disadvantage. Word Web App, Excel Web App, PowerPoint Web App, and OneNote Web App are stripped-down versions of Word, Excel, PowerPoint, and OneNote. The Office Web Apps don't have nearly as many features or amenities as their Office 2010 counterparts.

Office Web Apps: The Big Picture

To use Office Web Apps, start by setting up an account with Windows Live, a Microsoft Web site that offers Web-based applications and services. One of the services is called SkyDrive. Use it to create, store, and share Office Web App files. Windows Live (and SkyDrive) cost nothing to use. (See "Getting Ready to Use the Office Web Apps," later in this chapter.)

In SkyDrive, you can create folders for storing files online. You can also upload files from your computer to SkyDrive and download files from SkyDrive to your computer. (See "Managing SkyDrive Folders" and "Managing Your Files on SkyDrive.")

To create a document, worksheet, presentation, or notebook with an Office Web App, either start in a SkyDrive folder and choose the New command, or start on the File tab in Word, Excel, PowerPoint, or OneNote and choose Save & Send⇨Save to Web. (See "Creating an Office Web App file.")

The Office Web Apps — Word Web App, Excel Web App, PowerPoint Web App, and OneNote Web App — are abridged versions of their Office 2010 namesakes. Use the commands on the Ribbon and the tabs to create and perfect your document, worksheet, presentation, or notebook. To make use of a command in an Office program that isn't found in an Office Web App, click the Open In button (the rightmost button on the Ribbon). (See "Editing an Office Web App file, later in this chapter.")

To see how to use SkyDrive to collaborate online with other people, establish permissions for sharing folders, and issue invitations to your co-workers so that they can work alongside you in cyberspace, see "Sharing and Co-Authoring Files," later in this chapter.

SharePoint 2010: The other way to use the Office Web Apps

In this book, I describe how to run the Office Web Apps from a server located at Windows Live, a Microsoft Web site, but you can also run Office Web Apps without keeping your files at Windows Live. Using a software product called SharePoint 2010, you can run the Office Web Apps from a server on a local network. For example, you can run the applications from and store your files on a server that is owned and operated by the company you work for.

Keeping files on a network server close to home helps solve the privacy problem. Meddlers and spies who want to steal files have a harder time getting them from a server on a closed network than they do getting them from a Windows Live server on the Internet. To install a SharePoint 2010, however, you need a fair amount of technical expertise. If SharePoint 2010 interests you, see *SharePoint 2010 For Dummies*, by Vanessa L. Williams.

Getting Ready to Use the Office Web Apps

To start using the Office Web Apps, complete these tasks:

1. **Make sure you have the right Web browser.**

The Office Web Apps work with Internet Explorer, Firefox, and Safari, but not the Chrome or Opera browser. For all occasions, I recommend using Firefox, and you can download and install it starting at this address:

```
www.mozilla.com/firefox
```

2. **Install Microsoft Silverlight.**

Silverlight is an application that improves the delivery of media over the Internet. Installing Silverlight isn't mandatory, but Microsoft recommends it because the Office Web Apps work better and faster when Silverlight is installed. To download and install Silverlight, go to this address:

```
www.silverlight.net
```

3. **Sign up with Windows Live.**

Go to the address listed here to sign up. You are asked to provide your e-mail address and a password. If you have an account with Hotmail, the online e-mailing service, you can use your Hotmail address and password to sign into Windows Live. To sign up, you can create a Windows Live ID or use your e-mail address.

```
http://home.live.com
```

Signing In and Going to the SkyDrive Window

Sign in to Windows Live by going to the address shown here, entering your ID and password, and clicking the Sign In button:

```
http://home.live.com
```

The Home window at Windows Live opens, which is fine and dandy, but to use the Office Web Apps, you need to be on the SkyDrive window. As shown in Figure 8-2, you can use these techniques to get to the SkyDrive window:

✦ Click the More link on the Windows Live taskbar and choose SkyDrive on the drop-down list.

✦ Click SkyDrive on the Navigation bar (see Figure 8-2).

The SkyDrive window lists your folders and how much space the files in your folders occupy. (You can store up to 25GB of files.) To see all your folders rather than the ones you most recently opened, click the All Folders or View All link.

**Book VIII
Chapter 8**

Office Web Apps

Click SkyDrive on the Navigation bar. . .

Click to sign out

or click the More link and choose SkyDrive

Figure 8-2:
Going to the
SkyDrive
window at
Windows
Live.

When the time comes to sign out of Windows Live, click the Sign Out link in the upper-right corner of the screen.

Managing SkyDrive Folders

The SkyDrive window at Windows Live lists your top-level folders. Click a folder icon in the SkyDrive window to open a folder. Starting in the SkyDrive window, you can create folders, rename folders, and delete folders, as the following pages explain.

Creating a folder

SkyDrive gives you two folders for storing files. These folders are called My Documents and Public. (The Favorites folders are for storing shortcuts to Web sites.) Follow these steps to create a folder of your own:

1. **In the SkyDrive window, click the Create Folder link.**

   The Create a Folder window opens. If you want to create a subfolder (a folder inside another folder), open the parent folder before completing Step 1.

2. **In the Name box, enter a descriptive name for the folder.**

3. **On the Share With drop-down list, choose an option to make the folder public or private; then click the Next button.**

   The Share With options matter if you intend to share the files in your new folder with other people. For now, choose Just Me to create a private folder or Everyone to create a public folder. You can change Share With settings after you create a folder, as "Choosing Share With permissions" explains later in this chapter.

   The Add Files window appears.

4. **For each file that you want to upload from your computer to your new folder, click a Browse button, choose a file in the File Upload dialog box, and click the Open button.**

5. **Click the Upload button in the Add Files window.**

   Later in this chapter, "Uploading files to SkyDrive" explains how to add files to a folder you already created.

Going from folder to folder

The SkyDrive window shows, in big bold letters, the name of the folder you are currently viewing. Use these techniques go to from folder to folder:

✦ **Click a folder icon:** Clicking a folder icon opens the folder so that you can see its files and subfolders.

✦ **Use the Navigation bar:** The Navigation bar —located below the folder name — lists the path to the folder you're currently viewing. To backtrack, click SkyDrive or the name of a folder on the Navigation bar. For example, click SkyDrive to return to the SkyDrive window.

✦ **Click the Back or Forward button:** Click the Back or Forward button in your browser to return to a folder you previously visited.

When you're in a folder window, you can click the View link and choose Icons, Details, or Thumbnails on the drop-down list to get a better look at the files in that folder. In Details view, you can see when a file was last edited and its size. Click the Sort By link and choose an option on the drop-down list to arrange files by name, date, size, or type.

Renaming and deleting folders

To rename or delete a folder, start by opening it. Then use these techniques:

✦ **Renaming a folder:** Click the More link and choose Rename on the drop-down list, as shown in Figure 8-3. Then enter a name in the New Name text box and click the Save button.

✦ **Deleting a folder:** Click the More link and choose Delete on the drop-down list. Then click OK in the message box to delete the folder and all its contents.

You can't rename or delete a folder if you don't have permission to do so. For more information, see "Choosing Share With permissions," later in this chapter.

Figure 8-3: A folder window.

Creating and Editing Office Web App Files

To create a file with Word Web App, Excel Web App, PowerPoint Web App, or OneNote Web App, start by opening the folder where you want to keep the file. These pages explain how to create Office Web App files as well as how to open them, edit them, and find your way around the File window.

Creating an Office Web App file

I'm happy to report that creating an Office Web App file is quite easy. After signing in to Windows Live and going to the SkyDrive window, follow these steps to create an Office Web App file:

1. **Open the folder where you will keep the file.**

    See "Creating a folder," earlier in this chapter, if you need to create the folder or subfolder first.

2. **Click the New link and choose an option on the drop-down list, as shown in Figure 8-4.**

    The Word Web App, Excel Web App, PowerPoint Web App, or OneNote Web App opens so that you can create your worksheet, presentation, document, or notebook.

Figure 8-4:
Click New
to create a
workbook,
presentation,
document,
or notebook.

Opening Web App files

To open a Web App file, start by opening the folder where it is stored and
then click its icon. The file doesn't open right away. Instead, the File window
opens, as shown in Figure 8-5. The File window tells you everything you need
to know about a file. (The next section describes the File window in detail.)
Use these techniques to open a file from the File window:

✦ **Click the View link on the taskbar:** Clicking View opens the file in a
window so that you can view the file (but not edit it). If the file is being
shared and the file's owner has given you permission to edit the file in
an Office Web App, you can edit the file. Click the Edit in Browser button
after the file opens to edit the file in an Office Web App. (For more information, see "Editing an Office Web App file," later in this chapter.)

✦ **Click the Edit link on the taskbar:** Clicking Edit opens the file in an
Office Web App so that you can edit it. If the Edit link isn't available, the
file's owner has not given you permission to edit the file. (See "Choosing
Share With permissions," later in this chapter).

✦ **Click the file's icon:** Clicking a file icon opens the file so you can view it.
Clicking an icon gets the same results as clicking the View link.

Want to close an Office Web App file? Don't bother looking for a Close command, because you won't find one. To close a file, go to a different folder or
close your browser. Files are saved automatically when you close them.

All about the File window

The File window (refer to Figure 8-5) gives you many ways to see what a file
is all about before you view or edit it. Take heed of the activities you can do
in the File window:

✦ **View or edit the file:** On the taskbar, click View to open and examine
the file; click Edit to open the file in an Office Web App and be able to
edit the file as well as examine it.

Do file-related tasks

Open a different file in the folder

Figure 8-5:
The File
window,
where you
can do
all things
relating to a
file.

Read and write a description and comments

Get the Web address and embedding code

✦ **Do other file-related tasks:** Besides viewing and editing, visit the taskbar to download, delete, move, copy, rename, or share a file.

✦ **Read and enter a description and comments:** Especially if you intend to share the file with others, enter a description of the file so that others know what it is. Also, you can enter and read comments that explain what you or other users did to the file.

✦ **Examine a different file in the folder:** Click the Scroll Back or Scroll Forward arrow in the upper-right corner of the window to see the names of other files in the folder. Click a file's icon to go to its file window.

✦ **Get file information:** Glance at the right side of the File window to see who created the file, whether it is shared, and other information.

✦ **Copy the file's Web address:** One way to share a file is to copy its Web address and send it to other people. Under Information, you can copy the file's address from the Web Address box. For more information, see "Inviting others to a SkyDrive folder," later in this chapter.

✦ **Copy code for embedding:** You can also share a file by embedding code on a Web page such that others can click the hyperlink in the code and go to the file on SkyDrive. See "Inviting others to a SkyDrive folder," later in this chapter.

Editing an Office Web App file

The Office Web Apps are abridged versions of Word, Excel, PowerPoint, and OneNote. In the Office Web Apps, use the same techniques you use to edit a Word 2010 document (see Book II), an Excel 2010 worksheet (see Book V), a PowerPoint 2010 presentation (see Book VI), and a OneNote 2010 notebook (see Chapter 5 of this mini-book).

As well as edit an Office Web App file online, you can download it to your computer and edit it there. Both techniques are described forthwith.

You will not find a Save button in an Office Web App. The Save button is missing because changes you make to an Office Web App file are saved automatically. You don't have to bother clicking the Save button to preserve your work.

Editing in an Office Web App

To edit an Office Web App file in an Office Web App, click the Edit link in the File window (refer to Figure 8-5). The file opens in an Office Web App. If the Edit link isn't available, the file's owner has not given you permission to edit the file. See "Choosing Share With permissions," later in this chapter.

If you see the "This file cannot be edited" message, the file was created in an Office 2010 program, and you must save a copy of the file in order to edit it in an Office Web App. See the "Editing files created in Office 2010" sidebar.

Editing in an Office 2010 program

Yes, editing an Office Web App in an Office 2010 can be done. If you get frustrated editing an Office Web App file and you want to take advantage of the numerous commands in Word, Excel, PowerPoint, or OneNote, you can edit your file in an Office 2010 program by downloading the file and editing it offline. Follow these steps to edit an Office Web App File in an Office 2010 program:

1. **Open the Office Web App file (if it isn't already open).**

2. **Click the Open In button (in PowerPoint, for example, the button is called Open in PowerPoint).**

This button is located next to the File tab if you're viewing a file; it is located on the right side of the Ribbon if you're editing a file. When you click the button, the Open Document dialog box appears.

3. **Click OK to affirm that opening the file is okay.**

   An Office 2010 program — Word, Excel, PowerPoint, or OneNote — opens on your computer and the Connecting To dialog box appears.

4. **Enter your Windows Live ID and password; then click OK.**

   The file is downloaded and opened on your computer. Depending on your Windows settings, you may have to click the Enable Editing button to start editing. Be sure to save the file on your computer after you edit it.

Editing files created in Office 2010

As "Uploading files to SkyDrive" explains later in this chapter, you can upload Office 2010 files from your computer, store them on SkyDrive, and open them with an Office Web App. You can open them, but whether you can edit them is another matter.

As anybody who has spent more than five minutes with an Office Web App knows, the Office Web Apps don't offer as many features and doo-dads as their Office 2010 brethren. When it comes to editing files in an Office Web App that originated in Office 2010, you're out of luck if the original file contains features that the Office Web App doesn't support. For example, you can't enter comments in Excel Web App. If you upload and try to edit an Excel 2010 file that includes comments, the Excel Web App tells you that it can't be done unless you save a copy of the file.

Follow these steps to save a copy of an Office 2010 file so that you can edit it in an Office Web App:

1. **In the File window, click View on the taskbar.**

   The file opens, and if any features in the Office 2010 file are not supported, a "this file may not display as intended" message appears, as shown in the figure that follows these steps.

2. **On the File tab, choose Save a Copy.**

   A dialog box tells you which features in the Office 2010 file aren't supported by the Office Web App.

3. **Click Yes in the dialog box.**

   The Save As dialog box appears.

4. **Enter a new name for the file or select the Overwrite Existing Files check box.**

   Enter a new name of you want to keep the original Office 2010 file on hand; select the check box to delete the original file.

5. **Click the Save button.**

   Your Office Web App creates a stripped-down version of the Office 2010 file minus the features in the original file that are not supported.

Managing Your Files on SkyDrive

SkyDrive is first and foremost a means of organizing and managing files. You can take advantage of commands in a SkyDrive folder window to upload files to SkyDrive, download files from SkyDrive, and delete, rename, move, and copy files.

Uploading files to SkyDrive

To upload files from your computer to a folder you keep on SkyDrive, you can start in SkyDrive or in Word, Excel, PowerPoint, or OneNote:

✦ **Starting in SkyDrive:** Open the folder where you want to store the files and click the Add Files link. The Add Files window appears. Click a Browse button for each file you want to upload, choose a file in the File Upload dialog box, and click the Open button. Then Click the Upload button.

✦ **Starting in Word, Excel, PowerPoint, or OneNote:** With the file you want to upload to SkyDrive open, follow these steps to upload the file to SkyDrive:

1. On the File tab, choose Save & Send, and choose Save to Web. Save to Windows Live options appear.

2. Click the Sign In button, enter your Windows Live ID and password, and click OK. A list of folders you keep on Windows Live appears.

3. Select a folder and click the Save As button.

Later in this chapter, "Downloading files from SkyDrive to your computer" explains how to do move files in the other direction — from SkyDrive to your computer.

Moving, copying, renaming, and deleting files

Starting in a File window (refer to Figure 8-5), use these techniques to move, copy, rename, or delete a file:

✦ **Moving and copying:** Click the Move link or click the More link and choose Copy on the drop-down list. You see a window that lists your SkyDrive folders. Select a folder name and choose the Move or Copy command.

✦ **Renaming:** Click the More link and choose Rename on the drop-down list. Then enter a name in the New Name text box and click the Save button.

✦ **Deleting:** Click the Delete link and then click OK in the confirmation dialog box.

**Book VIII
Chapter 8**

Office Web Apps

Downloading files from SkyDrive to your computer

SkyDrive gives you the choice of downloading files one at a time or downloading all the files in a folder in a zip file:

✦ **Downloading a file:** In the File window (refer to Figure 8-5), click the Download link. You see the standard dialog box for downloading files from the Internet. Choose to open or save the file after you download it and click OK.

✦ **Downloading all the files in a folder:** In a Folder window (refer to Figure 8-3), click the More link and choose Download as .Zip File on the drop-down list. In the standard dialog box for downloading files, choose to open or save the file after you download it and click OK.

Sharing and Co-Authoring Files

As I mention at the start of this chapter, one of the great advantages of Office Web Apps is being able to share files with others. Microsoft uses the term *co-authoring* to describe what happens when more than one person works on a file in an Office Web App. As long as all parties have Windows Live accounts and all have permission to edit a file, they can edit it. These pages explain how to handle editing permissions, how to invite others to co-author a file, and what being invited to co-author a file entails.

Choosing Share With permissions

Whether others can open a folder on your SkyDrive page and view its files depends on which permissions the folder has been granted. Likewise, permissions determine whether others can add files to a folder, edit files, and delete files.

Types of permissions

If you intend to share files with others on Windows Live, you need to know how folder permissions work. Folder permissions fall into two broad categories:

✦ **Private folders:** Only the owner can open a private folder, view its files, add files, edit files, and delete files. The default My Documents folder is a private folder.

✦ **Public folders:** Everyone whom the owner invites to visit a public folder can visit it. The default Public folder that SkyDrive creates for you is an example of this type of folder. When others come to a public folder, they can do these tasks, depending (again) on which permissions the owner has given them:

  • *Public folder for viewing files only:* Visitors can open and view the files in the folder (but not edit or delete the files).

- *Public folder for viewing, adding, editing, and deleting files:* Visitors can view the files in the folder as well as add files to the folder, edit files, and delete files.

Editing a folder's permissions

When you create a new folder, SkyDrive asks you to choose an option on the Share With drop-down list to establish its permissions. At any time, however, you can follow these steps to establish folder permissions:

1. **In the Folder window (refer to Figure 8-3), click the More button and choose Edit Permissions on the drop-down list.**

You see the Edit Permissions window.

2. **Establish folder permissions.**

Choose whether to make the folder private or public, and if the folder is public, what visitors can do in the folder:

- *Private folder:* If the Edit Permissions folder says, "You're not sharing this folder," it is a private folder already. Click the Clear These Settings link to make the folder private if it is a public folder.

- *Public folder for viewing files only:* Select the Everyone (Public) check box.

- *Public folder for viewing, adding, editing, and deleting files:* For each person who will co-author files in the folder, enter an e-mail address and press Enter. Then, on the drop-down list beside the person's name, choose Can Add, Edit Details, and Delete Files.

3. **Click the Save button.**

If you entered e-mail addresses, SkyDrive asks whether to send e-mail notifications. The next topic in this chapter explains how to notify people that they can visit a public SkyDrive folder.

Inviting others to a SkyDrive folder

Starting in the Folder window (refer to Figure 8-3), you can invite others to visit a public SkyDrive folder by clicking the More button and choosing Send a Link. Then, in the Send a Link window, enter an e-mail address, a word or two, and click the Send button.

If the folder whose contents you want to share is a public folder for viewing files only, you can paste HTML code on a Web page or blog so that anyone can click a hyperlink and go to your folder on SkyDrive. To obtain the HTML code, click the More button and choose Share. Then copy the code from the Share in a Blog or Other Webpage window.

Visiting a SkyDrive folder by invitation

Invitations to visit a SkyDrive folder arrive in the form of an e-mail message. In the message, recipients can click the View Folder button to go to the Folder window on SkyDrive where the folder is located. From there, depending on the permission that they were given, they can view files or both view and edit files. Visitors can also create new Office Web App files by clicking the New link in the Folder window.

 If you share files with others, be sure to write comments in the File window describing what you did to the file you're sharing (see "All about the File window," earlier in this chapter). Comments help the people who work on a file understand when, where, and how changes were made.

Index

C

E

M

p

Business/Accounting & Bookkeeping

Bookkeeping For Dummies
978-0-7645-9848-7

eBay Business
All-in-One For Dummies,
2nd Edition
978-0-470-38536-4

Job Interviews
For Dummies,
3rd Edition
978-0-470-17748-8

Resumes For Dummies,
5th Edition
978-0-470-08037-5

Stock Investing
For Dummies,
3rd Edition
978-0-470-40114-9

Successful Time
Management
For Dummies
978-0-470-29034-7

Computer Hardware

BlackBerry For Dummies,
3rd Edition
978-0-470-45762-7

Computers For Seniors
For Dummies
978-0-470-24055-7

iPhone For Dummies,
2nd Edition
978-0-470-42342-4

Laptops For Dummies,
3rd Edition
978-0-470-27759-1

Macs For Dummies,
10th Edition
978-0-470-27817-8

Cooking & Entertaining

Cooking Basics
For Dummies,
3rd Edition
978-0-7645-7206-7

Wine For Dummies,
4th Edition
978-0-470-04579-4

Diet & Nutrition

Dieting For Dummies,
2nd Edition
978-0-7645-4149-0

Nutrition For Dummies,
4th Edition
978-0-471-79868-2

Weight Training
For Dummies,
3rd Edition
978-0-471-76845-6

Digital Photography

Digital Photography
For Dummies,
6th Edition
978-0-470-25074-7

Photoshop Elements 7
For Dummies
978-0-470-39700-8

Gardening

Gardening Basics
For Dummies
978-0-470-03749-2

Organic Gardening
For Dummies,
2nd Edition
978-0-470-43067-5

Green/Sustainable

Green Building
& Remodeling
For Dummies
978-0-470-17559-0

Green Cleaning
For Dummies
978-0-470-39106-8

Green IT For Dummies
978-0-470-38688-0

Health

Diabetes For Dummies,
3rd Edition
978-0-470-27086-8

Food Allergies
For Dummies
978-0-470-09584-3

Living Gluten-Free
For Dummies
978-0-471-77383-2

Hobbies/General

Chess For Dummies,
2nd Edition
978-0-7645-8404-6

Drawing For Dummies
978-0-7645-5476-6

Knitting For Dummies,
2nd Edition
978-0-470-28747-7

Organizing For Dummies
978-0-7645-5300-4

SuDoku For Dummies
978-0-470-01892-7

Home Improvement

Energy Efficient Homes
For Dummies
978-0-470-37602-7

Home Theater
For Dummies,
3rd Edition
978-0-470-41189-6

Living the Country Lifestyle
All-in-One For Dummies
978-0-470-43061-3

Solar Power Your Home
For Dummies
978-0-470-17569-9

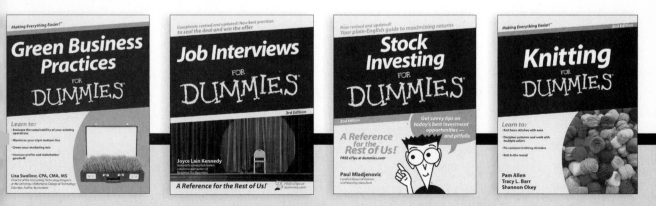

Available wherever books are sold. For more information or to order direct: U.S. customers visit www.dummies.com or call 1-877-762-2974.
U.K. customers visit www.wileyeurope.com or call (0) 1243 843291. Canadian customers visit www.wiley.ca or call 1-800-567-4797.

Internet

Blogging For Dummies,
2nd Edition
978-0-470-23017-6

eBay For Dummies,
6th Edition
978-0-470-49741-8

Facebook For Dummies
978-0-470-26273-3

Google Blogger
For Dummies
978-0-470-40742-4

Web Marketing
For Dummies,
2nd Edition
978-0-470-37181-7

WordPress For Dummies,
2nd Edition
978-0-470-40296-2

Language & Foreign Language

French For Dummies
978-0-7645-5193-2

Italian Phrases
For Dummies
978-0-7645-7203-6

Spanish For Dummies
978-0-7645-5194-9

Spanish For Dummies,
Audio Set
978-0-470-09585-0

Macintosh

Mac OS X Snow Leopard
For Dummies
978-0-470-43543-4

Math & Science

Algebra I For Dummies,
2nd Edition
978-0-470-55964-2

Biology For Dummies
978-0-7645-5326-4

Calculus For Dummies
978-0-7645-2498-1

Chemistry For Dummies
978-0-7645-5430-8

Microsoft Office

Excel 2007 For Dummies
978-0-470-03737-9

Office 2007 All-in-One
Desk Reference
For Dummies
978-0-471-78279-7

Music

Guitar For Dummies,
2nd Edition
978-0-7645-9904-0

iPod & iTunes
For Dummies,
6th Edition
978-0-470-39062-7

Piano Exercises
For Dummies
978-0-470-38765-8

Parenting & Education

Parenting For Dummies,
2nd Edition
978-0-7645-5418-6

Type 1 Diabetes
For Dummies
978-0-470-17811-9

Pets

Cats For Dummies,
2nd Edition
978-0-7645-5275-5

Dog Training For Dummies,
2nd Edition
978-0-7645-8418-3

Puppies For Dummies,
2nd Edition
978-0-470-03717-1

Religion & Inspiration

The Bible For Dummies
978-0-7645-5296-0

Catholicism For Dummies
978-0-7645-5391-2

Women in the Bible
For Dummies
978-0-7645-8475-6

Self-Help & Relationship

Anger Management
For Dummies
978-0-470-03715-7

Overcoming Anxiety
For Dummies
978-0-7645-5447-6

Sports

Baseball For Dummies,
3rd Edition
978-0-7645-7537-2

Basketball For Dummies,
2nd Edition
978-0-7645-5248-9

Golf For Dummies,
3rd Edition
978-0-471-76871-5

Web Development

Web Design All-in-One
For Dummies
978-0-470-41796-6

Windows Vista

Windows Vista
For Dummies
978-0-471-75421-3

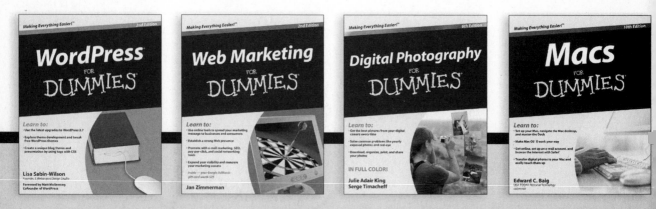